Emerging Technologies for the Evolution and Maintenance of Software Models

Jörg Rech
SAP Research, Germany

Christian Bunse
University of Applied Sciences Stralsund, Germany

Managing Director:	Lindsay Johnston
Senior Editorial Director:	Heather Probst
Book Production Manager:	Sean Woznicki
Development Manager:	Joel Gamon
Development Editor:	Hannah Abelbeck
Acquisitions Editor:	Erika Gallagher
Typesetters:	Brittany Metzel and Deanna Zombro
Print Coordinator:	Jamie Snavely
Cover Design:	Nick Newcomer

Published in the United States of America by
Information Science Reference (an imprint of IGI Global)
701 E. Chocolate Avenue
Hershey PA 17033
Tel: 717-533-8845
Fax: 717-533-8661
E-mail: cust@igi-global.com
Web site: http://www.igi-global.com

Library of Congress Cataloging-in-Publication Data

Emerging technologies for the evolution and maintenance of software models /
Jorg Rech and Christian Bunse, editors.
     p. cm.
  Includes bibliographical references and index.
   ISBN 978-1-61350-438-3 (hardcover) -- ISBN 978-1-61350-439-0 (ebook) --
ISBN 978-1-61350-440-6 (print & perpetual access) 1. Software maintenance--
Technological innovations. 2. Computer simulation--Technological innovations.
I. Rech, Jorg, 1972- II. Bunse, Christian.
  QA76.76.S64E48 2012
  005.1'6--dc23
                              2011038341

British Cataloguing in Publication Data
A Cataloguing in Publication record for this book is available from the British Library.

Manfred Broy, *Technical University Munich, Germany*
Manuel Wimmer, *Vienna University of Technology, Austria*
Mario Piattini, *University of Castilla-La Mancha, Spain*
Martina Seidl, *Johannes Kepler University Linz, Austria*
Matthias Riebisch, *Ilmenau University of Technology, Germany*
Michael Felderer, *University of Innsbruck, Institute of Computer Science, Austria*
Michel Hassenforder, *UHA / MIPS Laboratory / Haute Alsace University, France*
Miguel A. De Miguel, *Technical University of Madrid, Spain*
Petra Brosch, *Vienna University of Technology, Austria*
Philip Langer, *Johannes Kepler University Linz, Austria*
Qurat-ul-ann Farooq, *Ilmenau University of Technology, Germany*
Ricardo Pérez-Castillo, *University of Castilla-La Mancha, Spain*
Ruth Breu, *University of Innsbruck,Institute of Computer Science, Austria*
Sascha Kirstan, *Altran Technologies, Germany*
Serge Demeyer, *University of Antwerp, Belgium*
Sheridan Jeary, *Bournemouth University, School of Design, Engineering & Computing, UK*
Steffen Lehnert, *Ilmenau University of Technology, Germany*
Yu Sun, *University of Alabama at Birmingham, USA*
Zbigniew Huzar, *Institute of Informatics, Wroclaw University of Technology, Poland*

List of Reviewers

A. Cicchetti, *Malardalen University, Sweden*
A. Pierantonio, *University of L'Aquila, Italy*
Andrea Herrmann, *University Heidelberg, Germany*
Anne Keller, *University of Antwerp, Belgium*
Ayse Morali, *Ascure N.V., Belgium*
Bernhard Schätz, *fortiss, Germany*
Berthold Agreiter, *University of Innsbruck, Institute of Computer Science, Austria*
Bogumila Hnatkowska, *Institute of Informatics, Wroclaw University of Technology, Poland*
Charles-Georges Guillemot, *UHA / MIPS Laboratory / Haute Alsace University, France*
Christian Bunse, *University of Applied Sciences Stralsund, Germany*
Christian Seel, *Software AG, Germany*
Claudia Pereira, *UNICEN University, Tandil, Argentina*
Colin Atkinson, *University of Mannheim, Germany*
D. Di Ruscio, *University of L'Aquila, Italy*
D.S. Kolovos, *Department of Computer Science, The University of York, UK*
Dima Panfilenko, *German Research Center for Artificial Intelligence (DFKI), Germany*
Emilio Salazar, *Technical University of Madrid, Spain*
Florian Barth, *University of Mannheim, Germany*
Frederic Fondement, *UHA / MIPS Laboratory / Haute Alsace University, France*
Gerti Kappel, *Vienna University of Technology, Austria*
Helmut Krcmar, *Technical University Munich, Germany*
Ignacio García-Rodríguez de Guzmán, *University of Castilla-La Mancha, Spain*

Table of Contents

Section 1
Maintenance and Evolution of Software Models

Iwona Dubielewicz, Wroclaw University of Technology, Poland
Bogumila Hnatkowska, Wroclaw University of Technology, Poland
Zbigniew Huzar, Wroclaw University of Technology, Poland
Lech Tuzinkiewicz, Wroclaw University of Technology, Poland

Anne Keller, University of Antwerp, Belgium
Serge Demeyer, University of Antwerp, Belgium

Andrea Herrmann, University Heidelberg, Germany
Ayse Morali, Ascure N.V., Belgium

Yu Sun, University of Alabama at Birmingham, USA
Jeff Gray, University of Alabama, USA
Philip Langer, Johannes Kepler University, Austria
Gerti Kappel, Vienna University of Technology, Austria
Manuel Wimmer, Vienna University of Technology, Austria
Jules White, Virginia Tech, USA

Section 4
Miscellaneous

Foreword

As a researcher in the field of software engineering, I am actively contributing to the scientific research in software evolution and model-driven software engineering. Being the chair of the Software Evolution Working Group of the European Research Consortium for Informatics and Mathematics (ERCIM), I have the honor to write the foreword for this book. It was a real pleasure for me to take up this task as this book aims to reconcile two extremely relevant topics in today's software engineering research and practice: software evolution on the one hand, and model-driven software engineering on the other hand.

Software maintenance and software evolution have been considered as some of the most important challenges in software engineering since its origins in the late sixties. In fact, software maintenance was already coined as one of the crucial software engineering activities in the first NATO conference on software engineering in 1968. Since the early days, research progress in software evolution never ceased. Techniques, formalisms, tools, methods, and processes for software evolution slowly made it into mainstream programming practice, of which they are now an integral part. The general aim is to support software engineers in maintaining and evolving software-intensive systems in an effective manner without sacrificing quality. A fairly recent and comprehensive overview of the state-of-the-art in software evolution research can be found in the 2008 Springer book "Software Evolution."

Model-driven software engineering has also been around for quite a while. Even in the aforementioned NATO conference, the importance of design and supporting techniques was clearly stated. Since than, an enormous amount of modeling languages and methodologies have been developed and used in a wide variety of domains (data models, software models, hardware models, domain-specific models, etc.). Somewhere in the nineties, model-driven software engineering gained a renewed widespread interest, due to the effort of the Object Management Group to standardize the many existing software modeling languages into a new unified modeling language, known as the UML. The popularity increased even more by the introduction of OMG's Model-Driven Architecture method for developing software through the use of software models, and by annual scientific events such as the ACM/IEEE sponsored International Conference on Model Driven Engineering Languages and Systems (MoDELS) and Springer's SCI-indexed scientific journal on Software and Systems Modeling (SoSyM).

From a practical point of view, software evolution support for model-driven development environments and methodologies is still lagging behind. In 2005, together with several co-authors, we identified the 18 most pressing "Challenges in Software Evolution". These were presented in an article carrying the same name at IWPSE, the 8th International Workshop on Principles of Software Evolution (DOI: 10.1109/IWPSE.2005.7). Interestingly, "supporting model evolution" was identified as one of the key challenges. More precisely, the challenge was formulated as follows: "Software evolution techniques should be raised to a higher level of abstraction, in order to accommodate not only evolution of programs, but also evolution of higher-level artifacts such as analysis and design models, software architectures, requirements specifications, and so on."

I am therefore very pleased that the aim of this book is to present the emerging research techniques for software model evolution and maintenance. Jörg Rech and Christian Bunse, editors of this book, have done an excellent job in collecting high-quality contributing chapters focusing on a wide rage of different model evolution aspects:

- Model versioning, which aims to provide advanced version control support for software models
- Model-based testing, which aims to integrate automated tests in the model-driven software development process
- Model transformation to explore the use of transformation languages to evolve and manipulate software models
- Reusable models that help to develop new model-driven solutions through the reuse of existing modeling artifacts
- Model traceability and change impact analysis that allow to facilitate, and assess the effect of, propagating changes in models
- Model reverse engineering, which is used to reconstruct models from the program code, and these models can be used subsequently to re-engineer or modernize the system
- Model quality, which needs to be assured, preserved, and improved during model evolution
- As well as a wide variety of other emerging techniques that can aid in the model-driven development process, such as ontologies, social networks, and many more.

This book will provide a valuable source of information and inspiration for researchers and practitioners alike. Readers of this book will learn a lot about the interplay between the fields of software evolution and software modeling, and will get a good general picture of the current state-of-the-art.

I enjoyed reading this book, and I hope you will do so too. Happy reading!

Tom Mens
University of Mons, Belgium

__Tom Mens__ obtained his PhD in Science in 1999 at the Vrije Universiteit Brussel (Belgium). After that, he was a postdoctoral fellow of the Fund for Scientific Research – Flanders (FWO) for three years. In October 2003 he became a Lecturer at the Faculty of Sciences of the University of Mons (Belgium), where he founded and directs a research lab on software engineering. Since November 2008 he is full Professor. His main research interest lies in the underlying foundations of, and tool support for, modeling, developing, and evolving software. He published numerous peer-reviewed articles on this research topic in international journals and conferences. He has been co-organizer, program committee member, and reviewer of numerous international symposia and workshops on model-driven software engineering and software evolution. He has been involved in several interuniversity research projects and networks, and is founder and chair of the ERCIM Working Group on Software Evolution. In 2008 he co-edited the Springer book "Software Evolution" with S. Demeyer.

Preface

The success of software modeling languages and especially that of the Unified Modeling Language (UML) demonstrates a growing consensus in software industry that the general principles of abstraction, divide-and-conquer, and stepwise-refinement, enabled by modeling, are key in the development of large and complex software systems. This is also indicated by the recent advent of technologies such as component-based software systems, software product-lines, et cetera.

However, using technologies such as modeling, components, et cetera drastically alters the software development process and process organization. Today a software model tends to exists for a long time and will not be discarded when shipping the system. Thus, the maintenance, evolution, re-engineering, as well as reuse of software models gains importance for the practical application of model-based development. Furthermore, as technologies and tools mature, we face the challenge of shifting from short model-based sketches to complex models with a long lifespan that will likely appear in several versions of a system or even across multiple systems.

In the long-term, regarding those fine-grained software models, we have to address emerging questions regarding their maintenance, evolution, and re-engineering. This includes partitioning and maintaining of models, as well as managing their change. Systematic methods need to support the quality of software models, ways to define model libraries, techniques for impact analysis, and integration for varying domains.

EVOLUTION AND MAINTENANCE OF SOFTWARE MODELS

In general, the term "evolution" describes the process of change of groups or elements over generations and puts a specific focus on mutations, drift, and "natural selection." Following the ideas of Richta and Bloomfield, technology, as all elements, evolves. When used in the domain of software, and more specifically in software maintenance, evolution refers to the process of initially developing a software system and evolving/changing by various generations and reasons. Any (software) system with a significant complexity has to face changing conditions during its lifetime. Thus, modern software systems have to become flexible to "embrace" changes by either static or dynamic adaptation. Software evolution addresses this by putting the focus on adaptation and migration.

While substantial research from both industry and academia has been devoted to software evolution and maintenance, there has been only a limited number projects that studied software evolution in model-driven software development. Getting a better understanding of these concepts is important especially when putting the focus on evolution-in-the-large. The evolution of large-scale software systems is of increasing importance and often has an impact onto many technology areas. However, following Favre, regardless the technology used, recognizing the concepts of model and meta-models is important in this context.

OBJECTIVE OF THE BOOK

In this book, we have collected and connected the latest views from research and practice, in order to stimulate and support the development of research in the evolution, maintenance, and re-engineering of software models. In general, modeling is a means for mastering complexity by abstraction. A scientific model can provide a way to read elements easily which have been broken down to a simpler form. Therefore science uses a significant number of methods, techniques, and theory about all kinds of specialized scientific modeling. Within software development, specific modeling languages and diagram types are used throughout all development phases to express information/knowledge or systems in a structure that is defined by a consistent set of rules. Within this book the use of models, mainly based on UML, are used to support the maintenance and evolution of software systems. This covers meta-models to define or specify language extensions and semantics (e.g., of the UML), models that describe how systems or -parts (i.e., components) can be tested, or even test themselves when reused, and models that demonstrate the structure and semantics of systems that were designed for evolution.

In summary, this book provides an in-depth coverage of important issues, concepts, trends, tools, methodologies, and technology in the field of model evolution and maintenance and is targeted to become a premier reference resource that presents original academic work as well as experience reports from industry. The book therefore supports the installment of successful project organization structures that are based on model-driven development and reuse across projects. It therefore helps to broaden the view from single projects to project organizations. By understanding and applying the knowledge contained within this book, typical risks and failures - as found in many projects - can be avoided.

TARGET AUDIENCE

Model-driven development and reuse has already reached the mass adoption phase of technology transfer and is widely used throughout software industry. This not only has made the topic broad, but also created a constantly growing demand for technology support regarding the evolution and maintenance of software models. Unfortunately, model maintenance is not a simple question of tools and techniques. Its basic principles and concepts have to be known by all involved developers by heart.

This book provides a comprehensive overview to those who are interested in studying and learning in the field of model evolution and maintenance. However, the book is not meant to be a textbook that supports lectures or self-studies for the inexperienced. It is aimed at researchers, project managers, and developers with a sufficient background in model-driven development who want to learn about the current research trends and latest achievements.

In order to transfer as much knowledge as possible, we gave the authors the room to explain and document their research in a larger space and in more detail than workshops, conferences, and even journals allow.

ORGANIZATION OF THE BOOK / VOLUME OVERVIEW

The chapters of this book provide a comprehensive overview on the current state-of-the-art of model evolution and maintenance for the development of software. All chapters provide descriptions of innovative research and, if existing, practical or empirical evidence. As such, the book supports both research and practice. In detail, the book is organized as follows:

- Section 1 gives an overview to the emerging technologies for the evolution and maintenance of software models, which is presented in six chapters. The approaches described include quality-driven development methods, the usage semantics and ontologies, or change impact analysis techniques in order to support MER activities.
- Section 2 presents two techniques for the re-engineering or modernization of software systems using a model-driven approach.
- Section 3 covers the use of testing techniques to improve the quality and development of software models as well as the model-based testing of software systems.
- Section 4 presents two interesting approaches about the deployment of MDA artifacts and the versioning of software models.

CONCLUSION / WHAT WAS LEFT OUT

A book, even of the size of the one you currently hold in your hands is not large enough to cover all aspects of model-driven software development, evolution, and maintenance. We tried to collect the current state of the art in the field of evolution and maintenance of software models, however, much has to be left out and could not be covered.

For more detail, readers may want to refer to additional material that is given by the references of single chapters. Furthermore, the editors ask all interested readers to ask for more information by contacting the authors and/or editors.

Jörg Rech
SAP Research Center Karlsruhe, Germany

Christian Bunse
University of Applied Sciences Stralsund, Germany

Acknowledgment

Our vision for this book was to gather information about methods, techniques, and applications related to all aspects affecting the maintenance, evolution, and reengineering (MER) of software models as well as the long-term management of software models. Additionally, we want to share this information within the community and distribute it across projects and organizational boundaries.

During the course of realizing this vision, we received much support from people who spent a huge amount of effort on the creation and review process of the book. We would like to express our appreciation to all the projects and people involved in researching MER techniques for software models. We are especially grateful to the authors who provided us with deep insights into their projects and related results. This book would not exist without the hard and committed work of the chapter authors. We want to thank them for their contribution to build this book as a community of researchers in a new and interesting area. In addition, thanks go to all who provided constructive and comprehensive reviews.

Finally, we want to thank the team at IGI Global for their continuous support throughout the publication process. Deep appreciation and gratitude is due to Hannah Abelbeck, editorial assistant at IGI Global, who supported us and always ensured that the project was kept on schedule. She never complained even when we missed a deadline or answered late.

Jörg Rech
SAP Research, Germany

Christian Bunse
University of Applied Sciences Stralsund, Germany

Section 1
Maintenance and Evolution of Software Models

Chapter 1
Quality–Driven Software Development for Maintenance

Iwona Dubielewicz
Wroclaw University of Technology, Poland

Bogumila Hnatkowska
Wroclaw University of Technology, Poland

Zbigniew Huzar
Wroclaw University of Technology, Poland

Lech Tuzinkiewicz
Wroclaw University of Technology, Poland

ABSTRACT

Software maintenance is sometimes considered as a special kind of activity that is separated from a software development process. Meanwhile, the opposite is true; maintenance should be taken into account from the beginning of the software development process. Because a model-based software development is the prevailing software development paradigm, the maintainability should be considered within models that arise in software development process. We claim that the quality of the models arising in the software development process has a positive influence on their maintainability: the higher quality of the models, the more effective maintainability activity. The background for our consideration is MDA approach, and the scope of the consideration is limited to perfective maintenance only. The set of so called 6C quality characteristics is assumed to define a quality of MDA-models. Our selection of 6C quality characteristics is justified by the fact that they are related to activities performed on models within the maintenance. To assess MDA-models in the context of the maintainability, we define checklists for the 6C characteristics. These checklists are used for derivation of some measures which are useful in checking to what scope a given characteristics is satisfied. The main advantage of the approach is its independence of the knowledge of future changes of user requirements that trigger perfective maintenance. In the chapter, we demonstrate a simple example of how to assess the quality of PIM-models that are the realization of the CIM-model. Additionally, we discuss how to select, for further development, the best PIM-model from the set of possible solution.

DOI: 10.4018/978-1-61350-438-3.ch001

INTRODUCTION

Software maintenance is an integral part of a software life cycle. It means that software maintenance should not be considered without the context of software life cycle. The consequence is that "the main problem in doing maintenance is that we cannot do maintenance on a system which was not designed for maintenance" (Schneidewind, 1987). So, our basic assumption when dealing with maintenance is manifested by the phrase: *Don't think about software maintenance if you didn't think about it during software development process.*

Nowadays, dominating approaches to software development form the group called Model Development Engineering (MDE). It means that models are considered as basic artifacts elaborated within the software development process. One of the MDE approaches, Model Driven Architecture (MDA), (Kleppe, Warmer & Bast, 2004)) introduces three categories of models: Computer Independent Model (CIM), Platform Independent Model (PIM), and Platform Specific Model (PSM), and proposes the software development as a process of elaboration and transformation of the models according to the schema:

```
CIM → PIM → PSM → Code
```

It means that on the basis of initial CIM model, first PIM and next PSM models are elaborated, and finally PSM model is transformed into Code.

In the chapter, we follow the scheme of MDA. This pattern may be used repeatedly in the life of the software product. The first application of this scheme is associated with the initial development of the software product – with the issue of the first release of a software product. The subsequent application of the same scheme may result from the need of the product maintenance, and is concerned with the issue of a new release of the software product. The scope of subsequent applications of MDA scheme depends on the kind of maintenance.

ISO vocabulary (ISO/IEC 24765, 2009) defines three kinds of maintenance: adaptive, perfective and corrective. In the chapter, we concentrate on perfective maintenance, and we have omitted adaptive and corrective maintenance. The reasons are twofold. First, perfective maintenance covers about 60% of total maintenance costs (Canfora & Cimitile, 2000; Deissenbock, 2009), and is concerned with a change in the problem domain. Second, adaptive maintenance is concerned with the solution domain and corrective maintenance concentrates mainly on modification of code. Additionally, perfective maintenance entails modification of all MDA models, while adaptive maintenance entails modification of PSM model and code, and corrective maintenance entails only modification of code.

The MDA models may be defined in different ways depending on the applied software development methodology. There are many methodologies that are based on the MDA approach (Kleppe, Warmer & Bast, 2004). In the chapter, to define the MDA models we use Quality Driven Software Development (QUAD) methodology (Dubielewicz, Hnatkowska, Huzar & Tuzinkiewicz, 2010). QUAD belongs to the group of Unified Process methodologies. The main reason for QUAD selection is its specificity, i.e. the quality and evaluation models are applied to selected artifacts on each stage of software development. Maintainability is one of the quality characteristics defined in (ISO/IEC 9126-1, 2001), and models are the main artifacts of the developing software. Therefore, maintainability may be assessed in the same way as it has been proposed in QUAD methodology for software quality evaluation. The knowledge of QUAD is not necessary because the required elements are introduced and explained in further presentation.

Maintainability, similarly to other ISO quality characteristics (ISO/IEC 9126-1, 2001), may be considered from external and internal perspective of quality specification.

In general, it is very difficult to specify maintainability from external perspective. In practice, maintainability is usually not considered from external (i.e. contracting user) perspective, when the contract for the first release of a software product is agreed. The client realizes the problem of maintainability when there is a request to modify, usually to extend, the software product, and, in consequence, there is a need to sign a contract for the new release of the software product. In this situation the problem is how to extend the software product at minimum cost. The idea is to find a balance between the extent of changes and the cost of labor of the software developer. In such a context it is difficult to treat the maintainability similarly to other quality characteristics.

A precise specification of maintainability requires knowledge about the future changes of the product, which means that its possible extensions or modifications should be predicted. It explains why maintainability is rarely considered by future users at the stage of software product requirements.

Software developers are in a somewhat better position, because they anticipate a priori that the software product may undergo various modifications. So, they develop a software in such a way that it would be open and flexible to modifications, especially extensions, in a wide range.

Therefore, in the chapter, we concentrate on perfective maintenance from internal (i.e. developer perspective) quality perspective only. One can say that we follow the note from (ISO/IEC 9126-1, 2001, p. 6): "From the perspective of support staff, maintainability can be interpreted as a quality in use for the goal of maintaining the product: the degree to which a product meets needs to maintain the product with effectiveness, efficiency, safety and satisfaction in specific context of use".

We try to do all the best from the internal perspective for high quality of maintainability independently of external maintenance requirements. Our main claim is that the care about maintenance, perfective maintenance in particular, makes us to the care about the high quality of MDA-models, the code in particular.

Our working hypothesis is: the maintainability of MDA-models is measured by the quality of these models; the higher the quality of the MDA-models, the higher the effectiveness and efficiency of their maintainability.

Since the early 70's, it has been a well-known fact that the software quality is strongly related to the software evolution. This relationship was observed as a result of empirical study, and formulated as Lehmann's laws of software evolution. The law refers to the, so-called, e-systems (Koskinen, 2010). E-systems are considered as the systems that are actively used in real-world applications to solve specific domain problems. One of the laws says, that unless rigorously evolved to take into account changes in the operational environment, the quality of an e-type system will fall into a decline (Koskinen, 2010). The law may be interpreted as an appeal for careful, quality-driven software development. Based on our working hypothesis we expect that high quality MDA-models can be expressed in terms of measures for maintainability subcharacteristics, for example ISO measures (ISO/IEC 9126-3, 2003). The main objectives of the chapter are:

- To show that it is possible to take maintainability into consideration within software development process, especially to include the maintainability at the beginning stage of software development process, and;
- To demonstrate how it can be done for selected MDA models.

Because of the chapter size limitation, we discuss quality of PIM-models only. We assume that CIM-models as the initial models must be accepted in the form in which they are defined. Therefore, although possible, quality of CIM-models are not considered here. We discuss in more details how the change of a CIM-model influences the quality of a related PIM-model.

BACKGROUND

Let us remember that according to the various standards (IEEE Std. 1219-1998; ISO/IEC 24765, 2009) and authors of (Canfora & Cimitile, 2000);Pressman, 1992), perfective, adaptive and corrective maintenance are distinguished as three basic kinds of maintenance.

The activities related to these kinds of maintenance are characterized as follows (Deissenbock, 2009). Perfective maintenance activities change existing functionality or add new functionality to a software product. This type of maintenance is triggered from the problem domain, e.g. by changes to business processes or new user requests. With respect to the total maintenance costs this type of maintenance typically accounts for about 60% of the overall maintenance efforts.

Adaptive maintenance activities adapt a software to a changing environment. This type of maintenance is triggered from the solution domain, e. g. by changes to base technology like operating systems or changes to third party software systems. This type of maintenance is usually reported to account for about 20% of the maintenance efforts.

Corrective maintenance activities correct faults in a software product. This type of maintenance is triggered neither from the problem nor the solution domain but by defects in the product itself. This type of maintenance is usually reported to account for about 17% of the maintenance efforts. While efforts for adaptive and corrective maintenance are both close to 20%, most studies agree that more effort is spent on adaptive than on corrective maintenance.

Apart from corrective, adaptive, and perfective maintenance, sometimes preventive maintenance is considered (Agarwal, 2005; Deissenbock, 2009; Erdil et al., 2003). Preventive maintenance activities prepare a software product for prospective changes. This type of maintenance has no explicit trigger but is performed to enhance the efficiency of future maintenance tasks. Examples are restructuring (refactoring), consolidation or re-documentation. Currently, most organizations hardly perform any preventive maintenance. So, the efforts for this type of maintenance are often not reported. If they are, they typically account for about 4%.

The scope of maintenance activities, apart from preventive maintenance (which may be carried on each stage of software development), is described below on the background of MDA model. The scope of corrective maintenance is limited to the code, the scope of adaptive maintenance spreads throughout PSM, and code, while the scope of perfective maintenance, additionally to PSM and code, includes PIM.

Moreover, we have observed that classic MDA schema may be used repeatedly which leads to the proposal of the following cycle of software development and maintenance as well:

$$CIM_0 \rightarrow PIM_0 \rightarrow PSM_0 \rightarrow Code_0 \qquad (0)$$
$$CIM_1 \rightarrow PIM_1 \rightarrow PSM_1 \rightarrow Code_1 \qquad (1)$$
$$\dots\dots\dots\dots\dots\dots\dots\dots\dots\dots \qquad \dots$$
$$CIM_n \rightarrow PIM_n \rightarrow PSM_n \rightarrow Code_n \qquad (n)$$
$$\dots\dots\dots\dots\dots\dots\dots\dots\dots\dots \qquad \dots$$

This cycle consists of sub-cycles. The first one is the classic MDA software development cycle and it will be called software development sub-cycle. The subsequent sub-cycles will be called maintenance sub-cycles. The maintenance sub-cycle is similar to MDA development cycle except that there are extra constraints resulting from existing models and software product elaborated in its previous sub-cycle. The similarity between the development and maintenance processes is also noticed by (Agarwal, 2005; Erdil et al., 2003).

During exploitation of the software product, released after software development (initial) sub-cycle, new user needs may appear. The needs are the main reason for perfective maintenance, and they lead to new user requirements. User requirements are basic components of CIM model. So, the initial CIM_0 model should be replaced by CIM_1 model. CIM_1 is a modification of CIM_0 model, mostly CIM_1 is the extension of CIM_0 model. Now, having artifacts elaborated in the development sub-cycle PIM_0, PSM_0, and $Code_0$, and new CIM_1 model, we have to develop effectively PIM_1, PSM_1, and finally $Code_1$. In other words, we are faced with initiation of the maintenance sub-cycle. This sub-cycle completes with a new release of the developed software product. Next, the new release of the software product is exploited, and after that the described proceeding may repeat again and again.

During a software development within each of the sub-cycles, the problem is how to anticipate and take into account possible future changes of user requirements. Unfortunately, there is no general solution to the problem. So, instead of trying to solve this problem, we formulate the postulate: let us try to build MDA models that have the highest maintainability from the perspective of the software developer. The postulate means that:

- We consider maintainability problem from the software developer perspective, i.e., in the terms of ISO standard (ISO/IEC 9126-1, 2001), from the internal perspective, and
- T knowledge of future changes of client's requirements is not needed, and, in this sense, our considerations will be independent from these changes.

Now, two questions arise: how to define the maintainability for MDA-model, and how to assess this quality. According to the definition of quality models given in ISO (ISO/IEC 9126-1, 2001), we have to define quality characteristics. Additionally, to enable quantitative interpretation of the characteristics, we have to assign some measures to them. Measures are functions defined over the values of measurable models' attributes that yield results from some, usually numerical, sets.

As MDA-models play the role of intermediate artifact in the process of software product development they may be assessed from the ISO internal quality perspective. Beside this perspective, ISO defines two other perspectives for quality evaluation: quality in use and external perspectives. The maintainability is one of six quality characteristics defined for the internal and external perspectives. It would suggest that ISO quality model might be a good basis for our considerations. But it is not because the quality models representing different perspectives are strongly interrelated. The external quality model should be derived from the quality in use model while the internal quality model should take into account the characteristics from the external quality model. This means that we should not abstract from client's demands while our assumption is that the knowledge of future changes of client's requirements is not needed. Therefore, we have decided to define our quality model for maintainability basing on 6C model (Mohagheghi, Dehlen & Neple, 2009) comprising six quality characteristics: correctness, completeness, consistency, comprehension, confinement, changeability.

We claim that MDA-model may be considered as well-maintainable if the MDA-model has high quality in terms of 6C model.

Below, following (Mohagheghi, Dehlen & Neple, 2009) we give definitions of the 6C model together with our comments dealing with the interpretation of the characteristics.

C1-Correctness. Correctness is defined as (Mohagheghi, Dehlen & Neple, 2009, p. 1652):
  (a) "Including right elements and correct relations between them, and including correct statements about the domain;
  (b) Not violating rules and conventions; for example adhering to language syntax (well-formedness or syntactic correctness), style rules, naming guidelines or other rules or conventions."

In our approach, we consider correctness only from free-context syntax and context-sensitive syntax. Additionally, we demand that considered models are instantiable. This demand relates only to the models which consists of classifiers, for example class diagrams. Instantability means that the class diagram has object diagrams as its instances that are finite. Further, we will not devote separate attention to the correctness, since the context-free and context-sensitive correctness are usually checked by tools supporting modeling.

C2-Completeness. "Completeness is defined as having all the necessary information that is relevant and being detailed enough according to the purpose of modeling." (Mohagheghi, Dehlen & Neple, 2009, p. 1653)

The completeness of a target model is checked against the source model. Assuming that source and target models represent the software at different abstraction levels, we expect that:

- For each element in the source model there exists an element in the target model which is its representation (all features of the source model are mapped onto relevant features of target model). For example, for each use-case in CIM model should exist a use-case realization in PIM. This relationship is especially important in change impact analysis.
- Each element in the target model is expected to have a trace to some element(s) of the source model (coverage/traceability relationship). For example, a package in PIM model may be traced to a use-case in CIM model. The traceability relationship allows to check if the target model realizes everything what is expected and only what is expected in the source model (there are no useless elements in the target model).

C3-Consistency. "Consistency is defined as no contradictions in the model (…) It also covers semantic consistency between models; i.e., the same element does not have multiple meanings in different diagrams or

models." (Mohagheghi, Dehlen & Neple, 2009, p. 1653)

According to horizontal and vertical transformations between models (Mens & Vangorp, 2006; Nugroho & Chaudron, 2009), we distinguish horizontal and vertical model consistency. We defined them as:

- Horizontal consistency relates models at the same semantic level. It is understood as the lack of possibility to derive two contradictory statements. For example, let us consider a model consisting of two kinds of diagrams: a class diagram, and a state diagram associated with one of the classes from the class diagram. There is a contradiction if a state triggering call event on the state diagram is not represented by any respective method on the associated class diagram.
- Vertical consistency relates models written at different semantic levels. The relationship between two models may be considered as specification-implementation relationship between the models. The source model, at higher level of abstraction, may be considered as a specification for the target model, at lower level of abstraction. Following this approach, we expect that behavior defined by the source model will be consistent with behavior defined by the target model. Identifying behavior as a scenario, checking of behavior consistency may be reduced to scenario comparison. For example, scenarios generated by use-case realization in PIM model should be consistent to the textual specification of the use-case in CIM model.

C4-Comprehensibility. "Comprehensibility is defined as being understandable by the intended users; either human users or tools."

(Mohagheghi, Dehlen & Neple, 2009, p. 1653)

It takes into consideration aesthetics of diagrams, model simplicity or complexity, using the correct type of diagram for the intended audience.

C5-Confinement. "Confinement is defined as being in agreement with the purpose of modeling and the type of system; such as including relevant diagrams and being at the right abstraction level. A model is a description from which detail has been removed intentionally. A confined model does not have unnecessary information and is not more complex or detailed than necessary." (Mohagheghi, Dehlen & Neple, 2009, p. 1653)

Confinement is strongly dependent on an applied modeling methodology. The models constructed according to the QUAD methodology are guaranteed to be confined.

C6-Changeability. "Changeability is defined as supporting changes or improvements so that models can be changed or evolved rapidly and continuously." (Mohagheghi, Dehlen & Neple, 2009, p. 1653)

We associate changeability with modularity, which is defined as "the degree to which a system or computer program is composed of discrete components such that a change to one component has minimal impact on other components." (ISO/IEC 9126-1, 2001)

It should be emphasized that these definitions are informal, and they reflect only some intensions. Further, for our purposes, they will be interpreted according to the above comments.

In the literature, other approaches to the definitions of model quality characteristics can be encountered (Saeki & Kaiya, 2006; Mohagheghi & Dehlen, 2008; Sourrouille et al., 2009)). For example, Lange's framework for quality of UML models (Lange & Chaudron, 2005) defines quality characteristics organized by a specific purpose (e.g. modification or testing) associated with the context of the use of models: maintenance or development. The set of characteristics associated with development contains: complexity, balance, modularity, communicativeness, and correspondence. The other characteristics like esthetics, the degree of details, consistency, completeness, self-descriptiveness, conciseness, precision are associated with maintenance. Complexity is the only characteristic associated with both maintenance and development processes.

The number of characteristics is numerous, however, it is difficult to say why some of them are associated with only one purpose, e.g. self-descriptiveness is connected only with communication, when, in our opinion, it may also be connected with comprehension or analysis. It should be noted that in our approach, we do not distinguish quality characteristics usefulness from development or maintenance perspective, as we treat maintenance as a kind of software development.

In general, a mapping between some of Lange's framework characteristics and 6C model may be considered. For example: modularity from Lange's framework may be mapped to changeability from 6C model; consistency to consistency; completeness to completeness; communicativeness, esthetics, and self-descriptiveness to comprehension; balance, correspondence, conciseness, and the degree of details to confinement; precision to correctness. The last proposed mapping is not so obvious, as the meaning of precision is a little different than the meaning of correctness.

Having outlined quality characteristics for maintenance, we have to ask how to measure the characteristics and how to interpret the measured values. Although, there are many different measures defined for UML models, e.g. in (Unhelkar, 2005), their usefulness in the context of the selected set of quality characteristics is doubtful.

Most of them focus on model understandability (e.g. Piattini & Genero, 2002) or complexity and indirectly allow to assess model comprehensibility. Some of them consider coupling and cohesion, e.g. Martin's measures (Martin, 2006) and CBO (Chidamber & Kemerer, 1994), and can be used for the changeability assessing.

Our observation is that it is hard to propose valuable universal measures to check completeness, correctness, consistency, and confinement, as the possible measures strongly depend on the artifacts being the output of applied software development process, and their quality attributes. However, it seems reasonable to distinguish the characteristics for which all considered models should gain full quality acceptance.

Assuming the use of 6C model, we propose to divide its characteristics into two groups. The first one is the set of so called 'mandatory characteristics' as we believe that maintenance activities (understanding of a model and its required changes, making changes, and testing changes) should guarantee correctness, completeness and consistency of the evaluated MDA model. The second one is the set of so called 'improving characteristics'. It contains comprehensibility, confinement and changeability characteristics that should be interpreted in the following way: high quality assessment of a MDA model for these characteristics positively influences the quality of the model in the context of maintainability.

The partition of the set of the quality characteristics into two subsets is comparable with (Bobkowska, 2009), where two kinds of quality characteristics have been proposed:

- Characteristics associated with content substance, which have an impact on a solution, i.e. completeness, correctness with respect to goals of the software product, consistency, and be consistent with the vision of the product,
- Characteristics associated with an expression substance, which have an impact on

understanding i.e. understandability, precision, adequate symbols, simplicity, and adequate level of abstraction.

The content has a direct impact on the software product and these criteria can be used in order to predict the quality of software. The expression criteria are indirectly concerned with the product quality, but they indicate for possible problems with understanding by their users and resulting defects.

For the mandatory characteristics, we formulate a set of questions (check list) that should be satisfied by considered MDA models. For the improving characteristics, we assemble well-know measures and adopt them for evaluation of MDA models quality in the context of maintenance. For the improving characteristics, we also define check lists with the intension to use them in derivation of new measures.

QUALITY ASSESSMENT OF PIM MODELS IN THE CONTEXT OF PERFECTIVE MAINTENANCE

Introduction

In the case of model driven development, a quality of models is of crucial importance. Among MDA models, the quality of CIM and PIM seems to have the highest influence on the quality of the final product. As the quality of CIM must be checked by domain experts and this process cannot be automated, we concentrate on the quality of PIM model. PIM models present all important parts of the developed software product (a solution). This solution could be transformed to many platforms if necessary. There are some PIM-PSM transformations defined for specific platforms, for example to EJB, Web applications (e.g. (Kleppe, Warmer & Bast, 2004; UML Profile for Corba, 2008).

The quality of models needs to be assessed. According to (ISO/IEC 24765, 2009) an assessment is "an action of applying specific documented criteria to a specific software module, package or product for the purpose of determining acceptance or release of the software module, package or product". This process "compares quality characteristics with quality requirements in order to evaluate conformity" (Deissenbock, 2009).

Basing on the literature (Bobkowska, 2009; Nugroho & Chaudron, 2009) the following contemporary methods in model quality assessment may be distinguished:

1. Quality models for software models,
2. Design measurements (with thresholds),
3. Design inspections with the use of check lists,
4. Modeling conventions,
5. Formal methods,
6. Heuristics.

In our approach we combine the first four methods out of six mentioned above. We claim that high quality of MDA models entails their high quality in the context of maintainability.

As explained previously, we adopted the 6C model for that purpose. We divided the characteristics of the 6C model into two subsets – the mandatory and improving characteristics. In our opinion MDA models must fully satisfy the quality demands represented by the first subset, and should be as good as possible with respect to the second subset of characteristics.

The open question is how to define measures for particular characteristics. According to (Mohagheghi & Dehlen, 2009) existing model measures belong to three categories:

- Size measures,
- Design measures (OO measures), and
- Model-specific measures related to comprehensibility of models.

The examples of size measures are the number of classes or attributes of a model.

The examples of design measures are DIT (Depth of Inheritance Tree), NOC (Number of Children) or CBO (Coupling between object classes). Other measures refer to coupling and cohesion (e.g. Martin's measures (Martin, 2006; Chidamber & Kemerer, 1994), and therefore may be used for assessing changeability.

The examples of comprehensibility measures are the number of crossing associations or the number of relationships between classes and interfaces in the package. The latter measure is a typical size measure, however, at the same time it could be considered a complexity measure which influences comprehensibility of models (Esperanza, Cruz-Lemus, Genero & Piattini, 2009). Unfortunately, there are no commonly accepted threshold values for the measures that might be used to classify models either as "good" or "bad".

The measures mentioned above fit the set of improving characteristics. Unfortunately, the existing measures do not fit the first subset of quality characteristics. Analysis of meaning of these characteristics leads to difficult logical problems, and therefore one cannot expect that by calculating the value of some measures it is possible to decide on the MDA models' correctness, complexity or consistency. Of course, likewise to (ISO/IEC 9126-3, 2003), based on characteristics' definitions given in the previous Section, we can propose a measure for completeness as A/B, where A is the number of elements in a source model that do not have their representation in a target model, and B is the number of all elements in a source model. But in our opinion, the usefulness of such defined measure is low, especially in the case when the models are complex and consist of many views (diagrams), because of numerous relationships to be checked.

So, instead of trying to find such measures, it seems to be more reasonable to formulate some check lists for which negative answers will disqualify the quality of a model. Check lists for MDA models play the same role as test cases play for programs: they can falsify a model but not verify the model against given characteristics.

Check lists are very popular, and their application is a commonly accepted method of verifying quality of models (Deissenbock, 2009; Bobkowska, 2009; Chaudron, Gelhausen, Landhäußer & Körner, 2009). They can be adjusted to a specific kind of models being the output from a selected software development methodology. This way, we are able to check the desired features of a model, knowing from what type of elements it is built. In this case check lists are used for checking the obligatory demands, and all questions from the list must be answered 'Yes' to assume that the model is complete, correct, and consistent.

The check lists may also be used for checking PIM models against the second subset of quality characteristics, i.e. comprehensibility, confinement, and changeability. For example, some questions in check lists may address the problem of modeling conventions. However, in our approach they play an auxiliary role of a *Question* element in *Goal Question* approach (Basili, Caldiera & Rombach, 1994). This approach was defined in IEEE's Standard for a Software Quality s Methodology, (IEEE Std 1061™1998 (R2004)): "The GQM paradigm is a mechanism for defining and evaluating a set of operational goals, using measurement. The goals are defined in an operational, tractable way by refining them into a set of quantifiable questions that are used to extract the appropriate information from the models. The questions and models, in turn, define a specific set of metrics and data for collection and provide a framework for interpretation." The check lists serve as a base for definition of measures that better fit to check the extent to which a particular quality characteristics is satisfied by the PIM model. On the base of these measures we are able to assess the model quality, and what is more important, basing on the results of assessment functions we can compare its quality with the quality of another model, for example its alternative version.

CIM and PIM Models in QUAD Methodology

The PIM model in QUAD methodology consists of the following named elements visualized by respective UML diagrams:

- Software architecture model visualized by a package diagram,
- Conceptual data model visualized by a class diagram,
- Use-case realization model visualized by a class diagram and a set of sequence diagrams,
- Object life cycle of selected classes visualized by a state diagram.

The quality of a PIM model is assessed in the context of a CIM model. The CIM model is built according to QUAD methodology, and consists of the following elements:

- Definition of business rules that are organized according to von Halle classification (Halle, 2002) into terms, facts, and rules (constraints, action enablers, derivations, derivations including inferences and computations),
- Software requirement specification consisting of:
  - Use-case model visualized by a use-case diagram,
  - Use-case specification expressed by textual description presenting actor-system collaborations, and
  - Non-functional requirement specification expressed in natural language.

PIM Quality Evaluation Model

Correctness, Completeness and Consistency: Checklists

For each mandatory quality characteristics we define a check list containing questions grouped

Table 1. Check lists for PIM model

Characteristic	Artifact	Question
Correctness	Architecture model	1. Does the software architecture is defined according to any architecture pattern?
	Data Conceptual model	2. Is it possible to instantiate a data model for all non-abstract classes? 3. Does each class have some attributes defined? 4. Does each relationship between classes represented in only one way (either as an association or as an attribute)?
	Use Case Realization	5. Does the communication between objects meet assumed conventions (BCE pattern)? For example, do the instances of actors communicate to the system by objects of boundary classes?
	State Machine	6. Is state machine deterministic? 7. Are all states of state machine reachable?
Completeness	Architecture	8. Does each packet have a relevant CIM element which the package is traceable to?
	Conceptual Data Model	9. Does each class is traceable to a term (notion) in business rules of the CIM model? 10. Does each relationship is traceable from facts in business rules of the CIM model?
	Use Case Realization	11. Does each use-case from the CIM model have its representation as a use-case realization in the PIM model? 12. Does each interaction use-case realization is represented by at least one class diagram, and one sequence diagram? 13. Does each use-case realization involve all classes needed for use-case purpose?
	State Machine	14. Does it exist – for each transition – a use-case scenario that triggers it?
Consistency	Architecture	15. Is the architecture model consistent with the applied decomposition strategy to architecture definition, for example, a decomposition strategy based on actors, on use cases, business entities? 16. Do the dependence relationships between packages result from the existing relationships between classes in the class model?
	Conceptual Data Model	17. Does each class is traceable to a term (notion) in business rules of the CIM model? 18. Does each relationship is traceable from facts in business rules of the CIM model? 19. Does each multiplicity is traceable from constraints in business rules of the CIM model? 20. Is each class used at least in one use-case realization?
	Use Case Realization	21. Are all objects used in use-case realizations instances of classes from the class diagram (of the use-case realization)? 22. Does a sequence diagram (the sequence diagrams) realize the behavior presented in a use-case specification?
	State Machine	23. Does each state machine determine the behavior of a class from any of class diagrams? 24. Does each call event have its representation as the method in the class for which the diagram is shown?

according to the elements of the PIM model. Table 1 presents all of them.

Checklist development was conducted as systematic procedures based on qualitative research methodology. The checklists were elaborated following the five major steps:

1. A literature survey to identify existing checklists for UML models.
2. Merging all found checklist items into one list for one type of UML model (e.g. analysis model, design model).
3. Classification and refinement of checklist items according to characteristics of 6C model.
4. Checklist extension according to the author's own experiences.
5. Validation of the checklists in a BSc. student course.
6. Checklists update after validation.

The literature survey (step 1) resulted in the set of checklists proposed in e.g. (Martin, 2006; Unhelkar, 2005). The merged list of checklists (step

2) comprised more than 200 items. Each item was classified by two authors independently with respect to quality characteristics and was either connected with only one characteristic or removed from further consideration. Examples of checklist questions that the authors consider not to be useful (too general, too specific or checking first of all the syntax correctness) are as follows: "If the class is abstract, is it represented by its name shown in italics?", "Are notes added to clarify diagrams?" (Unhelkar, 2005) "Where several diagrams illustrate the use-case realization, the role of each is clear, and the diagrams are consistent with one another in their presentation of common behavior", "The analysis class name is unique", "The class's brief description captures the purpose of the class and briefly summarizes its responsibilities" (Rational Unified Process), "The derived class never needs to transmute to be an object in some other class" (Coad,1998).

Authors had also proposed – based on their own experiences – their own checklist questions (step 4). This step resulted in 36 items, 7 checklist's items for the correctness, 7 for completeness, 8 for consistency, 9 for comprehensibility, 3 for changeability, and 2 for confinement. Within each characteristic, the checklist items are distributed over 4 categories; each category is determined by one analysis model element (in the paper we show checklist for 4 elements i.e. conceptual data model described by UML class diagram, architecture defined by package diagram, use case realization described by class and sequence diagrams, class behavior expressed by a state machine diagram). The checklist was validated (step 5) in a BSc. student course, where 28 students applied the checklist in their software development after analysis phase. Each student reported which checklist items they found to be useful, and which ones they had trouble to understand. What's more, the authors of the checklist analyzed the answers given by the students for the checklists according to their accuracy. A major finding from the validation was that the first version of

the checklist was generally well-defined, some of items needed a small redefinition to gain a better understanding (step 6).

Comprehensibility, Confinement, Changeability: Measures and Assessment Functions

We follow *Goal Question Measure* approach (Basili, Caldiera & Rombach, 1994) to propose usable measures for model quality assessment. A quality characteristics is understood here as a *Goal* we want to achieve, and a check list question serves for a measure proposal. However, our assumption is that the measures should be fully controllable by developers. We want to have measures that are not only indicators of something (as most size and complexity measures defined for UML diagrams (Unhelkar, 2005), but which values could be directly interpreted, and on the base of this interpretation the measured model may be rebuilt. All introduced measures – see Table 2 – have the same normalized range of values from 0 to 1, where 1 means that the quality attribute is fully satisfied, and 0 means that it is not satisfied at all. The developers can change the measure values by improving (refactoring) the models.

The similar approach to measure selection is presented in (Voigt, Güldali & Engels, 2008). In this paper the authors presented how to obtain some useful measures for checking quality of state diagram. We adopted one measure from their work (i.e. meaningful state names).

A specific consideration must be given to changeability characteristics, as the definition proposed by (Mohagheghi, Dehlen & Neple, 2009) is far different from those proposed for example by ISO (ISO/IEC 9126-3, 2003), or SWEBOK (Guide to the Software Engineering Body of Knowledge (SWEBOK, 2004). In the latter documents changeability is defined as an effort associated with implementing a specified modification. So, to measure this effort we need to know a modification upfront. The problem is,

Table 2. Check lists, quality attributes and measures for PIM model artifacts

Char.	Artifact	Question	Quality Attribute	Measure
Comprehensibility	Architecture	1. Do all packages contain at least N elements?	Proper granularity of packages	M1 = A/B A – the number of packages containing at least N*) elements B – the number of all packages
		2. Is the package nesting level less than a given N?		M2 = 1 – when the nesting level is less than N*) 0 – otherwise
	Conceptual Data Model	3. Does each class name is a noun and start with a capital letter?	Proper naming conventions	M3 = A/B
		4. Does each attribute name is a noun and start with a small letter?		M4 = A/B A – number of classes/attributes following the naming convention B – number of all classes/attributes
		5. Are there no synonyms in the set of attributes of all classes (in the dictionary of attributes)?	Avoid misunderstandings	M5 = 1-A/B
		6. Are there no homonyms there is in the set of attributes of all classes (in the dictionary of attributes)?		M6 = 1-A/B A – the number of synonyms/homonyms in the dictionary of attributes B – the number of all attributes
	Use Case Realization	7. Does a sequence diagram model exactly one flow of events?	Avoid cognitive overloading	M7 =1/A A – the number of scenarios in a diagram
	State Machine	8. Do arcs not cross the boundary of states?	Proper transition modeling	M8 = 1-A/B A – the number of crossing transitions B – the number of all transitions
		9. Are the name of states meaningful?	Meaningful state names	M9 = A/B A – the number of states with meaningful name B – the number of all states

continued on following page

Table 2. Continued

	Architecture			M10 = 1
Confinement	Conceptual Data Model	10. Does the conceptual data model present only static properties, i.e. attributes, associations, compositions, aggregations, and generalizations?	Proper level of details	M11 = A/B A – the number of classes for which only static properties were presented B – the number of all classes on the diagram
	Use Case Realization	11. Is specification of messages synchronization omitted?	Proper level of details	M12 = A/B A – the number of messages for which the synchronization details are left unspecified B – the number of all messages on the diagrams
	State Machine			M13 = 1
Changeability	Architecture	12. Are there no cyclic dependencies between packages?	Acyclic dependency principle (Martin, 2006)	M14 = A/B A – the number of packages without cycles B – the number of all packages
		13. Do the packages dependencies support maintainability?	Stable dependency principle (Martin, 2006)	M15 = 1 - A/B A – the number of packages that breaks the Stable Dependency Principle (for which there exist dependencies leading from less stable to more stable packages, $I_1 \geq I_2$, the *I* measure from (Martin, 2006)) B – the number of all dependencies between packages
		14. Are packages as abstract as stable?	Stable abstraction principle (Martin, 2006)	M16 = A/B A – the number of packages which distance D from the main sequence (the measure defined in (Martin, R. C., 2006)) is less than a given N*); packages that belong to so called pain zone (Martin, 2006), are excluded from calculations B – the number of all packages
	Conceptual Data Model	None		M17 = 1
	Use Case Realization	None		M18 = 1
	State Machine	None		M19 = 1

that according to the definition presented in (Mohagheghi, Dehlen & Neple, 2009) and adopted by us, we need to measure the easiness of modification of an artifact without any knowledge of a planned change. This is a very difficult problem, and by now, we found only a few measures that can be applied to software architecture, and could help us in measuring changeability. For the rest of artifacts of a PIM-model for which changeability measures are not defined (and similarly for other quality characteristics), we decided to assign them the dummy measure with value 1, which means that these characteristics do not influence the overall quality of the artifact.

On the basis of the above proposed measures we are able to define different derived measures for artifact/model evaluation.

The formula for evaluating a specific artifact against specific characteristics:

Quality (characteristics, artifact)=

$$\frac{\sum_{i=1}^{n} measure_i^{characteristics}}{n} \quad (1)$$

where n is the number of measures for the selected characteristics.

The formula for evaluating specific artifact against three quality characteristics:

$$FinalQuality\left(artefact\right) = \sum_{c \in \{Confinement, Comprehensibility, Changeability\}} \frac{Quality\left(c, artefact\right)}{3} \quad (2)$$

The formula for evaluating the whole PIM model:

Final Quality(PIM)=

$$\sum_{artefact \in PIM}^{n} FinalQuality(artefact) / n \quad (3)$$

where n is the number of artifacts which constitute the PIM model.

Moreover, for a specific project, depending on some additional features, e.g. size, number of people involved, etc. we can define the minimal acceptance level for particular characteristics, e.g.

Quality(confinement, any) =
Quality(comprehensibility, any) =
Quality(changeability, any) = 0.8

where *any* means any artifact.

What is more important, we can easily define relative assessment functions, that allow us to compare quality of two different artifacts of the same type.

Final Compare (*art*1, *art*2) = Final Quality (*art*1) – Final Quality (*art*2) (4)

Eventually, we may compare entire PIM-models:

Final Compare(*PIM*1, *PIM*2) = Final Compare (*PIM*1) – Final Compare (*PIM*2) (5)

Having measures for particular artifacts, we are able to evaluate, and finally to assess both components of the PIM models, and the PIM models themselves, according to the Formulas (1) – (5).

EXAMPLE

Outline

To show how to develop models with maintenance in mind we have prepared a simple example. This example involves two sub-cycles (see previous section): software development sub-cycle, and maintenance sub-cycle. For the sake of simplicity the development sub-cycle delivers a software product with only few functionalities. The artifacts

Table 3.

Use-case name:	*<Entity> Management*
Template parameter:	*<Entity>*, *<entity data>*
Short description:	The use-case enables to add, modify, delete *<entities>*
Main scenario:	1. Actor wants to do something with an *<entity>* 2. System displays *<entity data>* for all entities (allows to filter and/or sort them) 3. An actor decides what to do (add, modify, delete)
Add scenario	
Pre-conditions:	Actor is authorized
Post-conditions:	An *<entity>* is added to a system
Main *Add* scenario:	1. Actor wants to add an *<entity>* 2. System asks for *<entity data>* 3. Actor delivers *<entity data>* 4. System validates *<entity data>* (see business rules) 5. System registers the *<entity>* Back to step 2 of the *Main* scenario
Delete scenario	
Pre-condition:	Actor is authorized
Post-condition:	An *<entity>* is deleted from a system
Main *Delete* scenario	1. Actor selects an *<entity>* to be deleted 2. System verifies that the deletion is possible (see business rules) 3. System deletes the selected *<entity>* and informs about it Back to step 2 of *Main* scenario
Modify scenario	
Pre-condition:	None
Post-condition:	An *<entity data>* are modified
Main *Modify* scenario	1. Actor selects an *<entity>* to be modified 2. System enables the *<entity data>* to be modified 3. Actor modifies the *<entity data>* 4. System verifies that the *<entity data>* are valid (see business rules) and remembers them Back to step 2 of *Main* scenario

Table 4.

Use-case name:	*Course Enrollment*
Short description:	The use-case enables a student to enroll in a course
Pre-conditions:	Actor is authorized
Post-conditions:	A student is enrolled in a course
Main scenario	1. Student wants to enroll in a course 2. System displays information about these courses, which the student previously was not enrolled in 3. Student selects interesting courses and ask for enrolling 4. System enrolls the student in the selected courses

elaborated during this sub-cycle are assessed with the use of pre-defined quality evaluation model – the assessment is limited to two artifacts, i.e. conceptual data model, and software architecture.

One extension to software functionality is defined in maintenance sub-cycle. The example shows how to use assessment functions to: (a) select better from alternative solutions, (b) manage the

Figure 1. PIM conceptual data model, development sub-cycle: (a) version 1, (b) version 2

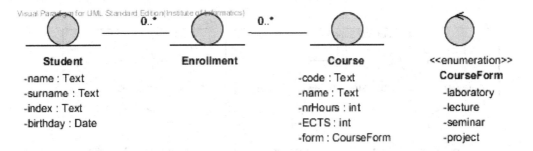

development process (the software model being the output of maintenance cycle shouldn't be worse than the original one).

The intended software product is used at the university. Its main functionality is to enable students to enroll in courses which are offered by the university. Of course, the main functionality must be supported by some administrative ones serving to register the students and the courses.

Development of Sub-Cycle

CIM Definition

CIM presentation is limited to business rules definition, and part of software requirement specification which has the crucial impact on PIM model, i.e.: use-case model, and use-case specifications.

Business Rules Definition

Terms:
- ◦ Course: the number of lectures or other matter dealing with a subject described by: code, name, number of hours, form, ECTS points.
- ◦ Student: a person who studies something described by: index, name, surname, birthday.

Facts:
- ◦ Enrollment – a student enrolls in a course.

Constraints:
- ◦ Context Course:
  - ▪ A code is unique,
  - ▪ All fields are obligatory,
  - ▪ A form is one of {lecture, seminar, laboratory, project},
  - ▪ A course can have many students enrolled
  - ▪ A course can be deleted only when no students are enrolled to it.
- • Context Student:
  - ◦ An index is unique,
  - ◦ All fields are obligatory,
  - ◦ A student can be enrolled in many courses,
  - ◦ A student can enrolled to a course only once.

Action enablers: none
Derivations: none

Use-Case Model

At the beginning only two actors were identified: *Administrator* and *Student*. *Administrator* has two use-cases assigned: *Course Management*, and *Student Management*, while *Student* – has only one use case assigned: *Course Enrollment*.

Figure 2. PIM software architecture (version 1): development sub-cycle

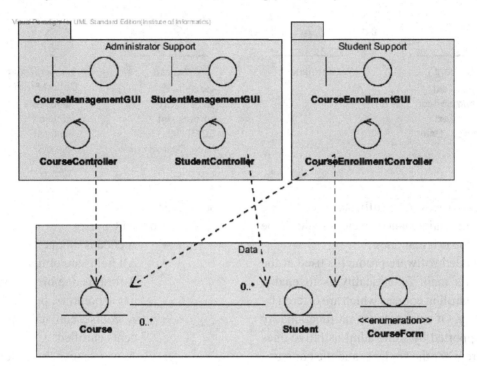

Figure 3. PIM software architecture (version 2): development sub-cycle

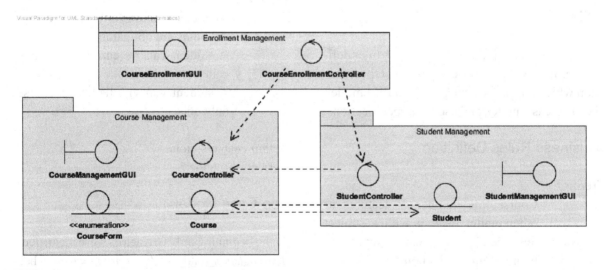

Use-Case Specifications

As the *Course Management*, and the *Student Management* are typical CRUD (Create, Retrieve, Update, Delete) use-cases, their description will be presented as one parameterized use-case *Entity Management*. The *Entity Management* use-case description involves many scenarios – each for a specific operation (C, R, U, D). (Table 3.)

Table 4 shows there is a specification of the *Course Enrollment* use-case.

PIM Definition

Conceptual Data Model and its Assessment Against Mandatory Characteristics

Based on business rules and having the textual specification of use-cases we are ready to propose a conceptual data model, being a part of PIM.

The first attempt resulted in a class diagram is presented in Figure 1 (a).

The conceptual data model should first of all be checked against all mandatory characteristics, i.e. correctness, completeness, and consistency. It must fully satisfy them to be regarded further.

The diagram is syntactically correct. Let us examine now its completeness. We check if all elements in the conceptual data model can be traced from selected type of elements from the CIM model (check list questions 9-10) – the answer is *No*, as the *Enrollment* class is not traced from the term description. To sum up, the class diagram from Figure 1 (a) is not a proper model of domain and must be replaced with any correct diagram.

The second attempt resulted in the diagram presented in Figure 1 (b).

In this new proposed diagram the *Enrollment* class was eliminated, which resulted in the better quality diagram (all questions from the check list for the conceptual data model are answered *Yes*). This diagram can be assessed against the rest of quality characteristics.

Software Architecture and its Assessment Against Mandatory Characteristics

Software architecture at PIM level is usually presented as a package diagram. We start with two alternative solutions presented on Figure 2, and Figure 3, each of which will be assessed with our measures.

The architecture presented in Figure 2 is a typical two layer architecture. Application layer

packages are traced from actors. All entities are gathered in *Data* package. Control and view classes (Guideline: Boundary Control Entity Pattern) are gathered in the upper layer packages.

The architecture satisfies all evaluation questions from the check lists.

In the Figure 3, we have one layer architecture in which the packages are traced from the use-cases. They gather all kinds of functionally related classes, i.e. view, control and entity classes. The assumption is that a control class in package A to access entities from the package B needs to communicate with the control class in B. The architecture contains one cycle, resulting from bidirectional association between *Course* and *Student* classes. All questions from the check list considering software architecture are answered *Yes*.

Remark: All the dependencies between the classes at the diagrams are presented in order to enable the supporting tool to execute accurate calculations.

PIM Assessment

Conceptual Data Model Measurement

Table 5 presents the measures of conceptual data model. All of them have the highest values, so at that moment, there is nothing to be corrected.

The measures were taken from SDs V2.2 tool – Demo version (SDMetrics). The tool accepts as

Table 5.

Characteristics	Measure	A	B	Value
Comprehensibility	M3	2	2	1
	M4	9	9	1
	M5	0	9	1
	M6	0	9	1
Confinement	M11	2	2	1
Changeability	M17	-	-	1

Table 6.

Characteristics	Version 1				Version 2			
	Measure	A	B	Value	Measure	A	B	Value
Comprehensibility	M1 (N=2)	3	3	1.00	M1 (N=2)	3	3	1.00
	M2 (N=3)	3	3	1.00	M2 (N=3)	3	3	1.00
Confinement	M10	-	-	1.00	M10	-	-	1.00
Changeability	M14	3	3	1.00	M14	2	3	0.66
	M15	0	3	1.00	M15	1	3	1.00
	M16 (D=0.2)	2	2	1.00	M16 (D=0.2)	1	3	0.33

Figure 4. Basic measures for software architectures taken with SDs tool

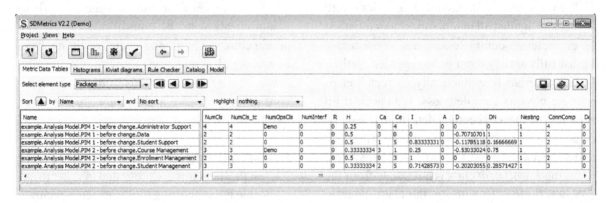

an input a UML model in the XMI format (for UML 2). It allows to measure the number of classes in a specific package as well as the number of attributes defined in classes (the <<enumeration>> classes are not taken into consideration). It checks also some naming conventions (e.g. if a class name starts with a small letter, if an attribute name starts with a capital letter). The other checks, especially addressing naming conventions (is each name of a class/an attribute a noun?) were done manually.

Software Architecture Measurement

Table 6 presents the result measures of two alternative versions of the software architecture. Three measures (M1, M2, and M16) need to be parameterized with specific N. The proposed values of *N* are:

- For M1 according to (Unhelkar, 2005) the recommended minimal number of classes within a package is equal to 3. However in a very early stage of development, the number of classes may be decreased, in the considered example, we assume $N = 2$.
- For M2, $N = 3$; this value is recommended by (Unhelkar, 2005)
- For M16, $N = 0.2$; this value is agreed to Pareto rule

The basic values for calculating M1, M2, M15 and M16 of alternative versions of the software architectures were taken with SDs tool – see Figure 4. The *Data* package (version 1) was agreed to belong to the pain zone (Martin, 2006), so it is why it is excluded from M16 calculation. It contains stable elements – data definitions and relationships between them and at the same time it does not include any abstract classes. Its distance from the main sequence (Martin, 2006) is maximal and equals 1 (see Figure 4).

The very useful mechanism for assessing the changeability characteristics for software architecture is rule checker available in the tool. It shows cyclic dependencies between packages as well as violations of Stable Dependencies Principle (Martin, 2006). The mechanism delivers data for calculating M14 and M15 measures.

Remarks

Let *cdm* be the abbreviation for conceptual data model, *sa_v1* the abbreviation for software architecture – version 1 (see the Figure 2), and *sa_v2* – the abbreviation for software architecture – version 2 (see the Figure 3). The evaluation of the artifacts quality is presented below:

Quality(confinement, cdm) =
Quality(comprehensibility, cdm) =

Quality(changeability, cdm) = 1 (application of the formula (1) for evaluating *cdm*)

FinalQuality(cdm) = 1 (application of the formula (2) for evaluating *cdm*)

The quality of conceptual data model is very high. At the moment nothing can be done.

Quality(comprehensibility, sa_v1) = 1 (application of the formula (1) for evaluating *sa_v1*)

Quality(confinement, sa_v1) = 1

Quality(changeability, sa_v1) = 1

FinalQuality(sa_v1) = 1 (application of the formula (2) for evaluating *sa_v1*)

The quality of the software architecture – version 1 meets all requirements. So, it is fully acceptable.

Quality(comprehensibility, sa_v2) = 1 (application of the formula (1) for evaluating *sa_v2*)

Quality(confinement, sa_v2) = 1

Quality(changeability, sa_v2) = 0.66

FinalQuality(sa_v2) = 0.89 (application of the formula (2) for evaluating *sa_v2*)

FinalCompare(sa_v1, sa_v2) = 1.00 – 0.89 = 0.11

(application of the formula (4) for comparing two versions of software architecture)

The software architecture – version 2 has lower quality than the version 1 (0.89 versus 1.00 what gives the difference 0.11), and it does not satisfy the requirements, especially against changeability demands. Therefore, it should be rejected from further development or refactor to obtain better marks. However, we decided to consider both versions to illustrate the consequences of selection of improper solution at this stage of software development.

Let us now consider the final quality of *PIM_v1*, and *PIM_v2* models. The models have the same conceptual data model, and different versions of the software architecture.

FinalQuality(PIM_v1) = (1 + 1)/2 = 1.00 (application of the formula (3) for evaluating *PIM_v1*)

FinalQuality(PIM_v2) = (1 + 0.89)/2 = 0.95 (application of the formula (3) for evaluating *PIM_v2*)

FinalCompare(PIM_v1, PIM_v2) = 1.00 – 0.95 = 0.05

(application of the formula (5) for comparing *PIM_v1* with *PIM_v2*)

Table 7.

Use-case name:	*History*
Short description:	The use-case enables a student to read the names of courses he/she is actually enrolled in as well as the names of courses together with final marks he/she has finished.
Pre-conditions:	Actor is authorized
Post-conditions:	None
Main scenario:	1. Student wants to see the names of all courses he/she is enrolled in or has been enrolled in 2. System displays the name of courses with the final mark (if it is available)
Use-case name:	*Giving Marks*
Short description:	The use-case enables a teacher to add/modify a final mark of a student who is enrolled in the course the teacher provides
Pre-conditions:	Actor is authorized
Post-conditions:	A final mark for a student from a specific course is stored
Main scenario:	1. Teacher wants to assign final marks 2. System displays information about all the teacher's courses 3. Teacher selects a specific course 4. System displays information about students enrolled in the course (see business rules) together with their final marks (if available) 5. Teacher registers/modifies final marks for selected students

Figure 5. PIM conceptual data model: maintenance sub-cycle

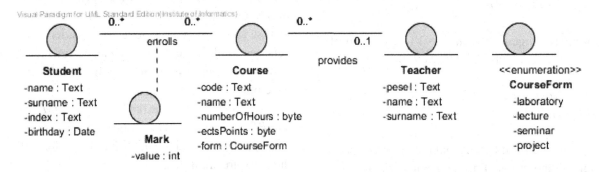

The final quality of *PIM_v*1 is better by 0.05 than the final quality of *PIM_v*2. It is a consequence of lower quality of software architecture component of *PIM_v*2.

MAINTENANCE SUB-CYCLE

CIM Definition

Our CIM model is extended with one new demand. We want to allow the teachers to assess students (to put final marks for them). Students should have the possibility to read the marks.

Business Rules

Business Rules – the presentation is limited to new elements only.

Terms:

- Mark: a value representing the assessment given to a student by a teacher in a course,

Figure 6. PIM software architecture (version 1): maintenance sub-cycle

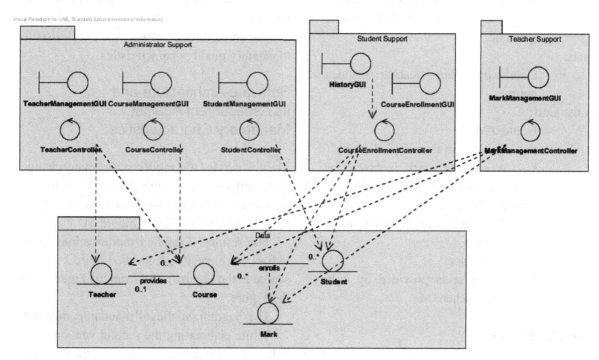

Figure 7. PIM software architecture (version 2): maintenance sub-cycle

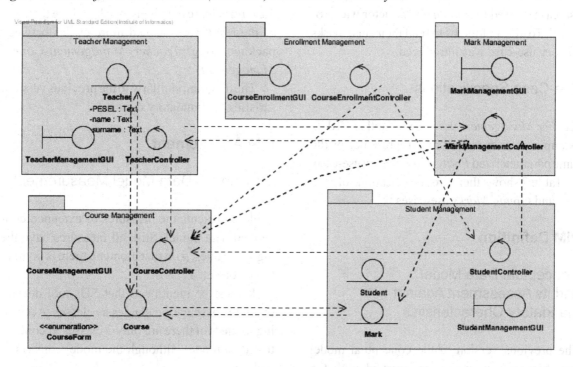

◦ Teacher: a person providing courses; described by: PESEL, name, surname.

Facts:

◦ Course providing – teacher provides courses.

Constraints:

◦ Context Mark:
  ▪ Value from the set {2, 3, 4, 5},
  ▪ A separate mark is given for each Student-Course pair.
◦ Context Teacher:
  ▪ A teacher can provide many courses.
◦ Context Course:
  ▪ A course is provided by only one teacher.

Use-Case Model

The extended version of the use-case diagram is described below. A new actor – *Lecturer* – has to be introduced together with *Giving Marks* use-case. To manage teachers data *Teacher Management* use-case offered to *Administrator* actor was proposed. To allow students to read their final marks *History* use-case was introduced.

Use-Case Specifications

Teacher Management use-case is another CRUD example, so its specification is represented by the same parameterized *Entity Management* use-case.

Table 7 shows there are specifications of *History* and *Giving Marks* use-cases.

PIM Definition

Conceptual Data Model and its Assessment Against Mandatory Characteristics

The previous version of the conceptual model (see Figure 1(a)) was supplemented with the *Teacher* class, and the *Mark* association-class – see Figure 5.

The changes don't violate the check lists for mandatory quality characteristics.

Software Architecture and its Assessment Against Mandatory Characteristics

The changes in CIM model caused many changes in the software architecture. We consider them for both previously presented versions of package diagram (see Figure 2 and Figure 3).

The results of applied modifications to the software architecture from the Figure 2 are presented in the Figure 6, and from the Figure 3 – in the Figure 7.

The diagram satisfies all mandatory demands.

While elaborating the second version of the software architecture, we encounter the following problem – where to place the *Teacher* class and the *Mark* class. Being consistent with the previous decisions the classes should be placed in the new packages, *Teacher Management* and *Mark Management* respectively. We had done that, and as the result we obtained more cycles between packages (e.g. *Teacher Management-Course Management*).

The diagram, similarly to the previous version, satisfies all mandatory demands.

PIM Assessment

Conceptual Data Model Measurement

Table 8 presents the measures of extended conceptual data model. Still, all measures have the highest values, so at that moment, there is nothing to be corrected.

It must be mentioned that SDs tool doesn't count the association classes as classes. According to the tool there are only 3 classes in conceptual data model, although the model consists of 4 classes.

Table 8.

Characteristics	Measure	A	B	Value
Comprehensibility	M3	4	4	1
	M4	4	4	1
	M5	0	13	1
	M6	0	13	1
Confinement	M10	4	4	1
Changeability	M16	-	-	1

Software Architecture Measurement

Table 9 presents the measures of extended versions of software architecture, calculated for two alternative versions of it. The *N* for M1 measure is now set to 3 as the development proceeds.

The measures were calculated with the usage of SDs tool.

Similarly to the previous calculations, *Data* package from software architecture (version 1) was agreed to belong to the pain zone and, in consequence, rejected from M16 calculation.

Remarks

Basing on the measures values, we are able to evaluate and assess the quality of the extended PIM models and theirs components. Used abbreviations in the following formulas have the same meaning as those used in *Remarks* of the previous subsection (in the development sub-cycle).

Quality(confinement, cdm) =
Quality(comprehensibility, cdm) =

Quality(changeability, cdm) = 1 (application of the formula (1) for evaluating *cdm*)

FinalQuality(cdm) = 1

The extension has no negative impact on the quality of conceptual data model.

Quality(comprehensibility, sa_v1) = 0.87 (application of the formula (1) for evaluating *sa_v1*)

Quality(confinement, sa_v1) = 1

Quality(changeability, sa_v1) = 1

FinalQuality(sa_v1) = 0.96 (application of the formula (2) for evaluating *sa_v1*)

The software architecture version 1 still meets all requirements. Its comprehensibility is a little worse than before, but we expect, that this will positively change during next maintenance sub-cycles. The expectation is based on the assumption that subsequent sub-cycles bring new classes.

Quality(comprehensibility, sa_v2) = 0.80 (application of the formula (1) for evaluating *sa_v2*)

Quality(confinement, sa_v2) = 1

Table 9.

Characteristics	Version 1				Version 2			
	Measure	A	B	Value	Measure	A	B	Value
Comprehensibility	M1 (N=3)	3	4	0.75	M1 (N=3)	3	5	0.60
	M2 (N=3)	4	4	1.00	M2 (N=3)	5	5	1.00
Confinement	M10	-	-	1.00	M10	-	-	1.00
Changeability	M14	4	4	1	M14	1	5	0.20
	M15	0	4	1	M15	1	5	0.80
	M16 (D=0.2)	3	3	1	M16 (D=0.2)	1	5	0.20

Quality(*changeability*, *sa_v2*) = 0.40

FinalQuality(*sa_v2*) = 0.73 (application of the formula (2) for evaluating *sa_v1*)

FinalCompare(*sa_v1*, *sa_v2*) = 0.96 – 0.73 = 0.23

(application of the formula (4) for comparison of *sa_v1* and *sa_v2*)

The software architecture version 2 still doesn't satisfy changeability demands (0.40 versus 0.66). The comprehensibility is now lower than previously obtained (0.8 versus 1). The overall assessment of software architecture is worse (0.73 versus 0.89).

The difference between the software architecture version 1, and version 2 is now bigger (0.23 versus 0.11).

Let us now make the final comparison of two different versions of PIM models.

FinalQuality(*PIM_v1*) = (1 + 0.96)/2 = 0.98

FinalQuality(*PIM_v2*) = (1 + 0.73)/2 = 0.87

FinalCompare(*PIM_v1*, *PIM_v2*) = 0.98 – 0.87 = 0.11

(application of the formula (5) for comparison of *PIM_v1* and *PIM_v2*)

The quality of *PIM_v1* (extended version) is decreased by 0.02 (0.98 versus 1.00), while the quality of *PIM_v2* (extended version) is decreased by 0.07 (0.87 versus 0.94). The difference in the quality of two considered versions of the PIM-models is greater than previously obtained (0.11 versus 0.05). The result of the comparison is in accordance with our expectation declared by the working hypothesis that low quality of the model at the beginning means worse quality, if the development proceeds.

CONCLUSION

The literature study (Agarwal, R., 2005; Canfora & Cimitile, 2000; Erdil et al., 2003) shows that maintainability is closely related to the software development process regardless of the used methodology. This means that maintainability should be considered at each stage of a software development. Software maintenance is classified as corrective, perfective, and adaptive maintenance. In this chapter we have restricted our discussion to the perfective maintenance which deals with adding new functionality or new non-functional demands to the existing system.

To present our approach to maintainability, we assumed the MDA as the background software development process. The MDA software development process can be perceived through the two activities:

- Modeling at different levels of abstraction, and
- Model transformations.

A final software product is a result of these modeling and transformations activities. So, the quality of the final product, including its maintainability, depends on the quality of preceding models, i.e. CIM, PIM and PSM models. Detailed definition of MDA models depends on specific methodology applied to software development. We have used QUAD methodology which was elaborated for quality-driven software development, and limit our considerations to PIM models only.

There are some proposals for quality of MDA models, but in general, the question, how to define quality of MDA models, is still open. We decided to adopt the so called 6C model. The adaptation led to the division of the characteristics of 6C model into two subsets: mandatory, and improving characteristics.

The first subset contains only the characteristics that are used to express necessary conditions for the maintainability. An artifact may be positively assed if all the answers to the questions from the check list are "Yes". The positive answers mean that the artifact may be considered as:

- Consisting of proper elements and correct relations between them including syntactic and static semantic correctness (*correctness*),
- Representing all the necessary information that is relevant and detailed enough according to the purpose of modeling (*completeness*),
- Not being in contradiction with other artifacts (*consistency*).

The second subset contains the characteristics and associated quality measures that are used to complete quality assessment of the PIM model maintainability. Noteworthy is how the measures for the second subset of characteristics are defined. All the measures take normalized values from the range [0..1]. If the value of the measure increases then the quality of the evaluated model is better. It allows to estimate model quality while taking into account the distance between the value and the boundary values 0 and 1. It also facilitates specifying quality acceptance threshold which can be individually specified for a given artifact by a project implementation team. We also defined assessment functions over the measures. For some of the assessment functions, we defined the threshold value that enable separating "good" from "bad" maintainable MDA-models. However, on the current stage of research it is not possible to give absolute interpretation of the final assessment of a given model.

The proposed quality and evaluation model is a base model than could be refined (especially the measures for *comprehensibility, changeability, confinement*). Its advantage is that it allows quality evaluation of the PIM models abstracting from the future system modifications.

The presented example shows how the quality model could be applied within the proposed approach to the assessment of a simple PIM model in the context of maintainability. It should be noted that the quality model, especially the measures, are very sensitive - it strongly depends on the number of model's elements (for tiny models a given assessment could rapidly change after a small change in the model).

The proposed approach to quality assessment of MDA models seems to be promising. In our opinion the approach is simple and understandable for both experienced as well as novice developers. The approach has been tested for three months by authors and students of the Institute of Informatics at the Wroclaw University of Technology. Our observations and students' opinions encourage us to continue our work in the subject-matter discussed and described in this chapter.

After conducting planned experiments and verifications of the quality and evaluation model presented in this paper, development of a quality product monitoring system is planned. This monitoring system will support decision making during the product development.

REFERENCES

Agarwal, R. (2005). *Software development vs. software maintenance*. Virginia Tech. Retrieved from http://www.irahul.com/workzone/pm/Software_Dev_vs_Maint.pdf

Basili, V. R., Caldiera, G., & Rombach, H. D. (1994). *The goal question approach*. Retrieved from ftp://ftp.cs.umd.edu/pub/sel/papers/gqm.pdf

Bobkowska, A. (2009). Integrating quality criteria and methods of evaluation for software models. In J. Rech & C. Bunse (Eds,), *Model-driven software development: Integrating quality assurance*. Hershey, PA: IGI Global

Brooks, F. P. Jr. (1987). No silver bullet. *IEEE Computer, 20*(4), 10–19.

Canfora, G., & Cimitile, A. (2000). *Software maintenance*. Retrieved from citeseerx.ist.psu.edu/viewdoc/download?doi=10.1.1.25.1678&rep

Chaudron, M., Gelhausen, T., Landhäußer, M., & Körner, S. (2009). Automatic checklist generation for the assessment of UML. In Chaudron, M. R. (Ed.), *Models in software engineering, Lecture Notes in Computer Science* (*Vol. 5421*, pp. 387–399). Berlin, Germany: Springer.

Chidamber, S. R., & Kemerer, C. F. (1994). A suite for object oriented design. *IEEE Transactions on Software Engineering, 20*(6), 476–493. doi:10.1109/32.295895

Coad, P., Mayfield, M., & Kern, H. (1998). *Java design: Building better apps and applets* (2nd ed.). Prentice Hall.

Deissenbock, F. (2009). *Continuous quality control of long-lived software systems*; Institut für Informatik der Technischen Universität München, Master thesis.

Dubielewicz, I., Hnatkowska, B., Huzar, Z., & Tuzinkiewicz, L. (2010). *Metodyka QUAD – Sterowane jakością wytwarzanie aplikacji bazodanowych (QUAD) – (Methodology for Quality-Driven Development of Database Applications)*. Wrocław, Poland: University of Technology Printing House. (in Polish)

Encyclopedia Britannica. (n.d.). *Online*. Retrieved from http://www.britannica.com/bps/dictionary?query=course

EPF. (n.d.). *Guideline: Boundary control entity pattern*. Retrieved from http://epf.eclipse.org/wikis/abrd/core.tech.common.extend_supp/guidances/guidelines/entity_control_boundary_pattern_C4047897.html

Erdil, K., Finn, E., Keating, K., Meattle, J., Park, S., & Yoon, D. (2003). *Software maintenance as part of the software life cycle*. Comp180: Software Engineering, Department of Computer Science Tufts University. Retrieved from http://www.hepguru.com/maintenance/Final_121603_v6.pdf

Esperanza, M. M., Cruz-Lemus, J. A., Genero, M., & Piattini, M. (2009). Empirical validation of measures for UML class diagrams: A meta-analysis study. In M. R. Chaudron (Ed.), *Models in software engineering, Lecture Notes in Computer Science* (pp. 303-313). Berlin, Germany: Springer-Verlag. doi: 10.1007/978-3-642-01648-6_32

ISO/IEC. (2001). *9126-1:2001(E), software engineering – Product quality – Part 1: Quality model.*

ISO/IEC. (2003). 9126-2:2003(E), software engineering – Product quality – Part 2: External metrics.

ISO/IEC(2003). 9126-3:2003(E), software engineering – Product quality – Part 3: Internal metrics.

ISO/IEC. (2005). 25000:2005(E), software engineering – Software quality and requirements evaluation (SQuaRE) guide to SQuaRE.

ISO/IEC. (2009). *24765:2009, systems and software engineering – Vocabulary.*

Kleppe, A., Warmer, J., & Bast, W. (2004). *MDA explained: The model driven architecture: Practice and promise*. Boston, MA: Pearson Education, Inc.

Koskinen, J. (2010). Maintenance. In Laplante, P. A. (Ed.), *Encyclopedia_of software engineering* (*Vol. 1*). CRC Press.

Lange, C. F. J., & Chaudron, M. R. V. (2005). Managing model quality in UML-based software development. In *Proceedings of the 13th IEEE International Workshop on Software Technology and Engineering Practice (STEP'05)* (pp. 7-16). Washington, DC: IEEE Compter Society.

Lientz, B. P., & Swanson, B. E. (1983). *Software maintenance management*. Reading, MA: Addison-Wesley.

Martin, R. C. (2006). *Agile software development: Principles, patterns, and practices in C.* Prentice Hall.

Mens, T., & Vangorp, P. (2006). A taxonomy of model transformation. *Electronic Notes in Theoretical Computer Science, vol. 152* (pp. 125-142). Elsevier. ISSN: 15710661; DOI: 10.1016/j.entcs.2005.10.021

Miller, J., & Mukerji, J. (2003). *MDA guide version 1.0.1*. Retrieved from http://www.omg.org/

Mohagheghi, P., & Dehlen, V. (2008). *A metamodel for specifying quality models in model-driven engineering.* Nordic Workshop on Model Driven Engineering NW-MoDE '08, Reykjavik Iceland.

Mohagheghi, P., & Dehlen, V. (2009). Existing model s and relations to model quality. *2009 ICSE Workshop on Software Quality* (pp. 39-45), ISBN: 9781424437238 DOI: 10.1109/WOSQ.2009.5071555

Mohagheghi, P., Dehlen, V., & Neple, T. (2009). Definitions and approaches to model quality in model-based software development: A review of literature. *Information and Software Technology, 15*, 1646–1669. doi:10.1016/j.infsof.2009.04.004

Nugroho, A., & Chaudron, M. (2009). *Managing the quality of UML models in practice.* In J. Rech & C. Bunse (Eds,), *Model-driven software development: Integrating quality assurance.* Hershey, PA: IGI Global

Oh, J. M. C., Feather, M. S., & Khorrami, M. A. (2009). *High-quality software models of the mid-infrared instrument for the James Webb space telescope.* In J. Rech & C. Bunse (Eds,), *Model-driven software development: Integrating quality assurance.* Hershey, PA: IGI Global

Piattini, M., & Genero, M. (2002). An empirical study with s for object-relational databases. *Lecture Notes in Computer Science*, 298–309.

Pressman, R. S. (1992). *Software engineering – A practitioner's approach.* New York, NY: McGraw-Hill.

Rational Unified Process. (n.d.). *FP6*. Retrieved from http://rup.hops-fp6.org/

Ross, R. G. (1997). *The business rule book* (2nd ed.). Houston, TX: Business Rules Solutions, Inc.

Saeki, M., & Kaiya, H. (2006). Model s and s of model transformation. *Proc. of 1st Workshop on Quality in Modeling*, (pp. 31-44).

Schieferdecker, & S. Goericke (Eds.), *Proceedings of the 11th International Conference on Quality Engineering in Software Technology* (CONQUEST 2008), (pp. 353-370).

Schneidewind, N. F. (1987). The state of software maintenance. *IEEE Transactions on Software Engineering*, *13*(3), 303–310. doi:10.1109/TSE.1987.233161

SDS. (n.d.). *LoM*. Retrieved from http://www.sds.com/LoM.html

Software Engineering Body of Knowledge (SWE-BOK). (2004). *Guide*. Retrieved from http://www.computer.org/portal/web/swebok/about

Std, I. E. E. E. (1998). *1219-1998: Standard for software maintenance*. Los Alamitos, CA: IEEE Computer Society Press.

UML. (2008). *Profile for Corba and Corba components specification*. (Version 1.0. formal/2008-04-07). Retrieved from http://www.omg.org/spec/CCCMP/1.0/PDF/

Unhelkar, B. (2005). *Verification and validation for quality of UML 2.0 models*. Hoboken, NJ: Wiley-Interscience. doi:10.1002/0471734322

Unified Process. (n.d.). *Wiki*. Retrieved from http://en.wikipedia.org/wiki/Unified_Process

Voigt, H., Güldali, B., & Engels, G. (2008). Quality plans for measuring the testability of models. In I.

von Halle, B. (2002). *Business rules applied: Building better systems using the business rules approach*. Wiley Computer Publishing.

ADDITIONAL READING

Behkamal, B., Kahani, M., & Akbari, M. K. (2009). Customizing ISO 9126 quality model for evaluation of B2B applications. *Information and Software Technology, 51*, 599–609. doi:10.1016/j.infsof.2008.08.001

Calero, C., Sahraoui, H. A., Piattini, M., & Lounis, H. (2002) Estimating Object-Relational Database Understandability Using Structural s. From www.springerlink.com/index/04jldq2uwenn5v90.pdf

Deissenboeck, F., Juergens, E., Lochmann, K., & Wagner, S. (2009). Software Quality Models: Purposes, Usage Scenarios and Requirements, In: *Proc. Seventh Workshop on Software Quality* (pp. 9-14), IEEE Computer Society.

Dubielewicz, I., Hnatkowska, B., Huzar, Z., & Tuzinkiewicz, L. (2006). Software Quality Metamodel for Requirement, Evaluation and Assessment, In: *Proceedings of Information, Simulation, Modeling. ISIM'06 Conference*. pp. 115–122. Prerov, Czech Republic:Acta Mosis No. 105.

Dubielewicz, I., Hnatkowska, B., Huzar, Z., & Tuzinkiewicz, L. (2006). An approach to software quality specification and evaluation (SPoQE). In Sacha, K. (Ed.), *Software engineering techniques: design for quality* (pp. 155–165). New York, Boston: Springer. doi:10.1007/978-0-387-39388-9_16

Dubielewicz, I., Hnatkowska, B., Huzar, Z., & Tuzinkiewicz, L. (2007). Quality-driven software development within MDA approach. *International Review on Computers and Software, 6*(2), 573–580.

Garvin, D. A. (1984). What does "product quality" really mean? [Los Alamitos, CA: IEEE Computer Society Press.]. *MIT Sloan Management Review, 26*(1), 25–43.

Genero, M., & Piattini, M. (2002) Empirical validation of measures for class diagram structural complexity through controlled experiments. from www.iro.umontreal.ca/~sahraouh/qaoose01/genero.pdf

Mohagheghi, P., & Aagedal, J. (2007). Evaluating Quality in Model-Driven Engineering. In: *International Workshop on Modeling in Software Engineering* (pp. 6), IEEE Computer Society, Washington, DC, USA.

Mohagheghi, P., & Dehlen, V. (2008). *Developing a Quality Framework for Model-Driven Engineering. Models in Software Engineering* (pp. 275–289). Heidelberg: Springer Berlin.

Piattini, M., Calero, C., Sahraoui, H., & Lounis, H. (2001). Object-relational database s. *L'Object. Edition Hermès Sciences, 17*(4), 477–498.

Piattini, M., & Genero, M. (2001). Empirical validation of measures for class diagram structural complexity through controlled experiments. from http://www.iro.umontreal.ca/~sahraouh/qaoose01/genero.pdf

Rech, J., & Bunse, C. (2008). *Model-Driven Software Development: Integrating Quality Assurance*. Information Science Reference. doi:10.4018/978-1-60566-006-6

Rosenberg, D., & Scott, K. (1999). *Use Case Driven Object Modeling With UML: A Practical Approach*. Reading, MA: Addison Wesley Longman, Inc.

Wagner, S., & Deissenboeck, F. (2007). An Integrated Approach to Quality Modelling, In: *Proceedings of the 5th International Workshop on Software Quality* (pp. 1), Washington, DC: IEEE Computer Society.

Wagner, S., Lochmann, K., Winter, S., Goeb, A., & Klaes, M. (2009). Quality Models in Practice: A Preliminary Analysis, In: *Proc. 3rd International Symposium on Empirical Software Engineering and Measurement* (pp. 464-467). IEEE Computer Society, Lake Buena Vista, FL, USA.

KEY TERMS AND DEFINITIONS

Checklist: "Items listed together for convenience of comparison […..]; an example is a list of items to be inspected that is created during quality planning and applied during quality control" (PMBOK® Guide, 2004).

Maintainability: "The ease with which a software system or component can be modified to change or add capabilities, correct faults or defects, improve performance or other attributes, or adapt to a changed environment" (ISO/IEC 24765, 2009), or "the capability of the software product to be modified" (IEEE 14764, 2006).

Model Driven Architecture (MDA): "An approach to system development…[that]… provides a means for using models to direct the course of understanding, design, construction, deployment, operation, maintenance and modification" (Kleppe, Warmer& Nast, 2003); this approach introduces specific levels of abstraction that enable separation of system functionality specification from the specification of the implementation of that functionality on a specific technology platform; system development is seen as a transformation of models that represent different viewpoints.

Perfective Maintenance: "Improvements in software's performance or functionality (for example, in response to user suggestions and requests)" (ISO/IEC 24765, 2009).

Quality Model: "Defined set of characteristics, and of relationships between them, which provides a framework for specifying quality requirements and evaluating quality" (ISO/IEC 25000,2005).

Software Development Cycle: Usually understood as the period of time that begins with the decision to develop a software product and ends when the software is delivered and typically includes a requirements phase, design phase, implementation phase, test phase, and sometimes, installation and checkout phase (ISO/IEC 24765,2009). We use it in a broader meaning i.e. the entire software life cycle.

Software Life Cycle: "The period of time that begins when a software product is conceived and ends when the software is no longer available for use" (ISO/IEC 24765, 2009).

Software Maintenance: "The process of modifying a software system or component after delivery, to correct faults, improve performance or other attributes, or adapt to a changed environment" (ISO/IEC 24765, 2009). Maintenance is categorized into adaptive maintenance, corrective maintenance, perfective maintenance.

(Software) Quality Evaluation: "Systematic examination of the extent to which a software product is capable of satisfying stated and implied needs" (ISO/IEC 25000, 2005).

Chapter 2
Change Impact Analysis for UML Model Maintenance

Anne Keller
University of Antwerp, Belgium

Serge Demeyer
University of Antwerp, Belgium

ABSTRACT

Software maintenance is generally considered to be the most costly phase in the software life-cycle. The software system to be maintained consists of numerous inter-dependent artifacts that inevitably undergo various changes during maintenance. What makes planning and executing these changes difficult is that each change may have severe "ripple effects" to other points of the system that are difficult to assess due to the inter-dependent nature of the artifacts. The goal of this chapter is to introduce a lightweight and accurate change impact analysis technique for UML models. Impact analysis rules are created that trace different relationships between UML model elements depending on the type of change applied. We will show that we can achieve good accuracy. To validate the technique, a change scenario that consists of changes that occur during the resolution of inconsistencies between different UML models (correc-tive maintenance) was chosen. The validation is performed on two case studies, which together contain approximately 5686 UML model element instances on which 3287 inconsistencies are resolved. The validation of the two case studies returns a mean precision and recall of (0.77, 0.95) and (0.97, 0.93).

INTRODUCTION

Software maintenance is generally considered to be the most costly phase in the software life-cycle (Morrissey, 1979). The software system to be maintained consists of numerous inter-dependent artifacts that, inevitably, undergo various changes during maintenance. In the model-driven engi-neering context, the artifacts are inter-dependent models and their model elements that describe the system at different levels of abstraction, show

DOI: 10.4018/978-1-61350-438-3.ch002

different views and can even use different formalisms (Kleppe, 2003).

What makes planning and executing these changes difficult, is that each change may have severe "ripple effects" to other points of the system that are difficult to assess due to the inter-dependent nature of the artifacts (Yau, 1978; Yau, 1979). Change impact analysis identifies "the potential consequences of a change" and estimates "what needs to be modified to accomplish a change" (Arnold, 1996). This information can be used to estimate the cost of the changes in terms of time, labor and money, reduce potential errors due to unexpected side effects, and finally, efficiently implement the change.

What change impact analysis techniques have in common is that they calculate a so-called *impact set* from a given *change set*. The change set contains the artifacts that are directly changed; the impact set contains the artifacts that require a subsequent change. In order to identify the impact set, the relationships of the artifacts of the change set to the rest of the system are analyzed. This analysis is done recursively starting from the original change set depending on the desired depth of analysis. The most basic change impact analysis techniques traverse all relationships, however, more elaborate change impact analysis techniques exploit knowledge about the planned changes and the actual relationships. For example, a change impact analysis technique might start from fine-grained, atomic changes (such as create, delete, modify) and chain those together in sequences of changes that have to be applied together. Other techniques require manual intervention of a software engineer to assess whether a change will propagate or not.

Since change impact analysis is an approximate technique, a validation of its accuracy is crucial (Hattori, 2008). Indeed, the danger of each change impact analysis technique is that it produces false-positives, that is, artifacts are identified, as belonging to the impact set, yet will not be affected once the planned change is applied.

False-negatives are likely as well, that is, artifacts are affected by a change; yet do not appear in the impact set. Therefore, validation of a change impact analysis is done by counting false-negatives and false-positives, or in information retrieval terms by computing the precision and recall. For this, an experiment must compare the impact set with the elements that are actually affected when applying the changes in the change set.

This chapter presents a lightweight change impact analysis technique for UML models, which makes use of a small, generic set of *impact analysis rules.*

The presented change impact analysis technique traces relationships between UML model elements (OMG, 2004). The kind of change (e.g., add, remove, modify) is used to reduce the amount of relationships to trace. For instance, to determine the impact for the creation of a UML model element, not all relationships but only the containment relationships to this UML model element are traced.

Through the exploitation of the UML metamodel and the type of change we can present a small, generic set of impact analysis rules.

Our change impact analysis technique does not require user interaction to apply the impact analysis rules, yet is reasonably accurate, as we will show in the validation section. Accuracy is crucial to judge the quality of the technique and a prerequisite for its acceptance in praxis. Another contribution of the small, generic set of impact analysis rules is that they can be adapted easily. This holds both for the case where the meta-model evolves as well as for the case where the impact analysis rules themselves need to be adjusted or extended. And finally, the small set of impact analysis rules makes it easy for tool builders interested in supporting change impact analysis for UML models to implement the rules.

This impact analysis technique was developed as part of a framework to support inconsistency resolution for UML models. Therefore, the change scenario chosen to validate the technique is changes that occur due to the resolution of inconsistencies between different UML models (corrective maintenance (Swanson, 1976)). The advantage of using inconsistency resolution is that we can naturally detect a large amount of inconsistencies on a given UML model. The resolutions offer a large set of different kinds of changes of varying complexity from a single change to several dependent composite changes. Since most inconsistencies occur several times in a UML model, the resolution changes can be applied several times at different UML model element instances. This allows us to validate the technique for a specific change set on these different UML model element instances and thereby investigate the influence the UML model element instances have on the accuracy of the technique.

The validation is performed on two case studies: an ATM machine ((Briand, 2003)) and a car rental system called EU-Rent ((Frias, 2003)). The case studies together contain approximately 5686 UML model element instances on which 3287 inconsistencies are resolved.

The chapter is structured as follows. Section 2 explains the background of change impact analysis concepts and how these are translated to concrete design decisions for the presented change impact analysis technique. Section 3 explains the technique in detail. Section 4 presents our results in terms of precision and recall for varying depths of analysis. Finally, Section 5 summarizes the results and points out avenues for future research.

BACKGROUND

In each change impact analysis technique the planned changes are used to populate a change set, which contains the artifacts that are directly changed. The relationships between the changed artifacts and the rest of the system are traversed and used to populate the impact set. Finally, the impact set is filtered to increase the relevance of the returned result.

According to Arnold et al. each impact analysis relies on the ability to: (i) create models of relationships among artifacts, (ii) capture the relationships in software and associated representations, (iii) translate a specific software change into the impacted objects and relationships, (iv) trace relationships and reasonably bound the search for impacts, and (v) translate the estimated affected objects back into software objects.

In this section we go into detail regarding the relationships between artifacts (i, ii), the identification and representation of change (iii), and performing impact analysis and bound the search for impacts (iv). But first, change impact analysis technique classifications are introduced to position the presented change impact analysis technique with respect to related techniques.

Related Techniques and Change Impact Analysis Classifications

Change impact analysis is a research topic that has been investigated quite deeply within software engineering research and is applied successfully to many different fields. Arnold et al. provide a broad overview of the field (Arnold, 1996). Some recent examples of the application of change impact analysis to different fields include Fisler et al. (Fisler, 2005) who apply change impact analysis for changes to access-control policies of online data. Zhang et al. (Zhang, 2008) who develop a change impact analysis technique for aspect-oriented software. Maule et al. (Maule, 2008) who use change impact analysis to determine the impact of database schema changes on object-oriented applications. And Ren et al. (Ren, 2005) who use change impact analysis to determine the effect of changes to java programs on the behavior of the tests. In the following we restrict ourselves to related work that deals with the different aspects of change impact analysis for maintenance at the modeling level.

Kung et al. (Kung, 1994) present a change impact analysis technique that is laid out to deal with the difficulties that object-orientation brings to change impact analysis developed for "traditional function-oriented programming". The goal of the change impact analysis technique is to support regression testing during maintenance by facilitating the retesting of only the parts of the system that are affected by a modification. The technique is based on reverse engineering the classes and their relationships from source code. This information is presented in a multigraph and is the basis for automatic identification of the changes and their effects.

Han (Han, 1997) presents a change impact analysis technique that is designed to support impact analysis and change propagation directly inside software engineering environments. The goal is to allow the application of change impact analysis both during software development as well during maintenance. The key of this technique is that change impact analysis is performed on the original representation of the software artifacts in the development environment rather than on an extracted model of the system. The technique can perform change impact analysis both on design documents (i.e., class diagrams and state transition diagrams) as well as on the implementation in C++.

Briand et al. (Briand, 2006) present a UML model-based change impact analysis technique. The target of the technique is to support large software development teams during maintenance by assessing the complexity and the side effects of changes. The technique identifies the changes based on a change taxonomy and determines the impact based on formally defined impact analysis rules. A prototype implementation of the change impact analysis technique is presented.

Chen et al. (Chen, 2009) present a holistic approach for change impact analysis to "maintain the consistency and integrity of the system". The change impact analysis technique is holistic, since it can handle four different kinds of artifacts, namely software components, design documents, external data, and requirements. A software system prototype called EPIC (Entire-Phase Identifier

of Change) is presented. To use EPIC with UML diagrams, the contents of class and object diagrams are regarded as software components and use cases can be regarded as requirement artifacts.

Different authors have classified change impact analysis techniques differently. In order to position the presented change impact analysis technique we draw upon these classifications.

Chen et al. (Chen, 2009) classify change impact analysis techniques based on the artifacts they are applied on. Implementation-based techniques are such that deal with software components and mostly perform change impact analysis by "static call-graphs of the program code". Model-based techniques deal with models of the system and perform change impact analysis at the object level in the diagrams. The classification also suggests that implementation-based techniques are usually performed during the coding and maintenance phase, while model-based techniques play a larger role in the analysis and design phase.

Briand et al. (Briand, 2009) classify change impact analysis techniques based on the levels of abstraction they span in UML-based iterative development. They distinguish between vertical and horizontal impact analysis. Vertical impact analysis deals with changes at one level of abstraction and their impact on another level of abstraction. Horizontal impact analysis deals with changes and impacts at one level of abstraction.

Arnold et al. (Arnold, 1996) distinguish between two major technology areas for change impact analysis: dependency analysis and traceability analysis. Dependency analysis gives a narrow perspective in form of source-code analysis while traceability analysis analyzes more broad relationships between different artifacts, e.g., documentation, requirements and design artifact. Additionally, a distinction is made for the kind of analysis performed, namely static and dynamic analysis. In static analysis, the static code structure is analyzed. In dynamic analysis, the software is executed in order to aid determining the impact.

Figure 1. Classification and positioning of the presented change impact analysis technique

Artifacts:	implementation-based		model-based	✓
Technology:	dependency analysis	✓	traceability analysis	
Kind of Analysis:	static	✓	dynamic	
Abstraction Level:	horizontal	✓	vertical	

Figure 1 shows where we position the presented change impact analysis technique with regard to the above classifications.

Relationships Between Artifacts

Each change impact analysis technique relies on relationships between artifacts that connect them in a meaningful way, that is, (i) create models of relationships among artifacts; (ii) capture the relationships in software and associated representations. For the presented change impact analysis technique we want to present a technique for the UML language and the defined diagram types. The artifacts used are therefore UML models and UML model elements defined by the UML meta-model (OMG, 2004).

The artifacts targeted by a specific change impact analysis technique influence how and what relationships are established. For example, Chen et al. (Chen, 2009) define four different types of relationships: RequirementToComponentLinkage, ComponentToComponentLinkage, ComponentToDataLinkage, and ComponentToDocumentLinkage. Through these relationships different attributes characterizing the different artifacts are connected and are traced once a change occurs. Han (Han, 1997) takes a different approach. A desired feature of this technique is to use the relationships between artifacts as defined and represented during artifact construction and

manipulation in the software development environment. While the definition of custom relationships allows optimization for the artifacts and problem at hand, reusing existing relationships facilitates more flexibility.

For the change impact analysis technique presented here, similarly to Han (Han, 1997), the artifacts and their relationships are directly used as provided by the UML meta-model. That is, the UML meta-model is used as a model of the relationships between the different artifacts, i.e., *UML model elements*. Figure 2 shows an excerpt of the UML meta-model. We use four different relationships from the UML meta-model: association (*assoc*), composition (*comp, compPart*) and the relationship between a UML model element and one of its attributes (*attrib*). An association is "a relationship that may occur between instances of classifiers" (OMG, 2003). An example of an association relationship (*assoc*) is the opposite association between two Property UML model elements shown in Figure 2. A composition describes "a form of aggregation which requires that a part instance be included in at most one composite at a time, and that the composite object is responsible for the creation and destruction of the parts" (OMG, 2003). We distinguish between two relationships for composition, on the one hand where the UML model element is the part (*compPart)* and on the other hand the relationship where the UML model element is the composite (*comp*).

Figure 2. Excerpt of the UML meta-model (OMG, 2004)

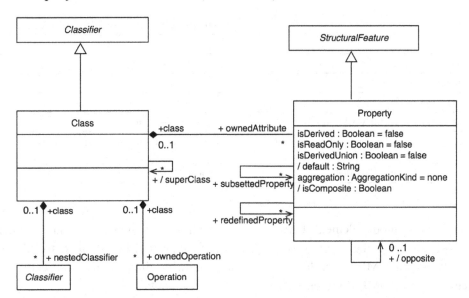

By using the relationships provided by the UML meta-model, we avoid an extra extraction step to create a model of the relationships. Another advantage is that the change impact analysis technique is applicable where ever the UML meta-model is used, e.g., as the basis of a domain specific language.

Change

A change impact analysis technique needs to specify how changes are defined, that is, translate a specific software change into the impacted objects and relationships, (iii). Briand et al. (Briand, 2006), for example, define a change taxonomy that is used to identify changes between different model versions and classify them. Each item in the change taxonomy represents one change applied to a specific model element. For each item in the change taxonomy, different impact analysis rules are used to determine the impact. Han (Han, 1997) distinguishes between "update, introduction and deletion" as types of changes, and define a change as a pair (obj, m_{type}) where obj is the changed object and m_{type} is the type of

change. Chen et al. (Chen, 2009), on the other hand, do not distinguish between different types of changes. Instead, each change affects different attributes of the involved artifacts. This way each change is treated equally and the different impacts are based on the defined relationships and attributes rather than the type of change.

We distinguish between seven different types of changes as shown in the first column of Table 1. The type of change is distinguished on the one hand by the change it poses on the UML model and on the other hand by the UML model element it is applied to. We distinguish between types of changes that applied on UML model elements as for example Class, Property, and Operation shown in Figure 2 and types of changes that are applied on the references of UML model elements. For example, when the opposite association is created between two instances of the Property UML model element, this is an *addRef* change.

Remove and *add* describe the removal and addition of a UML model element (UMLmodElem), and *modify* describes the modification of an attribute of a UML model element (UMLmodElem). *RemoveRef* describes the removal of a

Table 1. Types of change and impact analysis rules

Types of Change	Impact Analysis Rules
(*remove*, UMLmodElem)	{*remove*} → {*assoc, compPart*}
(*add*, UMLmodElem)	{*add*} → {*comp*}
(*modify*, UMLmodElem)	{*modify*} → {*attrib*}
(*removeRef*, UMLmodElem, ref)	{*removeRef*} → {*assoc*}
(*addRef*, UMLmodElem, ref, targetUMLModElem)	{*addRef*} → {*assoc*}
(*addRefToNewUMLmodElem*, newUMLmodElem, ref, targetUMLMod-Elem)	{*addRefToNewUMLmodElem*} → {*assoc*}
(*modifyRef*, UMLmodElem, ref, targetUMLModElem)	{*modifyRef*} → {*assoc*}

reference (ref) of a UML model element (UML-modElem). *AddRef* describe the addition of a reference (ref) between two UML model elements (UMLmodElem and targetUMLModElem). *Ad-dRefToNewUMLmodElem* describes the addition of a reference (ref) between a UML model element (targetUMLModElem) and a UML model element that is being created (newUMLmodElem). The case where this occurs is when a UML model element is added and afterwards a reference to this newly created UML model element is added. *ModifyRef* describes the modification of a reference, that is, referencing a different UML model element (targetUMLModElem) than before.

Performing Impact Analysis

With (iv) Arnold et al. (Arnold, 1996) state that a change impact analysis technique needs to be able to "trace and reasonably bound the search for impact". That is, the defined relationships are traced to determine the impact based on the change set. In order to increase the accuracy and to increase the number of relevant results the search needs to be bounded.

To trace the relationships, Han (Han, 1997) formulates *change patterns* in the form of: a typed modification on a typed object results in specific typed modifications on specific typed objects if a Boolean expression holds. Similarly, Briand et al. (Briand, 2006) define impact analysis rules for

each change applied to a model element of a specific type. The impact analysis rules are used to determine directly and indirectly impacted model elements.

For both techniques, the number of impact analysis rules depends on the number of specified changes and the number of artifact (model element) types recognized. For the UML, for example, which specifies over 275 model element types, the number of impact analysis rules can therefore be quite large. With the presented change impact analysis technique we focus on reducing the number of impact analysis rules in order to ease application and maintenance of the impact analysis rules by presenting impact analysis rules for each type of change only.

Figure 3 shows our conceptual meta-model of the impact analysis rules we define. Each impact analysis rule specifies the impact of a specific type of change. In order to determine the impact, different relationships are traced based on the type of change. That is, if a specific type of change is applied to a UML model element (*ModelElement*), then instead of tracing all relationships of this UML model element, only specific relationships of this UML model element are traced. The rules that determine which relationship to trace for which type of change are our impact analysis rules. Table 1 shows the impact analysis rules in the form of {*typeOfChange$_j$*} → {*rel$_1$,.., rel$_3$*} where rel$_i$ is a relationship from the relationships

Figure 3. Impact analysis rules conceptual model

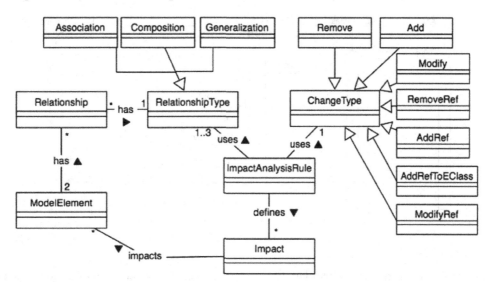

defined in Section 2.2 Relationships between Artifacts: *Rel* = {*assoc, comp, compPart, attrib*} and *typeOfChange$_j$* is a type of change that we specified in Section 2.3 Change *TypeOfChange* = { *remove, add, modify, addRef, removeRef, ad-dRefToNewUMLmodElem, modifyRef*}. In Section 3.2 Change Impact Analysis Technique we show on an example the reason behind the different impact analysis rules.

Impact analysis rules can be applied recursively, that is, an impact analysis rule is applied to the UML model elements that were found to be impacted by a previous application of the impact analysis rule. For each recursive application of the impact analysis rules, the distance of the change impact analysis is increased by one. However, depending on the distance of recursion a large amount of impacted UML model element instances can be returned. Therefore, the results should be bounded in order to increase the accuracy of the change impact analysis technique. This can be done manually by a user that determines which changes will be required as for instance done by Han (Han, 1997). Another approach is by defining a distance measure, as for instance done by Briand et al. (Briand, 2006). Since the impact distance

influences the accuracy, a technique must decide on the appropriate distance measure. The intuition is that the larger the distance the less likely it is that the UML model element will be impacted. At this stage we have investigated the results for different distances. In the **Discussion** section we show concretely how the distance influences the accuracy of our change impact analysis technique.

Change Impact Analysis Technique

Corrective Maintenance Example

As an example of corrective maintenance we use changes that resolve inconsistencies between UML models. Inconsistencies between UML models are violations of specific consistency rules. A consistency rule may for example be a *well-formedness rule*, an *application domain rule* or a *development process compliance rule* (see Spanoudakis et al. (Spanoudakis, 2001) for definitions of the different kinds of consistency rules and a more complete list).

These consistency rules should be checked on a regular basis to ensure that the UML models evolve correctly during maintenance. Once a

Figure 4. Sequence diagram with classless instance inconsistency

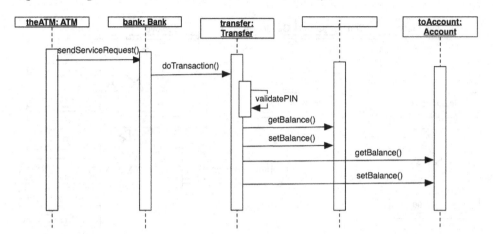

consistency rule is violated and scheduled for resolution, there are a number of resolutions that fix the inconsistency.

The example consistency rule we use throughout this paper is the *classless instance* consistency rule specified by Van Der Straeten (Van Der Straeten, 2005). This consistency rule is a good example because it is relatively simple, yet results in a number of resolutions with varying complexity and spanning different changes such as the addition, modification, and removal of UML model elements.

The consistency rule checks if an object in a UML sequence diagram (i.e., a UML *Lifeline*) is the instance of a class (i.e., a UML *Class*) that does not exist in the UML model or if the class of the object is not specified. In both cases the consistency rule is violated and an inconsistency is reported. Figure 4 shows one instance of the *classless instance* inconsistency in which the class of the unnamed object is not specified.

Figure 5 shows the resolutions applicable to the concrete inconsistency shown in Figure 4. Figure 5 presents 5 out of 20 concrete resolutions. The missing 15 resolutions are variations of the resolutions shown in the second row that reference other available classes from the ATM class diagram. The first column gives a short description

of the resolution, column two shows the concrete resolutions for the specific inconsistency shown in Figure 4 on UML model element instances, and the third column describes the resolution in terms of changes applied to the UML model elements.

Change Impact Analysis Technique

The main goal of the presented change impact analysis technique is to provide an accurate and lightweight account of the impacted UML model elements for UML model changes. Accuracy is crucial to judge the quality of the technique and a prerequisite for its acceptance in praxis. A lightweight technique is one that, on the one hand, requires little user interaction to create and apply the impact analysis rules. On the other hand, lightweight also describes that the technique relies on a small, generic set of impact analysis rules.

Figure 6 shows parts of the second resolution (Res2) of the *classless instance* inconsistency. (The resolution is expressed in the Epsilon Object Language - EOL (Kolovos, 2006).) In Res2 the classless instance inconsistency is resolved by linking the classless instance to an existing class in the model.

Figure 5. Resolutions for one instance of the classless instance inconsistency

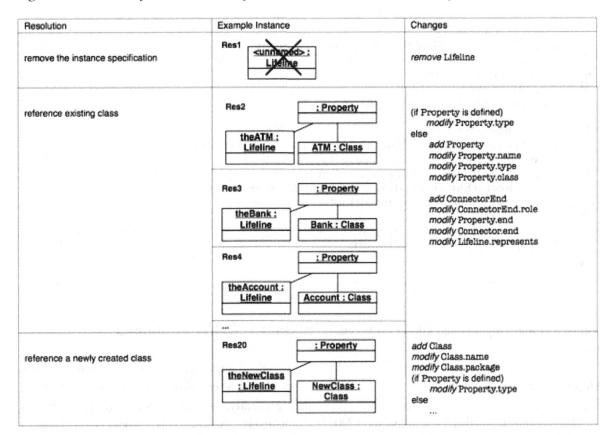

In the first paragraph (line 2-6) of Figure 6 one new UML model element of type Property is created and basic attributes and references are set. In paragraph two, a new UML model element of type ConnectorEnd is created (line 9-10). In line 11 and 13, the newly created connector end is added as reference to the prior created property and to the list of connector ends of a connector, respectively. Finally, paragraph 3 (line 16) adds the reference to the newly created property from the lifeline.

Basic Steps

To identify which UML model element instances would be impacted when a specific change is executed we use the following steps.

Step 1: Extract Changes

Input to the technique are types of changes applied to one or more UML model elements, the *change pairs*, cp_R=(*typeOfChange*, {UML-modElem,..}). A resolution as in Figure 6 is thus expressed by a set of change pairs: CP_R. In the following steps the set CP_R is input and serves as placeholder for the coded resolutions.

Step 2: Check Meta-Level Relationships

For each of the different changes we defined the relevant meta-model relationships that describe which UML model elements are impacted for this kind of change. In this step, we extract the impacted subset of the UML meta-model,

Figure 6. Classless instance inconsistency resolution2

```
1  //create new property
2  var newProperty := Model.createInstance(`Property');
3  newProperty.name := `newElement';
4  newProperty.isReadOnly := false;
5  newProperty.type := targetClass;
6  newProperty.class := impactedElem.interaction;
7
8  //create connector end
9  var newConnectorEnd := Model.createInstance(`ConnectorEnd');
10 newConnectorEnd.role := newProperty;
11 newProperty.end.add(newConnectorEnd);
12 //add connectorEnd to existing connector of interaction
13 Connector.end.add(newConnectorEnd);
14
15 //reference property from lifeline
16 Lifeline.represents := newProperty;
```

recursively applying this step allows for varying impact distance.

Step 3: Instance-Level Analysis

Here we check whether these impacted UML model elements are indeed instantiated in the current model, i.e., have UML model element instances, and are thus impacted by the specified change.

Result: The above steps result in a change set for each change pair of a resolution. To determine the impact for a complete resolution the impacted UML model element instances of each change pair are added to a final set of impacted UML model element instances I_R.

Note that the extraction of the change pairs and step 2 are independent of the UML model under study, hence could be computed in advance once the change is known. Step 3 is the only step that is specific to the UML model the change is acting upon.

Step 1: Extract Changes

A static change impact analysis technique needs to address how it deals with composite changes, specifically, with a) the repeated application of changes to the same UML model element and b) dependent composite changes.

The repeated application of a change to the same UML model element can be seen in line 3 and 4 of Figure 6 where two attributes of a Property are modified. Since change pairs are defined as a change to a UML model element these changes are not distinguishable and are thus simple repetitions of the same impact analysis. In order to make them distinguishable, one would have the choice to enhance the change pair definition by including the information of which attribute is modified. In order to keep a small and generic impact analysis rule set, we chose, however, not to record this additional information. This results in the lines line 3 and line 4 being expressed by the equivalent change pairs: (*modify*, newProperty) and (*modify*, newProperty). Additionally, we avoid duplicate change impact analysis of these change pairs by creating a *set* of change pairs and thus eliminating any duplicates.

This influences the definition of the technique to return impacted UML model element instances rather than the number of times a UML model element instance is impacted. Furthermore, avoiding duplicate application of the same impact analysis improves the overall performance of the technique. However, since performance is not subject of this paper, an analysis of the degree of improvement and possible further optimizations is left for further research.

Dependent composite changes are changes to different UML model elements that are dependent. For example, if a UML model element is created the subsequent referencing of another UML model element is considered dependent (line 2 and line 5-6 in Figure 6). For such dependent composite changes we capture each of these changes, however the order is not explicitly recorded, resulting in the first paragraph of Figure 6 expressed in change pairs as follows: CP_{res2}= {(*add*, newProperty), (*modify*, newProperty), (*addRef*, newProperty, type, targetClass), (*addRef*, newProperty, class, impactedElem.interaction)}.

Step 2: Check Meta-Level Relationships

In Table 2 the different impact analysis rules we created are shown. Here we motivate why for specific types of change only certain relationships are traced.

When a UML model element is removed (*remove*, UMLmodElem), all UML model elements that reference the removed UML model element and all UML model elements that are contained by the removed UML model element are impacted. That is, all references to the removed UML model element need to be updated and the contained UML model elements whose container is removed are removed from the model.

When a UML model element is added (*add*, UMLmodElem), all UML model elements that will contain this UML model element are impacted.

When a UML model element is modified (*modify*, UMLmodElem), only the UML model element itself is impacted since the changes are made to its own attributes.

In case the reference of a UML model element is removed (*removeRef*, UMLmodElem, ref), the UML model element containing the reference is added to the impact set. If the reference is bi-directional also the opposite UML model element is added to the impact set.

In case a reference is added (*addRef*, UMLmodElem, ref, targetUMLModElem), the UML model element containing the reference is added to the impact set as well as the UML model element the reference is created to (targetUMLModElem). The targetUMLModElem is only impacted if the reference is bi-directional.

In case a reference is created between a newly created UML model element and a target UML

Table 2. Impact analysis rules and description

Impact Analysis Rules	The impacted element...
{*remove*} → {*assoc, compPart*}	... is contained by the changed model element ... references the changed model element
{*add*} → {*comp*}	... contains the changed model element
{*modify*} → {*attrib*}	... is the changed model element
{*removeRef*} → {*assoc*}	... is opposite model element of the changed model element if bi-directional
{*addRef*} → {*assoc*}	... is opposite model element of the changed model element if bi-directional
{*addRefToNewUMLmodElem*} → {*assoc*}	... is opposite model element of the changed model element if bi-directional
{*modifyRef*}} → {*assoc*}	... is opposite model element of the changed model element if bi-directional

model element (*addRefToNewUMLmodElem*, newUMLmodElem, ref, targetUMLModElem), the newly created UML model element containing the reference is added to the impact set. The targetUMLModElem is only impacted if the reference is bi-directional.

In case a reference is modified (*modifyRef*, UMLmodElem, ref, targetUMLModElem), i.e., a reference is modified to reference a different UML model element, the UML model element containing the reference is added to the impact set. Further, if the modified reference is bi-directional, the formerly referenced UML model element is impacted as well as the newly referenced UML model element.

Following the example, for (*add*, newProperty) the composition relationships of the type of newProperty, namely Property, in the UML meta-model is checked, resulting in six potentially impacted UML model elements: Element via the owner reference, Property via the datatype reference, NamedElement via the namespace reference, ParameterableElement via the owningTemplateParameter reference, Property via the owningAssociation reference, and Property via the associationEnd reference.

Step 3: Instance-Level Analysis

After extracting the changes and extracting the impacted subset of the UML meta-model, the instance-level analysis makes sure that it is checked which of the impacted UML model elements are indeed instantiated in the model and are thus impacted by the change. E.g., for the removal of a class its operations and attributes are impacted according to the meta-model analysis. In this step, we check whether the concrete class contains operations and attributes and if so, how many.

Since the presented change impact analysis technique is a static technique, which means that the changes are not executed, the instance-level analysis is not straightforward when dealing with

the addition of UML model elements as well as dealing with composite changes.

For the addition of a UML model element (*add*, UMLmodElem) and the addition of a reference to this newly created UML model element (*addRefToNewUMLmodElem*, newUMLmodElem, ref, targetUMLModElem) the technique needs to predict the impact without the concrete UML model element instance of the added UML model element being available. Tackling this challenge with a lightweight solution, we use a heuristic, which checks whether *any* instance of one of the impacted UML model elements, generated in the meta-level analysis step, exists. For example, when a class is added the package into which it will be added is impacted according to the meta-model analysis step. Thus, if *any* package exists in the UML model, we assume that this package is impacted. I.e., since we do not have the information in which package the UML model element will be added into, we check that there is a package and count this as impacted. We show in the discussion section how this simple heuristic fares.

The fact that the changes are not executed can pose a problem for composite changes. That is, on the one hand, changes to the same UML model element cannot be considered and, on the other hand, a change that impacts a UML model element that is later changed can also not be considered. Since this is the case, we do not record the order of the changes and assume the pre-change UML model element instance for all changes. The change impact analysis is performed on those pre-change UML model element instances. The influence of composite changes on the accuracy of our change impact analysis technique is discussed in the following section.

Validation

In order to validate the accuracy of the change impact technique we compare the impact set with the actual change recorded when applying the change. Here we motivate and explain the experimental setup we used for the validation.

The main contribution of the technique is to use different relationships between UML model elements in order to predict the impact of different changes. Therefore, the validation needs to show that these relationships are generally relevant to predict the impact of changes. To do so, the experiment should provide a good coverage of different UML model elements (*meta-model coverage*). The units of analysis of the experiment are the different resolutions, i.e., the different changes, applied to the UML model. Thus, the experiment should take different resolutions with varying structure, i.e., composite changes as well as changes consisting of few and many change pairs into account (*resolution coverage*). And lastly, in order to explore if UML model element instances have an impact on the presented change impact analysis technique, we present the validation for different inconsistency instances (*instance coverage*).

We used two cases to observe inconsistencies and generate resolutions on: the Automatic Teller Machine (ATM) case, adapted from (Briand, 2003), and EU-Rent case, adapted from (Frias, 2003). The ATM model consists of one class diagram containing 18 classes, 15 use case diagrams, and 15 sequence diagrams. The EU-Rent case consists of 4 class diagrams containing about 75 classes, 12 object diagrams containing around 253 objects, one package diagram containing about 10 packages, 52 sequence diagrams containing around 164 lifelines, 3 state machine diagrams containing around 28 states, and 10 use case diagrams.

Table 3 shows the violated consistency rules, the number of times each consistency rule is violated and the number of resolutions executed. In the shown values we see that the consistency rules vary greatly in number of violations in the UML models and number of resolutions.

For the ATM case, we selected and checked 50 consistency rules that check consistency in

Table 3. Inconsistencies in ATM and EU-Rent case

Name of Consistency Rule	# of times violated	# of resolutions
classless instance inconsistency (Van Der Straeten, 2005)	5	20
dangling connectable association reference inconsistency (Van Der Straeten, 2005)	15	21
named element_3 well-formedness rule, no.3 (OMG, 2004)	107	125
namespace_1 well-formedness rule, no.1 (OMG, 2004)	61	7
operation_7 well-formedness rule, no.7 (OMG, 2004)	1	9
package_1 well-formedness rule, no.1 (OMG, 2004)	26	4
namespace_1 well-formedness rule, no.1 (OMG, 2004)	1242	6
classifier_3 well-formedness rule, no.3 (OMG, 2004)	3	5
multiplicity element_2 well-formedness rule, no.2 (OMG, 2004)	66	2
multiplicity element_3 well-formedness rule, no.3 (OMG, 2004)	70	7
property_1 well-formedness rule, no.1 (OMG, 2004)	480	751
pseudostate_1 well-formedness rule, no.1 (OMG, 2004)	5	11
transition kind_2 well-formedness rule, no.2 (OMG, 2004)	2	18
named element_2 well-formedness rule, no.2 (OMG, 2004)	74	2
named element_3 well-formedness rule, no.3 (OMG, 2004)	1022	1
classless instance inconsistency (Van Der Straeten, 2005)	15	3

class, sequence and use case diagrams from the consistency rule sets defined by (OMG, 2004) and (Van Der Straeten, 2005). Checking the consistency rules returned 215 inconsistencies from the violation of six consistency rules (row 2 to 7), shown in Table 3 (i.e., 44 consistency rules were not violated). The number of resolutions applicable to each inconsistency is shown in the third column of Table 3, these total to 187 resolutions. From the 90 UML model elements that describe class, sequence and use case diagrams (in the Classes, Interaction and Use Case package) 20 were covered by the resolutions (*meta-model coverage*). The resolutions contained 1 to 8 different change pairs (*resolution coverage*) and in total 924 single resolutions (number of resolutions per inconsistency instance) were used in the impact experiment on the ATM case (*instance coverage*).

For the EU-Rent case, 142 consistency rules checking consistency in class, object, package, sequence, state machine, and use case diagrams were checked ((OMG, 2004), (Van Der Straeten, 2005)). Checking the consistency rules returned 2979 inconsistencies from the violation of the 10 consistency rules presented in Table 3, row 8 to 17, (i.e., 132 consistency rules did not return inconsistencies). The number of resolutions applicable to each instance of the violated consistency rules is shown in the last column of Table 3. In total 806 different resolutions were checked. From the 106 UML model elements that describe the

above-mentioned diagrams of the EU-Rent case (in the Classes, Interaction, State Machine and Use Case package) 20 were covered by the resolutions (*meta-model coverage*). The resolutions contained 1 to 7 different change pairs (*resolution coverage*) and in total 369.875 single resolutions were checked (*instance coverage*).

The actual changes used as the baseline to compare our predictions against were captured using the *EMF change model* (Steinberg, 2009), which is distributed with the change plug-in of the *Eclipse Modeling Framework EMF* (Steinberg, 2009). It allows monitoring and recording the changes done to a model. The actual change is recorded for each resolution by executing the resolution for each inconsistency instance on the ATM model.

Precision and Recall

We validate the change impact analysis by calculating precision and recall. This is a standard validation for change impact, as among others described by Hattori et al. (Hattori, 2008). The impacted UML model elements are expressed by the set *I* and the actually changed UML model elements by the set *A*. Figure 7 illustrates this dependency.

Precision gives a measure for the amount of false positives, i.e., the UML model elements

Figure 7. Impacted elements I and actual change A

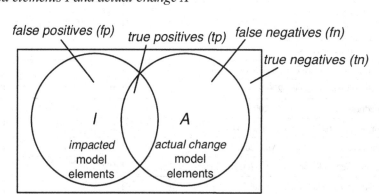

Figure 8. Class diagram of change impact analysis tool

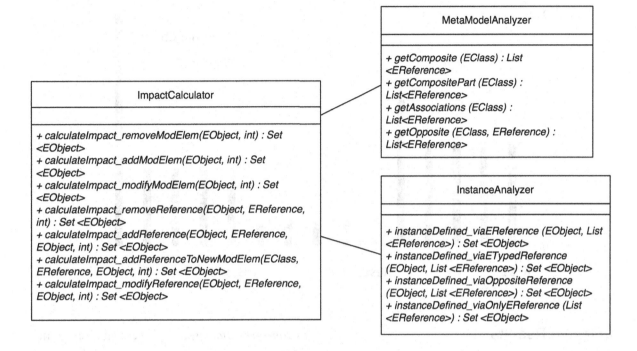

wrongly marked as impacted. It is calculated according to: $P = |I \cap A| / |I| = tp / (tp + fp)$.

Recall gives a measure for the false negatives, i.e., the UML model elements that are in the actual change but not found to be impacted and is calculated according to: $R = |I \cap A| / |A| = tp / tp + fn$

Implementation

As part of a larger effort to create an inconsistency resolution framework, a change impact analysis prototype tool was developed. The change impact analysis prototype tool is implemented as an Eclipse plug-in making use of the reflection and model persistence capabilities of the Eclipse Modeling Framework EMF (Steinberg, 2009). The UML models are created with UML2, which is an EMF-based implementation of the UML meta-model for the Eclipse platform.

The change impact analysis prototype tool gets as input the change pairs of a specific resolution and outputs a set of impacted elements for the given resolution. Figure 8 shows the class diagram of the change impact analysis part of the tool. The ImpactCalculator class contains the methods that represent the impact analysis rules presented in Table 2. These methods perform the change impact analysis for given UML model elements. The MetaModelAnalyzer class contains the methods necessary to perform *Step 2 Check Meta-level Relationships.* The InstanceAnalyzer class contains the methods necessary to perform *Step 3 Instance-level Analysis.*

To carry out the validation experiments, we build an additional tool that, additionally to generating a set of impacted elements for each resolution, also executes the resolution, records the changed UML model elements (via the EMF change model) and compares these to the set of impacted UML model elements. This tool then generates the precision and recall of the change impact analysis tool. This tool is also implemented for Eclipse making use of the EMF Eclipse Modeling Framework.

Figure 9. Impact and change in classless instance

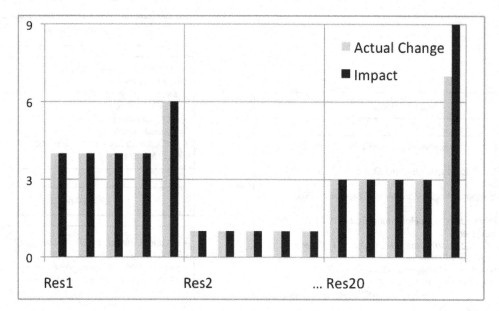

Selected Results

Figure 9 and Figure 10 show the number of changed UML model element instances when the resolution is executed (i.e., the *actual change*) compared to the number of impacted UML model element instances resulting from the change impact analysis (i.e., the *impact)* for the *classless*

instance and *namespace_1* inconsistency of the ATM case. Each pair of bars shows the actual change and the impact next to each other. There is one pair for each resolution of each inconsistency instance. The first set of bars, under the label *"Res1"*, shows the actual change and impact for the first resolution of the inconsistency for each inconsistency instance. The following sets of bars

Figure 10. Impact and change in namespace_1 inconsistency

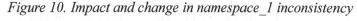

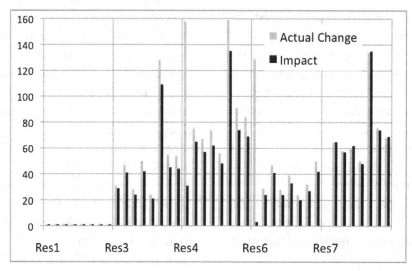

show the actual change and the impact for further resolutions applied to all inconsistency instances. The y-axis depicts the number of impacted and changed UML model element instances.

Without going into detail about the concrete numbers, these figures were chosen to illustrate two important points. On the one hand, both figures show cases of how the impact predicts the actual change accurately, as well as cases where it is above *and* below. We want to stress that the impact is not always only a worst-case assessment and therefore it is necessary to evaluate both precision and recall. Secondly, we emphasize the wide range of values for the impact. The smallest impact is 1, e.g., for Res1 in Figure 10, and the highest impact we encountered was 160 UML model element instances for Res4 in Figure 10.

Figure 11 shows precision (x-axis) and recall (y-axis) of the ATM case. The data points labeled with P/R represent a set of the precision and recall numbers we received for the 924 concrete resolutions. That is, duplicate results are represented by one data point mainly for visibility reasons. The data point mean shows the mean precision and recall for all 924 resolutions: (0.97, 0.93). Mean is calculated by averaging the mean precision and recall of each consistency rule. The reason for

this is to avoid bias of inconsistencies with many instances, as for example through the *named element_3* inconsistency that has 107 instances with both precision and recall of 1. The precision values do not drop below 0.5 (0.55 to be precise). The recall drops at 52 instances (out of 924) to 0.5 and below however with a precision of 1.

Figure 12 shows the precision and recall for the EU-Rent case. The EU-Rent case has a mean precision and recall of (0.77, 0.95).

Figure 13 and Figure 14 show histograms for recall and precision for both cases. Here it becomes clear how the recall and precision values are spread among the possible values and how the amount of occurrences of each value compares. We see that by far most precision and recall values are around 1.

The explanation for these results is discussed in the next section.

Discussion

Low Precision:
The Influence of Additions on Accuracy

We only encounter low precision (<1) in resolutions that contain additions of UML model ele-

Figure 11. Precision and recall scatter plot ATM case

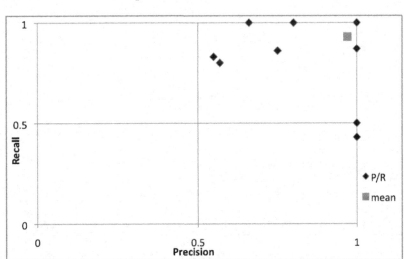

Figure 12. Precision and recall scatter plot EU-Rent case

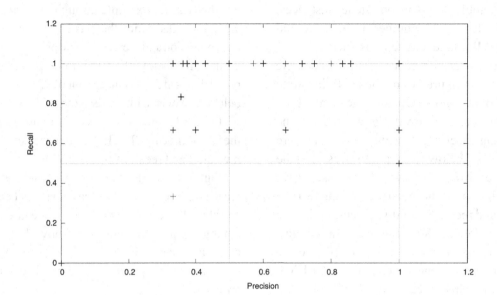

ments. However, it is important to note that not all resolutions with additions have a low precision. That means, when a UML model element is created, there is the possibility that UML model element instances are in the impact set that are not actually changed by the resolution. The reason for this is that during addition the UML model element is not actually created in the UML model and thus there is no way of checking whether the UML model element instances found as impacted would be in any dependency with the new UML model element instance. Thus, only relying on

Figure 13. Histogram recall for ATM and EU-Rent

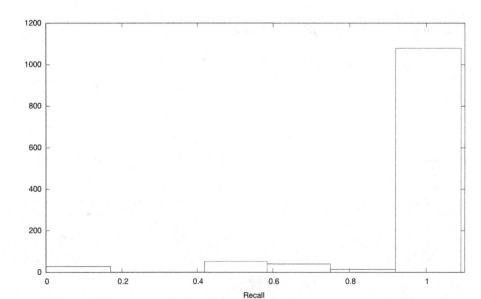

Figure 14. Histogram precision for ATM and EU-Rent

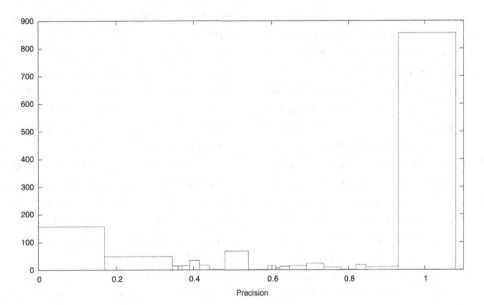

pre-change information is a clearly identified source for decreased precision. However, since the heuristic also returns correctly impacted UML model element instances and with a mean precision of 0.97 for the ATM case and 0.77 for the EU-Rent case we judge this to be a reasonable cost.

The Influence of Inconsistency Instances on Accuracy

In Figure 11 we noted that there is a small number of different precision and recall values. One reason for this is that 59% of the 924 resolutions in the ATM case have a precision and recall of (1,1). However, also the different inconsistency instances are responsible. That is, it is possible for resolutions to describe changes to supertypes, e.g., (*modify*, NamedElement). A supertype is "in a generalization relationship, the generalization of another type, the subtype", while a subtype is "in a generalization relationship, the specialization of another type, the supertype" (OMG, 2003). Thus, if an inconsistency is found on different subtypes of the one supertype, also the resolutions will be applied to the different types. For resolutions

describing changes to supertypes, we found only small changes in precision and recall for the different subtypes. Also, the different UML model element instances vary concerning the values of their attributes and references. And while for different UML model element instances of the same UML model element the concrete values of the attributes and references vary, this has no effect on the precision and recall.

Thus, the application of our technique on a resolution that, e.g., is applied on 26 different inconsistent UML model element instances of the same type, returns the same precision and recall for all UML model element instances. For the application of the technique to resolutions of different subtypes of the same supertype, small differences in precision and recall are found.

Low Recall: The Influence of Removals on Accuracy

We observe low recall mainly in resolutions that contain the removal of a UML model element. That is, there are UML model elements that are removed in the resolution, but are not detected as impacted by the technique. For example, for the *namespace_1* inconsistency the resolutions removed an Interaction from the UML model. An interaction represents behavior contained in a sequence diagram and contains UML model elements such as the lifelines representing the objects as well as messages sent between the lifelines. In a removal, contained UML model elements such as the lifelines and messages are removed from the UML model. These UML model elements were correctly impacted, however since the prediction technique was initially set to only check UML model elements at distance 1, UML model element contained in the removed UML model element were not predicted impacted. In this specific example this means, messages were impacted but their arguments not, and also connectors were impacted but the contained connector ends were not.

The Influence of Distance on Recall

To avoid low recall for removal of UML model elements and increase the overall recall of the technique, we investigated a distance measure. As described in Section *2.4 Performing Impact Analysis*, impact analysis rules can be applied recursively. For each recursive application of an impact analysis rule to the UML model element instances that were found impacted by the prior application, the distance is increased by 1. A distance measure defines how often an impact analysis rule is applied recursively and to which UML model element instances. In order to investigate the influence on the accuracy of different distance measures, we implemented two distance measures. The initial distance measure implementation recursively applies the impact analysis rules on *all* the impacted UML model element instances (*Brute Distance*). The second distance measure uses a simple heuristic to decrease the number of UML model element instances to re-check (*Heuristic Distance*). The heuristic analyses the reference to the UML model elements to re-check and only re-checks those that are marked as *"Required = true"*. *Required* is an attribute, which exists for references in the EMF-based implementation of the UML meta-model. If *Required* is set to true this means that at least one value is required for a valid instance. That is, that an instance of the reference is required to exists for the UML model to be valid.

Figure 15. Distance measures compared for instance of dangling connectable association reference inconsistency

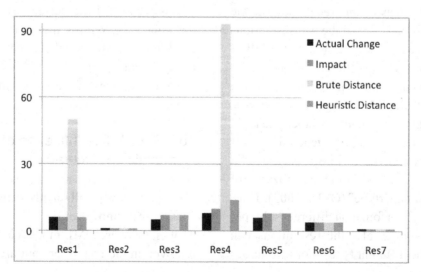

Figure 16. Precision and recall development for increase distance (remove element)

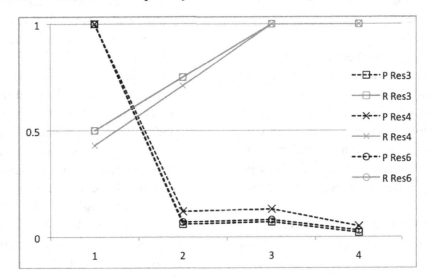

Figure 15 shows the number of impacted UML model element instances for increased distance (from distance 1 to a distance of 2 in this case). The figure shows the results for one instance of the *dangling connectable association reference* inconsistency.

Applying the two distance measures to the different resolutions we found that the *Heuristic Distance* that checks only required references nearly had no effect on the amount of impacted UML model element (e.g., Res3 in Figure 15). The main reason is that the specific UML model elements we checked do not have many references that are set as "Required". Therefore, the *Heuristic Distance* distance measure has no major impact on the recall, which we set out to increase with a distance measure. For the *Brute Distance* we found that the removal of UML model elements largely increases the number of impacted UML model element instances (e.g., Res1 and Res4 in Figure 15) and therefore can have an influence on the recall.

Figure 16 shows the precision and recall for the Brute Distance distance measure with increased distance for three different resolutions of the *namespace_1* inconsistency. We can see that the recall increases and the precision decreases for

a distance between 1 and 4 on. The dashed lines labeled with *P* represent precision and the lines labeled with *R* show recall. We see that while the recall increases in all cases at a distance of 3 to 1, the precision decreases dramatically. The reason why we only observe this behavior with the removal of UML model elements is that for additions the ATM model used for this study has a relatively flat hierarchy of UML model element instances and thus recursively re-checking containers quickly ends at the package or model level. And finally, for the creation and deletion of references the distance is only increased if the references are bi-directional and in general there are not many bi-directional references in the UML meta-model. Thus, if the target is to optimize the recall of the change impact analysis technique, the distance measure presents a viable solution. However, it does present a trade-off with the precision.

Threats to Validity

In this section we identify factors that may jeopardize the validity of our results and the actions we took to reduce or alleviate the risk. Consistent with the guidelines for case studies research (see

(Yin, 2002; Runeson, 2009)) we organize them into four categories.

Construct validity: do we measure what was intended? We define the impact of a resolution as the actual changes caused by it. However, the number of changes might not be a good indicator for the impact of a resolution, e.g., some changes may be more difficult than others. However, there is related work with the same approach such as (Briand, 2006).

The formulas for calculating precision and recall are taken from literature: Hattori et al. (Hattori, 2008).

Internal validity: are there unknown factors, which might affect the causal dependency? Since we had complete and fine-grained control over the changes applied to the system under study we can be certain that all observed effects are indeed caused by resolving a particular inconsistency.

External validity: to what extent it is possible to generalize the findings? Since this research was mainly a feasibility study ---investigating whether it is possible to exploit the UML meta-model to predict change impact--- external validity was not our primary concern. Nevertheless, we selected the cases to feature several UML diagrams, and we selected the consistency rules so that they cover different UML model elements (*meta-model coverage*), differently structured changes (*resolution coverage*), and different UML model element instances (*instance coverage*). As such, the case is sufficiently realistic for investigating the usage of the UML meta-model and the accuracy of the presented change impact analysis technique. However, since we choose two specific cases, these cases might display characteristics, which are specific to them and not to other projects. This should be tackled by future research,

which uses different cases for validation. Additionally, scalability remains an open issue; we will investigate larger models in the future.

Reliability: is the result dependent on the researchers and tools? We did several manual inspections of results to verify that our technique indeed worked as intended; in particular we compared the result set against the UML meta-model. The oracle against which we calculated the prediction and recall was obtained through the EMF change model. The result thus depends also on our implementation of the change model queries. Also here, we used manual inspections to ensure the validity.

Further, the validity of our results depends on the input used and the tools used to create the input. On the one hand, the UML editor used to create the models of the case studies influences the result by creating certain UML model elements in a certain way (we used the UML2 editor provided by the UML2 tools Eclipse plug-in). On the other hand, the specific inconsistencies used, their generation and the resolutions influence the validity. The inconsistencies we analyzed are both inconsistencies found in the initial version of the model as well as inconsistencies seeded in order to cover a larger amount of UML model elements. The resolutions were created based on our knowledge of the inconsistencies and the system. In order to ensure that the results can be reproduced with different input, we carefully document our decisions in this chapter.

CONCLUSION

In order to plan and execute changes during software maintenance it is important to assess the "ripple effects" that a change has to other parts of the system.

In this chapter, we presented a lightweight change impact analysis technique. We validated the predictions of the technique in terms of precision and recall against a baseline of actual changes obtained by the EMF change model. Based on our experiments, the change impact technique has a mean precision and recall of (0.97, 0.93) for the ATM case and a mean precision and recall of (0.77, 0.95) for the EU-Rent case. We also analyzed different decisions taken during construction in terms of their influence on the technique's accuracy, specifically precision and recall. From this we conclude that a lower precision is mainly due to the way we calculate the impact for addition of UML model elements and a lower recall can be attributed to the way we calculate the impact of removal of UML model elements. We also investigated the impact of recursively re-running the change impact analysis technique to specifically increase the recall for changes that remove a UML model element. We found that while the recall did indeed improve, with a simple recursive re-run, the precision quickly dropped below 0.1.

Compared to our previous work (see (Keller, 2009)) we improved the overall accuracy of the technique by a more fine-grained change definition.

REFERENCES

Arnold, R., & Bohner, S. (Eds.). (1996). *Software change impact analysis*. Wiley-IEEE Computer Society Press.

Briand, L. C., Labiche, Y., & O'Sullivan, L. (2003). *Impact analysis and change management of UML models* (SCE-03-01). Carleton University. Retrieved from http://www.sce.carleton.ca/Squall

Briand, L. C., Labiche, Y., O'Sullivan, L., & Sówka, M. M. (2006). Automated impact analysis of UML models. *J. Syst. Softw., 79*(3), 339--352. Doi: http://dx.doi.org/10.1016/j.jss.2005.05.001

Briand, L. C., Labiche, Y., & Yue, T. (2009). Automated traceability analysis for UML model refinements. *Information and Software Technology, 51*, 512–527..doi:10.1016/j.infsof.2008.06.002

Chen, C.-Y., & Chen, P.-C. (2009). A holistic approach to managing software change impact. *Journal of Systems and Software, 82*, 2051–2067.. doi:10.1016/j.jss.2009.06.052

Fisler, K., Krishnamurthi, S., Meyerovich, L. A., & Tschantz, M. C. (2005). Verification and change-impact analysis of access-control policies. In *Proceedings of the 27th International Conference on Software Engineering* (pp. 196--205). ACM. ISBN: 1-58113-963-2

Frias, L., Queralt, A., & Olivé, A. (2003). *EU-Rent Car rentals specification* (LSI-03-59-R). LSI Research Report.

Han, J. (1997). Supporting impact analysis and change propagation in software engineering environments. In *Software Technology and Engineering Practice, 1997. Proceedings., Eighth IEEE International Workshop on Incorporating Computer Aided Software Engineering* (pp. 172 -182).

Hattori, L., Guerrero, D., Figueiredo, J., Brunet, J., & Damásio, J. (2008). On the precision and accuracy of impact analysis techniques. *ACIS International Conference on Computer and Information Science*, (pp. 513-518). Doi: http://doi.ieeecomputersociety.org/10.1109/ICIS.2008.104

Keller, A., Schippers, H., & Demeyer, S. (2009). *Supporting inconsistency resolution through predictive change impact analysis*. In MODELS Workshop on Model-Driven Engineering, Verification, and Validation (MoDeVVa).

Kleppe, A. G., Warmer, J., & Bast, W. (2003). *MDA explained: The model driven architecture: Practice and promise*. Addison-Wesley Longman Publishing Co., Inc.

Kolovos, D. S., Paige, R. F., & Polack, F. A. (2006). The epsilon object language (EOL). *In Proc. of European Conference in Model Driven Architecture (EC-MDA)* Bilbao, Spain, (pp. 128-142). Retrieved from http://www.springerlink.com/content/r262468962017266/

Kung, D. C., Gao, J., Hsia, P., Wen, F., Toyoshima, Y., & Chen, C. (1994). Change impact identification in object oriented software maintenance. In *Proceedings of the International Conference on Software Maintenance* (pp. 202--211). IEEE Computer Society. ISBN: 0-8186-6330-8

Maule, A., Emmerich, W., & Rosenblum, D. S. (2008). Impact analysis of database schema changes. In *Proceedings of the 30th International Conference on Software Engineering* (pp. 451-460). ACM. ISBN: 978-1-60558-079-1

Morrissey, J. H., & Wu, L. S.-Y. (1979). Software engineering... an economic perspective. In *ICSE '79: Proceedings of the 4th International Conference on Software Engineering* (pp. 412–422). Piscataway, NJ: IEEE Press.

OMG - The Object Management Group. (2003). *Unified modeling language (UML) specification: Infrastructure*.

OMG - The Object Management Group. (2004). *UML 2.0 superstructure specification*. Retrieved from http://www.omg.org/cgi-bin/doc?ptc/2004-10-02

Ren, X., Ryder, B. G., Stoerzer, M., & Tip, F. (2005). Chianti: A change impact analysis tool for Java programs. In *Proceedings of the 27th International Conference on Software Engineering* (pp. 664--665). ACM. ISBN: 1-58113-963-2

Runeson, P., & Hųst, M. (2009). Guidelines for conducting and reporting case study research in software engineering. *Empirical Software Engineering, 14*(2), 131–164. doi:10.1007/s10664-008-9102-8

Spanoudakis, G., & Zisman, A. (2001). Inconsistency management in software engineering: Survey and open research issues. In Chang, S. K. (Ed.), *Handbook of software engineering and knowledge engineering* (*Vol. 1*, pp. 329–380).

Steinberg, D., Budinsky, F., Paternostro, M., & Merks, E. (2009). *EMF: Eclipse modeling framework 2.0*. Addison-Wesley Professional.

Straeten, R. V. D. (2005). *Inconsistency management in model-driven engineering: An approach using description logics. Unpublished doctoral disseration*. Vrije Universiteit Brussel.

Swanson, E. B. (1976). The dimensions of maintenance. In *ICSE '76: Proceedings of the 2nd International Conference on Software Engineering* (pp. 492-497). IEEE Computer Society Press.

Vallecillo, A. (2010). On the combination of domain specific modeling languages. In T. Kühne, B. Selic, M.-P. Gervais & F. Terrier (Eds.), *Modelling foundations and applications, vol. 6138* (pp. 305-320). Berlin, Germany: Springer. Retrieved from http://dx.doi.org/10.1007/978-3-642-13595-8_24

Yau, S., & Collofello, J. (1979). *Some stability measures for software maintenance* (pp. 674–679).

Yau, S., Collofello, J., & MacGregor, T. (1978). *Ripple effect analysis of software maintenance* (pp. 60–65).

Yin, R. K. (2002). *Case study research: Design and methods* (3rd ed.). Sage Publications.

Zhang, S., Gu, Z., Lin, Y., & Zhao, J. (2008). Change impact analysis for AspectJ programs. In *IEEE International Conference on Software Maintenance, ICSM 2008* (pp. 87 -96).

Chapter 3
Interplay of Security Requirements Engineering and Reverse Engineering in the Maintenance of Undocumented Software

Andrea Herrmann
University Heidelberg, Germany

Ayse Morali
Ascure N.V., Belgium

ABSTRACT

During software maintenance of security-relevant software, before changes are made, the impact analysis must be able to answer two questions: (1) How do changes in the (security) requirements affect the system's architecture and code? (2) How do changes in the code affect the system's requirements satisfaction, e.g. security?

A precondition to answer these questions reliably is that both requirements and code are documented and these models are linked traceably to each other. However, in practice, this often is not the case. In a situation where parts of this documentation are missing or outdated, in a first step, one needs methods for reconstructing and linking the models to each other. Such methods are known in the domains of requirements engineering and reverse engineering.

Requirements engineering and reverse engineering are two separate arts so far. However, as both solve parts of the same problem, we expect that combining methods from both domains can even better support the software documentation reconstruction and thus the impact analysis of security-relevant systems.

The contribution this chapter makes is to provide a literature overview on security requirements engineering methods as well as reverse engineering methods and to provide for categories to discuss how one can choose and link such methods to answer the two impact analysis questions.

DOI: 10.4018/978-1-61350-438-3.ch003

INTRODUCTION

Software maintenance includes the modification of a software system after its delivery in order to adapt it to changed requirements or to a changed environment or for the fault-correction (IEEE, 1998). This means that the requirements as well as the code evolve. It is important that before changes are made, their impact is analyzed, especially for security-relevant software.

The impact analysis must be able to answer two questions: (1) How do changes in the (security) requirements affect the system´s architecture and code?, and (2) How do changes in the code affect the system´s requirements satisfaction, e.g. security?

A precondition to answer these questions reliably is that both requirements and code are documented and these models are linked traceably to each other (Pfleeger and Bohner, 1990). These documentations must be complete and up-to-date. However, in practice, this often is not the case, as a survey has shown (Schier and Herrmann, 2010). In a situation where parts of this documentation are missing or outdated, in a first step, one needs methods for reconstructing and linking the models to each other. Only the second step can be to use these models for impact analysis and all other activities of model-driven software development.

So far, the analysis of security requirements engineering and reverse engineering play different roles during software maintenance:

The requirements engineering of security requirements identifies and models – in the form of requirements - what security means for different stakeholders, whether an existing software system is secure (i.e., whether it satisfies the security requirements) and how the security of this system can be improved. As security requirements are and must be specified from different viewpoints (like manager, user, architect and developer perspective), we claim that security requirements engineering can and should link these perspectives to each other (see Figure 1). Reverse

engineering "is the process of analyzing a subject system to identify the system's components and their interrelationships and create representations of the system in another form or at a higher level of abstraction" (Chikofsky and Cross II, 1990).

Requirements engineering and reverse engineering are two separate arts so far. (For instance, authors of requirements engineering articles do not cite reverse engineering articles and vice versa.) Requirements engineering belongs to the forward engineering process and usually proceeds top-down – from business objectives to user requirements. Reverse engineering vice versa proceeds bottom-up – from code to architecture models – as illustrated in Figure 1. However, as both solve parts of the same problem, we expect that combining methods from both domains can even better support the software documentation reconstruction and thus the impact analysis of security-relevant system.

In what follows, we focus on *security requirements*, where we believe that the topics treated in this chapter are most relevant. Also, we want to focus the literature overview, because security requirements engineering uses specific models which are often requirements engineering models adapted to security. Nevertheless, we expect that the framework we develop for to combine requirements engineering and reverse engineering methods can be applied to other software properties also, not only to security.

This chapter – based on the state of the art – discusses how methods from both disciplines can be combined during software maintenance in order to support the impact analysis. This chapter has the following structure: First, we start with some definitions needed in this chapter. Then, we develop categories which help to classify methods for the impact analysis and the model preparation for it. The subsequent two subchapters describe and classify the state of the art of security requirements engineering and reverse engineering methods. Finally, we summarize the state of the art and discuss how these methods can be chosen

Figure 1. Different perspectives in security engineering, examples of their artifacts, and the activities of forwards and reverse engineering

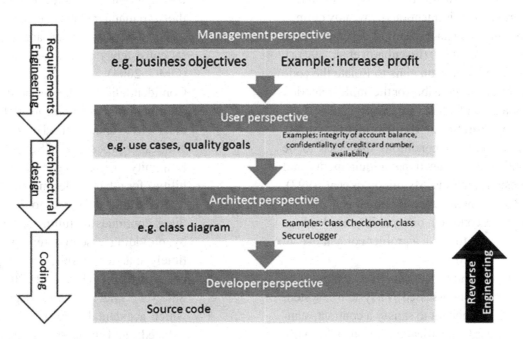

and combined, based on the categories found in the literature research.

Definitions

This subchapter gives some definitions which are needed later-on, in alphabetical order.

- **Aspect Mining:** Aspect mining is a research direction that tries to identify crosscutting concerns in already developed software systems, without using the aspect oriented paradigm. The goal is to identify them and then to refactor them to aspects, to obtain a system that can be easily understood, maintained and modified (Czibula et al., 2009).
- **Clone Detection** aims to detect code fragments that were replicated and slightly changed (Tonella et al., 2007).
- **Crosscutting Concern:** Crosscutting concerns are software system features whose implementation is spread across many mod-

ules as tangled and scattered code (Canfora et al., 2006), because it crosscuts the system´s decomposition into modular units (Bruntink et al., 2004).
- **Dynamic Analysis**, or the analysis of data gathered from a running program, has the potential to provide an accurate picture of a software system: e.g., in the context of object-oriented systems it can reveal object identities and occurrences of late binding (Cornelissen et al., 2008).
- **Execution Trace:** The execution trace lists the sequence of all performed calls (Eisenbarth et al., 2002). The execution trace can be visualized, for instance, as a matrix where time is presented on one axis and the files on the other axis. In the matrix fields, dark rectangles indicate which file was active at which point of time.
- **Execution Profile:** The execution profile of a given program is the set of all routines in the execution trace (Eisenbarth et al., 2002).

- **Feature:** A feature is a realized (functional as well as non-functional) requirement (the term feature is intentionally weakly defined because its exact meaning depends on the specific context) (Eisenbarth et al., 2001a).
- **Feature Location** aims to isolate the code portions responsible for the implementation of a given feature (Tonella et al., 2007).
- **Non-Functional Requirements** express constraints or conditions that need to be satisfied by functional requirements and design solutions (Myloupoulos et al.,1992).
- **Requirement:** A requirement is:
  (1) A condition or capability needed by a user to solve a problem or achieve an objective.
  (2) A condition or capability that must be met or possessed by a system or system component to satisfy a contract, standard, specification, or other formally imposed documents.
  (3) A documented representation of a condition or capability as in (1) or (2). (IEEE, 1990)
- **Scenario:** A scenario defines the context in which a feature is studied, for example, the sequence of the developer's actions with the program (Poshyvanyk et al., 2007).
- **Security:** Security is a software quality attribute with many facets. We define that security has the following factors:
  - Operational security: "Attributes of software that bear on its ability to prevent unauthorized access, whether accidental or deliberate, to programs and data." (ISO, 1991, section A.2.1.).
  - Availability: "Availability is the capability of the software product to be in a state to perform a required function at a given point in time, under stated conditions of use." (OMG, 2008).
  - Integrity: "The property that data has not been altered or destroyed in an unauthorized manner" (ISO, 1989);

data and programs are modified or destroyed only in a specified and authorized manner (Madan et al., 2002).
  - Coherence: concurrent and temporal consistency of data and functions (OMG, 2004).
  - Confidentiality: "The property that information is not made available or disclosed to unauthorized individuals, entities, or processes." (ISO, 1989).
  - Immunity: non-existence of vulnerabilities for attacks (Herrmann, 2007).
  - Survivability: "Degree to which a thing continues to fulfill its mission by providing essential services in a timely manner in spite of the presence of attacks" (Firesmith, 2003a).
  - Safety: "Safety is the degree to which accidental harm is prevented, reduced, and properly reacted to" (Firesmith, 2003b).
- **Static Code Analysis** is "based on the source code alone" (Tonella et al., 2007), without execution of the program.
- A **Tool** is an application which implements and supports the usage of one or more methods. Clearly, each method can be implemented or supported in different ways by several tools (Tonella et al., 2007).
- **Traceability:** The ability of a software to provide a thread from the requirements to the implementation, with respect to the specific development and operational environment (IEEE, 1998).

Categories

In this chapter, we present categories of models and steps which support the preparation and execution of impact analysis. These will later-on help to classify the methods found during our literature research. The categories defined in this chapter are the result of our literature research. We do not use the terms of any specific method but develop our own as an abstraction of what we found in literature. Where the methods we found make a difference – even if made implicitly – we also make a difference, because this category helps to classify the methods. For instance, we do not distinguish the four types of maintenance which the IEEE Standard (IEEE, 1998) knows – adaptive, perfective, corrective and emergency – because the methods identified during our literature research do not make a difference between these four. Rather, we classify changes according to whether they modify system vision (adaptive and perfective) or the real system (corrective and emergency).

We found the following dimensions of categories:

- **Perspectives** describe a specific stakeholder´s view, but also the level of abstraction of the models which this perspective uses.
- **Reality or vision:** The same models can document the system as it is or a vision of a system. Vision requirements describe what stakeholders want or need. It is not guaranteed that these requirements will be realized or even can be realized. They might contradict each other.
- **Steps** describe single steps which, starting from an undocumented software system lead to a documented system and its impact analysis.

In what follows, we define and describe the dimensions and their categories which we identified from the requirements engineering and reverse engineering literature.

The four perspectives (see Figure 1) we define as follows, top-down from high level of abstraction down to code with no abstraction:

- **Management perspective:** This perspective most often defines business objectives, which exist independently of the software

system, but the software system is part of a strategy to satisfy these objectives. The business objectives can form a hierarchy.
- **User perspective:** The user views the software system as a black box and is mostly interested in what happens at the interface between system and user. This not only includes functionality (functional requirements), but also quality of the system (non-functional requirements), that means not only what it does but also how it does it. We distinguish between functional and non-functional requirements. Both are treated differently by requirements engineering and reverse engineering methods. We make the note that while security is a non-functional requirement, when it is operationalized in more detailed requirements this leads to functional requirements.
- **Architect perspective:** The architect has a technical but abstract view on the software system and views it as a set of components and their interactions. The components can form hierarchies.
- **Developer perspective:** The developer reads the source code. No abstraction is made.

We cannot say whether all these perspectives are necessary when modeling a software system. That mainly depends on the stakeholders involved and their needs. We use these perspectives to categorize existing requirements engineering and reverse engineering models.

Reality or vision: One cannot say that some perspectives or models always belong to reality or vision. For instance, at the moment when a system is implemented, its requirements models can become a realistic documentation of the functionality and quality of the existing system. Whether a model describes reality or vision is an attribute which might change. Even code can be a vision, when it is in a prototypical status.

Our topic is the analysis of the impact of changes. These changes can originate either from high-level visions (adaptive and perfective maintenance) or from a change of the real code (corrective or emergency maintenance) (IEEE, 1998). It seems unrealistic that code vision is changed first, without serving a vision change on a higher level of abstraction, and also the requirements satisfaction is not modified without code change. Therefore, the impact analysis takes place in two directions - forwards and reverse:

- **Forwards impact analysis** (From high-level visions to real code): One wants to analyze the impact which new or modified business objectives or user requirements have on the existing system in terms of cost, architecture modifications and risk reduction or even risk increase.
- **Reverse impact analysis** (From real code to high-level visions): One wants to analyze the impact which code modifications have on the satisfaction of the security requirements. For instance: Will processes then work differently from user perspective, will security increase or decrease, how does performance change and will business objectives still be satisfied?

Consequently, it seems necessary, that there exists at least one vision model and real code documentation.

As we said in the introduction, **traceability** between the models is a precondition for being able to answer the impact analysis questions reliably. When our starting point is undocumented software, before analyzing impact, we must first reconstruct both models and traceability links.

During our literature research in the security requirements engineering and reverse engineering literature, we found the following **steps** for reconstructing the models for undocumented software and quantifying impact:

a) Elicitation of requirements from the stakeholders, including modeling them.
b) Qualitative forwards impact analysis: Reconstruction of traceability links between models top-down.
c) Quantitative forwards impact analysis: Quantifying impact of changes top-down.
d) Reconstruction of documentation of real code.
e) Qualitative reverse impact analysis: Reconstruction of traceability links between models bottom-up.
f) Quantitative reverse impact analysis: Quantifying impact of changes bottom-up.

Criteria for the quantification of change impact are cost, architectural modification, and risk.

We found method support for the steps (a) to (c) in the requirements engineering domain. These proceed top-down in the direction of forward engineering. The steps (d) to (f) proceed bottom-up in the direction of reverse engineering. The chronological order in which the steps are to be executed, should probably start with the reconstruction of the models (that means steps (a) and (d)) which are the precondition for the reconstruction of traceability links (steps (b) and (e)), which are the precondition for the quantitative impact analysis (steps (c) and (f)).

These are the categories which emerged from our analysis and comparison of the methods we found during our literature research. In what follows, we classify the results of this literature research according to these categories.

Forwards Impact Analysis

Requirements from both user and management perspective change as the software system environment changes, e.g. new business strategy, new legislations, new threats and new functionalities.

Additionally, code evolves by fault correction, restructuring, and extension, which influences the requirements satisfaction. Thus, models of the current system – vision as well as reality documentation - become often incomplete and out-dated.

The forward impact analysis has the objective to quantify the impact of changes in the system vision on the code. This includes three steps:

a) Elicitation of requirements from the stake-holders, including modeling them.
b) Qualitative forwards impact analysis: Reconstruction of traceability links between models top-down.
c) Quantitative forwards impact analysis: Quantifying impact of changes top-down.

Forward impact analysis is especially difficult for highly coupled software, i.e. software that responds to faults of other distributed software and hardware components, and when the software is not well modularized, e.g. when executing a functionality, many architectural components are concerned.

In this subchapter, typical security requirements engineering methods are described, in the subsequent subchapter, they are compared to each other. All of these methods are made for eliciting requirements from stakeholders and modeling these, i.e. they support step (a). Table 1 analyzes which perspectives each of the methods includes and how traceability links are modeled. The requirements engineering methods do not model the code, i.e. the developer perspective. However, the other three perspectives can be found to be supported: management perspective, user perspective and architect perspective. Those methods which support more than one perspective, usually also model traceability links between the perspectives, but they provide no support for the reconstruction of traceability links. So, step (b) is only partly supported. Table 1 also comments on how traceability links are modeled. Step (c), the

quantification of impact, is usually not supported, but the documentation of these impacts. Table 2 shows which method supports which of the three categories of impact: cost, architectural modification, and risk. Although requirements engineering methods have the purpose of modeling visions, they can also model reality, that means the real properties of a software system.

Some methods cover all three perspectives:

• Tropos is one of the most widely known goal-oriented software development methodology (Castro et al., 2002). Tropos adopts the i* (Yu, 1995) organizational modeling framework to model early and late requirements, as well as architectural and detailed design. They refine the goals of the actors of a system (stakeholders) down to the behavior of each architectural component.
• Fabian et al. (2010) give a state of the art overview on security requirements engineering methods and for doing so have developed a conceptual model which integrates those of many separate methods. Therefore, this model is more complete than other models.
• The Common Criteria (2009a, 2009b and 2009c) link business perspective, user perspective and architectural perspective and describe them using the same concepts, thus not clearly distinguishing between the perspectives.
• Secure Tropos (Mouratidis et al., 2003) is an extension of the Tropos method (Castro et al., 2002) by security related concepts, such as integrity and privacy, as well as by risk estimation concepts. The three layers of the model (assets, events, and treatments) correspond to the business, user and architectural perspective respectively.
• Combining Secure Tropos and UMLSec leads to a method that covers all three perspectives (Mouratidis and Jurjens, 2010).

Table 1. Comparison of security requirements engineering methods with respect to which perspectives they cover and how, and how they document links between them

Method	Management perspective	User perspective	Architect perspective	Link between perspectives
Tropos (Castro et al., 2002) and Secure Tropos (Mouratidis et al., 2003)	Actor goal	functional and non-functional requirement	Architectural component	Goal refinement
Conceptual model of Fabian et al. (2010)	Functional goal, non-functional goal, security goal	(Organizational) procedure and process, use, functional requirement, non-functional requirement, security requirement, stakeholder, asset, information, counter-stakeholder, circumstances, assumption (domain level), fact (domain level), resource, vulnerability, potential loss, risk, countermeasure, attack, threat, attacker, threat agent	Assumption (design level), facts (design level), specification (requirements which the machine can fulfill), design of the machine; Facts (implementation level), implementation of the machine (incl. deployment and configuration)	Specific relationships between the concepts in a conceptual model
Common Criteria (2009a, 2009b and 2009c)	Target of Evaluation (TOE); the evaluation context and audience to which the evaluation criteria are addressed; EAL = evaluation assurance level	asset, owner, threat agent, threat, risk, countermeasure, vulnerability, cause of vulnerability	Not considered	From threat to counter-measure
I* extension of Elahi and Yu (2009)	Design goal and objective, softgoal	actor, task, softgoal, resource, security-specific concepts (threat, vulnerability, attacker, malicious goal, attack, asset, security mechanism)	Not considered	goal contribution, goal decomposition, means-end-analysis
goal-risk model of Asnar et al. (2010)	asset layer: business object, goal, task	event layer: event with likelihood, impact with severity, risk	treatment layer: treatment	Arrows within layers and between layers
GSRM of Islam (2009), Islam and Houmb (2010)	Goal layer	risk-obstacle layer, assessment layer (likelihood, impact)	treatment layer	From goal via obstacle to treatment
Mayer et al. (2005 and 2007)	business asset	i*: actor, goal, task, resource, softgoal; security: security goal, risk, threat, vulnerability, impact, constraint, security requirement	information system asset, vulnerability, risk treatment	As "dependency" arrows in the graphical model
BSI Standards (BSI, 2008a), (BSI, 2008b), (BSI, 2008c)	Processes of security management, including personnel, data security concept, outsourcing, home office, server rooms and buildings; criticality of data and applications; damage quantification with respect to privacy, integrity and availability (normal/ high/ very high); threats with respect to privacy, integrity and availability	Not considered	Assets: data and application	damage is quantified from the business perspective and prioritizes threats and countermeasures; links between concepts are documented in tables
Abuse cases (McDermott and Fox, 1999)	Not considered	Abuse case	Not considered	

continued on following page

Table 1. Continued

Sindre and Opdahl (2001 and 20052005)	Not considered	mis-actor, misuse case (=name, summary, basic path, alternative path, capture point, extension point, extension point, trigger, assumption, precondition, postcondition, related business rule, potential misuser profile, stakeholder and threat, scope)	Not considered	
Firesmith (2004)	Not considered	security goal, security, policy, security requirement, quality factor, security mechanism, security risk, threat, attacker, attack, harm, vulnerability, asset	Not considered	
OMG model (OMG, 2004)	SWOT analysis, context submodel	Unwanted incident submodel, risk model	Not considered	
Elahi et al. (2010)	Not considered	asset, threat/ attack, effect, security impact, vulnerability, countermeasure, malicious task, malicious goal, malicious softgoal; i* concepts: actor, goal, softgoal, task, dependency, decomposition	Not considered	
Attack trees and attack patterns of Moore et al. (2001)	Not considered	attack tree consisting of attack goals and sub-goals; attack pattern: goal, precondition, steps of attack, postcondition		Graphical in the attack tree
EMPRESS (Dörr et al., 2003 and 2004)	value	Task, quality attribute, metric, means, functional requirement, non-functional requirement	Architectural requirement	Refinement in a quality model
Goal-oriented method (Lamsweerde, 2003)	Not considered	(soft)goal, agent, expectation, object, obstacle, vulnerability	requirement	Refinement within the goal tree, e.g. with AND and OR relationships
SecReq (Houmb et al., 2010)	Not considered	system objective, security target, target of evaluation, protection profile + security-related stereotype like security objective, security requirement	object and sequence diagrams, deployment diagram + security-related stereotypes	use case diagram -> activity diagram -> object and sequence diagrams, deployment diagram
SQUARE (Mead et al., 2005)	Not considered	threat, misuse case, incident, prevention, quantification: baseline risk, bypass rate, residual risk, net present value		Derivation of preventions from misuse cases, and risk quantification
Component-Bus-System-Properties (CBSP) Approach (Grünbacher et al., 2001)	Not considered	Requirement (any form)	Components and their interactions (modeled as connectors)	Manual categorization of requirements
NFR Framework (Chung et al. 2000, Cysneiros et al. 2003)	Not considered	NFR softgoals and their dependencies	Operationalization softgoal	refinement and decomposition in the softgoal interdependency graph (SIG): Operationalization softgoal contributes to (satisficing or denying) of NFR softgoal
Threat Modeling extension of the NFR Framework (Oladimeji et al., 2006)	System goal	NFR Softgoal, N-softgoal (negative softgoal = threat), asset, vulnerability, access point	Operationalizing softgoal (counter-measure)	refinement in the softgoal interdependency graph (SIG) and threat-SIG, additional contribution: inverse contribution relation = threat

continued on following page

Table 1. Continued

Security patterns (Yoshioka et al., 2008), (Yoder and Barcalow, 1997), (Dougherty et al., 2009), [CGI], [coresec]	Not considered	Not considered	Pattern = components and their interactions	It is assumed that using these patterns enhances<< security respectively avoid a security threat
Security patterns of Blakley et al. (2004)	Not considered	Not considered	Security patterns, elements: motivation, applicability, structure, participants, collaborations, consequences, implementation	
UMLsec (Jürjens, 2001, 2003 and 2005)	Not considered	Not considered	UML plus stereotypes (e.g. risk, crash/performance, value, guarantee, redundancy, safe links, safe dependency, critical, safe behavior, containment, error handling), tagged values (for security levels), and constraints	
RiskREP (Herrmann and Morali, 2010)	Business goals and business damages	Quality goals, quality deficiencies, misuse cases, countermeasures	Incident Propagation Paths, countermeasures	Top-down analysis; documentation in graphics on management perspective and in tables for the other two perspectives

- Risk-Based Requirements Elicitation and Prioritization (RiskREP) combines a top-down requirements analysis with a bottom-up, architecture-based risk analysis (Herrmann and Morali, 2010). Top-down, it prioritizes business goals, and from these derives security goals and then verifiable requirements. Bottom-up, it analyzes IT architectures in order to identify security risks in the form of critical components. Linking these critical components to security requirements helps to analyze the effects of requirements on architecture and vice versa, and also to prioritize the security requirements identified.

The link between business and user perspective is made by:

- The Goal-Driven Software Development Risk Management Model (GSRM) of Islam (Islam, 2009; Islam and Houmb (2010) which is an extension of KAOS, and
- Mayer et al. (2005 and 2007) who integrate requirements engineering (i*) and risk

management with the objective to improve business/IT alignment.
- To systematically elicit security requirements, Elahi and Yu (2009) propose to derive security requirements from high level goals by extending the i* framework.

The first work does not clearly separate between business and user perspective by using different concepts, while the second does.

Uniting business and architectural perspective without treating the user perspective explicitly is done by only one of our sources: The Standards of the BSI (Bundesministerium für Sicherheit in der Informationstechnik = German Minstery of Security in Information Technology) (BSI 2008a, 2008b, 2008c) integrate business perspective and architectural perspective. The Standard 100-1 (BSI 2008a) describes security purely from the business perspective in the form of processes and responsibilities in information security and risk management, where damage is quantified from the business perspective. Standard 100-2 (BSI 2008b) performs an analysis of the technical infrastructure, from the architectural perspective, while the criticality of data and damages which

Table 2. Comparison of security requirements engineering methods with respect to impact quantification

Method	Impact in terms of cost	Impact in terms of risk mitigation	Impact in terms of architectural modification
Tropos (Castro et al., 2002)	Not considered	Risk is considered as a non-functional requirement	Allows comparing two architectures depending on how well they satisfy the requirements
Conceptual model of Fabian et al. (2010)	Protection cost	Vulnerability mitigation and risk reduction	Not considered
Common Criteria (2009a, 2009b and 2009c)	Cost	Countermeasures reduce risk to assets; sufficiency of countermeasures	Not considered
Goal-Risk Framework (Asnar et al., 2010)	Cost and value of assets (goals) and resources are linked to business goals	Treatments impact on risk by reducing its likelihood or attenuating its severity	Not considered
GSRM (Islam and Houmb, 2010)	Cost is one of the risk treatment evaluation criteria (risk metric) among resource availability and goal of implementation	Consider risks related with each requirement by prioritizing them	Not considered
Mayer et al. (2005, 2007)	Suggests cost of countermeasures and value of business asset as requirements ranking criteria	Risk analysis is a core part of requirements engineering	Links business goals to system architecture over security requirements
BSI Standards (BSI, 2008a), (BSI, 2008b), (BSI, 2008c)	Cost and also other resources needed is specified	Measures are qualified according to the qualification level for which they are needed	Not considered
Abuse cases (McDermott and Fox, 1999)	Not considered	Not considered	Not considered
Sindre and Opdahl (2001 and 20052005)	Not considered	likelihood and cost of each misuse variant	Not considered
Firesmith (2004)	Not considered	Countermeasures are chosen in order to achieve an acceptable risk level	Not considered
OMG model (OMG, 2004)	Not considered	Risk reduction is quantified and also types of risk reduction are distinguished: avoid, reduce consequence, reduce likelihood, transfer, retain	Not considered
Security extended i* method (Elahi and Yu, 2009)	Assets have a value and security requirements protect this value. But cost of satisfying requirements is not considered	Determines the risk of security requirements based on the affected vulnerabilities	Not considered
Attack trees and attack patterns of Moore et al. (2001)	Not considered	Not considered	Not considered
EMPRESS (Dörr et al., 2003 and 2004)	Not considered	Not considered	Means can be architectural patterns
Goal-Oriented Requirements Engineering (Lamsweerde et al. 2003)	Not considered	Not considered	Not considered

continued on following page

Table 2. Continued

Secure Tropos (Mou-ratidis et al., 2003)	By evaluating different architectural alternatives complexity (the effort required for achieving a task) is considered.	Security is analyzed parallel to other goals; by evaluating different archi-tectural alternatives criticality (how the goals of actors will be affected if a task is not achieved) is considered	Allows comparing two architectures depending on how critical and complex they are
SecReq (Houmb et al., 2010)	Not considered	Not considered	Not considered
SQUARE (Mead et al., 2005)	Not considered	Analyzes risk (impact and likeli-hood) of the treats to the security of an IT system	Analyzes the effects of requirements on IT architecture
Component-Bus-Sys-tem-Properties (CBSP) Approach (Grünbacher et al., 2001)	Not considered	Not considered	Requirements are categorized according to their influence on architecture
NFR Framework (Chung et al. 2000, Cysneiros et al. 2003)	can be included as claim softgoal	Can be included as claim softgoal	Positive contribution and negative con-tribution
Threat Modeling extension of the NFR Framework (Oladimeji et al., 2006)	As claim softgoal	Qualitative, as "inverse contribution" relation, and as claim softgoal	Countermeasures are defined as "architec-tural mechanisms"
Security patterns (Yo-shioka et al., 2008), (Yoder and Barcalow, 1997), (Dougherty et al., 2009), [CGI], [coresec]	Can be described in the field "consequences"	Can be described in the field "conse-quences" or "motivation"	Security patterns mostly are architectural patterns
Security patterns of Blakley et al. (2004)	Can be described in the field "consequences"	Can be described in the field "conse-quences" or "motivation"	Can be described in the field "conse-quences" or "applicability"
UMLsec (Jürjens, 2001 and 2003)	Not considered	Using stereotype "value"	yes
RiskREP (Herrmann and Morali, 2010)	Is considered as a crite-rion for the choice of the optimal set of security requirements	Security requirements are defined in order to reduce risk; risk reduction is terms of reduction of ease and impact is quantified	Identifies critical architectural compo-nents and Incident Propagation Paths as basis for vulnerability and requirements identification

might be caused by security incidents are quanti-fied from a business perspective. The structural analysis documents the current status and then the protection need is analyzed, countermeasures are chosen, risk assessed. Finally, countermeasures are consolidated and realized. Standard 100-3 (BSI 2008c) adds quantitative risk analysis to this analysis.

From the user perspective, security incidents and their countermeasures are described in the form of abuse cases (McDermott and Fox, 1999), as misuse cases (Firesmith, 2004; Sindre and

Opdahl, 2001 and 20052005), in the OMG model for quality of service and fault tolerance (OMG, 2004), by the framework for security requirements elicitation and analysis centered on vulnerabilities of Elahi et al. (2010). Vulnerabilities in this work are weaknesses in the requirements, design, and implementation, which attackers exploit to com-promise the system.

Methods which analyze the user perspective in order to derive requirements on the architectural perspective have been found to be most frequent:

- The Component-Bus-System-Properties (CBSP) Approach (Grünbacher et al., 2001) offers a process for mapping requirements to architecture. It is not specific for security requirements, but can be applied to these. The CBSP is a lightweight approach of five steps. In the end, the requirements are categorized into the six CBSP dimensions: C, B, S, CP, BP, and SP. The architecture is described in the style of language C2, where components provide services and require services, and are linked via buses. A requirement is of category C, when it contains component-relevant information, and correspondingly for bus (connector)-relevant information (B). General (crosscutting) system requirements that affect a larger part of the architecture, are of category S. Non-functional requirements belong to the categories CP, BP, and SP, where "P" stands for "property". The requirements are categorized by voting of the stakeholders and reconciling their conflicting classifications, supported by the tool EasyWinWin.
- Models that combine user perspective and architect perspective without clear separation are the attack trees and attack patterns of Moore et al. (2001), and the misuse cases of the SQUARE method (Mead et al., 2005) (SQUARE = Security Quality Requirements Engineering). To reduce the effort needed to complete SQUARE researchers developed new versions of the method focusing on reusability, R-SQUARE (Christian, 2010) and SQUARE-Lite (Gayash et al., 2008).
- The NFR Framework (Chung et al. 2000, Cysneiros et al. 2003), the goal-oriented model of Lamsweerde (2003), the EMPRESS models (Dörr et al. 2003 and 2004) and the extended NFR Framework of Oladimeji et al. (2006) elicit user perspective concepts and architectural concepts separately, and model them in an integrated model.
- SecReq (Houmb et al., 2010) is a security requirements engineering methodology that combines three techniques: Common Criteria, heuristic, and UMLsec.

A pure architectural perspective is taken by:

- Security (design) patterns (Yoshioka et al., 2008; Yoder and Barcalow, 1997; Blakley et al., 2004; Dougherty et al., 2009; [CGI]; [coresec]) are high-level abstract structuring principles of an architecture, which describe how a system can be modularized in several components and their interaction. Architectures which implement a security pattern are known to be more secure than alternative ways of modularization and interaction. Often, it is defined which security vulnerability is avoided by using a specific security pattern.
- UMLsec is an extension of UML for modeling security requirements and also potential failure on the architectural level. The UML extension mechanisms used are stereotypes, tagged values, and constraints (Jürjens, 2001, 2003 and 2005).

Comparison of the Security Requirements Engineering Methods

The security requirements engineering methods described before, are now compared to each other in two dimensions:

1. **See Table 1:** With respect to which perspectives they model: management, user and/ or architecture perspective. (Requirements engineering methods never treat the developer perspective, but stay on an abstract level.) In the corresponding column, the method´s concepts are listed. We also make a hint on

how each method links the traceability links between perspectives top-down.

2. **See Table 2:** Methods are classified according to whether they quantify or model the quantification of the effects of requirements changes on cost of satisfying requirements, security risks and architecture.

As requirements get modified or new requirements are introduced one needs to reevaluate the cost and effectiveness of requirements. Such an evaluation requires estimating the security risks each requirement mitigates, considering the dependencies and trade-off among the requirements, as well as their costs and effectiveness. This is a very complex and costly process. Thus, a dynamic requirements engineering method with tool support is necessary that can dynamically reevaluate the new set of requirements each time there is a requirement added or modified. However, only some requirements engineering methods take into consideration the risk, as well as cost and effectiveness of requirements, and influence on architecture. Such methods are the extended i* approach presented in (Elahi and Yu, 2009), GSRM (Islam et al., 2010), the extended KAOS presented in (van Lamsweerde et al., 2003), the approach proposed by Mayer et al. (Mayer et al., 2007) and RiskREP (Herrmann and Morali, 2010). And to the best of our knowledge, none of them can reevaluate requirements automatically.

When applied together, requirements may contradict with each other or support each other. Elahi and Yu (2009), Mylopoulos et al. (2001), Mayer et al. (2007), and Asnar et al. (2010) consider these combined effects and prioritize the system requirements accordingly. ATAM (Architecture Tradeoff Analysis Method) (Kazman et al, 2000) also considers how countermeasures affect each other and point out the architectural tradeoffs.

The methods that model the impact of requirement modifications on architecture can be a potentially link to reverse engineering because reverse engineering produces such an architectural model.

The common property of risk-based approaches is that they first elicit requirements from business goals and prioritize them according to the risks they mitigate. However, not all of the risk-based approaches consider costs of requirements and the architectural modification into consideration. Table 2 presents an overview of the requirements engineering methods that we present above according these attributes.

According to Table 2: Comparison of security requirements engineering methods with respect to impact quantification. Table 2, there are only five methods that consider all three attributes: Secure Tropos (Mouratidis et al., 2003), the approach of Mayer et al. (Mayer et al., 2005), the NFR Framework (Chung et al. 2000, Cysneiros et al. 2003), its Threat Modeling extension (Oladimeji et al., 2006) and RiskREP (Herrmann and Morali, 2010).

However, although some methods model the impact in terms of both cost and risk, to the best of our knowledge, there is no method that reevaluates or even quantifies the requirements systematically and semi-automatically after a change in the requirements.

Reverse Impact Analysis

The reverse impact analysis has the objective to find out: If a certain piece of code is modified, which requirements and their degree of satisfaction are affected? By how much? Will processes then work differently from user perspective, will security increase or decrease, or how does performance change?

Reverse engineering methods analyze the code to reconstruct more abstract models of the code. In terms of perspectives, the developer perspective is the starting point, and the reverse engineering methods reconstruct the architect perspective and the link of this developer perspective to the architect or/ and user perspective.

Reverse engineering methods always analyze and model reality, not visions.

As was said before, we reviewed reverse engineering methods with respect to how they support the following three steps:

d) Reconstruction of documentation of real code.
e) Qualitative reverse impact analysis: Reconstruction of traceability links between models bottom-up.
f) Quantitative reverse impact analysis: Quantifying impact of changes bottom-up.

During our literature research, we found many methods which identify traceability links semi-automatically, using code analysis. However, it seems that the quantification of the impact has not been investigated at all so far. On the contrary, it has been emphasized that "just because artifacts are linked doesn't mean that a change will propagate. Engineering judgment is necessary for determining which impact-tree branches can be pruned or where you must add new branches because new artifacts are required" (Dick, 2005).

We identified six types of reverse engineering methods which support steps (e) and/ or (f):

- Manual code analysis, the so-called "grep" lexical text search method
- Static code analysis
- Dynamic code analysis of traces of execution
- Hybrid methods combining static and dynamic analysis
- Analysis of the development history
- Semantic code and text analysis

Typical examples of each type of methods are presented in what follows. In the end of the chapter, the method types are compared to each other.

Manual Code Analysis

Manual code analysis, the so-called "grep" lexical text search method, means that a developer manually searches for key words in the code, e.g. in variable names, function names and comments. As a starting point, he needs a hypothesis about the names of the variables and functions which implement a specific architectural component or requirement. He then tests this hypothesis by first searching for this key word and if he finds code with this word, he checks whether the code really implements the expected component or requirement. If he finds no code with the key word or if the code found implements something else, he creates a new hypothesis/ key word. This approach has been evaluated like this: "Grep and similar tools provide very fast search for text strings matching a given regular expression. The tool is used to search for relevant comments, variable names, and so on that the software engineer hypothesizes as being present in the code. Each segment that is found must be studied, and this study may give rise to new queries to look for additional comments, subroutines or variables. One problem with the grep method is that there is no obvious stopping point if a meaningful comment or code segment is not found quickly. Grep may find that variable A is used to set B and C, B is used to set D, D to set E and F, and so on. Taken to an extreme, the grep method may degenerate into an exhaustive search of the call or data flow graph of the program." (Wilde et al., 2003)

In this type of method, the abstract system model on architecture or user perspective is guessed by the executing person, and the traceability link identified manually also. No specific model is provided which documents the abstract model and the traceability links. On the other hand, all types of models can be combined with this procedure.

Static Code Analysis

A huge diversity of code properties can be analyzed in order to find links to more abstract models, e.g. requirements models. Usually, the type of analysis applied also constrains the type of requirements which can be located in the code.

- One can use *dependency graphs*, e.g. data flow or call flow, like Chen and Rajlich (2000), who search these graphs in order to locate the code that executes a specific feature or concept. Different search strategies are known and documented in a search graph.

- The Hierarchical Clustering Algorithm for Crosscutting Concerns Identification (HACO) uses dissimilarity metric respectively a *distance function* for object-oriented code, in order to identify crosscutting concerns in existing software (Czibula et al., 2009). They assume that methods from different crosscutting concerns are distant from each other and methods from the same crosscutting concern are close to each other.

- Cleland-Huang and Schmelzer (2003) define the EBTDP approach which uses *design patterns* as an intermediate concept when recovering traceability links between code and non-functional requirements. The approach is based on the idea that non-functional requirements are often implemented by or supported by design patterns. The user initially defines coarse-grained links, and the method dynamically generates fine-grained traceability links during system maintenance.

- Aspect mining by *clone detection* assumes that when concerns cannot be cleanly modularized, they are implemented by code duplication: Bruntink et al. (2004a, 2004b) successfully test three different clone detection techniques to identify crosscutting concerns like error handling. The three tools used here are: Axivion Bauhaus Suite clone detector 'ccdiml' (version 4.7.2) and CCFinder (version 7.1.1). Clone metrics help to distinguish between clones which

are less or more relevant for an aspect (Bruntink, 2004; Bruntink et al., 2004a).

- The approach of Zhang et al. (2006) for identifying use cases in source code is based on the observation that in procedural programming languages, *branch statements* are a primary mechanism to separate one use case from another in source code. Following this idea, they design a static representation of software systems through incorporating branch information into the traditional call graph, which is named the Branch-Reserving Call Graph (BRCG). First, the BRCG for the entire system is constructed by analyzing the source code. Second, the initial BRCG is pruned to get rid of irrelevant nodes (using an importance metric). Third, use cases are generated by traversing the pruned BRCG. Fourth, the generated use cases are reviewed to construct a use case model with some adjustment if necessary.

- Marin et al. (2007) use the *fan-in metric* for aspect mining and is supported by an Eclipse plug-in called FINT. A high fan-in characterizes methods that are called from many different places, which can be seen as a symptom of crosscutting functionality. The approach is semiautomatic, and consists of three steps: metric calculation, method filtering, and call site analysis. The method especially finds crosscutting concerns which are largely scattered.

Dynamic Code Analysis

The dynamic code analysis executes the code and analyses its behavior during execution. The execution is documented by traces of execution, what means that in a log file data is gathered as a protocol of what parts of the code have been used, when and how. Often, the code must be instrumented (i.e. additional code must be inserted which creates such a log file) before dynamic code analysis is possible. The following methods are typical examples of how dynamic code analysis helps to link code to more abstract models:

- **Software reconnaissance** and **feature location** methods map execution traces to test cases/ scenarios and these to features. The steps to be executed are: test case definition, code instrumentation, test case execution, analysis of the program's trace to view how program execution varies between test cases, comparison of traces from different test cases to extract those code pieces which are specific to one test case, map the code to features.
  - **Software reconnaissance** is a research topic at the University of West Florida. It has been executed for C programs (Lukoit et al., 2000), Fortran (Wilde et al., 2003) and for Ada (White and Wilde, 2001). Software reconnaissance is supported by two tools, RECON and TraceGraph. RECON3 is used to instrument C/C++ and Fortran code, with plans to include Ada and Java in the future (Fantozzi, 2002; Wilde, 2010). The visualization of the traces is done by the Trace Graph tool. TraceGraph shows time on the x-axis of a diagram and the traces on the y-axis. A piece of code is coloured grey if executed and black when executed for the first time (Lukoit et al., 2000).
  - Wong et al. (2000) use an execution slice-based technique to identify the basic blocks which are used to implement a program feature. They use three metrics to improve the mapping between program component and feature: the quantitative disparity between a program component and a feature, the concentration of a feature in a program component, and the

dedication of a program component to a feature.
  - The **Trace Analyzer** technique and tool presents execution traces in the form of a footprint graph. Rules are then used for mapping code nodes to model elements such as data flow, class, and use case diagrams. Starting with predefined hypothesized traces, the traceability recovery can happen fully automated, and can produce a complete set of traceability links, at the expense of also producing some incorrect ones (Egyed and Grunbacher, 1994; Egyed, 2001; Egyed and Grunbacher, 2002).
  - The **TraceScraper** compacts the feature execution traces into sets of source artifacts that participate in a feature's runtime behavior. The tool takes a two-sided perspective: feature perspective (which shows which and how often one computational unit is called by one feature) and computational unit perspective. Several feature views are offered: feature history views, feature addition views, feature intersection views, and feature evolution chart (Greevy and Ducasse, 2005; Greevy et al., 2006).
  - An approach specifically adapted to **distributed systems** is presented by Edwards et al. (2006). In distributed systems, feature location is difficult because distributed systems often exhibit stochastic behavior and because time intervals are hard to identify with precision. These authors define a weighting function which results in a component relevance index, which measures the relevance of a software component to a particular feature.
- Dynamic **aspect mining** identifies code which might implement crosscutting con-

cerns from execution information; an overview on aspect mining techniques is given in (Kellens and Mens, 2005), here we cite two typical methods:

- ○ DynAMiT: searches for dynamic patterns in the execution trace (Breu and Krinke, 2003), (Breu and Krinke, 2004)
- ○ Dynamo: a mining technique which applies formal concept analysis (FCA) to execution traces (Tonella and Ceccato, 2004)

- Feature location can be automated if **heuristics** are used to interpret execution traces. However, these heuristics must be defined manually and the quality of the result depends on the completeness and quality of the heuristics (Eisenberg and De Volder, 2005).

Combining Static and Dynamic Code Analysis

The results of static and dynamic code analysis are complementary and therefore are often combined in order to get less false positives in the results. Here, we name some examples:

- Eisenbarth et al. (2001a, 2001b, 2003) combine *static dependency graphs* and *execution profiles* in order to construct a concept lattice. It is also quantified how specific a piece of code is for a given feature. The tools used here are simple and available: The Gnu C compiler gcc, Gnu object code viewer nm, Gnu profiler gprof, graph editor Graphlet and a short Perl script.
- Antoniol and Gueheneuc (2005) combine *processor emulation, knowledge filtering, and probabilistic ranking*. First, they build a model of a program´s architecture. Second, they identify features to provide maintainers with subsets of the program architecture (e.g. classes, methods, and

fields). Third, they compare the different features, the architecture subsets, to highlight their differences. They associate events with features using a relevance index, and a ranking quantifying the probability that an event is relevant to a feature under study.

- Bohnet and Döllner (2006, 2008) extract the *function call graph* during feature execution (from the log file) and interpret it within the *static architecture*. Additionally, they exploit the function execution times, which give hints to feature-implementing functions: Functions with long execution times most likely induce the execution of other functions that implement calculation intensive functionality, i.e., typically the feature's core functionality.
- Poshyvanyk et al. (2006, 2007) in their method PROMESIR combine *Latent Semantic Indexing (LSI) with Scenario Based Probabilistic (SBP) ranking of events*, which are observed while executing a program under given scenarios. These authors in their case studies not only search for features, but also for bugs.
- Liut et al. (2007) in their method Single Execution Traces and Information (SITIR) combine the *dynamic analysis of execution trace with Latent Semantic Indexing* which indexes source code (comments and identifiers).
- LEarning and ANAlyzing Requirements Traceability (LeanART) (Grechanik et al., 2007) combines *program analysis, runtime monitoring, and machine learning*. It links program source code to elements of use case diagrams. Initial traceability links are automatically propagated and new traceability links are identified. Starting with 6% of all links, one can automatically obtain an average if 64% of all links.

Analysis of the Development History

The analysis of the development history as documented in version management systems can also help to analyze code and other documents. Often, such an analysis assumes that when model elements and pieces of code are repeatedly co-changed with high frequency over multiple versions, then these artifacts potentially have a traceability link between them. Two different approaches have been proposed: (1) When code lines are changed together, they might belong to the same requirement (e.g. a crosscutting concern), or (2) one can investigate co-change of code and other documents like the requirements specification.

- **Visualizations** of the code and document history are helpful, like the Evolution Matrix which presents the time line of the system's evolution (Lanza and Ducasse, 2001), or in CVSGrab (Voinea and Alexandru, 2006; VCN, 2010).
- **Metrics, e.g.** support and confidence, measure how often two files have been modified together. These numbers can be presented in a matrix (Burch et al., 2005; Weißgerber et al., 2007).
- Some aspect mining techniques analyze *line co-change*:
  - ○ Canfora et al. (2006) combine aspect mining by analyzing line co-change and clone detection to improve the performance achieved by the separate approaches. This is a promising approach, since often the sets of detected crosscuts have been found to be disjoint.
  - ○ The History-based Aspect Mining (HAM) method identifies code changes that are likely to be crosscutting concerns by predefined change patterns. They analyze timestamp, submitting developer, and method

calls. The method can identify crosscutting concerns with a precision between 36% and 54%. The precision increases with project size and history and was fond to be up to 90% (Breu and Zimmermann, 2006).
  - ○ Concern Mining using Mutual Information over Time (COMMIT) (Adams et al, 2010) analyzes the source code history to statistically cluster functions, variables, types and macros that have been changed together intentionally. The reported extracted is called a seed graph.
- **Co-change of code and other types of documents** can also be analyzed: A "heuristic-based approach that uses sequential-pattern mining is applied to the commits in software repositories for uncovering highly frequent co-changing sets of artifacts (e.g., source code and documentation)" was developed by Kagdi et al. (2007).

Semantic Code and Text Analysis

Semantic code and text analysis often uses heuristics, dictionaries, thesauri and information retrieval algorithms. These methods are based on the assumption that requirements (like crosscutting concerns) in the source code are reflected by the use of naming conventions.

- The process for traceability link recovery using an Information Retrieval method (Antoniol et al., 2002) includes two paths of activities: one to prepare the document for retrieval (document path) and the other to extract the queries from code (code path). In the approach of Antoniol et al., on the document path, documents are indexed based on a vocabulary that is extracted from the documents themselves. Antoniol et al. (2002) apply both the probabilistic model and a vector space model. Other information retrieval methods are a vector space model algorithm developed by Hayes et al. (2003) and Latent Semantic Indexing (Marcus and Maletic, 2003; Marcus et al., 2004; De Lucia et al., 2004 and 2008). Latent Semantic Indexing demands users to write queries relevant to the desired feature and to rank code elements based on their textual similarity to the query.

- The Aspect Mining Tool AMT helps to visualize search results based on user-defined queries (based on type usage and regular expressions) even for large software systems, displaying matching lines in specific colours (Hannemann and Kiczales, 2001).
- The DelfSTof tool applies formal concept analysis (Tourwé and Mens, 2004), (Ceccato et al., 2005); this method leads to false positives and false negatives, because the methods relies on coding conventions.
- One Natural Language Processing (NLP) method is lexical chaining (Shepherd et al., 2005).
- Poshyvanyk and Marcus (2007) combine Formal Concept Analysis (FCA) and Latent Semantic Indexing (LSI) for feature location. In this approach, LSI is used to map the concepts expressed in queries written by the programmer to relevant parts of the source code (and related documentation). The search results are presented as a list, ranked based on their similarity to the query. Given the ranked list of source code elements, the approach selects most relevant attributes from these documents and organizes the results in a concept lattice, generated via FCA.

In this book chapter, we give only a succinct overview on methods. For more detailed descriptions of the methods, please read the original references cited. We also recommend several method overviews:

- Bruntink (2004) gives an overview on aspect mining techniques using static code analysis.
- Spanoudakis and Zisman (2005) present traceability recovery methods.
- An overview on aspect mining techniques is given in (Kellens and Mens, 2005).
- Liu et al. (2007) give a tabular comparison of feature location approaches which use dynamic analysis.
- Kaur and Johari (2009) compare eight techniques for aspect mining.
- Ducasse and Pollet (2009) give a state of the art overview on reverse engineering methods which reconstruct architecture from code, i.e. the abstract components of the code and their relationships to each other and to the environment, and the principles guiding its design and evolution.

All the above approaches have been tested in larger examples, case studies or even industrial projects. They showed a sufficient gain of productivity of the developer, but also lead to false positives and false negatives in the results, so that most authors conclude that the method helps the developer to reduce the space which he has to investigate. The results of several methods can be disjoint (Ceccato et al. 2005). Combinations of methods have shown to improve the quality of the results, but still include false positives and false negatives. Full automatization of the reconstruction of backwards traceability links evidently is not possible and where the identification of traceability links is automated, either manually constructed input is needed or the results need a manual interpretation, usually for sorting out false positives and adding false negatives. All the above methods are specific to certain types of requirements. Some are also specific to certain programming languages or families of programming languages (e.g. for object-oriented languages). The languages covered are mostly C/

C++ or Java, but also Ada and Fortran programs have been analyzed.

While there are a variety of methods for identifying traceability links backwards from code to requirements, there is few work on the quantification of the impact which code modifications have on requirements satisfaction. Wilde and Casey report on their experiences when trying to do so: "We also tried creating a 'feature correlation measure' by counting the number of subroutines that contained code from each pair of features. We hoped that this correlation would show up interesting design patterns but the results did not show anything that was useful." (Wilde and Casey, 1996) Metrics so far are used in order to quantify how relevant some code is for a requirement, but not to quantify which impact a code change would have on the satisfaction of the requirement.

The prediction of change effort from traceability information is not straightforward, because the effort for implementing a requirement is not necessarily proportional to the number of code units to be modified. Some code elements do not need to be changed although there is a link to the new requirement, and different changes cause a different size of effort. Vice versa, the change of a code unit does not necessarily mean that related requirements are affected. It is possible that a code modification exclusively influences code quality, but not its functionality. We found no method which predicts whether a planned code change in fact will influence the requirement satisfaction. So, the traceability links help the developer to identify those requirements which might be affected by a code change. Consequently the links help him to not forget to consider one of the requirements, but this is only an input information for his manual impact analysis. Vice versa, of course, a change in the requirements usually will influence the code, except for the case where new requirements are added or modified where the system behavior should be as it is implemented and not as it had been specified. This means that a requirement change also does not necessarily mean that code

must be modified. Therefore, a manual step and human validation is necessary.

Comparison of the Reverse Engineering Methods

Table 3 classifies the method types according to the degree of potential automatization. Some methods can reconstruct traceability links to some types of requirements, but not to others. Table 4 classifies the methods according to how they consider architect and user perspective and how they reconstruct traceability links from code to architecture and user perspective. The developer perspective is always treated by the reverse engineering methods, while the management perspective never was found to be included.

Summary of State of the Art

For summarizing the state of the art, we revisit the categories defined in the beginning of this chapter.

In terms of perspectives, we found that:

- Security requirements engineering methods support one, two or all three of these: the management perspective, user perspective and architecture perspective, but not the developer perspective, while
- Reverse engineering methods always cover the developer perspective and user perspective, but not always the architect perspective and never the business perspective.

Reality or vision? While requirements engineering methods are made for modeling visions, they can also describe the real system on an abstract level. Reverse engineering, however, always analyzes existing code, and therefore its results describe reality.

The support of the steps identified before is incomplete:

a) Elicitation of requirements from the stake-holders, including modeling them: All security requirements engineering methods support this.

b) Qualitative forwards impact analysis, i.e. reconstruction of traceability links between models top-down: This activity must be done completely manually, but many methods support the documentation of these traceability links, see Table 1.

c) Quantitative forwards impact analysis, i.e. quantifying impact of changes top-down: As shown in Table 2, there are five methods which allow the documentation of the quantification of all three criteria - cost, risk reduction and architectural impact. However, these methods only support the documentation of such a quantification, the quantification itself must be done manually.

d) Reconstruction of documentation of real code: All reverse engineering methods allow this documentation.

e) Qualitative reverse impact analysis, i.e. reconstruction of traceability links between models bottom-up: Reverse engineering methods also support this, however, each method can identify traceability links to only specific types of model elements in the architecture and user perspective, see Table 4. However, this activity cannot be automatized completely. Either intitial proposals must be made or rules defined manually which are the basis for an automated analysis, or search results must be evaluated manually.

Table 3. Comparison of reverse engineering method types with respect to possible degree of automatization

Method type	Possible degree of automatization	Type of requirements	Remarks
Manual code analysis	Completely manual, supported by code editors	All types	Error-prone and probably not repeatable because results depend on the human executing the analysis; additionally, results depend on the code´s compliance to naming conventions
Dynamic code analysis of traces of execution	Semi-automated, but manual test case preparation and manual result interpretation	Functional requirements (i.e. features), which are visible to the user	Demands instrumentation of code, suitable test cases and a sufficient set of test data; produce large data sets with a lot of noise
Static code analysis	semi-automated, but manual result interpretation	All types, but there are restrictions; e.g. clone detection applies only to requirements which are already implemented and have been modified before	Usually, these methods "reduce the search space that the user needs to review" (Marcus et al., 2004)
Hybrid methods, combining static and dynamic analysis	semi-automated, but manual test case preparation and manual result interpretation	Functional requirements (i.e. features), which are visible to the user	Better than the corresponding static and dynamic methods alone
Analysis of the development history	semi-automated, but manual result interpretation	Requirements which are already implemented and have been modified before	Many false positives
Semantic code and text analysis	semi-automated, but usually manual definition of search queries and manual result interpretation needed, methods deliver only candidate links	All types	Result depends on the code´s compliance to naming conventions and on the algorithm used

Table 4. Comparison of reverse engineering methods with respect to perspectives supported

Method/ authors	Architect perspective	User perspective	Reconstruction of traceability links
Manual code analysis	any model supported	any model supported	Manually by testing hypotheses and search in the code
Static code analysis			
Chen and Rajlich (2000)	dependency graphs, e.g. data flow or call flow	Executable feature or concept	Manual search strategy
Hierarchical Clustering Algorithm for Crosscutting Concerns Identification (HACO) (Czibula et al., 2009)	methods	crosscutting concerns	Clustering algorithm using a distance metric
EBTDP approach (Cleland-Huang and Schmelzer, 2003)	design patterns	non-functional requirements	user initially defines coarse-grained links, and the method dynamically generates fine-grained traceability links
clone detection techniques (Bruntink et al. 2004a, 2004b)	Not considered	crosscutting concerns	Clone metrics help to distinguish between clones which are less or more relevant for an aspect
Zhang et al. (2006)	Branch-Reserving Call Graph (BRCG): a call graph including branch information	Use cases	Several steps
Marin et al. (2007)	Methods with their fan-in metric	crosscutting concerns	three steps: metric calculation, method filtering, and call site analysis
Dynamic code analysis			
Software reconnaissance and feature location methods (e.g. Lukoit et al., 2000)	Not considered	test cases/ scenarios which are linked to features	Execution of different test cases and comparison of the execution traces produced
Trace Analyzer (Egyed and Grunbacher, 1994; Egyed, 2001; Egyed and Grunbacher, 2002)	data flow and class diagram	use case diagrams	Starting with predefined hypothesized traces, the traceability recovery can happen fully automated
TraceScraper (Greevy and Ducasse, 2005; Greevy et al., 2006)	computational units (e.g. methods, classes and packages)	Features	Comparison of execution traces of different features
Edwards et al. (2006)	Software component, e.g. module, class	feature	weighting function which results in a component relevance index, which measures the relevance of a software component to a particular feature
Dynamic aspect mining (Kellens and Mens, 2005)	Not considered	crosscutting concerns	Automated analysis of the execution traces, e.g. search for patterns, formal concept analysis, cluster analysis, program slicing, metrics, heuristics, clone detection, pattern matching, etc.
Eisenberg and De Volder (2005)		features	Manually defined heuristics are used to interpret execution traces

continued on following page

Table 4. Continued

Combining static and dynamic code analysis			
Eisenbarth et al. (2001a, 2001b, 2003)	dependency graphs	feature	Documented in a concept lattice
Antoniol and Gueheneuc (2005)	program architecture (e.g. classes, methods, and fields)	feature	Combination of processor emulation, knowledge filtering, and probabilistic ranking
Bohnet and Döllner (2006, 2008)	static architecture and function call graph	feature	Exploit execution trace and function execution times
PROMESIR (Poshyvanyk et al., 2006, 2007)	developer-defined granularity level (that is, methods or classes)	feature	combine Latent Semantic Indexing (LSI) with Scenario Based Probabilistic (SBP) ranking of events
Single Execution Traces and Information (SITIR) (Liut et al., 2007)	methods	feature	combine the dynamic analysis of execution trace with Latent Semantic Indexing which indexes source code (comments and identifiers)
LEarning and ANAlyzing Requirements Traceability (LeanART) (Grechanik et al., 2007)	Not considered	use case diagrams	combines program analysis, runtime monitoring, and machine learning -> Initial traceability links are automatically propagated and new traceability links are identified
Analysis of the development history			
Analysis of co-change of code lines	Not considered	Crosscutting concerns	Graphical visualization, metrics or aspect mining techniques
Analysis of co-change of code and other types of documents (Kagdi et al., 2007)	Not considered	Any document and model	Heuristic-based pattern-mining
Semantic code and text analysis			
Semantic code and text analysis	Not considered	Any model	heuristics, dictionaries, thesauri and information retrieval algorithms

f) Quantitative reverse impact analysis, i.e. quantifying impact of changes bottom-up: We found no methods for quantifying this impact.

Why and How to Combine Security Requirements Engineering and Reverse Engineering Methods

As has been seen above, security requirements engineering methods and reverse engineering methods complement each other: Requirements engineering methods can model the management perspective and visions, what reverse engineering methods do not. The latter have their strength in visualizing the developer perspective and semi-automatized reconstruction of reality models on architect or user perspective from the code. The requirements engineering methods support the steps (a) to (c), however, they must all be done manually. The methods only support the results of such analyses. The reverse engineering methods support step (d) completely, (e) partly and (f) not at all. Step (e) is supported partly as only specific types of model elements in the architecture and user perspective can be treated and it can not be automatized completely.

So, it would make sense to combine a security requirements engineering method with one or several reverse engineering methods. Such a combination brings the advantage that more perspectives can be covered than with one method alone, visions and reality are both modeled, and more steps can be supported or at least their results be documented – both forwards impact analysis and reverse impact analysis.

How can these methods be combined in order to support impact analysis? First, the models are reconstructed (that means steps (a) and (d)) which are the precondition for the reconstruction of traceability links (steps (b) and (e)), which are the precondition for the quantitative impact analysis (steps (c) and (f)).

Step (a) plus (b) can be done using a top-down security engineering method for documenting the system as it is. The architectural components, user perspective model elements and traceability links identified by reverse engineering (step (d) plus (e)) can be included in the security requirements model. By doing so, security requirements and code are linked to each other. When a security requirements engineering method and a reverse engineering method are combined, the one proceeding top-down, the other bottom-up, they can only be integrated when they use one and the same model in the same perspective. This could be the architect perspective or the user perspective. The methods must then be chosen so that both support the same model on the same perspective, so the results of the top-down requirements elicitation and the bottom-up code analysis can be mapped to each other. Table 1 and Table 4 can help to choose the right model and methods.

As reverse engineering can locate only specific types of requirements in the code, several methods must be combined. In Table 4, we identify the following types of requirements: functional requirements (in the form of features or use case models), non-functional requirements and crosscutting concerns.

- Security requirements often are countermeasures which must detect or prevent an attack when it is attempted. This means that the security of a software system can be described and tested by attack scenarios including the system´s reaction. Dynamic analysis of the code during runtime can be used as a white box test for security, visualizing the propagation of a hacker´s activities throughout the system. This approach covers the user perspective of security. To link attack scenarios to architecture, one can Incident Propagation Paths, which are part of RiskREP (Herrmann and Morali, 2010), or the misuse case maps, a modeling technique which is similar to the use case map (Karpati, Sindre and Opdahl, 2010). It visualizes attacks in their architectural context. Architectural components are presented graphically and are nested to present hierarchies. The flow of scenario paths is drawn as lines.

- Security patterns are ways to implement security requirements and therefore can also be used for linking code pieces to security on the architectural level.

- Security requirements often are crosscutting concerns and must be implemented throughout the code consequently, like the check of authorizations when users access a data base. These accesses might be initiated by several pieces of code, and then this authorization check is a crosscutting concern, maybe even realized by code clones. Aspect mining techniques for identifying crosscutting concerns in code can be found by many methods presented in Table 4. They work on the developer level.

During software maintenance, traceability between requirements and code supports impact analysis, which includes the analysis how code changes might influence the satisfaction of security requirements and whether new or changed security requirements have unwanted side-effects. However, the quantification of these effects (steps (c) and (f)) cannot be automatized.

We use results of three of our RiskREP case studies for showing which types of requirements can appear in a security analysis and which are consequently important when choosing a method. Case study no. 1 has been published in (Herrmann and Morali, 2010), while the other two are still unpublished. In these three case studies, we applied RiskREP for the top-down analysis of security requirements. In case study no. 1, we started the analysis from the quality goal "availability of the system" and derived 10 requirements. In the two other case studies, 25, respectively, 38 requirements were identified. In these two case studies, the focus was on finding architecture-related security requirements.

In the results, we found the functional requirements (which describe what a software is expected to do) and architectural requirements (which describe requirements on how the architecture should be). Both could be either crosscutting or related to specific functionalities respectively to individual architectural components. Also, crosscutting non-functional requirements were found. The crosscutting architectural requirements, crosscutting functional requirements and crosscutting non-functional requirements, can be summarized as "crosscutting concerns". In Table 5, we classify the 73 countermeasures from the three case studies in order to see how frequent the requirements types were. The statistics are based on the countermeasures on the level where we stopped the analysis, because they were in the right form for discussing their implementation further. What we can see from these statistics is that almost half of the security requirements are not related to the code (instead, to software operation, software development, or the environment), but the others belong to types of requirements which can be related to code by methods of reverse engineering. Especially, crosscutting requirements are frequent and tool support can be helpful to analyze change impact for these requirements which are not easy to locate in the code manually.

When comparing the categories of requirements found in the case studies with those used in the chapter "Reverse Impact Analysis" (which are functional requirement, non-functional requirements and crosscutting concern), we conclude:

- Reverse engineering methods do not treat architectural requirements.
- Requirements engineering methods can model architectural requirements in an architecture model, however, there must then be two architecture models – one for the vision (requirements) and one for the documentation of the real architecture. There might be a gap between these two.
- The crosscutting concerns can be distinguished according to whether they are functional requirements (which belong to the user perspective), architectural requirements (which belong to the architect perspective) or non-functional requirements (which can and should be transformed into other types of requirements by further requirements analysis (Herrmann and Paech, 2008)). For the reverse engineering method, these categories make no difference, but for the requirements engineering, there is a difference because they must be modeled differently, on different perspectives and in different models.
- The crosscutting non-functional requirements in the TUgether case study was and could itself be analyzed and detailed further. However, as security was the focus of the analysis and the non-functional

Table 5. Statistics about countermeasures found in three RiskREP case studies

	case study no. 1	case study no. 2	case study no. 3	sum	%
crosscutting architectural requirement	3	8	5	16	22
architectural requirement		2	8	10	14
crosscutting functional requirement	1	5	2	8	11
functional requirement	2	1	3	6	8
crosscutting non-functional requirement	1		5	6	8
process requirement on the software operation	1	4	6	11	15
process requirement on software development		5	9	14	19
requirement on the environment	2			2	3
sum	10	25	38	73	
%	14	34	52		

requirements belonged to other software quality attributes, we did not do this.

- A security requirements analysis not only leads to software-related requirements, but also to requirements related to the process of software operation, software development and to the environment. These are outside the scope of this chapter.

SUMMARY AND CONCLUSION

This chapter discussed, based on the state of the art, how security requirements engineering and reverse engineering can interplay in order to support impact analysis in both directions – top-down from requirements to code and bottom-up from code to requirements. This is especially necessary because IT systems live in many cases longer than the period they are designed to live for. Thus during the life time of a system new requirements appear, available requirements get modified and the software changes due to code modifications.

Existing methods can be applied for identifying and modeling the traceability links between different perspectives on the software system. These methods all have been evaluated and tested before. The link reconstruction can be automatized only

partly, but demands human expertise at one step or the other. This is even more the case for the quantification of impacts, e.g. in terms of cost, risk, architecture modification or requirements satisfaction. The traceability links between requirements and architecture only document potential impact, but the size of this impact when requirements or code change, must be decided by an expert for each planned modification.

Security requirements engineering and reverse engineering can complement each other. We recommend to combine one requirements engineering method with several reverse engineering methods. They must share one model which they all use and where their analysis results can be integrated. Additionally, the methods must be chosen accordingly to complement each other in order to cover all perspectives and requirement types needed in the specific context.

In the security requirements engineering and reverse engineering methods, impact analysis results can be documented, but impact analysis is not actively supported. Therefore, these methods should probably also be complemented by impact analysis methods.

This chapter treats the situation when software is undocumented or at least partly undocumented or the documentation is outdated. The reconstruction of models and traceability links between these models not only supports impact analysis but also prepares the use of model-driven development approaches which execute other software engineering activities.

As the questions treated in this chapter are new and our present objective was mainly to provide for a literature overview, there is space for future research on the following topics:

- This chapter proposes that, why and how methods can be combined in order to support impact analysis during software maintenance better. Based on our recommendations, still many combinations of methods are possible. Which of these are better than the others, should be evaluated empirically in future work.

- During maintenance, one needs models of the existing software system, but also models of visions of the system´s future state. This means that for each model used, there should exist two versions: The one set of models documents reality and the other models vision. However, it is not clear how these models must be linked to each other. Tool and process support for managing two versions of all models and coping with their differences would be useful.

ACKNOWLEDGMENT

This research is supported by the research programs Sentinels and ASKS. Sentinels (http://www.sentinels.nl) is being financed by Technology Foundation STW, the Netherlands Organization for Scientific Research (NWO), and the Dutch Ministry of Economic Affairs. ASKS (Architekturbasierte Sicherheitsanalyse geschäftskritischer Software-Systeme = Architecture-based Security Analyses of critical Software Systems) is financed by the German Ministry of Education and Research.

REFERENCES

Adams, B., Jiang, Z. M., & Hassan, M. E. (2010) Identifying crosscutting concerns using historical code changes. *Proceedings of the 32nd ACM/IEEE International Conference on Software Engineering ICSE 2010,* Vol. 1.

Antoniol, G., Canfora, G., Casazza, G., De Lucia, A., & Merlo, E. (2002). Recovering traceability links between code and documentation. *IEEE Transactions on Software Engineering, 28*(10). doi:10.1109/TSE.2002.1041053

Antoniol, G., & Gueheneuc, Y.-G. (2005). Feature identification: A novel approach and a case study. *Proceedings of the 21st IEEE International Conference on Software Maintenance ICSM'05* (pp. 357-366).

Asnar, Y., Giorgini, P., & Mylopoulos, J., (2010). Goal-driven risk assessment in requirements engineering. *Requirement Engineering Journal,* 1-16.

Blakley, B., Heath, C., and members of The Open Group Security Forum. (2004). *Security design patterns.* Technical Report, The Open Group.

Bohnet, J., & Doellner, J. (2006). Visual exploration of function call graphs for feature location in complex software systems. *Proceeding of the ACM Symposium on Software Visualization SoftVis '06.*

Bohnet, J., & Doellner, J. (2008). Analyzing dynamic call graphs enhanced with program state information for feature location and understanding. *Proceedings of the 30nd ACM/IEEE International Conference on Software Engineering ICSE 2008.*

Breu, S., & Krinke, J. (2003) *Aspect mining using dynamic analysis.* Workshop on Software-Reengineering, Bad Honnef.

Breu, S., & Krinke, J. (2004). *Aspect mining using event traces.* Conference on Automated Software Engineering ASE.

Breu, S., & Zimmermann, T. (2006). Mining aspects from version history. *21ˢᵗ IEEE/ACM International Conference on Automated Software Engineering ASE* (pp. 221-230)

Bruntink, M. (2004). *Aspect mining using clone class metrics.* 1st Workshop on Aspect Reverse Engineering.

Bruntink, M. v. Deursen, A., v. Engelen, R., & Tourwé, T. (2004a). An evaluation of clone detection techniques for identifying crosscutting concerns. *Proceedings of the IEEE International Conference on Software Maintenance ICSM,* IEEE Computer Society Press.

Bruntink, M. v. Deursen, A., Tourwé, T., & v. Engelen, R. (2004b). An evaluation of clone detection techniques for crosscutting concerns. *Proceedings of the 20th IEEE International Conference on Software Maintenance* (pp. 200-209)

BSI. (2008a). *BSI-standard 100-1: Managementsysteme für Informationssicherheit* (ISMS) version 1.5. Retrieved from https://www.bsi.bund.de/cae/servlet/contentblob/471450/publicationFile/30749/standard_1001_pdf.pdf

BSI. (2008b). *BSI-standard 100-2 IT-Grundschutz-Vorgehensweise,* version 2.0. Retrieved from https://www.bsi.bund.de/cae/servlet/contentblob/471452/publicationFile/30758/standard_1002_pdf.pdf

BSI. (2008c). *BSI-standard 100-3 Risikoanalyse auf der Basis von IT-Grundschutz,* version 2.5. Retrieved from https://www.bsi.bund.de/cae/servlet/contentblob/471454/publicationFile/30757/standard_1003_pdf.pdf

Burch, M., Diehl, S., & Weißgerber, P. (2005). Visual data mining in software archives. *Proceedings of ACM Symposium on Software Visualization SOFT-VIS05,* St. Louis, USA

Canfora, G., Cerulo, L., & Di Penta, M. (2006). On the use of line co-change for identifying crosscutting concern code. *22nd IEEE International Conference on Software Maintenance ICSM'06,* Philadelphia, Pennsylvania (pp. 213-222).

Castro, J., Kolp, M., & Mylopoulos, J. (2002). Towards requirements-driven information systems engineering: The Tropos project. *Information Systems, 27,* 365–389. doi:10.1016/S0306-4379(02)00012-1

Ceccato, M., Marin, M., Mens, K., Moonen, L., Tonello, P., & Tourwé, T. (2005). *A qualitative comparison of three aspect mining techniques.* International Workshop on Program Comprehension IWPC.

CGI. (n.d.). *Website.* Retrieved from www.cgisecurity.com

Chen, K., & Rajlich, V. (2000) Case study of feature location using dependence graph. *Proceedings of the International Workshop on Program Comprehension* (pp. 241–249). IEEE Computer Society Press, Los Alamitos, CA.

Chikofsky, E., & Cross, J. II. (1990). Reverse engineering and design recovery: A taxonomy. *IEEE Software, 7*(1), 13–17. doi:10.1109/52.43044

Christian, T. (2010, September). *Security requirements reusability and the SQUARE methodology.* Technical Report CMU/SEI-2010-TN-027, Carnegie Mellon University, Software Engineering Institute, CERT Program.

Chung, L. K., Nixon, B. A., Yu, E., & Mylopoulos, J. (2000). *Non-functional requirements in software engineering.* Dordrecht, The Netherlands: Kluwer Academic Publishers.

Cleland-Huang, J., & Schmelzer, D. (2003). Dynamic tracing non-functional requirements through design patter invariants. *Proceedings of the 2nd International Workshop on Traceability in Emerging Forms of Software Engineering TEFSE 2003,* Canada.

Common Criteria. (2009a). *Common criteria for Information Technology security evaluation, part 1: Introduction and general model,* July 2009, version 3.1, revision 3, final. Retrieved from http://www.commoncriteriaportal.org/files/ccfiles/CCPART1V3.1R3.pdf

Common Criteria. (2009b). *Common criteria for Information Technology security evaluation, part 2: Security functional components,* July 2009, version 3.1, revision 3, final. Retrieved from http://www.commoncriteriaportal.org/files/ccfiles/CCPART2V3.1R3.pdf

Common Criteria. (2009c). *Common criteria for Information Technology security evaluation, part 3: Security assurance components,* July 2009, version 3.1, revision 3, final. Retrieved from http://www.commoncriteriaportal.org/files/ccfiles/CCPART3V3.1R3.pdf

coresec. (n.d.). *Website*. Retrieved from www.coresecuritypatterns.com

Cornelissen, B., Zaidman, A., Holten, D., Moonen, L., van Deursen, A., & van Wijk, J. J. (2008). Execution trace analysis through massive sequence and circular bundle views. *Journal of Systems and Software, 81*(12), 2252–2268. doi:10.1016/j.jss.2008.02.068

Czibula, I. G., Czibula, G., & Cojocar, G. S. (2009). Hierarchical clustering for identifying crosscutting concerns in object oriented software systems. *INFOCOMP Journal of Computer Science, 8*(3).

De Lucia, A., Fasano, F., Oliveto, R., & Tortora, G. (2004). Enhancing an artefact management system with traceability recovery features. *Proceedings of the 20th IEEE International Conference on Software Maintenance* (pp. 306-315)

De Lucia, A., Oliveto, R., & Tortora, G. (2008). ADAMS re-trace: Traceability link recovery via latent semantic indexing. *Proceedings of the 30th International Conference on Software Engineering ICSE '08.*

Dick, J. (2005). Design traceability. *IEEE Software, 22*(6), 14–16. doi:10.1109/MS.2005.150

Dörr, J., Kerkow, D., von Knethen, A., & Paech, B. (2003). Eliciting efficiency requirements with use cases. In *Proceedings of the 9ᵗʰ International Workshop on Requirements Engineering: Foundation of Software Quality - REFSQ 03*, Essener Informatik Beiträge Bd.8, Essen, (pp. 37–46).

Dörr, J., Punter, T., Bayer, J., Kerkow, D., Kolb, R., Koenig, T., et al. (2004). *Quality models for non-functional requirements.* IESE-Report Nr. 010.04/E.

Dougherty, C., Sayre, K., Seacord, R. C., Svoboda, D., & Togashi, K. (2009). *Secure design patterns.* Technical Report CMU/SEI-2009-TR-010, Software Engineering Institute, Carnegie Mellon University, March 2009; Updated October 2009.

Ducasse, S., & Pollet, D. (2009). Software architecture reconstruction: A process-oriented taxon. *IEEE Transactions on Software Engineering, 35*(4), 573–591. doi:10.1109/TSE.2009.19

Egyed, A. (2001). *A scenario-driven approach to traceability.* 23rd International Conference on Software Engineering ICSE'01, Toronto, Canada.

Egyed, A., & Grunbacher, P. (2002) Automating requirements traceability: Beyond the record & replay paradigm. *Proceedings of the 17th International Conference on Automated Software Engineering ASE*, Edinburgh, Scotland, UK (pp. 163-171).

Eisenbarth, T., Koschke, R., & Simon, D. (2001a). Feature-driven program understanding using concept analysis of execution traces. *Proceedings of the 9th International Workshop on Program Comprehension, IWPC 2001* (pp. 300-309).

Eisenbarth, T., Koschke, R., & Simon, D. (2001b). Aiding program comprehension by static and dynamic feature analysis. *Proceedings of the IEEE International Conference on Software Maintenance*, Florence, Italy (pp. 602-611).

Eisenbarth, T., Koschke, R., & Simon, D. (2002). Incremental location of combined features for large-scale programs. *Proceedings of the International Conference on Software Maintenance* (pp. 273-282).

Eisenbarth, T., Koschke, R., & Simon, D. (2003). Locating features in source code. *IEEE Transactions on Software Engineering, 29*, 210–224. doi:10.1109/TSE.2003.1183929

Eisenberg, A. D., & De Volder, K. (2005). Dynamic feature traces: Finding features in unfamiliar code. *21st IEEE International Conference on Software Maintenance ICSM'05,* Budapest, Hungary.

Elahi, G., & Yu, E. (2009). Modeling and analysis of security trade-offs: A goal oriented approach. *Data & Knowledge Engineering, 68*(7), 579–598. doi:10.1016/j.datak.2009.02.004

Elahi, G., Yu, E., & Zannone, N. (2010). A vulnerability-centric requirements engineering framework: Analyzing security attacks, countermeasures, and requirements based on vulnerabilities. *Requirements Engineering Journal, 15*(1), 41–62. doi:10.1007/s00766-009-0090-z

Fabian, B., Gürses, S., Heisel, M., Santen, T., & Schmidt, H. (2010). A comparison of security requirements engineering methods. *Requirements Engineering - Special Issue on RE'09. Security Requirements Engineering, 15*(1), 7–40. doi:10.1007/s00766-009-0092-x

Fantozzi, A. (2002). *Locating features in Vim: A software reconnaissance case study.* Technical Report of SERC, November 6, 2002. Retrieved December 21, 2010, from http://www.cs.uwf. edu/~wilde/publications/ReconVIM/ReconVIM. pdf

Firesmith, D. G. (2003a). *Analyzing and specifying reusable security requirements.* 11th IEEE International Requirements Engineering Conference RE'2003. Requirements for High Assurance Systems (RHAS) Workshop, Monterey, California, September 2003.

Firesmith, D. G. (2003b). *Common concepts underlying safety, security, and survivability engineering.* Technical Note CMU/SEI-2003-TN-033. Retrieved December 21, 2010, from http://www.sei.cmu.edu/pub/documents/03. reports/pdf/03tn033.pdf

Firesmith, D. G. (2004). Specifying reusable security requirements. *Journal of Object Technology, 3*(1), 61–75. doi:10.5381/jot.2004.3.1.c6

Gayash, A., Viswanathan, V., & Padmanabhan, D. (2008, June). *SQUARE-Lite: Case study on VADSoft project.* Technical Report CMU/SEI-2008-SR-017, Carnegie Mellon University, Software Engineering Institute, CERT Program.

Grechanik, M., McKinley, K. S., & Perry, D. E. (2007). *Recovering and using use-case-diagram-to-source-code traceability links.* 6th Joint Meeting of the European Software Engineering Conference and the ACM SIGSOFT Symposium on the Foundations of Software Engineering ESEC/FSE, Dubrovnik, Croatia.

Greevy, O., & Ducasse, S. (2005). Correlating features and code using a compact two-sided trace analysis approach. *Ninth European Conference on Software Maintenance and Reengineering CSMR* (pp. 314-323)

Greevy, O., Ducasse, S., & Gîrba, T. (2006). Analyzing software evolution through feature views. *Journal of Software Maintenance and Evolution: Research and Practice, 18*(6). doi:10.1002/smr.340

Grünbacher, P., Egyed, A., & Medvidovic, N. (2001). Reconciling software requirements and architectures: The CBSP approach. *5th IEEE International Symposium on Requirements Engineering RE´01* (pp. 202-211).

Hannemann, J., & Kiczales, G. (2001). *Overcoming the prevalent decomposition of legacy code.* Workshop on Advanced Separation of Concerns.

Hayes, J. H., Dekhtyar, A., & Osborne, J. (2003). Improving requirements tracing via information retrieval. *Proceedings of the 11th IEEE International Requirements Engineering Conference,* Monterey Bay.

Herrmann, A. (2007). Von Risiken zu Nutzen: Vorhersage von Risiken durch Schätzmethoden. *Proceedings of the Metrikon 2007,* 15th Nov. 2007, Kaiserslautern, Germany, (pp. 179-199).

Herrmann, A., & Morali, A. (2010). *RiskREP: Risk-based security requirements elicitation and prioritization (extended version).* Technical Report TR-CTIT-10-28, Centre for Telematics and Information Technology University of Twente, Enschede. ISSN 1381-3625

Herrmann, A., & Paech, B. (2008). MOQARE: Misuse-oriented quality requirements engineering. *Requirements Engineering Journal, 13*(1), 73–86. doi:10.1007/s00766-007-0058-9

Herrmann, A., & Schier, S. (2010). Die Spezifikation von Delta-Anforderungen. *OBJEKTspektrum, 6,* 10–13.

Houmb, S. H., Islam, S., Knauss, E., Jürjens, J., & Schneider, K. (2010). Eliciting security requirements and tracing them to design: An integration of Common Criteria, heuristics, and UMLsec. *Requirements Engineering - Special Issue on RE'09. Security Requirements Engineering, 15*(1), 63–93. doi:10.1007/s00766-009-0093-9

IEEE. (1990). *IEEE std 610.12-1990: IEEE standard glossary of software engineering terminology.* Washington, USA: IEEE.

IEEE. (1998). *IEEE standard 1219-1998: IEEE standard for software maintenance.* Washington, DC: IEEE.

Islam, S. (2009). Software development risk management model – A goal driven approach. Doctoral Symposium. In *Proceedings of the 7th ESEC/FSE.*

Islam, S., & Houmb, S. H. (2010). Integrating risk management activities into requirements engineering. In *Proceedings of the 4th International Conference on Research Challenges in Information Science (RCIS'10),* (pp. 299-310).

ISO (International Standards Organization). (1989). *ISO 7498-2:1989 "Information processing systems -- Open Systems Interconnection -- Basic Reference Model -- Part 2: Security Architecture"*

ISO (International Standards Organization). (1991). *International Standard ISO/IEC 9126. Information technology -- Software product evaluation -- Quality characteristics and guidelines for their use*

Jürjens, J. (2001). Towards development of secure systems using UMLsec. *Proceedings of the 4th International Conference on Fundamental Approaches to Software Engineering FASE 2001.*

Jürjens, J. (2003). *Developing safety-critical systems with UML.* UML 2003, San Francisco, Oct. 20–24.

Jürjens, J. (2005). *Secure system development with UML.* Heidelberg, Germany: Springer.

Kagdi, H., Maletic, J. I., & Sharif, B. (2007). *Mining software repositories for traceability links.* 15th IEEE International Conference on Program Comprehension ICPC '07.

Karpati, P., Sindre, G., & Opdahl, A. L. (2010). Visualizing cyber attacks with misuse case maps. *16th International Working Conference Requirements Engineering: Foundations for Software Quality REFSQ 2010,* Essen, Germany (pp. 262-275).

Kaur, A., & Johari, K. (2009). Identification of crosscutting concerns: A survey. *International Journal of Engineering Science and Technology, 1*(3), 166–172.

Kazman, R., Klein, M., Clements, P., & Compton, N. (2000). *ATAM: Method for architecture evaluation.* Technical Report CMU/SEI-2000-TR-004.

Kellens, A., & Mens, K. (2005). *A survey of aspect mining tools and techniques.* Technical Report 2005-08, INGI, UCL, Belgium.

Lanza, M., & Ducasse, S. (2001). A categorization of classes based on the visualization of their internal structure: the class blueprint. *Proceedings of the Conference on Object-Oriented Programming, Systems, Languages, and Applications OOPSLA,* (pp. 300-311). New York, NY: ACM Press.

Liu, D., Marcus, A., Poshyvanyk, D., & Rajlich, V. (2007). Feature location via information retrieval based filtering of a single scenario execution trace. *Proceedings of the 22nd IEEE/ACM International Conference on Automated Software Engineering ASE '07.*

Lukoit, K., Wilde, N., Stowell, S., & Hennessey, T. (2000a). *TraceGraph: Immediate visual location of software features.* SERC-TR-86-F, Software Engineering Research Center, Purdue University, February 2000.

Lukoit, K., Wilde, N., Stowell, S., & Hennessey, T. (2000b). TraceGraph: Immediate visual location of software features. *International Conference on Software Maintenance ICSM 2000,* San Jose, CA, USA.

Madan, B. B., Goševa-Popstojanova, K., Vaidyanathan, K., & Trivedi, K. S. (2002). Modeling and quantification of security. Attributes of software systems. *Proceedings of the International Conference on Dependable Systems and Networks DSN '02.*

Marcus, A., & Maletic, J. I. (2003). *Recovering documentation-to-source-code traceability links using latent semantic indexing.* 25th International Conference on Software Engineering ICSE'03, Portland, Oregon.

Marcus, A., Sergeyev, A., Rajlich, V., & Maletic, J. I. (2004). An information retrieval approach to concept location in source code. *Proceedings 11th Working Conference on Reverse Engineering* (pp. 214-223).

Marin, M., van Deursen, A., & Moonen, L. (2007). Identifying crosscutting concerns using fan-in analysis. *ACM Transactions on Software Engineering and Methodology, 17*(1). doi:10.1145/1314493.1314496

Mayer, N., Dubois, E., & Rifaut, A. (2007). *Requirements engineering for improving business/IT alignment in security risk management methods.* 3rd International Conference Interoperability for Enterprise Software and Applications (I-ESA'07).

Mayer, N., Rifaut, A., & Dubois, E. (2005). Towards a risk-based security requirements engineering framework. *11th International Workshop on Requirements Engineering: Foundation for Software Quality (REFSQ'05).*

Mead, N. R., Hough, E. D., & Stehney, T. R. (2005, November). *Security quality requirements engineering (SQUARE) methodology.* Technical Report CMU/SEI-2005-TR-009, Carnegie Mellon University, Software Engineering Institute, CERT Program.

Moore, A. P., Ellison, R. J., & Linger, R. C. (2001). *Attack modeling for information security and survivability.* Technical Report CMU/SEI-2001-TN-001, CMU Software Engineering Institute.

Mouratidis, H., Giorgini, P., & Manson, G. A. (2003). Integrating security and systems engineering: Towards the modelling of secure information systems. In J. Eder & M. Missikoff (Eds.), *15th International Conference on Advanced Information Systems Engineering, Lecture Notes in Computer Science, vol 2681,* (pp. 63–78).

Mylopoulos, J., Chung, L., Liao, S., Wang, H., & Yu, E. (2001). Exploring alternatives during requirements analysis. *IEEE Software, 18,* 92–96. doi:10.1109/52.903174

Mylopoulos, J., Chung, L., & Nixon, B. A. (1992). Representing and using non-functional requirements: A process-oriented approach. Special issue on Knowledge Representation and Reasoning in Software Development. *IEEE Transactions on Software Engineering, 18*(6), 483–497. doi:10.1109/32.142871

Oladimeji, E. A., Supakkul, S., & Chung, L. (2006). Security threat modeling and analysis: A goal-oriented approach. In *Proc. The 10th IASTED International Conference on Software Engineering and Applications (SEA 2006)*, Dallas, Texas, USA, November 13-15, 2006.

OMG (Object Management Group). (2008). *UML profile for modeling quality of service and fault tolerance characteristics and mechanisms*, version 1.1, April 2008, Retrieved December 21, 2010, from http://www.omg.org/spec/QFTP/1.1/

Pfleeger, S. L., & Bohner, S. A. (1990). A framework for software maintenance metrics. *Conference on Software Maintenance, IEEE Computer Society Press, Los Alamitos CA* (pp. 320–327).

Poshyvanyk, D., Gueheneuc, Y.-G., Marcus, A., Antoniol, G., & Rajlich, V. (2006). Combining probabilistic ranking and latent semantic indexing for feature identification. *14th IEEE International Conference on Program Comprehension ICPC 2006* (pp. 137-148)

Poshyvanyk, D., & Marcus, A. (2007). Combining formal concept analysis with information retrieval for concept location in source code. *15th IEEE International Conference on Program Comprehension ICPC '07* (pp. 37-48).

Poshyvanyk, D., Marcus, A., & Rajlich, V. (2007). Feature location using probabilistic ranking of methods based on execution scenarios and information retrieval. *IEEE Transactions on Software Engineering, 33*(6). doi:10.1109/TSE.2007.1016

Shepherd, D., Tourwé, T., & Pollock, L. (2005). *Using language clues to discover crosscutting concerns.* Workshop on the Modeling and Analysis of Concerns.

Sindre, G., & Opdahl, A. (2005). Eliciting security requirements with misuse cases. *Requirements Engineering Journal, 10*(1), 34–44. doi:10.1007/s00766-004-0194-4

Spanoudakis, G., & Zisman, A. (2005). Software traceability: A roadmap. In S. K. Chang (Ed.), *Handbook of software engineering and Knowledge Engineering, vol. 3: Recent advancements.* World Scientific Publishing Co.

Tonella, P., & Ceccato, M. (2004). *Aspect mining through the formal concept analysis of execution traces.* 11th IEEE Working Conference on Reverse Engineering.

Tonella, P., Torchiano, M., Da Bois, B., & Systa, T. (2007). Empirical studies in reverse engineering: State of the art and future trends. *Empirical Software Engineering, 12*(5). doi:10.1007/s10664-007-9037-5

Tourwé, T., & Mens, K. (2004). *Mining aspectual views using formal concept analysis.* Source Code Analysis and Manipulation Workshop SCAM.

van Lamsweerde, A., Brohez, S., De Landtsheer, R., & Janssens, D. (2003). From system goals to intruder anti-goals: Attack generation and resolution for security requirements engineering. *Proceedings of RHAS Workshop at RE'03*, Essener Informatik Beitraege, Bd.6 (pp. 49-56).

VCN. (2010). *Visual code navigator.* Retrieved December 21, 2010, from http://www.win.tue.nl/~lvoinea/VCN.html

Voinea, L., & Alexandru, T. (2006). Multiscale and multivariate visualizations of software evolution. *Proceedings of the 2006 ACM Symposium on Software Visualization*, Brighton, United Kingdom (pp. 115-124).

Weißgerber, P., Pohl, M., & Burch, M. (2007). Visual data mining in software archives to detect how developers work together. *Proceedings of Fourth International Workshop on Mining Software Repositories MSR'07,* ICSE (pp. 9-17).

White, L., & Wilde, N. (2001). Dynamic analysis for locating product features in Ada code. *Proceedings of the 2001 Annual ACM SIG Ada International Conference on Ada, 2001.*

Wilde, N. (2010). *University of West Florida: RECON tools for software engineers*. Retrieved December 21, 2010, from http://www.cs.uwf.edu/~recon/

Wilde, N., Buckellew, M., Page, H., Rajlich, V., & Pounds, L. (2003). A comparison of methods for locating features in legacy software. *Journal of Systems and Software, 65*, 105–114.

Wilde, N., & Casey, C. (1996). Early field experience with the software reconnaissance technique for program comprehension. *International Conference on Software Maintenance*, (pp. 312-318). IEEE Computer Society.

Wong, W. E., Gokhale, S. S., & Horgan, J. R. (2000). Quantifying the closeness between program components and features. *Journal of Systems and Software. Special Issue on Software Maintenance, 54*(2), 87–98.

Yoder, J., & Barcalow, J. (1998). Architectural patterns for enabling application security. *Pattern Languages of Programs, Monticello, IL*, 1998.

Yoshioka, N., Washizaki, H., & Maruyama, K. (2008). A survey on security patterns. *Special Issue: The future of software engineering for security and privacy. Progress in Informatics, 5*, 35–47. doi:10.2201/NiiPi.2008.5.5

Yu, E. S. K. (1995). *Modeling strategic relationships for process reengineering*. PhD Thesis, University of Toronto.

Zhang, L., Qin, T., Zhou, Z., Hao, D., & Sun, J. (2006). Identifying use cases in source code. *Journal of Systems and Software, 79*(11), 1588–1598. doi:10.1016/j.jss.2006.02.032

Chapter 4
A WYSIWYG Approach to Support Layout Configuration in Model Evolution

Yu Sun
University of Alabama at Birmingham, USA

Jeff Gray
University of Alabama, USA

Philip Langer
Johannes Kepler University, Austria

Gerti Kappel
Vienna University of Technology, Austria

Manuel Wimmer
Vienna University of Technology, Austria

Jules White
Virginia Tech, USA

ABSTRACT

Model evolution has become an essential activity in software development with the ongoing adoption of domain-specific modeling, which is commonly supported and automated by using model transformation techniques. Although a number of model transformation languages and tools have been developed to support model evolution activities, the layout of visual models in the evolution process is not often considered. In many cases, after a transformation is performed, the layout of the resulting model must be manually rearranged, which can be time consuming and error-prone. The automatic layout arrangement features provided by some modeling tools usually do not take a user's preferences or the semantics of the model into consideration, and therefore could potentially alter the desired layout in an undesired manner. This chapter describes a new approach to enable users to specify the model layout as a demonstrated model transformation. We applied the Model Transformation By Demonstration (MTBD) approach and extended it to let users specify the layout information using the concept of "What You See Is What You Get" (WYSIWYG), so that the complex layout specification can be simplified.

DOI: 10.4018/978-1-61350-438-3.ch004

INTRODUCTION

With the ongoing adoption of Domain-Specific Modeling (DSM) (Gray et al., 2007), models are emerging as first-class entities in many domains and play an increasingly significant role in every phase of software development (i.e., from system requirements analysis and design, to software implementation and maintenance). In the DSM context, whenever a software system needs to evolve, the models used to represent the system should evolve accordingly. For instance, system design models often need to be changed to adapt to new system requirements (Greenfield & Short, 2004). As an additional example, it is sometimes necessary to apply model refactoring (France et al., 2003) to optimize the internal structure of the implementation models (i.e., models used to generate implementation code through code generators). Furthermore, models used to control the deployment of a software system are occasionally scaled up for the purpose of improving performance (Sun et al., 2009a).

Although manual model evolution is often tedious and error-prone, automating complex model evolution tasks using model transformation technologies has become a popular practice (Gray et al., 2006). A number of executable model transformation languages (e.g., QVT (http://www.omg.org/cgi-bin/doc?ptc/2005-11-01, 2010), ATL (Jouault et al., 2008)) have been developed to enable users to specify model transformation rules, which take an input model and evolve it to produce an output model automatically.

Open Problems

Although the implementation of model evolution concerning the abstract syntax has been well-supported, the layout of models is rarely considered in the traditional model evolution process. Most evolution efforts focus only on the semantic aspects of the evolution (e.g., adding or removing necessary model elements and connections, modifying attributes of model elements), and often ignore model layout configuration concerns during the evolution (e.g., positions of model elements, font, color and size used in labels). For instance, executing a set of model transformation rules to add model elements and connections will sometimes lead to placing all the newly created elements in a random location in the model editor.

Ignoring the desired layout after model evolution has a strong potential to undermine the readability and understandability of the evolved model, and may even unexpectedly affect the implicit semantics under certain circumstances. For example, users may accidentally misunderstand the system because of a disordered layout (e.g., a sequence of actions to be executed is represented by a set of nodes with arrows indicating the sequence, but a disordered arrangement of the nodes may lead to a challenge in identifying the correct execution order). Furthermore, the positions of model elements and connections may correspond to special coordinates in the real world, such that an unoptimized layout could lead to unexpected problems for the actual system (e.g., the configuration of the actual hardware devices and cables might be based on the positions of model elements and connections representing them, or the color of the elements might represent the running status of the actual devices). It may be possible to incorporate the layout information related with the implicit semantics into the metamodel as part of the abstract syntax, but a change to the metamodel may trigger further model migration problems (Sprinkle, 2003). Although it is very direct to manually adjust the layout, it becomes a tedious, timing-consuming task when a larger number of model elements are involved in the model evolution process. Therefore, while the semantic concerns of model evolution have been implemented and automated, it is indispensible to realize the automatic configuration of the layout as part of the model evolution process.

The most commonly used approach to automatically arrange the layout of models is to apply layout algorithms (Battista & Tamassia, 1993; Misue et al., 1995) after the evolution process. A number of modeling tools (e.g., GMF (http://www.eclipse.org/modeling/gmf, 2011), GEMS (http://www.eclipse.org/gmt/gems, 2011), GME (Ledeczi et al., 2001), MetaCase+ (http://www.metacase.com, 2011)) provide automatic layout functionality in their model editors using specific algorithms. They can rearrange the layout of the models and make them more readable by avoiding the overlaps of model elements and connections, adding blank spaces among model elements, or grouping the same type of elements together. However, most of these algorithms do not consider the implicit semantics of the model elements and connections; the result being that a readable model does not necessarily result in an optimized system if part of the system implementation depends on the layout configuration. Furthermore, fixed layout algorithms usually cannot consider the underlying mental map of individual users (i.e., a user's understanding of the relationship between the entities in a diagram) (Misue et al., 1995) into consideration. Although a user might prefer to see different types of model elements grouped closely, the automatic layout algorithm might destroy the user's mental map by separating them. Although a few algorithms integrate implicit semantic issues or common mental maps (e.g., placing the parent model elements being extended above their children model elements), they are often fixed in the model editors and cannot be customized easily according to a user's preference, which is inadequate for handling various kinds of implicit semantic issues and mental maps.

An alternative to configuring the layout is to change the layout properties as part of the model evolution using a model transformation process. When specifying model transformation rules to evolve the semantic aspect of the model, extra rules may be given to handle the layout configuration. Although this offers a flexible way to enable users to customize the preferred implicit semantics and mental maps, some drawbacks exist. First of all,

it forces the layout to be a crosscutting concern that becomes coupled with the semantics of the model transformation. In addition, testing and debugging the layout configuration are done by running the transformation and checking the final model, which is not direct and convenient. Imagine configuring the positions of a large number of newly added elements, which may require a great deal of effort to finally confirm the precise and desirable coordinate values for all of the modeling elements. Finally, implementing model transformations usually requires the user to know a model transformation language and the metamodel definition of the domain. For general users who are not familiar with model transformation languages or abstract metamodel definitions, they may be prevented from configuring the desired layout for the models they are using.

Therefore, a desirable approach to configure the model layout concerns in model evolution tasks should include the following features:

1) It should enable users to customize the layout configuration flexibly in order to realize their desired implicit semantics and mental maps.
2) It should be separated clearly from the semantic aspect of the model evolution.
3) It should enable end-users to configure and test the result using the notation related to their domain.
4) It should be at a level of abstraction that is appropriate for end-user adoption, and not tied to low-level accident complexities of the transformation process.

Solution Approach: Configuring Model Layout in a WYSIWYG Style

This chapter presents an innovative approach to enable users to specify and customize the preferred layout information by directly showing and demonstrating the layout configuration.

This approach is based on the idea of Model Transformation By Demonstration (MTBD) (Sun et al., 2009; Langer et al., 2010), which aims to simplify the implementation of model transformations by demonstrating specific model transformation tasks on concrete examples, and then inferring the generic transformation patterns automatically. With MTBD, users do not need to know any model transformation languages and are fully isolated from abstract metamodel definitions. MTBD has already been applied successfully in a number of model evolution applications (Sun et al., 2009a; Sun et al., 2009b; Langer et al., 2010), showing improvement in the efficiency and simplicity of implementing model transformations.

By following and extending the concepts of MTBD, we have developed an approach that enables users to demonstrate the desired layout configuration in a graphical model editor. After demonstrating the semantic concerns of the model evolution using MTBD, users can continue to select target model elements and place them at the correct positions. At the same time, the underlying MTBD engine records all of the user's operations and then generates a transformation pattern that incorporates both the semantic evolution and the layout configuration. Various options can be applied when specifying the positions, such as when model elements are placed using absolute coordinates in the model editor. Users can also choose one or multiple elements as a reference to configure the relative coordinates, or the reference could be the whole model instance whereby users configure the relative coordinates to the boundary of the model. Moreover, other layout information such as the font, color and size used in the model editor can also be configured and integrated into the model transformation.

By demonstrating the layout configuration directly, rather than specifying it explicitly in model transformation rules, users are able to customize their desired layout and preserve their mental maps (or other implicit semantic issues) without knowing any model transformation language or metamodel definition. The approach also offers a more convenient environment to give precise positions as well as to test and debug the resulting layout transformation. The demonstration of layout configuration occurs after the demonstration of the semantic evolution, so that the two concepts are separated without being tangled as crosscutting concerns.

The rest of the chapter is organized as follows. We first illustrate the problems and challenges of layout configuration during model transformation using two motivating examples, followed by the analysis on the related model configuration techniques. Then, the MTBD framework is introduced, which is the basis for the layout configuration approach. To solve the two motivating examples, we will present the layout configuration extensions to MTBD and the implementation details. Finally, we offer concluding remarks and summarize future work.

MOTIVATING EXAMPLES

In this section, we illustrate the problems of layout configuration during model evolution using two motivating examples. For each example, we first explain the model evolution scenario as the underlying context, followed by showing what the model will look like after traditional model transformation is applied without layout configuration. We also explain why the fixed layout algorithms cannot handle most implicit semantic issues and user mental maps. Additionally, an excerpt of the model transformation rules written in a specific model transformation language will be given to explain why specifying the layout configuration explicitly with manually created model transformation rules is not a preferred approach.

Evolving Stochastic Reward Nets Models

Stochastic Reward Nets (SRNs) (Muppala et al., 1994) can be used for evaluating the reliability of complex distributed systems. SRNs have been used extensively for designing and modeling reliability and performance of different types of systems. The Stochastic Reward Net Modeling Language (SRNML) (Kogekar et al., 2006) was developed to describe SRN models of large distributed systems, which share similar goals with performance-based modeling extensions for the UML, such as the schedulability, performance, and time profiles. For example, the SRN model defined by SRNML in Figure 1a depicts the Reactor pattern (Schmidt et al., 2000) in middleware for network services, providing mechanisms to handle synchronous event demultiplexing and dispatching.

In the Reactor pattern, an application registers an event handler with the event demultiplexer and delegates the incoming events to it. On the occurrence of an event, the demultiplexer dispatches the event to its corresponding event handler by making a callback. An SRN model consists of two parts: the event types handled by a reactor (the top part of Figure 1a) and the associated execution snapshot (the bottom part of Figure 1a). The execution snapshot depicts the underlying mechanism for handling the event types, so any changes made to the event types will require corresponding changes to the snapshot.

Model Evolution Scenario in SRNML

A typical SRN model evolution scenario arises from the addition of new event types and connections between their corresponding event handlers. As shown in Figure 1d, when two new event types (*3* and *4*) need to be modeled, two new sets of event types and connections (i.e., from *A3* to *Sr3*, from *A4* to *Sr4*) should be added. Also, the snapshot model should be scaled accordingly by adding new *Snapshot Places* (i.e., *SnpLnProg3*,

SnpLnProg4), *Snapshot Transitions* from starting place to end place (i.e., *TStSnp3*, *TEnSnp3*, *TStSnp4*, *TEnSnp4*), *Snapshot Transitions* between each new place and each existing place (i.e., *TProcSnp3,1*, *TProcSnp1,3*, *TProcSnp3,2*, *TProcSnp2,3*, *TProcSnp4,1*, *TProcSnp1,4*, *TProcSnp4,2*, *TProcSnp2,4*, *TProcSnp3,4*, *TProcSnp4,3*), as well as all the needed connections between places and transitions.

A number of new elements and connections are created during this model evolution scenario. The creation process can be automated by executing model transformation rules or calling APIs provided by the modeling environment. Figure 1b shows the SRN model after executing the transformation rules defined in the Embedded Constraint Language (ECL) (Lin et al., 2008), which scale the model from 2 event types to 4. Although the correct number of elements (i.e., 26 model elements) are created and the correct connections are made (i.e., 38 connections), all the newly created elements and connections are placed randomly in the upper-left corner of the editor and overlapped with each other, which is unreadable without arranging the layout. However, manual layout arrangement is tedious and time-consuming, especially when the model is scaled to adapt a larger number of event types (e.g., over 100 new elements will be created when scaling a SRN model from 5 event types to 10, and over 150 connections are needed to connect them).

One option that avoids manual layout arrangement is to use the auto-layout functionality provided by the modeling tool. For instance, Figure 1c shows the scaled SRN model after applying the auto-layout function embedded in the GMF editor. Compared with Figure 1b, it can be seen that the overlaps of all the newly created elements are removed; the location of each element is changed so that the distances between each two elements are more similar; and all the elements connected are grouped together. A clear and readable model is obtained by a single mouse-click. However, a readable model does not necessarily preserve the

Figure 1. SRN models

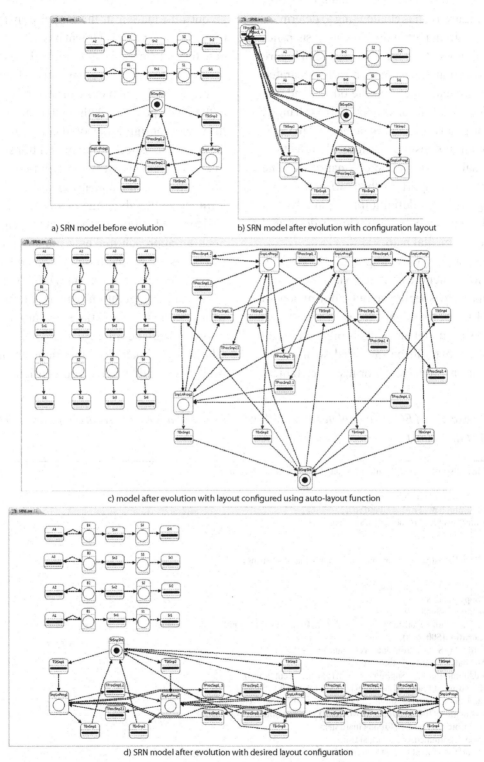

a) SRN model before evolution

b) SRN model after evolution with configuration layout

c) model after evolution with layout configured using auto-layout function

d) SRN model after evolution with desired layout configuration

implicit semantics and a user's mental map. As shown in Figure 1c, it is challenging to determine the corresponding part in the execution snapshot for each of the existing event types, and in Figure 1b the execution snapshot is clearly separated by different event types. On the other hand, the layout of event definitions in Figure 1c is changed from the original horizontal arrangement to vertical. Although it does not significantly affect the understandability or implicit semantics of the definitions, users might have their own preferences of placing the event definition horizontally, and the auto-layout functionality obviously destroyed this particular mental map.

An alternative layout configuration approach to address the problems associated with auto-layout algorithms is to specify layout information in the model transformation rules (i.e., the $<x, y>$ coordinates of model elements is often an inherent property that can be modified with model transformation languages). For instance, Table 1

shows an excerpt of the ECL code that configures layout information in the model transformation process. Each model element has a *Location* attribute that can be used to configure the coordinates of the element, and setting this attribute after adding the new element can result in placing it at the given position. Although users can control fully the configuration of the layout, it forces the semantic aspect of the model transformation rules to be entangled with layout concerns, the consequence being that any changes to the transformation rules about the model elements might lead to modifications on the layout configurations. Such an approach makes a transformation rule less cohesive. Furthermore, to test and debug the layout configuration, executing the rules and adjusting the configurations will have to be iterated, which is a tedious and time-consuming process. This task becomes more challenging when many relative coordinate configurations are involved. Additionally, adding the layout configuration in the

Table 1. An excerpt of ECL to complete the model evolution with integrated layout configuration (adapted from (Lin et al. 2006))

```
strategy addEvents(min_new, max_new: integer; TEnSnpGuardStr: string)
{
if (min_new <= max_new) then
addNewEvent(min_new, TEnSnpGuardStr);
addEvents(min_new+1, max_new, TEnSnpGuardStr);
endif;
}
strategy addNewEvent(event_num: integer; TEnSnpGuardStr: string)
{
declare start, stTran, inProg, endTran: atom;
declare TStSnp_guard: string;
start:= findAtom("StSnpSht");
stTran:= addAtom("ImmTransition", "TStSnp" + intToString(event_num));
stTran.setLocation(500, 600);
TStSnp_guard:= "(#S" + intToString(event_num) + " == 1)?1: 0";
stTran.setAttribute("Guard", TStSnp_guard);
inProg:= addAtom("Place", "SnpInProg" + intToString(event_num));
inProg.setLocation(stTran.getLocation().getX() + 100, 600);
endTran:= addAtom("ImmTransition", "TEnSnp" + intToString(event_num));
endTran.setLocation(100, getUpperMostAtom().getLocation().getY() + 100);
endTran.setAttribute("Guard", TEnSnpGuardStr);
addConnection("InpImmedArc", start, stTran);
addConnection("OutImmedArc", stTran, inProg);
addConnection("InpImmedArc", inProg, endTran);
addConnection("OutImmedArc", endTran, start);
}
...
```

transformation rules requires users to understand the model transformation language, the layout configuration APIs, as well as the metamodel definition. In many cases, when end-users (e.g., domain experts who are not familiar with model transformation languages) encounter the layout problems, it would be challenging for them to learn the languages and metamodel definitions.

The Administration of Cloud Computing Management Models

Another example is based on the Cloud Computing Management Modeling Language (C2M2L) (Sun et al., 2009a) - a domain-specific modeling language (DSML) constructed specifically to describe the deployment of application nodes in a cloud computing server that monitors the running status of each node. For instance, the top of Figure 2 shows a diagram of an EJB cloud application deployed in Amazon EC2 (http://aws.amazon.com/ec2, 2011), containing several Nodes, such as *Web Tier Instance*, *Middle Tier Instance*, *Data Tier Instance* all connected to the *Load Balancer*. *NodeServices* (not shown in the figure) are included in each Node (e.g., *Apache, Tomcat, MySQL, JBoss, OpenSSH*) to define the services needed for each tier instance. A list of properties can be configured for each *Node*, such as the name of the host (i.e., *HostName*), the running status of the Node (i.e., *IsWorking*), the load of the CPU (i.e., *CPULoad*), and the changing rate of the CPU load (i.e., *CPULoadRateOfChange*). The connections between Nodes indicate the data flows from the source *Node* to the target *Node*. This model configures the deployment and execution parameters of an application in a cloud computing server.

To facilitate the management of applications in the cloud, a causal relationship is built between the running applications and the model. Changes to the state of the cloud application must be communicated back to the modeling tool and translated into changes in the elements of the model, while changes from the model must also be pushed back into the cloud. Therefore, the models defined by C2M2L serve as an interface to deploy, monitor, and manage the applications in the cloud at runtime.

Model Evolution Scenario in C2M2L

One essential task in the management of applications in the cloud is to ensure that each node is handling a proper amount of work load without being overloaded. For instance, if the *CPULoad* of a certain Node is out of the normal range (e.g., *CPULoad > 100*), the *Node* will stop working, so the connection between the failed *Node* and the *NodeBalancer* needs to be removed. Furthermore, *Nodes* containing the same *NodeServices* and configuration, and the corresponding, connections need to be replicated in order to balance the work load, as shown in the bottom of Figure 2.

When managing the C2M2L models, layout configuration is also indispensible. For instance, when a failed *Node* is replaced with two new *Nodes*, the new *Nodes* should be placed under the original *Node* as illustrated in the bottom of Figure 2. Also, since the failed *Node* is no longer used, it is better to place it at the top of the editor rather than taking space among the working *Nodes*. To improve the management process and make it more illustrative, it is also desired to highlight the failed *Node* with a red background color, and to use the green for the newly added *Nodes*.

This layout configuration process will be challenging to accomplish manually, particularly when a large number of application *Nodes* are running in the cloud. Because the existing auto-layout functionality cannot preserve such kind of layout requirements, it is necessary to have an approach to automate the layout configuration process without using model transformation languages or knowing metamodel definitions.

Figure 2. A C2M2L model with three Nodes overloaded (top) and the model after removing and replicating the overloaded Nodes (bottom)

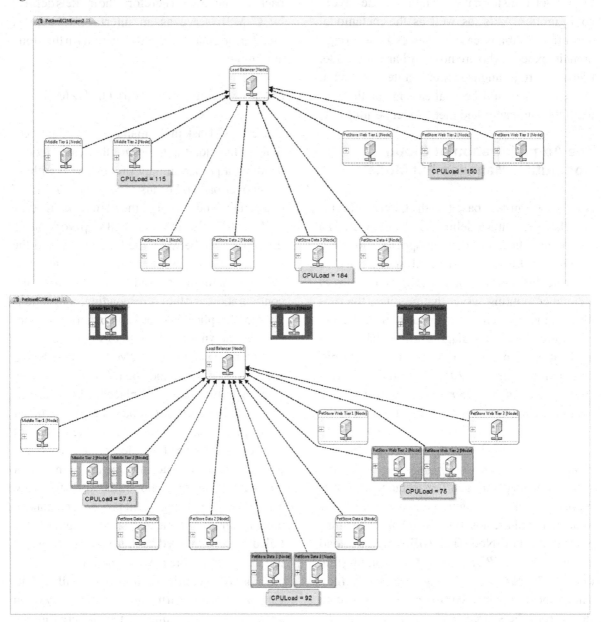

RELATED WORKS

A compact and readable diagram layout is vital for leveraging the full potential of graphical DSMLs. Because models are frequently subjected to evolution and transformation during their life cycles, techniques enabling the automatic adap-

tion of a model's diagram layout become crucial for retaining model compactness and readability.

Concerning the goal of the demonstration-based approach to layout configuration as presented in this chapter, we distinguish between two categories of related work: (i) approaches aiming to improve single diagram layouts, and

(ii) approaches for optimizing sequences of diagram layouts. In this chapter, we describe a novel technique for the latter category, i.e., deriving a new version of an existing diagram layout after its underlying model has been transformed. Nevertheless, one way of deriving a new version of a diagram layout is to simply apply single diagram layout algorithms after each change of the underlying model, which is often referred to as dynamic graph drawing in the literature (Di Battista et al., 1998).

Layout Configuration for Single Diagrams

Due to the graph-based nature of diagrams, algorithms for configuring the layout of diagrams are strongly related to algorithms solving the graph drawing problem (Di Battista et al., 1998). In this research area, several different approaches have been proposed. A popular representative of such approaches is the spring embedder layout (Fruchterman & Reingold, 1991), which is a force-driven layout algorithm. In particular, each node in a graph contains attractive and repulsive forces that either move an element toward or away from other nodes. Iteratively, each node is moved until the sum of all forces settles at a minimum. Although such algorithms are capable of largely avoiding overlapping nodes and edges in a diagram, due to their generic nature, they do not take type information of graph nodes and domain-specific layout preferences into account. However, domain-specific layout patterns, such as horizontal tree layouts for control flow languages, are commonly applied in practice to support users in understanding a diagram. Therefore, domain-specific layout algorithms have been developed which place nodes and edges according to certain layout constraints or layout rules. Hower and Graf (Hower & Graf, 1996) provided an extensive survey on constraint-based layout approaches in several application domains. More recently, Dwyer et al. proposed an authoring tool specifically

designed for network diagrams that also places elements according to domain-specific layout constraints (Dwyer et al., 2009). A constraint solver computes a solution for these declarative constraints to produce an improved diagram layout. Layout-based approaches employ domain-specific layout rules instead of constraints. As proposed by Maier and Minas (Maier & Minas, 2009), a rule consists of a condition and an action that is executed if the condition is fulfilled. For instance, a rule might be activated as soon as an element is too small for its compartments (condition) and induce a resizing of the element (action).

Generic, as well as domain-specific layout algorithms, also found their way into several graphical modeling tools. For instance, UML tools such as ArgoUML, Visual Paradigm, and Enterprise Architect, as well as meta-modeling tools such as GMF, GEMS, GME, and Meta-Case+ provide automatic layout functionality. Most modeling tools use domain-specific layout algorithms because they are tailored for specific modeling languages. Metamodeling tools usually provide generic layout algorithms for modeling editors that are created from metamodel specifications. Additionally, many model editors also offer extension points for attaching domain-specific layout facilities.

Layout Configuration for Diagram Sequences

The aforementioned approaches focus on establishing a diagram layout from scratch or improving an existing diagram layout, but they are not tailored to optimize the layout across sequences of diagrams. However, when a model is transformed, the diagram has to be adjusted to the evolved model. One major requirement in this task is to preserve the mental map (Misue et al., 1995) across one or more transformations of the diagram's underlying model. This aspect is the particular focus of the previous works (Jucknath-John et al., 2006; Pilgrim, 2007; Johannes & Gaul, 2009).

Jucknath-John et al. aim at layout graphs that are transformed by a sequence of endogenous graph transformations. The design rationale of their algorithm is to (i) achieve an optimal quality for each single graph layout, (ii) retain the mental map of a graph layout, (iii) consider its future extension, and (iv) identify the changes between two succeeding graph layouts by visually emphasizing the differences. To achieve these goals, the authors propose an iterative layout algorithm based on the aforementioned spring embedder layout (Fruchterman & Reingold, 1991). In particular, the spring embedder layout is extended by the concept of node aging and protection of the layout of senior nodes. By this, senior nodes (i.e., nodes that have been introduced earlier than others) are less likely to be repositioned by the algorithm than younger nodes in order to retain the mental map of the graph layout.

The focus of Pilgrim is to retain the mental map in exogenous model transformations. The transformation of the semantic model is applied using ATL (Jouault & Kurtev, 2005). The proposed algorithm takes the transformed input model, the input diagram layout, the output model, and the transformation trace as input to create a new diagram layout for the generated output model. Nodes representing elements in the output model are placed according to the position of nodes representing input model elements linked by the transformation trace in order to retain the mental map. The output diagram layout is optimized by scaling and adjusting the nodes to avoid overlaps. Furthermore, a 3D editor is used to display the source diagram and target diagram (and its correspondences in terms of traces) in a single window.

Johannes and Gaul considered diagram layout when composing domain-specific models. In their approach, the layout composition information is delivered through a graphical model composition script, which specifies how the semantic models should be composed. After the composed model is created, the diagrams of the composed model are merged into a new composed diagram according to the positions in the graphical model composition script. Johannes and Gaul also apply algorithms to adjust the final layout to remove overlaps.

All mentioned approaches for configuring the layout of diagram sequences particularly focus on retaining the mental map in endogenous or exogenous transformations. Pilgrim and Johannes and Gaul tackle this issue for exogenous transformations. Only Jucknath-John et al., as our approach, focus on endogenous transformations. In the approach of Jucknath-John et al., the position of existing nodes is protected by applying the concept of node aging, but in contrast to our approach, they do not consider transformation rule-specific layout preferences. With specific transformation rule layout preferences, the transformation engineer may regard certain aspects of a transformation in the resulting layout which enables users to understand a diagram better, especially in the context of a specific evolution task after the transformation has been performed. Only Johannes and Gaul partially consider this aspect because the resulting diagram layout is set up according to the positioning in the graphical composition script. However, they do not support the configuration of relative positioning of nodes to certain existing context nodes of a transformation. Additionally, all aforementioned approaches do not support the automatic assignment of other layout properties (e.g., background colors) after a transformation has been performed. Another major difference of our approach to these existing approaches is the adoption of the WYSIWYG technique to easily specify the desired layout after a transformation is created by demonstration.

INTRODUCTION TO MODEL TRANSFORMATION BY DEMONSTRATION

Our solution to the auto-layout customization problem is to use a demonstration-based technique to support specification of the layout configuration by automating the whole process as model transformations. The idea is based on our previous work on Model Transformation By Demonstration (MTBD), which is a new approach to implement endogenous model transformations, with the goal being to enable general users (e.g., domain experts or non-programmers) to realize transformation tasks without knowing model transformation languages or metamodel definitions. In this section, we introduce MTBD, and then explain how to use MTBD to support general model evolution tasks by using the motivating examples presented previously. The extensions to support layout configuration will be presented in the next section.

Overview of MTBD

The basic idea of MTBD is that rather than manually writing model transformation rules, users are asked to use concrete model instances and demonstrate how to transform a source model to a target model by directly editing and changing it. During the demonstration process, a recording and inference engine captures all of the user operations and automatically infers a transformation pattern that summarizes the desired evolution task

captured as a transformation. This generated pattern can be executed by the engine in any model instance to carry out the same evolution task on other parts of a model.

Figure 3 is an overview of the MTBD idea, which consists of the following main steps and components.

Step 1: User Demonstration and Recording

Users must first give a demonstration by directly editing a model instance (e.g., add a new model element or connection, modify the attribute of a model element, connect two model elements) to simulate an evolution task. During the demonstration, users are expected to perform operations not only on model elements and connections, but also on their attributes, so that the attribute evolution can be supported. An attribute refactoring editor has been developed to enable users to access all the attributes in the current model editor and specify the desired transformation (e.g., string and arithmetic computation). At the same time, an event listener monitors all the operations occurring in

Figure 3. Overview of MTBD

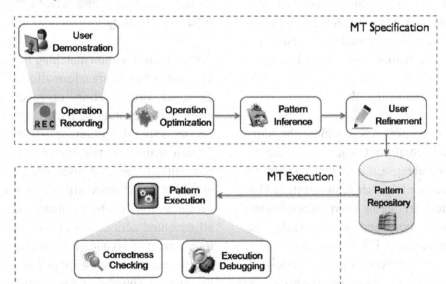

the model editor and collects the information for each operation in sequence.

Step 2: Operation Optimization

The list of recorded operations indicates how a model evolution should be performed. However, not all operations in the list are meaningful. Users may perform useless or inefficient operations during the demonstration. For instance, without a careful design, it is possible that a user first adds a new element and modifies its attributes, and then deletes it in another operation later, with the result being that all the operations regarding this element actually did not take effect in the transformation process and therefore are meaningless. Thus, after the demonstration, the engine optimizes the recorded operations to eliminate meaningless actions.

Step 3: Pattern Inference

With an optimized list of recorded operations, the transformation can be inferred. Because the MTBD approach does not rely on any model transformation languages, it is not necessary to generate specific transformation rules, although that is possible. Instead, we generate a transformation pattern, which summarizes the precondition of a transformation (i.e., where a transformation should be done) and the actions needed in a transformation (i.e., how a transformation should be done).

Step 4: User Refinement

The initial pattern inferred is specific to the demonstration and is usually not generic and accurate enough for general reuse, due to the limitation on the expressiveness of the user demonstration. Users are permitted to refine the inferred transformation by providing more feedback for the desired transformation scenario. For instance, users may give more restrictive preconditions on the desired evolution, such as "replace element A only if A has

no incoming or outgoing connections," or "add new element B in C only when the attribute value of C is greater than *200*." Users can also identify which operations should be generic (i.e., operations should be repeated as long as appropriate model elements are available, rather than being executed only once). All the user refinements are still performed at the model instance level without explicitly modifying the metamodel, after which a transformation pattern will be finalized and stored in the pattern repository for future use.

Step 5: Pattern Execution

The final generated patterns can be executed on any model instances. Because a pattern consists of the precondition and the transformation actions, the execution starts with matching the precondition in the new model instance and then carries out the transformation actions on the matched locations of the model. Notifications are made to users when the selected model fails to match the transformation pattern. Multiple transformation patterns can be executed in sequence on the same model, in order to apply some continuous evolution tasks. The same matching process is taken before executing each pattern.

Step 6: Correctness Checking and Debugging

Although the location matching the precondition guarantees that all transformation actions can be executed with necessary operands, it does not ensure that executing them will not violate the syntax, semantics definitions or external constraints. Therefore, the execution of each transformation action will be logged and model instance correctness checking is performed after every execution. If a certain action violates the metamodel definition, all executed actions are undone and the whole transformation is cancelled. An execution control component has been developed as part of MTBD to control the number of execution times, and enable the execution of multiple patterns together in sequence. A debugger is under development to enable end-users to track the execution of the transformation pattern without being exposed to low-level execution information.

Using MTBD, users are only involved in editing model instances to demonstrate the model transformation process including specific attribute configurations and giving feedback after the demonstration. All of the other procedures (i.e., optimization, inference, generation, execution, and correctness checking) are fully automated. No model transformation languages are used and the generated transformation patterns are invisible to users. One demonstration results in a transformation pattern. Therefore, users are completely isolated from knowing MTLs and the metamodel definition.

Admittedly, a user demonstration is not as expressive and powerful as specified rules, the result being that MTBD can only support a subset of tasks that can be realized using MTLs (e.g., QVT and ATL). For example, selecting the element with a certain maximum value can be specified directly with a function call, but it is challenging to demonstrate by mouse and keyboard. However, MTBD has been applied successfully in a number of model evolution tasks, such as model refactoring, aspect-oriented modeling, and model scalability. It has been shown in many cases to be a practical alternative to enable end-users to real-

Figure 4. The process of scaling a SRN model from two events to three events

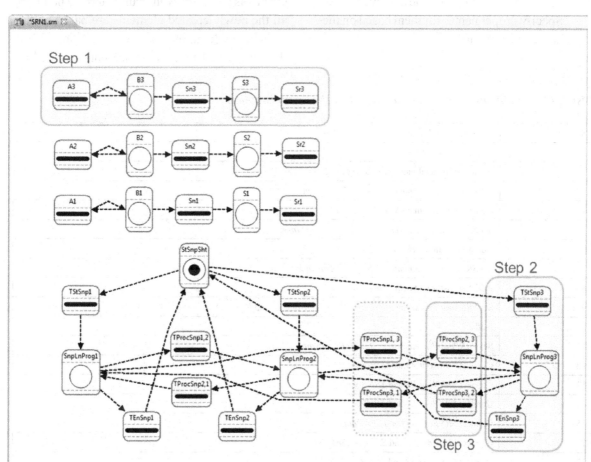

ize model evolution tasks without the knowledge of MTLs and metamodels.

Applying MTBD to the SRNML

To better illustrate the idea, we show how to use MTBD to demonstrate scaling of SRN models (the motivating example from an earler section) without configuring the layout. The demonstration illustrates how the transformation pattern can be generated and reused to automate the scaling process in other model instances.

By examining the scalability requirements of the example, the task of adding one more event type to an existing SRN model consists of the following three steps, as shown in Figure 4:

- Step 1. Create a new set of *Places*, *Transitions* and connections for the new event type. Specify proper names for them based on the name of the event.

- Step 2. Create the *TStSnp* and *TEnSnp Snapshot Transitions* and the *SnpInProg Snapshot Place*, as well as the associated connections.
- Step 3. For each pair of <existing *Snapshot Place*, new *Snapshot Place*>, create two *TProcSnp Transitions* and connect their *SnpInProg Places* to these *TProcSnp Transitions*.

To give this demonstration, we choose the 2-event SRN model as shown in Figure 1a. Then, we manually edit the model and demonstrate the task following the three steps. For Step 1, the operations shown in List 1 are performed.

All of these operations are used to create the new elements and necessary connections for the event definition (i.e., *A3*, *B3*, *Sn3*, *S3*, *Sr3*). Each event has a unique event name, and the names of all the newly created elements are based on this event name (e.g., the new event is called "3," so the places and transitions are named as "A3,"

List 1. Operations for step 1 of example 2.1 in the demonstration

Sequence	Operation Performed
1	Add a *Place* in *SRNRoot*
2	Create an artificial name with the value: *EventName* = *"3"*
3	Set *SRNRoot.Place.name* = *"A"* + *EventName* = *"A3"*
4	Add a *Transition* in *SRNRoot*
5	Set *SRNRoot.Transition.name* = *"B"* + *EventName* = *"B3"*
6	Add a *Place* in *SRNRoot*
7	Set *SRNRoot.Place.name* = *"Sn"* + *EventName* = *"Sn3"*
8	Add a *Transition* in *SRNRoot*
9	Set *SRNRoot.Transition.name* = *"S"* + *EventName* = *"S3"*
10	Add a *Place* in *SRNRoot*
11	Set *SRNRoot.Place.name* = *"Sr"* + *EventName* = *"Sr3"*
12	Connect *SRNRoot.A3* and *SRNRoot.B3*
13	Connect *SRNRoot.B3* and *SRNRoot.A3*
14	Connect *SRNRoot.B3* and *SRNRoot.Sn3*
15	Connect *SRNRoot.Sn3* and *SRNRoot.S3*
16	Connect *SRNRoot.S3* and *SRNRoot.Sr3*
17	Connect *SRNRoot.A3* and *SRNRoot.B3*

"B3," "Sn3,"). Therefore, Operation 2 is used to manually create a name for a certain value, which can be reused later in the rest of the demonstration to setup the desired name for each element. For instance, when setting up the attribute in operations 3, 5, 7, 9, 11, users just need to give the specific composition of the attributes by using the artificial names and constants, or simply select an existing attribute value in the attribute refactoring editor. After applying these operations, the model will have a new event type definition, as shown in Figure 4 (Step 1).

To finish Step 2, the necessary *Snapshot Places* and *Snapshot Transitions* are added for the new event type by performing the operations indicated in List 2. Figure 4 (Step 2) shows the model after these operations.

To demonstrate Step 3, two *Snapshot Transitions* for each <existing *Snapshot Place*, new *Snapshot Place*> need to be created. For example, *TProcSnp1,3* and *TProcSnp3,1* should be added between *SnpLnProg1* and *SnpLnProg3*, while *TProcSnp2,3* and *TProcSnp3,2* are needed between *SnpLnProg2* and *SnpLnProg3*. Because the number of the existing *Snapshot Place* varies in different model instances, instead of demonstrating the addition of *Snapshot Transitions* in every pair, we only need to demonstrate the process for one pair, followed by identifying the operations as generic in the user refinement step. This is needed so that the engine will generate the correct transformation pattern to repeat these operations when needed according to the different number of the existing *Snapshot Place*. The operations performed are shown in List 3. We select *SnpLnProg2* as the existing *Snapshot Place*, and demonstrate the creation of *Snapshot Transitions - TProcSnp2,3* and *TProcSnp3,2*.

When specifying the name attributes, complex String composition can be given using the Java APIs, as done in operations 29 and 31. After the demonstration is completed and generic operations are identified in the user refinement step, the inference engine automatically infers and generates the transformation pattern, which will be saved in the transformation repository.

After the pattern is saved, a user may select any model instance and a desired transformation pattern, and the selected model will be scaled by adding a new event type. The execution controller can be used to enable execution of a pattern multiple times. Figure 1b is the result of adding two event types using the inferred pattern automatically. Although the correct number of new

List 2. Operations for step 2 of example 2.1 in the demonstration

Sequence	Operation Performed
18	Add a *SnpPlace* in *SRNRoot*
19	Set *SRNRoot.SnpPlace.name* = "SnpLnProg"+EventName = "SnpLnProg3"
20	Add a *SnpTransition* in *SRNRoot*
21	Set *SRNRoot.SnpTransition.name* = "TStSnp" + EventName = "TStSnp3"
22	Add a *SnpTransition* in *SRNRoot*
23	Set *SRNRoot.SnpTransition.name* = "TEnSnp" + EventName = "TEnSnp3"
24	Connect *SRNRoot.StSnpSht* and *SRNRoot.TStSnp3*
25	Connect *SRNRoot.TStSnp3* and *SRNRoot.SnpLnProg3*
26	Connect *SRNRoot.SnpLnProg3* and *SRNRoot.TEnSnp3*
27	Connect *SRNRoot.TEnSnp3* and *SRNRoot.StSnpSht*

List 3. Operations for Step 3 in the demonstration of example 2.1

Sequence	Operation Performed
28*	Add a *SnpTransition* in *SRNRoot*
29*	Set *SRNRoot.SnpTransition.name* = *"TProcSnp"* + *SRNRoot.SnpLnProg2.name.subString(9)* + *","* + *EventName* = *"TProcSnp"* + *"2"* + *","* + *"3"* = *"TProcSnp2,3"*
30*	Add a *SnpTransition* in *SRNRoot*
31*	Set *SRNRoot.SnpTransition.name* = *"TProcSnp"* + *EventName* + *","* + *SRNRoot.SnpLnProg3.name.subString(9)* = *"TProcSnp"* + *"3"* + *","* + *"2"* = *"TProcSnp3,2"*
32*	Connect *SRNRoot.SnpLnProg2* and *SRNRoot.TProcSnp2,3*
33*	Connect *SRNRoot.TProcSnp2,3* and *SRNRoot.SnpLnProg3*
34*	Connect *SRNRoot.SnpLnProg3* and *SRNRoot.TProcSnp3,2*
35*	Connect *SRNRoot.TProcSnp3,2* and *SRNRoot.SnpLnProg2*

(* represents generic operations to be identified)

elements and connections has been created with consistent names, all of the elements are overlapped and randomly placed on the upper-left corner of the editor. To address the layout problem in model transformation, we extended MTBD to enable demonstration of layout configuration.

LAYOUT SUPPORT IN MTBD

The idea of supporting layout configuration using MTBD is based on an additional demonstration step. After demonstrating the basic model transformation task, users are able to demonstrate how to configure the layout (e.g., where to place each element, what layout properties to specify), so that the layout information can be summarized and integrated in the generated transformation pattern. Because the demonstration is performed on the concrete model instances in the model editor and the engine automatically records the low-level layout information (e.g., the specific coordinate values), users can configure the layout in a WYSIWYG manner without being aware of the implementation details.

Currently, we focus on configuring the layout from two perspectives: the location of the model elements and the appearance of model elements. Model connections are not considered in the current work, because in most modeling tools and editors, the layout of connections depends on the source and target model elements and cannot be customized by users, but the idea proposed in this chapter can be applied to connections as well.

Configuring Locations of Model Elements

The main layout of a model depends on the location of each model element. In most modeling tools, a *Location* attribute is attached to each model element internally, which specifies the coordinates of the element. In the editors, the *Location* attribute of an element changes automatically when it is moved. Therefore, by capturing moving operations (i.e., the drag-and-drop operation in most editors) in the demonstration, coordinate values can be recorded automatically by reading the updated location of the element. As model elements often need to be moved in the editor multiple times before reaching the desired location, rather than recording every moving operation, a confirmation location operation is provided for users to confirm the final desired location of a model element, which is recorded and integrated into the generated transformation pattern. The confirmation location operation can be based on either absolute coordinates or relative coordinates.

Absolute coordinates. The most direct and simplest layout configuration is to use absolute coordinates. Users can demonstrate where to place each element exactly in the editor. As shown in List 4, two kinds of operations are added to the editor to support locating and choosing the absolute coordinates of a certain element. When the transformation is executed, the chosen model elements will be placed in the exact same location as in the demonstration.

For example, in the top of Figure 5, the *Node* in the lower-right corner is selected and confirmed with an absolute coordinate for both X and Y in the demonstration. When the generated transformation pattern is executed, the *Node* is configured with the same coordinate values automatically as shown in the bottom of Figure 5.

While confirming the absolute coordinates, the actual coordinate values are not visible to users, so that users are separated from the low-level layout information. The recording engine reads the values, and saves them in the final generated transformation pattern. In the execution process, the execution engine loads the values and passes them as parameters to the location configuration process.

The absolute coordinates approach is easy to implement, but not flexible and practical in most model transformation scenarios. Unless the user is configuring the layout information for a single and unique model element (e.g., the root or folder of a domain model), using absolute coordinates cannot adapt the transformation to diverse model evolution scenarios. For example, if any model elements or connections exist or cross at certain absolute coordinates configured in the demonstration, placing a new element there will lead to overlaps. In addition, when applying a transformation pattern multiple times, all the newly created elements will be placed in the same location. Therefore, in many cases, configuring the layout using relative coordinates is more preferable.

Relative Coordinates to Model Boundary

Using relative coordinates needs a reference point. One type of reference is to consider all the model elements and connections as a whole rectangle (i.e., the minimum rectangle that includes all the current model elements and connections), and use the boundary of the rectangle as the reference. The coordinates can be relative to each side of the rectangle from either inside or outside. Thus, a total of eight operations can be extended, as shown in List 5.

Similar to using absolute coordinates, users may demonstrate the relative values by a drag-and-drop process in the editor without being aware of the low-level details. It is the recording engine that automatically captures the rectangle boundary in the current editor and calculates the specific relative values. During the execution process of the generated transformation, the execution engine will capture the boundary of the model again and set up the location attribute using the stored relative values. For instance, in the top of

List 4. Layout configuration operations using absolute coordinates

Operation Type	Description
Set X as Current	Set X in the current coordinates as the desired X
Set Y as Current	Set Y in the current coordinates as the desired Y

Figure 5. Using absolute coordinates in the demonstration (top) make the element be in the same location in every model evolution scenario (bottom)

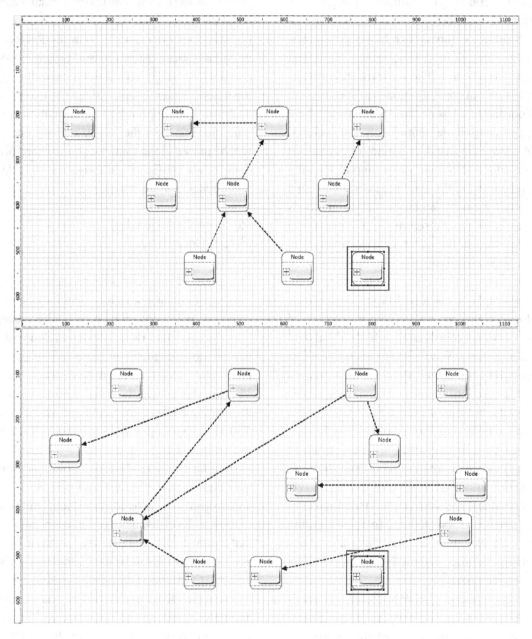

Figure 6, *Node1* and *Node2* are two newly created model elements. When configuring the layout in the demonstration, *Node1* is specified using *Set X Relative to Rightmost Outside*, and *Set Y as Current*, while *Node2* applies *Set X Relative to Leftmost Inside* and *Set Y Relative to Lowermost Inside*. The result is that when apply-ing the transformation in other models, *Node1* will always be placed to the right of the existing model, but at the same vertical level as in the demonstration; and *Node2* will always appear on the left-lower corner of the existing model, as shown in the bottom of Figure 6.

List 5. Layout configuration operations using relative coordinates to model boundary

Operation Type	Description
Set Y Relative to Uppermost (Inside/Outside)	Set the desired Y to be the current Y relative to the uppermost boundary of the current model from inside or outside
Set Y Relative to Lowermost (Inside/Outside)	Set the desired Y to be the current Y relative to the lowermost boundary of the current model from inside or outside
Set X Relative to Leftmost (Inside/Outside)	Set the desired X to be the current X relative to the leftmost boundary of the current model from inside or outside
Set X Relative to Rightmost (Inside/Outside)	Set the desired X to be the current X relative to the rightmost boundary of the current model from inside or outside

The relative coordinate to the model boundary proves to be useful in practice when a large number of new elements are created in the model evolution process or the same process is executed multiple times (e.g., the first motivating example). As the model is enlarged, it is always necessary to add new elements based on a layout pattern incrementally. However, when the model transformation focuses on modifying a small number of elements without adding many new elements (e.g., the second motivating example), relative coordinates to the boundary are not sufficient, and a different type of reference with improved granularity is needed.

Relative Coordinates to Model Element(S)

A more improved granularity and flexible reference is to set up the coordinates of a model element relative to other model element(s). As enumerated in List 6, users can configure X/Y based on the location of another model element.

In the current implementation, a model element selector has been developed that enables users to choose any element from the existing model instance, and set up the X or Y coordinate. Again, the recording engine calculates the relative value and stores it, while the execution engine loads the value and sets up the location. The calculated relative value can be either positive or negative according to the relative locations (i.e., the value will be negative if the element is to the left or above the reference element, and will be positive

if the element is to the right or below the reference element).

For example, at the top of Figure 7, several model elements (i.e., *Node1, Node2, Node3, Node4, Node5*) are involved in a model transformation scenario. Users configure the location of *Node3* using *Set X Relative to Model Element Node2*, and *Set Y Relative to Model Element Node1*, so that *Node3* will always be in the same horizontal level as *Node2* and have the same vertical distance to *Node1* no matter where *Node2* and *Node1* are located in different model instances. On the other hand, both X and Y of *Node4* are configured relative to *Node5*, the result being that *Node4* is always on the upper-left part of *Node5* with the same distance as illustrated in the bottom of Figure 7.

Relative coordinates to specific model elements provide more freedom for users to configure model element locations. When the reference element(s) were used in the demonstration of the semantic aspect of the evolution process, the recording and execution engine can save and load the values directly; but if the reference element(s) are not included in the previous demonstration about semantic aspect evolution (e.g., using the *Node* in the upper-left corner as a reference in the top of Figure 6), the element(s) will be automatically added to the generated transformation as a structural precondition, which means that the execution engine must match and find out the element in the model transformation to ensure the correct layout configuration using it.

Figure 6. Using coordinates relative to the boundary of the existing model in the demonstration (top) make the element be in the location relative to the existing model in every model evolution scenario (bottom)

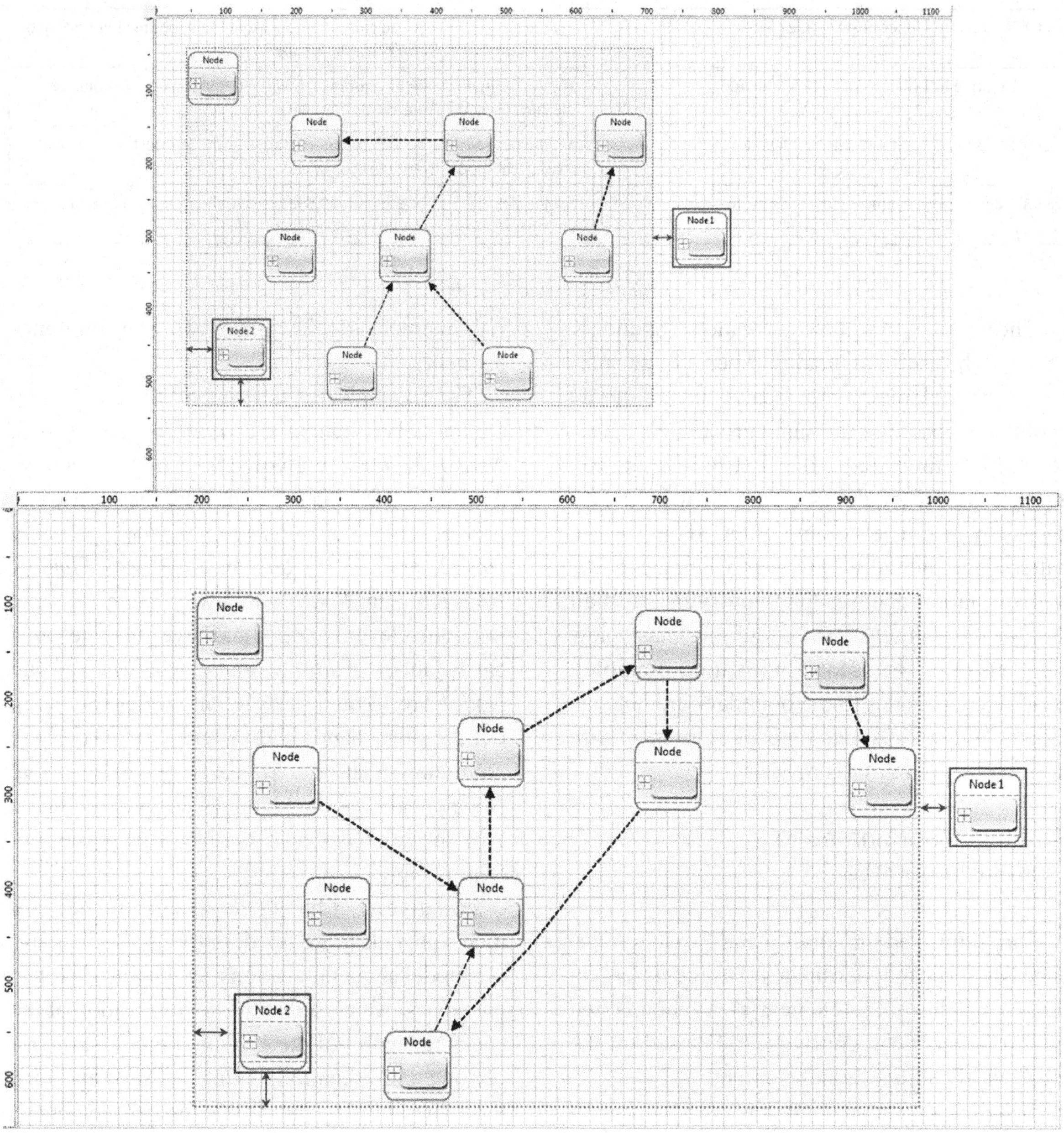

List 6. Layout configuration operations using relative coordinates to model element(s)

Operation Type	Description
Set X Relative to Model Element E	Set the desired X to be the current X relative to the X of the model element E
Set Y Relative to Model Element E	Set the desired Y to be the current Y relative to the X of the model element E

Figure 7. Using coordinate relative to the other model elements in the demonstration (top) make the element be in the location relative to the same model elements in every model evolution scenario (bottom)

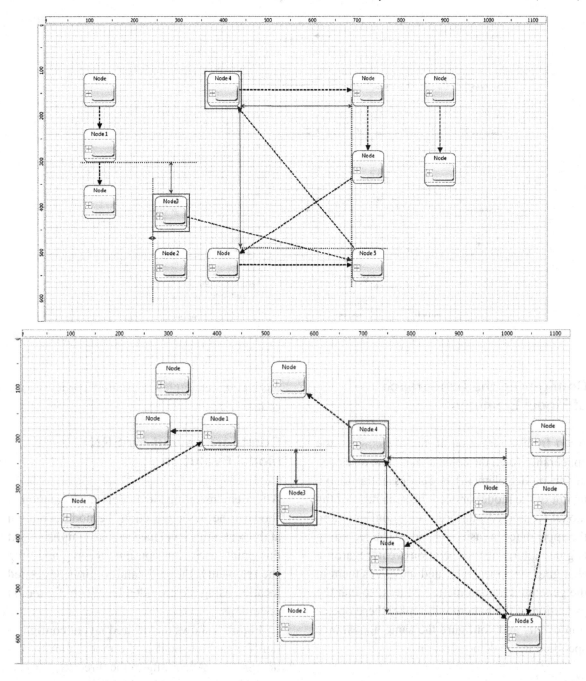

Figure 8. The layout demonstration in action for the first motivating example

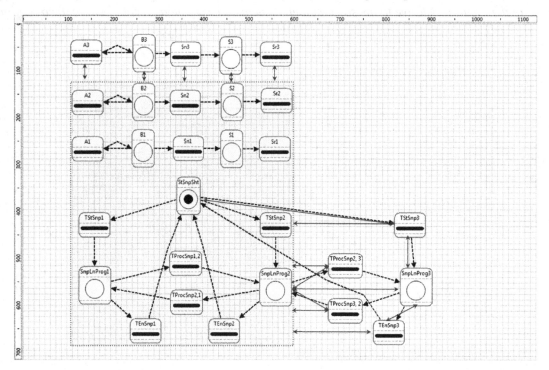

Configuring the Appearance of Model Elements

Apart from the location of model elements, the appearance (e.g., the color, shape, font, size used in the model element) is also essential to the layout of the model or even the semantics of the model. Compared with the location configuration, the appearance is easier to handle. The recording engine captures all the operation events regarding changing the appearance, and integrates them in the generated transformation pattern, so that the execution of the pattern will replay these operation events and configure the same appearance specified in the demonstration.

EXAMPLE LAYOUT DEMONSTRATION

In this section, we demonstrate the use of MTBD to automate the layout configuration for the two motivating examples presented earlier in the chapter.

Configure Layout for SRN Model Evolution

After demonstrating the model transformation as shown in the previous section, the model evolution at the semantics level has been accomplished. At this point, users can continue to drag-and-drop each element in the editor and confirm the desired location using the provided layout configuration operations.

Figure 8 shows the desired layout configuration for each element in the model transformation process. According to the three steps in this model evolution scenario, the newly created model elements and connections belong to three parts. The first part is the event definition (i.e., *A3, B3, Sn3, S3, Sr3*). Assume that most users prefer to place these elements always above the previous definitions. Therefore, they use the uppermost boundary of the existing model as the reference for

List 7. Operations to configure layout demonstration for part one of the motivating example

Sequence	Operation Performed
36	Set *SRNRoot.A3.Y* Relative to Uppermost Outside
37	Set *SRNRoot.A3.X* Relative to *A1.X*
38	Set *SRNRoot.B3.Y* Relative to Uppermost Outside
39	Set *SRNRoot.B3.X* Relative to *B1.X*
40	Set *SRNRoot.Sn3.Y* Relative to Uppermost Outside
41	Set *SRNRoot.Sn3.X* Relative to *Sn1.X*
42	Set *SRNRoot.S3.Y* Relative to Uppermost Outside
43	Set *SRNRoot.S3.X* Relative to *S1.X*
44	Set *SRNRoot.Sr3.Y* Relative to Uppermost Outside
45	Set *SRNRoot.Sr3.X* Relative to *Sr1.X*

(The layout demonstration is immediately after the model transformation demonstration)

List 8. Operations to configure layout demonstration for part two of the motivating example

Sequence	Operation Performed
46	Set *SRNRoot.TStSnp3.X* Relative to Rightmost Outside
47	Set *SRNRoot.TStSnp3.Y* Relative to *SrnRoot.StSnpSht.Y*
48	Set *SRNRoot.SnpLnProg3.X* Relative to Rightmost Outside
49	Set *SRNRoot.SnpLnProg3.Y* Relative to *TStSnp3.Y*
50	Set *SRNRoot.TEnSnp3.X* Relative to Rightmost Outside
51	Set *SRNRoot.TEnSnp3.Y* Relative to *SnpLnProg3.Y*

Y, and the X coordinate of each element in event type *1* for X. Users would generally perform the operations in List 7 in the layout demonstration.

For the new execution snapshot part definition (i.e., *TStSnp3, SnpLnProg3, TEnSnp3*), we set all the X to be relative to the rightmost boundary, and Y relative to the root of the execution snapshot *StSnpSht* (*TStSnp3.Y* is set to be directly relative to *StSnpSht.Y*, *SnpLnProg3.Y* is set to be relative to *TStSnp3.Y*, and *TEnSnp3.Y* to be relative to *SnpLnProg3.Y*), please see List 8 for the specific details. Finally, for the *Execution Snapshot Transitions*, the X is relative to the rightmost boundary, and Y is relative to the *Snapshot Place* it is connected to, please see List 9 for those details.

After the demonstration is completed, the recording engine calculates all the values and integrates them in the final generated transformation

List 9. Operations to configure layout demonstration for part three of the motivating example

Sequence	Operation Performed
52	Set *SRNRoot.TProcSnp2,3.X* Relative to Rightmost Outside
53	Set *SRNRoot.TProcSnp2,3.Y* Relative to *SrnRoot.StSnpSht.Y*
54	Set *SRNRoot.TProcSnp3,2.X* Relative to Rightmost Outside
55	Set *SRNRoot.TProcSnp3,2.Y* Relative to *TStSnp3.Y*

List 10. Operations in the demonstration for the second motivating example

Sequence	Operation Performed
1	Add a *Node* in *C2M2LRoot (Replicate the 1st Node)*
2	Set *Node.Name = MiddleTier2.Name =* "*MiddleTier2*"
3	Set *Node.AMI = MiddleTier2.AMI =* "*ami-45e7002c*"
4	Set *Node.Annotation = MiddleTier2.Annotation =* "*Middle Tier for PetStore*"
5	Set *Node.HeartbeatURI = MiddleTier2.HeartbeatURI =* "*http://ps01.aws.amazon.com/hb*"
6	Set *Node.HostName = MiddleTier2.HostName =* "*http://ps01.aws.amazon.com/hb*"
7	Set *Node.CPULoad =* *MiddleTier2.CPULoad / 2 = 115 / 2 = 57.5* ^{p1}*MiddleTier2.CPULoad > 100*
8	Add a *Node* in *C2M2LRoot (Replicate the 2nd Node)*
9	Set *Node.Name = MiddleTier2.Name =* "*MiddleTier2*"
10	Set *Node.AMI = MiddleTier2.AMI =* "*ami-45e7002c*"
11	Set *Node.Annotation = MiddleTier2.Annotation =* "*MiddleTier for PetStore*"
12	Set *Node.HeartbeatURI = MiddleTier2.HeartbeatURI =* "*http://ps01.aws.amazon.com/hb*"
13	Set *Node.HostName = MiddleTier2.HostName =* "*http://ps01.aws.amazon.com/hb*"
14	Set *Node.CPULoad =* *MiddleTier2.CPULoad / 2 = 115 / 2 = 57.5*
15	Remove the connection between *MiddleTier2* and *LoadBalancer*
16	Connect *MiddleTier2* (1st) and *LoadBalancer*
17	Connect *MiddleTier2* (2nd) and *LoadBalancer*

pattern. Executing the final pattern will result in the model shown in Figure 1d.

Configuring the Layout for C2M2L Model Evolution

Before addressing the layout problem in the second motivating example, we first demonstrate how to evolve the model at the semantics level by replicating the overloaded *Node*. The demonstration in this scenario is straightforward, which is based on an overloaded *Node* (e.g., the overloaded *Node* is defined as the *Node* having *CPULoad > 100*). Replicating a model element requires the creation of a new copy of the same type of element, as well as setting up all the attributes of the element to be the same as the one being replicated. Therefore, operations 1-8 and operations 9-14 in List 10 replicate two *Nodes* and copy all the attributes from the overloaded *Node - MiddleTier2*, except the *CPULoad* is balanced by dividing the original value. Operations 15-17 deal with the connections. The precondition is given after the demonstration in the precondition specification dialog, where users can choose any model element or connections involved in the demonstration and specify the precondition constraints.

Figure 9. Demonstrating the layout configuration for the C2M2L model

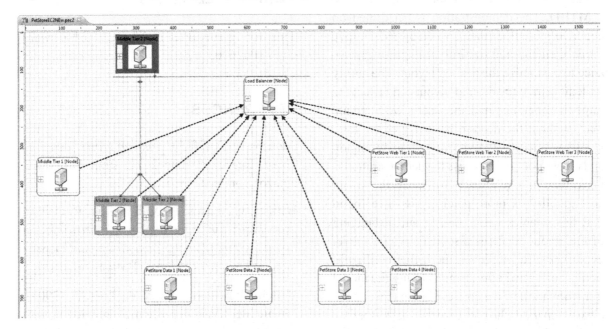

Layout demonstration comes after the traditional use of MTBD, which is based on demonstrating the operational parts of an evolution task. The desired layout as shown in Figure 9 uses the original location of the overloaded *Node* as a reference to set up the location for the two new *Nodes*. The overloaded *Node* is moved to the uppermost part of the editor (using its own *X* and relative *Y* to the *NodeBalancer*). Also, two different colors are configured for the new and old *Nodes*. Please see List 11 for details.

When the final generated pattern is applied to other model instances, all the overloaded *Nodes* can be detected automatically based on the precondition, and the required new *Nodes* can be created to replicate the old ones, with the location configured and colors highlighted.

CONCLUSION AND FUTURE WORK

This chapter presents a new approach for configuring model layout during model evolution, which

List 11. Operations to configure layout in the demonstration of the second motivating example

Sequence	Operation Performed
18	Set *MiddleTier2(1st).X* Relative to *MiddleTier2(overloaded).X*
19	Set *MiddleTier2(1st).Y* Relative to *MiddleTier2(overloaded).Y*
20	Set *MiddleTier2(2nd).X* Relative to *MiddleTier2(overloaded).X*
21	Set *MiddleTier2(2nd).Y* Relative to *MiddleTier2(overloaded).Y*
22	Set *MiddleTier2(overloaded).Y* Relative to *NodeBalancer.Y*
23	Set *MiddlerTier2(1st)* background color to *Green*
24	Set *MiddlerTier2(2nd)* background color to *Green*
25	Set *MiddlerTier2(overloaded)* background color to *Red*

is based on the demonstration-based technique – MTBD. The demonstration is performed on concrete model instances, whereby users move model elements and confirm locations or appearance to customize the desired layout. The ability to demonstrate the desired layout can reflect the implicit semantics and the user's own mental map, without the need to be aware of the low-level details associated with model transformation and metamodeling. Because the demonstration is performed in a WYSIWYG manner, the layout configuration is more precise. We have found that this enables easier testing and debugging of the layout concerns associated with a model evolution task. Moreover, the layout configuration is performed after demonstrating the model transformation of the core evolution task, which clearly separates the core evolution task from the model layout concerns, rather than being entangled together. Furthermore, no model transformation languages are used in the process, and users do not need to understand metamodel definitions, which enables general end-users and non-programmers to configure their desired layout in the model evolution process.

As future work, dealing with the overlaps of model elements in model evolution is our next goal. Although the relative coordinate configuration helps to avoid the overlaps, it cannot adapt to every scenario perfectly, particularly when model elements are used as references. Integrating overlap removal algorithms might solve the problem, but there is also a possibility that the implicit semantics and a user's mental map will be affected after applying the algorithm. Additionally, we plan to also implement the configuration of model layout for exogenous model transformations using MTBD (i.e., the model transformation between two different domains) so that the layout of a target model is set up based on the source model's layout.

ACKNOWLEDGMENT

This work is supported by NSF CAREER award CCF-1052616.

REFERENCES

Amazon EC2. (2011). *Amazon elastic compute cloud*. Retrieved June 2011, from http://aws.amazon.com/ec2/

Battista, G., Eades, P., & Tamassia, R. (1993). *Algorithms for automatic graph drawing: An annotated bibliography. Technical report*. Department of Computer Science, Brown University.

Bottoni, P., Guerra, E., & de Lara, J. (2006). Metamodel-based definition of interaction with visual environments. *In Proceedings of the 2nd International Workshop on Model Driven Development of Advanced User Interfaces (MDDAUI '06)*, CEUR Workshop Proceedings 214.

Di Battista, G., Eades, P., Tamassia, R., & Tollis, I. G. (1998). *Graph drawing: Algorithms for the visualization of graphs*. Prentice Hall.

Dwyer, T., Marriott, K., & Wybrow, M. (2009). Dunnart: A constraint-based network diagram authoring tool. *In 16th International Symposium on Graph Drawing (GD '08), LNCS 5417*, Hersonissos, Heraklion Crete, Greece, (pp. 384-389). Springer-Verlag.

Eclipse. (n.d.). *Generic Eclipse Modeling System* (GEMS). Retrieved from http://www.eclipse.org/gmt/gems/

Eclipse. (n.d.). *Graphical Modeling Framework* (GMF). http://www.eclipse.org/modeling/gmf/

France, R., Ghosh, S., Song, E., & Kim, D. (2003). A metamodeling approach to pattern-based model refactoring. *IEEE Software*, *20*(5), 52–58. doi:10.1109/MS.2003.1231152

Fruchterman, T., & Reingold, E. (1991). Graph drawing by force-directed placement. *Software, Practice & Experience, 21*, 1129–1164. doi:10.1002/spe.4380211102

Gray, J., Lin, Y., & Zhang, J. (2006). Automating change evolution in model-driven engineering. *IEEE Computer, 39*(2), 51–58.

Gray, J., Tolvanen, J. P., Kelly, S., Gokhale, A., Neema, S., & Sprinkle, J. (2007). Domain-specific modeling. In Fishwick, P. A. (Ed.), *Handbook of dynamic system modeling*. CRC Press. doi:10.1201/9781420010855.pt2

Greenfield, J., & Short, K. (2004). *Software factories: Assembling applications with patterns, models, frameworks, and tools*. John Wiley and Sons.

Hower, W., & Graf, W. H. (1996). A bibliographical survey of constraint-based approaches to CAD, graphics, layout, visualization, and related topics. [Elsevier.]. *Knowledge-Based Systems, 9*(7), 449–464. doi:10.1016/S0950-7051(96)01055-6

Johannes, J., & Gaul, K. (2009). Towards a generic layout composition framework for domain-specific models. *In Proceedings of the 9th OOPSLA Workshop on Domain-Specific Modeling*, Orlando, FL, 6 pages.

Jouault, F., Allilaire, F., Bézivin, J., & Kurtev, I. (2008). ATL: A model transformation tool. *Science of Computer Programming, 72*(1-2), 31–39. doi:10.1016/j.scico.2007.08.002

Jouault, F., & Kurtev, I. (2005). Transforming models with ATL. *In Proceedings of the International Conference on Model Driven Engineering Languages and Systems, LNCS 3844*, (pp. 128-138). Springer-Verlag.

Jucknath-John, S., Graf, D., & Taentzer, G. (2006). Evolutionary layout of graph transformation sequences. *In Proceedings of the Third International Workshop on Graph Based Tools (GraBaTs)*, Electronic Communications of the EASST, vol. 1.

Kogekar, A., Kaul, D., Gokhale, A., Vandal, P., Praphamontripong, U., & Gokhale, S. … Gray, J. (2006). Model-driven generative techniques for scalable performability analysis of distributed systems. *IPDPS Workshop on Next Generation Systems*, Rhodes Island, Greece, (pp. 292-292).

Langer, P., Wimmer, M., & Kappel, G. (2010). Model-to-model transformations by demonstration. In *Proceedings of International Conference on Model Transformation*, Malaga, Spain, (pp. 153-167).

Lédeczi, A., Bakay, A., Maróti, M., Völgyesi, P., Nordstrom, G., Sprinkle, J., & Karsai, G. (2001). Composing domain-specific design environments. *IEEE Computer, 34*(11), 44–51.

Lin, Y., Gray, J., Zhang, J., Nordstrom, S., Gokhale, A., Neema, S., & Gokhale, S. (2008). Model replication: Transformations to address model scalability. *Software, Practice & Experience, 38*(14), 1475–1497. doi:10.1002/spe.876

Maier, S., & Minas, M. (2009). Rule-based diagram layout using meta-models. In *Proceedings of the Workshop on Visual Languages and Computing 2009 (VLC 2009)*, San Francisco, USA. MetaCase+. (n.d.). *MetaCase+*. Retrieved from http://www.metacase.com/

Misue, K., Eades, P., Lai, W., & Sugiyama, K. (1995). Layout adjustment and the mental map. *Journal of Visual Languages and Computing, 6*(2), 183–210. doi:10.1006/jvlc.1995.1010

MOF. (2005). *Query/views/transformations specification (QVT)*. Retrieved from http://www.omg.org/cgi-bin/doc?ptc/2005-11-01

Muppala, J., Ciardo, G., & Trivedi, K. (1994). Stochastic reward nets for reliability prediction. *Communications in Reliability. Maintainability and Serviceability, 1*(2), 9–20.

Pilgrim, J. (2007). Mental map and model driven development. In *Proceedings of the Workshop on the Layout of (Software) Engineering Diagrams (LED)*, Electronic Communications of the EASST, vol. 7.

Schmidt, D., Stal, M., Rohnert, H., & Buschman, F. (2000). *Pattern-oriented software architecture – Volume 2: Patterns for concurrent and networked objects*. John Wiley and Sons.

Sprinkle, J. (2003). *Metamodel driven model migration*. PhD thesis, Vanderbilt University, Nashville, TN.

Sun, Y., Gray, J., Langer, P., Wimmer, M., & White, J. (2010). A WYSIWYG approach for configuring model layout using model transformations. *10th Workshop on Domain-Specific Modeling*, held at SPLASH 2010, Reno, NV, (pp. 20-25).

Sun, Y., Gray, J., & White, J. (2010). *MT-Scribe: A flexible tool to support model evolution*. Workshop on Flexible Modeling Tools (FlexiTools), held at SPLASH 2010, Reno, NV.

Sun, Y., White, J., & Gray, J. (2009b). Model transformation by demonstration. In *Proceedings of International Conference on Model Driven Engineering Languages and Systems*, Denver, CO, (pp. 712-726).

Sun, Y., White, J., Gray, J., & Gokhale, A. (2009a). Model-driven automated error recovery in cloud computing. In Osis, J., & Asnina, E. (Eds.), *Model-driven analysis and software development: Architectures and functions*. Hershey, PA: IGI Global.

KEY TERMS AND DEFINITIONS

Domain-Specific Modeling Language: One type of domain-specific language used to represent the various aspects of a system at a higher level of abstraction than general-purpose modeling languages, which requires fewer details and less effort to specify a system.

Model Layout Configuration: The specification of the properties related with the concrete representation of models in a model editor, such as position, color, and font.

Model Transformation by Demonstration: A new model transformation approach that enables general end-users to implement model transformation tasks without learning any model transformation languages or knowing the metamodel definitions.

Model Transformation Languages: Domain-specific languages to implement model transformation tasks.

Model Transformation: A core technology in Model-driven Engineering. It receives a source model that conforms to a given metamodel as input, and produces as output another model conforming to a given metamodel.

Model-Driven Engineering: A new software development methodology to increase software development productivity by raising the level of abstraction from traditional general-purpose programming languages to high-level problem domain concept models.

WYSIWYG: An acronym for "What You See Is What You Get", which in the context of model layout configuration, means the approach to specify the layout configuration by using the actual layout state of the models in the model editor.

Chapter 5
Enriching the Model–Driven Architecture with Weakly Structured Information

Dima Panfilenko
DFKI (German Research Center for Artificial Intelligence), Germany

Christian Seel
University of Applied Sciences Landshut, Germany

Keith Phalp
Bournemouth University, UK

Sheridan Jeary
Bournemouth University, UK

ABSTRACT

Most Model-Driven-Architecture (MDA) approaches are focussed on Platform Independent Models (PIM) and Platform Specific Models (PSM) and the transformation between them. The more conceptual Computation Independent Models (CIM) or even unstructured information is often neglected, despite the importance of requirements modelling at the CIM-level and the impact this has on the entire software development process. Almost every change that is done within the software development lifecycle, including maintenance triggers, is based on unstructured information in the early stages which then affects the CIM level, e.g. a change in a business process or a change in law that requires a change of software. Therefore unstructured or weakly structured information has to be included in any maintenance processes.

In order to introduce unstructured or weakly structured information to the MDA, we propose to enhance the MDA-levels by a pre-CIM-level for unstructured information, extend the modelling capabilities on CIM-level, and establish links between the objects on different levels that allows traceability of requirements into code.

DOI: 10.4018/978-1-61350-438-3.ch005

INTRODUCTION

Model-driven architecture (MDA) (OMG 2003) is becoming increasingly important in both the literature and in practice. However, most MDA approaches are focused on Platform Independent Models (PIM) and Platform Specific Models (PSM) and the transformation between them (Frankel 2003). The more conceptual Computation Independent Model (CIM) level or even the unstructured information which informs the models is often neglected (Mellor et. al. 2004); and this despite the importance of modelling of requirements at the CIM-level and the impact this has on the entire software development process. Almost every change that is done within a software development lifecycle including maintenance is based on unstructured information in the early stages which then affects the CIM level and is propagated to the PIM and PSM level beneath. There are various examples for unstructured or weakly structured information that influence the Model Driven Development (MDD), such as the change in a business process or a change of law like the introduction of the Sarbanes-Oxley-Act (SOX) (U.S. Government Printing Office 2002). This law can be regarded as unstructured information from a software engineering point of view, but it requires a change of many business processes at the CIM-level, which leads to changes and maintenance efforts in the derived software systems. The examples show how a change in law can trigger a software maintenance process. But if there is no relation between this unstructured information and the existing software, the entire software has to be regarded in order to find the places that need to be changed instead of concentrating directly on the parts of the software that require change.

Therefore, we propose to integrate weakly structured information into MDA and create a linkage between unstructured information and the CIM-level as the current top level of the MDA model stack (Kanyaru et. al. 2008). This leads to an extension of the MDA, which can be used to speed up maintenance and software development processes as the impact of weakly structured information on software is clearly defined, and shows transparently which change of weakly structured information leads to which part of the CIM-level model (Kanyaru et. al. 2008, Martin et. al. 2008).

In detail, this chapter proposes a way to deal with weakly structured information, an extended modelling language at the CIM-level and the means to describe the relation between them. The goal of our work is to keep track of changes that occur on a very high and abstract level and allow the stakeholder to visualise the effect of those changes. This will include finding related information on the CIM and PIM level immediately. This allows us to estimate and to achieve changes because of new requirements (which are usually a result of unstructured or weakly structured information) much better.

The pre-CIM level in MDA should keep the weakly structured information semi-formalised inside the software development lifecycle and visualised for the further use by business architects (Kanyaru et. al. 2008). Its role in getting the domain experts more involved in requirements modelling is vital for preserving the domain knowledge and thus aligning it with the software product throughout the various modelling levels of the software lifecycle.

For MDA's first level, CIM, we propose the specific CIM-modelling language called VIDE CIM Level Language ("VCLL") (VIDE 2007), which extends Business Process Modeling Notation (BPMN) (OMG 2006a) to give four integrated modelling views. The designed modelling language allows creation of business processes, relevant data, business rules, and organisational aspects. The VCLL focuses on the development of business applications and provides two entry points into MDA. First, our proposed modelling language can be used to describe the behaviour of one application (micro view). Second it can be used to orchestrate different applications (macro view). Furthermore, the VCLL provides a connection to a pre-CIM-level and reveals the relation of model elements with their origin in weakly structured information, like recorded interviews, forms, documents, etc.

Related Work

In recent years there has been a growing realisation of the role of the requirements phase within software development. Of particular importance is the work of Jackson (1995), where three distinct tasks are delineated, that of analysis (or requirements), which concentrates on description of the problem domain, design which describes the internal elements of the proposed solution system (referred to as the 'machine') and specification which acts as the interface between the problem domain and the machine (and thus spans the system boundary). Hence, models which are best suited to descriptions of machines, or designs, (software models) may not be appropriate for modelling the problem domain. In particular they may not allow us to capture the nuances of the domain or the perspectives of the various business stakeholders, when other modelling approaches (e.g., Soft Systems (Checkland, 1999), Role Activity Diagrams (Ould, 2005)) may provide far more suitable modelling alternatives. However, one of the issues with such alternatives is, in having very different notational concepts, that they often introduce a genuine mapping problem, which clearly detracts from the model driven intentions of providing transformations among phases.

The idea of MDA (Mellor et al. 2004; OMG 2003) is the translation of information models via different steps into finally executable code. According to the definition of MDA the process of creating software starts with information models on CIM level and transforms them into models on PIM level. These models on PIM level are enriched and then transformed into PSM which result in executable source code after the last transformation (Frankel 2003; OMG 2003). By a separation of concerns through creating CIMs

and PIMs before PSMs you reach a kind of interdependency from platforms, languages and systems. The transformation starts on a highly abstract level and gets more concrete with each step down. Enterprise Resource Planning (ERP) systems which support manufacturing processes are a very good example how to use MDA. Domain experts can be much more included in the software development process to bridge the gap between their requirements and the understanding of them by a software engineer. On the three different levels of MDA different modelling languages are used. Therefore commonly used modelling languages are regarded.

Event-driven Process Chains (EPC) (Keller at al. 1992) allow for creating semi-formal process models. This semi-formal notation is essentially a sequence of the successive events signalising the important occurrences in the process and functions dealing with the events and further information. It is suitable for a high level design of application systems or organizational structures, but it is not focused on the transformation into an IT system. The disadvantage of this methodology is that though it gives the business users the understandable idea of a business process and its possible paths, but at the same time there is no place for business rules that are standing for the decisions made at important steps in the process model.

Another modelling concept is Unified Modeling Language (UML) (OMG 2005). It gives the IT specialists one of the most substantial tools for modelling the target application systems in different aspects on the different levels of abstraction. At the same time, it is not that well suitable for business users for involving too much knowledge about the technical aspects of the system under construction. It also doesn't provide the mechanisms of dealing with business rules. Though UML can be combined with the Object Constraint Language (OCL) (OMG 2006b) it is in turn too formalized to be used on the requirements level for which the VCLL tool is providing support.

Probably the most extensively used language for modelling of the business processes is the Object Modeling Group (OMG) standard BPMN (OMG 2006a). It can be used on different levels of abstractions, firstly, and can also contain a sufficient amount of technical information, secondly. The technical aspects are needed for the lower level implementation of those processes into for example the Business Process Execution Language (BPEL) (OASIS 2007) (which is a machine readable, textual format without an easy-going way to sketch a process in a graphical way). The disadvantage of BPMN notation is its limitedness to one and only one view, namely the process view that is not always sufficient for the purposes of modelling the systems. It also doesn't provide the extended methodology for data and organization modelling, thus weaving the data and organization constructs into the process view directly.

ENHANCING THE MDA WITH UNSTRUCTURED INFORMATION[1]

The Pre-CIM Phase

As stated our contention is that the MDA approach would be improved by the addition of a further set of models in the stack and that this includes models at what we have termed a pre-CIM phase.

In this section we introduce our rationale for the term pre-CIM and attempt to describe the issues that these further (pre-CIM) models are intended to resolve. We explore the link between pre-CIM and maintenance before providing a description of one approach to pre-CIM, which attempts to tackle some of the issues raised and show a worked example using our pre-CIM modelling tool. (This will then be described later in the chapter when we move towards our, more conventional, CIM models). Finally, we also outline some empirical work which sought to gauge the efficacy of our approach.

The Need for Pre-CIM

One might well question both the intention and wisdom of introducing the term pre-CIM (which we originally coined for the MDABIZ workshop in 2008). On the one hand, as MDA is divided into CIM, PIM and PSM, it can be argued that CIM is, in essence, all that goes before PIM, and in that sense is unbounded, and thus could have a pre-CIM phase; anything within pre-CIM is just part of CIM. Our intention, was, of course, to be deliberately provocative, in order to highlight what we viewed as a difference in what CIM ought to be (or at least so it appeared to us, with an albeit process modelling and requirements perspective) and what is typically to be found within the CIM phase.

Whilst it is not our intention here to provide such critique in full, it is perhaps worth outlining some of the, inevitably intertwined areas, where the CIM phase is often lacking.

Clearly moving downstream from CIM, to PIM and PSM is understood (though, as an aside we note that transformations between PIM and PSM are far better supported than CIM to PIM tends to be). However, CIM models often seem to start some way down the development life-cycle. The inception and conception of software projects will involve much business activity of it as informal models (or sketches). For more managed processes where project goals (and requirements) may be aligned with strategic goals (such as within the BSCP approach (Bleistein et. al. 2006)), these upstream activities are generally neither recognised nor supported.

Hence, we suggest a need for the CIM phase to move further back upstream (further up the MDA modelling stack) in order to capture adequately the requirements of the user (or client), and note that this may require the support for rather less formal models (from a software engineering perspective) to capture ideas, draw upon other sources of information, and sketch informal models. In addition (as MDA advocates), we would still wish, in an ideal world, to support a managed transformation from such early sketches to our more traditional CIM models.

It is clearly of paramount importance to the validation of software or system requirements that stakeholder involvement is sought. Thus, those from the business, who genuinely understand the needs for the prospective system, can be active in the description of that proposed system. However, for such validation to be successful there are two related needs. The first, perhaps most obvious, is that the models to be validated must be understandable to that audience, so that they comprehend the notation, can see what is being represented, can find errors and can revise models accordingly. Related to this, is the perception that the stakeholder has of the model. That is, even, assuming suitable explanation, if models are comprehensible, adequate involvement of these people will only be achieved if they believe the models to be appropriate, accessible and meeting their needs.

In particular, we note that the models to be found within CIM do not best support the goals of increasing stakeholder involvement, especially for the less technical (in a software engineering sense) clients, as they are not accessible to those audiences.

The Link Between Pre-CIM and Maintenance

The importance of the process model (or CIM phase model) in maintenance is long established. For example, the ESPRC funded PROCESS project in the UK, specifically addressed the issue of mapping process models to existing (legacy) systems in order to improve the efficacy of software maintenance (Henderson, 94) and the EPSRC managed programme that followed again (Systems Engineering for Business Process Change) again focussed on the relationship between the business model and the legacy system (see Henderson, 2000).

In producing a mapping between the process (or within MDA the CIM) and the system we can consider not only the impact of change, indeed even whether such change will be cost-effective, but also plan the software development process accordingly. Phalp (1997) states: 'by understanding the relationship between the business process and the legacy system, such changes may be better compared, gauged and managed'.

Given that, particularly for data intensive systems (as was the focus of our VIDE project), the models of process and architecture might be somewhat orthogonal, small changes to process might represent significant and widespread changes within the supporting software system. A good example historically was the introduction of loyalty cards within supermarkets. While the impact on the process, of both customers and point of sale processes initially suggests that this would be a small change, the potential support implications, though positive in the long term, were significant, and were far less constrained in their impact.

Hence it is important for stakeholders to be able to consider the impact of changes to the business, not just in terms of their own strategy, goals and business processes, but also in terms of impact on existing software systems, particularly where (as is most often the case) there is existing legacy. That some form of experimentation can take place (process prototyping) as early as possible is clearly a goal.

With model driven development approaches, much of the opportunity for such experimentation and consideration is supported by the method. Given that we can maintain traceability through the modelling stages, from CIM to PIM to PSM, the method supports our understanding of the impact of change.

However, this further highlights the need for our CIM phase models to be accessible to the non-technical stakeholders. By allowing relatively informal modelling, (as we have demonstrated with our pre-CIM approaches), which is both simple and accessible, we allow for just those stakeholders to be part of the initial modelling effort. Therefore, right from the point of conceptual models (be they either new processes or changes to existing processes) we can produce our families of models, and, by maintaining traceability gauge the impact, and, thus, feasibility of suggested or proposed changes.

Furthermore, once satisfied that such changes are justified, these same mechanisms will allow for the production of the revised software systems in an effective and efficient manner, via to model driven toolset.

An Outline Solution

In suggesting a pre-CIM phase, we have, somewhat provocatively, noted the need to provide models which are amenable to the descriptions of the problem domain: support the early, often informal phases of development and, perhaps most importantly, to provide models which are accessible to the audience for the models. In addition, we wish the CIM phase internally to follow the model driven paradigm in attempting to support a guided or managed transformation through its internal modelling phases, and of course to then allow for CIM to PIM transformation as one might expect.

Scraps and Scrapbooks

In supporting the early parts of the development, our proposed pre-CIM allows users to organise, maintain and utilise (for modelling) a variety of informal sources or 'scraps' of information.

The information scrap, maybe textual, pictorial, or it could be folders that may in turn contain subfolders. The storage and organisation of domain information is useful for subsequent stages of development because it acts as a basis for validating subsequent artefacts. Customers, end-users,

or other stakeholders with knowledge regarding the problem domain can populate the scrapbook, using a range of sources such as existing procedure documents, forms, reports etc.

Secondary notation using both a traditional tree structure and a visual representation of the relationship between scraps can be used. Additional links could be made between these scraps of information providing further detail regarding any hidden dependencies

Consider a scenario where an organisation pursues business opportunities with prospective (or existing) clients. Such an opportunity elicitation process may require identifying possible clients, visiting the client and obtaining a lead. The organisation might want to store documents relating to previous successful opportunities, or unsuccessful ones with reasons to their success or lack of it. The MDA process does not provide a means to record such informal information. We propose the scrapbook concept to record and inter-relate artefacts that are built or elicited during problem domain analysis. Each item in the scrapbook model is a scrap item, which can be refined or expanded when further information comes to light.

Elicitation of problem domain information and the organisation of such information using the scrapbook concept provides a record of such information for use in the MDA process. There are a variety of issues and concepts that domain experts (or business users) identify from the scrapbook that may interest business and system analysts during the elicitation of problem domain information. For example, many business stakeholders will be familiar with their organisational hierarchy and with the roles and responsibilities of various stakeholders. In addition, they will have knowledge of which of these stakeholders produce or consume data, and indeed who has ownership of that data. All this information is of interest to the business and system analysts.

Roles, Activities, Data Objects and "Bloops"

In moving on from scraps we reach the stage where we wish to support informal modelling, though with the intention that such models will evolve through a process of revision and further consideration to become more formalised. Hence, we are moving from the merely conceptual and information gathering phases to what might be viewed as closer to traditional analysis. Domain analysis has been described as the process of identifying and classifying knowledge in the problem domain with the purpose of illustrating or providing solutions to those problems (Arango, 1989).

We need a notation which will be simple for both business expert and analyst to understand, but with low overheads in terms of learning to allow both expert and analyst to concentrate on the problems at hand. Many languages are cumbersome, presenting the business users with a large variety of constructs. Flowcharts (from 1958) had 6 basic constructs and 4 extended constructs whereas BPMN (in 2006) had 11 basic constructs and 39 extended constructs (zur Muehlen et. al. 2007). Wahl and Sindre (Wahl & Sindre, 2005) analyse BPMN according to the Semiotic Quality Framework and believe that the goal of the notation being understood by both non- technical domain experts and IT professionals is unrealistic. There are 23 different pre-defined elements to represent different types of events. Most of the concepts have their origin in the IT domain and not the business domain and are therefore not intuitive for the business user.

In contrast to such complex models we developed the Analysis Palette which provides a means for developing models of the domain using only a subset of notational elements; roles, activities, data objects and bloops. We use a visual notation to depict these concepts in order to construct such models as part of an initial input into the MDA development process. Activities are shown as rectangles with a letter **A** at the top left corner of the rectangle. Roles and data objects are depicted using a similar shape, with the indicative letters R and D at the top left corner of the rectangle.

The business user may be unclear about some of their processes at a low level, those very processes which are of interest to the business or systems analyst and thus analysis can be a very challenging. It may also be that the complexity of the problem domain may mean that the analyst incurs significant learning overheads in trying to understand the issues and problems that the business is facing; and there are likely thus, to be concepts that aren't clearly articulated or understood by either business users or analysts. However, there is likely to be a need to record them so that they can be clarified in a later iteration and are not forgotten or missed. We have called this unidentified concept a 'Bloop'. This use of the cloud as a metaphor, identifying something as yet unspecified or un-detailed is a familiar concept; it is found in network diagrams and in cloud computing where it acknowledges that the detail is unspecified. The use of bloops means the business analyst or domain specialist is not overburdened with choosing the specific or correct notation, but can model quickly and informally and more detail can be added at a later date.

These notations can be taken by the business analyst and a rich, business process model can be created at the CIM level using both their experience and the communication with the business user enabled by the pre-CIM level. The remainder of this chapter takes up the further CIM stages, again describing both rationale and our implementation (both models and tools) continuing the worked example.

The CIM Level and the VCLL

VIDE CIM Level Language

The VCLL aims at the integration of end users into the software development process, especially data intensive business applications, which demands certain requirements to be regarded. The language has to be as simple and as commonly understandable as possible for "non-IT-oriented" business domain experts. Furthermore the CIM-level language should be able to represent information that allows creating draft UML models on PIM-level. Finally larger business processes can result into more than one monolithic application. Therefore the orchestration of different (sub)-applications should be possible.

In order to create such a modelling language different established languages and notations were explored. For example the Business Process Modeling Notation (BPMN), the Business Process Execution Language (BPEL) OASIS 2007, and the Event driven Process Chain (EPC) Keller at al. 1992 have been analysed. It turned out that each has its advantages and disadvantages that can be viewed in "related work" section. Based on our research (VIDE 2007) (Seel 2010), BPMN offers the best starting point for creating the VCLL.

So, the BPMN meta-model was used as a basis and enriched by different items, partly gathered from other languages as well as newly created. For example, we introduced the concept of business rules, but it showed that, on conceptual design level, we only need decision rules and constraint rules (Scheer & Werth 2005).

Decision business rules are used to describe complex branches of the control flow, e.g. if the decision which activity is the next to execute depends on the combination of several subdecisions. Therefore decision business rules consist of one or more statements. Each statement consists of business variable values and one activity. If the business variables have the values which are described in the statement the activity, which is referred to in the statement, is executed. One decision business rule can consist of one or more statements, those having a logic relation between each other. Optionally, a last row can be added, which contains the keyword "else" as a condition. The action which is assigned to this row is executed if no other condition is true.

Constraint business rules can be annotated to any model element on the CIM level and state constraints from a business point of view. For example defining that an order process can be started by a phone call is not possible for new customers. Constraint business rules are constructs which are similar to natural language in order to make them easily accessible for business users. However, to avoid the ambiguity of natural language the parts of constraint business rules are further defined. For this purpose, the use of natural language has to be restricted to the use of standardised statements (Endl 2004). In addition to established approaches like RDF (W3C 2004a) or OWL (W3C 2004b), which both focus on semantic-web-technologies, the approach "Semantics of Business Vocabulary and Business Rules Specification" (SBVR) (OMG 2008), which is defined by the OMG, proves to be a well developed concept for describing business rules in an enterprise-context.

The people addressed by the SBVR-specification are mainly users from the business domain, who should be enabled to formulate rules in a structured but also easy comprehensible manner. There is also a focus on the necessary transformation of the formulated rules into IT-systems. The SBVR defines specifications for the used vocabulary as well as syntactical rules to allow a structured documentation of business vocabularies, business facts and business rules. Furthermore, the specification describes a XMI-scheme to share business vocabularies and business rules between organizations and IT-systems. The SBVR is designed to be interpretable in predicate logic with a small extension in modal logic. It also defines demands towards the behaviour of IT-systems regarding their ability to share vocabularies and rules that complies with the specification (OMG 2008).

The SBVR-approach uses three perspectives on business rules. The first perspective is derived from the business rules mantra (BRG 2006) and supports a simplified approximation towards a business rule. This perspective should support the communication with people who are not familiar with the approach, e.g. decision makers. The second perspective is the representation. It contains the specifications of SBVR which should be used to formulate vocabularies and rules. The third perspective is the meaning. It contains the underlying semantics of the used vocabularies and rules.

Figure 1 shows the graphical meta-model of the proposed CIM language. Beyond the business rule view we added three other views, namely a process, a data and an organizational view. The most extensively represented process view integrates the other views and consists of eight parts. Structuring objects are the top-level class the model contains. The control flow section introduces lane elements, which are connected to each other by flow objects. The connections section has two further types of connections between objects in a model. The annotated elements part of the meta-model shows model objects that are used to enrich activity objects with relevant information. The activity section tells which elements are representing actions in a model. The events section describes different types of events which tell what kind of triggers could be used in a model. Gateways explain how decisions of different types could be integrated into a VIDE CIM model. The enumerations section is the last section and it gives an overview of the complex types used in three different classes. Data, organizational and business rules views introduce interfaces to three further business process analysis scopes.

Figure 1. VCLL meta-model (VIDE 2007)

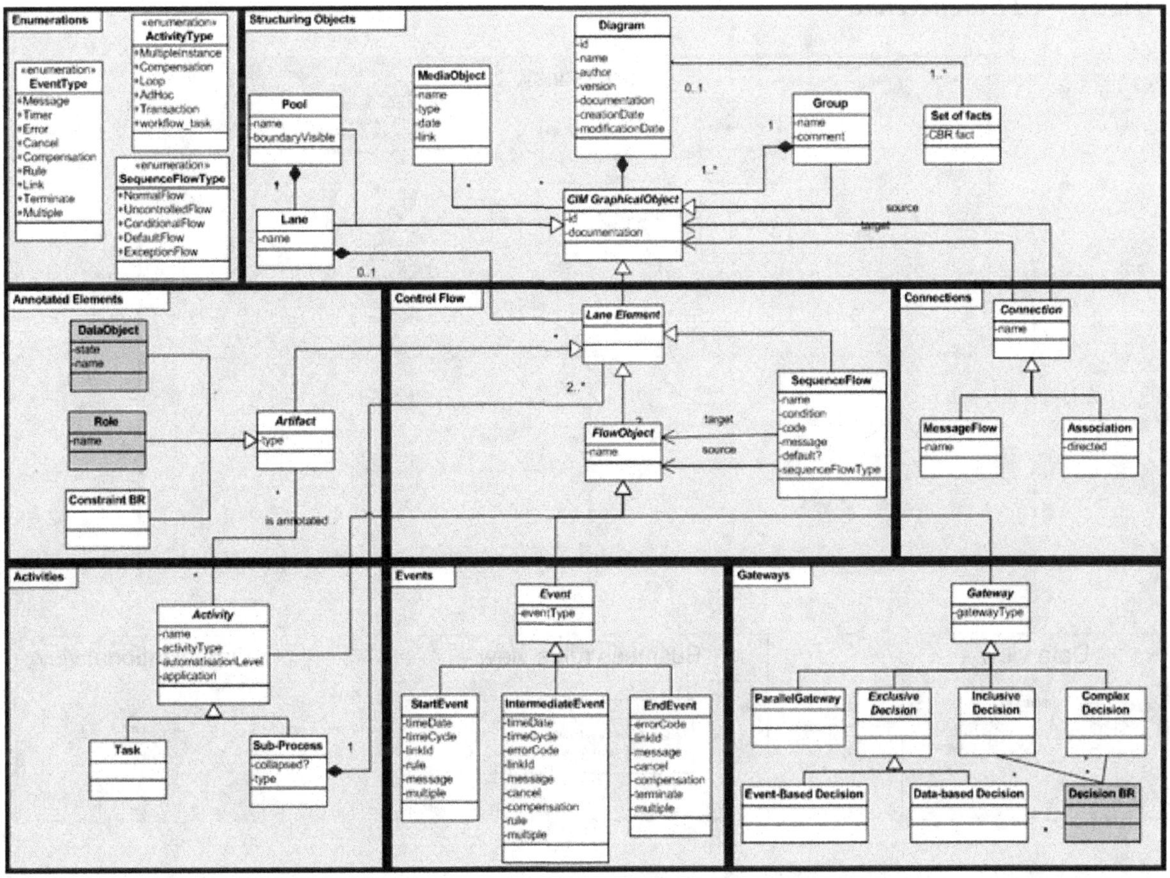

In Figure 2 you can see a simple example of the different views and their interconnection. Inside the data view there are two entities 'opportunity' and 'party', which are connected by a simply expressed association 'is offered to'. Then there is a business rule defining a branching condition and at least inside the organizational view a role 'sales director'. On top of the picture the process view shows the business logic as a flow of different functions. After the start event a function 'Identify opportunity' is executed, doing some work on a data object 'Opportunity' which is imported from the data view. Then the function 'Create opportunity' follows which is accomplished by a person who has the role 'Sales director'. After that, at the branch construct, it will be decided whether to stop the process in case of a negative condition or to go on with the opportu-nity process and 'Send a confirmation'. The shown information can then be used either focusing on the micro view, i.e. the definition of concrete PIM function or service, or on the macro view, i.e. controlling the calls of functions or services by a workflow system. For more information concerning the PIM transformation see Martin et al. 2008.

As the VCLL is compatible to BPMN 2.0, VCLL models can be used to generate XPDL documents that define the orchestration of different applications. So, VCLL models can be imported by all XPDL compatible workflow management systems. Furthermore a software tool has been developed that supports the import of unstructured requirements information (see Kanyaru et al. 2008), the creation of VCLL models and the export into draft UML models on PIM-level or XPDL files.

Figure 2. VCLL architecture

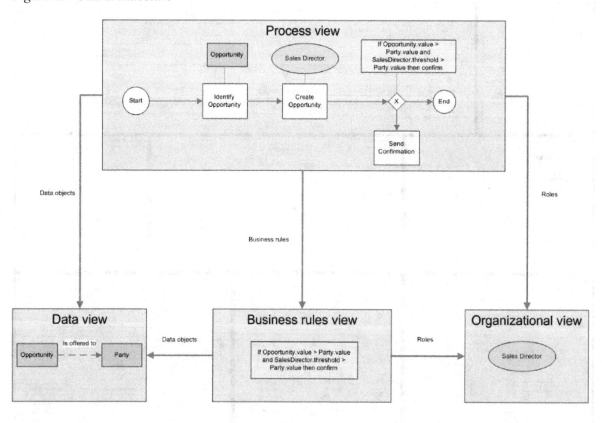

Business Process Support by VCLL

Classification of Business Processes

Business processes can be classified by different criteria. An important criterion for the use and especially the economic benefit of a software support for business processes is their repetition rate. The repetition rate as a criterion for the classification of business processes is proposed by several authors (Derszteler 2000; Giaglis 2001; Leymann & Roller 2000; Maurer 1996; Picot & Reichwald 1985; Rathgeb 1994; Reijers 2003; Schmidt 2002). Despite this criterion being very common the values that describe the repetition rate differ between different authors. In order to categorise different possible values we distinguish between three categories of repetition rate: singular, sometimes, frequently. Singular business process only executes once. These are business processes which are individual for each customer or are research and development processes which are not standardised. Business processes that are executed sometimes are not processes that occur in the daily business but occur more than once. An example would be the creation of a balance sheet once a year. The last category contains business processes that occur frequently. These are processes from daily business, which can include variants, but are standardised and documented.

A second criterion for the classification of business processes is their degree of structure. The degree of structure as classification criterion is used by several authors, e.g. (Aalst 1999; Deiters et al. 1996; Derszteler 2000; Maurer 1996; Picot & Reichwald 1985; Schmidt 2002; Sheth et al. 1997). The distinction between different degrees of structure is stated differently. Becker et al. 2002 differentiate between ad-hoc processes and structures, pre-defined activities but ad-hoc processes, and pre-defined processes. By ad-hoc processes they mean business processes that are not structured, planned and documented. Their run-time behaviour is defined not until their ex-ecution. The second category consists of planned activities, which can be aggregated to a business processes at runtime. The third category consists of planned, managed and standardised business processes, where each activity as well as the whole process is known at its build-time. The other references mentioned above describe the first category as hastily formed or unstructured. The second category is not mentioned in all references. The third one is described as structured or formally defined. In order to get an intuitive formulation the categories are described as unstructured, semi-structured and (fully) structured. Unstructured refers to business processes where the activities and the control flow of the business process is not defined at their build-time. The opposite are structured business processes. Business processes are classified as semi-structured if their activities or their control flow are partly defined at build-time.

The next criterion is the alignment of business processes to strategic levels (Heilmann 1994, Zhou & Chen 2003). Traditionally in economics three different levels are defined: the strategic, the tactical and the operational level. Strategic business processes serve the purpose of long-time planning and definition of goals. These business processes usually require creativity and are not standardised. In order to realise strategic goals the strategic business processes are refined into tactical business processes. They usually have a mid-time range. These tactical business processes are refined again into operational business processes. The operational business processes are executed in every-day work. The creation of business value is done by this type of processes.

The next criterion is the stability or *frequency of changes* of the business processes (Aalst & Hee 2002, Maurer 1996). Some business processes are have to be adapted frequently, e.g. for each project. Other are changed rarely and other are very stable. The last category e.g. describes business processes that are predefined by laws, which won't be changed for a long time.

Another attribute of business processes is their granularity (Becker et al. 1999; Sheth et al. 1997). The can be modelled in a very detailed manner, so that the activities of the processes can be further refined in a reasonable manner. Compounded business processes have parts that are detailed but other parts that can be refined by a detailed process. The highest granularity is aggregated business processes. They are often depicted as value chains. They show the relation and order of groups of process steps, e. g. that the marketing activities are done before the sales activities.

Additionally several authors classify business processes by the value they create (Leymann & Roller 2000). Authors distinguish between business processes of low and of high business value. Business processes that create a low value are mostly administrative and support processes. They are necessary in order to create goods or services but do not create saleable products. Business processes with a high value creation are customer-oriented core processes.

Furthermore business processes can be classified by their scope as intra- or inter-organisational (Becker et al. 2002, Hauser 1996). Intra-organisational business processes take place within one enterprise. All organisational units, hardware and software systems that take part in the processes belong to the same enterprise. Inter-organisational business processes take place between two or more different enterprises. This type of business processes requires interfaces between the application systems that are used in different enterprises. Judicial aspects have to be considered and security aspects have to be taken into account.

In addition, the use of persistent data of a business process can be different (Kalenborn 2000; Picot & Reichwald 1985). Business processes can just check information or transform a defined input into an output. This type of business process is very rare. They don't use any persistent data. The second type of business processes uses persistent data but does not create or change it. The largest group of business processes use, create and change persistent data.

A very important criterion for the classification of business processes is the level of automation (Derungs 1996, Sheth et al. 1997). Three levels are distinguished manual, semi-manual and automated. Manual business processes are executed by employees without using application systems, e. g. service or consulting processes. Semi-automated business processes are executed by humans but supported by application systems, e.g. an employee enters the personal data of a customer in an application and the system checks the consistency of data. Automated processes run without human interaction. They are performed completely by application systems, e.g. bookings on bank accounts from one bank to another, which run as batch job every night.

Two other attributes that classify business processes are the number of process participants (Sheth et al. 1997) and the number of parallel instances (Mentzas 1999). The number of processes participants is classified into two categories: high and low. The number of parallel instances can be one, which means there is no parallelism. It can be also some or many. Some means a small number of instances below ten.

Another attribute of a business processes is data-driven, referring to the data that is involved in the business process. It is the necessity of using transactions, which can either be required or not. If it is required the business process has to ensure that it will be completed successfully or comes back to the starting state again, e.g. the transfer of money from one bank account to another, has to be done completely and shouldn't stop after withdrawing the money from the first account and before in-payment to the second account.

The attributes for the classification of business processes and their possible values are summarised in as morphological box in Table 1.

Table 1. Morphological box for business process classification

Attribute	Value		
repetition rate	singular	sometimes	frequently
degree of structure	unstructured	semi-structured	structured
alignment	strategic	tactical	operational
frequency of changes	never	sometimes	often
granularity	detailed	compounded	aggregated
value creation	low	high	
process scope	intra-organisational	inter-organisational	
usage of persistent information	none	low	high
level of automation	manual	semi-automated	automated
# of process participants	low	high	
# parallel instances	one	some	many
transaction necessity	required	not required	

Criteria of Business Processes Supported by VCLL

After criteria for the classification of business processes have been presented, this section classifies the business processes that are supported by VCLL. For this purpose, for each category defined above, the supported business processes are classified.

For the repetition rate, VCLL is able to support all types of business processes. But in addition to other software development methodologies the software development is too expensive for a process which is only executed once in the same way. Therefore a software development project is only reasonable if there is a trade-off between the resources spent in software development and the benefit the developed software creates. As VCLL is aimed particularly at rapid software development, the software development is going to become less expensive and therefore more reasonable for business processes that are only executed sometimes.

Concerning the second criterion, only defined parts of a business process can be implemented. Therefore structured business processes are sup-

ported by VCLL. Semi-structured business processes can be treated with the VCLL methodology in two ways. If the control flow of the business process is completely available then it could be used for the orchestration of VCLL applications based on a workflow management system. Otherwise the structured and detailed activities can be implemented using the CIM-to-PIM transformation wizard that VCLL offers. Unstructured or ad-hoc business processes are not supported by VCLL as the logic of the business processes is too vague to create an executable description.

Regarding the strategic alignment of business processes VCLL could support all three levels. But an implementation for the support of creative decisions which have to be taken in strategic or tactical business processes are difficult to describe as business processes and to implement in software. Therefore VCLL supports especially the implementation of everyday business processes with relation to internal or external customers, which are located at the operational level.

Similar to the repetition rate the frequency of changes has an economic impact on the software development process. Business processes which are unchanged or rarely changed just need to be implemented once and can stay unchanged. Unfortunately changing business models, shorter product lifecycles, and new competitors in markets increase the need to change business processes and shorten the time in which they remain unchanged. Therefore the software that supports business processes has to be changed more often as well. As VCLL starts its MDA approach at the CIM level and keeps the relation between CIM and PIM objects the implementation of changes is relatively fast, because changes in business processes can be propagated to the PIM level. Therefore VCLL supports frequently changed and unchanged business processes as well. Nevertheless, it's not economically reasonable to implement business processes that are changed faster than it took to implement them.

Regarding the granularity of business processes, two types are supported. Detailed business processes, which cannot be further refined from a business perspective, can be transformed into PIM models. Compounded business processes can be used for orchestration. The activities which can be further refined are regarded as black boxes and an appropriate application is invoked by the Workflow Management Systems (WfMS).

The value creation also addresses economic issues. From an implementation point of view business processes with a low value creation as well as processes with a high value creation can be implemented with VCLL. But the benefit that arises from an implementation of a business processes with a low value creation can be less than the effort for the implementation. Therefore VCLL especially supports business processes with a high value creation.

The process scope that VCLL regards is on intra-organisational business processes. The modelling languages VCLL uses on CIM and PIM level don't consider special information such as the description of interfaces or mechanisms for information hiding between different enterprises. Because of the fact that modelling of inter-organisational business processes and

software is itself a field of research (Röhricht & Schlögel 2001; Schulz & Orlowska 2001; Schulz 2002), this kind of models is not in the scope of the project and the methodology being developed.

Concerning the usage of persistent information, VCLL is designed to handle persistent data. Most business applications use, create or manipulate data. Therefore the VIDE CIM level language has its own data view in order to describe data objects and their usage in the business process. PIM level language elements for data definition and queries on databases have been introduced. Therefore VCLL can handle all three types of business processes with regard to their usage of persistent data.

The level of automation that business processes possess is crucial for their implementability. VCLL supports business processes that are fully automated. They can be described at CIM and PIM level and/or be orchestrated in the sense of the VCLL approach. Semi-automated business processes can be described on the CIM level, because the CIM modelling language also allows for the description of activities that are executed manually. However, on the PIM level, manual activities cannot be described. Therefore in semi-automated business processes the whole business process is described at the CIM level but only the automated part is transferred to PIM level. Manual business processes can be described on the CIM level in VCLL, but are not implemented.

Regarding the number of participants and parallel instances that VCLL can support a limitation is only given by the target platform on PSM level. If the PSM level supports multiple instances and is able to handle a large number of users VCLL can be used for this kind of system.

Regarding the last classification criterion, the need of a business process for transaction support, VCLL partly supports transactions. As VCLL is based on databases, the transaction concepts of databases can be used. Therefore a transaction support for data is realised. But transaction support for the process steps itself is only partly possible.

The VIDE CIM level language offers the concept of compensation. This does not allow a roll-back to be done, but defines actions that have to be undertaken in order to undo an activity. Since the description of compensations on CIM level are done in the same way as the description of normal business processes, they can be implemented at the PIM level as well. Therefore VCLL offers a full transaction concept for data and compensations for business process activities. An overview of the type of business processes that are supported by VCLL gives the following table:

In general VCLL supports all types of executable business processes. The only requirement is that the business processes can be described by a set of actions, a control flow between them, and data objects the activities are working on. The type of business processes which are supported optimally are business processes which just display, create or change data. These actions are typically for administrative processes, such as booking a flight or the administration of a warehouse.

Other domains, such as real-time or embedded systems, are not in the focus of VCLL. Furthermore VCLL is not designed to depict very complex algorithms, such as those used in Artificial Intelligence systems, because these kinds of systems require a large number of loops, branches and case differentiation which are difficult to describe in the control flow of the VIDE CIM level language.

Traceability Within Pre-CIM and Relation Between CIM and Pre-CIM Level

A typical challenge for development of software systems is the traceability (Alexander, 2003) of information across phases. This is particularly relevant in the MDA process.

For example, existing MDA tools have no means to indicate to a developer where any elements of a PIM model are derived from within an associated CIM model. The richness associated with models created at the CIM level is lost in subsequent successive stages. We provide tool support that provides traceability between the scrapbook and the domain model, and the domain model and the subsequent CIM. A relationship is maintained between these informal model elements and their source in the scrapbook, such that if more detail

Table 2. Classification of business processes supported by VCLL

Attribute	Value		
repetition rate	singular	sometimes	frequently
degree of structure	unstructured	semi-structured	structured
alignment	strategic	tactical	operational
frequency of changes	never	sometimes	often
granularity	detailed	compounded	aggregated
value creation	low		high
process scope	intra-organisational		inter-organisational
usage of persistent information	none	low	high
level of automation	manual	semi-automated	automated
# of process participants	low		high
# parallel instances	one	some	many
transaction necessity	required		not required

is required the scrapbook can be interrogated to find the source of the information.

The use of a visual notation, rather than textual description in this setting has a number of advantages. Firstly, an analysis model of the problem domain that shows activities, the roles that perform those activities and the produced or used data is one that non-technical business stakeholders can identify with, and therefore validate. Secondly, the use of informal notations such as Bloops, or annotated rounded rectangles means that modelling is simple because there are no strict rules on using such elements. Thirdly, whereas the notational elements that depict the concepts of activities, roles, and data are informal, similar concepts are used in the MDA's CIM development phase. This suggests the possibility of one-to-one mapping between similar concepts between both pre-CIM and CIM.

The Domain Analysis Tool (DAT)

To demonstrate the use of the scrapbook and the analysis palette notations we developed a prototype tool as part of the VIDE project (VIDE, 2009b). The scrapbook part of the DAT works as a storage mechanism for a variety of scraps of information.

The scrapbook allows scraps to be organised and linked using an editor, with the left side of the screen showing a tree structure of the scrap items, including a preview of the scrap model. The elements in the scrapbook model can be associated based on the way in which a business user understands their domain. The links may be annotated to indicate the relationship between any two items. The main contribution of the scrapbook concept to the MDA process is that it allows the recording and organising of domain information, and affords non-technical users flexibility in creating very informal models of the storage and organisation of their information. Thus, the structure and inter-relationships between concepts

in the problem domain can be represented visually as an initial step in the MDA process

Specified information from the scrapbook is brought forward into the Analysis Palette section of the tool, where further refinement of the concepts and additional modelling can take place. The user can, as they bring in elements from the scrapbook, define the scrap of information as an activity, role or data, or if unsure specify it as a bloop.

A prevalence of bloops in an analysis model may be an indication that further analysis of the problem is needed. Identification of this issue so early in the development process highlights the value of this concept. Further analysis is likely to mean that bloops are broken down into the more clear concepts such as activities, roles or data objects.

A Worked Example

Consider a business situation where an enterprise seeks to manage their full sales process, it starts with the contacts made for enabling pursuit of opportunities, and production of quotations and then the opportunity has progresses to a business transaction. One might envisage a business user constructing their own informal model where these items regarding opportunities are shown along with their inter-relatedness, including any items that may not be clear. The full scenario is detailed in Figure 3.

This information is not likely to be stored in such a simple description within the company. On the contrary, it is likely to be gained from domain expert interviews and is unlikely to be such a clearly described process. The initial analysis by the business user, perhaps not accompanied by the analyst will to begin to make sense of the processes involved. They are likely to have to refer to organisational diagrams, perhaps videos, maybe some initial process flows. During this phase many ambiguities in the vocabulary will be identified and some initial thoughts on

Figure 3. The sales scenario (VIDE, 2009a)

> *The Sales Scenario focuses on sales processes of enterprises selling one or more products. It involves different aspects, ranging from opportunity management to quotations to customers, sales order processing and invoice processing.*
>
> *From a customers point of view the functionality of the Sales Scenario is described as follows:*
>
> *1.   A field representative of a manufacturer of computer hardware receives a message on his PDA, telling him that company X is planning to replace its complete system in the next quarter. The company has budgeted substantial financial resources for the replacement.*
>
> *2.   He immediately enters this information in the system, i.e., master data of the potential customer, including budget estimation, description of sales opportunity, sales volume, and timeframe of the opportunity.*
>
> *3.   The Opportunity object is created in the system and evolved by the assigned employee until it reaches a go/no go decision by sales management.*
>
> *4.   Another employee of the sales office creates an offer using the Quotation module, which automatically generates a quotation template based on the sales opportunity.*
>
> *5.   Based on the categorisation of the prospect in a Customer Group, estimated sales volume, and sales probability, the Individual Prices module is used to calculate a discount for the customer, which is included in the quotation.*
>
> *6.   After the sales office has contacted the customer and received an order, the system automatically converts the quotation into an order upon mouse click using the module Sales Processing.*
>
> *7.   To check the creditworthiness of the customer, a Credit Check is performed during sales processing by interacting with the Payment module.*
>
> *8.   An (optional) Availability Check is performed to check warehouse stock for required capacities.*
>
> *9.   The availability-to-promise check requires interaction with warehouse management (Stock). In case of Multiple Stocks only those warehouses sufficiently close to the shipping address are included.*
>
> *10.   In cooperation with the Delivery module, the order is split into separate orders for each involved warehouse, which have to be scheduled appropriately.*
>
> *11.   If Payment is to be integrated into the process, it would be activated automatically upon creating a binding sales order. Depending on the method of payment offered by the system and selected by the customer, an automatic debit transfer from the customer's account can be triggered (Payment Card), an invoicing document can be attached to the delivery (Cash On Delivery), or Invoicing is activated for later settlement.*
>
> *12.   The order status is set to "completed" by an employee as soon as it is delivered to the customer.*

requirements for any IT systems will start to be teased out.

The scraps that are likely to be selected in the example are those items that will have significance to the analysis process and are easily identified using noun/verb identification in the first instance. For the worked example these are shown below and illustrated in Figure 4.

- Product
- Opportunity
- Customer
- Check the creditworthiness
- Lead
- Evaluate opportunity
- Employee assignment
- Timeframe estimation

Figure 4. Selected scraps in scrap book editor (VIDE 2009a)

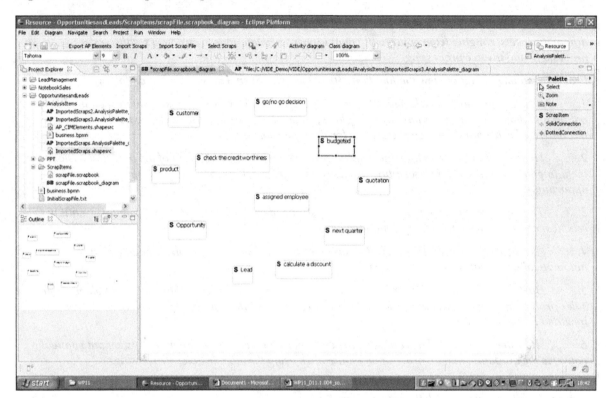

Figure 5. VIDE-informal model in analysis palette (VIDE 2009a)

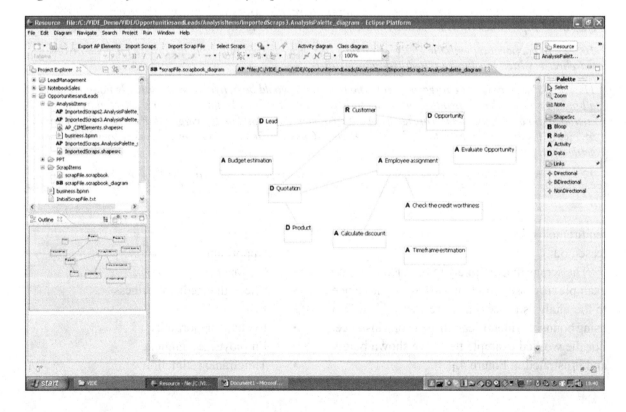

- Quotation
- Budget estimation
- Calculate discount

The identified scraps are then exported into the analysis palette part of the tool.

These scraps are further refined by the analyst in conversation with the business user in the Analysis Palette part of the DAT. Roles, activities, data objects and 'bloops' are identified, along with any links between them, thus allowing an informal model of the domain to be constructed. The resulting information is shown in Figure 5.

Once the informal pre-CIM model has been identified then the concepts can be exported into the next component of the MDA tool, giving the analyst a set of sound initial principles upon which to base their business process model. From the Domain Analysis Tool the information is represented as an initial process model that is used as

basis for finding additional process steps for the original process model. However, in contrast to modelling new applications from scratch, the scraps and their corresponding process steps represent new requirements needed to be combined with existing models.

After the refinement phase of the scraps into "things" and processes, the VCLL tool is used to formalise, still at the business analyst level, the processes as shown in Figure 6, for the whole Sales Process. Please note the VCLL tool is also uses to define organisational, business and data models at the CIM level, but as the most innovative part of VIDE is about behaviour, the focus is on the process model. First the existing models process models such as the Sales Process shown in Figure 6, are extended. One example of an existing process model – available as executable process and business component(s) with service interfaces

Figure 6. VIDE - Original process model (VIDE 2009a)

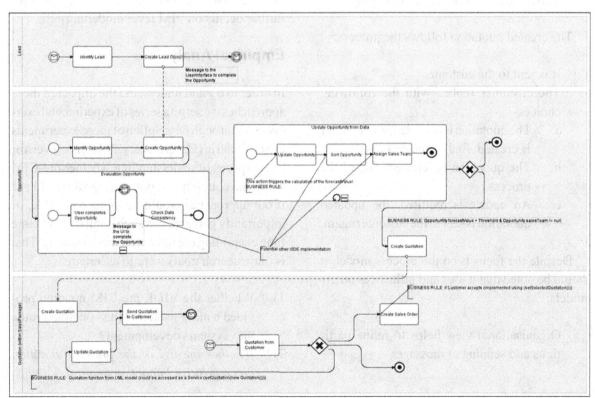

(double nature approach) from the VIDE VCLL tool is shown in Figure 6.

The whole process is split over 3 entities: Lead, Opportunity and Quotation.

The creation of an opportunity requires:

1. The identification and the creation of a lead associated to that opportunity,
2. The evaluation of the opportunity that is further refined into:
   a. Completion of the opportunity
   b. Check of data consistency
3. The update of the opportunity also refined into:
   a. Update of the opportunity which trigger the calculation of the forecast value according to the specified business rule
   b. Sort the opportunity in order to
   c. Assign it to a sales team
4. The creation of a quotation if, according to the business rule, the opportunity forecast value is high enough and there is someone in the sales team to manage that opportunity.

The created quotation follows the process:

5. It is sent to the customer
6. The customer replies with the following choices
   a. The quotation is accepted: a sales order is created. End of the process
   b. The quotation is rejected: end of the process
   c. An update is required: the updated quotation is sent to the customer again.

Despite the focus is on the process model, it should be noted that it uses and influences others models:

- Organisational view helps to refine partitions and sending of messages
- Data view helps to refine partitions also and production and consumption of data in the process model
- Business rules view helps to clarify and define process flows.

The process model along with the business model and the data model are the main contributions to the PIM model. The data model can even be imported in an UML modelling tool as a starting point because it follows the Ecore/XMI format. At this stage the process model can also be exported to OfficeObjects Workflow or any XPDL workflow engine thanks to the XPDL exporter. The XPDL controls workflow execution and further business behaviour can be implemented as business components via Web Services as described in Section 5 in VIDE 2009a. Therefore, the further focus would be on PIM level models for business component implementation. Next, the initial PIM level models would be created to extend the existing design. Those models are combined with the existing UML class model (see VIDE 2009a for further details on PIM level modelling).

Empirical Analysis

In order to try and understand the impact of these approaches we set up a series of experimental exercises. A thorough description of these experiments can be found in (Phalp & Jeary, 2010), however, for the purposes of understanding whether pre-CIM could have an impact, our main goal was to see if our approaches would be more accessible, or importantly perceived as such, whilst at the same time examining the impact on model quality. That is our research goals were to ascertain:

1) Whether the VIDE pre-CIM notation provided a more palatable (less onerous) route into systems development?
2) *Whether the use of the pre-CIM notation had a positive impact on quality?*

The experiment was conducted across two sets of subjects, one using the pre-CIM notation and one without. The subjects performed a set of sequential tasks mirroring the CIM phase and the tasks performed by the tool. Our hypotheses attempted to examine differences in overall model quality and perceived difficulty of tasks. For model quality we took both a positive and negative approach to quality, that is we scored positively for elements which one might expect in the perfect answer (e.g., keywords identified, objects identified) and also counted mistakes made (again across a number of attributes), each of these being then considered as a separate hypothesis relating to research question two (above). Interestingly we found that in all cases the pre-CIM notation group performed better. However, the genuinely significant finding was in terms of the perception of difficulty (our third hypothesis as reported in Phalp & Jeary, 2010). Our hypothesis relating to the perception of difficulty was stated as:

H: Group 1, using the pre-CIM notation perceived (rated) the tasks (Task 1 and 2) as easier (lower difficulty score) than group 2. The alternative hypothesis being

HA: Both groups rated the tasks as equally difficult.

As we have argued for models, often a graphical or visual representation tells the story most clearly. Figure 7 shows this for pre-CIM versus CIM, where the box plot not only shows that the that the group with pre-CIM fare much better, but also that there is little overlap, with the median for the group without pre-CIM close to the top of the box (75th percentile) for the group with pre-CIM.

Indeed, as one might expect, this was confirmed by the descriptive statistics (means) and by a t-test where the significance of the t-test (0.003) for 2 tailed, (0.0015 for single tailed) showed a highly significant (P<0.01) difference in the perceived

Figure 7. Box plots for hypothesis 3

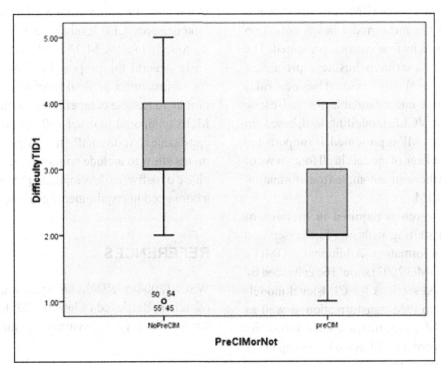

difficulty of the tasks (again see Phalp & Jeary, 2010 for a more detailed statistical analysis).

FUTURE RESEARCH DIRECTIONS

We have argued that among the issues with common application of the CIM phase of MDA are a lack of appropriateness for modelling the problem domain, insufficient scope for the very early aspects of development (where models are often informal) and, crucially, that models are often not best suited, indeed are inaccessible, to many of the stakeholders we are trying to entice into greater involvement in validation and modelling with MDA. In suggesting an enhancement to CIM, termed pre-CIM, we have outlined further requirements, such as the need to have traceability and to support managed transformations, and have described, in brief, our modelling approaches at this pre-CIM phase, introducing a worked example to do so.

The MDA approach is an effective way to create software systems to support business processes. But therefore a proper CIM-level language is needed. Thus the meta-model based definition of the VCLL and its four views is presented. The VCLL allows describing business processes, data, organisational structures and business rules in a way that is understandable for end users. Furthermore a VCLL modelling tool based on the framework GMF is presented. It supports the creation and linkage of models in all four views of the VCLL and the semi-automated transformation from CIM to PIM.

Further research is required in the area of CIM creation starting with non-formalised and unstructured information. Additionally OMG's MDA Guide (OMG 2003) should be enhanced by more elaborated sections for CIM-level modelling and CIM to PIM transformation as well as for PIM to CIM transformation and information propagation in order to fill the existing gap in the relation between these levels.

CONCLUSION

The Model Driven Architecture and Model Driven Development gained more and more importance as a Software Engineering approach. But the technical perspective on software development is still predominant. Therefore it was proposed in this chapter to introduce the pre-CIM level and enhance the CIM level by the VCLL as a new modelling technique, thus providing a more comprehensive unstructured information propagation to the CIM level of the MDA stack.

The pre-CIM level is capable to deal with unstructured information and enhances MDA approaches by unstructured but very important information. The empirical research presented above proves that the enhancement by a pre-CIM level and the proposed notation provides a more palatable (less onerous) route into systems development as well as positive impact on quality of the software development.

The enhancement of the CIM level with the VCLL as notation contains more relevant information than the BPMN standard and structures them into four different views. Furthermore it is linked the pre-CIM level above, which integrates it properly into the MDA model stack.

In general the proposed extension of MDA for unstructured or weakly structured information increases the competitiveness and quality of MDA compared to other software development approaches. Additionally the proposed enhancements allow to include domain expert in the early phase of software development process, which is a core need in requirements engineering.

REFERENCES

W3C. (2004a). *RDF/XML syntax specification (Revised)*. Retrieved 14 January, 2011, from http://www.w3.org/TR/rdf-syntax-grammar

W3C. (2004b). *OWL Web ontology language overview*. Retrieved 14 January, 2011, from http://www.w3.org/TR/owl-features

Alexander, I. (2003). Are there requirements for BPS? In J. Eder, R. Mittermeir & B. Pernici (Eds.), *Proceedings of Workshop on Requirements Engineering for Business Process Support* (REB-PS'03), *CAISE'03*, Klagenfurt/Velden, Austria.

Arango. (1989). Domain analysis: From art form to engineering discipline. *SIGSOFT Software Engineering Notes, 14*(3), 152-159.

Becker, J., zur Muehlen, M., & Gille, M. (2002). Workflow application architectures: Classification and characteristics of workflow-based Information Systems. In Fischer, L. (Ed.), *Workflow handbook 2002. Future strategies*. Lighthouse Point, FL.

Becker, J., & zur Mühlen, M. (1999). Rocks, stones and sand - Zur Granularität von Komponenten in Workflowmanagementsystemen. *Information Management & Consulting, 17*(2), 57–67.

Bleistein, S., Cox, K., Verner, J., & Phalp, K. (2006). B-SCP: A requirements analysis framework for validating strategic alignment of organisational IT based on strategy, context and process. *Information and Software Technology, 48*(9), 846–868. doi:10.1016/j.infsof.2005.12.001

Business Rules Group (Ed.). (2006). *Business rules manifesto: The principles of rule independence*. Retrieved January 14, 2011, from http://www.businessrulesgroup.org/brmanifesto.htm

Checkland, P. B. (1999). *Soft systems methodology in action*. John Wiley and Sons Ltd.

Deiters, W., Herrmann, T., Löffler, T., & Striemer, R. (1996). Identifikation, Klassifikation und Unterstützung semi-strukturierter Prozesse in prozeßorientierten Telekooperationssystemen. In Krcmar, H., Kewe, H., & Schwabe, G. (Eds.), *Herausforderung Telekooperation* (pp. 261–274). Berlin.

Derszteler, G. (2000). *Prozeßmanagement auf Basis von Workflow-Systemen: ein integrierter Ansatz zur Modellierung, Steuerung und Überwachung von Geschäftsprozessen*. Zugl. Berlin, Techn. Univ., Diss., 1999, Lohmar 2000.

Derungs, M. (1996). Vom Geschäftsprozess zum Workflow. In Österle, H., & Vogler, P. (Eds.), *Praxis des Workflow-Managements* (pp. 123–146). St. Gallen.

Endl, R. (2004). *Regelbasierte Entwicklung betrieblicher Informationssysteme.* ([). Eul, Lohmar et al.]. *Wirtschaftsinformatik,* 45.

Frankel, D. S. (2003). *Model driven architecture: Applying MDA to enterprise computing*. Indianapolis, IN: Wiley.

Giaglis, G. M. (2001). A taxonomy of business process modeling and Information Systems modeling techniques. *International Journal of Flexible Manufacturing Systems, 13*(2), 209–228. doi:10.1023/A:1011139719773

Hauser, C. (1996). *Marktorientierte Bewertung von Unternehmungsprozessen*. Zugl.: St. Gallen, Univ., Diss., 1996, Bergisch Gladbach 1996.

Heilmann, H. (1994). Workflow management: Integration von Organization und Informationsverarbeitung. *HMD, 31*(176), 8–21.

Henderson, P. (2000). *Software processes are business processes too*. Third International Conference on the Software Process. 1994. Reston, Virginia, USA: IEEE Computer Society Press. Systems Engineering for Business Process Change: Collected Papers from the EPSRC Research Programme, Springer (30 May 2000). ISBN-10: 1852332220

Jackson, M. (1995). *Software requirements & specifications: A lexicon of practice, principles and prejudices*. Addison-Wesley.

Kalenborn, A. (2000). *Prozeßorganization und Workflow-Management. Organizationstheoretisches Konzept und informationstechnische Umsetzung*. Zugl.: Trier, Univ., Diss., 1998, Aachen, 2000.

Kanyaru, J., Coles, M., Jeary, S., & Phalp, K. (2008). Using visualisation to elicit domain information as part of the Model Driven Architecture (MDA) approach. In *Proceedings of the 1st International Workshop on Business Support for MDA co-located with TOOLS EUROPE 2008*, Zurich, Switzerland, July 3.

Keller, G., Nüttgens, M., & Scheer, A.-W. (1992). Semantische Prozeßmodellierung auf der Grundlage "Ereignisgesteuerter Prozeßketten (EPK)". In A.-W. Scheer (Eds.), *Veröffentlichungen des Instituts für Wirtschaftsinformatik*, vol. 89. IWi, Saarbruecken.

Leymann, F., & Roller, D. (2000). *Produktion workflow. Concepts and techniques*. Upper Saddle River, NJ: Prentice Hall.

Martin, A., Seel, C., Jeary, S., Coles, M., Kanyaru, J., & Phalp, K. (2008). Generating software support for industrial business processes. *Proceedings of the 10th International Conference on The Modern Information Technology in the Innovation Processes of the Industrial Enterprises.*

Maurer, G. (1996). *Von der Prozeßorientierung zum Workflow Management. Teil 2: Prozeßmanagement, Workflow Management, Workflow-Management-Systeme. Arbeitspapiere WI - Nr. 10/1996. Lehrstuhl für allgemeine BWL und Wirtschaftsinformatik*. Mainz: Universität Mainz.

Mellor, S. J., Scott, K., Uhl, A., & Weise, D. (2004). *MDA distilled: Principles of model-driven architecture*. New York, NY: Addison-Wesley.

Mentzas, G. N. (1999). Coupling object oriented and workflow modeling in business and information process reengineering. *Information - Knowledge - System Management, 1,* 63-87.

OASIS07. (2007). *Web services business process execution language version 2.0*. Retrieved 14 January, 2011, from http://docs.oasis-open.org/wsbpel/2.0/OS/wsbpel-v2.0-OS.pdf

OMG. (2003). *MDA guide version 1.0.1*. Retrieved January 14, 2011, from http://www.omg.org/cgi-bin/doc?omg/03-06-01.pdf

OMG. (2005). *Unified modeling language (UML) 2.0 infrastructure and superstructure*. Retrieved 14 January, 2011, from http://www.omg.org/spec/UML/2.0/Infrastructure/PDF and http://www.omg.org/spec/UML/2.0/Superstructure/PDF

OMG. (2006a). *Business process modeling notation specification*. Retrieved 14 January, 2011, from http://www.bpmn.org/Documents/OMG_Final_Adopted_BPMN_1-0_Spec_06-02-01.pdf

OMG. (2006b). *Object constraint language (OCL) 2.0*. Retrieved 14 January, 2011, from http://www.omg.org/spec/OCL/2.0/PDF/

OMG. (2008). *Semantics of business vocabulary and business rules specification*. Retrieved 14 January, 2011, from http://www.omg.org/spec/SBVR/1.0/PDF/

Ould, M. A. (2005). *Business process management: A rigorous approach*. Swindon, UK: British Computer Society.

Phalp, K., & Jeary, S. (2010). *An empirical investigation of the utility of 'pre-CIM' models*. Paper presented at the 18th International Software Quality Management Conference.

Phalp, K. T. (1998). The CAP framework for business process modelling. *Information and Software Technology, 40*(13).

Picot, A., & Reichwald, R. (1985). *Bürokommunikation: Leitsätze für den Anwender*. 2. edit., München.

Rathgeb, M. (1994). Einführung von Workflow-Management-Systemen. In Hasenkamp, U., Kirn, S., & Syring, M. (Eds.), *CSCW - Computer Supported Cooperative Work. Informationssysteme für dezentralisierte Unternehmensstrukturen* (pp. 45–66). Bonn, Germany: Addison-Wesley.

Reijers, H. A. (2003). *Design and control of workflow processes*. New York, NY: Springer-Verlag, Inc.doi:10.1007/3-540-36615-6

Röhricht, J., & Schlögel, C. (2001). *cBusiness – Erfolgreiche Internetstrategien durch Collobarotive Business am Beispiel mySAP.com*. Munich, Germany: Addison-Wesley.

Scheer, A.-W., & Werth, D. (2005). Geschäftsprozessmanagement und Geschäftsregeln. In A.-W. Scheer (Ed.), *Arbeitsberichte des Instituts für Wirtschaftsinformatik*, vol. 183. IWi, Saarbrücken.

Schmidt, G. (2002). *Prozessmanagement. Modelle und Methoden*. 2. edit., Berlin.

Schulz, K. (2002). *Modelling and architecting of cross-organizational workflows*. Diss. 2002, University of Queensland, Australia.

Schulz, K., & Orlowska, M. (2001). Architectural issues for cross-organisational B2B interactions. In *Proceedings of the International Workshop on Distributed Dynamic Multiservice Architectures (DDMA)*.

Seel, C. (2010). Reverse method engineering. Methode und Softwareunterstützung zur Konstruktion und Adaption semiformaler Informationsmodellierungstechniken. *Berlin*.

Sheth, A., Georgakopoulos, D., Joosten, S. M. M., Rusinkiewicz, M., Scacchi, W., Wileden, J., & Wolf, A. L. (1997). Report from the NSF workshop on workflow and process automation in information systems. *ACM SIGSOFT Software Engineering Notes*, *1*, 28–38. doi:10.1145/251759.251825

U.S. Government Printing Office. (2002). *An act to protect investors by improving the accuracy and reliability of corporate disclosures made pursuant to the securities laws, and for other purposes*. Retrieved from.http://frwebgate.access.gpo.gov/cgi-bin/getdoc.cgi?dbname=107_cong_bills&docid=f:h3763enr.tst.pdf

van der Aalst, W. M. P. (1999). Formalization and verification of event-driven process chains. *Information and Software Technology*, *41*(10), 639–650. doi:10.1016/S0950-5849(99)00016-6

van der Aalst, W. M. P., & van Hee, K. M. (2002). *Workflow management: Models, methods, and systems*. Cambridge, MA: MIT.

VIDE. (2007). *Deliverable number 7.1: Metamodel and notation of the VIDE process modeling language, requirements concerning process model*. Retrieved 14 January, 2011, from http://www.vide-ist.eu/extern/VIDE_D7.1.pdf

VIDE. (2009a). *Deliverable 11.1: Framework 6 EU Commission IST033606STP*.

VIDE. (2009b). *Visualize all model driven programming*. FP6-IST-2004-033606. Retrieved 14 January, 2011, from http://www.vide-ist.eu/index.html

Wahl, T., & Sindre, G. (2005). *An analytical evaluation of BPMN using a semiotic quality framework*. Paper presented at the 10th International Workshop Exploring Modelliong Methods in Systems Analysis and Design (EMMSAD '05), Porto, Portugal.

Zhou, Y., & Chen, Y. (2003). The methodology for business process optimized design. In *The 29th Annual Conference of the IEEE Industrial Electronics Society*, vol. 2 (pp. 1819-1824).

zur Muehlen, M., Recker, J. C., & Indulska, M. (2007). *Sometimes less is more: Are process modelling languages overly complex?* Paper presented at the 3rd International Workshop on Vocabularies, Ontologies and Rules for The Enterprise, Annapolis, Maryland.

Chapter 6
Model Evolution Leads by Users Interactions

Charles-Georges Guillemot
Upper Alsace University, France

Frederic Fondement
Upper Alsace University, France

Michel Hassenforder
Upper Alsace University, France

ABSTRACT

Reuse has long proven its interest in software engineering. It is also useful while modeling: reusable elements can be concepts in a meta-model, or modeling elements in libraries, as libraries of components, or of activities to be used in frameworks. Choosing among those elements implies a compromise between modeling needs and provided services. Some authors have proposed to describe such services by means of models. However, this description is rarely available in practice. We propose here to let users improve these specifications by themselves in a participative way by merely tagging the reusable elements. Tags express how the elements can be used, or how to compare the elements together. To do so, questions, which depend on a model, are automatically asked to the user while working. Answers, provided under the form of tags or keywords, are processed in order to evolve the model.

INTRODUCTION

Modelling is an activity that everyone performs everyday. Indeed, it is the normal functioning for our brain: We all associate a mental image with each person or item around us. This image is a model, made of concepts and relations between them, which describes that entity in order to men-
tally simulate its behaviour. Einstein (Einstein & Infeld, 1967) illustrates the model notion in the form of a metaphor:

"Physical concepts are free creations of the human mind, and are not, however it may seem, uniquely determined by the external world. In our endeavor to understand reality we are somewhat like a man trying to understand the mechanism of a closed watch. He sees the face and the moving hands, even

DOI: 10.4018/978-1-61350-438-3.ch006

Figure 1. Simple image preparation with a view to counting the number of cells

hears its ticking, but he has no way of opening the case. If he is ingenious he may form some picture of a mechanism which could be responsible for all the things he observes, but he may never be quite sure his picture is the only one which could explain his observations. He will never be able to compare his picture with the real mechanism and he cannot even imagine the possibility or the meaning of such a comparison."

The creation of such models is an intuitive step, and is not necessarily made explicit by describing it in a document written in a formalized or even natural language. However, such formalizations may become necessary as soon as one needs to reuse or share such models. So in recent years, Model-Driven Engineering (MDE) (Schmidt, 2006) tends to play an increasingly significant role in various domains, and in particular in the software development. Indeed, all software aspects are defined by models and thus when a software system needs evolve, his models must evolve accordingly. Although many model transformation languages (MOF, 2010) (Jouault and al., 2008) have been developed, this task remains time-con-

suming, tedious, and error-prone. Consequently, if a user of one software has a need which is not describes in the model, he will have to choose an other software or wait an update, hoping that this update takes account of his need.

We will illustrate this situation with a simple example of image processing (Figure 1). This process prepares a picture with a view to counting the number of cells which are inside. The first action allows to delete objects which are not cells and keeps only good candidates. Secondly, we successively erode and expanse all remaining objects to remove all latest artifacts. Then the picture is ready to be analyzed. But this scenario is completely determined by the source picture. A modification of this picture type could modify a part or all of the process.

For instance, we will apply the same processing over a different picture, which include intensity skips. In this picture type the previous process will not produce correct results, because intensity skips could interfere with filter actions. So, various activities (Figure 2) must be applied to delete these skips, and get a correct result.

Figure 2. Modified previous scenario

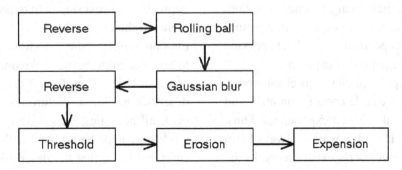

Various works try to solve this problem. We can cite Y. Saidali (Saidali, 2002, 2003) who proposes an acquisition and consultation platform of image processing. It is made up of an ontology which stores a set of image processing scenarios. These scenarios are a sequence of image processing operators in order to accomplish a fixed purpose, and they are created by experts who describe their aim and the concatenation of operators to use. At the end, users can search one possible solution of their problem among this list of scenarios. So, if the model does not take account of this modification, the appropriate scenario will not be suggested and the image processing will give false results. And even if a user knows the correct adjustments to do, he is not able to modify the model and, therefore he will not be able to modify the previous processing.

One solution is summarized by this guiding principle formulated by Eistein (1955, p.1):

"The object of all science, whether natural science or psychology, is to co-ordinate our experiences and to bring them into a logical order."

Enrst Von Glasersfeld (2001) noted this principle forms the core of the constructivist epistemology and determines the constructivist view, not only of the result of scientific endeavor but also of all the ordinary knowledge we glean from everyday experience. Like the ingenious observer in Einstein's metaphor, scientists invent theoretical models of mechanisms and test their viability in repeated and controlled experiments, while non-scientists gather rules of them and attempt to apply them in their living practice. For both the actual purpose is not to obtain a true picture of an observer-independent reality, but to provide tools for the management of experience.

Based on this point of view, this chapter present an approach to enable users to maintain and evolve models thanks to their experiences. Thus, tools will evolve in such a way to always be in a position to manage user's experiments. In the

following, we will apply our proposal about the image processing domain. An application of image processing is composed by a sequence of image processing operators. So, one possible mean to modelize them is to use a workflow language. Indeed the "wysiwyg" nature of graphical interfaces of workflow softwares makes them an attractive tool, because users do not need specific knowledge about workflows to work. Workflows are made of interconnected activities, which all represent processing steps. To formulate a workflow, a user thus needs to choose the activities in a predefined list and connect them together. In the rest of this chapter, this user will be called model-designer, because a workflow represents the model of a process, which is likely to be repeated often. For instance, to process a picture, a workflow may contain instances of compression or edge detection activities. Choosing those possible activities among a list of all possible ones must be performed carefully (Jazéquel, 1997) depending on functional and non functional properties. The model-designer can make his choice according to the data to process, the expected results, the activities features (as the speed or the efficiency), or other personal criteria. Such criteria can be modelled in a knowledge base by mean of an ontology. Thus, the semantic of activities can be captured and used to help model-designers to create workflows easier. For example, Bowers and Ludäscher (2004) are able to perform automatically syntactic adaptations of data when their semantic are known and compatible. Other, like Renouf (2007), use an ontology to help the model-designer while creating workflows. In this approach, the first step is to express the requirements of the desired model with the concepts of the ontology, and the workflow is found thanks to an association between the ontology and concrete activities. Therefore, if the model-designer describes his initial picture and his processing goal, all activities, which composed the suited workflow, may be automatically found on the strict condition that the description of his input data (initial picture and processing purpose) were beforehand stored in the ontology.

To apply such approaches, one needs both a library of all the possible activities, and an ontology whom concepts allow to express the activities features and how they can influence the model. But this approach raises two issues. The first one lies in the fact that it requires a complete ontology of the domain. Indeed, the ontology must be entirely determined before creating a model if the model-designer wants to describe his search criteria and compare the resulting activities. Adding new concepts in an existing knowledge base requires an expert or group of experts. This task, whose the cost can be prohibitive and time-consuming, makes hard to maintain and evolve the knowledge base. The second issue is that all elements of the library must be described, and these descriptions must be stored in the ontology. In theory, this task is devoted to activities designers but, actually, they do it very rarely. This is easily explained by the fact that they are expert in their domain thus implying both that they may not be also experts in knowledge engineering, and that they don't need any help about how to use the activities they have designed.

We aim at capture in an ontology the knowledge of model-designers, rather than the knowledge of the designers of activities. However, model-designers do not necessarily have the cognizance to handle the ontology directly. Thus, we have put in place a social tagging system, which allows model-designers to describe activities using simple tags. Questions, concerning by the choice of one activity among others, are asked to the model-designer. All given answers enrich a folksonomy, which is a knowledge base resulting of the social tagging system and that is not as formal as an ontology. In the end, the folksonomy will help in growing the ontology, on the one hand increasing concepts, and on the other hand improving the description of the activities.

The rest of this chapter is organized as follows. Section two fixes the vocabulary. In section three, we present our proposal, its issues and the related works. We illustrate it by a case of study on workflows in image processing and discuss the work done on the knowledge capitalization in the section four. In section five, we present future research direction that it will interesting to follow up and finally we give the conclusion in section six.

BACKGROUND

Workflows

Workflows represent in general the modeling and computer management of the set of tasks and/or actors from which a process is composed. Their final aim is to automate at best the works process. Commonly, the word "workflows" represents as well the modelled process as the system used to his modeling. Therefore, in order to differentiate both meanings, and in accordance with the vocabulary of the WorkFlow Management Coalition, we will use the word "procedure" to talk about the process and "workflow" to designate the software which performs his modeling. Two main kind of workflows exist, the business and the scientific workflows.

The business workflows appeared in the 70's, and their definition we retain is given by the Work-Flow Management Coalition (Specification, W. M. C.): "The automation of a business process, in whole or parts, where documents, information or tasks are passed from one participant to another to be processed, according to a set of procedural rules." They allow to automate the work processes within enterprises, which used to be handmade. These workflows are tasks oriented and allow to perform complex processes with a significant control-flow. The notion of task oriented means that all entities handled by the user within a business workflow represent a task which must be realized by any actor (human or computer system).

The scientific workflows are a various form of the business workflows. They are so relatively similar but the scientific workflows have various functionalities which the business workflows do not have. The definition we retain of these workflows is given by B. Ludäscher and al. (2006): "These are networks of analytical steps that may involve, e.g., database access and querying steps, data analysis and mining steps, and many other steps including computationally intensive jobs on high perform cluster computer." This kind of workflows mainly targets scientists and, therefore, is able to meet their specific needs, by providing a mean to model, control, and analyze of processes. A process defined as a scientific workflow is defined by a model which is made of activities and relations between them. The model of computation of scientific workflows is based on a data-flow model while the one of business workflows is a control-flow model.

But in the recent years, to be met with the passion for the workflows and the arising of new needs, an other kind of workflows appeared. We name it adaptive workflows, flexible workflows, or Workflows-Driven Ontologies (Salayandia, 2006). The main property of this kind of workflows is to offer the possibility to modify the structure of one process during its execution. This provide a new flexibility for the user as some decisions are taken during the execution of their processes. The heart of these workflows is a notion that we going to tackle and which is the ontologies.

Ontologies

The concept of ontology is a notion which is difficult to characterize. Indeed, ontologies are used in many different domains, such as philosophy, linguistic, or artificial intelligence, and each one of them proposes its specific definition. Etymologically speaking, the word ontology comes from the Greek "onto" meaning "is, what is it" and "logos" meaning "speech, treaty". Initially, this term has been introduced into philosophy during the nineteenth century and refers to a discipline of the philosophy, field of metaphysic, which studies the nature and the organization of the being. The communities of artificial intelligence and knowledge engineering have adopted this term during the 1990's. They write the word ontology with an initial lower-case in order to differentiate their context from the original where Ontology is written with an initial upper-case.

Even if the definition of ontology has evolved over time, the more commonly accepted is that one defined by Gruber (1993): "a formal and explicit specification of a conceptualization". This definition is the continuation of previous works (Gruber, 1991) which described ontologies as "the definition of terms and basic relations including as well the domain vocabulary as the rules which allow to combine them in order to expand this vocabulary". This view of ontology was extended by Studer (1998): "Ontology is a formal, explicit specification of a shared conceptualization".

In order to understand this definition, it is important to explain the meaning of all used words. Thus, the term "conceptualization" indicates that the whole pertinent concepts of the target domain and their properties are identified and hierarchically organized in an abstract model. A "concept" is defined such as a notion generally expressed using a term, or more generally a sign. It represents a group of objects or entities sharing a set of characteristics which allow us to recognize them as a part of this group (Gandon, 2002). "Explicit specification" implies that concepts and their constraints are explicitly defined. The use of the term "formal" emphasizes that this conceptualization must be understood and interpreted not only by humans but by machines too. Finally, the notion "shared" means that the ontology captures consensual knowledge, which are not restricted to one individual, but shared by a group.

More formally, Renouf (2007) has defined ontology as the sum of several sets:

- A set of concepts;
- A set of relations between these concepts;
- A set of axioms (e.g. transitivity, reflexivity,...).

But the formal nature of ontologies makes them difficult to bring about some change. So, all modifications require an expert or group of expert. To allow model-designers to add their knowledge themselves in an ontology, we must have recourse to a less formal knowledge base form than an ontology. One possible mean to do this is to use a social tagging system.

Social Tagging

With the advent of semantic web, social tagging is booming. It is also known as folksonomy (Vander Wal, 2007), which is a neologism resulting of the concatenation of "folk" and "taxonomy", or collaborative tagging system (Tanasescu & Streibel, 2007). Social tagging qualifies the practice of describing objects using freely chosen keywords (tags). Many social resource sharing systems on the web implement this mechanism, such as Flickr for photos galleries, del.icio.us for bookmarks or CiteULike for scientific publications.

Social tagging systems can be represented (Tanasescu & Streibel, 2007) as a tripartite graph with hyper edges where the set of vertexes is partitioned into three disjoint sets:

$$A = a_1, a_2, a_n$$

$$C = c_1, c_2, ..., c_n$$

$$O = o_1, o_2, ..., o_n$$

A, C, and O correspond to actors (users), concepts (keywords or tags), and annotated objects (resources). Users tag objects with concepts and they create a ternary association between the user, the object and the concept. This association

is named a tagging and it is thus an element of T, where:

$$T \subseteq A \times C \times O$$

Finally, the hypergraph formed by this collaborative tagging is the tripartite hyper graph F, where:

$$T(F) = <V, E>$$

with vertexes $V = A \cup C \cup O$ and edges $E\{\{a, o, c\} \mid (a, o, c) \in T\}$

These systems are an opportunity to acquire knowledge about resources from model-designers who handle them. It is important to note that the results of these social tagging systems are lightweight knowledge representations. Indeed, these keywords cannot be considered as vocabulary, which is the simplest form of an ontology (Smith & Welty, 2001), and no semantic links can be found directly in these systems, because none of the conditions of the semantic emergence (Aberer & Ouksel, 2004) is fulfilled.

MAIN FOCUS

Related Works

Some workflows can be executed even before they are fully specified. Such workflows are named flexible workflows (Halliday, 2001), adaptive workflows, dynamic workflows (Chun & Atluri, 2003), or ontology-driven workflows (WDOs) (Salayandia, 2007). Workflow ontologies are at the core of these approaches. Almeida and al. (2004) explains these ontologies represent relationships between abstract and concrete workflows, resources and users. The relationships between abstract and concrete processing steps are explored by a mechanism for choosing alternatives. So, a flexible workflow can use semantic proximity properties to find semantically equivalent sub-workflows, semantically equivalent resources, and/or a user with equivalent capacities.

Renouf (2007) uses this approach to image processing applications. His ontology is a formal representation of the problem, that the process-designer wants to resolve, and is independent from the solution. First is specified the goals to be reached, i.e. users needs, and then data to process are described, i.e. the picture class. These formulations contain all required information to create the solution matching with the initial specifications, and so to generate the corresponding program.

Our idea is complementary to the Renouf's proposal. He uses an ontology to generate a program, and his ontology is build by an expert. It is a difficult task which costs much time and asks some skills. In our case, we propose to facilitate this task and to build this ontology (semi-) automatically. Indeed, the model-designers will not be limited by an expert for integrating new knowledge into the ontology, because they will do it themselves. To do so, we turn toward Semantic Web and folksonomy usages.

However, the folksonomies introduce some issues and a lot of research attempt to compensate them by trying to learn semantic relations from these knowledge representations in order to close the gap between ontologies and folksonomies. We can discern and put them away into two main categories of researches: a-posteriori analysis, and tagged analysis of folksonomies. The first analyzes the structure of folksonomies in order to get a representation of the semantic structure defined by the community. This represents the alleged first step of the process to elaborate an ontology. Thus, Mika (2005) proposes to build lightweight ontologies from folksonomies analysis. He uses a folksonomies tripartite model where instances are web resources associated by a user to a list of concepts. He performs analysis methods of social networks to establish graphs representing links between concepts. He can deduce from those graphs groups of tags or even subsumption relationships between tags. Moreover, from a graph linking activities and concepts, he can find semantic possible links and he may deduce generalization relationships between the groups of tags. Other approaches pick the folksonomies tripartite model of Mika up again and use data mining methods to extract information about the folksonomies structure.

Thus, Jaschke and al. (2008) use formal analysis methods to discover users subsets sharing a same conceptualization on the same resources. Schmitz and al. (2006) use other data mining techniques to extract association rules in the folksonomies such as: users, whom associate the tags of the set C_A to a set of resources, associate often the tags of the set C_B to the same resources. This type of rules could be applied to a system of tags recommendations.

With our proposal, the model-designers specify themselves the semantic of the relationships which exist between the tags. They can indicate that a tag does the same thing, or is more efficient or fast than an other. As these relationships are provided by freely chosen tags, model-designers can invent and create all tags they desire or can reuse existing tags. Thus, the relationships between tags are explicit, and the model-designer expressiveness is not limited to the subsumption relations.

Tanasescu and Streibel (2007) propose another method to structure the folksonomies. They suggest to engage more users in the social tagging system and allow them to tag the tags themselves or relationships between tags. These tags can be expressed with triplets, what allow use them with search engines of the semantic web. They suggest to equip the community in order to sort out the problem of the provided information pertinence too. The aim of this equipment is to encourage the users contributions. So, users might appreciate or depreciate a tag, or else tags could win points according to their uses.

On the contrary of Tanasescu, we distinguish tags and resources. We go further distinguishing in tags, the set of relation tags, which describes relationships between tags, and the set of domain tags, which qualifies the resources or the tags. Our system provides also to appreciate or depreciate a tagging. To do so, the model-designers can tag the tagging with a tag. But, they are allowed also to tag a tagging with another tagging for justifying their mind.

The second category of techniques to close the gap between folksonomy and ontologies consists in bringing a formal base to the folksonomies. Thus, Passant (2007) suggests to structure the folksonomy during the annotation of a post in a business blog. In this case, a tag is assimilated to a concept's property of an controlled ontology. The ontology leads the annotation by piloting the choice of the tag. In fact, the user handles existing labels or proposes a new label to designate a concept. The user can also propose a new concept and the corresponding label to the administrator, when the concept does not exist. The interest of this approach is to remove the ambiguity of tags compared to the concepts they designate.

Good and al. (2007) lead the same reasoning than Passant and propose a system which makes coexist freely chosen terms and controlled ontologies terms. They suggest to exploit the set of annotations in order to deduct existing relations between these two types of terms.

For his part, Gruber (2005) says there is not an opposition between ontologies and folksonomies. He proposes to build an ontology of folksonomies, called tagOntology, which will permit to formalize the action of annotation. Four entities are used in this ontology: the resource or tagged object; the tag, i.e. the keyword used; the user tagging the resource with the tag; and the domain in which the tagging is realized. Gruber is doing more than Passant. Indeed, for Passant the tag is just a string of characters linked to concepts of formal ontologies. Gruber considers each tag as an object and proposes the user to tag the tags to avoid spams or ambiguities.

Like Gruber, we think it does not exist oppositions between an ontology and a folksonomy. Our system refines the gruber's ontology and extends

the entities which composed it. Our ontology supplies tools to model-designers in such a way as to lead them to give the most possible of their knowledge during their works.

Issues

Our proposal is to combine advantages of both approaches to enhance an ontology using the knowledge contained in a folksonomy fed by model-designers This approach inherits of the constructivist epistemology, because we believe that a knowledge base should not represent a closed world. Knowledge of each person evolve according to their experiments and our ontology must to be able to manage these changes. Moreover, if build and maintain an ontology is a difficult task for one person, we believe the best solution is to have it done by a group. This point of view is keeping with a main property of ontologies which is they should be shared by a group. The result will be a compromise between the whole of users and it will benefit from their knowledge to represent as accurately as possible their domain. So, questions are posed to the final users of a system to improve the ontology used. These questions are about the choices made when using this system. "What performs this component?", "Why do you use this rather than that?" are examples of questions that users will be led to answer. The given answers will be saved and processed to help in the enrichment of the knowledge base.

But the establishment of such proposal requires to solve several issues. The first of them is to find good questions to capture as much information as possible without overloading process-designers. A second issue is how to accept incomplete, or even inconsistent information. Indeed, if the process-designer is questioned too much, there might have no answers. He wants make his job and it is understandable that he does not want to waste one's time to answer questions. The third and last issue is to find how combine ontologies and folksonomies. If ontologies are fine at representing knowledge, their formal structure makes them hard to build and maintain. Therefore, ontology-based systems are limited by the expression ability of their ontology (Draper, 1996) and it will be very hard to do evolve it. On the contrary, a folksonomy takes advantage of a lack of formal definition in order to be easily described. But paradoxically, even if a folksonomy offers advantages as flexibility, adaptability, simplicity, and easiness of use, this lack of formality makes the organization of the taggings by users chaotic (Mathes, 2004). Main limitations of folksonomies are ambiguity, and variability in writing tags which are supposed equivalent. They can thus be a source of "info-pollution" (Sutter, 1998) since they have no semantic. As tags of folksonomies are not chosen from a dedicated and reliable thesaurus, many confusions and disturbing polysemies are introduced.

Solution

To solve these limitations, we have defined our own ontology which formalizes the action of tagging. Such an ontology is also called tagOntology in the literature (Gruber, 2005). Like a standard folksonomy, this ontology allows model-designers to tag resources. Moreover, the classical model of tagging (i.e. the relation between a tag and a tagged element such as a resource) is extended making possible to tag the tags, the relations between tags, and even the taggings themselves. Thus, they can explicitly disambiguate introduced tags by tagging them. They can also describe the semantic relationship between two elements by tagging them, especially when this relation can not be deduced by another way such as mika's method (Mika, 2007). Moreover, tagging the taggings can be a mean for system-designers to appreciate or depreciate taggings, and to motivate such taggings by new taggings.

Our formalization of the tagOntology provides model-designers, on the one hand, a greater expressiveness and on the other hand, a structured non-specialized framework to express and capitalize their knowledge. Taggings and tags are individuals of the ontology and users are be able using them to clearly describe their activities and/or processes. If a term does not exist, users could easily insert it into the ontology as they could do it using the social tagging. From this point of view, knowledge is merely represented by a set of tags, while the users actually manipulate an ontology without know that.

We distinguish two kinds of tags: Relation tags, which qualify relations between individuals, and description tags, which qualify individuals (tags, taggings, or resources). The description tag class is made up of two subclasses. The first is the value tag class which contains all tags about data values, and the domain tag class. This last class is the root of the target domain ontology and that the model-designer wants to enrich.

In our proposal, a folksonomy is described by the following model:

$$F: (U, T, R, \prec, \leq)$$

where:

U = the set of the users who participate in the tagging activity

T = the set of the tags

R = the set of resources

$\prec$ = the set of taggings for tags or resources, i.e.: $U \times (R \cup T) \times TR \times (R \cup T)$

$\leq$ = the set of taggings for taggings, i.e.: $U \times \pi \times TR \times (\prec \times TD)$

with

$T = (TR \cup TD)$

TR = a subset of T which includes the tags to qualify the relations between two entities (e.g. faster-than)

TD = a subset of T which includes the tags to describe an entity (e.g. data-compressor)

Figure 3. The model of our ontology of tagging

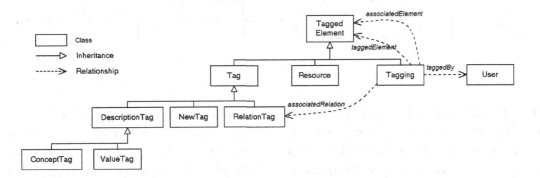

To better visualize it, the Figure 3 depicts an glimpse of the architecture of our tagOntology.

Concerning the implementation of our system, we have decided to use the OWL-DL language (W3C, 2009) which is based on the description logics and is widely used by communities of the knowledge engineering and of the Semantic Web. Moreover this language is a W3C recommendation and is characterized by formal semantics and RDF/XML-based serializations. As RDF, OWL-DL is a tripartite language, in sense that it allows each operator two arguments of the form subject/ verb/object. This is a major feature, because we modelize each tagging by a set of four elements. Thus, to get around this problem, instead of creating one quaternary relationship, we will create 4 ternary relationships.

To validate our proposal, we have modelized it with the B Method (Abrial, 1996). The B Method is a formal specification method which allows the development of software which is contractually guaranteed to be fault-free. We express accurately, thanks to an adequate language, the properties required by specifications and one can then mathematically prove in a fully automated fashion that these properties are unambiguous, coherent and are not contradictory. So we have used B to make an abstract modelling of our ontology in order to verify its coherence with an activity of formal proofs. The resulting model is in keeping with our needs and matches with our proposal. It generates seventeen proof obligations and all of these proofs are automatically proven by the atelier B, which is one of the major B tools and that allows for the operational use of the B Method in the development of proven software.

A CONCRETE APPLICATION

Nowadays, multi-dimensional microscopic imagery systems are complex image processing systems, which handle a large amount of data. These systems are able to implement a set of imaging operations, such as capture, transformation, transmission, and display of images. The results of the combination of these operations are image processings, whose the pertinence depends on the orchestration of the used operations. However, the knowledge necessary to build these orchestrations are often the result of experimentations, where data are wrong formalized.

Indeed, model-designers, who process images, are experts on their domain, but they do not necessarily know the subtleties of the tools or the programming languages they use. So, in most cases an image processing is a monolithic program of tens, hundreds of lines, or more. The set of knowledge required to well-form an orchestration is entirely contained in this set of sequential instructions. Thus, existing orchestrations are difficult to understand, and therefore they are difficult to reuse and adapt. To realize a new image processing, a model-designer must in

Figure 4. An image processing which improves a picture

the most of cases, create a new orchestration from scratch. The formalization being a main issue in the image processing domain, we have included a short list of significant works about this question in the additionnal reading section.

To illustrate our approach, we apply it on a simple example of image processing (Figure 4), whose the purpose is to improve a picture. In the rest of this section, we will describe the behaviour of our system during the creation of this workflow.

Thus, we depict on the Figure 5 our ontology of tagging at the beginning of our process. The ontology owns only one registered model-designer (user1) and the relation *is-a*. This relation is used to structure the capitalization of the new knowledge, indicating the membership class of each new tag. Our ontology of tagging is also coupled with a target domain ontology in order to own basic knowledge about this domain.

In this example, the domain ontology is a subset of the ontology proposed by Renouf (2007) regarding image processing tasks (①).

When the model-designer uses the *Open_Picture* and since this activity does not exist as a resource of the ontology, it is automatically created. Then model-designer can describe its behaviour, beginning by specify the task performed by this activity. Its task is not an image processing task, but rather a manage task. Therefore, he could create the new task category to represent it. He creates the new tag *ManageTask* and a new tagging which explains this tag is a subclass of *DomainTag*. This step is depicted on the Figure 6. In the same way, he specifies that the task *Open picture* is a subclass of *ManageTask*. He creates also the relation *perform* which allows to specify the task performed by a resource. (For reasons of readability, we will not represent resulting taggings of these additions in the following Figures).

Now, the model-designer can describe what task is performed by *Open picture*. He selects in a dialog box the resource *Open picture*, the tag *Open* describing the activity and the relation which explains the semantic of the link between them.

Figure 5. The state of our ontology at the beginning of the process

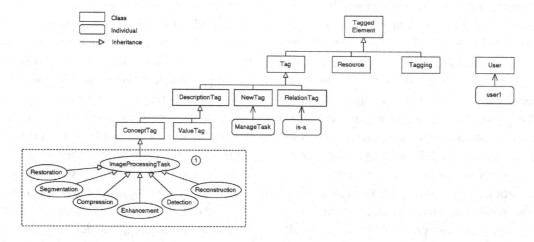

Figure 6. Capitalization of a new knowledge: create a new tag

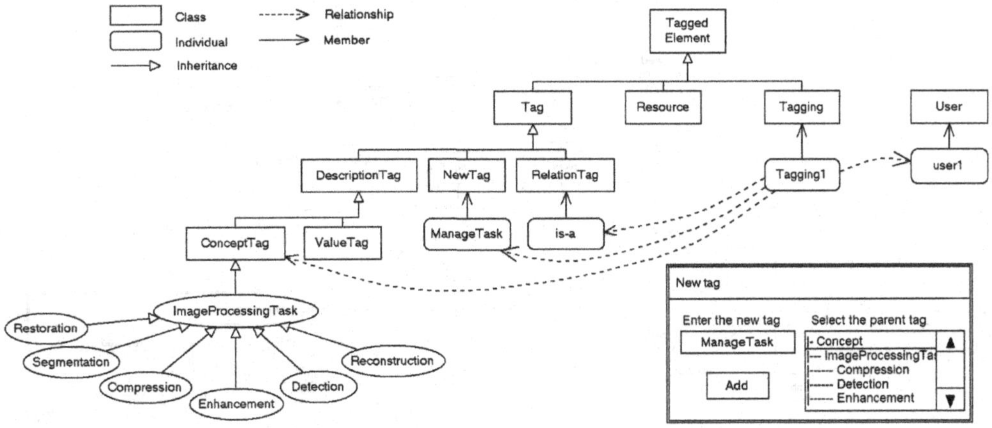

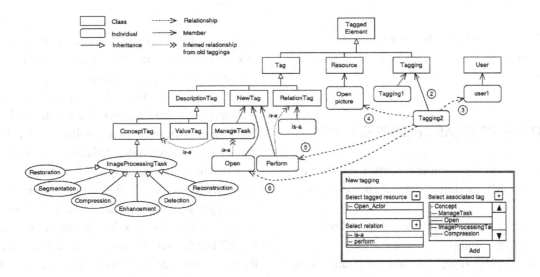

Figure 7. Capitalization of a new knowledge: Create a new tagging

This action is depicted on Figure 7 and will create at first the tagging *tagging2* ②, and the relation ③ with the user *user1* which is the author of this tagging. Then, the relation ④, indicating what resource is tagged, is created. Next, the semantic existing between the resource and the tag is specified by the link ⑤. Finally, the relation ⑥ indicates the task performed by the resource. So, the next time a model-designer will use this actor, the system will know why he wants to use it and it will be able to propose alternatives if our ontology owns resources with a similar semantic.

However, it is possible that a model-designer does not agree with an other. In order to express his disagreement, in the same way he performed to tag a resource by a tag, he can tag taggings themselves. The principle is to add a tag indicating he does not agree with this tagging, but he can also tag it by a new tagging to justify his opinion and to indicate why he is not agree. This step is depicted on the Figure 6 where the model-designer specifies he is not agree with the *tagging2*. Then, he tags that he thinks being the trust tagging (*tagging3* ⑦) and indicates his disagreement by

Figure 8. Capitalization of a new knowledge: tag a tagging by a tagging

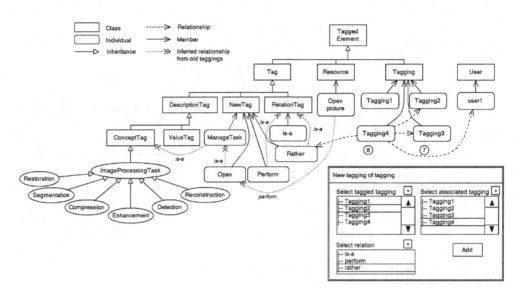

tagging *tagging2* with the *tagging4* and the relation *rather* ⑧ (relation that he must previously create).

FUTURE RESEARCH DIRECTIONS

As expressed by Limpens (2008), interesting issues for information systems community are:

- Merge some structures of a folksonomy and an ontology;
- Explicitly represent and maintain these junction points;
- Manage the frictions between the two life cycles;
- Assist and automate the least intrusive possible exchanges between these two objects

We are agree with his point of view and that is why our proposal is positioned in the same perspective and tries to provide answers to these issues.

For us, the social nature of knowledge exchange is not incompatible with the possibilities offered by formal ontologies systems. Indeed, there is no reason to oppose ontologies and folksonomies, because it appears that these two approaches are often complementary. In our approach, we take advantage of the use of formal representations, but also informal representations in everyday interactions of individuals to attempt to avoid the bottleneck of knowledge acquisition we can have when we want to create and maintain an ontology.

Currently, we develop the tool which corresponds to our proposal in order to improve an ontology of image processing domain. We combine our approach with a workflow management system to facilitate the work of users. Indeed, they can easily create and execute their image processings and we can capitalized some information directly by studying their behavior when they use the software. For the other information, we ask them questions through the use of dialog boxes, but in order to not overloading them or boring them, we are planning to explore mechanisms which motivate users to answer. As our purpose is to improve a domain ontology, we also plan to find a mean to evaluate the information capitalized with our system in order to know the trust that we can have in the reusable elements which are tagged by the users.

CONCLUSION

In this article, we have presented our proposal which is the coupling of a domain ontology with an ontology of tagging. Our approach completes the work of Renouf (2007), which helps model-designers to create a workflow using ontologies. We propose to create these ontologies by social tagging. But this approach requires to solve two issues. The first is to find good questions to capture as much information as possible without overloading model-designers. The second issue is to be able to accept incomplete, or even inconsistent information. To solve these issues, we have proposed to use our ontology of tagging as a blotting ontology to filter incoherences before enrich the domain ontology. Then, it's up to model-designers themselves to evaluate the tagging following principles of social tagging.

Our reasoning breaks down into three steps. The first is the processing of the available reusable modeling elements, which are all considered as resources. In addition, our ontology of tagging might also be initialized with an existing domain ontology in order to get an initial vocabulary. During the second step, users, who tag the reusable elements they use, capitalize their knowledge into our tagOntology, where can coexist incoherent information. The next and final step consists in processing the capitalized knowledge in order to manage these conflicts and to enrich the domain ontology. This proposal offers the advantage of greatly easing the work of users and also storing their knowledge easily for future uses and potential shares.

We finally emphasize that our ontology of tagging is not bound to a domain in particular. Thus, the approach exposed in this paper may be easily applied to other domains which are a large library of reusable elements, such as component frameworks.

REFERENCES

W3C. (2009). *OWL 2 Web ontology language.* Retrieved April 30, 2011, from http://www.w3.org/TR/owl2-overview/

Aberer, K., Cudré-Mauroux, P., Ouksel, A. M., Catarci, T., Hacid, M. S., & Illarramendi, A. … Neuhold, E. J. (2004). *Emergent semantics principles and issues.* Technical report, Zaragoza.

Abrial, J. R. (1996). *The B-book: Assigning programs to meanings.* Cambridge University Press. doi:10.1017/CBO9780511624162

Almeida, T., Vieira, S. C., Casanova, M. A., & Ferrão, L. G. (2004). An ontology-driven architecture for flexible workflow execution. In *OSEA'04: Proceedings of the workshop on Ontologies as Software Engineering Artifacts*, (pp. 70-77).

Bowers, S., & Ludascher, B. (2004). *An ontology-driven framework for data transformation in scientific workflows* (pp. 1–16).

Chun, S. A., & Atluri, V. (2003). *Ontology-based workflow change management for flexible eGovernment service delivery.*

Draper, B., Hanson, A., & Riseman, E. (1996). Knowledge-directed vision: Control, learning, and integration. *Proceedings of the IEEE, 84*(11), 1625–1681. doi:10.1109/5.542412

Einstein, A. (1955). *The meaning of relativity.* Princeton, NJ: Princeton University Press.

Einstein, A., & Infeld, L. (1967). *Evolution of physics.* Touchstone.

Gandon, F. (2002). *Ontology engineering: A survey and a return on experience.* Technical Report RR-4396, INRIA.

Good, B. M., Kawas, E. A., & Wilkinson, M. D. (2007). *Bridging the gap between social tagging and semantic annotation.* ED, the Entity Describer. Retrieved on September 26, 2007, from http://precedings.nature.com/documents/945/version/2

Gruber, T. (1993). A translation approach to portable ontology specifications. *Knowledge Acquisition*, *5*(2), 199–220. doi:10.1006/knac.1993.1008

Gruber, T. (2005). Ontology of folksonomy: A mash-up of apples and oranges. In *MTSR'05: The First Online Conference on Metadata and Semantics Research*. Retrieved November 30, 2010, from http://tomgruber.org/writing/ontology-of-folksonomy.htm

Gruber, T., Neches, R., Fikes, R., Finin, T., Patil, R., Senator, T., & Swartout, W. R. (1991). Enabling technology for knowledge sharing. *AI Magazine*, *12*(3), 36–56.

Halliday, J. J., Shrivastava, S. K., & Wheater, S. M. (2001). Flexible workflow management in the OPENflow system. In *EDOC'01: Proceedings of the International Conference on Enterprise Distributed Object Computing*, (pp. 82-92).

Jaschke, R., Hotho, A., Schmitz, C., Ganter, B., & Stumme, G. (2008). Discovering shared conceptualizations in folksonomies. *Web Semantics: Science. Services and Agents on the World Wide Web*, *6*(1), 38–53.

Jazequel, J. M., & Meyer, B. (1997). Design by contract: The lessons of Ariane. *Computer*, *30*(1), 129–130. doi:10.1109/2.562936

Jouault, F., Allilaire, F., Bézivin, J., & Kurtev, I. (2008). ATL: A model transformation tool. *Science of Computer Programming*, *72*(1-2), 31–39. doi:10.1016/j.scico.2007.08.002

Limpens, F., Gandon, F., & Buffa, M. (2008). Rapprocher les ontologies et les folksonomies pour la gestion des connaissances partagées: Un état de l'art. In Prié, Y., & Prié, Y. (Eds.), *Actes d'IC* (pp. 123–134). Institut National Polytechnique de Lorraine.

Ludascher, B., Altintas, I., Berkley, C., Higgins, D., Jaeger, E., & Jones, M. (2006). Scientific workflow management and the Kepler system. *Concurrency and Computation*, *18*(10), 1039–1065. doi:10.1002/cpe.994

Mathes, A. (2004). *Folksonomies - Cooperative classication and communication through shared metadata*. Retrieved January 30, 2007, from http://www.adammathes.com/academic/computer-mediated-communication/folksonomies.html

Mika, P. (2007). Ontologies are us: A unified model of social networks and semantics. *Web Semantics: Science. Services and Agents on the World Wide Web*, *5*(1), 5–15. doi:10.1016/j.websem.2006.11.002

OMG. (2011). *MOF 2.0 query/views/transformations specification*. Retrieved April 30, 2011, from http://www.omg.org/spec/QVT/1.1/

Passant, A. (2007). Using ontologies to strenghten folksonomies and enrich information retrieval in weblogs: Theoretical background and corporate use-case. In *ICWSM'07: Proceedings of the International Conference on Weblogs and Social Media*, Boulder, CO.

Renouf, A. (2007). *Modélisation de la formulation d'applications de traitement d'images*. Doctoral thesis, University of Caen, France

Saidali, Y. (2002) *Modélisation et acquisition de connaissances: Application à une plate-forme de traitement d'images*. PhD thesis, University of Rouen Mont Saint Aignan.

Saidali, Y., Trupin, E., & Labiche, J. (2003) Aide à l'acquisition de connaissances en traitement d'images: Une approche basée sur la gestion d'historiques de scénarios. In *IAPR'03: Proceedings of the International Conference on Image and Signal Processing*, (pp. 138–144). Agadir, Morocco.

Saidali, Y., Trupin, E., Labiche, J., Baudouin, N., & Holzem, M. (2002). Incremental modelling and acquisition of image processing knowledge. In *Proceedings of the IADIS International Conference WWW/Internet*, (pp. 184–190). Lisbon, Portugal.

Salayandia, L., da Silva, P. P., Gates, A. Q., & Salcedo, F. (2006). Workflow-driven ontologies: An Earth sciences case study. e-*science, 17*.

Salayandia, L., Pinheiro da Silva, P., & Gates, A. Q. (2007). *WDO-It! A tool for building scientific workflows from ontologies*. (Technical Report: UTEP-CS-07-50).

Schmidt, D. C. (2006). Model-driven engineering. *Computer, 39*(2), 25–31. doi:10.1109/MC.2006.58

Schmitz, C., Hotho, A., Jaschke, R., & Stumme, G. (2006). Mining association rules in folksonomies. *Data Science and Classication*, 261–270.

Smith, B., & Welty, C. (2001). FOIS introduction: Ontology—towards a new synthesis. In *FOIS'01: Proceedings of the International Conference on Formal Ontology in Information Systems*. New York, NY: ACM.

Specification, W. M. C. (1999). *Workflow Management Coalition terminology & glossary (Document No. WFMC-TC-1011)*. Workflow Management Coalition.

Studer, R., Benjamins, R. V., & Fensel, D. (1998). Knowledge engineering: Principles and methods. *Data & Knowledge Engineering, 25*(1-2), 161–197. doi:10.1016/S0169-023X(97)00056-6

Sutter, E. (1998). Pour une écologie de l'information. *Documentaliste – Sciences de l'information, 35*(2), 83-86.

Tanasescu, V., & Streibel, O. (2007). Extreme tagging: Emergent semantics through the tagging of tags. In *ESOE'07: Proceedings of the International Workshop on Emergent Semantics and Ontology Evolution*, (pp. 84-94).

Vander Wal, T. (2007). *Folksonomy coinage and definition*. Retrieved November 30, 2010, from http://www.vanderwal.net/folksonomy.html

von Glasersfeld, E. (2001). The radical constructivist view of science. *Foundations of Science, 6*(1), 31–43. doi:10.1023/A:1011345023932

ADDITIONAL READING

Bloehdorn, S., Petridis, K., Saathoff, C., Simou, N., Avrithis, Y., Siegfried, H., et al. (2005). Semantic annotation of images and videos for multimedia analysis. In *In Proceedings of the 2nd European Semantic Web Conference, ESWC 2005*, volume 3532:592–607.

Bombardier, V., Lhoste, P., & Mazaud, C. (2004). Modélisation et intégration de connaissances métier pour l'identification de défauts par règles linguistiques floues. *Traitement du Signal, 21*(3), 227–247.

Clouard, R., Porquet, C., Elmoataz, A., & Revenu, M. (1993). Resolution of image processing problems by dynamic planning within the framework of the blackboard model. In SPIE Int. Symposium: Intelligent Robot and Computer Vision XII: Algorithms and Techniques, 2056:419–429, Boston, USA.

Crevier, D., & Lepage, R. (1997). Knowledge-based image understanding systems: a survey. *Computer Vision and Image Understanding, 67*(2), 160–185. doi:10.1006/cviu.1996.0520

Dejean, P., & Dalle, P. (1996). Image analysis operators as concept constructors. In IEEE Southwest Symposium on Image Analysis and *Interpretation*:66–70, San Antonio, Texas (USA)

Draper, B. A., Bins, J., & Baek, K. (1999). ADORE: Adaptive object recognition. In *ICVS'99: Proceedings of the International Conference on Computer Vision Systems*:522–537.

Hasegawa, J. I., Kubota, H., & Toriwaki, J. I. (1986). Automated construction of image processing procedures by sample-figure presentation. In *ICPR '86: Proceedings of the International Confer-ence for Pattern Recognition*:586–588.

Liu, Y., Zhang, D., Lu, G., & Ma, W. Y. (2007). A survey of content-based image retrieval with high-level semantics. *Pattern Recognition*, *40*(1), 262–282. doi:10.1016/j.patcog.2006.04.045

Nouvel, A. Dalle. P. (2002). An interactive ap-proach for image ontology definition. In *13ème Congrès de Reconnaissance des Formes et Intel-ligence Artificielle*:1023–1031, Angers, France.

Petridis, K., Bloehdorn, S., Saathoff, C., Simou, N., Dasiopoulou, S., & Tzouvaras, V. (2006). Knowledge representation and semantic annota-tion of multimedia content. IEE Proceedings on Vision, Image and Signal Processing - Special issue on the Integration of Knowledge. *Semantics and Digital Media Technology*, *153*(3), 255–262.

KEY TERMS AND DEFINITIONS

Business Workflow: The automation of a business process, in whole or parts, where docu-ments, information or tasks are passed from one participant to another to be processed, according to a set of procedural rules.

Constructivism: A theory of knowledge that argues that humans generate knowledge and mean-ing from an interaction between their experiences and their ideas.

Crowdsourcing: Outsourcing a task to an undefined, generally, large group.

Folksonomy: Neologism resulting of the concatenation of "folk" and "taxonomy" and are lightweight knowledge representations.

Ontology: A formal, explicit specification of a shared conceptualization.

Scientific Workflow: These are networks of analytical steps that may involve, e.g., database access and querying steps, data analysis and mining steps, and many other steps including computationally intensive jobs on high perform cluster computer.

Social Tagging: The practice of describing (annotating) objects using freely chosen keywords (tags).

Section 2
Reengineering of Software Models

Chapter 7
Software System Modernization:
An MDA–Based Approach

Liliana Favre
*Universidad Nacional del Centro de la Provincia de Buenos Aires, Argentina & Comisión de
Investigaciones Científicas de la Provincia de Buenos Aires, Argentina*

Liliana Martinez
Universidad Nacional del Centro de la Provincia de Buenos Aires, Argentina

Claudia Pereira
Universidad Nacional del Centro de la Provincia de Buenos Aires, Argentina

ABSTRACT

*System modernization requires the existence of technical frameworks for information integration and
tool interoperation that allow managing new platforms technologies, design techniques, and processes.
The Model Driven Architecture (MDA) is aligned with this requirement. It is an evolving conceptual
architecture to achieve cohesive model-driven technology specifications. MDA distinguishes the following models: Computation Independent Model (CIM), Platform Independent Model (PIM), and Platform
Specific Model (PSM). The integration of classical reverse engineering techniques with the MDA initiative will play a crucial role in software system modernization. In light of these issues, this chapter
describes a framework for MDA-based reverse engineering that integrates static and dynamic analysis,
meta-modeling, and formal specification. The essential idea is to combine static and dynamic analysis
to generate software models (PSM and PIM) from code, and to analyze the consistency of these transformations by using meta-modeling techniques and formal algebraic specification. The chapter shows
how to use reverse engineering to create PSM and PIM (that are expressed in terms of UML models)
from object oriented code. More specifically, the chapter emphasizes the bases of a reverse engineering
approach and describes how to reverse engineer class diagram, state diagram, activity diagram, and
use case diagram within the context of MDA initiative.*

DOI: 10.4018/978-1-61350-438-3.ch007

INTRODUCTION

Reverse Engineering is the process of analyzing available software artifacts such as requirements, design, architectures, code or byte code, with the objective of extracting information and providing high-level views on the underlying system.

Reverse engineering is an integral part of the modernization of legacy systems whose aging can or will have a negative impact on the economy, finance and society. These systems include software, hardware, business processes and organizational strategies and politics. Many of them may be written for technology which is expensive to maintain and which may not be aligned with current organizational politics, however they resume key knowledge acquired over the life of an organization. Important business rules are embedded in the software and, may not be documented elsewhere and the way in which legacy systems operate is not explicit. There is a high risk to replace them because they are generally business-critical systems (Sommerville, 2004).

Reverse engineering techniques are used as a mean to design software systems by evolving existing software systems for the purpose of adapt them to new requirements or technologies. 20 years ago, they focused mainly on recovering high-level architectures or diagrams from procedural code to face up to problems such as comprehending data structures or databases or the Y2K problem. By the year 2000, many different kinds of slicing techniques were developed and several studies were carried out to compare them. Basically, the initial reverse engineering techniques were based on static analysis and the concept of abstract interpretation, which amounts the program computations using value descriptions or abstract values in place of actual computed values. Abstract interpretation allows obtaining information about run time behavior without actually having to run programs on all input data.

When the object oriented languages emerged, a growing demand for reengineering object oriented systems appeared on the stage. New approaches were developed to identify objects into legacy code (e.g. legacy code in COBOL) and translate this code into an object oriented language. Object oriented programs are essentially dynamic and present particular problems linked to polymorphism, late binding, abstract classes and dynamically typed languages. For example, some object oriented languages introduce concepts such as the reflection and the possibility of loading dynamically classes, although these mechanisms are powerful, they affect the effectiveness of reverse engineering techniques. During the time object oriented programming, the focus of software analysis moved from static analysis to dynamic analysis, more precisely static analysis was complemented with dynamic analysis (Fanta & Rajlich, 1998; Systa, 2000).

When the Unified Modeling Language (UML) comes into the world, a new problem was how to extract higher level views of the system expressed by different kind of UML diagrams. Relevant work for extracting UML diagrams (e.g. class diagram, state diagram, sequence diagram, object diagram, activity diagram and package diagram) from source code was developed (Tonella & Potrich, 2005).

Nowadays, software and system engineering industry evolves to manage new platform technologies, design techniques and processes and a lot of challenges still need to be done. New technical frameworks for information integration and tool interoperation such as the Model Driven Development (MDD) created the need to develop new analysis tools and specific techniques. MDD refers to a range of development approaches that are based on the use of software models as first class entities. The most well-known is the OMG standard Model Driven Architecture (MDA), i.e., MDA is a realization of MDD (MDA, 2005).

MDA can be viewed as an evolution of OMG (Object Management Group) standards to support model centric development increasing the degree of automation of processes such as source code translation, reverse engineering, forward engineering and data reengineering. The outstanding ideas behind MDA are separating the specification of the system functionality from its implementation on specific platforms, managing the software evolution from abstract models to implementations increasing the degree of automation and achieving interoperability with multiple platforms, programming languages and formal languages.

Models play a major role in MDA which distinguishes the following:

- Computation Independent Model (CIM): a model that describes a system from the computation independent viewpoint that focuses on the environment of and the requirements for the system. In general it is called domain model.
- Platform Independent Model (PIM): a model with a high level of abstraction that is independent of any implementation technology.
- Platform Specific Model (PSM): a tailored model to specify the system in terms of the implementation constructs available in one specific platform.

Some authors also distinguish Implementation Specific Model (ISM) as a description (specification) of the system in source code (Brown, 2004; Favre, 2009).

MDA is carried out as a sequence of model transformations. We can distinguish different kinds of transformations. A refinement is the process of building a more detailed specification that conforms to another that is more abstract. Refactoring means changing a model leaving its behavior unchanged, but enhancing some non-functional quality factors such as simplicity, flexibility, understandability and performance. The relevant transformation involved in reverse engineering processes refers to the process of extracting from a more detailed specification (or

code) another one, more abstract, that is conformed by the more detailed one.

The initial diffusion of MDA was focused on its relation with UML as modeling language. However, there are UML users who do not use MDA, and MDA users who use other modeling languages such as Domain Specific Languages (DSL). The essence of MDA is MOF that allows different kinds of software artifacts to be used together in a single project. MOF provides two metamodels EMOF (Essential MOF) and CMOF (Complete MOF). EMOF favors simplicity of implementation over expressiveness. CMOF is a metamodel used to specify more sophisticated metamodels. The MOF 2.0 Query, View, Transformation (QVT) metamodel is the standard for expressing transformations. QVT has an hybrid declarative/imperative nature, with the declarative part of QVT structured into a two-layer architecture: Relations and Core, both including a metamodel and a language. In addition to the declarative parts, the imperative part includes one standard language Operational Mapping and one non-standard Black-Box (QVT, 2008).

The success of MDA depends on the existence of CASE (Computer Aided Software Engineering) tools that make a significant impact on the automation of round-trip engineering processes that provide generation of source code from models (forward engineering) and generation of models from source code (reverse engineering) (CASE Tools, 2011; CASE MDA, 2011). For instance, one or more PSM would be generated from a PIM using tools for automatic generation of platform details or, different PSM would be generated from object oriented code.

Commercial MDA tools have recently begun to emerge. In general, UML preexisting tools have been extended to support MDA. The current techniques available in these tools provide forward engineering and limited facilities for reverse engineering. Few MDA-based tools support the execution of QVT language and yet use their own transformation languages.

Validation, verification and consistency are crucial activities in the modernization of legacy systems that are critical to safety, security and economic profits. Reasoning about models of systems is well supported by automated theorem provers and model checkers, however these tools are not integrated into CASE tools environments. OMG is involved in the definition of standards to successfully modernize existing information systems and one of the main challenges is reverse engineering (ADM, 2010; KDM, 2011).

In light of the above-mentioned issues, this chapter describes an approach for MDA-based reverse engineering that integrates classical compiler techniques, metamodeling techniques and formal specification.

We propose to combine static and dynamic analysis to generate software models (PSM and PIM in particular) from code and, to analyze the consistency of these transformations by integrating metamodeling and formal specification. The bases of our approach are:

- The integration of static analysis, dynamic analysis, metamodeling techniques and formal specification.
- The definition of a formal Domain Specific Language (DSL) for defining metamodels and transformations.
- The automation of bridges between MOF metamodels and the DSL.

The chapter describes in detail code-to-model transformation based on static and dynamic analysis and their specification in terms of metamodeling techniques and algebraic specification. It includes a detailed description of reverse engineering of PSM and PIM from object oriented code. Class Diagram and State Diagram are considered at PSM level. Use Case Diagram and Activity Diagram are considered at PIM level. As an example, we analyze the reverse engineering of Java code, however the bases of our approach can be easily applied to other object oriented languages.

BACKGROUND

Related Work

Many works contributed to reverse engineering object oriented code. In (Muller, Jahnke, Smith, Storey, Tilley, & Wong, 2000) a roadmap for reverse engineering research for the first decade of the 2000s is presented. An overview of the state-of-the-art of reverse engineering techniques may be found in (Angyal, Lengyel, & Charaf, 2006). A more recent survey of existing work in the area of reverse engineering is (Canfora & Di Penta, 2007) that compares existing work, discusses success and provides a road map for possible future developments in the area.

Fanta and Rajlich (1998) describe the reengineering of a deteriorated object oriented industrial program written in C++. In order to deal with this problem, they designed and implemented several restructuring tools and used them in specific reengineering scenarios. Systa (2000) describes an experimental environment to reverse engineer Java software that integrates dynamic and static information. Demeyer, Ducasse, and Nierstrasz (2002) distinguish a variety of techniques for object oriented reengineering based on patterns.

In (Greevy, Ducasse & Girba, 2005) a novel approach to analyze the evolution of a system in terms of features reflecting how the functional roles of software artifacts change is described. They introduce visualizations to support reasoning about the evolution of a system from a feature perspective.

Tonella and Potrich (2005) provide a relevant overview of techniques that have been recently investigated and applied in the field of reverse engineering of object oriented code. They describe the algorithms involved in the recovery of UML diagrams from code and some of the techniques that can be adopted for their visualization. The algorithms deal with the reverse engineering of the following diagrams: class diagram, object and interaction diagram, state diagram and package diagram. The underlying principle in this approach is that information is derived statically by performing propagation of proper data in a data flow graph.

The increased use of data warehouse and data mining techniques had motivated an interest in data reverse technologies. In general, reverse engineering of persistent data structure of software systems is more specifically referred to as database reverse engineering. Kagdi, Collard and Maletic (2007) provide a survey and taxonomy of approaches for mining software repositories in the context of software evolution. The term Mining Software Repositories (MSR) describes a broad kind of research into the examination of software repositories including artifacts that are produced and stored during software evolution. The main contribution of this article is to present a layered taxonomy identifying four dimensions in order to objectively describe and compare the different existing approaches.

Novel approaches analyze the evolution of a system in terms of features. A feature in a program represents some functionality that is accessible by and visible to the developers, and usually captured by explicit requirements. The process of identifying the parts of code that correspond to specific functionality is called feature (or concept) location and it is part of the incremental change process. Pohyvanyk et al. (2007) analyze feature location using probabilistic ranking of methods based on execution scenarios and information retrieval and, proposes a new technique for feature location which combines an information retrieval technique with dynamic analysis.

Nowadays, software industry evolves to manage new platform technologies, design techniques and processes. There is an increased demand of modernization systems that are still business-critical in order to extend their useful lifetime. The success of system modernization depends on the existence of technical frameworks for information integration and tool interoperation like MDA.

Many works are linked to MDD-based reverse engineering. Qiao, Yang, Chu and Xu (2003) present an approach to bridging legacy systems to MDA that includes an architecture description language and a reverse engineering process. Koehler, Hauser, Kapoor, Wu, and Kumaran (2003) describe a method that implements model driven transformations between particular platform-independent (business views) and platform-specific (IT architectural) models. On the PIM level, they use business process models and on the PSM level, the IT architectural models are service-oriented and focus on specific platform using Web service and workflows. Gueheneuc (2004) proposes a study of class diagram constituents with respect to their recovery from object oriented code. Boronat, Carsi and Ramos (2005) describe MOMENT, a rigorous framework for automatic legacy system migration in MDA. MacDonald, Russell, and Atchison (2005) report on a project that assessed the feasibility of applying MDD to the evolution of a legacy system. Deissenboeck and Ratiu (2006) show the first steps towards the definition of a metamodel that unifies a conceptual view on programs with the classical structure-based reverse engineering metamodels. Reus, Geers and van Deursen (2006) describe a feasibility study in reengineering legacy systems based on grammars and metamodels.

OMG is involved in the definition of standards to successfully modernize existing information systems. The OMG Architecture-Driven Modernization (ADM) Task Force is developing a set of specifications and promoting industry consensus on modernization of existing applications. ADM refers to the process of understanding and evolving existing software assets for the purpose of software improvement, modifications, interoperability, refactoring, restructuring, reuse, porting, migration and MDA migration (ADM, 2010). Current work involves building a Knowledge Discovery Meta-model (KDM) to facilitate the exchange of existing meta-data for various modernization tools. Subsequent standards will address analysis, visualization, refactoring and transformation related to OMG standards (KDM, 2011). KDM is defined as a metamodel for describing knowledge related to various key aspects of enterprise software.

Case Tools and Reverse Engineering

Many reverse engineering tools have been implemented to reverse engineering code written in procedural programming languages such as C and Cobol (Antoniol, Fiutem, Lutteri, Tonella & Zanfei, 1997). Examples of tools include CIA (Chen, Nishimoto, & Ramamoorthy, 1990) and the Software Refinery that used an object database, called Refine, to store artifacts in the form of an attribute Abstract Syntax Tree (Markosian, Newcomb, Brand, Burson, & Kitzmiller, 1994). At the time of the Y2K problem many different tools for extracting intermediate representations from the source code and storing it into databases were built.

Bellay and Gall (1998) evaluate the capabilities of reverse engineering tools by applying them to a real-world embedded software system which implements part of a train control system. The selected tools were Refine/C (Markosian, Newcomb, Brand, Burson, & Kitzmiller, 1994), Imagix4D (Imagix4D, 2000), SNiFF+ (SNiFF+, 1996) and Rigi (Muller & Klashinsky, 1988).

Amstrong and Trudeau (1998) examined tools focusing on the abstraction and visualization of system components and interactions. The five tools they examine were: Rigi (Muller & Klashinsky, 1988), the Dali workbench (Kazman, & Carriere, 1999), the Software Bookshelf (Finnigan, Holt, Kalas, Kerr, Kontogiannis et al, 1997), CIA (Chen, Nishimoto, & Ramamoorthy, 1990) and SNiFF+ (SNiFF+, 1996).

When the Unified Modeling Language (UML) emerged, a new problem was how to extract higher level views of the system expressed by different kind of diagrams (CASE Tools, 2011). The article (Dwyer, Hatcliff, Joehanes, Laubach, Pasareanu, Robby, Zheng, & Visser, 2001) describes

an integrated collection of program analysis and transformation components, called Bandera that enables the automatic extraction of safe, compact finite-state models from program source code.

The reverse engineering tool RevEng extracts UML diagrams from C++ code. Among the diagrams that RevEng extracts are class diagram, object diagram, state diagram, sequence and collaboration diagrams and package diagram (Potrich & Tonella, 2005).

Mansurov and Campara (2005) describe a tool-assisted way of introducing models in the migration towards MDA. They propose to automatically extract architecturally significant models (called Container models) and subsequently refactoring them to achieve models in higher-level of abstraction.

The Fujaba Tool Suite project is suited to provide an easy to extend UML, Story Driven Modeling and Graph Transformation platform with the ability to add plug-ins (FUJUBA, 2011). It combines UML static diagrams and UML behavior diagrams (Story Diagrams). Furthermore, it supports the generation of Java code. Fujaba is configured with plug-ins for Reverse Engineering and Design Pattern recognition.

The success of MDA depends on the existence of CASE tools that make a significant impact on software processes such as forward engineering and reverse engineering processes. All of the MDA tools are partially compliant to MDA features. They provide good support for modeling and limited support for automated transformation in reverse engineering. They generally support MDD from the PIM level and use UML class diagrams for designing PIM. As an example we can mention ArcStyler, one of the first products to embrace MDA using the relevant technology standards and providing model transformation. The main MDA Case tools and their facilities are described in (CASE MDA, 2011).

Techniques that currently exist in MDA CASE tools provide little support for validating models in the design stages. Reasoning about models of systems is well supported by automated theorem provers and model checkers, however these tools are not integrated into CASE tools environments. Another problem is that as soon as the requirements specifications are handed down, the system architecture begins to deviate from specifications. Only research tools provide support for formal specification and deductive verification. As an example, we can mention Use 3.0 that is a system for specification of information systems in OCL. Use allows snapshots of running systems can be created and manipulated during an animation, checking OCL constraints to validate the specification against non-formal requirements (Use, 2011). Many CASE tools support reverse engineering, however, they only use more basic notational features with a direct code representation and produce very large diagrams. Reverse engineering processes are facilitated by inserting annotations in the generated code. These annotations are the link between the model elements and the language. As such, they should be kept intact and not be changed. It is the programmer's responsibility to know what he or she can modify and what he or she cannot modify.

The Eclipse Modeling Framework (EMF) (Eclipse, 2011) was created for facilitating system modeling and the automatic generation of Java code. EMF started as an implementation of MOF resulting Ecore, the EMF metamodel comparable to EMOF. EMF has evolved starting from the experience of the Eclipse community to implement a variety of tools and to date is highly related to Model Driven engineering (MDE). For instance, ATL (Atlas Transformation Language) is a model transformation language in the field of MDE that is developed on top of the Eclipse platform (ATL, 2011). Commercial tools such as IBM Rational Software Architect, Spark System Enterprise Architect or Together are integrated with Eclipse-EMF (CASE MDA, 2011; Eclipse, 2011).

Few MDA-based CASE tools support QVT or at least, any of the QVT languages. As an example, IBM Rational Software Architect and Spark System Enterprise Architect do not implement QVT. Other tools partially support QVT, for instance Together allows defining and modifying transformations model-to-model (M2M) and model-to-text (M2T) that are QVT-Operational compliant.

Medini QVT partially implements QVT (Medini, 2011). It is integrated with Eclipse and allows the execution of transformations expressed in the QVT-Relation language. Eclipse M2M, the official tool compatible with of Eclipse 3.5 and EMF 2.5.0, is still under development and implements the specification of QVT-Operational. MoDisco (Modisco, 2011) provides an extensible framework to develop model-driven tools to support use-cases of existing software modernization. It uses EMF to describe and manipulate models, M2M to implement transformation of models into other models, Eclipse M2T to implement generation of text and Eclipse Java Development Tools (JDT).

A FRAMEWORK FOR REVERSE ENGINEERING

We propose to reverse engineering MDA models from object oriented code starting from the integration of compiler techniques, metamodeling and formal specification. Figure 1 shows a framework for reverse engineering that integrates static and dynamic analysis, metamodeling and formal specification. It distinguishes three different abstraction levels linked to models, metamodels and formal specifications.

The model level includes code, PIM and PSM. A PIM is a model with a high level of abstraction that is independent of an implementation technology (MDA, 2005). A PSM is a tailored model to specify a system in terms of specific platform such J2EE or.NET. PIM and PSM are expressed in UML and OCL (UML, 2010a) (UML, 2010b) (OCL, 2010). The subset of UML diagrams that

Figure 1. Framework for MDA-based reverse engineering

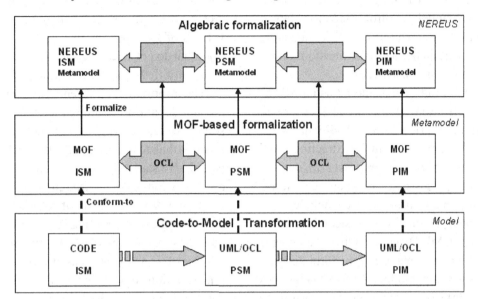

are useful for PSM includes class diagram, object diagram, state diagram, interaction diagram and package diagram. On the other hand, a PIM can be expressed by means of use case diagrams, activity diagrams, interactions diagrams to model system processes and, state diagrams to model lifecycle of the system entities. An ISM is a specification of the system in source code.

At model level, transformations are based on classical compiler construction techniques. They involve processes with different degrees of automation, which can go from totally automatic static analysis to human intervention requiring processes to dynamically analyze the resultant models. All the algorithms that deal with the reverse engineering share an analysis framework. The basic idea is to describe source code or models by an abstract language and perform a propagation analysis in a data-flow graph called in this context Object Flow Graph (OFG) (Tonella & Potrich, 2005). This static analysis is complemented with dynamic analysis supported by tracer tools.

The metamodel level includes MOF metamodels that describe the transformations at model level (MOF, 2006). A metamodel is an explicit model of the constructs and rules needed to construct specific models. MOF metamodels use an object modeling framework that is essentially a subset of UML 2.3 core (UML, 2010a). The modeling concepts are classes which model MOF metaobjects, associations, which model binary relations between metaobjects, data types which model other data, and packages which modularize the models. At this level MOF metamodels describe families of ISM, PSM and PIM. Every ISM, PSM and PIM conforms to a MOF metamodel. Metamodel transformations are specified as OCL contracts between a source metamodel and a target metamodel. MOF metamodels "control" the consistency of these transformations.

The level of formal specification includes specifications of MOF metamodels and metamodel transformations in the metamodeling language NEREUS that can be used to connect them with different formal and programming languages (Favre, 2006) (Favre, 2009).

To sum up, in the level of models, instances of ISM, PSM and PIM are generated by applying static and dynamic analysis. Static analysis builds an abstract model of the state and determines how the program executes to this state. Dynamic analysis operates by executing a program and evaluating the execution trace of the program. Contracts based on MOF-metamodels "control" the consistency of these transformations and NEREUS facilitates the connection of the metamodels and transformations with different formal languages.

Our work could be considered as an MDA-based formalization of the process described by Tonella and Potrich (2005). Additionally, we propose a different algorithm for extracting UML State diagrams and new processes to recover PIM including Uses cases Diagram and Activity Diagram. We also propose to include OCL specifications (preconditions, postconditions and invariants) in UML Diagrams. Other advantages are linked to the automation of the formalization process and interoperability of formal languages (Favre, 2009a) (Favre, 2009b) (Favre, Martinez & Pereira, 2009).

The following sections describe reverse engineering at three different levels of abstraction corresponding to code-to-model transformation, MOF-metamodel formalization and algebraic formalization.

CODE-TO-MODEL TRANSFORMATIONS

At model level, transformations are based on static and dynamic analysis. Static analysis extracts static information that describes the structure of the software reflected in the software documentation (e.g., the text of the source code) while dynamic analysis information describes the structure of the run-behavior. Static information can be extracted by using techniques and tools based on compiler techniques such as parsing and data flow algorithms. On the other hand, dynamic information can be extracted by using debuggers, event recorders and general tracer tools.

We describe the process for recovering PIM and PSM from code. Figure 2 shows the different phases. The source code is parsed to obtain an abstract syntax tree (AST) associated with the

source programming language grammar. Next, a metamodel extractor extracts a simplified, abstract version of the language that ignores all instructions that do not affect the data flows, for instance all control flows such as conditional and loops.

The information represented according to this metamodel allows building the OFG for a given source code, as well as conducting all other analysis that do not depend on the graph. The idea is to derive statically information by performing a propagation of data. Different kinds of analysis propagate different kinds of information in the data-flow graph, extracting the different kinds of diagrams that are included in a model.

The static analysis is based on classical compiler techniques (Aho, Sethi & Ullman, 1985) and abstract interpretation (Jones & Nielson, 1995). The generic flow propagation algorithms are specializations of classical flow analysis techniques. Because there are many possible executions, it is usually not reasonable to consider all state of the program. Thus, static analysis is based on abstract models of the program state that are easier to ma-

Figure 2. Reverse engineering at model level: Static and dynamic analysis

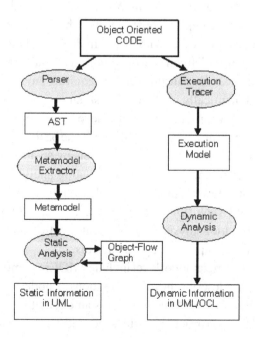

nipulate, although lose some information. Abstract interpretation of program state allows obtaining automatically as much information as possible about program executions without having to run the program on all input data and then ensuring computability or tractability.

The static analysis builds a partial model (PIM or PSM) that must be refined by dynamic analysis. Dynamic analysis is based on testing and profiling. Execution tracer tools generate execution model snapshots that allow us to deduce complementary information. Execution models, programs and UML models coexist in this process. An object oriented execution model has the following components: a set of objects, a set of attributes for each object, a location for each object, each object refers to a value of an object type and, a set of messages that include a name selector and may include one or more arguments. Additionally, types are available for describing types of attributes and parameters of methods or constructors. On the other hand, an object oriented program model has a set of classes, a set of attributes for each class, a set of operations for each class, and a generalization hierarchy over classes.

The combination of static and dynamic analysis can enrich reverse engineering process. There are different ways of combination, for instance performing first static analysis and then dynamic analysis or perhaps iterating static and dynamic analysis. Different kinds of analysis propagate different kind of information in a dataflow graph. This is built by parsing the source code described by a grammar.

Static Analysis

The concepts and algorithms of data flow analysis described in (Aho, Sethi & Ullman, 1985) are adapted for reverse engineering object oriented code. The data flow analysis can be viewed as the transmission of useful relationships from all parts of the code to the places when the information can be used.

The basic representation of the static analysis is the Object Flow Graph (OFG) that allows tracing information of object interactions from the object creation, through object assignment to variables, the storage of objects in attributes or their use in messages (method invocations). OFG is defined as an oriented graph that represents all data flows linking objects.

The static analysis is data flow sensitive, but control flow insensitive. This means that programs with different control flows and the same data flows are associated with the same analysis results. The choice of this program representation is motivated by the computational complexity of the involved algorithms. On the one hand, control flow sensitive analysis is computationally intractable and on the other hand, data flow sensitive analysis is aligned to the "nature" of the object oriented programs whose execution models impose more constraints on the data flows than on the control flows. For example, the sequence of method invocations may change when moving from an application which uses a class to another one, while the possible ways to copy and propagate object references remains more stable.

A consequence of the control flow insensitivity is that the construction of the OFG can be described with reference to a simplified, abstract version of the object oriented languages in which instructions related to flow control are ignored. A generic algorithm of flow propagation working on the OFG processes object information. In the following, we describe the three essential components of the common analysis framework: the simplified abstract object oriented language, the data flow graph and the flow propagation algorithm.

A Simplified Object Oriented Language

All instructions that refer to data flows are represented in the abstract language, while all control flow instructions such as conditional and different iteration constructs are ignored. To avoid name conflicts all identifiers are given fully scoped names including a list of enclosing packages, classes and methods. The abstract syntax of simplified language (Tonella & Potrich, 2005) is as follows:

(1) $P ::= D*S*$
(2) $D ::= a$
(3) $| \ m \ (p_1, p_2, \ldots, p_j)$
(4) $| \ cons \ (p_1, p_2, \ldots, p_j)$
(5) $S ::= x = new \ c \ (a_1, a_2, \ldots a_j)$
(6) $| \ x = y$
(7) $| \ [x =] \ y.m \ (a_1, a_2, \ldots, a_j)$

Some notational conventions are considered: non-terminals are denoted by upper case letters; a is class attribute name; m is method name; $p_1, p_2 \ldots p_j$ are formal parameters; x and y are program locations; $a_1, a_2 \ldots a_j$ are actual parameters; *cons* is class constructor and c is class name.

A program P consists of zero or more declarations (D*) concatenated with zero or more statements (S*). The order of declarations and instructions is irrelevant. The nesting structure of packages, classes and statements is flattened, i.e. statements belonging to different methods are merged and identified by their fully scope names. The process of transformation of an object oriented program into a simplified language can be easily automated.

There are three types of declaration production: attribute declarations (2), method declarations (3) and constructor declaration (4). An attribute declaration is defined by the scope determined by the list of packages, classes, followed by the attribute identifier. A method declaration consists in its name followed by a list of formal parameter $(p_1, p_2 \ldots p_j)$. Constructors have a similar declaration.

There are three types of statement production: allocation statements (5), assignments (6) and method invocation (7). The left hand side and the right hand side of all statements is a program location. The target of a method invocation is also a program location. Program locations are either, local variables, class attributes or method parameters.

Object Flow Graph (OFG)

OFG is a pair (N, E) where N is a set of nodes and E is a set of edges. A node is added for each program location (i.e. formal parameter or attribute). Edges represent the data flows appearing in the program. They are added to the OFG according to the rules specified in (Tonella & Potrich, 2005, pp. 26). Table 1 describes the rules for constructing OFG from Java statements.

When a constructor or method is invoked, edges are built which connect each actual parameter a_i to the respective formal parameter p_i. In case of constructor invocation, the newly created object, referenced by *cons.this* is paired with the left hand side x of the related assignment. In case of method invocation, the target object y becomes *m.this* inside the called method, generating the edge *(y, m.this),* and the value returned by method m (if any) flows to the left hand side x (pair *(m.return, x)*).

Some edges in the OFG may be related to the usage of class library. Each time a library class introduces a data flow from a variable x to a variable y an edge *(x,y)* must be included in the OFG. Containers are an example of library classes that introduce external data flows, for instance, any

Table 1.

(1)	$P ::= D*S*$	{ }
(2)	$D ::= a$	{ }
(3)	$| \ m \ (p_1, p_2, \ldots, p_j)$	{ }
(4)	$| \ cons \ (p_1, p_2, \ldots, p_j)$	{ }
(5)	$S ::= x = new \ c \ (a_1, a_2, \ldots a_j)$	$\{(a_1, p_1) \in E, ..(a_j, p_j) \in E, (cons.this, x) \in E\}$
(6)	$| \ x = y$	$\{(y, x) \in E\}$
(7)	$| \ [x =] \ y.m \ (a_1, a_2, \ldots, a_j)$	$\{(y, m.this) \in E, (a_1, p_1) \in E, ..(a_j, p_j) \in E, (m.return, x) \in E\}$

Java class implementing the interface Collection or the interface Map.

Object containers provide two basic operations affecting the OFG: *insert* and *extract* for adding an object to a container and accessing an object in a container respectively. In the abstract program representation, insertion and extraction methods are associated with container objects. Other cases require that data flows are modeled semi-automatically in a similar way as done for the class libraries, for instance dynamic loading and the access to code written in other programming languages.

Flow Propagation Algorithm

Next, we show a pseudo-code of generic forward propagation algorithm that is a specific instance of the algorithms applied to control flow graph described in (Aho, Sethi & Ullman, 1985):

```
for each node n ∈N
in[n] = {};
out[n]= gen[n] U (in[n] - kill[n])
endfor
while any in[n] or out[n] changes
for each node n ∈N
in[n] = U_p∈pred(n) out[p];
out[n] = gen[n] U(in[n] - kill[n])
endfor
endwhile
```

Let *gen[n]* and *kill[n]* be two sets of each basic node n ∈ N. *gen[n]* is the set of flow information entities generated by *n*. *kill[n]* is the set of definition outside of *n* that define entities that also have definitions within *n*. There are two sets of equations, called data-flow equations that relate incoming and outgoing flow information inside the sets *in[n]* and *out[n]*:

```
in[n] = U_p∈pred(n) out[p]
out[n] = gen[n] U (in[n] - kill[n])
```

Each node *n* stores the incoming and outgoing flow information inside the sets *in[n]* and *out[n]*, which are initially empty. Each node *n* generates the set of flow information entities included in *gen[s]* set, and prevents the elements of *kill[n]* set from being further propagated after node *n*. In forward propagation *in[n]* is obtained from the predecessors of node *n* as the union of the respective *out* sets.

In some cases, it may be appropriate to propagate information in reverse order by collecting the incoming information from the out sets of the successors.

The OFG constructed in based on the previous rules is "object insensitive". An object sensitive OFG might improve the analysis results. It can be built by giving all non-static program names an object scope instead a class scope and object can be identified statically by their allocation points. Thus, in an object sensitive OFG, non-static class attributes and methods with their parameters and local variables, are replicated for every statically identified object.

Dynamic Analysis

Dynamic analysis allows generating execution snapshot to collect life cycle traces of object instances and reason from tests and proofs. Ernst (2003) argues that whereas the chief challenge of static analysis is choosing a good abstract interpretation, the chief challenge of performing good dynamic analysis is selecting a representative set of test cases. A test can help to detect properties of the program, but it can be difficult to detect whether results of a test are true program properties or properties of a particular execution context.

Integrating dynamic and static analysis seems to be beneficial. For instance, the static analysis is not enough to determine the actual method invocations due to polymorphism. This is only possible by analyzing the behavior. The static and dynamic information could be shown as separated views or merged in a single view. In general, the dynamic behavior could be visualized as a scenery diagram which describes interaction between objects. To extract specific information, it is necessary to define particular views of these sceneries. Although, the construction of these views can be automated, their analysis requires some manual processing in most cases.

Dynamic analysis is based on object oriented execution model and object oriented program model. The first includes a set of objects, a set of attributes for each object, a location and a value for each object, and a set of messages.

The information that must be available from the execution traces to support the construction of diagrams consists of:

- Object identifiers which are computed within the execution of class constructors,
- Identifier of the current object and of the object on which each invocation is issued, which are included to the execution traces.
- Time stamps linked with method calls which are produced and traced.

The processing of the execution trace provides a diagram for each trace executed and depends on the quality of the test cases.

Maoz and Harel (2010) present a powerful technique for the visualization and exploration of execution traces of models that is different from previous approaches that consider execution traces at the code level. This technique belongs to the domain of model-based dynamic analysis adapting classical visualization paradigms and techniques to specific needs of dynamic analysis. It allows relating the system execution traces and its models in different tasks such as testing whether a system run satisfies model properties. We consider that these results allow us to address reverse engineering challenges in the context of model-driven development.

FROM CODE TO MODELS

Recovering Class Diagram

A class diagram is a representation of the static view that shows a collection of static model elements, such as classes, interfaces, methods, attributes, types as well as their properties (e.g., type and visibility). Besides, the class diagram shows the interrelationships holding among the classes (UML, 2010a; UML, 2010b).

Reverse engineering of class diagram from code is difficult task that cannot be automated due to certain elements in the class diagram carry behavioral information that cannot be inferred just from the analysis of the code. By analyzing the syntax of the source code, internal class features such as attributes and methods and their properties (e.g. the parameters of the methods and visibility) can be recovered. From the source code, associations, generalization, realizations and dependencies may be inferred too. However, to distinguish between aggregation and composition, or to include OCL specifications (e.g. preconditions and postconditions of operations, invariants and association constraints) we need to capture system states through dynamic analysis.

Figure 3 shows relationships that can be detected statically between a Java program and a UML class diagram.

Dynamic analysis allows generating execution snapshot to collect life cycle traces of object instances and reason from tests and proofs. Execution tracer tools generate execution model snapshots that allow us to deduce complementary information, for instance to detect compositions. A composition is a particular aggregation in which the lifetime of the part is controlled by the whole (directly or transitively) and we can identify it by generating tests and scanning dependency configurations between the birth and the death of a part object according to those of the whole. In the same way, the execution traces of different in-

Figure 3. Java constructs versus class diagram constructs

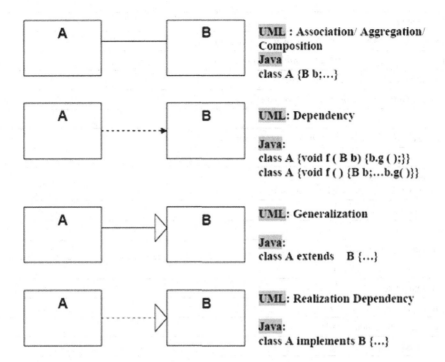

stances of the same class or method, could guide the construction of invariants or pre- and post-conditions respectively.

Recovering State Diagram

A state transition diagram describes the life cycle of objects that are instances of a class from the time they are created until they are destroyed. Object state is determined by the value of its attributes and possibly by the variables involved in attribute computations. The basic elements of a state diagram are states, identified as equivalence classes of attribute values and, transitions triggered by method invocation.

In our context, an abstract interpretation performs method invocation using abstract domains instead of concrete attribute values to deduce information about the object computation on its actual state from the resulting abstract descriptions of its attributes. This implies to abstract equivalence classes that group attribute values

corresponding to the different states in which the class can be and the transitions among state equivalence classes. The key is to define when two states s and t are equivalent, that is, for any input sequence, the paths from s and t labeled by that sequence of labels lead to state equivalence class. The recovery algorithm should iterate over the following activities: the construction of a finite automaton by executing abstract interpretations of class methods and the minimization of the automaton for recovering approximate state equivalence classes.

A taxonomy of finite-state automata minimization can be found at (Watson, 1995) and (Daciuk, 1998). The main characteristic of these algorithms is that they are incremental. The minimization algorithm should compare incrementally the equivalence between pairs of states to determine whether they can be merged in an only state. Table 2 shows the pseudo code of the proposed recovery algorithm based on an incremental minimization

Table 2. Algorithm for recovering state diagrams

	/* initialization of different sets*/
(1)	set-of-states initialStates = {}; /*states defined by class constructors*/
(2)	set-of-states pendingStates ={};/*set of states pending of analysis*/
(3)	set-of-states allStates = {};/*set of all states*/
	/*definition of initial states for the objects of the class*/
(4)	**for** each class constructor c
	/*executing an abstract interpretation of each class constructor*/
(5)	state s = abstractInterpretationState (c, {});
(6) (7)	initialStates = initialStates ∪ {s}; pendingStatesPending = pendingStates ∪ {s};
(8)	allStates = allStates ∪{s}
	endfor
	/*initialization of set-of-bins*/
(9)	set-of-bins b = empty-set-of-bins
(10	**while** |pendingStates| > 0
	/*initialization of transition set*/
(11)	set-of-transitions transitionSet = {};
(12)	state r = extract (pendingStates);
(13)	pendingState = pendingStates – {r};
(14)	**for** each transformer class method m
	/*generating transitions of the state r*/
(15)	s = abstractInterpretationState (m, r);
(16	**if** s ∉ allStates
(17)	pendingStates = pendingStates ∪ {s};
(18)	allStates = allStates ∪ {s}
	endif
(19)	transitionSet = transitionSet ∪ abstractInterpretationTransition (m,r,s)
	endfor
	/*updating subsets of transformer methods*/
(20)	b = modifyBins (r, transitionSet, allStates);
(21)	**for** each e ∈ b
(22)	**if** s ∈ b {/*defining equivalence of states and merging equivalent states*/
(23)	**for** each q ∈ b and s<> q
(24)	**if** equivalents (s, q) mergeStates (transitionSet, allStates, s, q) **endif**
	endfor
	endif
	endfor
	endwhile

each time a state is candidate to be added to the automaton.

This algorithm assumes that an abstract domain for the class attributes and variables involved in the attribute computations has been defined. Considerable human interaction to select which abstract interpretations should be executed is required. First of all, the algorithm initializes three sets: *initialStates*, *pendingStates* and *allStates*. *initialStates* includes the initial states defined by class constructors, in which any object of the class can be; *pendingStates* refers to the set of states pending of analysis and *allStates* is the set of "all" states the diagram. The initialization of the three sets is implemented by lines 1, 2 and 3. The first iteration (line 4) executes an abstract interpretation of each class constructor. The state *s* (line 5) obtained at the exit of each constructor is a possible initial state and is included in *initialStates* (line 6). Each state obtained by execution of class constructors is a possible starting point for method invocation and then must be inserted in the *pendingState* set (line 7). Next, it is added into the *allState* set (line 8). *transitionSet* is a set of transitions (line 9). An abstract interpretation for transitions is defined. Note that the labels of the transitions are linked only to methods that yields new instances of the interest class from existing instances of it (and possible instances of other types). In this context, this kind of method is called "transformer" distinguishing it from the query methods which yield properties of instances of the interest class. To optimize the comparison of pairs of states, states are classified according to their emerging transitions. Let *m* be a bound of the number of transformer methods of a class, the idea is to generate subsets of the set of transformer methods. Initially, *set-of-bins* contains one bin for each subset of transformer methods (line 10). The subset of emerging transitions of a new state belongs, in a particular snapshot, to one of them. Two states are candidates to be equivalent if they belong to the same subset of bins. Then, it is sufficient to compare all the pairs composed

by the state and one element of the respective subset.

To ensure tractability, our algorithm proposes an incremental minimization every time a state is candidate to be added to the automaton. The algorithm iterates over each pending states (line 10), generating a set of transitions for each method transformer (lines 11 to 19). Next, the algorithm updates the subset of bins (line 20). When it is detected that two states are equivalents, they are merged in an only state (lines 20 to 24). This could lead to modification of the parts of the automaton that had been previously minimized.

As an example, Figure 4 a shows a diagram including states $(s_1, s_2.., s_8)$ and transitions $(m_1, m_2, ... , m_6)$. Figure 4 b shows a simplified snapshot of the automaton when a transition to s_5 is added. Then, the shaded states could belong to the same equivalence state class. s_8 belongs to the same subset of s_4 and an equivalence analysis is carried out concluding that s_8 and s_4 can be merged (Figure 4.c, Figure 4.d). Figure 4.e shows the successive transformations.

Recovering Activity Diagram

Activity diagrams model the dynamic aspects of a system. They show the flow from activity to activity within a system. Activity diagrams may stand alone to visualize, specify, construct, and document the dynamics of a society of objects, or they may be used to model the flow of control of an operation. This process makes sense if the operation is complex enough, that is to say, it involves many activities.

The OFG represents all data flows involving objects and allows tracing the flow of information about objects from the object creation by allocation statements, trough object assignment to variables, up until the storage of objects in class fields or their usage in method invocation. A generic flow propagation algorithm working on the OFG is used to infer properties about the program objects. The following pseudo-code of generic

Figure 4. Recovering minimum state diagram

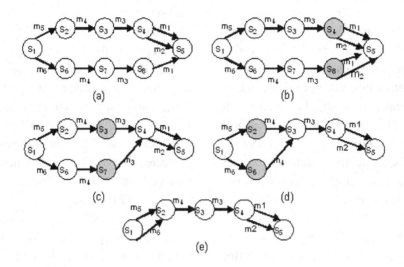

flow propagation algorithm is a specific instance of the algorithms applied to control flow graph:

```
for each node n ∈ OFG
in[n] = {};
out[n] = gen[n] U (in[n] -kill[n])
endfor
while any in[n] or out [n] changes
foreach node n ∈ OF
in[n] = U_{p∈pred(n)} out[p];
out[n] = gen[n] U (in[n]- kill[n])
endfor
endwhile
```

Each node *n* of the OFG stores the incoming and outgoing flow information respectively inside the sets *in[n]* and *out[n]*, which are initially empty. Moreover, each node *n* generates the set of flow information items contained in the *gen[n]* set, and prevents the elements in the *kill[n]* set from being further propagated after node *n*. Incoming flow information is obtained from the predecessors of node *n* as the union of the respective out sets (forward propagation).

To recovery activity diagram which model the operation workflow, the following diagram elements are required:

Action states: They represent the execution of an action, typically the invocation of an operation. An action represents a single step within an activity. Actions are deduced from method calls. For instance:

Class A f () {... p.g(); // this --- g ---> p }

this, instance of A, sends the message *g* to object *p*. *p* may be a variable of *f* or a class attribute.

The message *g* represents an action carried out by *p*.

1. *Swimlanes*: They are partitions on an interaction diagram to organize responsibilities for actions. They are inferred from the classes that implement the action.

2. *Transitions*: They represent the flow of control among consecutive action states. These are determined by dynamic analysis.

3. *Objects*: They are deduced from local variables and parameters of the operation. These objects are connected using a dependence relationship to the action or transition that creates, destroys or modifies them. This use of dependency relationships and objects is

called an object flow, it represents the participation of an object in a control flow.

The recovery of activity diagram elements that model the operation workflow is done in two steps:

1. Apply the algorithm of object flow propagation on the OFG constructed from the abstract code of the operation,
2. Execute the activity resolution algorithm for each call expression in the operation abstract code. Next, the pseudocode of the algorithm is shown:

```
resolveActivity (expr: 'p.g(a₁,…
,aₖ)'): Pair
A = class (scope(expr));
f = method (scope(expr));
objects = {};
if p is a class attribute
swimlanes = types(out [A.p]);….
else swimlanes = types(out [A.f.p])
endif
for each i in 1≤ i ≤ k
objects = objects ∪ in[A.f.aᵢ]
endfor
return (swimlanes, objects)
```

resolveActivity is applied to a call expression of the form $p.g(a_1, ..., a_k)$ inside a method f of class A. As a result, this algorithm returns a pair of sets, swimlanes and objects, containing types and object identifiers respectively. The swimlanes set is obtained by the types of the objects referenced by the location p (*out[A.f.p]* or *out[A.p]* in case p is a class attribute). More complex Java expressions involving method calls can be easily reduced to the case reported in *resolveActivity*. For instance, if a chain of attribute accesses precedes the method call, as in $p.q.g()$, the invocation targets are obtained from the last involved attribute: *out[B.q]*, where B is the class of the attribute q accessed

through p. The objects set is obtained from the objects referenced by the location a_i (*in[A.f.a_i]*).

Once activity diagram elements have been obtained, dynamic analysis allows determining the call flow (sequential, concurrent or alternative) through the execution traces generated by executing the code on a set of test cases. Moreover, dynamic analysis can be used to detect functionality that may never be executed.

Next, the activity diagram is obtained drawing an action for each call expression in the corresponding swimlane. The transitions are drawn among action states based on the information obtained through the dynamic analysis. The diagram is complemented with the objects and object flow. Tonella and Potrich (2005) exemplify reverse engineering by using the Java program *e-Lib* that support the main library functions. We exemplify the steps of the activity diagram recovery process in terms of this example (Figure 5). Figure 5 a and 5 b show Java code and abstract code of method *addLoan* of the class Library respectively. Figure 5 c shows the portion of OFG that contain the information obtained from applying the algorithm of object flow propagation, which is required to apply the activity resolution algorithm. Finally, Figure 5 d shows objects and swimlanes for each method call inside the method *addLoan* which are obtained by the *resolveActivity* algorithm. From this information, it is straightforward to build the activity diagram for the method *addLoan* (Figure 5 e).

Recovering Use Case Diagram

Use case diagrams model the dynamic aspects of a system being central to model the behavior of a system, a subsystem, or a class. Each diagram shows a set of use cases, actors and their relationships.

To recover use cases the following diagram elements are required:

Figure 5. Recovering activity diagram from Java code

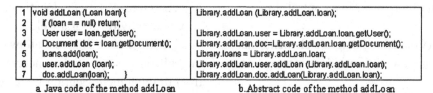

1	void addLoan (Loan loan) {	Library.addLoan (Library.addLoan. loan);
2	if (loan = = null) return;	
3	User user = loan.getUser();	Library.addLoan.user = Library.addLoan.loan.getUser();
4	Document doc = loan.getDocument();	Library.addLoan.doc=Library.addLoan.loan.getDocument();
5	loans.add(loan);	Library.loans = Library.addLoan.loan;
6	user.addLoan (loan);	Library.addLoan.user.addLoan (Library.addLoan.loan);
7	doc.addLoan(loan); }	Library.addLoan.doc.addLoan(Library.addLoan.loan);

a. Java code of the method addLoan   b. Abstract code of the method addLoan

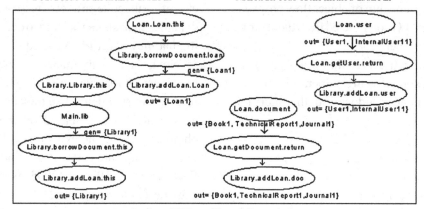

c. Portion of OFG used for activity resolution

Line	Calls	Swimlanes	Objects
1	Library.addLoan (Library.addLoan.loan)	Library	Loan1
3	Library.addLoan.loan.getUser ()	Loan	
4	Library.addLoan.loan.getDocument()	Loan	
6	Library.addLoan.user.addLoan (Library.addLoan.loan)	User, InternalUser	Loan1
7	Library.addLoan.doc.addLoan (Library.addLoan.loan)	Book, TechnicalReport, Journal	Loan1

d. Swimlanes and object returned by the algorithm

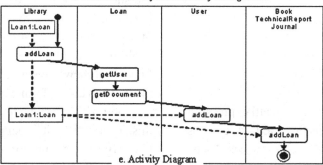

e. Activity Diagram

1. *Use case*: It is a description of a set of sequences of actions that a system performs to yield an observable result of value to an actor. Basic use cases are extracted analyzing public methods. Each public method of a class corresponds to a basic use case whose name is the same as the method name.

2. *Generalization*: It is a relationship where the child use case inherits the behavior and meaning of the parent use case; the child may add to or override its parent's behavior. For each pair of same-name methods which are members of different classes with a generalization between them, a generalization between use cases corresponding to these methods is generated. To determine the right kind of the relationship, either redefine or

enrichment, the expertise of the software engineer is needed.

3. *Dependency*: It is a using relationship between two use cases in which a change to one use case (the independent use case) may affect the semantics of the other use case (the dependent use case). For each public method of a class, the method calls are analyzed to extract dependence relationships among basic use cases. Each message sent to an object corresponds to a dependence relationship between use cases. The kind of relationship, either *include* or *extend*, may be inferred by a dynamic analysis.

4. *Actor*: It represents a coherent set of roles that users of use cases play when interacting with these use cases. Actors are not actually part of the system. They live outside despite being used in the models. Hence, actors cannot be automatically inferred.

Reverse engineering of the use case diagrams is done in three steps.

1. Generate abstract code from Java code.
2. Execute the algorithm for static recovery. It is executed on the abstract code, and it returns three sets containing use cases, dependences and generalizations. These sets are statically determined and allow obtaining relevant information to recover diagrams. Once these sets have been initialized as empty sets, the first step of the algorithm is to obtain the use case set. For each public method in the abstract code, a new use case is generated and included in the set. If there are methods with the same name, each method name is prefixed by the class name.

The second step is to obtain the dependence set. For each expression '*p.g()*' included in a public method *m* on the abstract code, if *g* is a public method, a dependence relationship between the use cases corresponding to *m* and *g* is included

in the set. Finally, the algorithm obtains the generalization set. For each pair of same-name use cases that correspond to methods of different classes that have a generalization relationship between them, a generalization between the use cases corresponding to these methods is generated. Algorithm 1 summarizes this step.

3. Perform dynamic analysis to determinate the kind of dependence relationship between use cases in the dependence set. Each initial use case obtained during static analysis corresponds to a method. For each of these methods, the system is executed to recover all possible threads, primary flow and alternative paths. The common sub-thread reflects primary flow and allows detecting possible include relationships between use cases whereas other sub-threads may correspond to extend relationships. The software engineer is required to accomplish this task. Moreover, dynamic analysis allows detecting functionality that may never be executed. In this case, the knowledge and expertise of the software engineer will be required to determine irrelevant use cases.

Figure 6 exemplifies the steps of the recovery process in terms of the *e-Lib* example described in (Tonella & Potrich, 2005). Figure 6.a and 6.b partially show Java code and abstract code. Figure 6.c shows outputs of the algorithm to recover use case diagrams. From this information, it is straightforward to build the use case diagrams (Figure 6.d). The proposed recovery process allows obtaining use case diagrams that correspond to a low-level functional view. To obtain higher-level views, use cases may be clustered in single abstract use case by applying simple heuristics. For instance, if a use case includes or extends exclusively a group of use cases, the use cases are clustered in a single abstract use case shown in a separate diagram.

Algorithm 1.

```
/* initialization of sets*/
useCases = { };
dependences = { };
generalizations = { };
/*generating useCases set*/
for each public method m
useCases = useCases ∪ { m }
endfor
/*generating dependences set*/
for each expr: 'p.g()' / g is a public method
m = method(scope(expr));
dependences = dependences ∪ { (m, g) }
endfor
/*generating generalizations set*/
for each mᵢ in useCases
  for each mₖ <>mᵢ in useCases
    if name(mₖ) = name(mᵢ)
      if class(mₖ) is parent of class (mᵢ)
        generalizations = generalizations ∪ { (mᵢ,mₖ) }
      else if class (mᵢ) is parent of class (mₖ)
              if class (mᵢ) is parent of class (mₖ)
                  generalizations = generalizations ∪ { (mₖ,mᵢ) }
              endif
            endif
      endif
    endif
  endfor
endfor
```

MOF-BASED FORMALIZATION

From Java to PSM

Metamodel transformations impose relations between a source metamodel and a target metamodel, both represented as MOF-metamodels. The transformations between models are described starting from the metaclass of the elements of the source model and the metaclass of the elements of the target model. The models to be transformed and the target models will be instances of the corresponding metamodel. Transformation semantics is aligned with QVT, in particular with the QVT Core. QVT depends on EssentialOCL (OCL, 2010) and EMOF (MOF, 2006). EMOF is a subset of MOF that allows simple metamodels to be defined using simple concepts. Essential OCL is a package exposing the minimal OCL required to work with EMOF.

We partially exemplify a transformation from an ISM-Java to a PSM Java including, for instance, Class Diagram and State Diagram. This transformation uses both the specialized

Figure 6. Recovering use case diagram from Java code

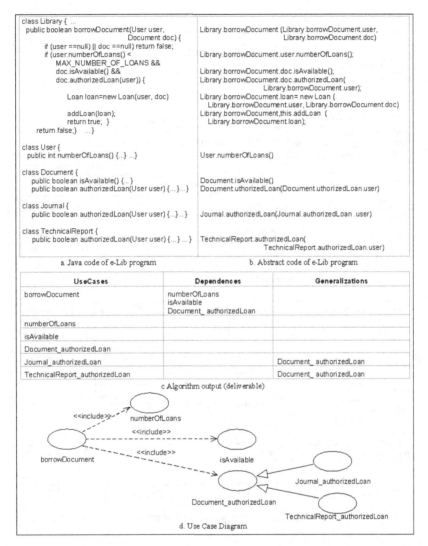

UML metamodel of Java code (Figure 7.b) and the UML metamodel of a Java platform (Figure 7.a, Figure 8.b) as source and target parameters respectively. The transformation specification is an OCL contract that consists of a name, a set of parameters, a precondition and postconditions. The precondition states relations between the metaclasses of the source metamodel. The postconditions deal with the state of the models after the transformation.

The ISM-Java metamodel includes constructs for representing classes, field and operations. It also shows different kind of relationships such as composition and generalization. For example, an instance of *JavaClass* could be related to another instance of *JavaClass* that takes the role of superclass or, it could be composed by other instances of *JavaClass* that take the role of *nested-Class* (Figure 7.b). Figure 7.a shows partially a PSM-Java metamodel that includes constructs for representing classes, field, operations and association-ends. It also shows different kind of relationships such as composition and generalization. For example, an instance of *JavaClass* could be

Figure 7. PSM and Java metamodels

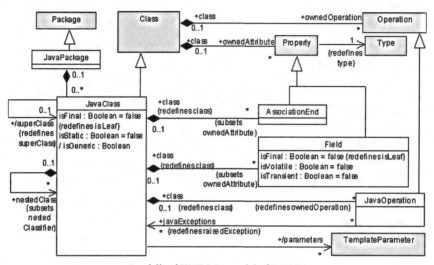

a. Specialized UML Metamodel of PSM Java

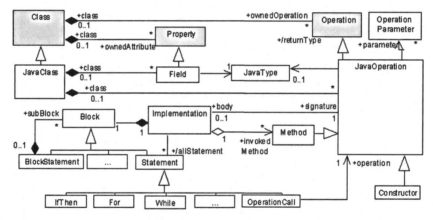

b. Specialized UML Metamodel of ISM Java

related to another instance of *JavaClass* that takes the role of superclass or, it could be composed by other instances of *JavaClass* that takes the role of *nestedClass*. The main difference between a Java-ISM and a Java-PSM is that the latter includes constructs for associations.

The State Diagram metamodel (Figure 8.b) defines a set of concepts than can be used for modeling discrete behavior through finite state transition systems such as state machines, state and transitions. OCL can be used to attach consistency rules to metamodel components. The rules

in Table 3 could be attached to the State-Diagram metamodel.

The transformation specification guarantees that for each class in Java code there is a class in the PSM-Java, both of them with the same name, the same parent class, equivalent operations and so on. Besides, the PSM-Java has a 'stateMachine' for each class having a significant dynamic behavior. Table 4 shows partially specify a code-to-model transformation between an ISM-Java and a PSM-Java.

Figure 8. Use case diagram, state diagram and activity diagram metamodels

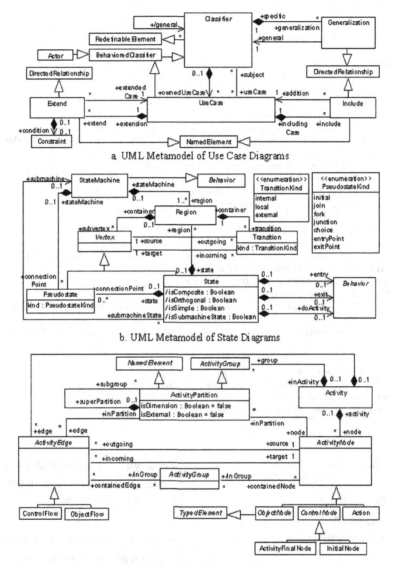

a. UML Metamodel of Use Case Diagrams

b. UML Metamodel of State Diagrams

c. UML Metamodel of Activity Diagrams

Table 3.

Context Statemachine /*The connection points of a state machine are pseudostates of kind entry point or exit point*/ conectionPoint -> forAll (c | c.kind = #entryPoint or c.kind = #exitPoint)
Context PseudoState /*An initial vertex can have at most one ongoing transition*/ (self.kind = #initial) implies (self.outgoing -> size <= 1)
Context Region /*A region can have at most one initial vertex*/ self.subvertex -> select (v |v.oclIsKindOf (Pseudostate)) -> select (p:Pseudostate |p.kind = #initial) -> size () <=1

Table 4.

Transformation ISM-JAVA-to-PSM-JAVA
parameters
sourceModel: ISM-JAVA-Metamodel:: JavaPackage
targetModel: PSM-JAVA-Metamodel:: JavaPackage
postconditions
/*for each class 'sourceClass' in the sourceModel*/
sourceModel.ownedMember -> select (oclIsTypeOf (JavaClass)) -> forAll (sourceClass |
/*there is a class 'targetClass' in the targetModel so that both classes have the same name,*/
targetModel.ownedMember -> select (oclIsTypeOf (JavaClass)) ->
exists (targetClass | targetClass.name = sourceClass.name **and**
/*if 'sourceClass' has an extends relation, targetModel has a superclass so that both superclasses are equivalent*/
sourceClass.extends -> size () = 1 **implies** (targetClass.superClass -> size () = 1 **and** targetClass.superClass.**classMatch**(sourceClass.extends)) **and**
/*for each operation of 'sourceClass' there is an operation in targetClass so that both operations are equivalent*/
sourceClass.javaOperation -> forAll (sourceOp | targetClass.javaOp -> exists (targetOp | targetOp.**operationMatch** (sourceOp))) **and**
/*for each field in 'sourceClass' whose type is a primitive type there is a field in 'targetClass' so that:*/
sourceClass.field -> select (f | f.javaType.oclIsTypeOf (Primitive)) ->
forAll (sourceField | targetClass.field -> exists (targetField |
/* 'targetField' and 'sourceField' have the same name, type,... */
targetField.name = sourceField.name **and** targetField.type = sourceField.javaType...)) **and**
/*for each field in 'sourceClass' whose type is a user defined type there is an association end in "targetClas" so that:*/
sourceClass.field -> select (f | f.javaType.oclIsTypeOf (UserJavaClass)) ->
forAll (sourceField | targetClass.associationEnd -> exists (targetAssocEnd |
/* 'targetAssocEnd' and 'sourceField' have the same name, type,... */
targetAssocEnd.name = sourceField.name **and** targetAssocEnd.opposite.type = sourceField.javaType **and...**) **and...**
/*If 'sourceClass' has some significant dynamic behavior, targetModel has a 'stateMachine' so that:*/
sourceClass.**hasSignificantDynamicBehavior() implies** targetModel.ownedMember -> select(oclIsTypeOf(JavaStateMachine))-> exists (targetMachine |
/* 'targetMachine' and 'sourceClass' have the same name and*/
targetMachine.name = sourceClass.name and
/*for each modifier operation in the 'sourceClass' there is a transition in 'targetClass'*/
sourceClass.javaOperation -> select (op | op.**isModifier** ()) ->
forAll (op | targetMachine.region.transition -> exists(t | t.**isCreatedFrom**(op))))) **and ...**

From Java to PIM

Specifying Code-to-Model Transformations Between Java and Activity Diagram

To specify reverse engineering of activity diagrams at metamodel level, source and target metamodels are specified. The source metamodel corresponds to the Java language (Figure 7.b). The target metamodel corresponds to the UML activity diagram, which is partially shown in Figure 8.c. The metamodel defines a set of concepts that can be used for modeling dynamic aspects of system such as activities, transitions and object flow (UML, 2010b). Table 5 shows partially specify a transformation between ISM-Java and Activity Diagram:

Specifying Code-to-Model Transformations Between Java and Use Case Diagram

To specify reverse engineering of use case diagrams at metamodel level, source and target metamodels are specified. The source metamodel corresponds to the Java language which is depicted in Figure 7.b. The target metamodel corresponds to the use cases UML metamodel, which is partially shown in Figure 8.a.

The Use Case metamodel defines a set of concepts that can be used for modeling dynamic aspects of a system, a subsystem or a class such as use cases, actors and their relationships. A UseCase is a kind of behaviored classifier that represents a declaration of an offered behavior. Each use case specifies some behavior that the

Table 5.

Transformation JavaCode-to-ActivityDiagram
parameters
source: Java-Code-Metamodel: Method
target: ActivityDiagram-UML-Metamodel: Activity
postconditions
/* the first generated node has the name of the 'source' method and contains an incoming edge from an initial node. Each parameter of the method corresponds to an object node. ... */
...
/*for each sentence Call of the implementation of the method 'source' */
source.implementation.allStatement ->select (sentence | sentence.oclIsTypeOf(OperationCall)
/* there is a node ActivityNode so that sentence corresponds to node*/
target.node -> exists (node | sentence.oclAsType(OperationCall).**operationCallMatch**(node)))
/*for each sentence IfThen of the method 'source' */
source.implementation.allStatement ->select (sentence | sentence.oclIsTypeOf(IfThen)
/*there is a node DecisionNode so that sentence corresponds to node*/
target.node -> exists (node | sentence.oclAsType(IfThen).**conditionalMatch**(node)))
...
/*for each pair of consecutive sentences in the method there is a transition in the activity diagram*/
... local operations
Java-Code-Metamodel::OperationCall:: **operationCallMatch**
(node:ActivityDiagram-UML-Metamodel**::ActivityNode): Boolean operationCallMatch (node)** =
/*operationCallMatch verifies that a call sentence in source corresponds to an activity node in target by checking the following properties:-the type of node is Action*/ node.oclIsTypeOf(Action) and
/* node and 'self' have the same name*/
node.name = self.operation.name and
/* node is contained in a partition whose name is the same as the class that owns 'self'*/
node.inPartition.name = self.operation.class and
/* the number of the incoming edges is equal to the number of 'self' parameters*/
node.incoming->select(inc| inc.oclIsTypeOf(ObjectFlow))->size() = self.operation.parameter->size() and ...

---

subject can perform in collaboration with one or more actors. A use case may be related to others through generalization, extend or include relationships (UML, 2010b).

Table 6 shows the transformation JavaCode-to-UseCaseDiagram:

ALGEBRAIC FORMALIZATION OF METAMODEL TRANSFORMATIONS

The concept of formal metamodel has contributed significantly to some of the core principles of MDA. In the context of MDA, a central problem is how to define metamodels correct and aligned with MOF. Inconsistencies in a metamodel specification will affect models and their implementations. The semantic of MOF is specified in OCL. Although OCL is a textual language, OCL expressions rely on UML class diagrams, i.e., the syntax context is determined graphically, OCL expressions cannot occur in isolation. OCL has a denotational semantics that has been implemented in tools that allow dynamic validation of snapshots.

A formal specification technique must at least provide syntax, some semantics and an inference system. The syntax defines the structure of the text of a formal specification including properties that are expressed as axioms (formulas of some logic). The semantics describes the models linked to a given specification; in the formal specification context, a model is a mathematical object that defines behavior of the realizations of the specifications. The inference system allows defining deductions that can be made from a formal specification. These deductions allow new formulas to be derived and checked. So, the inference system can help to automate testing, prototyping or verification. The formalization of the

Table 6.

```
Transformation JavaCode-to-UseCaseDiagram
parameters
source: JavaCode-Metamodel: Package
target: UseCaseDiagram-UML-Metamodel: Package
postconditions
/* for each public method of package 'source'*/
source.ownedMember ->select (oclIsTypeOf(Method) and visibility = #public) -> forAll (meth |
/* there is a basic use case 'ucase' in package 'target' that correspond to 'meth'*/
target.ownedMember -> select (oclIsTypeOf(UseCase)) ->
exists (ucase | ucase.oclAsType(UseCase).correspondTo
(meth.oclAsType(Method))))
/*for each public method of package 'source' and*/
source.ownedMember ->select (oclIsTypeOf(Method) and visibility = #public) -> forAll (meth |
/* for each invoked method in the 'meth' implementation,*/
meth.oclAsType(Method).implementation.invokedMethod ->select (visibility = #public) ->
forAll (invokedMeth |
/* there is a pair of use cases in package 'target', 'ucase1' and 'ucase2', so that*/
target.ownedMember -> select (oclIsTypeOf(UseCase)) -> exists (ucase1, ucase2 |
/* they correspond to the methods and*/
ucase1.oclAsType(UseCase).correspondTo
(meth.oclAsType(Method)) and ucase2.oclAsType(UseCase)correspondTo
(invokedMeth) and
/* there is a dependence relationship between 'ucase1' and 'ucase2' */
ucase1.clientDependency.supplier = ucase2)))
...
local operation
UseCaseDiagram-UML-Metamodel::UseCase::correspondTo
(JavaCodeMetamodel::Method:meth): Boolean;
correspondTo(meth)=
/*the use case 'self' and the method 'meth' have the same name*/
self.name = meth.name and
...
```

metamodel level implies to formalize metamodels and links among them.

In light of these issues, we define a special-purpose language NEREUS to provide extra support for metamodeling. NEREUS takes advantage of existing theoretical background on formal methods, for instance, the notions of refinement, implementation correctness, observable equivalences and behavioral equivalences that play an essential role in model-to-model transformations. The type system of NEREUS was defined rigorously in the algebraic framework.

The semantics of MOF metamodels (that is specified in OCL) can be enriched and refined by integrating it with NEREUS. This integration facilitates proofs and tests of models and model transformations via the formal specification of metamodels and metamodel transformations.

Some properties can be deduced from the formal specification and could be re-injected into the MOF specification without wasting the advantages of semi-formal languages of being more intuitive and pragmatic for most implementers and practitioners.

Our approach has two main advantages linked to automation and interoperability. On the one hand, our approach shows how to generate automatically formal specifications from MOF metamodels. Due to scalability problems, this is an essential requisite. On the other hand, our approach is the only one that focuses on interoperability of formal languages. Considering that there are many formal algebraic languages, NEREUS allows any number of source languages such as different Domain Specific Languages (DSLs) and target languages (different formal language) could be connected without having to define explicit metamodel transformations for each language pair.

Another advantage of our approach is linked to pragmatic aspects. NEREUS is a formal notation closed to MOF metamodels that allows meta-designers who must manipulate metamodels to understand their formal specification.

NEREUS allows specifying metamodels such as the Ecore metamodel, the specific metamodel for defining models in EMF (Eclipse Modeling Framework) (Eclipse, 2010). Today, we are integrating NEREUS in EMF.

Like MOF, NEREUS consists of several constructs to express classes, associations and packages and a repertoire of mechanisms for structuring them.

NEREUS is an intermediate notation open to many other formal languages such as algebraic, logic or functional. We define its semantics by giving a precise formal meaning to each of the constructs of the NEREUS language in terms of the CASL language (Bidoit & Mosses, 2004). A detailed description of NEREUS may be found at (Favre, 2009).

The specification in NEREUS of the State Diagram Metamodel shown in Figure 8.a is shown in Table 7.

Integrating MOF Metamodels with NEREUS

We define a bridge between EMOF- and Ecore-metamodels and NEREUS. The NEREUS specification is completed gradually. First, the signature and some axioms of classes are obtained by instantiating reusable schemes. Associations are transformed by using a reusable component ASSOCIATION. Next, OCL specifications are transformed using a set of transformation rules and a specification that reflects all the information of MOF metamodels is constructed.

The OCL basic types are associated with NEREUS basic types with the same name. NEREUS provides classes for collection type hierarchies. The types *Set*, *Bag* and *Sequence* are subtypes of *Collection(x)*.

The transformation process of OCL specifications to NEREUS is supported by a system of transformation rules. By analyzing OCL specifications we can derive axioms that will be included in the NEREUS specifications. Preconditions written in OCL are used to generate preconditions in NEREUS. Postconditions and invariants allow us to generate axioms in NEREUS. We define a system of transformation rules that only considers expressions based on Essential OCL. The following metaclasses defined in complete OCL are not part of the EssentialOCL: *MessageType*, *StateExp*, *ElementType*, *AssociationClassCallExp*, *MessageExp*, *and UnspecifiedValueExp*. Any well-formed rules defined for these classes are consequently not part of the definition of the transformation rule system.

The system includes a small set with around fifty rules. It was built by means of an iterative approach through successive refinements. The set of rules was validated by analyzing the different OCL expression attached to the UML metamodels, MOF and QVT.

As an example we show a few rules of the system. A detailed description of the system may be found at (Favre, 2010a). In each rule the shaded text denotes an OCL expression that can be translated by the non-shaded text in NEREUS. (Table 8)

The shaded axioms in the specification of Package *StateDiagramMetamodel* correspond to the translation of the OCL constraints attached to the metamodel.

A detailed description of formalization of metamodels and MDA transformation in NEREUS may be found at (Favre, 2009; Favre, 2006; Favre, 2010a; Favre, 2010b).

Table 7.

```
PACKAGE StateDiagramMetamodel
IMPORTS TransitionKind, PseudoStateKind
CLASS StateMachine
IS-SUBTYPE-OF UML::CommonBehaviors::BasicBehaviors::Behavior
ASSOCIATES
<< StateMachine-State>>
<< StateMachine-PseudoState >> ...
AXIOMS a: StateMachine-PseudoState; sm:StateMachine
forAll(c) (get_connectionPoint(a,sm),[kind(c) = #entryPoint or kind(c) = #exitPoint) ...
END-CLASS
CLASS Region
IS-SUBTYPE-OF UML::Classes::Kernel::Namespace
ASSOCIATES
<< State-Region>>
<< StateMachine-Region>>
<< Region-Vertex >>...
AXIOMS a: Region-Vertex; r: Region
size (select(p) (select (v) (get_subvertex(a, r), oclIsKinfOf (v,PseudoState) ]),
[kind (p) = #initial ])) <= 1
END-CLASS
CLASS PseudoState
IS-SUBTYPE-OF Vertex,...
ASSOCIATES
<<Vertex-Transition-1>>
<<Vertex-Transition-2>>
<< StateMachine-PseudoState>>...
ATTRIBUTE
kind: PseudoState -> PseudoStateKind
AXIOMS ps: PseudoState; a: Vertex-Transition-1
kind (ps) = #initial implies size (get_outgoing (a, ps)) <=1...
END-CLASS
ASSOCIATION stateMachine-PseudoState
IS Composition-2 [StateMachine: class1; PseudoState: class2;stateMachine: role1; conectionPoint: role2; 0..1: mult1; *: mult2; +: vis-
ibility1;+: visibility2]
CONSTRAINED-BY StateMachine: subsets namespace;
PseudoState: subsets ownedMember
END-ASSOCIATION
ASSOCIATION Region-Vertex
IS Composition-2 [Region: class1; Vertex:class2; container: role1; subvertex: role2; 0..1: mult1; *: mult2; +: visibility1; +: visibility2]
CONSTRAINED-BY Vertex: subsets ownedMember
END-ASSOCIATION
END-PACKAGE
```

FUTURE RESEARCH DIRECTIONS

Reverse engineering techniques are used as a mean to design software systems by evolving existing ones based on new requirements or technologies. Software evolution is multidimensional and is composed of different types of entities/concepts or artifacts that come from specifications, designs and architectures to source code, test cases and documentation. Each of them depends on other artifacts embodied in the implementation such as

user interfaces, components, patterns and so on. The different ways and rates that these artifacts change, lead to unreliable software and cause many problems associated with software maintenance.

MDA can help to develop and support a common application framework for software evolution that raises issues such as common exchange formats, tool integration and interoperability. When the system evolves, MDA maintains the interrelation between software entities accom-

Table 8.

Rule	OCL NEREUS
R1	v. operation(parameters) operation($Translate_{NEREUS}$(v), $Translate_{NEREUS}$ (parameters))
R2	v->operation (parameters) operation($Translate_{NEREUS}$(v), $Translate_{NEREUS}$ (parameters))
R3	v.attribute attribute (v)
R4	**context** Assoc object.rolename *Let a:Assoc* get_rolename (a, object)
R5	e.op e: expression op($Translate_{Nereus}$(e))
R6	exp1 infix-op exp2 $Translate_{Nereus}$(exp1)$Translate_{Nereus}$(infix-op) $Translate_{Nereus}$(exp2) $Translate_{Nereus}$(infix-oper) ($Translate_{Nereus}$(exp1), $Translate_{Nereus}$(exp2))
R7	T-> operationName (v:Type | bool-expr-with-v) OperationName::= forAll | exists | select | reject T::= Collection|Set|OrderedSet|Bag operationName (v) ($Translate_{NEREUS}$ (T), [$Translate_{NEREUS}$ (bool-expr-with-v)])

modating the evolution of higher level artifacts together with the code in a consistent way.

A challenge on software evolution is the necessity to achieve co-evolution between different types of software artifacts or different representations of them. MDA allows us to develop and relate all different artifacts in a way that ensures their inter-consistency. MDA raises the level of reasoning to a more abstract level and therefore even more appropriate. It places change and evolution in the center of software development process. To give a few examples, in the context of MDA co-evolution is needed between source code and models at levels of PSM and PIM, structural and behavioral models at levels of PSM, structural and behavioral models at levels of PIM and, code and CIM.

Existing formal methods provide a poor support for evolving specifications and incremental verification approaches. In particular, with the existing verification tools, simple changes in a system require to verify its complete specification again making the cost of the verification propor-

tional to its size. To use formal methods that place change and evolution in the center of the software development process is another challenge.

Refactoring is an important step for evolving models in reverse engineering processes however CASE tools provide limited facilities for refactoring only on source code through an explicit selection made for the designer but do not provide support for model refactorings.

Another research trend of reverse engineering is design pattern identification to understand the design considerations promoting reuse and quality of different software artifacts. Pattern identification allows measuring quality of software reverse engineering, because pattern and anti-pattern can help to discover weakness of code or models.

MDA approach is useless without tools automating the model transformation. To date, commercial Case tools might be able to support forward engineering and partial round trip engineering between PIM and code. Little support for reverse engineering PIM and PSM from code is provided for the existing CASE tools. These tools should also handle dynamic information. The idea is to determine, on the one hand what information need to be collected at run time, and then checking that the contracts are satisfied when the program run or, on the other hand inferring constraints that may be added to the artifact specification. Besides, there is a need to develop tools for new software architecture that have characteristics of being extremely dynamic, highly distributed, self-configurable and heterogeneous. The integration between ontologies (that are essentially CIMs) and MDA will occupy a central place in MDD. A new type of MDA tools that do a more intelligent job will arise in light of the evolution of ADM standards such as KDM. Probably, the next generation of tools might be able to recover the behavior of software systems in terms of domain models and translate it into executable programs on distributed environment.

In summary, a lot remains to be done to provide support for MDA-based reverse engineering and software evolution:

- Research on formalisms and theories to increase understanding of reverse engineering and software evolution processes,
- Development of methods, techniques and heuristics to provide support for software changes,
- New verification tools that embrace change and evolution as central in software development processes
- Development of new sophisticated tools to develop industrial size software systems
- Definition of standards to evaluate the quality of evolved artifacts/systems.

Besides, the adoption of reverse engineering and software evolution should be favored by educating future generations of software engineers, i.e., integrating background on software evolution into the computer science curriculum.

CONCLUSION

This chapter describes MDA reverse engineering processes based on the integration of traditional reverse engineering techniques, advanced metamodeling techniques and formal specification. A framework to reverse engineering MDA models from object oriented code that distinguishes three different levels of abstraction linked to models, metamodel and formal specification is proposed.

At model level, transformations are based on classical compiler construction techniques. They involve processes with different degrees of automation, which can go from totally automatic static analysis to human intervention requiring processes to dynamically analyze the resultant models. All the algorithms that deal with the reverse engineering share an analysis framework. The basic idea is to describe source code or models by an abstract language and perform a propagation analysis in an object-flow graph. This static analysis is complemented with dynamic analysis supported by tracer tools.

The metamodel level includes MOF metamodels that describe the transformations at model level. MOF metamodels describe families of ISM, PSM and PIM. Every ISM, PSM and PIM conforms to a MOF metamodel. Metamodel transformations are specified as OCL contracts between a source metamodel and a target metamodel. These contracts "control" the transformation consistency.

The level of formal specification includes specifications of MOF metamodels and metamodel transformations in the metamodeling language NEREUS that can be used to connect them with different formal and programming languages. NEREUS, like MDA, was designed for improving interoperability and reusability through separation of concerns. It is suited for specifying metamodels based on the concepts of entity, associations and systems. Formal specification can be automatically generated by using reusable schemes and a system of transformation rules for translating OCL specification into NEREUS. Although, we use some specific notation, the underlying ideas of our approach are independent of NEREUS and the proposed rule transformational system from MOF to NEREUS. The following are the bases of our approach:

- The integration of compiler techniques, metamodeling and formal specification.
- The definition of a formal Domain Specific Language (DSL) for defining metamodels and transformations.
- The automation of bridges between MOF metamodels and the DSL.

In this context, we describe reverse engineering of PSM and PIM expressed in terms of UML diagrams such as Class Diagram, State Diagram, Use Case Diagram and Activity Diagram.

REFERENCES

ADM. (2010). *Architecture driven modernization roadmap*. ADM Task Force. Retrieved April 2011 from adm.omg.org

Aho, A., Sethi, R., & Ullman, J. (1985). *Compilers: Principles, techniques, and tools* (2nd ed.). Reading, MA: Addison-Wesley.

Amstrong, M., & Trudeau, C. (1998). Evaluating architecture extractors. In *Proceedings of the 5th Working Conference on Reverse Engineering (WCRE 98)*. Honolulu, Hawaii, USA (pp. 30-39).

Angyal, L., Lengyel, L., & Charaf, H. (2006). An overview of the state-of-the-art reverse engineering techniques. In *Proceedings of the 7th International Symposium of Hungarian Researchers on Computational Intelligence* (pp. 507 - 516).

Antoniol, G., Fiutem, R., Lutteri, G., Tonella, P., & Zanfei, S. (1997). Program understanding and maintenance with the CANTO environment. In *Proceedings of the International Conference on Software Maintenance,* Bari, Italy (pp. 72-81).

ATL. (2011). *ATL documentation*. Retrieved April 2011 from www.eclipse.org/m2m/atl/documentation

Bellay, B., & Gall, H. (1998). An evaluation of reverse engineering tool capabilities. *Journal of Software Maintenance: Research and Practice, 10*, 305–331. doi:10.1002/(SICI)1096-908X(199809/10)10:5<305::AID-SMR175>3.0.CO;2-7

Bidoit, M., & Mosses, P. (2004). *CASL user manual- Introduction to using the common algebraic specification language, LNCS 2900*. Heidelberg, Germany: Springer-Verlag.

Boronat, A., Carsi, J., & Ramos, I. (2005). Automatic reengineering in MDA using rewriting logic a transformation engine. In *Proceedings of the Ninth European Conference on Software Maintenance and Reengineering (CSMR'05)* (pp. 228-231). Los Alamitos, CA: IEEE Computer Society.

Brown, A. (2004). *An introduction to model driven architecture*. Retrieved April 2011 from www.ibm.com/developerswork/rational/library/3100.html

Canfora, G., & Di Penta, M. (2007). New frontiers of reverse engineering. In *Proceedings of Future of Software Engineering (FOSE 2007)* (pp. 326-341). Los Alamitos, CA: IEEE Press.

CASE. (2011). *MDA*. Retrieved April 2011 from http://www.objectbydesign.com/tools/umltools_byCompany.htmlCASE. (2011). *Tools*. Retrieved April 2011 from http://case-tools.org/mda.html

Chen, Y., Nishimoto, M., & Ramamoorthy, C. (1990). The C information abstraction system. *IEEE Transactions on Software Engineering, 16*(3), 325–334..doi:10.1109/32.48940

Daciuk, J. (1998). *Incremental construction of finite-state automata and transducers, and their use in the natural language processing*. Ph. D. Thesis. Technical University of Gdansk.

Deissenboeck, F., & Ratiu, D. (2006). A unified meta model for concept-based reverse engineering. In *Proceedings of 3rd International Workshop on Metamodels, Schemes, Grammars, and Ontologies for Reverse Engineering*. Retrieved April 2011 from http://planet-mde.org/atem2006/atem06Proceedings.pdf

Demeyer, S., Ducasse, S., & Nierstrasz, O. (2002). *Object oriented reengineering patterns*. Amsterdam, The Netherlands: Morgan Kaufmann.

Dwyer, M., Hatcliff, J., Joehanes, R., Laubach, S., Pasareanu, C. R., Zheng, H., & Visser, W. (2001). Tool-supported program abstraction for finite-state verification. In *Proceedings of the International Conference on Software Engineering* (pp. 177-187).

Eclipse. (2011). *The Eclipse modeling framework*. Retrieved on April 2011 from http://www.eclipse.org/emf/

Ernst, M. (2003). Static and dynamic analysis: Synergy and duality. In *Proceedings of ICSE Workshop on Dynamic Analysis (WODA 2003)* (pp. 24-27).

Fanta, R., & Rajlich, V. (1998). Reengineering object oriented code. In *Proceedings of International Conference on Software Maintenance* (pp. 238-246). Los Alamitos, CA: IEEE Computer Society.

Favre, L. (2006). A rigorous framework for model driven development. In Siau, K. (Ed.), *Advanced topics in database research* (*Vol. 5*, pp. 1–27). Hershey, PA: Idea Group Publishing. doi:10.4018/978-1-59140-935-9.ch001

Favre, L. (2009). A formal foundation for metamodeling. ADA Europe 2009. []. Heidelberg, Germany: Springer-Verlag.]. *Lecture Notes in Computer Science, 5570,* 177–191. doi:10.1007/978-3-642-01924-1_13

Favre, L. (2010a). *Model driven architecture for reverse engineering technologies: Strategic directions and system evolution.* Hershey, PA: IGI Global. doi:10.4018/978-1-61520-649-0

Favre, L. (2010b) Foundations for QVT transformation. In *Proceedings 2010 International Conference on Software Engineering Research and Practice (SERP 2010)* (vol. 1, pp. 58-64), CSREA Press, USA.

Favre, L., Martinez, L., & Pereira, C. (2009). *MDA-based reverse engineering of object oriented code. Lecture Notes in Business Information Processing* (*Vol. 29*, pp. 251–263). Heidelberg, Germany: Springer-Verlag.

Favre, L., Pereira, C., & Martinez, L. (2009). Foundations for MDA CASE Tools. In Khosrow-Pour, M. (Ed.), *Encyclopedia of Information Science and Technology* (2nd ed., pp. 159–166). Hershey, PA: IGI Global.

Finnigan, P., Holt, R., Kalas, I., Kerr, S., Kontogiannnis, K., & Muller, H. (1997). The software bookshelf. *IBM Systems Journal, 36*(4), 564–593. doi:10.1147/sj.364.0564

FUJUBA. (2011). *Fujuba tool*. Retrieved April 2011 from www.fujuba.de

Greevy, O., Ducasse, S., & Girba, T. (2005). Analyzing software evolution through feature views. *Journal of Software Maintenance and Evolution. Research and Practice, 18*(6), 425–456.

Gueheneuc, Y. (2004). A systematic study of UML class diagram constituents for their abstract and precise recovery. In *Proceedings of 11th Asia-Pacific Software Engineering Conference (APSEC 2004)* (pp. 265-274). Los Alamitos, CA: IEEE Computer Society.

IMAGIX4D. (2000). *Imagix Corp*. Retrieved April 2011 from http://www.imagix.com

Jones, N., & Nielson, F. (1995). Abstract interpretation: A semantic based tool for program analysis. In Gabbay, D., Abramsky, S., & Maibaum, T. (Eds.), *Handbook of logic in computer science* (*Vol. 4*, pp. 527–636). Oxford, UK: Clarendon Press.

Kagdi, H., Collard, M. L., & Maletic, J. (2007). A survey and taxonomy of approaches for mining software repositories in the context of software evolution. *Journal of Software Maintenance and Evolution: Research and Practice, 19*, 77–131.. doi:10.1002/smr.344

Kazman, R., & Carriere, S. (1999). Playing detective: Reconstructing software architecture from available evidence. *Journal of Automated Software Engineering, 6*(2), 107–138.. doi:10.1023/A:1008781513258

KDM. (2011). *Knowledge discovery meta-model*, version 1.3-beta 2, March 2011. OMG specification formal 2010-12-12. Retrieved on April 2011 from http://www.omg.org/spec/kdm/1.3/beta2/pdf

Koehler, J., Hauser, R., Kapoor, S., Wu, F., & Kumaran, S. (2003). A model-driven transformation method. In. *Proceedings of Seven IEEE Enterprise Distributed Object Computing Conference, EDOC, 2003*, 186–197..doi:10.1109/EDOC.2003.1233848

MacDonald, A., Russell, D., & Atchison, B. (2005). Model driven development within a legacy system: An industry experience report. In *Proceedings of the 2005 Australian Software Engineering Conference (ASWEC 05)* (pp. 14-22). Los Alamitos, CA: IEEE Press.

Mansurov, N., & Campara, D. (2005). Managed architecture of existing code as a practical transition towards MDA. []. Heidelberg, Germany: Springer-Verlag.]. *Lecture Notes in Computer Science, 3297*, 219–233. doi:10.1007/978-3-540-31797-5_22

Maoz, S., & Harel, D. (2010) On tracing reactive systems. *Software & System Modeling*. Springer-Verlag. DOI 10.1007/510270-010-0151-2

Markosian, L., Newcomb, P., Brand, R., Burson, S., & Kitzmiller, T. (1994). Using an enabling technology to reengineer legacy systems. *Communications of the ACM, 37*(5), 58–70.. doi:10.1145/175290.175297

MDA. (2005). *The model driven architecture*. Retrieved April 2011 from www.omg.org/mda

Medini. (2011). *Medini QVT*. Retrieved April 2011 from http://projects.ikv.de/qvt

Modisco. (2011). Retrieved on April 2011 from http://www.eclipse.org/Modisco

MOF. (2006). *MOF: Meta object facility (MOF ™) 2.0*. OMG Specification formal/2006-01-01. Retrieved April 2011 from www.omg.org/mof

Muller, H., & Klashinsky (1988). Rigi- A system for programming in the large. In *Proceedings of the 10th International Conference on Software Engineering (ICSE)* (pp. 80-86). Los Alamitos, CA: IEEE Computer Society Press.

Muller, H., Jahnke, J., Smith, D., Storey, M., Tilley, S., & Wong, K. (2000). Reverse engineering: A roadmap. In *Proceedings of the 22nd International Conference on Software Engineering (ICSE 2000), Limerick, Ireland*. ACM Press. Retrieved April 2011 from http://www.cs.ucl.ac.uk/staff/A.Finkelstein/fose/finalmuller.pdf

OCL. (2010). *OCL: Object constraint language, version 2.2*. OMG: formal/2010-02-01.Retrieved April 2011 from www.omg.org

OCL. (2011). *Use*. Retrieved April 2011 from http://www.db.informatik.uni-bremen.de/projects/USE

Pohyvanyk, D., Gueheneuc, Y.-G., Marcus, A., Antoniol, G., & Rajlich, V. (2007). Feature location using probabilistic ranking of methods based on execution scenarios and information retrieval. *IEEE Transactions on Software Engineering*, *23*(6), 420–432..doi:10.1109/TSE.2007.1016

Qiao, B., Yang, H., Chu, W., & Xu, B. (2003). Bridging legacy systems to model driven architecture. In *Proceedings of 27th Annual International Computer Aided Software and Applications Conference* (pp. 304-309). Los Alamitos, CA: IEEE Press.

QVT. (2008). *QVT: MOF 2.0 query, view, transformation*. Formal/2008-04-03. Retrieved April 2011 from www.omg.org

Reus, T., Geers, H., & van Deursen, A. (2006). Harvesting software system for MDA-based reengineering. [Heidelberg, Germany: Springer-Verlag.]. *Lecture Notes in Computer Science*, *4066*, 220–236. doi:10.1007/11787044_17

SNiFF+ (1996). *SNiFF+: User guide and reference, Take-Five software*. Retrieved April 2011 from www.takefive.com

Sommerville, I. (2004). *Software engineering* (7th ed.). Reading, MA: Addison Wesley.

Systa, T. (2000). *Static and dynamic reverse engineering techniques for Java software systems*. PhD Thesis, University of Tampere, Report A-2000-4.

Tonella, P., & Potrich, A. (2005). *Reverse engineering of object oriented code. Monographs in Computer Science*. Heidelberg, Germany: Springer-Verlag.

UML. (2010a). *Unified modeling language: Infrastructure*. Version 2.3. OMG Specification formal/ 2010-05-03. Retrieved April 2011from www.omg.org.

UML. (2010b). *UML: Unified modeling language: Superstructure*. Version 2.3. OMG Specification: formal/2010-05-05. Retrieved April 2011 from www.omg.org

Use. (2011). *Use 3.0*. Retrieved April 2011 from http://www.db.informatik.uni-bremen.de/projects/USE

Watson, B. (1995). *Taxonomies and toolkits of regular language algorithms*. PhD thesis. Eindhoven University of Technology, The Netherlands.

KEY TERMS AND DEFINITIONS

Architecture Driven Modernization (ADM): The process of understanding and evolving existing software assets of a system of interest in the context of the Model Driven Architecture (MDA).

CASE Tool: Computer Aided Software Engineering (CASE); a tool to aid in the analysis and design of software systems.

Forward Engineering: The process of transforming a model into code through a mapping to a specific implementation language.

Knowledge Discovery Metamodel (KDM): A metamodel from the Object Management Group (OMG) for representing existing software, its elements, associations and operational environments that is related to software assurance and modernization.

Metamodel: A model that defines the language for expressing a model.

Meta-Object Facility (MOF): A meta-metamodel from the Object Management Group (OMG) that defines a common way for capturing the diversity of modeling standards and interchange constructs involved in MDA.

Model Driven Architecture (MDA): An initiative of the Object Management Group (OMG) for the development of software systems based on the separation of business and application logic from underlying platform technologies. It is an evolving conceptual architecture to achieve cohesive model-driven technology specifications.

Object Constraint Language (OCL): A notational language for analysis and design of software systems that allows software developers to write constraints and queries over object models such as UML models.

Query, View, Transformation (QVT): A metamodel from the Object Management Group for expressing transformation in MDA-based processes.

Reverse Engineering: The process of analyzing available software artifacts, such as requirements, design, architectures, code or byte code, with the objective of extracting information and providing high-level views on the underlying system.

Unified Modeling Language (UML): A unified modeling language from the Object Management Group (OMG) for visualizing, specifying, constructing, and documenting the artifacts of a software-intensive system.

Chapter 8
Model-Driven Reengineering

Ricardo Pérez-Castillo
University of Castilla-La Mancha, Spain

Ignacio García Rodríguez de Guzmán
University of Castilla-La Mancha, Spain

Mario Piattini
University of Castilla-La Mancha, Spain

ABSTRACT

Legacy information systems entail a risk for companies because, on the one hand, they cannot be thrown away since valuable business knowledge becomes embedded in them over time, and on the other hand, they cannot be easily maintained at a moderate cost. Over the last two decades, reengineering has been the solution to these problems, since it supports the evolutionary maintenance of legacy information systems whilst simultaneously preserving the knowledge embedded within them. Unfortunately, traditional reengineering is facing new challenges concerning its formalization and automation as a consequence of legacy information systems being increasingly larger and more complex. A new software engineering approach known as Model-Driven Reengineering has consequently emerged to deal with these limitations. Model-Driven Reengineering does not replace traditional reengineering, but incorporates the model-driven development principles; i.e., this approach treats all software artifacts as models and establishes transformations between these models at different degrees of abstraction. The objective of this chapter is to provide an overview of the emerging concepts and standards related to Model-Driven Reengineering. This chapter also discusses how Model-Driven Reengineering deals with typical challenges that emerge when LISs are evolved, in order to mitigate the negative effects of the software erosion phenomenon, preserve the embedded business knowledge, and reduce maintenance costs.

DOI: 10.4018/978-1-61350-438-3.ch008

INTRODUCTION

Although software is an intangible object, the quality of software diminishes over time in a similar way to that of material objects. Lehman's first law states that an information system must continually evolve or it will become progressively less suitable in a real-world environment (Lehman et al., 1998). Companies currently have an enormous amount of large legacy systems which undergo the phenomenon of software erosion and software ageing. This means that existing information systems become progressively less maintainable (Polo et al., 2003). The negative effects of software erosion can be dead code, clone programs, missing capacities, inconsistent data and control data (coupling), among others (Visaggio, 2001).

On the one hand, software maintenance is part of the software erosion problem, since software erosion is due to maintenance itself and to the uncontrolled evolution of the system over time. On the other hand, software maintenance is also part of the solution to software erosion. The successive changes in information systems transform them into Legacy Information Systems (LIS), and a new and improved system must therefore replace the previous one when the maintainability levels diminish below acceptable limits (Mens, 2008). Nevertheless, the wide replacement of these systems from scratch is a key challenge since it makes a great impact on the technological, human and economic aspects of companies (Sneed, 2005). Firstly, the entire replacement of LISs affects technological and human aspects, since it usually involves retraining all the users in order for them to understand the new system and/ or the new technology. Secondly, the new system may have a lack of specific functionalities that are missing as a result of technological changes. Thirdly, the economic aspect of companies is also affected, since the replacement of an entire LIS, by implementing a new system from scratch, implies a low Return of Investment (ROI) with regard to the old system. In addition, the development or purchase of the new system might exceed a company's budget.

In order to understand why a complete replacement from scratch in not an appropriate solution to the software erosion phenomenon, the following example, adapted from (Pérez-Castillo et al., 2011), is provided: Let us imagine a transmission belt in a car engine. This piece deteriorates progressively over time. When this piece is damaged, or its quality decreases considerably, it may become a threat to the overall performance of the motor. This transmission belt must consequently be replaced immediately, and the engine will therefore operate normally after the replacement. The solution in this case is easy, but an information system used in a company is more complicated. When an information system ages, it cannot simply be replaced by another new system for two important reasons: (i) a transmission belt costs a few dollars while an enterprise information system costs thousands of dollars, but in addition, (ii) while the environment of the belt (i.e. the motor) does not change, a considerable amount of business knowledge becomes embedded in the aged system over time in order to address the changes in the company's environment. This embedded knowledge is lost if the aged information system is replaced in its entirety, since this knowledge is not present anywhere else. A company with a new system may not therefore work normally, unlike the car engine.

An alternative to an entire replacement from scratch is another solution to software erosion that provides better results: software evolution. Software evolution is a kind of software maintenance which is also termed as evolutionary maintenance. In general, the maintenance process can perform four categories of modifications in the existing software (ISO/IEC, 2006):

- **Corrective maintenance**, which modifies a software product after delivery in order to correct any problems discovered.

- **Preventive maintenance**, which modifies a software product after delivery in order to detect and correct latent faults in the software product before they become effective faults.
- **Adaptive maintenance**, which modifies a software product after delivery in order to keep a software product usable in a changed or changing environment;
- **Perfective maintenance**, which modifies a software product after delivery in order to improve its performance or maintainability.

Evolutionary maintenance is a particular type of maintenance that focuses on adaptive and perfective modifications. Indeed, according to (Ghazarian, 2009), 78% of maintenance changes are corrective or behavior-preserving. Moreover, (Mens et al., 2008) states that a legacy system must be evolved when it *"operates in or addresses a problem or activity of the real world. As such, changes in the real world will affect the legacy system and require adaptations to it"*. Software evolution can be considered as a process by which to enhance LISs in order to deal with software erosion problems.

Nevertheless, the software erosion phenomenon is caused by the maintenance process itself. Thus, according to the software entropy law, evolutionary maintenance could trigger more software erosion problems over the long term (Jacobson et al., 1992).

"The software entropy law states that a closed system's disorder cannot be reduced, it can only remain unchanged or increase. A measure of this disorder is entropy. This law also seems plausible for software systems; as a system is modified, its disorder, or entropy, always increases. This is known as software entropy". (Jacobson et al., 1992)

Evolutionary maintenance must therefore improve LISs without discarding the existing systems, thus minimizing the software erosion effects. Evolutionary maintenance consequently makes it possible to manage controllable costs and preserves the valuable business knowledge embedded in the legacy system.

Over the last two decades, reengineering has been the principal technique used to address the evolutionary maintenance of legacy systems (Bianchi et al., 2003). Reengineering preserves the systems' legacy knowledge and makes it possible to change software easily, reliably and quickly, resulting in a maintenance cost that is also tolerable (Bennett et al., 2000).

The reengineering is the examination and alteration of a subject system to reconstitute it in a new form and the subsequent implementation of the new form [...] This may include modifications with respect to new requirements not met by the original system.(Chikofsky et al., 1990)

However, according to (Sneed, 2005), over 50% of reengineering projects fail. This is the result of at least two principal problems when dealing with specific challenges:

- The reengineering of large complex legacy information systems is very difficult to automate (Canfora et al., 2007a), and the maintenance costs may therefore grow significantly
- Traditional reengineering lacks formalization and standardization (Kazman et al., 1998), signifying that different reengineering tools that address specific tasks in the reengineering process cannot be integrated or reused in different reengineering projects.

As a consequence of these problems, the software industry is demanding reengineering through the evolutionary maintenance of legacy systems in an automatic and standardized manner. Model-driven engineering principles have become a valuable solution by which to meet reengineering's traditional demands (Khusidman, 2008), i.e., these principles make it possible to model all the legacy software artifacts as models and establish model transformations between models at different abstraction levels. Traditional reengineering has therefore shifted to what has been denominated as Model-Driven Reengineering. The main advantages of Model-Driven Reengineering compared to traditional reengineering are that it:

- Revitalizes legacy information systems, making them more agile.
- Reduces maintenance and development costs.
- Extends the useful life of legacy information systems, whilst also improving the ROI of these systems.
- Can be easily integrated with other systems and other environments such as Service-Oriented Architecture (SOA).

The objective of this chapter is to provide an overview of the emerging concepts and standards related to Model-Driven Reengineering. This chapter also discusses how Model-Driven Reengineering deals with typical challenges that emerge when LISs are evolved, in order to mitigate the negative effects of the software erosion phenomenon.

The remaining parts of this chapter are organized as follows. The second section summarizes the state-of-the-art of traditional reengineering along with the most important concepts addressed in this chapter. The third section provides a detailed account of Model-Driven Reengineering. The fourth section discusses the most important model-awareness challenges that must be addressed to achieve appropriate Model-Driven Reengineering processes from traditional reengineering. The fifth section briefly presents some projects and tools in which Model-Driven Reengineering has been successfully applied. Finally, the last section presents a summary of the chapter, along with future and emerging trends related to Model-Driven Reengineering.

Traditional Reengineering

Most companies manage a wide variety of existing information systems which are considered to be *Legacy Information Systems* (LIS) because the code in these systems was written long ago and may now be technologically obsolete. According to (Paradauskas et al., 2006), *"a legacy information system is any information system that significantly resists modification and evolution to meet new and constantly changing business requirements"*. (Ulrich, 2002) states that *"legacy systems are defined as any production-enabled software, regardless of the platform it runs on, language it is written in, or length of time it has been in production"*. (Hunt et al., 2002) go further by stating that the *"code becomes legacy code just about as soon as it's written"*.

The software industry has instilled a false belief that *"anything new is beautiful and that everything old is ugly"* and software customers have therefore become *"victims of a volatile IT industry"* (Sneed, 2008). Despite the fact that LISs may be obsolete, this type of system usually has a critical, or at least necessary, mission within the company and represents a valuable asset for companies, since LISs embed a lot of business logic and business rules that are not present anywhere else (Sommerville, 2006). The meaningful business knowledge embedded in LISs results from the fact that companies maintain their legacy systems over time. This maintenance adds increasingly more functionalities to legacy systems, thus supporting the company's operation and activities. However, maintenance is carried out in an uncontrolled manner and modifications are not reported. As a result, the companies cannot discard their LISs, but they must deal with a set of emerging problems related to the software erosion of their LISs (Paradauskas et al., 2006):

- Legacy systems are typically implemented with obsolete technology which is difficult and expensive to maintain.
- The lack of documentation leads to a lack of understanding of the legacy systems, making the maintenance of these systems a slow and expensive process.
- A great effort must be made to integrate a legacy system together with other systems in the company, since the interfaces and boundaries of the legacy system are not usually well defined.

Two decades ago, the reengineering of LISs became one of the most successful practices for dealing with the software erosion phenomenon. Reengineering methods do not discard the whole system, but enhance LISs and simultaneously preserve most of the business knowledge embedded in them. The reengineering processes therefore make it possible to carry out the evolutionary maintenance of LIS by assuming low risks as well as low costs (Sneed, 2005).

The traditional reengineering process consists of three stages: reverse engineering, restructuring and forward engineering (Chikofsky et al., 1990).

- **Reverse engineering** is the first stage, which must not be confused with the reengineering term, the overall process. The reverse engineering stage analyzes the legacy system in order to identify different components of an LIS and the interrelationships between them. The reverse engineering stage then builds one or more representations of the LIS at a higher degree of abstraction.
- **Restructuring**, also known as refactoring or modification, is the second stage of the traditional reengineering process. The restructuring stage takes the previous system's abstract representation and transforms it into an enhanced representation of the LIS at the same abstraction level. This

stage preserves the external behavior of the LIS.

- **Forward engineering** is the third stage of the traditional reengineering process. The forward engineering stage generates physical implementations of the target system at a low abstraction level from the previously restructured representation of the system.

The *horseshoe model* (Kazman et al., 1998) organizes the three stages of the whole reengineering process (see Figure 1). The reverse engineering stage that increases the abstraction level is represented by the left side of the horseshoe; the restructuring stage preserves the same abstraction level and is thus represented by the curve of the horseshoe; and the last part, on the right side of the horseshoe, is the forward engineering stage that instantiates the target system.

Reengineering Examples

Various reengineering practices have been applied in several fields other than that of software engineering, such as the hardware industry and business process management. Specifically, the software industry has successfully applied reengineering to many domains. This section briefly shows some examples of these applications.

Reengineering has traditionally been used to carry out technological changes or migrations to another programming language. One example is the transformation of an LIS that was developed by following a structured paradigm in an object-oriented system. This reengineering process also involves rewriting the code written in a structured programming language such as COBOL or C in another object-oriented language such as JAVA or C++.

Reengineering has also been used to modify the design of LISs in order to improve their maintainability, efficiency, and other design aspects. Let us imagine, for example, an LIS based on the JAVA platform. Firstly, in the reverse engineering

Figure 1. Example of a horseshoe reengineering model to improve the maintainability of a LIS

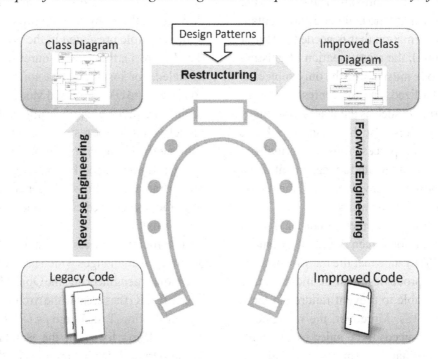

stage software engineers could analyze the legacy source code and recover the design of the LIS, i.e., a set of class diagrams depicting the LIS (see Figure 1). In the restructuring stage the software engineers could then modify the design of the systems by adding well-defined design patterns (see Figure 1) such as the patterns proposed by (Gamma et al., 1995), which would improve the maintainability of the LIS. Finally, the new source code from the improved class diagrams could be generated by means of forward engineering (see Figure 1).

Another software industry field in which re-engineering has been applied is that of database reengineering. In this respect, (Hainaut et al., 1996) propose reengineering as a mechanism with which to design relational databases. While the database design from scratch requires concep-tual design, logical design and physical design, the reengineering approach requires only data structure extraction and data structure conceptu-alization to obtain a design of a legacy database. This approach makes it possible to migrate legacy databases towards relational databases by using old data models.

Reengineering Limitations

Reengineering has been a successful practice in the software industry, but more than half of traditional reengineering projects currently fail (Sneed, 2005). The most important threats to traditional reengineering are the standardization and automation of the reengineering process used to deal with large and complex LISs.

• **Standardization** constitutes a key problem since the reengineering process has been typically carried out in an ad hoc manner. This means that engineers create and man-age particular artifacts with specific nota-tions throughout the traditional horseshoe reengineering model for each project that is carried out. Reengineering projects must focus their efforts on a better definition of the process, and standard representations for legacy software artifacts. Owing to the fact that "the code does not contain all the information that is needed" (Müller et al., 2000), the representation of existing source code must not be the only subject to be standardized, and the representation of other artifacts such as databases, user interfaces, etc. must also be standardized The reengineering process must be formalized to ensure an integrated management of all of the knowledge involved in all the different legacy software artifacts.

- **Automation** is another important limitation of traditional reengineering. (Canfora et al., 2007b) state that the traditional reengineering processes must be more mature and repeatable to prevent failures in large complex LISs. Moreover, the reengineering process needs to be aided by automated tools so that companies can avoid cost overruns and ensure certain paybacks in their reengineering projects (Sneed, 2005). The automation challenge is partially a consequence of the standardization limitation, since standardization and the formalization of the process are necessary requirements to provide mature tools with which to automate reengineering activities, which can be reused in various reengineering projects and different scenarios.

These limitations, together with the emergent trends from the model-driven engineering field, make Model-Driven Reengineering a more appropriate solution to the software erosion phenomenon since standardization and automation challenges are dealt with.

Model-Driven Reengineering

The traditional reengineering concept has evolved into Model-Driven Reengineering, which advocates for modeling all the legacy software artifacts as models and establishing model transformations

between models at different abstraction levels throughout the reengineering process. According to the example presented in the previous section (see Figure 1), the legacy source code would be modeled, for instance, as a source code model conforming to UML (Unified Modeling Language) during the reverse engineering stage. The code model would then be restructured into an improved code model by means of a model transformation using a domain-specific language. Finally, the model transformation would generate source code from the restructured code model through model transformations.

In order to address the standardization and automation challenges which have emerged from traditional reengineering, the Object Management Group (OMG) has created the Architecture-Driven Modernization Task Force (ADMTF). The ADMTF's efforts focus on the standardization of Model-Driven Reengineering defined by the OMG as Architecture-Driven Modernization (ADM) (OMG, 2007). According to (OMG, 2003), ADM is the concept of modernizing LISs with a focus on all aspects of the current system's architecture and the ability to transform current architectures into target architectures. ADM advocates carrying out reengineering processes by following the MDA (Model-Driven Architecture) standard (Miller et al., 2003). MDA is the particular standard of the OMG which supports the Model-Driven Development (MDD) principles within the wide term of Model-Driven Engineering (MDE) that is applied to various areas of engineering (and not only to software engineering) (see Figure 2).

ADM deals with the standardization and automation challenges of traditional reengineering by carrying out reengineering processes through the consideration of *model-driven development* principles. However, ADM does not replace traditional reengineering, but rather improves it. The MDA standard as proposed by the OMG defines two main principles: (i) modeling all the software artifacts as models at different abstraction levels;

Figure 2. Standardization and terminology concerning Model-Driven Reengineering (MDR)

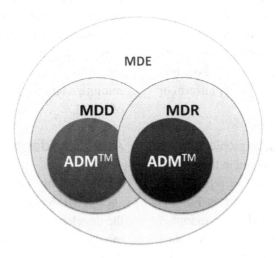

and (ii) establishing model transformations between them (Miller et al., 2003).

The horseshoe reengineering model has consequently also been adapted to ADM and is denominated as the horseshoe modernization model (also known as the horseshoe Model-Driven Reengineering model) (see Figure 3). There are three kinds of models in the horseshoe modernization model (Miller et al., 2003):

- **Computation Independent Model (CIM)**, which is a view of the system from the computation independent viewpoint at a high abstraction level. A CIM does not

show details of the system's structure. CIM models are sometimes called domain models and play the role of bridging the gap between the domain experts and experts in the system's design and construction.

- **Platform Independent Model (PIM)**, which is a view of a system from the platform independent viewpoint at an intermediate abstraction level. A PIM has a specific degree of technological independence in order to make it suitable for use with a number of different platforms of a similar type.

Figure 3. Horseshoe modernization model

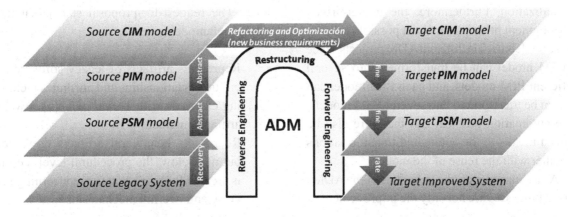

- **Platform Specific Model (PSM)**, which is a view of a system from the platform specific viewpoint at a low abstraction level. A PSM combines the specifications in the PIM with the details that specify how that system uses a particular type of platform or technology.

ADM solves the formalization problem since it represents all the artifacts involved in the reengineering process as models, which are represented in accordance with specific metamodels. For this purpose, Meta Object Facility (MOF), an adopted OMG standard, is used to provides a metadata management framework, and a set of metadata services to enable the development and interoperability of model and metadata driven systems. MOF has contributed significantly to some of the core principles of the MDA as well as ADM.

ADM therefore treats all software artifacts homogenously, i.e., as models that can be transformed into other models using deterministic transformations. These transformations can be formalized, for example, by means of the QVT (Query / Views / Transformations) standard proposed by the OMG (OMG, 2008). The QVT specification consists of two distinct but related languages: (i) the *QVT-Operational* language, which is procedural in nature, and (ii) *QVT-Relations*, a declarative language. QVT makes it possible to define transformations between models at the same abstraction level or at a different level. The model transformations can consequently be automated in addition to their formalization. Furthermore, the model-driven development principles make it possible to reuse those models used in different ADM projects, since a CIM model can be transformed into several different PIM models, and each PIM model can in turn be transformed into several PSM models. The automation problem can therefore also be solved thanks to the automated transformations together with the reuse of the models.

As a consequence, the outcomes of the ADM-based processes are not only the improvement or evolution of a particular LIS, but also that LISs are represented through a set of models at different abstraction levels that can be reused in future maintenance processes. The negative effects of the software erosion phenomenon are therefore minimized through software evolution by means of ADM.

ADM Standards

ADM not only adopts other existing standards such as MDA and QVT, but has also spearheaded the development of a set of standards with which to address the different challenges that appear in the modernization of legacy information systems (OMG, 2009b).

In June 2003, the OMG formed a Task Force in order to model software artifacts in the context of legacy systems. The group was initially called the Legacy Transformation Task Force and was then renamed the Architecture-Driven Modernization Task Force (ADMTF). In July 2003, the ADMTF issued a software modernization whitepaper (OMG, 2003). In November 2003, the ADMTF issued the request-for-proposal of the Knowledge Discovery Metamodel (KDM) specification. KDM aims to be an initial metamodel that allows modernization tools to exchange application metadata across different applications, languages, platforms and environments. The objective of this initial metamodel was to provide a comprehensive view of the application structure and data, but it does not represent software below the procedure level. The request-for-proposal stated that the KDM metamodel:

- Represents artifacts of legacy software as entities, relationships and attributes including external artifacts with which software artifacts interact.
- Represents behavioral artifacts down to, but not below, the procedural level, i.e., it is created for representation concerning reverse engineering mechanisms.

- Supports a variety of platforms and languages, i.e., it consists of a platform and language independent core, with extensions where needed.
- Defines a unified terminology for legacy software artifacts by describing the physical and logical structure of legacy systems.
- Can aggregate or modify, i.e., it refactors the physical system structure to facilitate tracing artifacts from the logical structure back to the physical structure.

In May 2004, six organizations responded to the request-for-proposal. However, throughout 2004 and 2005 more than 30 organizations from 5 different countries collaborated in the development and review of the KDM standard. In May 2006, KDM was adopted by the OMG and moved into the finalization stage of the adoption process. In March of 2007, the OMG presented the recommended specification of KDM 1.0. In April 2007, the OMG began ongoing maintenance of the KDM specification. In January 2009, the recommended specification of KDM 1.1 became available in the OMG (OMG, 2009a), and in turn, the OMG began the revision of that version. Recently, in March 2009, KDM was recognized as a draft international standard, specifically ISO/IEC 19506 (ISO/IEC, 2009).

KDM is the first fulfilled standard and is the cornerstone of the set of standards proposed by the ADMTF of the OMG. However, the ADMTF is currently defining the remainder of the standards planned around the KDM, although some of these standards are still at the approval or development stage (OMG, 2009b):

- **Abstract Syntax Tree Metamodel (ASTM)**, which is a specification built under KDM to represent software below the procedural level by means of abstract syntax tree models. The ASTM and the KDM are two complementary modeling specifications which fully represent applications

and facilitate the exchange of granular metadata across multiple languages. In 2009 the ADMTF proposed the first specification of ASTM 1.0.
- **Software Metrics Metamodel (SMM)**, which defines a metamodel with which to represent measurement information related to software, its operation, and its design. The specification is an extensible metamodel that is used to exchange software-related measurement information concerning legacy software artifacts: designs, implementations, or operations. In 2009, the ADMTF also proposed the first specification of SMM 1.0.
- **ADM Pattern Recognition specification** is a standard to facilitate the examination of structural metadata with the intent of deriving patterns concerning legacy systems. These patterns can be used to determine refactoring and transformation requirements and opportunities that could be applied to one or more systems. This specification was issued in 2009.
- **ADM Visualization specification**, which focuses on the different ways in which to show application metadata stored within the KDM models. In 2009 there was no target date for this proposal.
- **ADM Refactoring specification**, which seeks to define ways in which the KDM specification can be used to refactor applications by means of structuring, rationalizing, modularizing, and so on. In 2010 there was no target date for this proposal.
- **ADM Transformation specification**, which seeks to define mappings between KDM, ASTM and target models. In 2010 there was no target date for this proposal.

Figure 4 shows the set of ADM standards contextualized in the horseshoe modernization model, along with other OMG business modeling standards related to ADM-based processes.

Figure 4. The ADMTF standards within the horseshoe modernization model

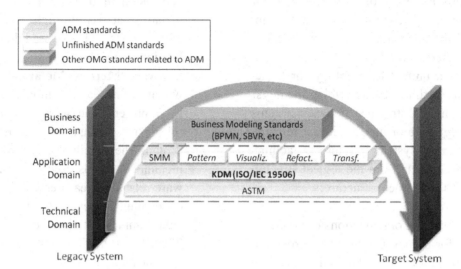

Model-Awareness Challenges

To date, model-driven development principles have normally been used in the forward engineering stage. Model-driven generative techniques are used in the forward engineering stage to obtain source code from different kinds of models, such as UML models. Indeed, some researchers consider that MDD is only applicable to forward engineering. However, MDD principles can be applied to the entire reengineering process, i.e., they can also be effectively applied in the reverse engineering and restructuring stages. However, achieving model-awareness from traditional reengineering implies certain challenges that must be addressed. Firstly, the representation and management of the knowledge recovered during the reverse engineering stage must be carried out appropriately. Anyway, to have code represented in a model is not the main objective, but it is a necessary means to achieve other maintenance goals. Secondly, refactoring techniques must be adapted to be applied to the retrieved models during the restructuring stage. Thirdly, Model-Driven Reengineering must facilitate the attainment of the maximum abstraction level, i.e., it must be able to recover and manage the business knowledge

embedded in LISs. The first sub-section shows an example concerning a modernization software project, which allows us to illustrate all the challenges involved. The following sub-sections provide a detailed explanation of these model-awareness challenges.

A Software Modernization Example

This section shows an example which is used to illustrate the model-awareness challenges and to understand how Model-Driven Reengineering works. The example considers a small *Java* application implementing a reselling process. The application is based on the product order process described by *Weske* (Weske, 2007). This process allows registered customers to place orders. In parallel, customers receive the products and the invoice to pay for the products. Figure 5 shows the structure of the application, which follows the traditional decomposition into three layers (Eckerson, 1995): (i) the *domain* layer supports all the business entities and controllers; (ii) the *persistence* layer handles the data access; and (iii) the *presentation* layer deals with the user interfaces (see Figure 5 left). The *ResellerController* class

Figure 5. Structure of an example product order application

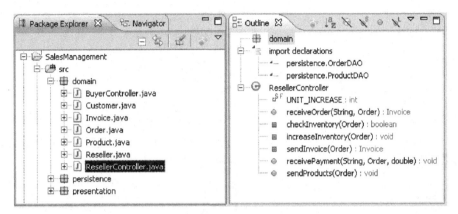

contains most of the logic of the application (see Figure 5 right).

Let us imagine that this application is undergoing the negative effects of software erosion as a consequence of the maintenance carried out in recent years. A software modernization project has therefore been planned by evolving the application to make it fit the reseller company's current situation. This means that the application must be re-implemented by preserving the embedded business knowledge. The following sections show the guidelines regarding how this application can be modernized whilst addressing the model-awareness challenges.

Representing and Handling the Recovered Knowledge

The first challenge involved in shifting from traditional reengineering to Model-Driven Reengineering concerns the representation and management of the recovered knowledge. In Model-Driven Reengineering the knowledge recovered from an LIS during the reverse engineering stage must be represented in models. A set of PSM models that can represent one or more software artifacts of the LIS is obtained. These models are represented according to specific metamodels that specify how a software artifact uses a particular type of platform or technology.

The proposed example only considers source code as a legacy software artifact, and a code model represented according to the Java metamodel should thus be represented. A parser could be used to statically analyze the legacy source code and generate the code model. The parser takes the Java source file as input (see Figure 6, left-hand side) and obtains the abstract syntax tree representing the java code model (see Figure 6, right-hand side). The parser obtains a *CompilationUnit* element for each of the java source files analyzed, and then adds the *PackageDeclaration* and *ImportDeclaration* elements. The parser subsequently generates a *ClassOrInterfaceDeclaration* element for the class, which contains a *ClassOrInterfaceBodyDeclaration* element for each method. Each method is represented through a *MethodDeclaration* with *ResultType*, *MethodDeclarator* and *Block* of *Statement* elements. The *Statement* element is, in turn, specialized into several kinds of elements: *ReturnStatement, IfStatement, Expression,* and so on. The right-hand side of Figure 6 shows the elements used to represent the business logic implemented in the 'receiveOrder' method.

LISs are becoming increasingly more complex, and the development and management of these systems already require a significant effort. However, it is possible that an even greater effort is needed to understand the complex legacy information systems in the reverse engineering stage.

Figure 6. An example transformation obtaining a code model for a product order system

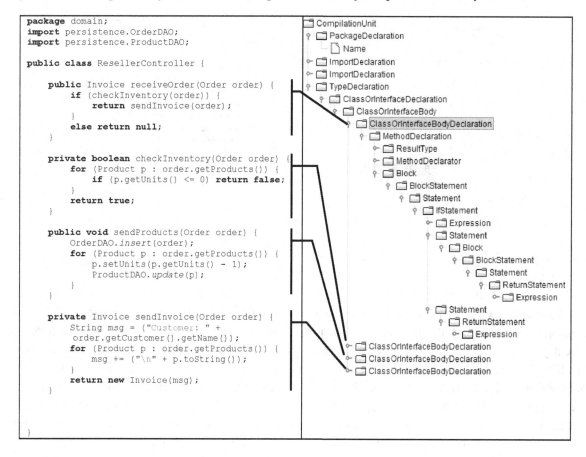

Model-Driven Reengineering, or most parts of it, must therefore be automated by means of reverse engineering tools. The KDM standard must thus be used to represent all software artifacts involved in a particular LIS, since it makes it possible to model all the artifacts of the legacy system in an integrated and technological-independent manner, i.e., it is a PIM model. The KDM model is obtained in an integrated manner because it works as a KDM repository that can be progressively populated with knowledge extracted from the different information systems of an organization. KDM can be compared with the UML standard (OMG, 2009c): While UML is used to generate new code in a top-down manner, a process involving KDM starts from the existing code and builds a higher level model in a bottom-up manner (Moyer, 2009).

The KDM standard changes the way in which reverse engineering tools are built and used. Traditional reverse engineering tools have been built as silos from which each tool recovers and analyzes different proprietary content in a single silo (see Figure 7, left). In the proposed example, a reverse engineering tool would be used for the source code and another tool would be used for the legacy database. At the end of the process we would consequently have two proprietary and independent models, a source code model and a database model, which would also have to be analyzed independently.

The KDM standard also makes it possible to build reverse engineering tools in a KDM ecosystem (see Figure 7, right). Here, the reverse engineering tools recover different knowledge related to different artifacts, but this knowledge

Figure 7. Reengineering tools: silo solutions (left) and KDM ecosystem (right)

is represented and managed in an integrated and standardized manner through KDM. The software analysis tools can thus analyze the KDM repository and generate new knowledge. Furthermore, in the future more software analysis tools can be homogeneously plugged into the KDM models to generate even more valuable knowledge.

To continue with the proposed example, in order to establish the model transformation between the code model (the PSM model) and the KDM code model (the PIM), we use QVT to define a model transformation. The example transformation specifically uses the QVT-Relation language, since the implementation of the transformation in a declarative manner is easy. This is owing to the fact that the structures of the Java metamodel and KDM code-action metamodel are very similar.

Figure 8 shows the most important metaclasses in the code and action packages of the KDM metamodel. According to the KDM code metamodel, each of the LISs analyzed must be represented as an instance of the *CodeModel* metaclass, which is the root metaclass. A *CodeModel* is composed of *AbstractCodeElements*, a metaclass that represents an abstract parent class for all KDM entities that can be used as *CallableUnit*, *StorableUnit*, and so on. The *CodeElement* metaclasses are also interrelated by means of *AbstractCodeRelationships* (*action* package),

a metaclass representing an abstract parent for all KDM relationships that can be used to represent the code relationships such as *Flow*, *Calls*, *Reads*, *Writes*, and so on.

A QVT transformation consists of several relations focusing on the transformation of specific elements. Each relation defines at least two domains of elements: (i) the source domain, tagged as *checkonly*, which evaluates whether the specific configuration of elements in the input metamodel (Java metamodel) exists, and the target domain, tagged as *enforce*, which evaluates the configuration of elements in the output metamodel (KDM) and creates or destroys elements to satisfy the rules of the relation. A QVT relation can also have *when* are *where* clauses which establish pre- and post-conditions of execution. Exhibit 1 shows a fragment of the proposed QVT transformation: the *'class2compilationUnit'* and *'method2callableUnit'* QVT relations. The *'class2compilationUnit'* relation transforms all the instances of the *Class* metaclass in the Java code model into instances of *CompilationUnit* in the KDM model. The relation also examines the *Method* instances belonging to the *Class* instance in the where clause (see Exhibit 1), and the *'method2callableUnit'* relation is triggered. The *'method2callableUnit'* relation is in charge of the transformation of the instances of the *Method*

Figure 8. Overview of action and code packages of the KDM metamodel

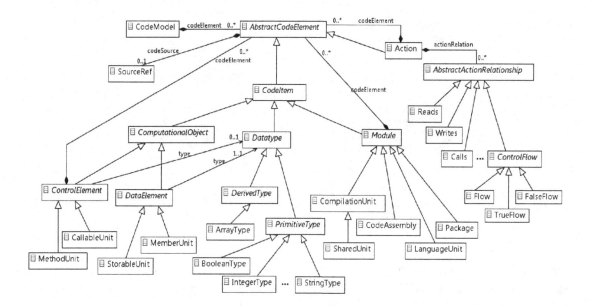

metaclass into *CallableUnit* instances with the same name and type. All the different kinds of statements in the Java code model are then transformed into *codeElement* instances by means of various QVT relations triggered in the where clause.

To continue with the example, Figure 9 shows the KDM model obtained after the execution of the proposed QVT transformation for the product shipping system. The KDM model contains a *Package* instance named *'domain'* with a nested *CompilationUnit* instance named *'Reseller'*. The *CompilationUnit* is obtained from the *Class* instance of the Java code model. The *'Reseller'* *CompilationUnit* instance contains an instance of the *CallableUnit* metaclass for each Java method.

Each *CallableUnit* instance is also defined by means of different *CodeElement* and *ActionElement* instances. For example, the *'receiveOrder'* method is modeled as a *CallableUnit* containing (see Figure 9): (i) an *EntryFlow* instance that defines the first KDM action in the unit (the first Java statement, since a model's sequentiality of actions is not clearly defined); (ii) a *Signature*

instance that defines the parameters of the unit; and finally (iii) an *ActionElement* instance that represents the *if* statement in the Java method. The remaining *CallableUnit* instances have a similar structure.

Model-Driven Refactoring

Besides representing the information recovered in the reverse engineering stage from software artifacts in models in accordance with certain metamodels, it is also necessary to apply restructuring and refactoring techniques to the models. This entails another important model-awareness challenge if appropriate Model-Driven Reengineering processes are to be attained.

The restructuring stage must therefore consist of model transformations from the input model (as is) to obtain a target model (as will be). Model-based restructuring or refactoring has certain advantages with regard to traditional refactoring: (i) model-based refactoring allows researchers to define language- and platform-independent refactoring techniques; (ii) a restructuring trans-

Exhibit 1. QVT relations to transform Java code models into KDM models

```
transformation Java2KDM (java:java, kdm:code){
   ...relation class2compilationUnit {
      className : String;
      checkonlydomain java jc : java::classifiers::Class {
            name = className
      };
      enforcedomain kdm kp : KDM_MetaModel::code::Package {
            codeElement = kcu : KDM_MetaModel::code::CompilationUnit {
               name = className
            }
      };
      where {
            jc.members->forAll (jm:java::members::Method | jm.oclIsKindOf(java
::members::Method)
                  implies method2callableUnit (jm, kcu));
      }
   }
   relation method2cllableUnit {
      methodName : String;
      methodType : String;
      checkonlydomain java jm : java::members::Method {
            name = methodName,
            typeReference = jtr : java::types::TypeReference {
               name = methodType
            }
      };
      enforcedomain kdm kcu : KDM_MetaModel::code::CompilationUnit {
            codeElement = cu : KDM_MetaModel::code::CallableUnit {
               name = methodName,
               type = t : KDM_MetaModel::code::Datatype {
                  name = methodType
               }
            }
      };
      where {
            jm.parameters->forAll(jp:java::parameters::Parameter | jp.oclIsKin
dOf(java::parameters::
                  Parameter) implies parameter2codeElement(jp, cu));
            jm.members->forAll(js:java::statements::Statement | js.oclIsKindOf
(java::statements::
                  ExpressionStatement) implies expressionStatement2codeElement
(js, cu));
```

continues on following page

Exhibit 1. Continued

```
            jm.members->forAll(js:java::statements::Statement | js.oclIsKindOf
(java::statements::
                    Conditional) implies conditional2codeElement(js, cu));
...
            jm.members->forAll(js:java::statements::Statement | js.oclIsKindOf
(java::statements::
                    Return) implies return2codeElement(js, cu));
        }
    }
    ...
}
```

formation could be implemented as a model itself, thus allowing the transformation to be reused; (iii) model-based refactoring makes it possible to define generic or domain-specific refactoring techniques in an easy manner; (iv) it improves the feature location since the traceability throughout

corresponding models at different abstraction levels is better.

According to the proposed example, once the KDM model has been obtained during the reverse engineering stage, there is an opportunity to clean up the design of the product order application. This

Figure 9. A KDM model obtained from the code model of a product order system

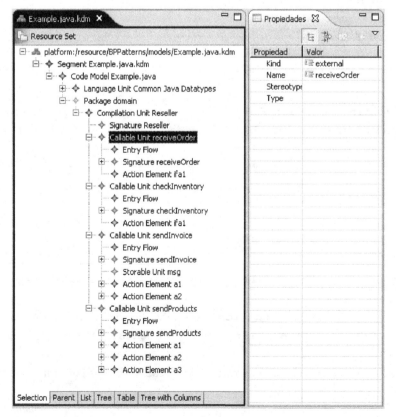

refactoring task may be difficult, particularly if the code is very poorly structured. For instance, there are large Java classes with extremely large methods (e.g, the *BuyerController* class). In this case, a small pattern in the KDM model can be defined to recognize large classes, which can be split. These classes can be redefined by extracting some methods and putting them into another class.

In Model-Driven Reengineering the pattern matching task used to recognize large classes must be supported through a model transformation and implemented by, for example, using QVT-Relations. The model transformation must inspect the KDM model and obtain an improved KDM model. For each instance of the *CompilationUnit* metaclass, that represents a large Java class, the transformation generates two or more instances of *CompilationUnit* metaclass. Each new *CompilationUnit* instance has some of the methods (represented in the KDM model as *CallableUnit* instances) of the original java class. Since the restructuring stage is also formalized by using the model-driven principles, this stage can be automated and reused in different modernization projects.

Business Process Archeology

According to (Koskinen et al , 2005), changes in business processes are one of the most important software modernization decision criteria. The recovery and preservation of the business knowledge embedded in LISs using model-driven principles

is, therefore, another important model-awareness challenge.

According to the horseshoe modernization model, the ADM-based process can be categorized into three kinds of modernization processes (Khusidman et al., 2007). These depend on the abstraction level reached in the reverse engineering stage. The reverse engineering stage is probably the most important stage in the horseshoe modernization model. This is owing to the fact that this activity conditions the abstraction level achieved in each kind of modernization process and, therefore, the resources provided and possibilities to restructure LISs. A higher abstraction level usually implies a greater amount of knowledge and rich information which provide the modernization process with more restructuring possibilities.

Figure 10 shows the three kinds of modernization processes depending on the maximum abstraction level reached during the reverse engineering stage.

- **Technical Modernization.** This kind of modernization considers the lowest abstraction level and is historically that which is most commonly applied to legacy systems. A company carries out a technical modernization project when it wishes to deal with platform or language obsolescence, new technical opportunities, conformance to standards, system efficiency, system usability or other similar modernization factors. This is sometimes not strictly considered to be a modernization

Figure 10. Three kinds of horseshoe modernization models (adapted from (Khusidman et al., 2007))

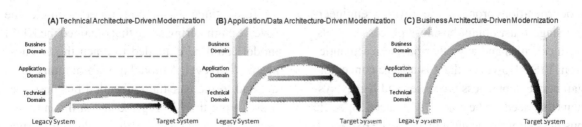

process since it focuses solely on corrective and preventive modifications, but in any case it addresses adaptive or perfective modifications according to the modernization definition.

- **Application/Data Modernization.** This kind of modernization considers an intermediate abstraction level since it focuses on restructuring a legacy system at the level of application and data design to obtain the target system. This kind of modernization is driven by several modernization factors such as improving the system reusability, reducing the delocalized system logic or system complexity, and applying design patterns. There is a fine line between this kind of modernization and the previous one, but that line is crossed when there is some impact on the system design level.

- **Business Modernization.** This kind of modernization increases the abstraction level to the maximum. The restructuring stage therefore takes place at the level of business architecture, i.e., the business rules and processes that govern a legacy system in the company. Apart from technical models and application/data models, this kind of modernization also incorporates business semantic models which are a key asset in (i) preserving the business knowledge embedded in legacy systems; and (ii) aligning the company's business requirements with the future target systems.

The reverse engineering stage is the key activity, particularly when a business modernization process is being carried out. In the third kind of modernization process, the reverse engineering stage must obtain business process models, business rules and any other business semantics from LISs. However, there is a large conceptual gap between business processes and legacy systems that needs to be gradually reduced. Specific business knowledge must therefore be extracted, although in many cases it must also be inferred or deduced from previous knowledge. This becomes an important challenge that must be addressed if appropriate Model-Driven Reengineering processes are to be carried out.

The reverse engineering stage can also be seen as a business process archeology procedure during the modernization process. Traditional archeologists investigate several artifacts and situations and attempt to understand what they are looking at, i.e., they must understand the cultural and civilizing forces that produced those artifacts. In the same way, a business process archeologist analyzes different legacy artifacts such as source code, databases and user interfaces and then tries *"to understand what they* (the business experts and systems analysts) *were thinking to understand how and why they wrote the code the way they did"* (Hunt et al., 2002). The business process archeology procedure therefore consists of analyzing different software artifacts by means of reverse engineering techniques and tools in order to obtain very abstract models that depict not only the legacy systems, but also the company and/or the company operation supported by this system, e.g., business process models.

Few attempts at business process archeology have been made to date. This might be owing to the fact that the mapping paradigms between business and IT lack the standardization needed to modernize LISs, and it is for this reason that the standardization effort by the ADMTF is so important. ADM facilitates the business process archeology procedure by means of KDM, since this standard makes it possible to represent all software artifacts involved in a certain legacy system in an integrated and standardized manner.

To continue with the proposed example, the reverse engineering stage that obtained the KDM model could be extended to reach the business abstraction level. A model transformation can be defined to recover the embedded business processes from the LIS represented at this moment as a KDM model. Firstly, the model transforma-

Figure 11. BPMN metamodel

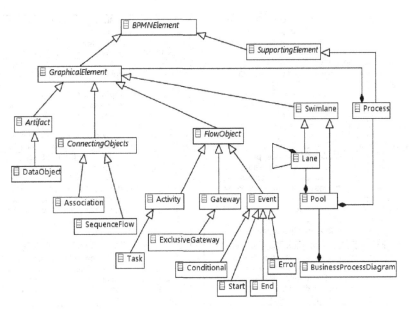

tion establishes a set of business patterns (Pérez-Castillo et al., 2010a), which define which pieces of the source code (represented in a KDM code model) are transformed into the specific structures of a business process.

Business process models are represented according to the Business Process Modeling and Notation (BPMN) metamodel. Figure 11 provides a sample view of the BPMN metamodel, which represents *business process diagrams* (BPD) that involve four kinds of elements: (i) flow object elements such as *events*, *activities* and *gateways*; (ii) connecting object elements such as *sequence flows*, *message flows* and *associations*; (iii) artifact elements such as *data objects*, *groups* and *annotations*; and (iv) swim lane elements for grouping elements such as *pools* and *lanes*.

The set of patterns are defined in terms of KDM and BPMN elements, and this transformation is thus independent of the program language and platform of the LIS in contrast to the previous transformations used in the example. This signifies that the set of proposed patterns could also be used with other systems in addition to Java-based systems. Figure 12 presents the set of busi-

ness patterns proposed by (Pérez-Castillo et al., 2010a). Each pattern consists of (i) a source configuration or structure of elements in the input KDM model, and (ii) a target structure of elements to be created in the output BPMN model.

In order to support the set of patterns, a model transformation is implemented using QVT-Relations, which supports the pattern matching process (Pérez-Castillo et al., 2010b). Each QVT relation searches for instances of the source structures defined by each pattern. The QVT relations, which are defined in a declarative manner, then enforce the creation in the business process model of instances of the target structures of the pattern for each input instance found in the KDM model.

Exhibit 2 shows a fragment of the QVT transformation: the *'Package2Pool'* and *'CallableUnit-2Task'* relations. Firstly, the *'Package2Pool'* relation transforms each instance of the *Package* metaclass into a *Process* instance nested in a *Pool* instance with the same name. This transformation builds the business process diagram skeleton in the business process model according to the *P1* pattern (see Figure 12). The *where* clause addition-

Figure 12. Summary of the set of business patterns

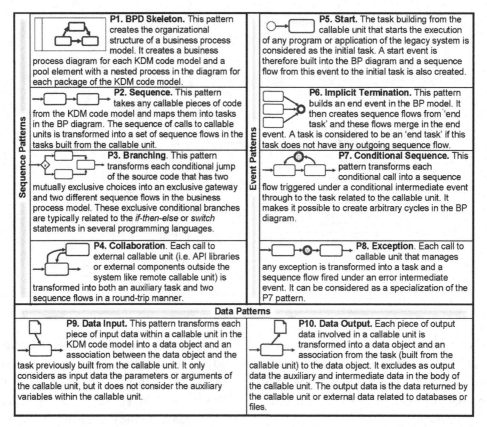

P1. BPD Skeleton. This pattern creates the organizational structure of a business process model. It creates a business process diagram for each KDM code model and a pool element with a nested process in the diagram for each package of the KDM code model.	**P5. Start.** The task building from the callable unit that starts the execution of any program or application of the legacy system is considered as the initial task. A start event is therefore built into the BP diagram and a sequence flow from this event to the initial task is also created.
P2. Sequence. This pattern takes any callable pieces of code from the KDM code model and maps them into tasks in the BP diagram. The sequence of calls to callable units is transformed into a set of sequence flows in the tasks built from the callable unit.	**P6. Implicit Termination.** This pattern builds an end event in the BP model. It then creates sequence flows from 'end task' and these flows merge in the end event. A task is considered to be an 'end task' if this task does not have any outgoing sequence flow.
P3. Branching. This pattern transforms each conditional jump of the source code that has two mutually exclusive choices into an exclusive gateway and two different sequence flows in the business process model. These exclusive conditional branches are typically related to the *if-then-else* or *switch* statements in several programming languages.	**P7. Conditional Sequence.** This pattern transforms each conditional call into a sequence flow triggered under a conditional intermediate event through to the task related to the callable unit. It makes it possible to create arbitrary cycles in the BP diagram.
P4. Collaboration. Each call to external callable unit (i.e. API libraries or external components outside the system like remote callable unit) is transformed into both an auxiliary task and two sequence flows in a round-trip manner.	**P8. Exception.** Each call to callable unit that manages any exception is transformed into a task and a sequence flow fired under an error intermediate event. It can be considered as a specialization of the P7 pattern.

Data Patterns

P9. Data Input. This pattern transforms each piece of input data within a callable unit in the KDM code model into a data object and an association between the data object and the task previously built from the callable unit. It only considers as input data the parameters or arguments of the callable unit, but it does not consider the auxiliary variables within the callable unit.	**P10. Data Output.** Each piece of output data involved in a callable unit is transformed into a data object and an association from the task (built from the callable unit) to the data object. It excludes as output data the auxiliary and intermediate data in the body of the callable unit. The output data is the data returned by the callable unit or external data related to databases or files.

ally triggers the *'CallableUnit2Task'* relation for each *CallableUnit* nested in a *CompilationUnit* that belongs to the Package instance. Secondly, the *'CallableUnit2Task'* relation transforms the *CallableUnit* instances into *Task* instances within the business process diagram supporting the *P2* pattern (see Figure 12). In the where clause, this relation calls, among others, the *'WritesStorableUnit2DataObject'* relation, which implements the *P6* pattern which is called for each piece of data written by the callable unit.

According to our example, the proposed transformation would obtain a first sketch of the business process diagram from the KDM model. Figure 13 shows the graphical representation of the business process model obtained after the execution of the QVT transformation. This model contains 10 tasks in total, although only 4 tasks are related to the four *CallableUnit* instances in the KDM model (compare Figure 13 and Figure 9), which are obtained by applying the *'P2.Sequence'* pattern. The gateways are also created by applying the *'P3. Branching'* pattern. 6 other tasks are also obtained by applying the *'P4.Collaboration'* pattern (see Figure 12). This pattern is applied to the three *ActionElement* instances of the *CallableUnit* instance named *'sendProducts'* in the KDM model (compare Figure 13 and Figure 9). These action elements represent calls to methods not defined in the same Java source file (e.g. *'update'*, *'setUnits'* and *'insert'*), and these calls are thus represented as external calls, which are transformed into six tasks with a round-trip sequence flow from the previous tasks.

The recovered business process (see Figure 13) could then be used to refactor the organization's business process at the highest abstraction level. A recent 2010 study developed by the SEI

Figure 13. An example of business process models recovered for a product order application

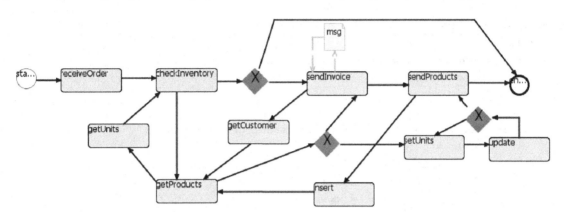

(Software Engineering Institute) (Lewis et al., 2010) states that business process recovery is needed to modernize LISs towards SOA systems. The restructuring stage could thus focus on obtaining an SOA model representing the system as a set of services. The business process restructured towards SOA would then be used at the beginning of the forward engineering stage as a valuable artifact involved in the requirements analysis task. Finally, several web services could be implemented to support the operation of the modernized system. The business process archeology challenge would consequently be addressed by following a strategy similar to that of the example presented.

Success Experiences on Model-Driven Reengineering

Despite being a relatively new approach, Model-Driven Reengineering has acquired great relevance within the academic and industrial communities. A great research effort has been carried out last years by academicians. In addition, various international projects and tools, which address the demands and challenges detected in the academic context, have flourished to achieve the appropriate transfer of technology in the industrial context.

Projects

The aim of certain international projects such as MOMOCS (MOMOCS, 2008) and Model-Ware (ModelWare, 2006) is to lead towards the industrialization of ADM and also to ensure its successful adoption by industry. Both projects are funded by the European Commission under the Information Society Technologies in the 6th Framework Program. These projects combine innovations in modeling technologies, engineering processes and methodologies, tool development, standardization, experimentations and change management.

The MOMOCS project studies how large and complex LISs can be modernized with a focus on some of their specific software portions, with the goal of *"keeping up with a very fast changing business and technical environment taking human beings as the centre of the interaction"* (MOMOCS, 2008). The MOMOCS project defines a modernization methodology that is applied to complex systems and makes it possible to reengineer software architectures, data heterogeneities and processes in order to make systems' behavior more predictably in terms of performance, stability and maintainability.

The ModelWare project has developed a complete infrastructure which is required for the

Exhibit 2. QVT relations to implement a business process archeology transformation

```
transformation patterns (kdm:code, bpmn:bpmn){
... relation Package2Pool {
xName : String;checkonlydomain kdm pk : code::Package  {
             name = xName
      };

      enforcedomain bpmn bpd: bpmn::BusinessProcessDiagram  {
             Pools = p : Pool {
                     name = xName,
                     ProcessRef = pr : bpmn::Process {
                              Name = xName
                      }
              }
       };
      where {
             pk.codeElement->forAll (c:code::AbstractCodeElement |
             c.oclAsType(code::CompilationUnit).codeElement->forAll(m:code::Abstra
ctCodeElement |
             (m.oclIsKindOf(code:: CallableUnit) and m.oclIsUndefined() and
m.oclAsType(code::
             CallableUnit).name<>'main')  implies   CallableUnit2Task (m, pr)));
...
      }
   }
... relation CallableUnit2Task {
      xName : String;
      checkonlydomain kdm m : code::CallableUnit {
             name = xName
      };
      enforcedomain bpmn pr : bpmn::Process {
             GraphicalElements = t : bpmn::Task {
                    Name = xName,
                    Status = bpmn::StatusType::None,
              }
       };
      where {
             m.codeElement->forAll (a: AbstractCodeElement | a.oclAsType (Actio-
nElement).actionRelation->forAll (w:AbstractActionRelationship |
             (w.oclIsKindOf(Writes)) and w.oclAsType(Writes).to.oclIsKindOf
(StorableUnit) implies WritesStorableUnit2DataObject (w, t, pr)));
             ...
       }
   }
}
```

large-scale deployment of model-driven development strategies, and this infrastructure has been validated in several business domains including the modernization of LISs (ModelWare, 2006). While the ModelWare project focuses on most parts of model-driven development, the MOMOCS project particularly addresses the activities and techniques of the software modernization approach.

Another relevant project is REMICS (Mohagheghi et al., 2010) which specifies, develops and evaluates a tool-supported model-driven methodology for migrating legacy applications to interoperable service cloud platforms. The migration process consists of understanding the legacy system in terms of its architecture and functions, designing a new SOA application that provides the same or better functionality, and verifying and implementing the new application in the cloud.

Moreover, in 2009 the OMG organized an *Architecture Driven Modernization Case Studies Workshop*. Some relevant works were presented at this event, which consist of real world case studies involving the automated transformation of information systems from legacy source code into modernized languages and platforms. For example, *DelaPeyronnie et al.* (DelaPeyronnie et al., 2010) present an ADM-based project for modernizing the EATMS system, an air traffic management system used at 280 airports worldwide. This project was carried out in a platform migration scenario, since the main objective was the transformation of the legacy system from the *Ada* language into the high-performance, real-time *Java* language. Another successful case study was the modernization project presented by *Barbier et al.* (Barbier et al., 2010), which focuses on how PIM models can be automatically generated from COBOL-based legacy systems.

In 2010, a study by the Standish Group (The Standish Group, 2010) reported the results of a modernization project involving an order processing application that takes orders from around the world, 24/7. According to this study, it was estimated that the LIS was costing the company

$5000 a day in lost orders, extra labor, and additional inventory. The study compares the option of carrying out a modernization project face to face with the options of rewriting the application from scratch or purchasing an application package. On the one hand, the average budget for the modernization project choice was $3.5 million for a one-and-a-half-year project. On the other hand, the estimated budget for a new development was $10 million for a three-year project, while the average cost for the purchase of an application package was $5 million and a two-year implementation project. The modernization choice was finally chosen. The modernization project was successfully carried out on time with a minimal cost overrun, in comparison to the estimations for the other two options. In addition, the expected ROI was higher for the modernization option.

Tools

At this time, there are no tools supporting a complete modernization process, i.e., the reverse engineering, restructuring and forward engineering stage. However, various tools are available to deal with certain ADM challenges. KDM SDK 2.0 is an Eclipse™ EMF plug-in which provides a set of tools for working with KDM. KDM SDK 2.0 is an adoption kit to help understand the KDM specification that facilitates mapping design from proprietary internal representation in the KDM metamodel and jump starts development of the KDM tools (KDM Analytics, 2008).

MoDisco is another important tool that consists of an Eclipse™ plug-in for model-driven reverse engineering. With MoDisco, practical extractions of models can be made from various kinds of legacy systems. In addition, MoDisco proposes a generic and extensible metamodel-driven approach to model discovery (MoDisco, 2008).

Agility™, from the Obeo company, is a tool that can be used to re-document, migrate, refactor or redesign any kind of program. Agility™ supports Ada, Java, C, C++, Forte, Cobol, Oracle

Forms and Visual Basic, among other types of programs (Obeo, 2007b). Furthermore, Obeo offers Acceleo™, another commercial tool that can be used together with Agility™. Acceleo™ is a code generator for transforming models into code by following the MDA approach (Obeo, 2007a). This tool therefore makes it possible to complete a whole modernization process based on the horseshoe model.

Modernization Workbench™ makes it possible to extract technical and business knowledge from existing application portfolios. This tool creates a centralized, always-current warehouse of business and technical intelligence regarding the applications that run in the business (Micro Focus, 2009).

BLU AGE™ (BLU AGE, 2010) focuses on the reverse engineering and forward engineering stages. On the one hand, this tool facilitates the generation of PIM models from different platforms and languages, and on the other hand it provides a module with which to automatically generate the source code of modernized systems.

Another core concept of ADM is transformation between models. There are many tools that make it possible to transform models using QVT: Medini QVT (ikv++, 2008) is an Eclipse™ application with which to transform models using QVT Relation, the declarative language of QVT; another tools is SmartQVT (France Telecom R&D, 2008), which provides an Eclipse™ plug-in to perform transformations according to QVT Operational (this tool was partly financed by the ModelWare project). These tools are not alone, since many other similar tools exist. Indeed, there are other tools that enable model transformations by following other transformation languages, such as ATL (ATLAS Transformation Language) (INRIA, 2005), TXL (Turing eXtender Language) (Queen's University et al., 2009), among others.

Finally, MARBLE, a non-commercial tool based on the Eclipse™ platform, can also be used to recover business processes from legacy systems in order to carry out business modernization processes (Pérez-Castillo et al., 2009). This tool obtains business processes through three transformations: firstly, the tool recovers PSM models from different legacy software artifacts; secondly, the tool integrates these models into a single PIM model according to the KDM metamodel; and finally, MARBLE recovers a business process model by applying a set of business patterns in the KDM model (Pérez-Castillo et al., 2010a).

CONCLUSION

As the history of software engineering reveals, information systems are not static entities that are unchangeable over time. Information systems deteriorate and age, which is known as the software erosion problem. This problem can be compared with the deterioration of any material object whose quality diminishes with use and time. However, the nature of software makes it impossible to replace an information system in the same way that a material object can be replaced. In fact, the wholesale replacement of a legacy information system has devastating economic and technical consequences.

LISs must therefore evolve to enhance versions of themselves, preserving the embedded business knowledge in order to extend the lifespan and improve the ROI of these legacy systems. This new software engineering approach is known as Model-Driven Reengineering, which allows LISs to be modernized and to evolve by considering the model-driven development principles, i.e., all the artifacts are treated as models and each model can be transformed into another model at a different abstraction level. Model-Driven Reengineering is also known as ADM (proposed by the OMG). KDM is the first and most important standard of ADM and defines a common metamodel with which to represent legacy software artifacts throughout the reverse engineering stage. KDM makes the integration between different reverse engineering tools and techniques possible.

Model-Driven Reengineering provides several key benefits: it enables business agility through software agility; better ROI value can be obtained in LISs by means of improving software development productivity and reducing maintenance efforts and costs; and the useful life of LISs can be extended. Indeed, ADM and Model-Driven Reengineering in general have acquired a certain degree of importance within academic and industrial communities, and there are several ongoing modernization projects and a wide variety of modernization tools.

FUTURE RESEARCH DIRECTIONS

In the future, software modernization will need *"to be addressed as a business issue as well as a technology issue, and therefore it is fundamentally interdisciplinary"* (Bennett et al., 2000). Model-Driven Reengineering will change how software and society interact, how software will be used, how software will behave, and how software will be developed. However, the biggest challenge for Model-Driven Reengineering is currently its more widespread adoption in the software industry. Indeed, modernization tools cannot be effective if they are not used.

Therefore, while the launch of a modernization effort is important, the sustainability and business adoption of these efforts are equally important. Thus, the communication of the added value of a certain Model-Driven Reengineering effort is also a main challenge (Ulrich, 2010).

On the other hand, in the software industry at this time, *"there is a pressing need for software on demand. This means that the basic functionality should be available before it is even required"* (Sneed, 2008). SOA environments can help to provide software as services on demand, but the problem is that an entire LIS cannot be thrown away, and must thus be modernized towards SOA environments (Lewis et al., 2010). Model-Driven Reengineering will be the cornerstone of SOA

transformations since the ADM standards help in the following way (OMG, 2006):

- They facilitate the identification of redundant, inconsistent and segregated functionalities that need to be refactored to create services.
- They also identify the interfaces that could serve as prototypes for the creation of a service that wraps a legacy system.
- They can discover and extract business logic from legacy systems as service candidates.
- They enable necessary refactoring across multiple platforms and languages.

In another research direction, ADM will address the most important problems related to the business process archeology challenge: those of *delocalization* and *interleaving*. These problems lie in the fact that pieces of knowledge are usually scattered between many LISs and a single LIS contains several pieces of business knowledge (Ratiu, 2009). Therefore, in the future, KDM should support the recovery, management and deduction of different knowledge from several LISs in an integrated and homogeneous manner.

LIST OF ABBREVIATIONS

ADM: Architecture-Driven Modernization
ASTM: Abstract Syntax Tree Metamodel
CIM: Computation Independent Model
KDM: Knowledge Discovery Metamodel
MDA: Model-Driven Architecture
MDR: Model-Driven Reengineering
OMG: Object Management Group
PIM: Platform Independent Model
PSM: Platform Specific Model
QVT: Query/View/Transformation
SMM: Software Metrics Metamodel
UML: Unified Modeling Language

REFERENCES

Analytics, K. D. M. (2008). *Knowledge discovery metamodel (KDM) software development kit 2.0 Eclipse plugin*. KDM Analytics, Inc. Retreived from http://www.kdmanalytics.com/kdmsdk/ KDMSDK_brochure.pdf

Barbier, F., Eveillard, S., Youbi, K., Guitton, O., Perrier, A., & Cariou, E. (2010). Model-driven reverse engineering of COBOL-based applications. In Ulrich, W. M., & Newcomb, P. H. (Eds.), *Information Systems transformation: Architecture driven modernization case studies* (pp. 283–299). Burlington, MA: Morgan Kauffman.

Bennett, K. H., & Rajlich, V. T. (2000). Software maintenance and evolution: A roadmap. *Proceedings of the Conference on The Future of Software Engineering*. Limerick, Ireland, ACM.

Bianchi, A., Caivano, D., Marengo, V., & Visaggio, G. (2003). Iterative reengineering of legacy systems. *IEEE Transactions on Software Engineering, 29*(3), 225–241. doi:10.1109/TSE.2003.1183932

BLUAGE. (2010). *BLUAGE - Agile model transformation*. Netfective Technology S.A.

Canfora, G., & Di Penta, M. (2007a). *New frontiers of reverse engineering. 2007 Future of Software Engineering* (pp. 326–341). IEEE Computer Society.

Canfora, G., & Penta, M. D. (2007b). *New frontiers of reverse engineering. 2007 Future of Software Engineering*. IEEE Computer Society.

Chikofsky, E. J., & Cross, J. H. (1990). Reverse engineering and design recovery: A taxonomy. *IEEE Software, 7*(1), 13–17. doi:10.1109/52.43044

DelaPeyronnie, J., Newcomb, P. H., Morillo, V., Trimech, F., Nguyen, L., & Purtill, M. (2010). Modernization of the Eurocat air traffic management system (EATMS). In Ulrich, W. M., & Newcomb, P. H. (Eds.), *Information Systems transformation: Architecture driven modernization case studies* (pp. 91–131). Burlington, MA: Morgan Kauffman.

Eckerson, W. (1995). Three tier client/server architecture: Achieving scalability, performance and efficiency in client server applications. *Open Information Systems, 10*(1), 3.

France Telecom R&D. (2008). *SmartQVT. An open source model transformation tool implementing the MOF 2.0 QVT-Operational language*. Retrieved from http://smartqvt.elibel.tm.fr/

Gamma, E., Helm, R., Johnson, R., & Vlissides, J. (1995). *Design patterns: Elements of reusable object-oriented software*. Boston, MA: Addison Wesley, Longman Publishing Co.

Ghazarian, A. (2009). A case study of source code evolution. In R. Ferenc, J. Knodel & A. Winter (Eds.), *13th European Conference on Software Maintenance and Reengineering (CSMR'09)*. Fraunhofer IESE, Kaiserslautern, Germany, IEEE Computer Society, (pp. 159-168).

Hainaut, J.-L., Henrard, J., Hick, J.-M., Roland, D., & Englebert, V. (1996). Database design recovery. *Proceedings of the 8th International Conference on Advances Information System Engineering*, (pp. 463-480). Springer-Verlag.

Hunt, A., & Thomas, D. (2002). Software archaeology. *IEEE Software, 19*(2), 20–22. doi:10.1109/52.991327

ikv++. (2008). *Medini QVT*. Retrieved from http://www.ikv.de/index.php?option=com_ content&task=view& id=75&Itemid=77

INRIA. (2005). *ATL transformation description template,* ver. 0.1. ATLAS Group. Retrieved from http://www.eclipse.org/m2m/atl/doc/ATL_Transformation_Template%5Bv00.01%5D.pdf

ISO/IEC. (2006). *ISO/IEC 14764:2006. Software engineering - Software life cycle processes - Maintenance.* Retrieved from http://www.iso.org/iso/catalogue_detail.htm?csnumber=39064

ISO/IEC. (2009). *ISO/IEC DIS 19506. Knowledge discovery meta-model (KDM), v1.1: Architecture-driven modernization.* Retrieved from http://www.iso.org/iso/iso_catalogue/catalogue_ics/catalogue_detail_ics.htm?ics1=35&ics2=080&ics3=&csnumber=32625

Jacobson, I., Christerson, M., Jonsson, P., & Övergaard, G. (1992). *Object-oriented software engineering: A use case driven approach.* Addison-Wesley.

Kazman, R., Woods, S. G., & Carrière, S. J. (1998). Requirements for integrating software architecture and reengineering models: CORUM II. *Proceedings of the Working Conference on Reverse Engineering (WCRE'98)* (pp. 154-163). IEEE Computer Society.

Khusidman, V. (2008). *ADM transformation White Paper. DRAFT V.1.* Retrieved from http://www.omg.org/docs/admtf/08-06-10.pdf.

Khusidman, V., & Ulrich, W. (2007). *Architecture-driven modernization: Transforming the enterprise, draft v.5.* Retrieved from http://www.omg.org/docs/admtf/07-12-01.pdf

Koskinen, J., Ahonen, J. J., Sivula, H., Tilus, T., Lintinen, H., & Kankaanpää, I. (2005). Software modernization decision criteria: An empirical study. *European Conference on Software Maintenance and Reengineering* (pp. 324-331). IEEE Computer Society.

Lehman, M. M., Perry, D. E., & Ramil, J. F. (1998). Implications of evolution metrics on software maintenance. *Proceedings of the International Conference on Software Maintenance,* (pp. 208-217). IEEE Computer Society.

Lewis, G. A., Smith, D. B., & Kontogiannis, K. (2010). *A research agenda for service-oriented architecture (SOA): Maintenance and evolution of service-oriented systems.* Software Engineering Institute.

Mens, T. (2008). Introduction and roadmap: History and challenges of software evolution. In Mens, T., & Denmyer, S. (Eds.), *Software evolution* (Vol. 1, pp. 1–11). Berlin, Germany: Springer. doi:10.1007/978-3-540-76440-3_1

Mens, T., & Demeyer, S. (Eds.). (2008). *Software evolution.* Berlin, Germany: Springer-Verlag.

Micro Focus. (2009). *Modernization workbench™.* Retrieved from http://www.microfocus.com/products/modernizationworkbench/

Miller, J., & Mukerji, J. (2003). *MDA guide,* version 1.0.1. Retrieved from www.omg.org/docs/omg/03-06-01.pdf

ModelWare. (2006). *ModelWare.* Project co-funded by the European Commission under the "Information Society Technologies" Sixth Framework Programme (2002-2006). Retrieved August 24, 2009, from http://www.modelware-ist.org/

MoDisco. (2008). KDM-to-UML2 Converter. MoDisco Eclipse incubation project. IST European MODELPLEX project (FP6-IP 34081). Retrieved from http://www.eclipse.org/gmt/modisco/toolBox/KDMtoUML2Converter/

Mohagheghi, P., Berre, A., Henry, A., Barbier, F., & Sadovykh, A. (2010). REMICS- REuse and migration of legacy applications to interoperable cloud services. In Di Nitto, E., & Yahyapour, R. (Eds.), *Towards a service-based Internet, LNCS 6481* (pp. 195–196). Berlin, Germany: Springer. doi:10.1007/978-3-642-17694-4_20

MOMOCS. (2008). *MOdel driven modernisation of complex systems is an EU-project.* Retrieved from http://www.momocs.org/

Moyer, B. (2009). Software archeology: Modernizing old systems. *Embedded Technology Journal, 1,* 1–4.

Müller, H. A., Jahnke, J. H., Smith, D. B., Storey, M.-A., Tilley, S. R., & Wong, K. (2000). Reverse engineering: A roadmap. *Proceedings of the Conference on The Future of Software Engineering.* Limerick, Ireland, ACM.

Obeo. (2007a). *Acceleo™.* Obeo Model Driven Company. Retrieved from http://www.obeo.fr/pages/acceleo/en

Obeo. (2007b). *Agility™.* Obeo Model Driven Company. Retrieved from http://www.obeo.fr/pages/agility/en

OMG. (2003). *Why do we need standards for the modernization of existing systems?* OMG ADM Task Force.

OMG. (2006). *Architecture-driven modernization scenarios.* Retrieved November 2, 2009, from http://adm.omg.org/ADMTF_Scenario_White_Paper%28pdf%29.pdf

OMG. (2007). *ADM task force by OMG.* Retrieved June 15, 2009, from http://www.omg.org/

OMG. (2008). *QVT. Meta object facility (MOF) 2.0 query/view/transformation specification.* Retrieved from http://www.omg.org/spec/QVT/1.0/PDF

OMG. (2009a). *Architecture-driven modernization (ADM): Knowledge discovery meta-model (KDM), v1.1.* Retrieved January 2, 2009, from http://www.omg.org/spec/KDM/1.1/PDF/

OMG. (2009b). *Architecture-driven modernization standards roadmap.* Retrieved October 29, 2009, from http://adm.omg.org/ADMTF%20Roadmap.pdf

OMG. (2009c). *UML (Unified Modeling Language). Superstructure specification,* version 2.2. Retrieved June 24, 2009, from http://www.omg.org/spec/UML/2.2/Superstructure/PDF/

Paradauskas, B., & Laurikaitis, A. (2006). Business knowledge extraction from legacy Information Systems. *Journal of Information Technology and Control, 35*(3), 214–221.

Pérez-Castillo, R., García-Rodríguez de Guzmán, I., Ávila-García, O., & Piattini, M. (2009). MARBLE: A modernization approach for recovering business processes from legacy systems. *International Workshop on Reverse Engineering Models from Software Artifacts (REM'09).* Lille, France, Simula Research Laboratory Reports, (pp. 17-20).

Pérez-Castillo, R., García-Rodríguez de Guzmán, I., Ávila-García, O., & Piattini, M. (2010a). Business process patterns for software archeology. *25th Annual ACM Symposium on Applied Computing (SAC'10).* Sierre, Switzerland, (pp. 165-166). ACM.

Pérez-Castillo, R., García-Rodríguez de Guzmán, I., & Piattini, M. (2010b). Implementing business process recovery patterns through QVT transformations. *International Conference on Model Transformation (ICMT'10), LNCS 6142* (pp. 168-183). Málaga, Spain. Springer-Verlag.

Pérez-Castillo, R., García Rodríguez de Guzmán, I., & Piattini, M. (2011). Architecture-driven modernization. In Dogru, A. H., & Bier, V. (Eds.), *Modern software engineering concepts and practices: Advanced approaches* (pp. 75–103). Hershey, PA: IGI Global.

Polo, M., Piattini, M., & Ruiz, F. (2003). *Advances in software maintenance management: Technologies and solutions.* Hershey, PA: Idea Group Publishing.

Queen's University. NSERC, & IBM. (2009). *Turing eXtender Language* (TXL). Retrieved from http://www.txl.ca/

Ratiu, D. (2009). Reverse engineering domain models from source code. *International Workshop on Reverse Engineering Models from Software Artifacts (REM'09)*. Lille, France, Simula Research Laboratory, (pp. 13-16).

Sneed, H. M. (2005). *Estimating the costs of a reengineering project*. IEEE Computer Society.

Sneed, H. M. (2008). Migrating to Web services. In De Lucia, A. (Ed.), *Emerging methods, technologies and process management in software engineering* (pp. 151–176). Wiley-IEEE Computer Society Press.

Sommerville, I. (2006). *Software engineering* (8th ed.). Addison Wesley.

The Standish Group. (2010). *Modernization. Clearing a pathway to success*. The Standish Group International, Inc.

Ulrich, W. M. (2002). *Legacy systems: Transformation strategies*. Prentice Hall.

Ulrich, W. M. (2010). Launching and sustaining modernization initiatives. In Ulrich, W. M., & Newcomb, P. H. (Eds.), *Information Systems transformation: Architecture driven modernization case studies* (pp. 403–418). Burlington, MA: Morgan Kauffman.

Visaggio, G. (2001). Ageing of a data-intensive legacy system: symptoms and remedies. *Journal of Software Maintenance, 13*(5), 281–308. doi:10.1002/smr.234

Weske, M. (2007). *Business process management: Concepts, languages, architectures*. Leipzig, Germany: Springer-Verlag.

Section 3
Testing and Software Models

Chapter 9
Model–Driven Testing with Test Sheets

Michael Felderer
University of Innsbruck, Austria

Colin Atkinson
University of Mannheim, Germany

Florian Barth
University of Mannheim, Germany

Ruth Breu
University of Innsbruck, Austria

ABSTRACT

Test Sheets provide a new way of representing tests that combines the ease-of-use of tabular test description approaches with the expressiveness of programmatic approaches. Since they are semantically self-contained, and thus executable, they offer a more compact and easy-to-understand approach to test specification than code-level representations of tests. Nevertheless, since they still define tests at a relatively low-level of detail, they can be difficult to develop, and can become quite complex when describing large testing scenarios. Model driven testing approaches on the other hand support high level, graphical views of tests and provide methodological support for deriving tests from system models. However, they invariably rely on code to describe executable versions of tests, and tend to depict the different ingredients of tests in separated, isolated views. The development of test sheets is therefore likely to be significantly simplified by the support of a suitable model-driven testing approach, while model driven testing approaches are likely to be enhanced by the availability of compact, executable representations of tests in the form of tests sheets. In this chapter we therefore explore the synergy between test sheets and model-driven development in the context of the test stories methodology. This is an advanced standards-compliant method that covers the whole test development process from abstract requirements to concrete executable tests, but in the context of programming languages as implementation vehicles. In this chapter we present a case study in which we apply the test stories methodology using test sheets as the test description, execution, and reporting vehicle.

DOI: 10.4018/978-1-61350-438-3.ch009

INTRODUCTION

Model-driven testing has gained widespread acceptance in the last few years and today is not only an active research area but is also a regular component of mainstream software engineering projects. This was perhaps inevitable because the benefits of using high-level, (semi-) formal models to assist in the analysis and design of tests are similar to the benefits of using them for the analysis and design of application code. In fact, in the early stages of system specification the same models cover the behaviour of both because the specification of a software system describes the required behaviour of the main application code as well as the tests designed to check it. Most approaches for model-driven testing are therefore derived from mainstream modelling approaches such as the UML (e.g. UML2 Testing Profile (OMG, 2005), (Baker et al., 2007)) or SDL (e.g. TTCN-3 (Willcock et al., 2005)).

Although model-driven testing methods can significantly enhance the testing process, however, just like the models used to develop the main application functionality they always need to be mapped into code at the end of the development process. In other words, a model is still a means to an end rather than an end in itself, and cannot usually be used to drive tests without at least some code being written by hand. Another weakness of the models supported by today's model-driven testing approaches is that they are only able to capture one isolated aspect of a test and provide little support for an integrated view of how a system should behave. More specifically, the models used in today's model-driven development methods typically focus either on the test data (input and expected values), the execution logic or the result data. This makes them ideal for understanding key aspects of test while they are being analysed and designed, but less suitable for executing and documenting them.

Test sheets, on the other hand, have the opposite mix of strengths and weaknesses. They were designed to address the above problems by providing compact, executable description of tests that are nevertheless easy-to-write and understand. They are therefore comparable to test code in that they are executable, yet they are comparable to models in that they are relatively user friendly and platform independent. Nevertheless, like any executable specifications, writing test sheets is greatly simplified by the support of a high-level analysis and design models backed up by an accompanying methodology. The premise of this chapter, therefore, is that model-driven testing and test sheets are highly complementary, and that the latter providing an ideal vehicle for capturing the knowledge and insights gained in the former. The goal of this chapter is to present this potential synergy and illustrate how test sheets and model-driven testing complement each other. The model-driven development method that we use for the investigation is the Telling TestStories (TTS) methodology (Felderer, Breu et al., 2009). Although it primarily uses graph-based models, certain key views of the TTS approach are tabular.

However, the integration of a model-driven testing approach like TTS with test sheets has to fulfil several requirements:

- The approach supports the automatic validation and quality assurance of designed test cases.
- The approach emphasizes the uses of user-friendly models backed up by rigorous specification, validation and quality assurance techniques.
- The approach guarantees traceability between tests, requirements, system elements and the artefacts of the system under test.
- The approach has an operational semantics and a semantically self-contained tabular test notation.
- The approach has a self-contained semantics for all its artefacts.

- The approach supports iterative, incremental, model-driven, and test-driven development.
- The approach has an abstract and user-friendly test definition format supporting test design by customers and domain experts.
- The approach supports an understandable and comprehensive way of representing test results
- The approach has one user-friendly tool implementation that integrates test sheets and model-driven testing.
- The approach and its tool implementation are compatible with existing modelling and testing standards.
- The approach supports system testing for arbitrary service technologies.

After discussing background on testing and model-driven testing in the next section, we first present the Test Sheets and the Telling TestStories approach separately. We then describe a running case study that we use to discuss the integration of the two approaches – a real-life telephony example from the automobile domain. We then start the comparison process by presenting the artefacts that are used to describe the same tests in each approach. Afterwards we compare and contrast test sheets and TTS, pointing out their strengths and weaknesses and identifying where they may reinforce each other. We discuss some concrete strategies for using the two technologies together and of obtaining a synergy between them that fulfil the requirements stated before. Finally, we conclude and present future research directions.

BACKGROUND

Testing is the evaluation of software by observing its execution (Ammann & Offutt, 2008). The executed system is called the *system under test* (SUT). Software testing consists of the *dynamic*

verification of the behaviour of a program on a *finite* set of test cases, suitably *selected* from the usually infinite execution domain, against the *expected* behaviour (Bourque & Dupuis, 2004). In a test case, the actual and intended behaviour of a SUT are compared with each other and *verdict* created. Generally, verdicts can be either of *pass* (behaviours conform), *fail* (behaviours don't conform), and *inconclusive* (not known whether behaviours conform) (ISO/IEC, 1994). A *test oracle* is a mechanism for determining the verdict. Testing comprises several activities. According to the generic test process of the International Software Testing Qualification Board (Black, 2008) testing involves the activities: planning and control, analysis and design, implementation and execution, evaluation and reporting, plus test closure activities. Test sheets and Telling TestStories focus on the activities design, implementation, execution, evaluation and reporting of tests but do not consider test management activities any further.

According to the level of detail, we can distinguish *unit testing* which is applied to the smallest unit of program code, *module testing* which tests the conformance of distinct components of a system, and *system testing* which is applied to a complete system. System testing in our respect is based on the system requirements. We therefore do not consider acceptance testing as separate testing category because acceptance testing is requirements testing from the customer's perspective and an extension of system testing focusing on usability requirements (Bertolino & Marchetti, 2005).

In principle, any form of software testing can be seen as model-based. The tester always forms a mental model of the system under test before engaging in activities such as test case design (Binder, 1999). The term *model-based testing* (MBT) is applicable when these mental models are documented and subsequently used to generate tests, to execute tests or to evaluate their results (Hartmann et al., 2005). There are many definitions of MBT (Roßner et al., 2010) but each contains at least one of the two aspects modelling of tests and generation of tests from models. The topic of model-based testing is well-covered in the literature (see (Broy et al., 2005) for an overview) and many tools are already on the market supporting model-based approaches (Goetz et al., 2009). According to (Zander et al., 2005a) we define model-driven testing as testing-based model-driven architecture (MDA) (OMG, 2003). Model-driven testing therefore comprises the derivation of executable test code from test models and can be considered as a specific type of model-based testing. Full automated generation of executable test can only be done in certain limited cases, however.

Abbors et al., (Abbors et al., 2009) define a requirements model and a system model similar to our approach based on domains models, used and required interfaces, and state machines. But in that approach only the mapping to Qtronic (Conformiq, 2009), a tool for automated test design, and not traceability or the relationship between the system and an independent test model are considered.

A model-driven approach to testing SOA with the UML 2.0 Testing Profile (OMG, 2005) is defined in (Baker et al., 2007). It focuses on web services technology and uses the whole set of UML 2.0 Testing profile (U2TP) concepts. Our approach can be mapped to that approach but additionally it is designed for arbitrary service technologies, provides a service-centric view on tests, supports

the tabular definition of tests and guarantees traceability between all involved artefacts.

In (Zander et al., 2005b) model-driven testing is defined and implemented by mapping test models in U2TP to test code in TTCN-3. The focus of the chapter is on the transformation of test models to executable code whereas TTS focuses on the relationship between requirements, test models and system models.

In (Margaria & Steffen, 2004) a system testing method whose test model is based on test graphs similar to our test stories is presented. Therein consistency and correctness is validated via model checking but the relationship to system models and traceability such as in our approach are not considered.

Overview of Test Sheets

The goal of test sheets is to provide a simple, concise and easy-to-understand description of tests that is, at the same time, directly executable (Atkinson et al. 2008, Atkinson et al. 2010). They achieve this by combining the tabular test definition metaphor of approaches such as FIT (Framework for Integrated Test) (Mugridge and Cunningham 2005) with the imperative programming style of mainstream programming languages.

The basic form of test sheets is shown in Figure 1. Each row represents one invocation of the SUT. This can be a complete software system, a component or a single object in a programming

Figure 1. Format of a basic test sheet

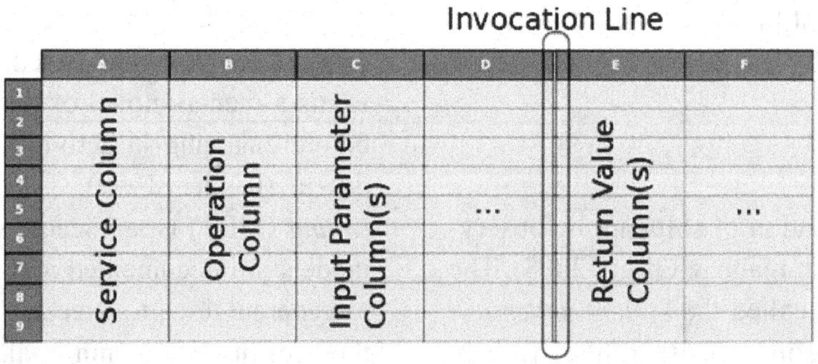

language such as Java. The first cell in each row identifies the target of the invocation while the second cell identifies the invoked operation. This is similar to method calls in a regular object oriented program. The remaining cells contain the input and output parameters (results) of the operation invocation. Those to the left of the so called invocation line (highlighted by a double lined boundary) contain the input parameters while those to the right of the invocation line contain the output parameters (or the results). If the entity under test is written in a mainstream object-oriented programming language such as Java there can be only one such column to the right of the invocation line because methods in java can only return one value. However, other languages and technologies such as web services support more than one return value.

Figure 2 shows a simple test sheet that verifies the behaviour of a calculator object. This compo-

nent is initialised in the first row and some of the basic operations are tested in the following rows. All cells in a test sheet maintain their state during the execution of the test. In rows 2 and 3, the identifier of the cell in which the initialised Calculator object was initially returned ("E1") is used to identify it as the target for ensuing invocations. Furthermore, the result of the second row is used as a parameter in the third row. Values specified in the result column represent expected values that need to be checked against those actually returned by the SUT during the test. Since test sheets maintain the state of all objects during their execution it is possible to add a value to the memory of the Calculator and verify the correct retrieval of this value in rows 4 and 5.

The results of test sheet executions are displayed using the same metaphor in the form of so called result test sheets. More specifically, information from the input test sheet is enhanced

Figure 2. Example input test sheet

	A	B	C	D	E
1	Calculator	init			
2	E1	add	2	7	9
3	E1	subtract	E2	5	4
4	E1	store	0.0		
5	E1	retrieve			C4

Figure 3. Example result test sheet

	A	B	C	D	E
1	Calculator	init			:Calculator
2	E1	add	2	7	9
3	E1	subtract	E2	5	4
4	E1	store	0		
5	E1	retrieve			0 / -1

Figure 4. Deterministic non-linear test sheet

	A	B	C	D
1	Calculator	init		
2	D1	store	random uniform()[1...1...100]	
3	D1	retrieve	C2	
4	D1	store	0	error
5	-> 6 / 1			
6	[#2 <= 10] -> 6 / 2	[#2 == 10] -> 7 / 3		
7	100% -> 8 / 4			
8				

with data from the execution of the test to produce a corresponding result test sheet. Figure 3 shows a result test sheet generated by applying the input test in Figure 2 to a Calculator object. The main difference is that the result columns now contain the values that have been returned by the SUT. Furthermore, in cells where expected values were specified in the input test sheet, the equivalence of the specified values to the actual returned values is indicated by a red/green colouring scheme. If the two values matched, the cell is coloured green and if they did not, both the expected and returned values are displayed, and the latter is coloured red, as illustrated in Figure 3. Note that in the grey scale versions of this chapter, green cells appear grey while red cells appear black with white text.

The test sheets shown so far are "linear" test sheets since the rows within them are executed sequentially from top to bottom. To support the description of more complex kinds of tests, non-linear tests sheets can also be defined in which the order of the execution of the rows is controlled by an additional "behaviour specification". This appears in an extra section of the tests sheet under the operation invocation rows, separated from them by a double line similar to the invocation line. Basically, the rows in this behavioural specification represent a state machine that can be either deterministic or probabilistic. Figure 4 shows a non-linear test sheet for the aforementioned Calculator. The first row represents the starting state of the state machine. Each behavioural cell represents a possible transition to another (or the same) state and defines the conditions

Figure 5. Probabilistic multi-scenario test sheet

	A	B	C	D	E
1	Calculator	init			
2	E1	add	random uniform()[1...1...10000]	random uniform()[1...1...10000]	C2+D2
3	E2	subtract	random uniform()[1...1...10000]	random uniform()[1...1...10000]	C3-D3
4	E3	multiply	random uniform()[1...1...10000]	random uniform()[1...1...10000]	C4*D4
5	E4	divide	random uniform()[1...1...10000]	random uniform()[1...1...10000]	C5/D5
6	-> 7 / 1				
7	30% -> 7 / 2	20% -> 7 / 3	25% -> 7 / 4	15% -> 7 / 4	10% -> 8
8					

Figure 6. Parameterized test sheet

	A	B	C	D
1	Calculator	init		
2	D1	store	random uniform()[1...1...100]	
3	D1	retrieve	C2	
4	D1	store	0	error
5	-> 6 / 1			
6	[#2 <= ?C] -> 6 / 2	[#2 == ?C] -> 7 / 3		
7	100% -> 8 / 4			
8				

under which it is selected, the next state after the transition has completed and the rows that are executed during the transition. For example, the first transition in the sixth row will be chosen if the number of executions of the second row up to that point, indicated by "#2", is less than or equal to 10. Then it will transition to the state represented by row 6 while executing row 2. The example in Figure 4 verifies the correct behaviour of the memory of the Calculator when implemented as a Stack. After adding ten values to the memory, a value is retrieved and validated. After this, a memory overflow is simulated by adding another value to the Stack and expecting an Exception to be raised, as indicated by the keyword "error".

Figure 5 shows another example of a non-linear test sheet that is based on a Markov model rather than a deterministic state machine. This stimulates the SUT based on a probabilistic behavioural model that can represent a realistic usage profile. The basic operations of the Calculator are invoked with random values based on the probabilistic distribution defined in row 7.

Another important enhancement of basic test sheets is provided by so called parameterized and higher order test sheets. Figure 6 is a slightly modified version of the test sheet in Figure 2 in which the values that control the number of values to be added to the memory have been replaced by a parameter "?C" that is supplied by a so called higher order test sheet.

Figure 7 shows a higher-order test sheet (in this case a second order test sheet) that twice invokes the first-order test sheet in Figure 6, once with the actual value 10 for the ?C parameter and once with the value 100. The result of a parameterized test sheet is a Boolean indicating the success of the test. Successful invocations of lower order tests are therefore expected to return "true" as the result value. Each invocation in the higher-order test sheet creates one execution of, thus one instance of, the lower-order test sheets. The result test sheets for these instances are also available after the test has been executed and can be analysed to discover the source of any failures that are detected.

Using parameterized and higher-order test sheets it is possible to organize test sheets into hierarchies that reflect complex tests suites. The key thing to note about test sheets is that although they are directly executable (after automated transformation into code) and no programming knowledge is required to write or understand them. Moreover they combine the definition of the invoked operations and test execution algorithms with a definition of the input parameters (test data), the expected return values and the actual test results. No other executable test specification

Figure 7. Higher order test sheet

	A	B	C	D
1	MemoryTest	test	10	true
2	MemoryTest	test	100	true

to our knowledge integrates all this information into a single view.

Overview of "Telling Teststories"

"Telling TestStories" (TTS) is a model-driven testing method for service-centric systems. The term *test story* was introduced in (Felderer, Breu et al., 2009) to emphasize the analogy with the term "user story" used in agile development to define a manageable requirement associated with acceptance tests. Like all testing methods it defines the activities and steps that make up the testing process and the artefacts that are generated, manipulated and used during this process. To provide an overview of the approach, in the next subsection we first describe the artefacts involved in the model-driven testing process and the relationships between them. In the subsequent subsection we then describe the main activates and steps involved in the process. A more detailed overview which discusses also the underlying meta models is presented in (Felderer, Breu et al., 2009).

TTS System and Testing Artefacts

Figure 8 depicts the artefacts involved in TTS and the relationships between them. Informal artefacts are depicted by clouds, (semi-) formal models by graphs, code by transparent blocks and running systems by filled blocks.

Based on the *Informal Requirements*, a *Requirements Model* is defined. Its model elements are traceable to model elements of the *System Model* and the *Test Model*. The system model is needed for validation, coverage checks and generation of the test model. The test model is used for validating the system model. From the test model *Test Code* is generated. The test code is executed by the *Test Controller* using *Adapter* classes to invoke operations on the *System Under Test*. The transformation from the system model to the system under test is symbolized by the dashed line in Figure 8, but this is not considered further in this chapter as it is not the focus of the discussion.

Requirements Model

The Requirements Model contains the functional and non-functional requirements for system development and testing. Its structured part consists of a requirements hierarchy. The requirements are based on informal requirements depicted as a cloud. The requirements model provides a way to integrate textual descriptions of requirements needed for communication with non-technicians into a modelling tool.

System Model

The system model describes the system structure and system behaviour in a platform independent way. Its *static structure* is based on the notion of services. Each (business) service or even each operation is assigned to a requirement. We assume that each service in the system model corresponds to an executable service in the running system to guarantee traceability. Additionally, configuration services for configuring the system or modifying

Figure 8. Overview of TTS artefacts and their relationship

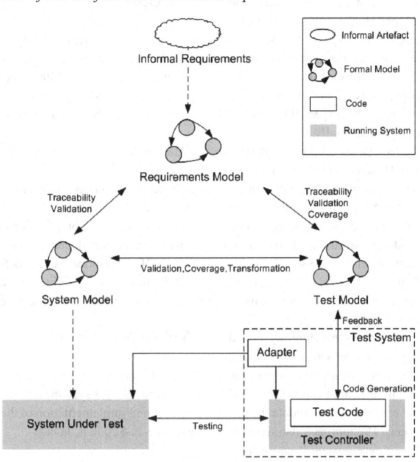

types and information services providing information about the business objects may be defined. The latter two types of services do not correspond to requirements. Nevertheless, all requirements, (business) services and executable services are traceable. The *dynamic structure* is based on local processes controlled by a specific service that correspond to an orchestration, and global processes which integrate several services and correspond to a choreography.

Test Model

The test model defines the test requirements, the test data and the test scenarios as so called test stories. We use the terms "test story" and "test" interchangeably in this chapter depending on

the context. To convey the more abstract view, we use the term "test, and to convey the more application-oriented and process-oriented view we use the term "test story". *Test stories* (i.e. tests) are controlled sequences of service operation invocations defining the interaction of services and assertions for computing verdicts. Tests may be generic in the sense that they do not contain concrete objects but variables which refer to test objects provided in tables. Tests can also invoke configuration services for the system setup and tear down. The concept of a test is in principle of its representation. We apply UML sequence diagrams (Felderer et al., 2010) and UML activity diagrams (Felderer, Zech et al., 2009) but are not restricted to these notations. Tests include references to a table of test data including values for all free parameters of the test. Each line in this table defines test data for one test case. The test data elements are stored in a *data pool*. *Test Requirements* can contain global arbitrations that define when a test is successful by restrictions on the verdicts, or coverage constraints that define what parts of a model have to be inspected by a test.

If tests are designed manually, the test stories tool has to guarantee that the tests are consistent with each other and that the set of tests in the test model fulfils some coverage criteria with respect to the system model. Alternatively, if the system model is complete, then tests can be generated by a model-to-model transformation between the system and the test model. If the system model is not complete, then the test model can be regarded as an integrated part of the system specification, a so called *partial system specification*. This model-driven approach can therefore be applied in a system-driven way by deriving tests from the system model or in a test-driven way by integrating tests into the system. In all application scenarios, the system model can be used to validate the test model and vice versa. The approach also supports classical *test-driven development* because from test models and adapters it is possible to derive executable tests even before the system implementation has been finished. Tests are linked to requirements and associated with services of the systems by service calls. Tests can additionally be transformed from an abstract workflow representation to a concrete test representation from which test code can be generated.

Each test is linked to a requirement and can therefore be regarded as an executable requirement by analogy with FIT tests (Mugridge & Cunningham, 2005). Tests in our sense can also be used as testing facets (Canfora & Di Penta, 2008) defining built-in test cases for a service that allows potential actors to evaluate the service. Together with appropriate requirements the tests may serve as executable SLAs.

Test Code

The test code is generated by a model-to-text transformation from the test model as explained in (Felderer, Fiedler et al., 2009). The transformation generates test code by a model-to-text transformation that can be executed by a test controller.

Adapters

Adapters are needed to access the operations provided and required by components of the system under test. For a service implemented as a web service, an adapter can be generated from its WSDL description. Adapters for each service are the link for traceability between the executable system, the test model and the requirements.

Test Controller

The test controller executes the generated test code and accesses the system services via adapters. The current implementation of the test controller executes test code in Java.

Test System

The test controller, the adapter and the test code form the test system.

System Under Test

The system under test (SUT) is a service-centric system with service interfaces that provide and require operations.

In TTS, traceability is guaranteed between all artefacts. Requirements, tests and services are associated on the model level via links between model elements. Each modelled service is associated with an executable service in the system. The adapter link service calls in the model to executable services. Every service invocation is thereby traceable to a requirement.

TTS Testing Process

Based on the artefacts presented in the previous section, in this subsection we define the stages of the TTS testing process and the affected artefacts. The process, depicted in Figure 9, consists of *design*, *validation*, *generation*, *execution* and *evaluation* phases performed in an iterative way. Initially, the process is triggered by requirements for which services and tests have to be defined.

The first step is the definition of requirements. Based on the requirements, the system model containing services and the test model containing tests are designed. The test model design includes the data pool definition and the definition of test requirements. The system model and the test model, including the tests, the data pool and the test requirements, can be validated for consistency and completeness and checked for coverage. In a system-driven approach tests can be gener-

ated from the system model by model-to-model transformations, and in a test-driven approach tests can be integrated in the system model. These validity checks facilitate iterative improvement of the system and test quality. In principle, the testing process can also be viewed as a test model-driven development process. The methodology does not consider the system development itself but is based on traceable services offered by the system under test. As soon as adapters are available for the system services, which may be generated (semi-) automatically or manually, depending on the technology, the process of test selection and test code generation (i.e. model-to-text transformation) can take place. The generated test code is then automatically compiled and executed by a test controller which logs all occurring events into a test log. Test evaluation is done offline by a test analysis tool which generates test reports and creates annotations to those

Figure 9. Model-driven testing process

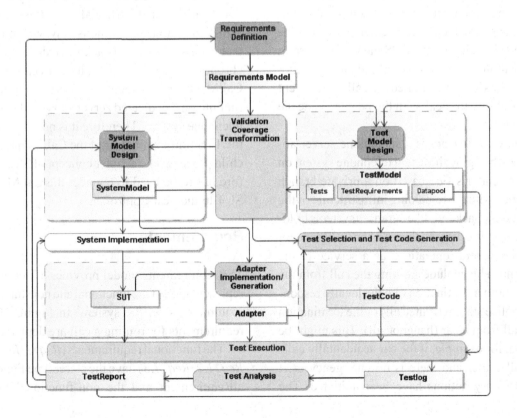

elements of the system and test model influencing the test result. Test reports and test logs are implementation artefacts that are not important for the overall process but for the practical evaluation process. Therefore, test reports and test logs are not considered further in the discussion.

The Case Study

To compare the TTS and test sheet approaches and discuss how they can be used together we will use the CallManager case study. The CallManager is an application in the area of Computer Telephony Integration (CTI) and parts of it have already been tested with unit tests. But the whole application can currently only be tested by manual tests. The CallManager application is a telematics system for the automotive industry developed for a big German car vendor. The application has been developed according to the European Union *eCall* rules that require any newly homologated car to be equipped with a technical device automatically initiating emergency calls when an accident happened. In this context, car specific information has to be transmitted to the call center answering the phone call including the GPS data of the current car position or the number of fired airbags. After the data has been transmitted the call center agent has the ability to speak with the people inside the crashed car.

The CallManager is a standalone server application bridging the actual telephone system on the car vendor's side based on a private branch exchange with the remaining infrastructure of the car vendor (Backend) like database systems holding car specific data. To this end, the CallManager provides several operations as a service to the Backend. This includes routing the call from the car to another destination like the locally responsible police station (routeCall) or the termination of a call from a car (hangupCall). This might be needed, for example, if the car accidentally calls the call center and there is no emergency or if all necessary actions have been initiated. The CallManager application connects the telephone system with the remaining backend of the car vendor, including the actual call center in order to fully handle the call.

In almost all scenarios the car executes the initial call so the CallManager is equipped with an asynchronous notification mechanism to inform the Backend of incoming calls or the termination of the call may be due to signal loss. Not only the initial notification but all service calls are asynchronous due to the nature of telephone systems. As already mentioned, the CallManager has a wide variety of possible use cases. In this case study, we focus on the following concrete scenario: We assume a car has an accident, collects all necessary data and initiates a call to the call center. This brings the CallManager into action and it performs its internal procedure of collecting the transmitted data and notifying the Backend of an incoming call. After the initial call has been received the call is routed to another destination such as the local police station. Afterwards the Backend decides to terminate the call by hanging up. As mentioned earlier all communication is achieved in an asynchronous way, which means that each service call is acknowledged by asynchronous events. As an additional challenge the CallManager is a standalone server application running on a dedicated server separated from the telephone system. Therefore it is not possible for the TTS framework to start the CallManager as a child process. The adapter concept of TTS therefore has to be used to connect the CallManager SUT to the Test Controller.

Requirements

The requirements model provides a hierarchical representation of the functional and non-functional requirements on the system. In Figure 10, the requirements for routing a call are depicted.

The functional requirements (*Req_1, Req_1.1, Req_1.2, Req_1.3*) have the stereotype FunctionalRequirement and the non-functional perfor-

Figure 10. Requirements of the CallManager application

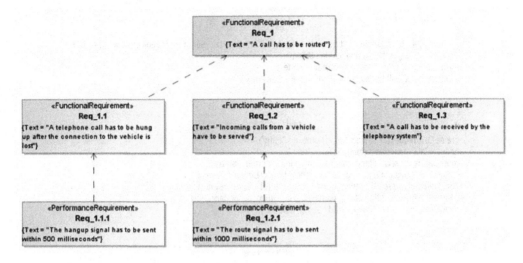

mance requirements (*Req_1.1.1, Req_1.2.1*) have the stereotype PerformanceRequirement which is a subtype of the meta model element NonFunctionalRequirement.

System

The system model of the CallManager defines amongst other things types representing the system, the services and the processes.

Types

The services have concrete interfaces. These interfaces use Java standard types such as primitive types and String (which are not modelled explicitly) and user defined types such as the complex type *ByteArray* and the enumeration type *ErrorTypes*.

Services and Interfaces

The system consists of four services providing and requiring interfaces. The services are depicted in Figure 11 and the interfaces in Figure 12.

The system provides the following services:

- The *VehicleService* represents the car that has an integrated telephone to initialize a call or to hang it up.

Figure 11. Service of the CallManager application

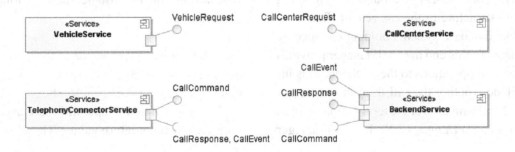

Figure 12. Interfaces of the CallManager application

- The *CallCenterService* represents a call center that receives routed calls from the vehicle via a telephone system.
- The *TelephonyConnectorService* is the service under test and models the CallManager. Technically, the CallManager is a stand-alone server application bridging the actual telephone system on the car vendor's side based on a private branch exchange.
- The *BackendService* models the remaining infrastructure of the car vendor (Backend) like database systems holding car specific data. To this end the CallManager provides several operations to the Backend. This includes routing the call from the car to another destination or the termination of a call from a car (*hangupCall*). The CallManager

application bridges the Telephony System with the remaining Backend of the car vendor, including the actual call center in order to fully control the handling of the call. The Backend is the only service without an underlying telephony infrastructure.

Each operation may have a precondition and a postcondition represented in OCL. The operation *initiateCall* for instance has the following precondition.

```
callerNumber.size>=0 and calledNum-
ber.size>=0 and callId.size>=0 and
callerNumber <> calledNumber
```

In this example the operations are asynchronous calls without return values. Therefore there are no postconditions defining a relationship between input and output parameters. In general failed preconditions indicate an irregularity in the environment and failed postconditions indicate irregularities in the operation under test (Meyer et al., 2009). We do not need the full capabilities of pre- and postconditions in our example we just use them to automate the application of oracles by evaluating assertions. Therefore in our implementation, if a precondition of a service call evaluates to false we assign it an inconclusive verdict, and if a postcondition evaluates to false we assign it a failed verdict. Additional pre- and postcondition based testing techniques for test generation are not considered in this chapter but can in principle be integrated into the framework.

Processes

A local process for the *VehicleService* is modelled as a state machine. The local process defines two internal states (*Ready* and *Calling*) for the vehicle. If the operation *hangupCall* is executed in state *Calling* then the state machine goes to state *Ready*. If the operation *initiateCall* is executed in state *Ready* then the state machine goes to state *Calling*. A global process for routing a call can be represented by a UML activity diagram. We do not consider a global workflow here but in other scenarios global workflows can be the basis for the generation of tests or for checking the consistency of tests.

Figure 13. Test for RouteCall

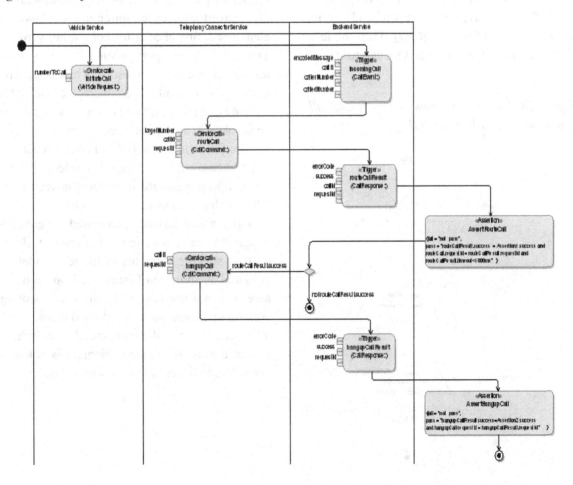

Test Artifacts for the Case Study

In this section we illustrate the artefacts that would be generated using the two different approaches under consideration in this chapter, TTS and test sheets, to develop and apply tests for the CallManager application.

Test Stories Artefacts

The test model for the CallManager example based on the requirements and system model defined in the previous section is represented in terms of UML activity diagrams and the corresponding data tables. Figure 13 depicts one parameterized test *RouteCall* that is referred to in the test *TestSuite* depicted in Figure 14 and fed with data defined in the test data table of Table 1.

In the test *RouteCall*, a call is initiated (*initiateCall*), and a trigger in the backend service receives the call (*incomingCall*). Then the telephone call is routed via the service call *routeCall*

and the trigger *routeCallResult*, and finally the telephone call is terminated via the service call *hangupCall* and the trigger *hangupCallResult*. Assertions check whether the routing and hangup return the expected values and react in time. The test *CallManagerTestSuite* calls the parameterized tests *RouteCall, ConnectCall*, and *RerouteCall* with the corresponding test data tables *RouteCallTestData, ConnectCallTestData*, and *RerouteCallTestData*.

The assertions check that the percentage of passes is *100%* for *RouteCall*, more than *90%* for *ConnectCall*, and that the average time for passed test cases is below 100 milliseconds for *RerouteCall*. Basically, the tests define activity flows of the system. The attached stereotypes define its operational semantics. Servicecall elements are invoked by the test execution engine on specific services depicted by lifelines, Trigger elements are invoked on the test execution engine and Assertion elements define checks for computing verdicts. The test *CallManagerTestSuite* is the top-level test containing all other tests in a hierarchy. This test may have an attached coverage constraint to indicate that all operations of the system have to be invoked in at least one service call.

The following table (table 1) defines data for two test cases. It also uses a data selection function *genInt* to generate an integer between 1 and 100 which serves as request identifier.

After a test has been executed a verdict is assigned to each assertion of the test run. Based on that, specific elements of the test model are coloured as shown in Figure 15. If at least one assertion in a test case fails, the corresponding column in the test table is coloured black, and if all assertions pass, the corresponding column is coloured gray. A sequence element is coloured according to the result of its arbitration.

Figure 14. Overall test sequence for RouteCall, ConnectCall and RerouteCall

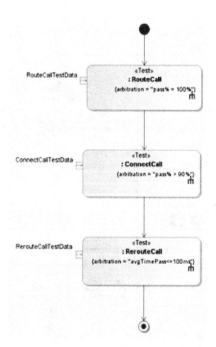

Table 1. Test data for RouteCall

Parameter	Test 1	Test 2
initiateCall.numberToCall	SIP:1234	SIP:1234
routeCall.requested	genInt(1,100)	genInt(1,100)
routeCall.callId	incomingCall.callId	incomingCall.callId
routeCall.targetNumber	SIP:transfer	SIP:invalid
Assertion1.success	True	False
hangupCall.requestId	routeCallResult.requestId	
hangupCall.callId	routeCallResult.callId	
Assertion2.success	true	

Test Sheet Artefacts

Each test in TTS can basically be mapped into a test sheet. The basic input test sheet for the test of *RouteCall* (see Figure 13) is depicted in Figure 16.

Each row of the test sheet represents a call to the system's functionality. The input parameters and output values are always separated into two distinct areas separated by the so called invocation line depicted by the vertical double line between the columns E and F in Figure 16.

In the lines 1 to 3, objects for the *Vehicle*, the *TelephonyConnector* and the *Backend* are created. They correspond to the partitions in TTS. In line 4 the object created by *Vehicle.create()* is referenced by F1 and the operation *initiateCall* with the input

literal ``*SIP:1234*'' is invoked on it. The calls of *incomingCall* and *routeCall* are similar - *rand() [1...100]* generates a randomized integer number between 1 and 100. The call *getRouteCallResult* in line 7 has a timeout with value 1000 as input parameter. In lines 8, 9 and 10 the values for the variables *callId*, *success*, and *requestId* are retrieved and compared to the expected return values in column F. These checks correspond to three assertions *routeCall.CallId=routeCallResult. CallId, routeCall.requestId=routeCallResult.requestId*, and *routeCallResult.success=Assertion1. success*. After the invocation of *hangUpCall*, the values for *success* and *requestId* are retrieved and checked by comparison to the lines 8 to 10. The Backend provides the operations *getRouteCallRe-*

Figure 15. Test result representation in TTS

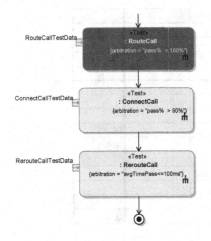

Paramter	Test1	Test2
initiateCall.numberToCall	SIP:1234	SIP:1234
routeCall.requestId	genInt(1,100)	genInt(1,100)
routeCall.callId	incomingCall.callId	incomingCall.callId
routeCall.targetNumber	SIP:transfer	SIP:invalid
Assertion1.success	true	false
hangupCall.requestId	routeCallResult.requestId	
hangupCall.callId	routeCallResult.callId	
Assertion2.success	true	

Figure 16. Input test sheet RouteCallTest for testing RouteCall

	A	B	C	D	E	F
1	'Vehicle	create				
2	'TelephonyConnector	create				
3	'BackendMock	create				
4	F1	initiateCall	"SIP:1234"			
5	F3	incomingCall				
6	F2	routeCall	"SIP:transfer"	F4	rand()[1...100]	
7	F3	getRouteCallResult	1000			
8	F7	getCallId				D6
9	F7	getSuccess				true
10	F7	getRequestId				E6
11	F2	hangUpCall	D4	rand()[1...100]		
12	F3	getHangupCallResult				
13	F12	getSuccess				true
14	F12	getRequestId				D11

sult and *getHangupCallResult* to retrieve objects that provide access to the variables *success, requestId*, and *callId* provided by the corresponding asynchronous service calls. A result test sheet for the execution of the test sheet in Figure 16 might have the form shown in Figure 17.

Each return value in column F is coloured gray if the expected value of the variables *callId, success*, or *requestId* matches the actual returned value (see lines 8,9,10,14). Otherwise the expected value and the black coloured return value are shown (see line 13).

The test sheet in Figure 17 is linear because it describes a single execution scenario based on the linear execution of their rows. Figure 18, in contrast, shows a multi-scenario test sheet that takes the condition in the test *RouteCall* into account.

Line 15 defines two deterministic transitions from state 15, each controlled by mutually exclusive guard conditions. After the execution of the lines 1 to 10, the value of the variable *success* reflected by the return value of the operation *getSuccess* in cell F9 is checked. If it is true, then the call is terminated and another call is initiated, otherwise the execution terminates at line 14.

Figure 19 shows a higher-order test sheet for routing a call.

Figure 17. Result test sheet for RouteCallTest

	A	B	C	D	E	F
1	'Vehicle	create				
2	'TelephonyConnector	create				
3	'BackendMock	create				
4	F1	initiateCall	"SIP:1234"			
5	F3	incomingCall				
6	F2	routeCall	"SIP:transfer"	F4	rand()[1...100]	
7	F3	getRouteCallResult	1000			
8	F7	getCallId				D6
9	F7	getSuccess				true
10	F7	getRequestId				E6
11	F2	hangUpCall	D4	rand()[1...100]		
12	F3	getHangupCallResult				
13	F12	getSuccess				true false
14	F12	getRequestId				D11

Figure 18. Multi-scenario test sheet MultiScenarioRouteCallTest for testing RouteCall

	A	B	C	D	E	F
1	'Vehicle	create				
2	'TelephonyConnector	create				
3	'BackendMock	create				
4	F1	initiateCall	"SIP:1234"			
5	F3	incomingCall				
6	F2	routeCall	"SIP:transfer"	F4	rand()[1...100]	
7	F3	getRouteCallResult	1000			
8	F7	getCallId				D6
9	F7	getSuccess				true
10	F7	getRequestId				E6
11	F2	hangUpCall	D4	rand()[1...100]		
12	F3	getHangupCallResult				
13	F12	getSuccess				true
14	F12	getRequestId				D11
15	100% -> 16 / 1 2 3 4 5 6 7 8 9 10					
16	[F9 == true] -> 15 / 11 12 13 14	[F9 != true] -> 17				
17						

The higher order test sheet contains two calls of the lower order test sheet *LowerOrderRouteCallTest*, calling its *test()* operation with three input parameters, i.e. the free parameters of the lower-order test sheet, and the expected return values *true* in column F.

Figure 20 shows the corresponding lower-order test sheet *LowerOrderRouteCallTest* for the higher-order test sheet of Figure 19.

The test sheet *LowerOrderRouteCallTest* has the same behaviour as the test sheet *RouteCallTest* in Figure 16 but is parameterized. It contains three parameters, indicated by *?C*, *?D*, and *?E*. The concrete values are the input values retrieved from the invoking higher-order test sheet.

Comparison and Integration

The various testing artefacts exemplified in the two previous sections illustrate the strengths and weaknesses of the TTS and Test sheets approaches, and highlight the potential synergy between them. In this section we discuss the pros and cons of each approach and then explain how they could be used together to create a more powerful approach to testing than either one individually.

Not surprisingly, the strength of the TTS approach stem from its clear and user-friendly representation of control flows due to its use of activity diagrams. These diagrams are immediately intuitive for users to understand and apply, and dovetail seamlessly with the manual analysis and design activities involved in the development of the applications software as well as the tests. Another major advantage of using activity diagrams to describe the flow of control in tests is that they are naturally (de)composable. This ability is utilized in Figure 13 and Figure 14 where the individual step, test *RouteCall*, in Figure 14 is elaborated into a full set of substeps in Figure 13.

Figure 19. Higher-order test sheet HigherOrderRouteCallTest for testing RouteCall

	A	B	C	D	E	F
1	'LowerOrderRouteCallTest	test	"SIP:1234"	"SIP:transfer"	true	true
2	'LowerOrderRouteCallTest	test	"SIP:1234"	"SIP:invalid"	false	true

Figure 20. Lower-order test sheet LowerOrder RouteCallTest for testing RouteCall

	A	B	C	D	E	F
1	'Vehicle	create				
2	'TelephonyConnector	create				
3	'BackendMock	create				
4	F1	initiateCall	?C			
5	F3	incomingCall				
6	F2	routeCall	?D	F4	rand()[1...100]	
7	F3	getRouteCallResult	1000			
8	F7	getCallId				D6
9	F7	getSuccess				?E
10	F7	getRequestId				E6
11	F2	hangUpCall	D4	rand()[1...100]		
12	F3	getHangupCallResult				
13	F12	getSuccess				true
14	F12	getRequestId				D11

For large test scenarios, this ability is obviously invaluable for breaking the overall test logic down into separately tractable parts.

The aforementioned advantages stem simply from using activity diagrams to describe the algorithms underpinning the test scenarios. However, the TTS infrastructure provides several significant enhancements that boost the value of activity diagrams for testing purposes. The first is the use of colour annotations to indicate which particular step in a test's flow of control caused a failure. The second is the built-in support for integrity checks which verify an activity diagram's consistency with the interface and method signatures provided by the tested artefacts. These not only help to improve the quality of the tests but also of the analysis and design models themselves. Finally, the third strength is the traceability support for keeping track of the relationships between the steps in a test scenario and the design models for the application as a whole.

The main weakness in the TTS approach is related to the so called "test data" tables. The first problem with these tables is their confusing semantics. Although they are called "test data" tables, in fact they actually contain much more information than just the test data. In addition to the pure test data (i.e. the input values for the parameters associated with the steps in the activity diagrams), test data tables also contain:

1. Definitions of the relationships that are expected to hold between values input to, or received from, the steps in a test scenario. For example, the first two rows in the test data table for the *routeCall* test shown in Table 1 contain simple input data, but the third row defines a relationship between the *callId* values passed to the *routeCall* step and the *callId* value returned from the *incomingCall* step. This has nothing to do with input data but defines a core relationship between values appearing at different parts of the test scenario and is thus a core part of the logic of the test,

2. The correctness of the relationships defined within the table is crucially dependent on the order in which the rows of the table are defined. If the rows were defined in a different order, the relationships would no longer necessarily be true. In this example, for the value returned from *incomingCall* to be the same as the value supplied to *routeCall*, it is essential that the former be executed after the latter,

3. Test data tables not only assume that the rows are defined in a particular order therefore,

they also assume that state is maintained between the invocations. In fact the first assumption essentially depends on the second assumption. The order in which the rows of the table are defined is important precisely because the state of the system has an impact on the validity (or not) of the defined relationships.

The second weakness of test data tables is the simple use of adjacent rows to define different sets of inputs to test scenarios. In general, of course, there will be many possible sets of input data for a given test scenario (i.e. activity diagram) but because the test data cannot be separated from the relationships and ordering information, the whole test data table has to essentially be duplicated for each set of test data.

Test sheets address exactly these aforementioned problems of test data tables. First, they have well defined execution semantics which explicitly handle the order in which rows are executed and the way in which state is maintained between the invocations of rows. They also highlight the occurrence of expected relationships between the values appearing at different points in the execution of a scenario. For example, in row 8 of the input test sheet in Figure 17, the cell F8 highlight the fact that the value returned from the invocation of the *getCallId* operation of the *BackendMock* objects is expected to be the same as that supplied to the prior invocation of the *routeCall* operation of the *TelephonyConnector* object in line 6.

Second, tests sheets explicitly support the separation of test logic, in terms of expected logical relationships between values appearing at different points in a scenario, from the pure input data. This is illustrated in Figure 19 and Figure 20. Figure 20 shows a parameterized test sheet in which the input data values have been defined as parameters, and Figure 19 shows a corresponding second order test sheet which supplies the actual values for these parameters. Each row of the second order test sheet essentially represents

an invocation of the first order parameterized test sheet, and supplies different actual values for the parameters. This second order test sheet in Figure 19 actually comes much closer to capturing the intuitive idea of a data table than TTS data tables because it is genuinely free of any test logic and really only contains input data used to drive the test scenario with different values. The order in which the rows of Figure 19 appear is therefore completely irrelevant. Because the tests sheet composition mechanism is completely hierarchic and can be nested to arbitrary levels it is possible to factor out different groupings of information in a way that best matches the needs of the scenario. The notion is also able to capture multiple scenarios (i.e. multiple sets of input data) in a much more compact and concise way than TTS test data tables.

The final advantage of tests sheets is that they provide much more fine grained information about where errors occur. While the colouring of activity diagrams shows which individual step in a test scenario gave rise to a test failure, it is not able to show which individual relationship was violated. This information could in principle be shown in test data tables, but in the current implementation it is not available because of the policy of assigning colours to columns rather than individual cells. The colouring scheme of test sheets, on the other hand, explicitly operates at the level of individual cells, and thus can show which logical relationships have been violated.

The disadvantage of test sheets is very clear, on the other hand – they provide absolutely no support for graphical diagrams and have no relationship to analysis and/or design information. They describe tests in an executable way akin to code. The potential synergy between the two approaches is therefore obvious. We propose to integrate the two approaches by replacing the test data tables of the TTS approach with tests sheets. This will result in a clean, comprehensive test methodology that supports all phases of the test development process, from analysis and design through to implementation and verification, in a systematic and traceable way. Moreover, the mapping of TTS concepts to test sheet concepts is fairly straightforward. ServiceCall and Trigger elements correspond to invocation rows. Nested tests and data lists with more than two rows correspond to higher-order test sheets. Decision elements can be mapped to multi-scenario test sheets, basic Assertion elements comparing values for equality can be mapped to output values. Finally, although Arbitration and Coverage elements are not considered in basic test sheets, at least the integration of arbitrations into the higher-order test sheet mechanism is straightforward.

FUTURE RESEARCH DIRECTIONS AND CONCLUSION

Techniques for defining, applying and analysing tests have progressed tremendously in recent years, and today a variety of different languages are used to provide different views of tests across the full testing lifecycle. Test developers are therefore no longer confined to working at the code level to describe and visualize the semantics of tests. This not only increases their productivity, it also opens up test specifications to a wider range of stakeholders in the software development processes.

Two approaches have been particularly instrumental in raising the levels of abstraction at which test are manipulated, and have recently received a great deal of attention in the recent community – model-driven approaches, based on the kinds of graphical models used to develop normal application code, and table driven approaches that uses tables to represent various aspects of tests. To date, however, these two approaches have only been used together in rather limited and ad hoc ways, and the potential synergies between them have not been significantly explored. In this chapter we have addressed this problem by investigating the relationship between two leading representatives of each group – the "Telling Test Stories" (TTS) approach from the University of Innsbruck and the Test Sheets approach from the University of Mannheim – and by proposing a way of using them together.

The proposed synergy essentially boils down to using test sheets as the final representations format in the test development process, building on the strengths of the TTS approach in the analysis and design phases. By replacing the simplistic and semantically obtuse "test data" tables used in the current TTS approach with the semantically self-contained and more flexible test sheet notation, a much cleaner separation is attained and a more orthogonal set of test views is made available to the tester. At the time of writing TTS and Test Sheets are both available in the Eclipse environment, but as separate plugins. We are currently working on integrating these two platforms to provide a single, integrated realization of the unified vision outline in this chapter.

ACKNOWLEDGMENT

This work is sponsored by the MATE project (FWF project number P17380) and QE LaB - Living Models for Open Systems (FFG 822740).

REFERENCES

Abbors, F., Paajarvi, T., et al. (2009). *Transformational support for model-based testing - From UML to QML*. 2nd Workshop on Model-based Testing in Practice.

Atkinson, C., Barth, F., & Falcone, G. (2010). *Software testing using test sheets*. International Workshop on Test-driven Development, Co-located with ICST 2010, Paris, France

Atkinson, C., Brenner, D., Falcone, G., & Juhasz, M. (2008). Specifying high assurance services. *IEEE Computer, 41*(8).

Baker, P., Dai, P. R., et al. (2007). *Model-driven testing - Using the UML testing profile.*

Canfora, G., & Di Penta, M. (2008). Service-oriented architectures testing: A survey. In L. Andrea De & L. C. Filomena Ferrucci (Eds.), *ISSSE, 5413,* 78-105.

Conformiq. (2009). *Qtronic.* Retrieved December 6, 2010, from http://www.conformiq.com

Felderer, M., Agreiter, B., et al. (2010). *Security testing by telling TestStories.*

Felderer, M., Breu, R., et al. (2009). Concepts for model-based requirements testing of service oriented systems. *Proceedings of the IASTED International Conference,* (pp. 152-157).

Felderer, M., Fiedler, F., et al. (2009). *Flexible test code generation for service oriented systems.*

Felderer, M., & Zech, P. (2009). Model-driven system testing of a telephony connector with telling test stories. Software Quality Engineering. *Proceedings of the CONQUEST, 2009,* 247–260.

Margaria, T., & Steffen, B. (2004). Lightweight coarse-grained coordination: A scalable system-level approach. *International Journal on Software Tools for Technology Transfer, 5,* 107–123. doi:10.1007/s10009-003-0119-4

Meyer, B., & Fiva, A. (2009). Programs that test themselves. [Los Alamitos, CA.]. *Computer, 42,* 46–55. doi:10.1109/MC.2009.296

Mugridge, R., & Cunningham, W. (2005). *Fit for developing software: Framework for integrated tests.*

OMG. (2005). *UML testing profile,* version 1.0.

Willcock, C., Deiss, T., et al. (2005). *An introduction to TTCN-3.*

Zander, J., Dai, Z. R., et al. (2005). *From U2TP models to executable tests with TTCN-3 - An approach to model driven testing.* TestCom.

KEY TERMS AND DEFINITIONS

Model-Driven Testing: Software testing inspired by model-driven engineering which applies UML based models for the definition and generation of tests.

System Testing: Testing a system for compliance with specified requirements. System Testing performed by customers is called acceptance testing.

Service-Centric System: A system consisting of a set of independent peers offering services that provide and require operations; a service-centric system is an abstraction from a SOA or a cloud.

Telling Teststories: A tabular and model-driven testing methodology for service-centric systems. Test Sheets: A tabular test design approach that is semantically self-contained and executable.

Chapter 10
Model–Based Regression Testing:
Process, Challenges and Approaches

Qurat-ul-ann Farooq
Ilmenau University of Technology, Germany

Matthias Riebisch
Ilmenau University of Technology, Germany

ABSTRACT

Evolution is the consequence of the continuous changes a software system has to perform due to changes in requirements and various maintenance activities. Regression testing provides a means to assure the wanted properties of the system after the introduction of the changes; however, testing requires high effort. Model-based regression testing (MBRT) has the potential to perform test tasks with a much better efficiency. MBRT uses analysis and design models for identifying changes and their corresponding test cases to retest the system after modifications. MBRT promises reduction in cost and labour by selecting a subset of the test cases corresponding to the modifications. However, the identification of modifications in a system and the selection of corresponding test cases is challenging due to interdependencies among models.

This chapter aims to provide a detailed insight into MBRT, how it is related to the general software lifecycle, and what are the challenges involved. We evaluate the state of the art in MBRT with a detailed analysis of the strengths and weaknesses of the existing approaches. For the analysis, we develop a set of comprehensive analysis criteria based on the identified challenges. Furthermore, we demonstrate the applicability of MBRT by presenting our state-based MBRT approach as an example. The chapter targets researchers and practitioners who want to achieve a detailed comprehension of the field and want to know the strengths and weaknesses of the existing approaches in MBRT. This chapter also identifies the areas within MBRT which require further attention by the researchers.

DOI: 10.4018/978-1-61350-438-3.ch010

To improve is to change; to be perfect is to change often (Winston Churchill)

INTRODUCTION

Evolution is inherent to the software systems. Due to the growing size and complexity of modern systems, the evolving nature of a system can cause adverse side effects and even system failures. Besides many other measures to prevent these unintended effects of evolution, it is essential to test a system after modifications; often referred to as *Regression Testing*. Regression testing is performed during the software maintenance phase and during various maintenance activities including *corrective*, *perfective* and *adaptive* maintenance (Wu & Offutt, 2003).

When a software system is modified, repeating the entire testing activity is a very costly task. A large system may have a huge number of test cases and test-execution requirements. Executing all these test cases is generally not a economically feasible option. Hence, it is necessary for regression testing to select a subset of the test cases corresponding to modifications. This is known as the selective strategy for regression testing and is a more feasible solution in terms of cost and time (Binder, 1999).

Another important issue during regression testing is scalability. Conventional code-based regression testing approaches fail to deal with the huge size of modern software systems. Model-based regression testing is a potential solution to this problem, because it offers several advantages compared to the conventional code-based regression testing approaches. This includes *better scalability*, *better complexity management* and *better comprehension* of the system, the relevant test suites and test cases. In model-based testing, the testing activity can be started in early phases of software development allowing *early regression planning and estimation* (Briand, Labiche, & He, 2009). This results in *effort reduction* in terms of time and labour. Furthermore, traceability

maintenance between test cases and models is relatively easier to accomplish as compared to the code-based approaches (Briand, Labiche, & He, 2009). Due to the use of models as primary artefact in the MBRT, static and dynamic *interactions are more visible* in design models and no static and dynamic analysis is required to determine the dynamic bindings as in code based approaches. Finally, *portability* and *platform independence* is a major benefit for evolving systems to adopt the rapid changes in technology and operational environment.

Besides all these benefits, there are some limitations of model-based regression testing as well. One of the major limitations is the potential impact of incomplete and outdated design models on the creation of effective regression test suites and plans. Moreover, since the test cases are generated from the design models, they are more abstract than test cases generated from code. This abstraction, sometimes make the test execution more difficult as the test cases should be adapted according to the implementation environment. However, considering the benefits of model-based regression testing, these limitations can be somehow compromised.

In this chapter, we try to not only give a broad overview of the area but also discuss all the main steps and key challenges involved in model-based regression testing. We discuss the role and place of MBRT in the classical software development lifecycle and identify the major steps involved in the MBRT phase. We also identify and discuss the challenges associated with model-driven regression testing approaches which are relatively novice approaches and are influenced by the concepts of model-driven architecture (MDA, 2011). We present our state-based regression testing approach with a demonstrating example to apply the regression testing steps identified previously and give a detailed insight of how practical regression testing can be performed to the reader. As the major contribution of the chapter, we provide a comparative analysis of the existing

MBRT approaches. For this analysis we develop comprehensive evaluation criteria and evaluate the approaches based on the criteria. Our analysis not only shows the strengths and weaknesses of the MBRT approaches but also highlights the areas which still require attention of the researchers and developers. By reading this chapter, researchers and practitioners can get a thorough picture of the area and state of the approaches available in the area. They will also get an insight into how practical MBRT can be performed and what are the major challenges in the field. The rest of the chapter is organized as follows.

Section II provides an overview of model-based regression testing. It discusses the MBRT in the context of the traditional software development lifecycle and also elaborates the major steps involved in the regression testing phase.

Section III presents a state-based regression testing approach developed by the authors as an example, together with a demonstrating case study to explain the approach. The approach and the discussed example provide an insight how the regression testing steps can be performed in practical scenarios.

Section IV discusses the challenges involved in MBRT in detail. These challenges include change identification, the notion of change propagation, the difficulties associated with baseline test suite generation, the risk of invalid test cases after regression test selection and the challenge of test automation. The challenges guide the analysis and classification of the state of the art presented in the section VI.

Section V extends the discussion of challenges of the previous section by those of model-*driven* regression testing approaches.

Section VI contains a comprehensive analysis and classification of existing MBRT approaches. It discusses the research questions identified, the comparison criteria and later the detailed analysis based on those criteria.

Section VII finally concludes the chapter and sums up its contents and findings.

MODEL-BASED REGRESSION TESTING: THE BIG PICTURE

In the traditional Software Development Life Cycle (SDLC), MBRT is the part of the testing activity in the maintenance phase. If we consider the simple waterfall development model, the regression testing will be performed in the maintenance phase when a change request is triggered. The following figure depicts the place of regression testing in the classical waterfall style SDLC. However, this figure is just for understanding the concept, in reality MBRT is applicable to all major SDLC,s for example RUP[1], SCRUM[2] etc.

According to Figure 1, a software system is constructed using the steps of any regular software development life cycle. When a change request is triggered probably due to a changed requirement, the maintenance activities are performed to entertain it. Once this new requirement is implemented, the system should be tested to detect the faults introduced by the changes. Model-based regression testing is used in this phase to test the changed software system.

As depicted in Figure 1, model-based regression testing constitutes of several steps shown in the last row. We discuss these steps in detail in the following sub sections.

Steps Involved in Model-Based Regression Testing Phase

As depicted in Figure 1, we identified 6 major steps, which constitute the MBRT phase. Before discussing those steps in detail, we first discuss a pre-requisite of MBRT in the next section i.e. establishment of baseline test suite. The sections afterward provide a discussion of the steps of the MBRT phase.

Baseline Test Suite Establishment

Before performing the actual regression testing, we need to have an existing test suite of the stable

Figure 1. MBRT: The big picture

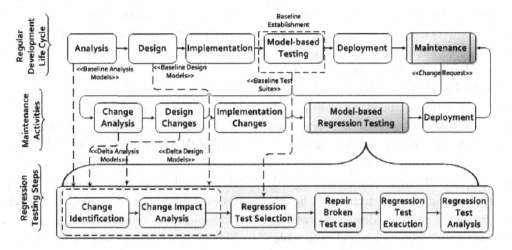

version of the system (the so-called baseline system). This test suite is often referred to as a baseline test suite. The test selection during regression testing is then performed by using this test suite. The establishment of a baseline test suite is a necessary activity because if there is no formal baseline test suite available, no regression testing can be performed.

Baseline test suites are often constructed using model-based testing approaches as shown in Figure 1. However, an important aspect while establishing the baseline test suite is preserving the relationships between the constituents of the test suites and the systems models. Otherwise, it will be hard to identify the affected test cases corresponding to affected elements of the models. This concept is a core concept in the field of model-based regression testing and is discussed in detail in section IV.B. In the next sections, we discuss the regression testing steps depicted in the lower part of Figure 1.

Change Identification

Change identification is the first step of regression testing performed after establishing the baseline test suite. This step aims at the identification of the delta–the changes introduced in the new system. In

MBRT this delta identification is often performed by comparing various design and architecture models. A more detailed discussion on change identification is available in section IV.A.

Change Impact Analysis

After obtaining the delta, the next step in MBRT is *Change Impact Analysis.* Several relationships and dependencies exist between different elements of the system. An impact analysis is necessary to identify the elements affected due to these relationships and dependencies. In context of model-based development several models of a system represent different views of the system and hence, are related to each other to give a complete picture of the system. The aim of change impact analysis in MBRT is to determine the impact of change in one model on other models of the system. It helps to identify the parts of the models/system which are indirectly affected by the changes. This topic is discussed in detail in section IV.B

Regression Test Selection

Regression test selection is performed after identifying the changed and impacted elements in the system. In this step, the changes and their impact (already determined in the previous steps) is used to select a subset of the test suite for regression testing. Relationships between elements in the model and test cases are established for performing test selection. As discussed earlier, these relationships are either established at the time of baseline test suite establishment or they need to be discovered later by applying heuristics to discover such relations. Test cases are classified against the added, deleted and changed parts of the system. A very famous test suite classification often adopted by several regression testing techniques in the literature by Leung et al. divides the regression test suite into obsolete, reusable and re-testable test cases (Leung & White, 1989). Test cases may also be prioritized based on cost and risk factors (Chen & Probert, 2003).

Repair Broken Test Cases

A lot of test cases become inapplicable due to the changes introduced to the system. After performing the test selection, it is necessary to identify such test and repair them for further use.

Regression Test Execution

Once all the test cases have been selected and broken test cases are repaired, the next step is execution of these test cases. This step does not require any special tools and techniques, as existing test execution methodologies, environments and engines used for testing the base line can be adapted during the regression test execution as well.

Regression Test Analysis

The last step is to analyze the test results and evaluate the test verdicts to determine the regression defects. Existing test analysis approaches for baseline test analysis can also be used in this step. If some defects are uncovered during the test analysis, some rework is often required to

correct the system. In the proceeding section we discuss an example state-based regression testing approach to demonstrate the applicability of the steps discussed above.

A PRACTICAL STATE-BASED MBRT APPROACH: A DEMONSTRATING EXAMPLE

In this section, we present a state-based approach for model-based regression testing developed by the authors, together with an illustrating example. This approach provides a practical demonstration of all the MBRT steps discussed in Section II.A. It is also included later in our analysis of the MBRT approaches.

Our approach uses UML class diagrams and state machines as input. The dependencies between both types of artefacts are discovered and change impact analysis is performed based on these dependencies. Figure 2 presents the overview of the approach. According to Figure 2, first of all the baseline version of both state machine and class diagram are compared for change identification and impact analysis. These artefacts are stored in a model repository for the version control. The set of changes obtained after the comparison is used to select the regression test cases from the baseline test suite. Before we discuss these activities in detail in following sections, we explain how the baseline test suite was established in the next section.

Baseline Test Suite Establishment in the State-Based MBRT Approach

As mentioned earlier baseline test suite construction is a prerequisite for regression testing. We constructed our state-based base line test suite using the transition tree methodology (Binder, 1999). Figure 3, depicts the partial transition tree of the state machine corresponding to the Student class presented in Figure 5. The dashed lines in

Figure 2. State-based regression testing process

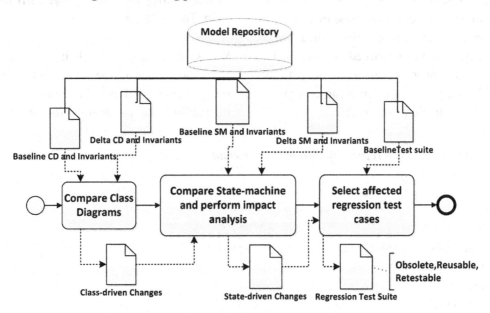

Figure 3. Partial transition tree for baseline student state machine

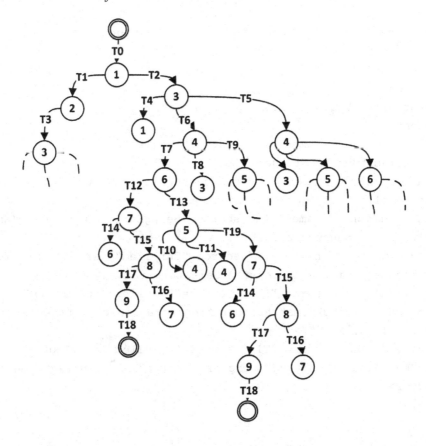

the figure represent an ongoing path which is not shown in due to the huge size of the tree.

The concrete test representation is in a XML format, where each block marked as Test case in the XML document represents a distinct path in the transition tree. Listing 1 depicts an excerpt of the test suite contacting two cases.

Traceability Between System Models and Test Cases

We use the concept of implicit traceability to discover the relationship between class diagrams and state machines and then the test cases. In implicit traceability, the traceability information is not

Listing 1. The concrete test representation in XML format

```
<?xml version="1.0" encoding="UTF-8"?>
<xmi:XMI xmi:version="2.1" xmlns:uml="http://schema.omg.org/spec/UML/2.0"
xmlns:xmi="http://schema.omg.org/spec/XMI/2.1">
<Test case name="TC1" TestContext="StudentClass">
<TestComponents>
<TestComponent name="RegistrarTestComponent"/>
</TestComponents>
     <TestTransition    name= "T0" source="Initial"
target="RegisteredStudent" trigger=""/>
     <TestTransition    name= "T2" source="RegisteredStudent"
target="BeingEnrolled" trigger="registrar.enrollInCourse"/>
     <TestTransition    name= "T4" source="BeingEnrolled"
target="RegisteredStudent" trigger="self.status==unsuccessful"/>
</Test case>
<Test case name="TC2">
<TestComponents>
<TestComponent name="RegistrationTestComponent"/>
</TestComponents>
     <TestTransition    name= "T0" source="Initial"
target="RegisteredStudent" trigger=""/>
     <TestTransition    name= "T2" source="RegisteredStudent"
target="BeingEnrolled" trigger="registrar.enrollInCourse"/>
     <TestTransition    name= "T6" source="BeingEnrolled" target="Enrolled"
trigger="self.status==unsuccessful"/>
     <TestTransition    name= "T7" source="Enrolled" target="Enrolled |
Studying" trigger="registration.currentSemester.status==Study"/>
     <TestTransition    name= "T12" source="Enrolled | Studying"
target="Enrolled | GivingExams" trigger="registration.currentSemester.
status==midTerm||finalExam"/>
     <TestTransition    name= "T14" source="Enrolled | GivingEx-
ams" target="Enrolled | Studying" trigger="registration.currentSemester.
status==Study"/>
</Test case>
</xmi:XMI>
```

already available and made explicit. To discover the relationship between class diagrams and state-machines, we apply heuristics based on similarity of the names and the ID's of model elements.

Discovering the relationship between state machines and test cases is simpler in our approach. During the test suite generation every test case contains the id of the corresponding transition in the state machine. These ID's are used later to trace the test cases corresponding to the affected transitions.

Performing Change Identification and Impact Analysis on the State-Based MBRT Approach

The first step of our MBRT approach is change identification and impact analysis. According to Figure 2, at first the changes in the class diagram are obtained by comparing the baseline and the delta versions of class diagrams along with class invariants and operation contracts. A change set is obtained after this comparison and is referred to as "Class-driven Changes". Change computation is performed by comparing the properties of all the elements of the class model such as classes, operations and attributes, after parsing both class diagrams.

After computing the class-driven changes the next activity is state machine comparison. Changes in both versions are detected and class-driven changes are used to obtain the affected elements of the state machine. For example, a state transition will be marked as affected if it uses any changed attribute or operation of the corresponding class in its guards, events or actions. The set of these changes is referred to as state-driven changes.

To elaborate the methodology, let us consider Student Enrolment System as an example. Figure 4 represents an excerpt of the class diagram of the Student Enrolment System.

In the class diagram shown in Figure 4, we have state machine corresponding to two state-full classes; the Student class and the Course class.

Figure 4. Baseline version class diagram of the example student enrolment system

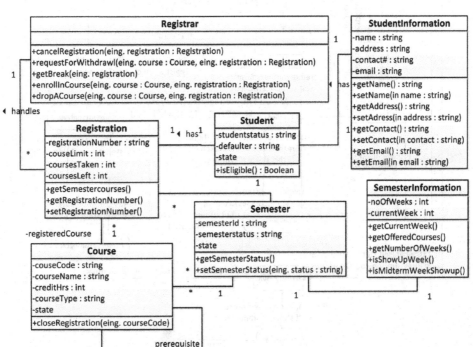

Figure 5 depicts the state machine of the baseline version of the student class.

Following corrective changes are introduced in the new version of the system.

1. The defaulter attribute of student class is modified. Its type is changed from *String* to *Boolean*.
2. State 2 and transition T1 and T3 are no more in the state machine of student class.

During the class diagram comparison process, the defaulter attribute is identified as modified and inserted in the set of class-driven changes. In the state machine comparison process, the state 2 and transition T1 and T3 are marked as

deleted. However, an additional transition is also marked as modified. The transition T5 is using the defaulter attribute of the student class in its guard condition "[self.defaulter="false"]", hence T5 is also marked as a modified transition

Listing 2 contains two sample change impact rules for the modified transition. It is important to note that such change models and change impact rules are defined for every model element in the state machine meta-model.

Regression Test Selection

Finally, the set of affected test cases from the baseline test suite are selected by tracing the state-driven changes to the corresponding test

Figure 5. Base line version state machine of the of the student class

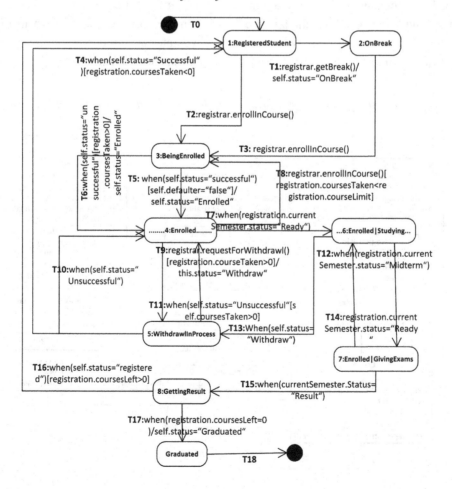

Listing 2. Example change impact rules for ModifiedTransition

1. A transition is modified if the event associated with the transition is modified.
    a. A call event is modified if its corresponding operation/Operation Contract defined in the class diagram is modified
    b. A signal event is modified if its corresponding operation /Operation Contract defined in the class diagram is modified
    c. A Change Event or a Time Event is modified if it uses a variable defined as class attribute in the class diagram and that variable is modified.
2. A transition is modified if its guard conditions are modified
    a. A guard condition is modified if it uses a variable or operation defined in the corresponding class and that variable or operation is modified.

cases. As discussed earlier, the test cases contain the information about the ID's of the transitions they correspond. The ID,s of the affected transitions are matched with the test cases to identify the affected test cases. Our test suite is classified into three types of test cases; obsolete, reusable and re-testable (Leung & White, 1989).

This classification is adopted by several regression testing techniques in the literature. Obsolete test cases are no more valid for the delta version. They usually correspond to elements in the system that are deleted and are not accessible in the delta version. Re-testable test cases need to be executed for regression testing as they correspond to modified parts of the system.

Table 1 summarizes the results of the case study. According to the table, the baseline test suite of the Course and Student class consists of 723 and 58 test cases respectively.

After performing the test suite classification for regression test selection, the total number of re-testable test cases that are required to execute during regression testing for the Course and Student class are 447 and 15 respectively. 29 test cases of the student class are also marked as obsolete and cannot be executed to test the delta version of the system.

CHALLENGES IN MODEL-BASED REGRESSION TESTING

In this section gives a general introduction to the challenges in research and industrial application of model-based regression testing. These challenges guide the analysis and classification in section VI.

Change Identification

Change identification is a crucial part of regression testing. As discussed earlier, change identification in MBRT is the process of calculating the change given one of more models of baseline and delta version of the system. Model comparison is a key concept while dealing with change identification in MBRT. Unfortunately, most of the existing approaches in MBRT do not place much focus on this aspect (see section VI.D.3).

However, in a few approaches [(Briand, Labiche, & Soccar, 2002), (Farooq, Z., Malik, & Nadeem, 2007)] change identification is explicitly covered. These approaches focus on elementary change types; *addition* of a model element, *deletion* of a model element and *modification* (*changed/added/deleted* property) of a model element. However, there can be more complex and fine grained changes. The so-called modular

Table 1. Results of the student enrolment case study

Test Classes	Total base-line test cases	Reusable	Re-testable	Obsolete
Course	723	276	447	0
Student	58	14	15	29

Figure 6. A Taxonomy of changes for change identification between models

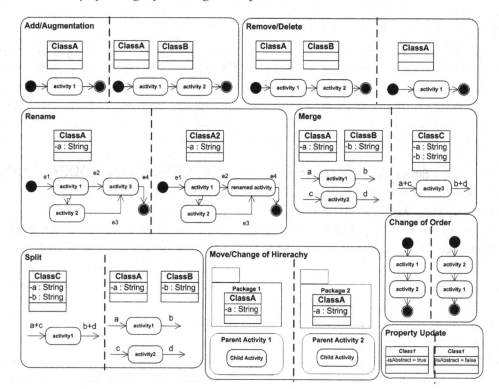

operators discussed by Baldwin and Clarke (Baldwin & Clarke, 1999) can be used as a foundation for understanding complex change types. These modular operators are *splitting*, *substituting*, *augmenting*, *excluding*, *inverting* and *porting*. Mäder et al. (Mäder, Gotel and Phillipow, 2009) also presented an interesting taxonomy of complex change types for traceability maintenance. These change types are *add*, *delete*, *move*, *merge*, *split*, and *replace*.

In Figure 6, we present a taxonomy of elementary and complex model changes for comparison of models for change identification during regression testing. The figure contains the change types from Baldwin and Clark, and Mäder et al. and some other additional change types relevant to model comparison. All the change types/operators are presented with a demonstrating example of a structural model (class diagram) and a behavioural model (activity or process diagram). In Figure 6, left hand side of the containers separated with a

dashed line show the original models and right hand side shows the modified models. The name of the container depicts the name of the change type/operator applied. We discuss these change types/operators in the following.

Add/Augmentation, Delete/Remove

The first two change types in Figure 6 are *add* and *delete* or according to Baldwin *Augmentation* and *remove*. This change type/or operator adds a new model element or removes an existing model element from a model. In the corresponding example in Figure 6 a new class and activity is added in the class diagram and activity/process diagram.

Rename

Rename is a change type/operator which changes the name of a model element in a model. *Rename* is quite similar to the property *update* change type; however, we separated it because name is often a unique and most significant property of a model element and the effect of this change type will normally different in regression testing as compared to the update property change type.

Split and Merge

The change-types *split* splits a model element into n number of model elements; whereas, *merge* merges n number of model elements into 1 respectively. In Figure 6, two classes A and B are merged into 1 class C. It is to notice that after merge properties of both classes are part of the merged class.

Similarly in case of an activity/process diagram example in Figure 6, input and output of the merged process are a combination of both processes it merged. Normally, changes like *merge* and *split* are hard to detect and require very strong heuristics and change detection rules.

Move/Change of Hierarchy

We combined the *move* and *change of hierarchy* change types/operators because, if we move any model element from one place to another, it will be placed from one container to another, which is a form of change in hierarchy as well. However, in some cases change of hierarchy can also be separated from move. For example, in a class diagram, if a new parent class is added or an existing parent class of a class is deleted then it will also cause change of hierarchy without application of move change type/operator.

Change of Order

Change of order occurs in the behavioural models. In the corresponding example in Figure 6, one the order of activities in the activity/process diagram is changed. Such changes are also hard to detect and also require strong heuristics and change detection rules.

Property Update

Property update is a change in which any attribute/property of a model element is changed. This is also a form of elementary change. Figure 6 contains an example of a *property update*, where a property value of the attribute isAbstract of a class is changed from true to false.

We think that the above mentioned change types are very interesting for change identification in MBRT and the investigation of the impact of such change type during regression test selection is a very interesting research question.

In the following sections we will discuss the types of model comparison approaches and the available tools and technologies for model comparison

Type of Model Comparison Approaches

There are two basic types of model comparison techniques. We discuss them in the following subsections.

Offline/State-Based Change Detection

In offline/state-based change detection, two states of the models are compared. The state before change (baseline models) and the state after change (delta model). Models are often compared to detect the added and deleted elements and changed properties of these elements. All the regression testing techniques discussed in the literature so far are using offline change detection.

Online/ Event-Based Change Detection

In contrast to the offline change detection, each change operation performed by a modeller is recorded in online/event-based change detection. This event capturing mechanism is built-in in the modelling tool and produces chains of recorded events. These event chains are then processed to extract the complex change type based on mod-eller's intentions by applying heuristics. Online change detection is used in many fields such as traceability maintenance and conflict resolution [(Mäder, Gotel and Phillipow, 2008); (Gerth et al., 2010)]. However, none of the regression testing techniques discussed in the literature so far uses on-line change detection. It is an interesting research question how these change operation chains can be processed to compute complex changes and then how they can affect the regression testing. At present, using online change detection for MBRT to answer these questions is a work in progress and the authors of this chapter are working on it.

Recent Tools and Technologies for Model Comparison

In this section, we discuss some recent tools and technologies developed in the field of model comparison.

EMF Compare (Generic Model Comparison Tool)

EMFCompare is a generic tool for comparing EMF based models (EMFCompare, 2011); hence, the tool is able to compare any model expressed in EMF. It focuses on the elementary change types add delete and update/change during model comparison. A very interesting feature of EMF-Compare is its ability of change visualisation in form of a model.

ECL (Epsilon Comparison Language)

Another interesting concept in model comparison introduced recently is of ECL (ECL, 2011). ECL is a rule-based language to specify the comparison logic; hence, complex change types can be speci-fied. However; more case studies are required to evaluate the comparison strengths and weaknesses and scalability of ECL.

Model Comparison Using Model Transformations

In such comparison approaches, comparison logic is specified using model transformation lan-guages. The examples available at the website of ATL (Atlas Transformation Language) for model comparison and model merging are examples of such comparison (ATL, 2011).

The approaches discussed in this section can be used in the change identification phase of MBRT because most of the MBRT approaches do not focus on change identification, as mentioned earlier. It is an interesting research question how regression testing techniques can use these new approaches for change identification, and consider the changes mentioned above.

Change Propagation

After the identification of changes, their conse-quences on tests have to be determined. A change in one artefact affects other related artefacts, for example test cases. This phenomenon is often re-ferred to as *Change Propagation*. In model-based development, several artefacts are covered by different views, which represent different aspects of the system. These views are inter-related as they represent the whole system. It is necessary to consider the relationships and dependencies between the artefacts and model elements, to analyze the change propagation phenomenon for effective regression testing. Two concepts are important when dealing with change propagation; *"Traceability"* for the establishment and mainte-nance of the relationships, and *"Change Impact"* for the determination of the affected artefacts. In the following sub sections, we will discuss both concepts in detail.

Traceability

According to a definition by Gotel and Finkelstein (Gotel & Finkelstein, 1995), traceability refers to the ability to describe and follow those aspects that are of interest. Traceability deals with the relationships among entities of interest. A traceability link expresses a dependency between two or more entities, which has been passed during a development activity. By definition, a dependency constitutes a relation between two artefacts of which the one has to be adapted if the related artefact changes. For MBRT, relations between artefacts from all development phases such as requirements, design, implementation, deployment, and test are of relevant.

Different artefacts relate with each other in a different context. This context determines the type of the relationship, the type of the artefacts, which can be related, and rules for completeness and consistency. The context, however, is determined by the problem to be solved by the modelling, and thus the goal of the modelling. There is no need to analyse other aspects such as the actual development activity, the design methodology applied, and the problem domain are related to the context in a minor degree, because the goal of the modelling is influenced by them. For example for a modelling of time behaviour, artefacts with a regard to time such as events, tasks and semaphores are relevant. The relevant types of relationships between them comprise all relationships with influence on the time behaviour such as *after*, *before*, *waits-for* and *similar*.

If the analysis of change propagation constitutes the goal of the modelling, all those artefacts are relevant that are influenced by a change, for example use cases and conceptual models as part of requirements models; systems, components, and interfaces as part of the structural view of architectural and design models; the various elements from behavioural models, and the elements of implementation and deployment models. The set of relevant types of relationships comprise all dependencies, for example the relationships *use*, *implements*, *part-of*, *is-a*, *instance-of*, and many more.

The relationship type of dependencies and traceability links is important for its evaluation and utilization. Using the relationship type, rules for consistency checks can be established, and methods for impact analysis can be developed. Unfortunately, there is no standard classification of types of dependencies. Moreover, Antequi et al. argue that it is not possible to foresee all relationship types for dependencies (Anquetil, et al., 2008). However, it is helpful for impact analysis to classify relationship types according to their nature in order to establish rules for impact evaluation for theses classes. Since the goal of modelling determines the relevant relationships, a classification should be made according to the purpose they serve. For testing, the issue analysed by a test determines the relevant dependency types. For example, if functional or structural properties are validated by a test, then component relations such as *part-of*, *kind-of*, and *instance-of* have to be evaluated to determine the need for a retest of a component after a change of a related component.

In literature, different characteristics for relationships are mentioned. Bachmann outlines basic dependency characteristics (Bachmann, Bass, & Klein, 2002):

Symmetricity explains the existence of names for both directions (e.g. *verify* − *isTestedBy*).

Semantic dependencies cannot be broken with intermediaries, only weakened by abstractions.

Dependencies are independent of specific changes to a model − dependencies remain despite modifications of modules. Pornpit et al. 2008 present a categorization of relationship types in an ontology, which we can transfer to the determination of impact relevant for tests (Wongthongtham, Chang, Dillon, & Sommerville, 2009): *generalisation*, *association*, *include* relationship, and *extend* relationship.

Furthermore, there is a category of dependencies between problem description and solution, or even between model elements towards a solution. Dependencies of the types *implements* and *realizes* fall into this category. Since, executable software is the subject, dependencies such as *uses*, *defined-by*, and *asserts* can help to evaluate the fact that on artefact has impact on another one. For tests regarding quality issues however, other types of dependencies are relevant according to the type of quality issue to be evaluated. For tests regarding security, safety, and dependability, all dependencies of the types *caused-by*, *Agent-Actor*, *harms*, and *failure-prevented-by* have to be analyzed. Summarizing we have to state that the relevance of a type of dependencies is related to the aspect one wants to test.

Change Impact Analysis

Determining the effect of a change to a software system is commonly referred to as Impact Analysis (Bohner & Arnold, 1996). Caused by dependencies between different software artefacts (e.g. classes), the effect of a change is able to spread across the entire software system, causing new changes and resulting in unwanted side effects.

Many different techniques to uncover such ripple-effects have been proposed in literature within the last years of research. The overall goal is to assist developers who are responsible for planning and implementing changes, allowing them to evaluate the effects of proposed changes before actually performing the change.

Impact Analysis can as well be used to [(Kabaili, Keller, & Lustman, 2001); (Orso, Apiwattanapong, & Harrold, 2003)] identify those test cases which must be executed after implementing a change and therefore assist regression testing. As MBRT is concerned with abstract system representations such as a systems architecture, Impact Analysis techniques developed for abstract models, such as (Briand L., Labiche, O'Sullivan, & Sowka, 2006), can be used to identify possible candidates for retesting.

Apart from dependencies between different artefacts, change couplings offer an additional source for conducting Impact Analysis. Change couplings can be inferred by observing historical change data, i.e. examining version control systems for patterns or clusters of co-changing artefacts (Xing & Stroulia, 2004), as a change to one artefact of a cluster is very likely to cause changes to the entire cluster of artefacts.

Baseline Test Suite Generation

As mentioned earlier, it is a prerequisite for regression testing approaches to have an existing baseline test suite used to test the stable version of the system. However, baseline test suite generation is very crucial, since model-based test generation approaches are still not very mature. Most of the test suite generation activities are often manual and only a few approaches for automated test generation in the domain of model-based testing are available.

Moreover, most of the approaches use ad-hoc specification languages for test specification. There are a very few approaches using test specific languages and even these approaches are not mature enough to be applied in different domains and in larger development contexts (Baker et al., 2008).

Moreover, maintenance of traceability and preserving the relationship between models and test cases is also often overlooked during baseline test suite generation. This makes the regression testing activity more difficult.

Validity of Test Cases

As mentioned earlier, due to introduction of changes, many test cases often become invalid and they therefore, must be identified and repaired prior to regression test execution. How these test cases can be automatically repaired is a very interesting research question which is completely neglected by existing MBRT approaches.

Test Automation

Like other model-based testing approaches, test automation is also a big challenge for model-based regression testing approaches. The standard conformance of these tools is another major issue, caused by rapidly changing modelling standards. Moreover, integration of model-based regression testing tools with other tools, especially baseline test generation tools and test execution environments is also a necessity which is often overlooked. Since MBRT relies heavily on models precise definitions of models (meta-models) and their implementation is required for tool implementation. Such meta-models are often not available for many domain specific languages. However, they are increasingly made available for example the UML and BPMN meta-model implementation for eclipse platform which is a positive sign for MBRT tool developers [(UML2Eclipse, 2011); (BPMNEclipse, 2011)].

In the next section, we discuss a practical approach for state-based MBRT. We are demonstrating the approach with the help of an example for the sake of brevity. The approach is discussed in context of the MBRT steps and challenges discussed above.

MODEL-DRIVEN REGRESSION TESTING: CHALLENGES AND EMERGING APPROACHES

Due to the increasing adaptation of model-driven development in the industry, researchers are investigating the possibilities of introducing MDA practices during regression testing as a next step after MBRT. The core of MDA lies in raising the level of abstraction by introducing models in all the development stages, compared to model-based techniques. Model transformations are the key concept in MDA which allows transformations of models between different or same abstractions.

Recently some researchers proposed ideas in the dimension of Model-driven regression testing (referred in this chapter as MDRT).

Challenges in Model-Driven Regression Testing

Maturity of Model-Driven Testing (MDT) Approaches

For the application of regression testing approaches, well defined model-driven test generation approaches are required. Due to the fact that MDT itself is a quite new research area, the number of sophisticated MDT approaches is very limited. MDRT approaches depend on the test-suites generated by MDT approaches; hence, it is difficult to perform the regression testing without existing test generation methodologies.

Maturity of Transformation Languages

For the application of MDT and MDRT approaches, transformation languages area core requirement. However, a lot of available transformation languages are not mature enough. They lack sophisticated development environments, sometimes they do not support the required modelling languages and sometimes they lack the important development facilities such as debugging etc.

Maturity of Test Modelling Languages

MDRT should use test modelling languages to conform to the MDA ideology. However, the support for test modelling is also very limited. Very few test modelling languages are available for example AGEDIS (AGEDIS, 2002), Tela (Pickin, 2001) and U2TP (U2TP1.0, 2005). However, AGEDIS and Tela are abandoned project and no more support is available for them. Although U2TP is a standard by OMG, it still lakes proper semantics and tool support for U2TP is also very limited.

Platform Independence

By definition of model-based and model-driven approaches, they should provide platform independence. However, its a big challenge to provide platform independence at every level during regression testing. For example, as discussed earlier, test modelling is another way to introduce the platform independence for test specification but due to immaturity of test modelling language it is hard to make the test specification platform independent.

Various Dimensions of Evolution

Due to the fact that in MDA models are available at different levels of abstractions, there are CIM (Computation Independent Models), PIM (Platform Independent Models) and PSM (Platform Specific Models). Hence, evolution is performed both vertically and horizontally as compared to the traditional model-based development where evolution is normally horizontal (Briand, Labiche, & Yue, 2009).

Another important aspect is meta-model evolution. In MDA every model should conform to some meta-model. In case the meta-model is changed or extended, it can create version compatibility issues. Another type of evolution is platform and technical infrastructure evolution where chains of code generators, runtime environments, dependency tools are changed. The effect of such evolution can be same as meta-model evolution (Visser, Warmer, & Deursen, 2007).

Models as Code

Emerging Approaches in the Field of Model-Driven Regression Testing

As discussed earlier, MDRT is about introducing MDA practices such as model transformations, platform independent models for test generation and platform independent models for test specifi-

cations. The approaches mentioned here are recent and most of them only present research ideas. The application of these ideas is still a work to be done.

Naslavsky et al's approach is to use traceability and model transformations for regression test selection (Naslavsky, Ziv, & Richardson, 2010). They used sequence diagrams for baseline test suite generation. The idea was in a preliminary phase and no results are reported for the success of the approach. Pilskalns et al. discuss another interesting approach for regression testing the designs models directly instead of testing the implementation (Pilskalns, Uyan, & Andrews, 2006). This means that the test cases corresponds directly to the model and will be executed on the design models instead of the code.

Silva et al. present a concern-based approach for model-driven system; however, they do not discuss the use of model transformation languages or model-based test specification in their approach (Silva, Budnik, Hasling, McKenna, & Subramanyan, 2010). We are evaluating the above mentioned approaches in our analysis in Section VI.

Another recent approach is by one of the authors of this chapter and it is a work in progress. The idea consists of using the MDA transformations for the baseline test suite generation with the integrated traceability. However, instead of ad-hoc test suite representations as adopted by other approaches, we are using U2TP[3] (U2TP1.0, 2005), a test modelling language, for the test specification. Use of a test modelling language not only increases the portability of the test suites but also the traceability maintenance is easy between design models and test models rather than test code. Another important aspect is that dedicated test specification languages cover several aspects of test specification such as test architecture, test time and test data modelling; hence, the impact analysis is fine grained and covers various aspects of test suites.

EVALUATION OF MODEL-BASED REGRESSION TESTING APPROACHES

In this section, we present a comprehensive evaluation of the existing MBRT approaches. Considering the challenges identified in the previous sections, it is very important to evaluate the ability of the existing MBRT approaches to deal with all these challenges. This will help the researches working in the field of MBRT to identify the weaknesses of the existing approaches and to further continue the research in those areas to improve those weaknesses. For the practitioners, however, this evaluation can help to select the approach that suites their particular needs and project's requirement. For the tool developers, the analysis provides a guideline to identify the state of automation in the field and it provides the motivation to build new tools to address the need of testers during software maintenance.

Before performing the analysis, we identified some research questions and formulated detailed evaluation criteria to address these research questions. We discuss them in the subsequent sections. The criteria presented here is equally applicable to MDRT approaches as well; hence, we include the MDRT approaches discussed in V.B in our analysis as well.

There are some existing surveys on model-based regression testing (Fahad & Nadeem, 2008), (Mahdian, Andrews, & Pilskalns, 2009), (Engstroem, Runeson, & Skoglund, 2010). However, the major difference of the survey presented in this chapter is the level of detail. We identified a set of research questions for each criterion to have a better understanding of weakness and strengths of approaches in certain areas. The criteria presented in this chapter are very comprehensive as compared to any other criteria developed to evaluate model-based regression testing techniques in the literature. It contains *9 criteria* and *27 inquiries* corresponding to them. Our criteria are discussed in detail in Section VI.C. Moreover, before the

comparison, we divided the approaches into 6 different sets for better understanding. These sets are explained in the start of VI.D.

Research Questions

According to the challenges discussed in section IV, we identified the following important research questions.

1. How much support is available for each regression testing step discussed in section II.A?
2. Whether the techniques provide strong support for change identification and impact analysis to deal with change propagation or not?
3. How much platform independence the existing techniques provide?
4. Do the techniques provide adequate test suite classification and how much reduction they promise?
5. How mature are the approaches in the field and how much support for the users they provide?
6. How much automation is supported by the model-based regression testing techniques?

Besides the research questions related to the challenges discussed earlier, we added two more research questions for better understand the techniques.

1. How many approaches exist for each testing level, i.e. unit, integration and system level?
2. What is the tendency of coverage of structural and behavioural models by the available model-based regression testing techniques?

In the next section we explain how we selected the studies for our analysis. We eliminate the irrelevant studies by establishing study selection criteria.

Study Selection

To eliminate the irrelevant studies before performing the analysis we used the following two filters.

1. All the approaches we considered are from the year 2000 and onwards. The reason is that the studies before that do not use mature modelling languages and are not applicable to the present scenarios.
2. We consider only those approaches that use models as input; hence, ignoring the approaches that use source code or specification and design artefacts other then models.

In the following sub sections, we discuss the study selection process and the eliminated studies.

Selected Studies

Initially the research papers were selected on the basis of title and abstract relevance. To search for the relevant papers we relied mostly on the existing knowledge of the authors in the field; hence, the initial papers were mostly already known by the authors. To make our search more reliable, we also thoroughly searched the references of all available papers and finally to get confidence on a complete coverage we searched the most popular databases IEEE digital Library, ACM Digital Library, SpringerLink and ScienceDirect using different combinations of following keywords.

"Regression Testing, Models, UML, Design Models, Model-driven, Model-based, specification-based, evolution".

After applying the initial selection filters and filtering them based on abstract and title relevance we obtained total 17 studies corresponding to 31 research papers. The list of these selected studies and their corresponding references are given in Appendix A.

Excluded Studies

We excluded all those approaches from our analysis which are published before year 2000. Interested readers can have a look on these studies in additional readings section in Appendix XI. Some other studies are excluded because the input used by these approaches was not models, they were either textual requirements or version data modelled using OCL. The list of these studies is also included in the additional reading section.

Analysis Criteria

In this section, we discuss the analysis criteria we developed to answer the above mentioned research questions. The criteria contain a set of further questions/inquiries satisfying the criteria. Table 2 presents each criterion and the inquiries related to the criterion.

A very important criterion to evaluate the regression testing techniques was presented by Rothermel & Harrold. This criterion includes 5 parameters, Inclusiveness, Precision, Efficiency, Generality, and Accountability (Rothermel & Harrold, 1994).

According to the criteria, inclusiveness is the extent to which modification revealing test cases are added in the regression test suite and Precision is the extent to which non-modification revealing test cases are omitted from the regression test suite. To determine inclusiveness is not possible without an experimental evaluation. For us experimental evaluation of 18 approaches was not possible due to time, resources and non-availability of detailed information for all the approaches. However, inclusiveness and precision in our case can be deduced by considering criterion 4 and 5 in Table 2.

Efficiency, according to Rothermel & Harrold, is determined by considering space and time requirements of the regression testing techniques. This criterion also cannot be determined without experimental evaluations. We defined efficiency as the reduction capability of regression testing

Table 2. Analysis criteria for MBRT approaches

1. Criteria name:*Testing Level*
Inquiries **Inq-1:** What is the testing level addressed by the approach?
2. Criteria Name:*Model Coverage*
Inquiries **Inq-2:** The approach covers structural modelling diagrams, behavioural modelling diagrams or both? Structural only Behavioural only Both structural and behavioural **Inq-3:** What are the input models used by the approach? **Inq-4:** What is the test specification language used by the approach?
3. Criteria Name: Support for Regression Testing Steps (RTS)
Inquiries **Inq-5:** Baseline test suite establishment **Inq-6:** Change identification (see Criteria 4) **Inq-7:** Change impact analysis (see Criteria 5) **Inq-8:** Regression test selection (see Criteria 7) **Inq-9:** Repair broken test cases **Inq-10:** Test result analysis
4. Criteria Name:*Change Identification*
Inquiries **Inq-11:** Does the approach provide sound change definitions for modifications in the system? **Inq-12:** How many change types were considered by the approach? **Inq-13:** Does the approach discusses the change detection mechanism and rules for change detection between different versions of the system?
5. Criteria Name:*Impact Analysis*
Inquiries **Inq-14:** How the traceability between several design and test artefacts was established? (Traceability Support) Explicit Traceability Implicit Traceability No traceability **Inq-15:** Does the approach perform impact analysis? (Inter-model) Impact Analysis within several models (Intra-model) Impact analysis within 1 model No Impact Analysis **Inq-16:** Does the approach consider the dependency types?
6. Criteria Name:*Platform Independence*
Inquiries **Inq-17:** Does the approach use platform independent specification and design models (input models) or they are polluted with implementation specific concerns. **Inq-18:** Does the approach support platform independent test modelling? **Inq-19:** Does the Tool support/implementation provided by the approach is specific to some platform?
7. Criteria Name:*Efficiency*
INQUIRIES **Inq-20:** how much reduction is achieved? (We are collecting the data provided by the authors and are not measuring the reduction ourselves) **Inq-21:** Does the approach provide some effective classification for the regression test selection? Modified test cases are identified Obsolete test cases are identified The elements for which new test cases are required are identified

continued on following page

Table 2. Continued

8. Criteria Name: *Maturity and Support*
Inquiries **Inq-22:** Is the approach evaluated on any case study or does any experimental evaluation was present? No: 0 Just an example (only some example diagrams are used) Small case study (Less than 100 Test cases OR less than 10 components) Medium case study (100-500 test cases OR 5-20 Components) Large case study(More than 500 test cases OR more than 20 Components) **Inq-23:** Is the approach compliant to the standards for input models? Complete compliance with a standard Partial Compliance (Notations and extensions applicable to standards) No standard compliance **Inq-24:** Is the approach compliant to the standards for test specifications? Complete compliance with a standard Partial Compliance (Notations and extensions applicable to standards) No standard compliance **Inq-25:** What is the degree of documentation and support? Just a paper Detailed Method description Plus Tutorials, templates and examples
9. Criteria Name: *Automation and Tool Support*
Inquiries **Inq-26:** Were the ideas defined by some algorithmic details or not? **Inq-27:** Does the approach provide tool support or not? Full tool support Prototype tool No tool support

techniques and ability to classify the original test suite for regression testing effectively. The criterion 7, in Table 2 presents this criterion. Rothermel & Harrold defined generality as the ability to function in a wide and practical range of solutions. In our case, generality can be deduced by considering the inquiries in criterion 1.

Harrold et al defined Accountability as the extent to which regression testing approaches promote structural coverage criteria. To us, application of a structural coverage is concerned mostly with test prioritization approaches and most of the regression testing approaches do not deal with application of structural coverage criteria; hence, we do not consider this in our analysis. Another very important issue is scalability of the approaches. Scalability can be deduced by considering criterion 1 and 2 in Table 2.

Detailed Analysis of MBRT Approaches

In this section, we present the detailed analysis of the selected studies for each criterion. We classified the approaches into 5 different categories according to the models they are using. Following is the classification of the approaches.

Specification Level Activity-Based Approaches

These are approaches with use specification models like use cases and activity diagrams as input for regression testing.

Approaches Involving Both Specification and Design Artefacts

These approaches either perform system level testing or involve multiple testing levels such as unit, integration and system levels. They take both specification and design models as input.

Design Level State-Based Approaches

These approaches take event-based models as input for regression testing. Most of these approaches take variants of finite state machines as input.

Design Level Component-Based Approaches

These approaches are specific for component-based regression testing.

Design Level Approaches Using Sequence and Class Diagrams

These approaches take sequence and class diagrams as input for regression testing.

Design Level Miscellaneous Approaches

These approaches are the design level approaches which do not fall into any above mentioned category.

In the following, we present the analysis of each criterion using for each classification of approaches mentioned above. Each criterion contains a corresponding analysis table and a "critical Issues" section highlighting the major findings of the analysis of the criterion.

Analysis of Criterion 1 & 2: Testing Level & Model Coverage

The criteria states which input models and test specification language the approaches use, and what levels of testing the approaches address? The inquiries other then inquiry 4 are more elaborative then analytical. These are used to understand the nature of the approaches better. Table 3 presents the analysis of the selected approaches for these

criteria. According to Table 3, from the total 17 approaches selected for the analysis, 7 of the approaches deal with system level testing, 2 approaches are about component-based testing, 4 approaches are integration level approaches and 7 approaches can be applied at unit level.

Most of the approaches do not use any particular test specification language for the test representation. Most of the approaches specify test in their custom styles. However, one approach uses JUnit for test specification and one use a XML-based representation of the test cases. The corresponding critical issues section contains the critical points extracted in the light of analysis.

Critical Issues: Testing Level and Model Coverage

The existing MBRT approaches use no standard test specification language such as TTCN or U2TP. They only use ad-hoc test representations and in most of the cases test specifications are very abstract and how these abstract test cases will be later mapped to the concrete test cases is unclear.

Analysis of Criterion 3: Support for Regression Testing Steps

This criterion shows how much support for the regression testing steps discussed in section II.A is provided by the existing MBRT approaches. Table 4 presents the analysis of the selected MBRT approaches for the inquiries of the criterion. For the discussion on the critical findings of the analysis please refer to the corresponding critical issues section.

Critical Issues: Support for RTS

1. The existing regression testing approaches do not consider two important steps of the regression testing; how the selected test should be repaired and analyzed.

Table 3. Analysis of model-based regression testing approaches for the criterion "testing level" & "model coverage"

Approaches▼	Study ID▼	Inq-1: What is the testing level addressed by the approach?	Inq-2: The approach covers structural modelling diagrams, behavioural modelling diagrams or both	Inq-3: What are the input models used by the approach?	Inq-4: What is the test specification language used by the approach?
		Testing Level	**Model Coverage**		
Specification Level Approaches (Activity-based)	Study-1: (Gorthi et al., 2008)	System Level	Behavioural Only	Structured Activity diagram	None
	Study-2: (Chen et al., (a), 2002,2003)	System Level	Behavioural only	Activity Diagram	None
	Study-3: (Silva et al., 2010)	Functional Testing using Category partition	Both structural and behavioural	Main artefact(Activity diagram) others (Class Diagram and Sequence Diagram)	None
Approaches involving Both Specification and Design Artefacts	Study-4: (Mansour et al., 2007,2011)	Unit, Integration and System Level	Behavioural and Structural both	Interaction Overview Diagram, Sequence Diagram, Class Diagram	None
	Study-5: (Briand et al., 2002,2003,2009)	System Level	Behavioural and Structural both	Use case Diagram, Sequence Diagram, Class Diagram	None
	Study-6: (Deng et al., 2004)	Black-box system testing	Behavioural and Structural both	Use case Diagram, Class Diagram, Sequence Diagram, Activity Diagram, State Chart	None
Design Level Approaches (State-based)	Study-7: (Chen et al., (b), 2007, 2009)	Unit Level	Behavioural Only	EFSM (Extended Finite State Machine), SDL	None
	Study-8: (Korel et al., 2002)	Unit Level	Behavioural Only	EFSM	None
	Study-9: (Beydeda et al., 2000)	Unit Level	Behavioural Only	Class State Machine and	None
	Study-10: (Farooq et al., 2007,2010)	Unit and Integration Level	Behavioural and Structural both	Class Diagram, State Machine	XML

continues on following page

Table 3. Continued

Approaches ▼	Study ID ▼	Inq-1: What is the testing level addressed by the approach?	Inq-2: The approach covers structural modelling diagrams, behavioural modelling diagrams or both	Inq-3: What are the input models used by the approach?	Inq-4: What is the test specification language used by the approach?
Design Level Approaches (Sequence diagram and Class diagram)	**Study-11: (Ali et al., 2007)**	System Level	Behavioural and Structural both	Class Diagram, Sequence Diagram	None
	Study-12: (Pilskalns et al., 2006)	System Level Testing of UML designs	Behavioural and Structural both	Class Diagram, Sequence Diagram,	None
	Study-13: (Naslavsky et al., 2007,2009,2010)	Unit and Integration Level	Behavioural and Structural both	Class Diagram, Sequence Diagram	JUnit for concrete test representation.
	Study-14: (Jeron et al., 1999, 2000)	Integration Testing	Structural	Class Diagram	None
Design Level (Component-based)	**Study-15: (Muccini et al., (b), 2005, 2006, 2007)**	Component-based Testing	Behavioural and Structural both	Sequence Diagram, Component Diagram, State Machine (FSP Algebra)	None
	Study-16: (Wu & Offet, 2003)	Component Level	Behavioural and Structural both	Class Diagram, State Chart, Collaboration Diagram	None
Design Level Approaches (Miscellaneous)	**Study17: (Martins et al., 2005)**	U nit Testing	Behavioural Only	Activity Diagram for a class implementation logic	None

2. A lot of the approaches provide limited support for change identification and impact analysis as well (see criterion change identificationVI.D.3 and impact analysis VI.D.4 for further details.)

Analysis of Criterion 4: Change Identification

Change identification is an important activity in regression testing. This section provides the analysis of the inquiries corresponding to the change identification for the selected MBRT approaches. The analysis is presented in Table 5.

For the critical issues refer to the corresponding critical issues section.

Critical Issues: Change Identification

1. Most of the approaches do not provide the sound change definitions to detect the changes in the models. If a change is not defined it cannot be detected later.

2. The existing MBRT approaches only consider the primary change types (Add, Delete, and Property Modification) and the effect of other complex change types discussed in section II.A.2 is not considered by any of the approaches.

Table 4. Analysis of MBRT approaches for the criterion "support for regression testing steps"

Approaches ▼	Study ID ▼	Inq-5: Baseline test suite establishment	Inq-6: Change identification (see Criteria 4)	Inq-7: Change impact analysis (see Criteria 5)	Inq-8: Regression test selection (see Criteria 7)	Inq-9: Repair broken test cases	Inq-10: test result analysis
Specification Level Approaches (Activity-based)	**Study-1: (Gorthi et al., 2008)**	Not discussed	Not discussed	No Impact Analysis	Yes (risk and cost based)	No	No
	Study-2: (Chen et al., (a), 2002,2003)	Not discussed	Not discussed	No Impact Analysis	Yes (risk and cost based)	No	No
	Study-3: (Silva et al., 2010)	Functional test cases generated by TDE-UML using category partitioning method	Yes (online change identification)	Yes	Yes (obsolete, reusable, re-testable)	No	No
Approaches involving Both Specification and Design Artefacts	**Study-4: (Mansour et al., 2007,2011)**	Not discussed	Partial(Change Definitions not provided)	Yes	Partial (only affected)	No	No
	Study-5: (Briand et al., 2002,2003,2009)	Yes it is referred to a previous approach	Yes	Yes	Yes	No	No
	Study-6: (Deng et al., 2004)	Rules for All branch, boundary and Faulty testing are discussed	No	Very Limited	No	No	No
Design Level Approaches (state-based)	**Study-7: (Chen et al., (b), 2007, 2009)**	Yes (As the work is a continuation of Korel et al. technique)	No	Yes(Partial, only intra model)	Yes (Only affected test cases are identified)	No	No
	Study-8: (Korel et al., 2002)	Yes	No	Yes (Partial only intra-model)	Yes (Only affected test cases are identified)	No	No
	Study-9: (Bey-deda et al., 2000)	Yes	No	Only between specification and source code	Yes (Only affected test cases are identified)	No	No
	Study-10: (Farooq et al., 2007,2010)	Yes, but manual test generation using transition tree method	Yes	Yes	Yes (obsolete, reusable, re-testable)	No	No

continues on following page

Table 4. Continued

Approaches ▼	Study ID ▼	Inq-5: Baseline test suite establishment	Inq-6: Change identification (see Criteria 4)	Inq-7: Change impact analysis (see Criteria 5)	Inq-8: Regression test selection (see Criteria 7)	Inq-9: Repair broken test cases	Inq-10: test result analysis
Design Level Approaches (Sequence diagram and Class diagram)	**Study-11: (Ali et al., 2007)**	Not discussed	Partial	Yes	Yes	No	No
	Study-12: (Pilskalns et al., 2006)	Yes, UML design testing producing UML test cases	yes	Yes	Yes (obsolete, reusable, new)	No	No
	Study-13: (Naslavsky et al., 2007,2009,2010)	Sequence diagram based test generation.	yes	Yes	yes	No	No
	Study-14: (Jeron et al., 1999, 2000)	Integration testing using test dependency graph	No	No	Limited Discussion	No	No
Design Level Approaches (Component-based)	**Study-15: (Muccini et al, 2005,2006, 2007)**						
	Study-16: (Wu & Offet, 2003)	Not discussed	No	Partial (Intra-model only)	New, retestable	No	No
Design Level Approaches (Miscellaneous)	**Study17: (Martins et al., 2005)**	Paths of a Behavioral Control Flow Graph (BCFG)	yes	No	Yes	No	No

3. A lot of approaches also do not discuss the rules for change identification between two versions of the system.

Analysis of Criterion 5: Impact Analysis

As discussed earlier, impact analysis is one of the most important activities in the regression testing. This section presents the analysis of the selected approaches for their capabilities to support impact analysis. Table 6 presents the analysis of the MBRT approaches for different inquiries corresponding to the impact analysis. The corresponding critical issues section discusses the critical findings of the analysis.

CRITICAL ISSUES: IMPACT ANALYSIS

1. Most of the regression testing approaches do not support the concept of explicit traceability, i.e., traceability is not maintained at the time of test generation so that it could be used to perform impact analysis later during regression testing.

2. Some approaches provide the traceability, most of them use ID and name comparison to find the relations which is a week approach and might miss many relations.

3. A lot of MBRT approaches either do not support impact analysis or support impact analysis within one diagram. The relations

Table 5. Analysis of the MBRT approaches for the criterion "change identification"

Approaches ▼	Study ID ▼	Inq-11: Does the approach provide sound change definitions for modifications in the system?	Inq-12: How many change types were considered by the approach?	Inq-13: Does the approach discusses the change detection mechanism and rules for change detection between different versions of the system?
Specification Level Approaches (Activity-based)	Study-1: (Gorthi et al., 2008)	No	Add, delete, modify	No
	Study-2: (Chen et al., (a), 2002,2003)	No	Modify	No
	Study-3: (Silva et al., 2010)	No	Add, delete, modify	Yes (using time stamps and edit time monitoring)
Approaches involving Both Specification and Design Artefacts	Study-4: (Mansour et al., 2007,2011)	No	Modify	Yes
	Study-5: (Briand et al., 2002,2003,2009)	Yes	Addition of elements, Deletion of elements, Modifications of element properties	
	Study-6: (Deng et al., 2004)	No	Modify	No
Design Level Approaches (state-based)	Study-7: (Chen et al., (b), 2007, 2009)	No	Add, delete, modify	No
	Study-8: (Korel et al., 2002)	No	Add, delete	No
	Study-9: (Beydeda et al., 2000)	No	Modify	No
	Study-10: (Farooq et al., 2007,2010)	Yes	Add, delete, modify	Yes
Design Level Approaches (Sequence diagram and Class diagram)	Study-11: (Ali et al., 2007)	Yes (Only a limited set)	Modify	No
	Study-12: (Pilskalns et al., 2006)	Yes	Add, delete, modify	Yes
	Study-13: (Naslavsky et al., 2007,2009,2010)	Yes	Add, delete, modify (using EMFCompare)	Yes
	Study-14: (Jeron et al., 1999, 2000)	No	No	No
Design Level Approaches (Component-based)	Study-15: (Muccini et al, 2005,2006,2007)	Yes	Add, delete, modify	
	Study-16: (Wu & Offet, 2003)	No	Add, delete, modify	No
Design Level Approaches (Miscellaneous)	Study17: (Martins et al., 2005)	No	Add, Remove	Yes

Table 6. Analysis of the MBRT approaches for the criterion "impact analysis"

Approaches ▼	Study ID ▼	Inq-14: How the traceability between several design and test artefacts was established	Inq-15: Does the approach perform impact analysis?	Inq-16: Does the approach consider the dependency types?
Specification Level Approaches (Activity-based)	**Study-1: (Gorthi et al., 2008)**	No Traceability	No Impact Analysis	None
	Study-2: (Chen et al., (a), 2002,2003)	Explicit (Traceability Matrix)	No Impact Analysis	None
	Study-3: (Silva et al., 2010)	Explicit traceability links are established	Supported using traceability links (between artefacts, models and test cases)	Not discussed
Approaches involving Both Specification and Design Artefacts	**Study-4: (Mansour et al., 2007,2011)**	Implicit Traceability	Between class diagram, IOD and SD	
	Study-5: (Briand et al., 2002,2003,2009)	Implicit, (using sequence matching)	Between CD, SD and UC	
	Study-6: (Deng et al., 2004)	No Traceability	Very few and abstract rules for impact analysis	None
Design Level Approaches (state-based)	**Study-7: (Chen et al., (b), 2007, 2009)**	No Traceability	Intra-model	
	Study-8: (Korel et al., 2002)	No Traceability	Intra-model	
	Study-9: (Beydeda et al., 2000)	No Traceability	Intra-model	
	Study-10: (Farooq et al., 2007,2010)	Implicit Traceability	Inter-model (Between CD and SM)	
Design Level Approaches (Sequence diagram and Class diagram)	**Study-11: (Ali et al., 2007)**	Implicit Traceability	Between CD and SD	
	Study-12: (Pilskalns et al., 2006)	Implicit traceability	Inter model (CD, SD OMDG, test cases)	Use dependency
	Study-13: (Naslavsky et al., 2007,2009,2010)	Explicit Traceability (in form of a traceability model).	Between SD and CD	Not discussed
	Study-14: (Jeron et al., 1999, 2000)	None	No Impact Analysis	Contractual and Implementation Dependencies
Design Level Approaches (Component-based)	**Study-15: (Muccini et al, 2005,2006, 2007)**	Implicit		
	Study-16: (Wu & Offet, 2003)	No Traceability	Intra Model	Control and data dependencies (within same model)
Design Level Approaches (Miscellaneous)	**Study17: (Martins et al., 2005)**	Implicit traceability	No Impact Analysis	None

between several diagrams are considered only in a few approaches.

4. Most of the approaches do not consider different types of dependencies. The type of dependency can affect the way selected test should be treated later. Only a few approaches consider control and data dependencies for intra-model impact analysis.

Analysis of Criterion 6: Platform Independence

This section provides the analysis of selected approaches for the criterion Platform independence. The criterion considers the platform independence of input models and test specification models and the implementation platform. Table 7 presents the analysis of the criterion for the selected approaches. Further issues are discussed the corresponding critical issues section.

Critical Issues: Platform Independence

1. The concept of test modelling which supports platform independent test suites is not supported by the existing model-based regression testing techniques.
2. Almost all the prototype implementations provided by the approaches are compliant to the Java platform and support for other platforms is not provided by the approaches

Analysis of Criterion 7: Efficiency

This criterion analyzes the efficiency of the approaches by analyzing the reduction capabilities and by considering the ability of test suite classification of the selected approaches. Table 8 presents the analysis of the selected approaches for the corresponding inquiries. The corresponding critical issues section highlights the general issues

considering the evaluation of the approaches for efficiency.

Critical Issues: Efficiency

Although some MBRT approaches report the reduction achieved by applying their approaches on the case studies. However this reduction depends on how much modifications they considered and how complex were the case studies. To evaluate the reduction capabilities of the approaches, the approaches should be empirically analysed with the same set of the approaches.

Analysis of Criterion 8: Maturity and Support

This criterion evaluates the maturity and support provided by the MBRT approaches by focusing on three main issues; case studies or evaluations, standard compliance and available documentation and support. Table 9 shows the results of the analysis of the selected approaches. We discuss the critical issues related to this criterion in the corresponding critical issues section.

Critical Issues: Maturity and Support

1. Although some cases studies are available for evaluating MBRT approaches for their applicability; however, most of the studies do not evaluate the approaches for efficiency and reduction. Unavailability of comparative evaluations is also a major issue in MBRT.
2. Standard compliance, especially for test specification is a major deficiency in the existing MBRT approaches.
3. The degree of documentation and support is very limited in the existing MBRT approaches. The only support material available for most of the approaches is a conference or a workshop paper. Very few

Table 7. Analysis of the MBRT approaches for the criterion "platform independence"

Approaches▼	Study ID▼	Inq-17: Does the approach use platform independent specification and design models?	Inq-18: Does the approach support platform independent test modelling?	Inq-19: Does the Tool support/ implementation provided by the approach is specific to some platform?
Specification Level Approaches (Activity-based)	**Study-1: (Gorthi et al., 2008)**	Yes (Extended Activity Diagram)	Test Modelling not discussed (Only test paths which are platform Independent)	No implementation
	Study-2: (Chen et al., (a), 2002,2003)	Yes (Activity Diagram)	Test Modelling not discussed (Only test paths which are platform Independent)	No implementation
	Study-3: (Silva et al., 2010)	Yes (Activity, sequence and Class diagram)	Test Modelling not supported (Custom test procedures, containing test steps and data bindings)	TDE/UML developed in Java, also available as in-house eclipse plug-in by SIEMENS corporation
Approaches involving Both Specification and Design Artefacts	**Study-4: (Mansour et al., 2007,2011)**	Yes (UML)	Test Modelling is not supported (test paths depicting sequence of methods)	No Implementation
	Study-5: (Briand et al., 2002,2003,2009)	Yes (UML)	Test Modelling not supported (Tests are in form of action sequence triplets)	Java 2 Platform, POET Object Server Suite, However UML meta model implementation is developed internally
	Study-6: (Deng et al., 2004)	Yes (UML)	Test Modelling not supported and form of the test cases is not discussed	No Implementation
Design Level Approaches (state-based)	**Study-7: (Chen et al., (b), 2007, 2009)**	Yes, SDL is platform Independent	Test Modelling is not discussed (Probably in form of SDL sequences)	No Implementation
	Study-8: (Korel et al., 2002)	Yes	Test Modelling is not discussed (Probably in form of sequences)	No Implementation
	Study-9: (Beydeda et al., 2000)	No (CSC is not a standard artefact and CSIG is constructed using both source code and specification)	Tests are not platform independent, contain source code information	No Implementation
	Study-10: (Farooq et al., 2007,2010)	Yes (UML)	Yes XML representation of state test sequences	Java based Implementation in Eclipse platform, UML2 plug-in for Eclipse

continues on following page

Table 7. Continued

Approaches ▼	Study ID ▼	Inq-17: Does the approach use platform independent specification and design models?	Inq-18: Does the approach support platform independent test modelling?	Inq-19: Does the Tool support/ implementation provided by the approach is specific to some platform?
Design Level Approaches (Sequence diagram and Class diagram)	**Study-11: (Ali et al., 2007)**	Yes (UML)	Test Modelling is not supported (test paths depicting paths of CCFG)	No Implementation
	Study-12: (Pilskalns et al., 2006)	Yes (UML)	Test Modelling not supported (test cases are in form of graph tuples)	No Implementation
	Study-13: (Naslavsky et al., 2007,2009,2010)	Yes (UML)	Test Modelling is not supported. Abstract test cases are sequences of sequence diagram.	Java-based implementation using Eclipse plugins. (EMFCompare, ATL and UML2 Plugins for Eclispe)
	Study-14: (Jeron et al., 1999, 2000)	Yes UML	Test Modelling not supported	No Implementaion
Design Level Approaches (Component-based)	**Study-15: (Muccini et al,2005,2006, 2007)**			
	Study-16: (Wu & Offet, 2003)	Yes (UML)	Test Modelling not supported	No Implementation
Design Level Approaches (Miscellaneous)	**Study17: (Martins et al., 2005)**	Yes(UML)	Test Modelling not supported	No Implementation

approaches also publish their results in a journal paper which contains relatively more detailed information. However, none of the approaches provide tutorials or other artefacts to support their approach. Most of the approaches also do not provide any other kind of documentation and tutorials for their tools and methodology.

Analysis of Criterion 9: Automation and Tool Support

This criterion evaluates the degree of automation and tool support by the existing MBRT approaches. Table 10 presents the analysis of the selected approaches for two further inquiries. The approach

provides the algorithmic details of the ideas or not and the ideas or implemented in a tool or not. The corresponding critical issues section discussed the critical findings of the analysis.

Critical Issues: Automation and Tool Support

Existing model-based regression testing approaches provide very limited tool support. Most of the tools are not mature and also not available online.

Discussions

In the above section, we presented a detailed analysis of the existing MBRT approaches. The

Table 8. Analysis of the MBRT approaches for the criterion "efficiency"

Approaches ▼	Study ID ▼	Inq-20: how much reduction is achieved?	Inq-21: Does the approach provide some effective classification for the regression test selection?
Specification Level Approaches (Activity-based)	Study-1: (Gorthi et al., 2008)	Not Discussed	(Added, Affected) test cases
	Study-2: (Chen et al., (a), 2002,2003)	Approx 70%	(Added, affected and Prioritized safety tests)
	Study-3: (Silva et al., 2010)	Not discussed	Obsolete, Reusable, Retestable &New
Approaches involving Both Specification and Design Artefacts	Study-4: (Mansour et al., 2007,2011)	92-100%	Affected
	Study-5: (Briand et al., 2002,2003,2009)		Obsolete, reusable and retestable
	Study-6: (Deng et al., 2004)	Not Discussed	Not Discussed
Design Level Approaches (state-based)	Study-7: (Chen et al., (b), 2007, 2009)	83-99.09%	Affected
	Study-8: (Korel et al., 2002)	83-99%	Affected
	Study-9: (Beydeda et al., 2000)	Not Discussed	Affected
	Study-10: (Farooq et al., 2007,2010)	Up to 63%	Obsolete, reusable and retestable
Design Level Approaches (Sequence diagram and Class diagram)	Study-11: (Ali et al., 2007)	Not Discussed	
	Study-12: (Pilskalns et al., 2006)	93%	New, Reusable, Obsolete
	Study-13: (Naslavsky et al., 2007,2009,2010)	Not discussed	Obsolete, Reusable and Retestable
	Study-14: (Jeron et al., 1999, 2000)	Not discussed	Affected
Design Level Approaches (Component-based)	Study-15: (Muccini et al, (a), 2005, 2006)		Retestable, New
	Study-16: (Wu & Offet, 2003)	Not Discussed	Modified and New
Design Level Approaches (Miscellaneous)	Study17: (Martins et al., 2005)	Varies version to version	Reusable, Retestable, Obsolete

Table 9. Analysis of the MBRT approaches for the criterion "maturity and support"

Approaches ▼	Study ID ▼	Inq-22: Is the approach evaluated on any case study or does any experimental evaluation was present?	Inq-23: Is the approach compliant to the standards for input models?	Inq-24: Is the approach compliant to the standards for test specifications?	Inq-25: What is the degree of documentation and support?
Specification Level Approaches (Activity-based)	**Study-1: (Gorthi et al., 2008)**	retail system case study, 342 Test cases MEDIUM	Partial Compliance (Activity like notation with extensions)	No Standard Compliance	One Conference Paper
	Study-2: (Chen et al., (a), 2002,2003)	3 IBM WEB SPHERE Components, 306 test cases): MEDIUM	Partial Compliance (Activity like notation with extensions)	No Standard Compliance	Two Conference Papers One Master's Thesis
	Study-3: (Silva et al., 2010)	None	Activity diagram with extended properties	No Standard Compliance	One Conference Paper
Approaches involving Both Specification and Design Artefacts	**Study-4: (Mansour et al., 2007,2011)**	(Evaluation on three different case studies. Max Test suite size is 90 MEDIUM)	UML 2.0 (full Compliance)	No Standard Compliance	A conference paper A journal paper
	Study-5: (Briand et al., 2002,2003,2009)	LARGE(596 test cases)	UML(full Compliance)	No Standard Compliance	A Conference Paper A journal Paper A technical Report
	Study-6: (Deng et al., 2004)	No case study and evalutaion	UML (Version unknown)	No standard compliance	A conference paper
Design Level Approaches (state-based)	**Study-7: (Chen et al., (b), 2007, 2009)**	LARGE (Models: 6 SDL models max No of test case: 1691)	SDL (Full Compliance)	No Standard Compliance	One Conference Paper One Journal Paper
	Study-8: (Korel et al., 2002)	Just an example	Partial Compliance (State machine)	No Standard Compliance	Conference Paper
	Study-9: (Beydeda et al., 2000)	Just an example (Class Account)	Partial Compliance (State machine)	No Standard Compliance	Conference Paper
	Study-10: (Farooq et al., 2007,2010)	LARGE (723 test cases Enrolment system Case study)	UML(full Compliance)	No Standard Compliance	One Conference Paper One Workshop Paper Masters Thesis Tool source code

continues on following page

Table 9. Continued

Approaches ▼	Study ID ▼	Inq-22: Is the approach evaluated on any case study or does any experimental evaluation was present?	Inq-23: Is the approach compliant to the standards for input models?	Inq-24: Is the approach compliant to the standards for test specifications?	Inq-25: What is the degree of documentation and support?
Design Level Approaches (Sequence diagram and Class diagram)	**Study-11: (Ali et al., 2007)**	(Just an example of ATM system No TC: 6)	UML (Full Compliance)	No Standard Compliance	A conference paper
	Study-12: (Pilskalns et al., 2006)	Transcoder Component of Battik toolkit 32 Classes and sequence diagrams and 52 test cases	UML (Version Unknown)	No Standard Compliance	A conference Paper
	Study-13: (Naslavsky et al., 2007,2009,2010)	PIMS), and the Aqualush case studies. Number of component, diagrams or test cases are not discussed	UML (Version 2)	Non standard test specifications (Abstract test cases are written in Custom format. For concrete test cases JUnit is used.)	3 Conference Papers
	Study-14: (Jeron et al., 1999, 2000)	SMDS Server case study in Telecommunication domain containing 38 classes	UML (Applicable to any version of class diagram)	No Standard Compliance	1 journal paper and one conference
Design Level Approaches (Component-based)	**Study-15: (Muccini et al, 2005,2006, 2007)**	(15 Components, number of test cases not specified MEDIUM)	Charmy Language		
	Study-16: (Wu & Offet, 2003)	An Example of ATM system.	UML	No Standard Compliance	A conference paper
Design Level Approaches (Miscellaneous)	**Study17: (Martins et al., 2005)**	Common C++ Library casestudy (2 classes having 16 and 8 methods) 6 versions of each class are considered	UML (Version Unknown)	No Standard Compliance	A conference Paper

critical issues corresponding to each analysis criterion are identified and discussed. The critical issues highlight the areas within MBRT which require further attention from the researchers. In general, the analysis shows that there is a need of better support of change identification and impact analysis. Moreover, test automation, standard conformance repair of broken test cases and test result analysis are the areas where further research is required.

MBRT approaches need to be mature by providing support in form of tutorials and more help materials to perform the approaches practically. Further, there is a strong need of comparative empirical evaluations of different categories of MBRT approaches to determine their comparative reduction capabilities and other factors discussed in section VI.C.

In the next section, we discuss an example of our state-based regression testing approach to demonstrate how MBRT can be practically ap-

Table 10. Analysis of the MBRT approaches for the criterion "automation and tool support"

Approaches ▼	Study ID ▼	Inq-26: Were the ideas defined by some algorithmic details or not?	Inq-27: Does the approach provide tool support or not?
Specification level MBRT Approaches	**Study-1: (Gorthi et al., 2008)**	Yes	No
	Study-2: (Chen et al., (a), 2002,2003)	Yes	No
	Study-3: (Silva et al., 2010)	Yes	Yes (TDE/UML) by Siemens Inc.
Approaches involving Both Specification and Design Artefacts	**Study-4: (Mansour et al., 2007,2011)**	Yes	No
	Study-5: (Briand et al., 2002,2003,2009)	Yes	Prototype (RTS Tool)
	Study-6: (Deng et al., 2004)	Yes	No
Design Level Approaches (state-based)	**Study-7: (Chen et al., (b), 2007, 2009)**	Yes	No
	Study-8: (Korel et al., 2002)	Yes	No
	Study-9: (Beydeda et al., 2000)	Yes	No
	Study-10: (Farooq et al., 2007,2010)	Yes	Prototype tool (START)
Design Level Approaches (Sequence diagram and Class diagram)	**Study-11: (Ali et al., 2007)**	Yes	No
	Study-12: (Pilskalns et al., 2006)	Yes	No
	Study-13: (Naslavsky et al., 2007,2009,2010)	yes	Eclipse-based prototype tool, For model comparison EMFCompare is used.
	Study-14: (Jeron et al., 1999, 2000)	Yes	No
Design Level Approaches (Component-based)	**Study-15: (Muccini et al, 2005,2006, 2007)**		A plugin inside Charmy environment
	Study-16: (Wu & Offet, 2003)	No	No
Design Level Approaches (Miscellaneous)	**Study17: (Martins et al., 2005)**	Yes	No

plied. Although, we are not resolving the above mentioned issues in the discussed example but we believe that this example can be useful to understand the basic concepts of MBRT.

CONCLUSION

In this chapter, we discussed the model-based regression testing (MBRT), its core concepts, challenges, the state of the art and the emerging trends. We also demonstrated how MBRT fits in the software development life cycle and we demonstrated the steps involved in MBRT phase. We discussed the challenges, which MBRT has to overcome to reach a more widespread application in the industrial practice. Moreover, we give an overview over the challenges of the emerging model-driven regression testing approaches, which are still in an early stage of development.

The main contribution of the chapter is provision of a comparative analysis and classification of the existing MBRT approaches. First we classified the approaches based on the artefacts they use and whether they are specification-based or design-based MBRT approaches. For this analysis, we developed comprehensive analysis criteria which contain 9 major evaluation criterions consisting of 27 inquiries (research questions). The criteria is based on the challenges in MBRT, we identified earlier in this chapter. We selected 17 studies from the MBRT literature consisting of 31 research papers. We applied the analysis criteria to compare the selected studies in detail. We identified the critical issues in existing MBRT approaches for each criterion after our analysis. In total, we identified 16 major issues that need to be improved by the MBRT approaches. This analysis can provide the researchers the reasons to do further research in the area of MBRT and to choose the issues they should address in their research. For the practitioners as well, the analysis provides a thorough insight of the strengths and weaknesses for different classes of the approaches.

Furthermore, we presented our own approach for state-based regression testing as a concrete example on how MBRT works in practical scenarios. To conclude we suggest, based on the analysis presented in this chapter, that the lack of tool support, standard conformance especially for test specification, limited focus on the impact analysis and change identification, and the lack of documentation are the major hindrances in the practical application of MBRT and the utilization of its full potential. Research should be conducted in the above mentioned areas to improve the quality and applicability of model-based regression testing approaches.

ACKNOWLEDGMENT

We want to thank our colleague Steffen Lehnert for his contribution to the change impact analysis section and for his valuable comments. This work was partly funded by Deutscher Akademischer Austauschdienst DAAD under the grant A/09/98224.

REFERENCES

U2TP1.0. (July 2005). *UML2 testing profile*. Retrieved from http://www.omg.org/spec/UTP/

Abramson, D., Sosic, R., & Brisbane, K. R. (1996). A debugging and testing tool for supporting software evolution. *Journal of Automated Software Engineering, 3*, 369–390. doi:10.1007/BF00132573

AGEDIS. (2002). *Automated generation and execution of test suites for distributed component-based software*. Retrieved from http://www.agedis.de/downloads.shtml

Ali, A., Nadeem, A., Iqbal, M. Z. Z., & Usman, M. (2007). Regression testing based on UML design models. *IEEE Pacific Rim International Symposium on Dependable Computing,* (pp. 85-88).

Anquetil, N., Grammel, B., da Silva, G. L., Noppen, J. A. R., Khan, S., & Arboleda, H. (2008, June). Traceability for model driven, software product line engineering. In *Proceedings of EC-MDA Traceability Workshop,* (pp. 77-86).

Arnold, R., & Bohner, S. (1996). *Software change impact analysis* (1st ed.). Wiley-IEEE Computer Society Press.

Bachmann, F., Bass, L., & Klein, M. (2002). *Illuminating the fundamental contributors to software architecture quality.* Pittsburgh: Technical Report, Carnegie Mellon Institute.

Baker, P., Dai, Z. R., Grabowski, J., Schieferdecker, I., & Williams, (2008) *Model-driven testing using UML testing profile.* Springer Verelag. ISBN 978-3-540-72562-6

Baldwin, C. Y., & Clark, K. B. (1999). *Design rules: The power of modularity* (*Vol. 1*). Cambridge, MA: MIT Press.

Beydeda, S., & Gruhn, V. (2001). Integrating white- and black-box techniques for class-level regression testing. *In Proceedings of 25th Annual International Computer Software and Applications Conference,* Chicago, Illinois, (p. 357).

Binder, R. V. (1999). *Testing object-oriented systems: Models, patterns, and tools.* Addison-Wesley Professional.

Bohner, S. A., & Arnold, R. S. (1996). *Software change impact analysis.* Wiley-IEEE.

BPMNEclipse. (2011). *UML meta-model implementation for Eclipse.* Retrieved from http://www.eclipse.org/modeling/mdt/?project=bpmn2

Briand, L., Labiche, Y., O'Sullivan, L., & Sowka, M. (2006). Automated impact analysis of UML models. *Journal of Systems and Software, 79,* 339–352. doi:10.1016/j.jss.2005.05.001

Briand, L., Labiche, Y., & Soccar, G. (2002). Automating impact analysis and regression test selection based on UML designs. *In Proceedings of the International Conference on Software Maintenance,* (p. 252). IEEE Computer Society.

Briand, L. C., Labiche, L., Buist, K., & Soccar, G. (2003). *Automating impact analysis and regression test selection based on UML designs.* Software Quality Engineering Laboratory, Carleton University, Technical Report, TR SCE-02-04.

Briand, L. C., Labiche, Y., & He, S. (2009). Automating regression test selection based on UML designs. *Information and Software Technology, 51*(1), 16–30. doi:10.1016/j.infsof.2008.09.010

Briand, L. C., Labiche, Y., & Yue, T. (2009). Automated traceability analysis for UML model refinements. *Information and Software Technology, 51,* 512–527. doi:10.1016/j.infsof.2008.06.002

Chen, Y. (2002). *Specification-based regression testing measurement with risk analysis.* School of Graduate Studies and Research, Carleton University, PhD Thesis.

Chen, Y., & Probert, R. (November 2003). A risk-based regression test selection strategy. In *Proceeding of the 14th IEEE International Symposium on Software Reliability Engineering,* (pp. 305-306).

Chen, Y., Probert, R. L., & Sims, D. P. (2002). Specification-based regression test selection with risk analysis. In *Proceedings of the 2002 Conference of the Centre for Advanced Studies on Collaborative Research.* IBM Press.

Chen, Y., Probert, R. L., & Ural, H. (2007). Regression test suite reduction using extended dependence analysis. In *Proceedings of Fourth International Workshop on Software Quality Assurance: In Conjunction with the 6th ESEC/FSE Joint Meeting,* (pp. 62-69). ACM.

Chen, Y., Probert, R. L., & Ural, H. (2007). Regression test suite reduction using extended dependence analysis. In *Fourth International Workshop on Software Quality Assurance: In Conjunction with the 6th ESEC/FSE Joint Meeting (SOQUA '07),* (pp. 62-69). New York, NY: ACM.

Chen, Y., Probert, R. L., & Ural, H. (2009). Regression test suite reduction based on SDL models of system requirements. *Journal of Software Maintenance and Evolution: Research and Practice, 21*(6), 379–405. doi:10.1002/smr.415

Chittimalli, P. K., & Harrold, M. J. (2008). Regression test selection on system requirements. *In Proceedings of the 1st India Software Engineering Conference,* (pp. 87-96). ACM Computer Society Press. ISBN: 0818673842

Deng, D., Sheu, P.-Y., & Wang, T. (2004). Model-based testing and maintenance. In *Proceedings of the IEEE Sixth International Symposium on Multimedia Software Engineering,* (pp. 278-285).

ECL. (2011). *Epsilon comparison language.* Retrieved from http://www.eclipse.org/gmt/epsilon/doc/ecl/

EMFCompare. (2011). *Model comparsion tool.* Retrieved from http://www.eclipse.org/emf/compare/

Engstroem, E., Runeson, P., & Skoglund, M. (2010). A systematic review on regression test selection techniques. *Information and Software Technology, 52*(1), 14–30. doi:10.1016/j.infsof.2009.07.001

Fahad, M., & Nadeem, A. (2008). A survey of UML based regression testing. In *Intelligent Information Processing, IV,* (pp. 200-210).

Farooq, Q.-U.-A. (November 2007). *An approach for selective state-machine based regression testing.* Mohammad Ali Jinnah University, Islamabad, Pakistan Masters Thesis. Retrieved from http://www.theoinf.tu-ilmenau.de/~qurat/publications.htm

Farooq, Q. U.-A. (2010). A model driven approach to test evolving business process based systems. *In Proceedings of Doctoral Symposium in MODELS 2010,* (pp. 19-24).

Farooq, Q.-U.-A., Iqbal, M. Z. Z., Malik, Z. I., & Nadeem, A. (2007). An approach for selective state machine based regression testing. *In Proceedings of the 3rd International Workshop on Advances in Model-Based Testing,* (pp. 44-52). ACM.

Farooq, Q. U.-A., Iqbal, M. Z. Z., Malik, Z. I., & Riebisch, M. (2010). A model-based regression testing approach for evolving software systems with flexible tool support. *In Proceedings of the 2010 17th IEEE International Conference and Workshops on the Engineering of Computer-Based Systems,* (pp. 41-49).

Filho, R. S. S., Budnik, C. J., Hasling, W. M., McKenna, M., & Subramanyan, R. (2010). Supporting concern-based regression testing and prioritization in a model-driven environment. *IEEE 34th Annual Computer Software and Applications Conference Workshops (COMPSACW),* (pp. 323-328).

Gerth, C., Küster, J. M., Luckey, M., & Engels, G. (2010). Precise detection of conflicting change operations using process model terms. In *Proceedings of the 13th International Conference on Model Driven Engineering Languages and Systems: Part II (MODELS'10),* (pp. 93-107). Berlin, Germany: Springer-Verlag.

Gorthi, R. P., Pasala, A., Chanduka, K. K., & Leong, B. (2008). Specification-based approach to select regression test suite to validate changed software. *In Proceedings of the 2008 15th Asia-Pacific Software Engineering Conference,* (pp. 153-160). IEEE Computer Society.

Gotel, O., & Finkelstein, A. (1995). Contribution structures requirements artifacts. *Proceedings of the Second IEEE International Symposium on Requirements Engineering,* (pp. 100-107).

Kabaili, H., Keller, R. K., & Lustman, F. (2001). A change impact model encompassing ripple effect and regression testing. *In Proceedings of the Fifth International Workshop on Quantitative Approaches in Object-Oriented Software Engineering,* (pp. 25-33). Budapest, Hungary.

Kolovos, D. S., Paige, R. F., & Polack, F. A. C. (2006). Model comparison: A foundation for model composition and model transformation testing. In *Proceedings of the 2006 International Workshop on Global Integrated Model Management (GaMMa '06),* (pp. 13-20). New York, NY: ACM.

Laski, J., & Szermer, W. (1992). Identification of program modifications and its applications in software maintenance. In *Proceedings of Conference on Software Maintenance,* (pp. 282-290).

Leung, H. K. N., & White, L. (1989). Insights into regression testing-software testing. In *Proceedings of Conference on Software Maintenance,* (pp. 60-69).

Mader, P., Gotel, O., & Philippow, I. (2008). Enabling automated traceability maintenance by recognizing development activities applied to models. In *Proceedings of the 23rd IEEE/ACM International Conference on Automated Software Engineering (ASE '08)* (pp. 49-58). Washington, DC: IEEE Computer Society.

Mäder, P., Gotel, O., & Philippow, I. (2009). Enabling automated traceability maintenance through the upkeep of traceability relations. In *Proceedings of the 5th European Conference on Model Driven Architecture - Foundations and Applications (ECMDA-FA '09),* (pp. 174-189). Berlin, Germany: Springer-Verlag.

Mahdian, A., Andrews, A. A., & Pilskalns, O. J. (2009). Regression testing with UML software designs: A survey. *Journal of Software Maintenance and Evolution, 21*(4), 253–286. doi:10.1002/smr.403

Mansour, N., & Takkoush, H. (2007). UML based regression testing for OO software. In Jeffrey E. Smith (Ed.), *Proceedings of the 11th IASTED International Conference on Software Engineering and* Applications *(SEA '07),* (pp. 96-101). Anaheim, CA: ACTA Press.

Mansour, N., Takkoush, H., & Nehme, A. (2011). UML-based regression testing for OO software. *Journal of Software Maintenance and Evolution: Research and Practice, 23,* 51–68. doi:10.1002/smr.508

MDA. (2011). *Model driven architecture.* Retrieved from http://www.omg.org/mda/

Model Comparison, A. T. L. (2011). *Meta-model comparison and model migration.* Retrieved from http://www.eclipse.org/gmt/amw/usecases/compare/

Muccini, H. (2007). Using model differencing for architecture-level regression testing. In *Proceedings of the 33rd EUROMICRO Conference on Software Engineering and Advanced Applications (EUROMICRO '07),* (pp. 59-66). Washington, DC: IEEE Computer Society.

Muccini, H., Dias, M., & Richardson, D. J. (2005). Reasoning about software architecture-based regression testing through a case study. In *Proceedings of the 29th Annual International Conference on Computer Software and Applications Conference (COMPSAC-W'05)*, (pp. 189-195). Washington, DC: IEEE Computer Society.

Muccini, H., Dias, M., & Richardson, J. D. (2006). Software architecture-based regression testing. *Journal of Systems and Software, 79*(10), 1379–1396. doi:10.1016/j.jss.2006.02.059

Muccini, H., Dias, M. S., & Richardson, D. J. (2005). Towards software architecture-based regression testing. *SIGSOFT Software Engineering Notes, 30*(4), 1–7. doi:10.1145/1082983.1083223

Naslavsky, L., & Richardson, D. J. (2007). Using traceability to support model-based regression testing. *In Proceedings of the Twenty-second IEEE/ACM International Conference on Automated Software Engineering (ASE '07)* (pp. 567-570). New York, NY: ACM.

Naslavsky, L., Ziv, H., & Richardson, D. J. (2009). A model-based regression test selection technique. *IEEE International Conference on Software Maintenance ICSM*, (pp. 515-518).

Naslavsky, L., Ziv, H., & Richardson, D. J. (2010). MbSRT2: Model-based selective regression testing with traceability. In *Proceedings of the 2010 Third International Conference on Software Testing, Verification and Validation (ICST '10)* (pp. 89-98). Washington, DC: IEEE Computer Society.

Orso, A., Apiwattanapong, T., & Harrold, M. J. (2003). Leveraging field data for impact analysis and regression testing. In *Proceedings of the 9th European Software Engineering Conference held jointly with 11th ACM SIGSOFT International Symposium on Foundations of Software Engineering (ESEC/FSE '03)*, Helsinki, Finland, (pp. 128-137).

Pickin, S., Jard, C., Heuillard, T., Jézéquel, J. M., & Desfray, P. (2001). A UML-integrated test description language for component testing. In *Workshop of the pUML-Group held together with the UML 2001 on Practical UML-Based Rigorous Development Methods - Countering or Integrating the eXtremists*, (pp. 208-223).

Pilskalns, O., Uyan, G., & Andrews, A. (2006). Regression testing UML designs. *22nd IEEE International Conference on Software Maintenance ICSM '06*, (pp. 254-264).

Pretschner, A., & Philipps, L. J. (2001). Model based testing in evolutionary software development. In *Proceedings of the 12th International Workshop on Rapid System Prototyping (RSP '01)*, (p. 155). Washington, DC: IEEE Computer Society.

Rothermel, G., & Harrold, M. J. (1994). A framework for evaluating regression test selection techniques. In *Proceedings of the 16th International Conference on Software Engineering* (ICSE '94), (pp. 201-210). Los Alamitos, CA: IEEE Computer Society Press.

Stallbaum, H., Metzger, A., & Pohl, K. (2008). An automated technique for risk-based test case generation and prioritization. In *Proceedings of the 3rd International Workshop on Automation of Software Test (AST '08)* (pp. 67-70). New York, NY: ACM.

Traon, Y. L., Jeron, T., Jezequel, J. M., & Morel, P. (2000). Efficient object-oriented integration and regression testing. *IEEE Transactions on Reliability, 49*(1), 12–25. doi:10.1109/24.855533

UMLEclipse. (Last accessed: April 2011). *BPMN meta-model implementation for Eclipse*. Retrieved from http://www.eclipse.org/modeling/mdt/?project=uml2

Visser, E., Warmer, J., & Deursen, A. V. (2007). Model-driven software evolution: A research agenda. In *Proceedings of International workshop on Model-driven Sofware Evolution held with ECSMR 2007.*

Wu, Y., & Offutt, J. (2003). Maintaining evolving component-based software with UML. In *Proceedings of the Seventh European Conference on Software Maintenance and Reengineering (CSMR '03),* (p. 133). Washington, DC: IEEE Computer Society.

Xing, Z., & Stroulia, E. (2004). Understanding class evolution in object-oriented software. *In Proceedings of the 12th IEEE International Workshop on Program Comprehension (IWPC'04),* (pp. 34-43).

Zhang, J. (2004). Supporting software evolution through model-driven program transformation. *In Companion to the 19th Annual ACM SIGPLAN Conference on Object-oriented Programming Systems, Languages, and Applications (OOPSLA '04),* (pp. 310-311). New York, NY: ACM.

ADDITIONAL READING

Biswas, S., Mall, R., Satpathy, M., & Sukumaran, S. (2009). A model-based regression test selection approach for embedded applications. *SIGSOFT Software Engineering Notes, 34,* 1–9. doi:10.1145/1543405.1543413

Harrold, M. J. (1998). Architecture-Based Regression Testing of Evolving Systems. *Proceedings of the International Workshop on the Role of Software Architecture in Testing and Analysis (ROSATEA 1998),* 73-77.

Hsia, P., Li, X., Kung, D. C., Hsu, C.-T., Li, L., & Toyoshima, Y. (1997). A technique for the selective revalidation of OO software. *Journal of Software Maintenance, 9,* 217–233. doi:10.1002/(SICI)1096-908X(199707/08)9:4<217::AID-SMR152>3.0.CO;2-2

Kung, D., Gao, J., Hsia, P., Toyoshima, Y., Chen, C., & Kim, Y.-S. (1995). Developing an object-oriented software testing and maintenance environment. *Communications of the ACM, 38*(10), 75–87. doi:10.1145/226239.226256

Kung, D., Gao, J., Hsia, P., Wen, F., Toyoshima, Y., & Chen, C. (1994). Change impact identification in object oriented software maintenance. *In Proceedings of the International Conference on Software Maintenance,* 202-211.

Lindvall, M., & Runesson, M. (1998). The visibility of maintenance in object models: an empirical study. *In Proceedings of the International Conference on Software Maintenance,* 54-62.

M., A. S., & Wibowo, B. (2003). Regression Test Selection Based on Version Changes of Components. *In Proceedings of the Tenth Asia-Pacific Software Engineering Conference Software Engineering Conference,* IEEE Computer Society, 78.

Mayrhauser, A. v., & Olender, K. (1993). Efficient testing of software modifications. *In Proceedings of the IEEE International Test Conference on Designing, Testing, and Diagnostics,* 859-864.

Memon, A., Nagarajan, A., & Xie, Q. (2005). Automating regression testing for evolving GUI software: Research Articles. *Journal of Software Maintenance and Evolution, 17*(1), 27–64. doi:10.1002/smr.305

Memon, A. M., & Banerjee, I. Hashmi, & N., Nagarajan, A. (2003). DART: A Framework for Regression Testing "Nightly/daily Builds" of GUI Applications. *In Proceedings of 19th IEEE International Conference on Software Maintenance*, 410-419

Onoma, A., Tsai, W., Poonawala, M., & Suganuma, H. (1998). Regression testing in an industrial environment. *Communications of the ACM, 41*(5), 81–86. doi:10.1145/274946.274960

Sajeev, A., & Wibowo, B. (2003). UML Modeling for Regression Testing of Component Based Systems. *Electronic Notes in Theoretical Computer Science, 82*(6), 190–198. doi:10.1016/S1571-0661(04)81037-5

Winter, M. (1998). Managing Object-Oriented Integration and Regression Testing (without becoming drowned). *In Eurostar (Ed.)*.

KEY TERMS AND DEFINITIONS

Abstract Test Cases and Concrete Test Cases: Abstract test cases are often extracted from the specification of the system. They cannot be executed often due to the fact that they are derived from a representation which is at a higher level of abstraction then the actual system code. They need to be translated to the executable from (concrete test cases) for execution on the system under test.

Baseline and Delta Versions: A baseline is a stable and tested version of the system. The test suite which was used to test the baseline is often referred to as baseline test suite. A delta version of the system is one in which new changes are introduced. It has to be tested using the regression testing approaches.

Change Impact Analysis: Change impact analysis is the process to identify the impact of change in one artefact on the other related artefacts. The impact analysis is performed by considering the various dependencies that exists between artefacts in a system.

Model-Based and Model-Driven Testing: Model-based testing uses analysis and design models of a system as input to identify the changes between different versions of a system. Model-driven testing is a type of Model-based testing which uses MDA principles such as Platform independent models and platform specific models as input and model transformations for test generation. Additionally Model-driven regression testing approaches should also use platform independent test suites and should support the concept of test modelling.

Model-Based Regression Testing (MBRT): Is a type of regression testing that uses analysis and design models of baseline and delta versions of the software system for the change identification. The analysis and design models of the baseline and delta versions are compared to identify the changes between different versions of the systems. The changes are used later to select the regression test cases.

Regression Testing: Regression testing is a testing activity which is performed after a change is introduced into the system. The aim of the regression testing is to reveal the defects introduced after the changes. The changes introduced in the system are the result of the software evolution. Changes are often identified by comparing the baseline and delta versions of the system. After the change identification, the test cases corresponding to the changes are identified from the baseline test suite to retest the system.

Traceability: Traceability is ability to specify and preserve the relationship between two entities of interest. Traceability is often categorized as implicit and explicit traceability. Implicit traceability is the traceability which exists between two model elements but is not made explicit. Explicit traceability is the traceability which is discovered and stored/persisted for further reuse.

ENDNOTES

1 http://www-01.ibm.com/software/awdtools/rup/#

2 http://scrummethodology.com/

3 U2TP (UML 2 Testing Profile) is a standard test specification language by Object Management Group (OMG). The preliminary building blocks of U2TP are "Test Architecture", "Test Behaviour", "Test Data" and "Test Time". The current available version of U2TP is 1.0; however, the next revisions are also in progress.

4 Although this paper consider testing of UML designs itself not the source code but we are not considering any particular representation of SUT. It can be either source code or executable model; hence, we are including this study in our analysis as well

APPENDIX

Table 11. The list of selected studies for the analysis

Selected Studies	Corresponding Research Papers
Study-1: (Gorthi et al., 2008)	(Gorthi R. P., Pasala, Chanduka, & Leong, 2008)
Study-2: (Chen et al., (a), 2002,2003)	(Chen, Probert, & Sims, 2002), (Chen Y., 2002) (Chen & Probert, 2003)
Study-3: (Silva et al., 2010)	(Silva, Budnik, Hasling, McKenna, & Subramanyan, 2010)
Study-4: (Mansour et al., 2007,2011)	(Mansour & Takkoush, 2007) (Mansour, Takkoush, & Nehme, 2011)
Study-5: (Briand et al., 2002,2003,2009)	(Briand, Labiche, & He, 2009) (Briand L., 2003) (Briand, Labiche, & Soccar, 2002)
Study-6: (Deng et al., 2004)	(Deng, Sheu, & Wang, 2004)
Study-7: (Chen et al., (b), 2007, 2009)	(Chen, Probert, & Ural, 2007), (Chen, Probert, & Ural, 2009)
Study-8: (Korel et al., 2002)	(Korel, Tahat, & Vaysburg, 2002)
Study-9: (Beydeda et al., 2000)	(Beydeda & Gruhn, 2000)
Study-10: (Farooq et al., 2007,2010)	(Farooq, Q., 2007) (Farooq, Z., Malik, & Nadeem, 2007), (Farooq, Iqbal, Malik, & Riebisch, 2010) Tool Source code: (http://www.theoinf.tu-ilmenau.de/~qurat/projects. htm)
Study-11: (Ali et al., 2007)	(Ali, Nadeem, Iqbal, & Usman, 2007)
Study-12: (Pilskalns et al., 2006)	(Pilskalns, Uyan, & Andrews, 2006)[4]
Study-13: (Naslavsky et al., 2007,2009,2010)	(Naslavsky, Ziv, & Richardson, 2010) (Naslavsky, Ziv, & Richardson, 2009) (Naslavsky & Richardson, 2007)
Study-14: (Jeron et al., 1999, 2000)	(Traon, Jeron, Jezequel, & Morel, 2000), (Jaeron, Jaezaequel, Traon, & Morel, 1999)
Study-15: (Muccini et al., 2005,2006, 2007)	(Muccini(b), Dias, & Richardson, 2005) (Muccini(a), Dias, & Richardson, 2005) , (Muccini, Dias, & Richardson, 2006) (Muccini, 2007)
Study-16: (Wu & Offet, 2003)	(Wu & Offutt, 2003)
Study17: (Martins et al., 2005)	(Martins & Vieira, 2005)

Chapter 11

State-Based Evolution Management of Risk-Based System Tests for Service-Centric Systems

Michael Felderer
University of Innsbruck, Austria

Berthold Agreiter
University of Innsbruck, Austria

Ruth Breu
University of Innsbruck, Austria

ABSTRACT

For various reasons, service-centric systems are subject to continuous evolution. Therefore, regular adaptations to their tests are essential to keep, or even improve, their quality of service. This chapter presents a model-based approach to manage tests for evolving service-centric systems. We do so by attaching state machines to all model elements of our system model and test model to manage the consistent evolution of the system and its tests. In our approach, a modification to an arbitrary model element is propagated to related model elements. As a consequence, also these model elements may change their state. The process integrates continuous risk assessment which enables the prioritization of tests for optimized test selection and subsequent test execution. Our system and test evolution management process is demonstrated in a case study from the home-networking domain.

DOI: 10.4018/978-1-61350-438-3.ch011

INTRODUCTION

A software system must evolve, or it becomes progressively less satisfactory (Lehman, 1980). Although evolution has been investigated for model-driven system development (R. Breu, 2010), such aspects have been neglected for model-driven *system testing* so far. Nevertheless, testing is very important during evolution (Moonen, Deursen, Zaidman, & Bruntink, 2008), and maintenance of test models is a key factor to make model-driven testing applicable at all. The evolution of a system provides additional information that supports the selection of test models and therefore the generation of an optimal test suite by analogy to classical regression testing (Rothermel & Harrold, 1998).

In many application domains, testing has to be done under severe pressure due to limited resources with the consequence that only a subset of all relevant test cases can be executed. In this context, *risk-based testing* (RBT) (Amland, 2000) is more and more applied to prioritize test cases based on assigned risks, i.e., the chance of damage determined by its probability and impact. The results of a test run are then used to reassess risks for future test prioritization. Risk-based testing can be integrated into a system and test evolution management process in a natural way.

In this chapter, we present a state-based evolution management methodology for dynamically evolving service-centric systems that integrates risk-based testing techniques for the prioritization of test cases. We put the main focus on how the evolution influences tests so to be able to build optimal test suites, and on how risk-based testing can be considered in the evolution process to have a further criterion for test selection. We enhance our previous evolution management approach (M. Felderer, B. Agreiter, & R. Breu, 2011) by risk-based testing to provide additional information for optimized test selection. Our approach is based on a state-model based computation of

test models and allows for regression testing of service-centric systems.

Arising application scenarios have demonstrated the power of service-centric systems. This ranges from the exchange of health related data among various stakeholders in healthcare, over the cross-linking of traffic participants, to home-network control systems. Taking the latter as an example, consider only a few device types are initially integrated in the scenario and will successively be extended by new actor instances, improved underlying infrastructure or new resp. modified functionality. The importance for systematically managing the evolution of service-centric systems is also reflected by a special volume on continual service improvement within the ITIL standard for service management (OGC, 2007).

In our methodology, each changeable artifact, i.e., a model element, has a state machine attached that describes its current state and possible future states of the artifact. The state machine triggers resp. receives events to compute the new state of its corresponding artifact. Consequently, we work with a model where any change may influence multiple model elements. The states of the model elements describe their condition, e.g., whether a service is executable, or whether a requirement is associated with a test.

Following the widely used classification in (Leung & White, 1989), the *type of a test* can be *evolution* for testing novelties of the system, *regression* for testing non-modified parts ensuring that evolution did not impact parts supposed not to be modified, *stagnation* for ensuring that evolution did actually take place and changed the behavior of the system, and *obsolete* for tests which are not relevant anymore. The type of a test is computed by the state machines mentioned before. Based on this type, and the risk value of a test and the test requirement, a test suite is determined. This supports safe regression testing (Rothermel & Harrold, 1998), which identifies all test cases in the original test set that can reveal one or more faults in the modified program, in a natural way.

Currently, the toolset operating on system models and test models is mostly unconnected, i.e., when certain parts of the system are modified, these modifications need to be manually traced in the system model, risk model, test model, etc. The various stakeholders, like test engineers, system architects, developers, risk analysts, etc., need to overlook the whole system to ensure that changes are traced to *all* affected parts. With a growing number of stakeholders and model elements, this becomes an increasingly complex issue, and can result in inconsistent views of the system. Our approach provides assistance for keeping track of evolution steps by using state machines as *executable* artifacts, which propagate changes immediately to all affected model elements.

Our approach acts on the assumption that multiple stakeholders are working on the same model but different parts of it. The contribution at hand is focusing on tracing changes on any part of the model, under consideration of a risk assessment. By this research we want to be able to define optimized test suites after system modifications. This means that our approach should allow for selecting exactly these tests which are of importance under specific selectable conditions. Tool support for consolidating the changes by different stakeholders, and the actual *interpretation* of state machines is described elsewhere (Trojer, Breu, & Löw, 2010), (M. Breu, Breu, & Löw, 2010).

This chapter is structured as follows. In the next section we provide background for this book. Then, in the following section we explain the underlying metamodel, and afterwards, we define our test evolution process. Before concluding the chapter we apply the approach to an industrial case study, and finally we draw conclusions and highlight future work.

Background

Evolution of software has attained much attention in the last years. Many approaches consider the evolution of the system either focusing on the source code or on the system model (Mens & Demeyer, 2008). However, only few approaches highlight the role of tests in the evolution process. In (Moonen et al., 2008), the interplay between software testing and evolution is investigated considering the influence of evolving tests on the system. That chapter introduces *test-driven refactoring*, i.e., refactoring of production code induced by the restructuring of the tests. As in (Moonen et al., 2008), we consider the relationship of tests and system evolution but on the model-level, and not on the code-level.

Model-based testing applies model-based design for the modeling of test artifacts or the automation of tests activities (Goetz, Nickolaus, Rossner, & Salomon, 2009). Most of today's model-based testing approaches test the functional behavior of systems by black-box techniques. But if testing is generally considered to be based on abstract models of the software or its source code (Ammann & Offutt, 2008), model-based testing can be performed for any type of test. According to (Zander, Dai, Schieferdecker, & Din, 2005) *model-driven testing* can be defined as testing-based Model Driven Architecture (OMG, 2003), i.e., the derivation of executable test code from test models. Telling TestStories (Felderer, Zech, Fiedler, & Breu, 2010) is a model-driven testing approach for service centric-systems that has been extended for test evolution management (M. Felderer et al., 2011; Michael Felderer, Berthold Agreiter, & Ruth Breu, 2011). The topic of model-based testing is well-covered in the literature (see (Broy, Jonsson, Katoen, Leucker, & Pretschner, 2005) for an overview) and many tools are already on the market supporting model-based approaches (Roßner, Brandes, Götz, & Winter, 2010), (Utting & Legeard, 2006).

Regression testing is the selective retesting of a system or component to verify that modifications have not caused unintended effects and that the system or component still complies with its specified requirements (IEEE, 1990). Regression testing can also be performed for any type of test independent of its level of detail, its characteristics and its accessibility. Regression testing is one major activity to maintain evolving systems (Gorthi, Pasala, Chanduka, & Leong, 2008). Rothermel and Harrold have published a detailed survey paper on regression test selection techniques (Rothermel & Harrold, 1996). In that survey, several techniques, e.g., dependency graphs or symbolic execution have been evaluated according to their inclusiveness, precision, efficiency, and generality. Most regression testing approaches are code-based (Von Mayrhauser & Zhang, 1999). Only a few model-based regression testing approaches have been considered.

Model-based regression testing approaches determine impacts of system model changes on the baseline test suite. UML-based system models typically consider class models and a specific type of behavior models, such as state machines in (Farooq, Iqbal, Malik, & Nadeem, 2007), sequence diagrams in (Briand, Labiche, & He, 2009) or activity diagrams in (Chen, Probert, & Sims, 2002).

In the approach of Chen et al. (Chen, Probert, & Ural, 2007), regression test suites are generated from extended finite state machines. A dependency analysis searches for the effects of changes expressed as elementary modifications, and creates test cases for the changed parts of the system.

The method presented in (Vaysburg, 2002) works similarly on extended finite state machines, and its focus is to reduce an existing regression test suite.

Fraser et al. (Fraser, Aichernig, & Wotawa, 2007) define an approach to regression testing and test suite update with model checkers.

Felderer et al. (Michael Felderer et al., 2011) define a test evolution management methodol-

ogy. In this approach state machines are attached to all model elements. The evolution process is then initiated by adding, modifying or deleting model elements which trigger change events and fire transitions in state machines. The model is then changed manually or automatically until it is consistent and executable. Based on a test requirement considering the actual state of model elements, a test suite is selected and executed. The evolution management methodology considers tests for evolving security requirements in (M. Felderer et al., 2011).

Under consideration of the modeling effort, model-based regression test selection has several advantages to test selection on the code level (Briand et al., 2009). The effort for testing can be estimated earlier, tools for regression testing can be largely technology independent, the management of traceability at the model level is more practical because it enables the specification of dependencies at a higher level of abstraction, and no complex static and dynamic code analysis is required. Models have the advantage that they are smaller referred to the size of modifiable elements because they are more abstract. Elbaum et al. (Elbaum, Malishevsky, & Rothermel, 2000) analyze several selection criteria to prioritize test cases for regression testing, e.g., random ordering or total statement coverage prioritization with the conclusion that even simple approaches can improve the rate of fault detection. However, the performance overhead of more sophisticated approaches is relatively high.

Risk-based testing (Amland, 2000) is a type of software testing that considers risks for designing, evaluating, and analyzing tests. Risk-based testing improves the selection of tests based on the assessment of risks for a system and provides decision support for evolution management. This is particularly true for regression testing where results of previous test runs can additionally be used to reassess risks. Risk-based testing techniques have rarely been applied on the model level. RiteDAP

(Stallbaum, Metzger, & Pohl, 2008) is a model-based approach to risk-based system testing that uses annotated UML activity diagrams for test case generation and prioritization. But risk-based testing techniques have so far not been integrated into a model-driven system plus test evolution process and not been applied for model--based regression testing.

Basically, a *service--centric system* consists of a set of independent peers providing and calling services (R. Breu, 2010) following the architectural style of a service-oriented architecture (SOA) (Engels et al., 2008). Orchestration and choreography technologies allow for a flexible composition of services to workflows (OASIS, 2007), (W3C, 2005). Recently, many methods (Canfora & Di Penta, 2006) and tools (Bertolino, De Angelis, Frantzen, & Polini, 2008) for testing service-centric systems have been developed but only a few classical regression testing approaches focusing on service-centric systems have been developed. For instance, Di Penta et al. (Di Penta, Bruno, Esposito, Mazza, & Canfora, 2007) present a regression testing strategy for web services considering service changes. The approach focuses on the minimization of service invocations by reusing monitoring data. In our approach not only service changes but also changes to the requirements and tests are considered.

Metamodel

Our static metamodel is based on the abstract system and test metamodel defined in (Felderer, Breu, Chimiak-Opoka, Breu, & Schupp, 2009). It describes requirements, tests, the system with its infrastructure, and risks in service-oriented systems. Based on this metamodel the evolution process is defined in the next section.

The metamodel consists of the packages *Requirements, System, Infrastructure, Test,* and *Risk.* In the remainder of this contribution we also refer to them as requirements, system, test, and risk model, respectively. The requirements model

defines a hierarchy of Requirement elements, describing which functionality should be supported by the system. Requirements are linked to Service and Test elements, and have an Impact assigned. This impact element describes the influence of a requirement to the whole system. This means, if a requirement with a high impact value is not met by the system, this may have serious consequences to the business or company assets as compared to a requirement with a low impact value.

The package *System* defines Service elements which contain provided and required Interface elements. Each interface consists of Operation elements which refer to classes. Service and Requirement elements can be associated to each other to denote which requirement is implemented by which service.

The package *Infrastructure* defines the deployed services and their deployment environment by the elements RunningService and InfrastructureElement. To keep the description of our approach clean, we do not consider choreographies and orchestrations in the metamodel because they trigger change operations by analogy to plain services. Consequently, our view represents such workflows as Service elements.

The package *Test* defines all elements needed for testing service centric systems. A TestSuite is a collection of Test elements. It is attached to TestRequirement elements, e.g., to select tests or define test exit criteria, and to TestRun elements assigning Verdict values to assertions. A Test has a Type, which can be either *evolution, stagnation, regression,* or *obsolete,* and consists of SequenceElement artifacts. A SequenceElement is either an Assertion defining how a verdict is computed or a Call element invoking a service operation and has some data assigned to the free variables of its assertions or calls.

The package *Risk* contains a very basic risk model. It links the impact of not meeting a requirement and the probability that a service does not work properly together in order to compute a risk value. The computed risk value is associated to a

Test element where it is used for the prioritization of tests. Further, as we will describe later, a test run can lead to a modification of the Probability element.

The model elements Requirement, Service, Test, Impact, and Probability have a special importance because changes on these elements trigger further changes on other model elements. Each of these three types of model elements has a state machine attached which describes their current condition. This state and the state transitions are later used for computing test suites. The current state of a model element is stored in an attribute state not depicted in Figure 1. The mechanism of mutual triggers by using these state machines is discussed in detail in the following section.

Evolution Process

This work investigates a method to keep a test model in-sync with a system model to be able to build optimal test suites. In this section we show how modifications to different model elements affect risk values, tests and vice versa. Additionally we show, how tests can be managed based on these modifications. The evolution process presented here defines the steps that an arbitrary modification of the model induces to obtain an

executable test suite for the updated model, and that fulfills certain test requirements. Because our metamodel defines connections among the requirements model, the system model, the test model, and the risk values we are able to propagate modifications to other relevant parts of the model along these connections. This is done via events and effects of state machines assigned to model elements. For example, if a service is undeployed, this mechanism allows to locate all calls referring to this service, and mark the according tests as ``*not executable*''. In the following, we first explain the overall evolution process, and then we present every single process step in more detail.

Process Overview

The *evolution process* is initiated by a change of a model element (cf. Figure 2), i.e., adding, modifying or removing a model element. A *change* is an event that triggers transitions in the state machines attached to model elements. The state machines *propagate the change* to all affected model elements. Afterwards, *risks have to be assessed* on the changed model. To present our evolution process in an understandable way, changes of model elements and the corresponding risk assessment are conducted consecutively. In

Figure 1. Metamodel for requirements, system, infrastructure and test, and including a basic risk model

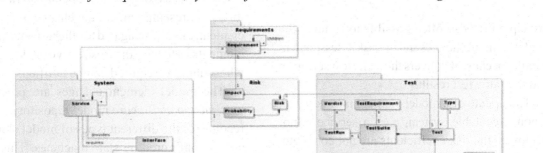

Figure 2. Risk-based evolution process for model element changes

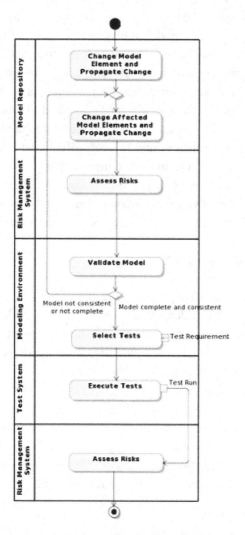

principle it is also often possible to conduct the model element changes and the risk assessment in parallel because it delivers the same test selection and the same test result.

The update of a model element may result in a non-executable system, e.g., a service is not deployed, the risk coefficients are not complete, or the model is inconsistent because operation signatures are not compatible to their calls. Therefore, the model needs to be validated, and possibly changed until the test model is consistent and complete. The validation checks, and poten-

tial modifications, are conducted in the modeling environment. Afterwards, based on certain test requirements, *tests are selected* from the test model. Finally, the selected *tests are executed* which includes the generation of executable test code. Based on the test result the *risks are reassessed*. The reassessment of risks may then initiate new changes to model elements. The sketched evolution process is carried out iteratively as long as changes are applied.

The different actions of the evolution process in Figure 2 are implemented by different tool sets. Because the process is *change-driven* (R. Breu, 2010), a *model repository* and a *modeling environment* are used for constructing a consistent and complete model. While the model repository manages changes and always provides the most current version of the model, the modeling environment consists of a set of modeling tools for manipulating plus validating models, and for selecting tests. A *risk management system* manages the assessment of risks. This is also a kind of modeling environment, however with a specific focus on the probabilities of faults or weaknesses. A *test system* is then responsible for executing tests conforming to a specific test requirement. The different tool sets interact via models and are interchangeable. The process can therefore be implemented by arbitrary model repositories, risk management systems, modeling environments and test systems as long as they operate on the same model representation. On the change of a model element, this is propagated to other affected model elements. Hence, the respective stakeholders whose input is required can be notified.

The model element changes are processed by a *metamodel-aware* model repository, which recognizes the different types of model element, and is configured by state machines. This way, every change is recorded in the repository, and because of its metamodel-awareness, it is able to identify the kind of modification. Consequently, the model repository is responsible for keeping various parts of the model in-sync by firing the corresponding transitions in state machines upon modifications. This part of our approach realizes the integration of different models and allows the various stakeholders to collaborate effectively. Preliminary achievements of such a model repository are discussed in (Trojer et al., 2010) and (M. Breu et al., 2010).

We assume that whenever a new service is created, an initial probability value is assigned, and when a new requirement is created, an initial impact value is assigned.

Change of Model Elements and Change Propagation

All model elements of the packages *Requirements*, *System* and *Test* can be subjects to modifications. Changes can be either the creation of a model element (*add--operations*), the deletion of a model element (*remove-operations*), or the modification of a model element (*modify-operations*).

The typical test design process starts with the definition of a new requirement. Afterwards, the requirement is assigned to tests. The test definition may also induce changes to the system model due to its connections to the system model via which its services are used. Hence, an additional requirement may have impact on the rest of the model and raise the need for further changes. This describes a test-driven development approach where the alignment of the requirement, test and system model is crucial to keep the whole model consistent. Note that any part of the model can be changed, and we also cover such cases, e.g., updates of infrastructural components or bug fixes to services.

Although changes may occur on all types of model elements of the metamodel depicted in Figure 1, in the sequel we only consider changes to instances of Requirement, Service, Test, Impact, and Probability. We do so because any change can be reduced to a change on one of these element types. Test suites, resp. test runs, are computed in the test selection resp. test execution phase, but

are not changed by state transitions considered in this step.

We define state machines describing how the states of these elements change. Each state transition defines a *trigger*, an optional *guard* condition and an optional *effect*, i.e., behavior to be performed when the transition fires. Hence, the structure of transitions is of the following form: *trigger() [guard] / effect*. The effect part is used here to propagate change, which means it may trigger further state transitions in other state machines. Simply put, the state machines show under which conditions a state transition occurs and which other elements are potentially affected.

Whenever a model element is removed, the Type variable of the assigned test is set to *obsolete*. In order to keep the state machines in this chapter more readable, we omit the transitions to the state *obsolete* when removing model elements.

In the following we describe the state machines for the model elements mentioned before, so that the reader gets an understanding for how change propagation takes place.

Requirements

Figure 3 depicts the states of Requirement elements. When a new requirement *r* is created, it is first in state defined. As soon as the requirement is assigned to a test *t*, its state changes to assigned. The requirement can only reach the state underTest if all of its associated sub-requirements are also in the same state, the requirement is *assigned* to at least one test and all assigned tests are *executable*. This transition can be fired either by assigning a test to *r* or by modifying assigned tests or their services so that all tests become executable. The condition also takes into account that requirements are organized hierarchically. When *r* is modified in state assigned or underTest the compatibility to all assigned tests has to be checked. If the requirement and a test are not compatible anymore, the connection among the two is removed, i.e., the *unassignTest()*-operation is triggered. The trigger

Figure 3. State machine describing the lifecycle of Requirement elements

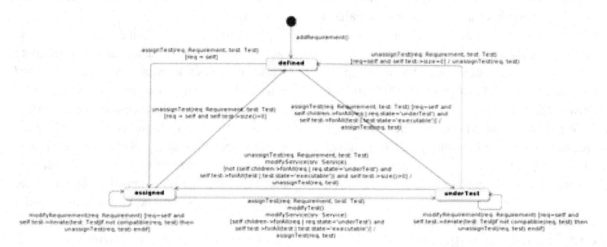

modifyRequirement further fires transitions in the state machine of tests as depicted in Figure 7. The implications of this trigger are described in the section on tests. Furthermore, a requirement under test must always be *assigned* to at least one test. In case this is not fulfilled anymore, its state changes back to defined. In the subsequent semi--formal definitions, we determine the predicates *assigned* and *compatible* used as guards in the state machines. In doing so, we write R for the set of all requirements, S for the set of all services, and T for the set of all tests.

Definition 1 (Test--Requirement Assignment)

The tuple set TR ⊆ R × T denotes all assignments of tests to requirements. For every tuple $(r, t) \in$ TR we say that t is *assigned* to r. When a requirement r is assigned to a test t, the tuple (r, t) is added to the set TR. We further define the function

assigned$_{TR}$ as follows:

assigned$_{TR}$: R × T → *Bool*, where *assigned*$_{TR}(r, t)$:=**true** if $(r, t) \in$ TR and **false** otherwise.

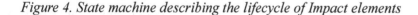

Figure 4. State machine describing the lifecycle of Impact elements

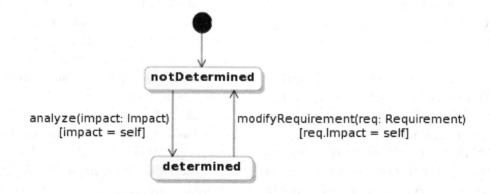

Definition 2 (Test Compatibility)

A test *t* ∈ T and a requirement *r* ∈ R are *compatible* if the test *t* validates the requirement *r*.

The assessment whether a test validates a requirement is a manual task because the requirements are always specified in an informal way.

To conduct a risk assessment, an impact value has to be assigned to each requirement. The determination of this impact value is also controlled by a state machine. Figure 4 shows this state machine. It only consists of two states because the impact value is either *determined*, in the case a risk management system evaluates the requirements and assigns appropriate impact values which is triggered by *analyze(impact:Impact)*, or *notDetermined*, in the case the requirement was newly defined or modified. The trigger *modifyRequirement()* causes a transition to the state *notDetermined* of assigned Impact elements whenever a requirement is modified. By this, the risk management system is always able to follow which requirements need to be analyzed. Details

on the risk assessment itself are explained in a later section.

Services

Similar to requirements, every service *s* ∈ S has a state. Figure 5 depicts the life cycle of services and its state transitions.

When a service is newly defined, it is in state new. The state changes to specified as soon as an interface is added to the service, because from that point on it can be referenced by tests. After a service is implemented, it can be deployed, which changes the state of the service to executable. However, deployment is only allowed if the service provides at least one interface. The deployment transition further triggers the operation *modifyService* which allows other model elements to react on the deployment of the service. Note that this operation has the current service object (self) as parameter. Before the interface or the infrastructural elements of a service can be modified again, the service has to be undeployed. Executable services always provide at least one

Figure 5. State machine describing the lifecycle of Service elements

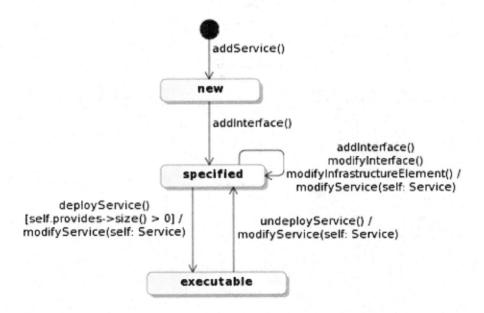

Figure 6. State machine describing the lifecycle of Probability elements

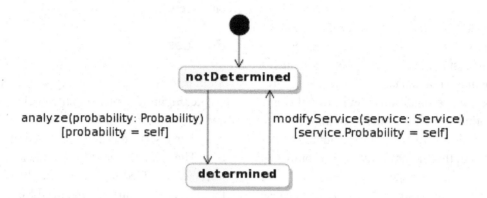

interface. Every modification to a service, its provided or required Interface elements, or to subordinate services being part of this service is propagated to *assigned* tests via the trigger *modifyService*.

Similar to requirements, also services are relevant to risk assessment. Every Service element is assigned a Probability element. The determination

of this probability value is controlled by a state machine. Figure 6 shows this state machine. Like the Impact state machine, also this one only consists of two states because the probability value is either *determined*, in the case a risk management system evaluates the service and assigns appropriate values, which is triggered by *analyze(probability:Probability)*, or *notDetermined*, in the

Figure 7. State machine describing the lifecycle of Test elements

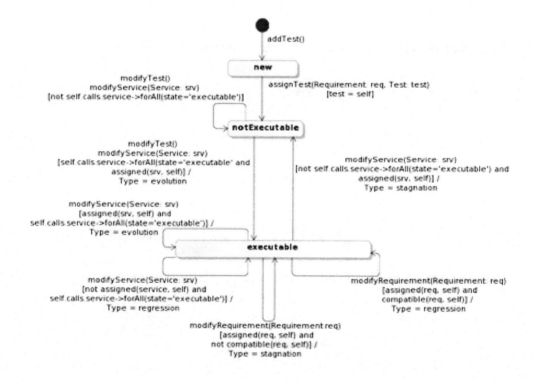

case the service was newly defined or modified. The trigger *modifyService()* causes a transition to the state *notDetermined* of assigned Probability elements whenever a service is modified. Again, this supports the risk analyst to always be able to follow which services need to be analyzed.

Tests

Every test $t \in$ T has a state. As explained above, state transitions of tests are not only caused by direct modifications to elements of type Test but can also be triggered by requirements and services. The possible states and transitions of tests are depicted in Figure 7.

Definition 3 (Test--Service Assignment)

The tuple set TS $\subseteq$ S $\times$ T denotes all assignments of tests to services. When a Call element, contained in a test $t \in$ T, is associated to an Operation element of a service $s \in$ S, the tuple *(s, t)* is added to TS. We say that *s* is *assigned* to *t* if *(s, t)* $\in$ TS.

We further define the function *assigned*$_{ST}$ as follows:

assigned$_{ST}$: S $\times$ T $\rightarrow$ *Bool*, where *assigned*$_{ST}$*(s, t):=***true** if *(s, t)* $\in$ TS and **false** otherwise.

Note that Call elements can only be associated to Operation elements if their signature is compatible in terms of parameters and data types.

A test is in state new as long as it has no requirements assigned by the operation *assignTest*. Note that the same operation is also a trigger in the Requirement state machine, i.e., this assignment causes a state transitions for both, tests and requirements. After the assignment of a requirement, a test is in state *notExecutable* until all *assigned* Service elements are in state executable. When a test or an *assigned* service is modified such that all *assigned* services of a test are in state executable, the test also gets the state executable. A guard condition checks for adherence to this rule.

Types of Tests

Test elements have an attribute Type. It describes the kind of a test regarding the last evolution step and is used for test selection. There exist four different test suites, namely *evolution*, *obsolete*, *regression*, and *stagnation*. Depending on the modifications to the model, the Type of a test is updated. If a test transitions from *notExecutable* to executable its Type is set to *evolution* because the test is the result of an evolution step. The same is true if a test is currently in state executable and one of its assigned services is subject to a modification. On the other hand, if a service is modified but the current test under consideration is not assigned with that service, the Type of the test is changed to *regression* because the test should not be affected by this modification.

Also the modification of requirements influences the Type attribute of executable tests. When a requirement assigned to a test *t* is modified such that *t* and the requirement are incompatible, the type is set to *stagnation* because the test *should* fail now. If, on the other hand, the requirement and the test are still compatible, the type is set to *regression*.

Change of Affected Model Elements

The changes to model elements may cause state changes of affected model elements, e.g., based on a service modification, a test may change its state from executable to *notExecutable*. This may induce further changes to get consistent and executable models. Furthermore, such changes are later used for the definition of test suites.

Risk Assessment

In the risk assessment phase, risk coefficients, i.e., numerical structures representing risks, are assigned to all tests. The risk coefficient of a test is computed dynamically based on the probability values of the services and the impact values of the requirements assigned to a test. The assignment of a probability value to a service is triggered by a function *analyze(probability:Probability)* of the risk management system, and the assignment of an impact value to a requirement is triggered by a function *analyze(impact:Impact)* of the risk management system. By a value assignment, the respective state machine of Impact elements in Figure 4 and of Probability elements in Figure 6 transitions to the state determined. As soon as the impact value and the probability value of a risk are determined, the risk coefficient can be assigned by the risk management system. Similar to the other model elements, any necessary stakeholder intervention is automatically determined by the state machines.

The probability considers technical factors that determine the likelihood of a failure, e.g., the code complexity, the architectural complexity or the usage rate and is assigned to services. Depending on the factors, the probability may be computed manually by a risk analyst, semi-automatically, or automatically. The impact considers business factors that determine the cost if a requirement is not fulfilled. The impact is determined manually.

The probability and impact values are then aggregated to risk coefficients by specific aggregation functions. We do not consider the computation of risk coefficients in detail because to this contribution it is only relevant that a risk coefficient is assigned but not how it has been computed.

Risks are assigned at two different places in the process: after the changes of model elements, and after test runs (see Figure 2). For instance, if all tests pass, then their risk coefficient can be reduced by a specific factor.

Risk coefficients can, in general, be arbitrary complex structures, e.g., pairs of a probability value and an impact value. In this publication we simply define a risk coefficient as a real number between 0 and 1 because this suffices to select and prioritize tests.

The risk assessment phase typically involves several roles. At least a technical expert, e.g., a software developer or architect, who is responsible for the determination of probability values, and a business expert, e.g., a customer or a domain expert, who is responsible for the determination of impact values, are involved in the risk assessment. In some settings, the determination of probability values and the risk assessment based on the test results can even be automated. In our respect, we abstract from the concrete roles performing parts of the risk assessment and the degree of automation by introducing a risk management system which manages and represents a concrete risk assessment process.

Model Validation

The process of changing tests, requirements and services is repeated until the overall model is *consistent*, i.e., it contains no internal contradictions, and *complete*, i.e., it contains all essential information. A consistent and complete test model is the prerequisite that test code can be generated and executed.

The consistency and completeness of models can be checked by OCL constraints. For instance, the consistency check shown in Exhibit 1 validates whether the parameters of all calls are compatible with the parameters of the referred operations.

Consistency checks can directly address the executability of tests. The query shown in Exhibit 2 validates whether all tests in a set of tests defined by the predicate *test_requirement* are in the state executable, which is the prerequisite that the generated test code is executable.

The completeness check shown in Exhibit 3 validates whether all risk coefficients of all tests are set. Additionally, it checks whether the set value is between 0.0 and 1.0.

Exhibit 1.

```
context Model:    Call::allInstances.parameters    ->forAll{ param | param.
data.class = self.operation.class }
```

Exhibit 2.

```
context Model:    Tests::allInstances->select{ t | test_requirement(t) }
->forAll{ t | t.state='executable'}
```

Exhibit 3.

```
context Model:    Tests::allInstances->forAll{ t | t.risk.oclIsDefined()    and
t.risk>=0.0 and t.risk<=1.0 }
```

Test Selection

Test selection is the process where an actual test suite is computed from the set of all tests based on test requirements. Test requirements define test selection criteria in OCL and typically consider the type of a test and the state of other model artifacts. A very general regression test could for example be based on the test selection criterion (see Exhibit 4), which selects all tests that are supposed to pass, i.e., tests of type *evolution* or *regression*.

A more specific test selection criterion would be the OCL query (Exhibit 5), which selects all tests of type *evolution* that are associated to a specific service, called *HomeGateway* in the example. We assume that calls resp. service operations are available to get all calls of a test resp. all services referenced in calls.

A more fine-grained test selection criterion can also consider risk coefficients of tests. The selection criterion in Exhibit 6 selects all tests with a risk coefficient greater than 0.5.

OCL criteria as listed above can be used to define *safe regression test suites*, selecting all tests in the original test suite that can reveal failures or *minimal regression test suites*, selecting

Exhibit 4.

```
context Model:    Test::allInstances->select{ t |    t.type='evolution' or
t.type='regression' }
```

Exhibit 5.

```
context Model:    Test::allInstances->select{ t |       t.type='evolution' and
t.calls.services       ->includes{s | s.name='HomeGateway'}
```

Exhibit 6.

```
context Model:    Test::allInstances->select{ t |       t.type='evolution' and
t.risk > 0.5 }
```

a minimal number of tests covering specific criteria.

Test Execution

In the test execution phase a test suite is executed. The risk coefficients of the tests can be used to control the test execution by executing a set of tests in order of descending risk coefficients. The result of the test execution is a test run which assigns verdicts to all assertions in the test suite. We abstract from the technical steps to make test models executable which includes the transformation of test to executable test code and its execution against the running services. The transformation of tests as modeled in our approach to executable test code and its execution is explained in (Felderer, Fiedler, Zech, & Breu, 2009). If the test result is not as expected, e.g., if a test in the stagnation suite passes, the test model changes and the evolution process is executed iteratively.

CASE STUDY

In this section we demonstrate our test evolution methodology by a home gateway application. We provide only a short overview of the application as far as needed to discuss evolution scenarios in the following sections. In (Felderer, Agreiter, Breu, & Armenteros, 2010), the system is presented in more detail.

A home gateway is an appliance connected to an operator's network and providing certain services to customers, e.g., internet connection or video surveillance of rooms. As a service-centric system, it consists of the peers *Access Requestor* (AR), *Home Gateway* (HG), *Policy Enforcement Point* (PEP) and the *Policy Decision Point* (PDP). Following service-centric principles (Erl, 2005), each peer can be considered as a service providing and requiring interfaces which define the contents of information exchange. The AR is the client application which establishes the connection to a HG and uses its functionalities. The HG is a device installed at the home of a customer to control access to different resources. The enforcement of who is allowed to access which resources on the network is made by an internal component of the HG called PEP. The PEP receives the policy it has to enforce for a specific AR by the PDP.

In the sequel, we provide representative examples for different evolution types, namely the creation of requirements, the modification of requirements, and the modification of services. The first example *adds* a new requirement, whereas the remaining two *modify* existing elements. The examples are intended to demonstrate how the different modifications on the model propagate, and especially how they affect risks and tests.

We assume that a model of the system does already exist. Furthermore, a risk assessment has been performed beforehand and also the risk values are assumed to be available. The examples should clarify how evolution steps are handled in our approach and how they propagate to other elements of the system, like Risk and Test.

Creation of a Requirement

In this section we consider the creation of a functional and a non-functional requirement. The requirements diagram containing the new requirements is depicted in Figure 3.

A new functional requirement with the ID number 2 is added. This action triggers the event *addRequirement* for this requirement, which is then in state defined. After assigning a test, similar to the one depicted in Figure 9, the requirement transitions to state assigned or, if the test is already executable, to *underTest*. This scenario reflects the test-driven development process which our testing methodology is based on, because assigning a test to a requirement triggers modifications to the system model. In this case, a service *AirConditioning* for setting the temperature has to be added to make the test fully executable.

Now, consider a new non-functional requirement "The AR establishes a connection to the HG within 100 ms" which is added with the ID 1.1. The requirement is assigned to a test similar to the one for the agent-based scenario depicted in Figure 9 but with an additional time assertion. The requirement is then in state *underTest*.

Both requirements are newly added, which means that the impact value has to be determined for both Requirement elements because the assigned Impact elements are both in the state *notDetermined*. Since we do not propose a specific risk assessment method, an arbitrary manual or automatic procedure can be used to determine the necessary values. However, what our approach

provides is a reference usable by the risk management system showing which Impact elements possibly need to be adapted. In this example, the risk management system would determine the according impact value by the method of one's own choice so that both assigned Impact elements reach the state determined.

Modification of a Requirement

In this scenario we assume that the functional requirement with ID 1 of Figure 8, which already has an executable test assigned, is modified by changing the network control from agent-based to agent-less. The modification of the requirement triggers the *modifyRequirement* event, but the requirement is then still in state *underTest*. The event *modifyRequirement* further triggers a transition in the state machine of assigned tests. Now, the modified requirement and the test for the agent-based scenario are not compatible anymore because the agent-less scenario needs an additional network filter service. Therefore, the type of test switches to *stagnation* because it is expected to fail. The assigned test is still in state executable because no service has been modified.

The test depicted in Figure 9 checks for agent-less network control, integrating the new service *NetworkFilter*. It is assigned to the requirement with ID 1 in a new evolution process after the test has been added. Then the test is in state *notExecutable* until all its service calls are executable. As soon as the new service *NetworkFilter* has been specified and is executable the event *modifyService* triggers the transition of the test to the state executable and its type is *evolution*.

Also in this case, the modification of the requirement signals to the risk management system that the according Impact element possibly needs to be adjusted because it is in state *notDetermined*. Furthermore, because a new service is added, the probability of the service to fail in realizing the modified requirement has to be determined. When the Probability and the Impact elements

Figure 8. Requirements of the home gateway application

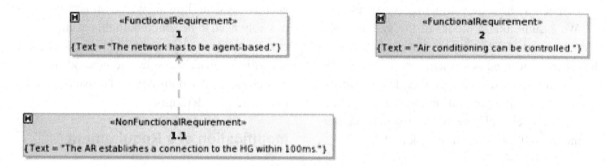

Figure 9. Test for the agent-less network control

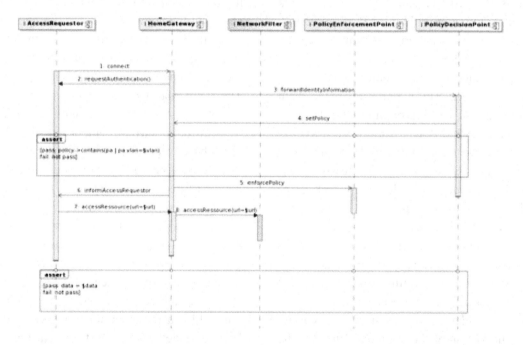

are in state determined, the risk values of all tests, to which the modified Service and Requirement elements are assigned, can be computed. If the risk values for tests with modified requirements are high, then this property can be considered for the selection of tests.

Modification of a Service

A typical modification of a service is the adaptation of an interface. For instance, the parameter *temperature* of an operation *setTemperature* of the

interface *AirConditioning* is changed from *integer* to *float*. The service interface has already been defined, and we assume that the corresponding service *AirConditioning* is in state specified and the assigned test *t* of the requirement with ID 2 in state *notExecutable*. The event *modifyInterface* triggers the action *modifyService* and leaves the service in state specified. *t* is not executable and therefore a second change iteration has to be applied to make the model executable. In the second iteration the service *AirConditioning* is deployed with the event *deployService* and the effect *modi-*

fyService which then triggers the transition from the state *notExecutable* to the state executable in the test *t*. By this step the type of *t* is set to *evolution*. The test *t* and the service *AirConditioning* are now consistent and executable.

Modifications of services can also be triggered by changes on the infrastructure as in the following scenario. The functionalities of the HG are provided on an OSGi infrastructure (OSGi-Alliance, 2010), a dynamic module system and service platform for Java. Before the OSGi infrastructure is changed, all services running on it are undeployed and then in state specified. The change of the infrastructure is reflected by a *modifyInfrastructureElement* event firing a transition. The affected services are then deployed (*deployService*) and move to state executable triggering *modifyService* events with the effect that the type of all assigned tests is set to *regression*. A *modifyService* action implies that the Probability element assigned to the service goes to the state *notDetermined* and has to be analyzed.

In all of the three scenarios we presented above, risk assessment is integrated into the evolution management and regression test process. The modification or addition of services or requirements triggers a risk assessment by the state transition to *notDetermined* in the state machine of an Impact or a Probability element. This is also true if the service or requirement has not directly been modified but the update has been caused by a modification on a different element. Furthermore, when a test is finally executed, the test results are used to reassess the risk values of tests to reflect the test outcome.

FUTURE RESEARCH DIRECTIONS AND CONCLUSION

We have presented a methodology to maintain risk-based test models in dynamically evolving service-centric systems by attaching state machines to all model elements. The evolution process is initiated by adding, modifying or deleting model elements which trigger change events and fire transitions in state machines. The model is then changed manually or automatically, and risks are assessed until the model is complete and consistent. Based on a test requirement considering the actual state of model elements and the risk values of tests, a regression test suite is selected and executed. Based on the test results, risks are reassessed. The test result or the reassessment of risks may initiate new changes. We have demonstrated our methodology in a home-networking case study. Compared to other model-based approaches to regression testing, we model tests separately from the system. With the additional assignment of risk values, this enables a very specific test selection and a development cycle where also test model changes can be integrated. Our methodology keeps the test model consistent and optimal. We have shown that the interplay between system evolution and software testing is twofold: On the one hand, if the system evolves, then tests have to co-evolve, making the evolution more difficult and time-intensive but manageable with our state machine based approach. On the other hand, many software evolution operations can only take place safely with adequate test models that allow to generate and execute safe regression test suites. Generally, test models provide a flexible and efficient way to manage the evolution of service-centric systems and to perform regression tests. Risk-based testing can be integrated into this process in a natural way. By the application of the evolution process on various changes in the home-networking case study, we have demonstrated how system evolution can effectively be managed on the model level under the consideration of tests and risks. The effects of changes on the model level have so far been traced manually and can be automated based on a model repository (Trojer et al., 2010), (M. Breu et al., 2010) as future work.

As a model-based approach to regression test selection our approach has several advantages to test selection on the code level (Briand et al.,

2009). The effort required for regression testing can be estimated earlier which is an important part of impact analysis and tools for regression testing can be largely technology independent. The management of traceability at the model level is more practical because it enables the specification of dependencies at a higher level of abstraction, and no complex static and dynamic code analysis is required. However, model-based regression test selection presumes that the system and test models are complete, internally consistent, and up-to-date which is considered in our methodology.

To employ our regression testing methodology in established industrial processes, it has to be integrated with existing standards for testing such as IEEE 829 (IEEE-SA-Standards-Board, 1998) for software test documentation. Because we consider test specifications, test logs and test reports as in IEEE 829 but do not define a concrete format for these artifacts, the future integration of our approach with IEEE 829 should be straightforward.

Based on the evolution management process for security requirements tests presented in (M. Felderer et al., 2011), we plan to apply our risk-enhanced evolution management process for risk-based testing of negative security requirements of dynamically evolving service-centric systems. In this case study we will also implement our proposed risk assessment procedure that integrates manual, semi-automated and automated determination of probability and impact factors.

The evolution process is based on state machines attached to all artifacts of the requirements, system, and test model which trigger changes to all affected model elements in an iterative way. As soon as the test model is consistent, tests can be selected based on selection criteria, transformed to test code which is then executed.

ACKNOWLEDGMENT

This work is sponsored by the SecureChange project (EU grant number ICT-FET-231101), the MATE project (FWF project number P17380), and QE LaB - Living Models for Open Systems (FFG 822740).

REFERENCES

W3C. (2005). Web services choreography description language version 1.0.

Amland, S. (2000). Risk-based testing: Risk analysis fundamentals and metrics for software testing including a financial application case study. *Journal of Systems and Software, 53*(3), 287–295. doi:10.1016/S0164-1212(00)00019-4

Ammann, P., & Offutt, J. (2008). *Introduction to software testing*. Cambridge, UK.

Bertolino, A., De Angelis, G., Frantzen, L., & Polini, A. (2008). *The PLASTIC framework and tools for testing service-oriented applications*. Paper presented at the ISSSE.

Breu, M., Breu, R., & Löw, S. (2010). *Living on the move: Towards an architecture for a living models infrastructure*.

Breu, R. (2010). *Ten principles for living models - A manifesto of change-driven software engineering*. Paper presented at the Proc. CISIS 2010, The Fourth International Conference on Complex, Intelligent and Software Intensive Systems.

Briand, L. C., Labiche, Y., & He, S. (2009). Automating regression test selection based on UML designs. *Information and Software Technology, 51*(1), 16–30. doi:10.1016/j.infsof.2008.09.010

Broy, M., Jonsson, B., Katoen, J. P., Leucker, M., & Pretschner, A. (2005). *Model-based testing of reactive systems, LNCS 3472*. Springer.

Canfora, G., & Di Penta, M. (2006). Testing services and service-centric systems: Challenges and opportunities. *IT Professional, 8*(2), 10–17. doi:10.1109/MITP.2006.51

Chen, Y., Probert, R. L., & Sims, D. P. (2002). *Specification-based regression test selection with risk analysis.* Paper presented at the CASCON 2002.

Chen, Y., Probert, R. L., & Ural, H. (2007). *Model-based regression test suite generation using dependence analysis.*

Di Penta, M., Bruno, M., Esposito, G., Mazza, V., & Canfora, G. (2007). Web services regression testing. In Baresi, L. (Ed.), *Test and analysis of Web services* (pp. 205–234). doi:10.1007/978-3-540-72912-9_8

Elbaum, S., Malishevsky, A. G., & Rothermel, G. (2000). Prioritizing test cases for regression testing. *ACM SIGSOFT Software Engineering Notes, 25*(5), 102–112. doi:10.1145/347636.348910

Engels, G., Hess, A., Humm, B., Juwig, O., Lohmann, M., Richter, J.-P., et al. (2008). *A method for engineering a true service-oriented architecture.*

Erl, T. (2005). *Service-oriented architecture: Concepts, technology, and design.* Prentice Hall PTR.

Farooq, Q., Iqbal, M. Z. Z., Malik, Z. I., & Nadeem, A. (2007). *An approach for selective state machine based regression testing.* Paper presented at the A-MOST 07.

Felderer, M., Agreiter, B., & Breu, R. (2011). Evolution of security requirements tests for service–centric systems. *International Symposium on Engineering Secure Software and Systems,* (pp. 181-194).

Felderer, M., Agreiter, B., & Breu, R. (2011). *Managing evolution of service centric systems by test models.* Paper presented at the IASTED International Conference on Software Engineering.

Felderer, M., Agreiter, B., Breu, R., & Armenteros, A. (2010). *Security testing by telling test stories.*

Felderer, M., Breu, R., Chimiak-Opoka, J., Breu, M., & Schupp, F. (2009). Concepts for model-based requirements testing of service oriented systems. *Proceedings of the IASTED International Conference, 642,* 18.

Felderer, M., Fiedler, F., Zech, P., & Breu, R. (2009). *Flexible test code generation for service oriented systems.*

Felderer, M., Zech, P., Fiedler, F., & Breu, R. (2010). *A tool-based methodology for system testing of service-oriented systems.* Paper presented at the The Second International Conference on Advances in System Testing and Validation Lifecycle (VALID 2010).

Fraser, G., Aichernig, B. K., & Wotawa, F. (2007). Handling model changes: Regression testing and test-suite update with model-checkers. *Electronic Notes in Theoretical Computer Science, 190*(2), 33–46. doi:10.1016/j.entcs.2007.08.004

Goetz, H., Nickolaus, M., Rossner, T., & Salomon, K. (2009). iX Studie Modellbasiertes Testen.

Gorthi, R. P., Pasala, A., Chanduka, K. K. P., & Leong, B. (2008). *Specification-based approach to select regression test suite to validate changed software.*

IEEE. (1990). *Standard glossary of software engineering terminology.* IEEE.

IEEE-SA-Standards-Board. (1998). *IEEE standard for software test documentation.* IEEE.

Lehman, M. M. (1980). Programs, life cycles, and laws of software evolution. *Proceedings of the IEEE, 68*(9), 1060–1076. doi:10.1109/PROC.1980.11805

Leung, H. K. N., & White, L. (1989). *Insights into regression testing (software testing).*

Mens, T., & Demeyer, S. (2008). *Software evolution.* Springer Verlag.

Moonen, L., Deursen, A., Zaidman, A., & Bruntink, M. (2008). On the interplay between software testing and evolution and its effect on program comprehension. In T. Mens & S. Demeyer (Eds.), *Software evolution*, 173-202.

OASIS. (2007). Web services business process execution language version 2.0 - OASIS standard.

OGC. (2007). *ITIL lifecycle publication suite books, 2nd impression*. TSO.

OMG. (2003). *MDA guide,* version 1.0.1.

OSGi-Alliance. (2010). *OSGi service platform,* release 4 version 4.2.

Roßner, T., Brandes, C., Götz, H., & Winter, M. (2010). *Basiswissen modellbasierter Test*. dpunkt. verlag.

Rothermel, G., & Harrold, M. J. (1996). Analyzing regression test selection techniques. *IEEE Transactions on Software Engineering, 22*(8), 529–551. doi:10.1109/32.536955

Rothermel, G., & Harrold, M. J. (1998). Empirical studies of a safe regression test selection technique. *IEEE Transactions on Software Engineering, 24*(6), 401–419. doi:10.1109/32.689399

Stallbaum, H., Metzger, A., & Pohl, K. (2008). *An automated technique for risk-based test case generation and prioritization*. Leipzig, Germany.

Trojer, T., Breu, M., & Löw, S. (2010). *Change-driven model evolution for living models*. Paper presented at the 3rd Workshop on Model-Driven Tool and Process Integration.

Utting, M., & Legeard, B. (2006). *Practical model-based testing: A tools approach*. San Francisco, CA, USA.

Vaysburg, B. (2002). *Model based regression test reduction using dependence analysis*.

Von Mayrhauser, A., & Zhang, N. (1999). Automated regression testing using DBT and Sleuth. *Journal of Software Maintenance Research and Practice, 11*(2), 93–116. doi:10.1002/ (SICI)1096-908X(199903/04)11:2<93::AID-SMR188>3.0.CO;2-5

Zander, J., Dai, Z. R., Schieferdecker, I., & Din, G. (2005). *From U2TP models to executable tests with TTCN-3 - An approach to model driven testing*.

KEY TERMS AND DEFINITIONS

Change-Driven Process: A software development process is change-driven if it is driven by change events, the state of the model elements and their interrelationships with other model elements.

Evolution Management: Evolution management is the integrated management of changes on requirements, services and tests of a service-centric system.

Model-Driven Testing: Model-driven testing considers the derivation of executable test code from test models by analogy to Model Driven Architecture (MDA) (OMG, 2003).

Regression Testing: Regression testing is the selective retesting of a system or component to verify that modifications have not caused unintended effects, and that the system or component still complies with its specified requirements.

Risk Assessment: In the risk assessment phase, risk values are determined and assigned to tests.

Risk-Based Testing: Risk-based testing considers risks for the design, selection, execution, and evaluation of tests.

Security Testing: Security testing is software testing of positive and negative security requirements.

Service-Centric System: A service-centric system consists of a set of independent peers providing and calling services.

System Testing: System testing comprises methods for validating the system's compliance with its specified requirements.

Chapter 12
A Test–Driven Approach for Metamodel Development

A. Cicchetti
Malardalen University, Sweden

D. Di Ruscio
University of L'Aquila, Italy

A. Pierantonio
University of L'Aquila, Italy

D.S. Kolovos
The University of York, UK

ABSTRACT

Model Driven Engineering (MDE) is increasingly gaining acceptance in the development of complex systems as a mean to leverage the abstraction level and render business logic resilient to technological changes. Metamodels precisely define the constructs and underlying well-formedness rules for modeling languages. However, the definition of a metamodel is intrinsically complex since it must be precisely tailored according to the specific purpose the models must have.

The paper proposes a test-driven development process for metamodels, where models are used a) to validate metamodel expressiveness in the early stages of their definition, and b) to convey feedback to designers as a guidance for further refinement and evolution.

INTRODUCTION

Model Driven Engineering (MDE) (Schmidt, 2006) is increasingly gaining acceptance as a mean to leverage abstraction and render business logic resilient to technological changes. Coordinated

DOI: 10.4018/978-1-61350-438-3.ch012

collections of models and modelling languages are used to describe software systems on different abstraction layers and from different perspectives. In general, domains are analysed and engineered by means of *metamodels*, i.e., coherent sets of interrelated concepts. A model is said to *conform* to a metamodel, or in other words it is expressed by the concepts encoded in the metamodel, and model transformations occur when models are translated into other artifacts such as other models, code and documentation.

Metamodels are vital entities for designers and tool implementors as they define useful standards that enable tools and models to work together portably and effectively. Since almost any artifact involved in a model-driven development process is depending on the considered metamodels (Kurtev, Berg, & Jouault, 2006), defining a metamodel as a whole with little or no feedback is practically unrealistic. In fact, the expressiveness of the metamodel, i.e., the amount of detail which has to be captured for each concept, depends predominately on the kind of applications (e.g., model-to-model and model-to-code transformations) the designer is aiming at.

Little guidance exists on creating modeling languages (Kelly & Pohjonen, 2009). Designing and implementing a metamodel in a consistent manner requires an in-depth understanding of the problem domain and enough solution domain expertise to foresee the necessary information that instance models will need to capture. In practice, a metamodel often evolves towards a final form only after it undergoes an iterative restructuring and refinement process. Each iteration consists of extending and refining the set of available features and adapting the corresponding model transformations and tools which are tightly coupled with the metamodel. Possible shortcomings, such as the inability to correctly generate an artifact fragment, must be conveyed to the designer in order to enhance the metamodel. Moreover, such a step-wise process also continues after the first delivery, based on user feedback.

Test-driven development (Beck, 2000) (TDD) is an increasingly popular approach for building systems with reliability, understandability, and maintainability requirements. In this paper, we present an iterative bottom-up approach to metamodel development based on TDD where models are considered as test cases that are validated against incremental metamodel imple-

mentations. In fact, a model can be seen as an unambiguous requirement that the metamodel and its implementation must satisfy: *a)* once the current version of the metamodel successfully captures the model *b)* the designer can then take a step back, survey the landscape that was created *c)* refactor and then move on to the next requirement. As such, the metamodel development process consists of small incremental steps which provide crucial feedback. These small steps eventually lead to the definitive metamodel with a better and more verifiable formalization. In contrast with similar approaches (Paige, Brooke, & Ostroff, 2004), which mainly focus on formally checking terminal models against a metamodel for conformance, the proposed technique aims at consistently defining a metamodel at a level of abstraction which is the most appropriate for the envisioned goals. The approach has been validated by defining and implementing the beContent metamodel, a full-scale domain-specific modeling language for data-intensive Web applications (Cicchetti, Di Ruscio, Eramo, Maccarrone, & Pierantonio, 2009; Cicchetti, Di Ruscio, Iovino, & Pierantonio, 2011).

The remainder of the paper is structured as follows. The motivation for this work is discussed in the next section. Section 3 presents the TDD-based approach, and an agile framework for metamodel development alongside the necessary underlying infrastructure. Then, in Section 4 a real-world application of the process is discussed. Finally, the work is compared with related research in the field of language engineering and development and some conclusions are drawn.

MOTIVATING SCENARIO

In the MDE vision (Bézivin, 2005) abstractions are provided by models, which are intended to be approximations of reality: each application is described by means of domain-specific models which are refined step-by-step to obtain the implementation. The refinement steps are automated by means of model transformations. An abstraction reaches its usefulness if it is complete and unambiguous to the purpose it has been conceived. In other words, given a specific domain and a model, it should be interpreted in a unique way without leaving any questions or assumptions. The more models are precise, the more transformations will be able to derive correct mappings and produce useful artefacts and effective analyses. In the same way a grammar is specified to describe a programming language, a metamodel can be given to define correct models.

In the following we outline a typical MDE development process which includes also the definition of metamodels (see Section 2.1). Section 2.2 outlines the problems that might occur when an already defined metamodel is refined to satisfy unforeseen requirements.

MDE DEVELOPMENT PROCESS

Traditionally, a development process (see Figure 1) requires the designer to incrementally extend and refine both metamodels and transformation rules. In particular, if the model Ms is given in terms of the constructs specified by the metamodel MMs,

then the subsequent generation of target models Mt encompasses the application of several model transformations. Like any other software artifacts, the definition of models, metamodels and transformations is a strenuous task and relies on an iterative approach in which the produced artifacts are continually refined with respect to feedback that can be generated at any level. Especially, the lower the level of abstraction at which the feedback is collected, the more difficult it is to use it to refactor artifacts at a higher level of abstraction – and in particular the source metamodels. Therefore, a practical approach would rely on an iterative design process in which both the language designers and users participate in refining the current version of the metamodel as early as possible. In fact, developers could validate new features against their own design intentions, while users would be kept up-to-date with the new features. Unfortunately, none of the currently available frameworks offers some form of analysis, especially able to deal with partially implemented versions of a certain model-driven infrastructure (Kleppe, 2008). Therefore, both the designers and the users are able to test and validate the outcome of the development phase only after a stable revision of the metamodel has been reached, which in general translates to an extensive and

Figure 1. An exemplification of the MDE development process

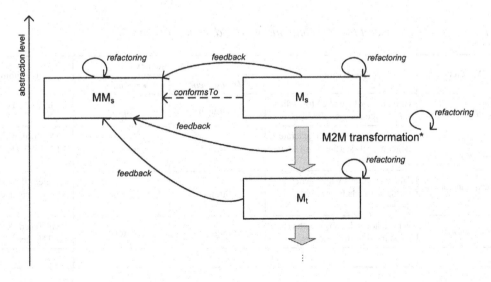

labour-intensive refactoring of all the surrounding artifacts, such as editors and transformations (Fowler, 2005).

CO-EVOLUTION PROBLEMS

As mentioned above, almost any artifact involved in a model-driven development process somehow depends on the considered metamodels. Dependencies can emerge at different times during the metamodel life-cycle, and with different degrees of causality depending on the nature of the considered artifact. Table 1 outlines the different types of dependencies that can occur between metamodels and tools/artifacts by distinguishing among development and evolution time, although this work mainly focuses on the former. In particular, any form of model-to-model and model-to-text transformations can *strongly* drive the definition of the metamodel (Kurtev et al., 2006) as the rule-based decomposition of a model transformation is tightly coupled with the structural definition of the *source* metamodels. By contrast, other kinds of tools (e.g., graphical and textual editors, model repositories, etc.) are affected by the metamodel definition but do not typically influence its design. In any case, metamodel refinements impact on existing artifacts in terms of co-evolution problems, i.e. the latter ones

have to be kept synchronized and well-formed with the set of concepts provided by the current version of the language. Being more precise, metamodels may evolve in different ways: some changes may be additive and independent from the other elements, thus requiring no or little cochanges. However, in other cases metamodel manipulations introduce incompatibilities and inconsistencies which cannot be easily (and automatically) resolved. For instance, in the case of metamodel/model co-evolution, metamodel manipulations can be classified by their corrupting or not-corrupting effects on existing models (Wachsmuth, 2007):

- *Non-breaking changes*: changes which do not break the conformance of models to the corresponding metamodel;
- *Breaking and resolvable changes*: changes which break the conformance of models even though they can be automatically co-adapted;
- *Breaking and unresolvable changes*: changes which break the conformance of models which can not automatically co-evolved and user intervention is required.

In these cases, in order to apply proper model adaptation strategies, it is necessary to identify the operated metamodel changes. This is preparatory

Table 1. Dependencies between metamodels and model-driven tools/artifacts

Tool/Artifact	Description	Dependency		Technology
		development	*evolution*	
graphical and textual editors	Graphical or textual editors which support the editing of models	Marginal	Strong	GMF, TCS, TGE, etc
model-to-model transformations	Transformations which generate target models starting from source ones	Strong	Medium	ATL, Epsilon, QVT, VIATRA2, etc
model-to-text transformations	Transformations which generate textual artifacts from source models	Strong	Medium	Acceleo, JET, MOF-Script, Xpand, etc
model repositories	Persistency solutions which can be adopted to store models	Marginal	Strong	EMF Teneo, XMI, HUTN, etc
...	...	...	...	...

for defining corresponding co-changes to be performed on the affected models in order to recover their conformance relation with the new version of the considered metamodel. Also the calculation of the differences between two subsequent versions of the same metamodel is a difficult task. In fact, it relies on model matching which can be reduced to the graph isomorphism problem (Read & Corneil, 1977), i.e., to the problem of finding correspondences between two given graphs. Theoretically, the graph isomorphism problem is NP-hard (Lin, Gray, & Jouault, 2007; Kolovos, Di Ruscio, Paige, & Pierantonio, 2009) and the available approaches tend to deal with the computational complexity by providing solutions which are metamodel specific or are able to approximate the exact solution.

Similarly to models, metamodel changes can give place to model transformation inconsistencies, which are those elements in the considered transformation that do not longer satisfy the *domain conformance* (Méndez, Etien, Muller, & Casallas, 2010). For instance, a sample domain conformance constraint might state that the source elements of every transformation rule must correspond to a metaclass in the source metamodel (Rose et al., 2010). Consequently, when a concept is removed from a metamodel, existing transformations that use the removed concept are no longer domain conformant with the evolved metamodel.

In order to reduce co-evolution problems outlined above, which can occur during metamodel development activities, especially in the early stages of its definition, this paper proposes a practical process for developing metamodels which anticipates the feedback collection. In particular, the work proposes an agile implementation process for metamodels, which treats models as test-cases.

PROPOSED METAMODEL DEVELOPMENT APPROACH

In this section, we present a test-driven development process for metamodels, and the techniques

necessary to support it. TDD enables high reliability by gradually amortising testing throughout the development process, and by focusing on short code-and-test increments. TDD has three steps in its micro-process: write a test (without worrying if it does not compile); write enough code to make the test pass; and refactor the code to eliminate redundancies and other design flaws introduced by making the test pass – thus, tests act as specifications that drive the design process (Beck, 2000). Such a metamodel definition process is described in Section 3.1, whereas Section 3.2 introduces an agile infrastructure supporting it. Section 3.3 describes a strategy for integrating the proposed approach with existing modeling platforms such as EMF.

TDD Based Metamodel Definition Process

Metamodels are the outcome of an evolutionary process consisting of two main steps *i)* elicitation of concepts from the domain to the metamodel *ii)* validation of the formalization of the concepts by describing parts of real systems. However, the real application of such a process requires an agile and flexible infrastructure which permits the designer to put more effort on the metamodel definition and less on the other artifacts. The metamodel development process given in Figure 2 is based on a variant of TDD that considers executable models as tests. Therefore, in our proposal a test is a model containing desired features that are exploited to verify metamodel expressiveness. A test fails if the metamodel version taken into account is not able to support a particular desired characteristic, or in other words whenever its expressive power is not able to provide needed details to obtain the required execution behaviour.

By going into more details, concepts are elicited from the analyzed domain (step **a** in the figure) and are in turn formalized by means of the agile infrastructure described in Section 3.2. The implementation of the concepts and their

Figure 2. Metamodel definition process

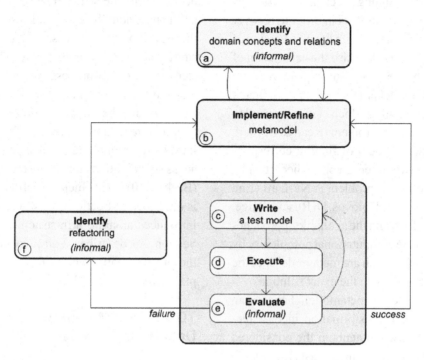

interrelationships (step **b**) forms a *virtual machine* capable of executing encoded models (steps **c** and **d**). The outcome of the execution serves to collect feedback (step e) which is used to refactor the implementation (semantics) and refine/revise the metamodel (syntax) (step **f**). The proposed process consists of a sequence of actions which tends to modify the metamodel syntax and its intended semantics in terms of subsequent refinements, as illustrated in Figure 3. Once the process is terminated, the designers and users obtain a code fragment encoding the validated metamodel which can be in turn represented by means of a proper

metamodel specification, e.g., in KM3 (Jouault & Bézivin, 2006). This operation, which is part of the proposed metamodel definition process, is named *metamodel injection* and is described in Section 3.3. This enables building-up the complete development environment, by eventually specifying the concrete syntax and the required model transformations, which can also be partially extracted from the metamodel implementation – as discussed in the sequel.

The direct implementation of the metamodel, in contrast with the more traditional approach of chaining model transformations (as in Figure 1),

Figure 3. Metamodel refinements

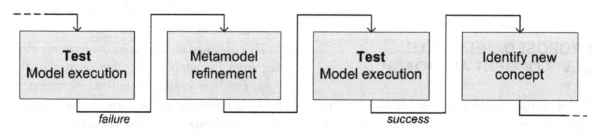

presents the advantage of having an early valida-tion of the expressiveness of the metamodel. It is important to stress how, during the process, the models used as tests are not necessarily conform-ing to the metamodels being defined, since they might express a requirement (how the designer ideally conceives the modeling language) which is not satisfied yet. Nevertheless, the implementa-tion of the metamodel requires a basic infrastruc-ture which facilitates the encoding of the metamodel constituent parts, such as meta-classes and meta-associations, as described in the next section.

AGILE INFRASTRUCTURE

As described so far, the proposed method is based on an agile infrastructure for implementing metamodels and executing tests. In particular, models are encoded in an object-oriented language which either provides built-in agent/closure con-structs or can be augmented with such without much effort as shown later in this section. Agents are a way to encapsulate operations in objects; the operation can then be invoked on collections (e.g., a set or linked list) when necessary. For instance, in Eiffel[2] two built-in agents are for_all and there_exists, which can be used to implement quantifiers over finite data structures and therefore are a mean to navigate the models. Apart from this, no restrictions are imposed on the choice of the language, although certain languages may be more suitable than others in given application domains.

The basic infrastructure which is used to em-bed a metamodel in a given host language mainly consists of the MetaClass and MetaAssociation in Figure 4: the former is a template for any meta class in the metamodel, whereas the latter permits to realize associations among instances. It is important to stress that this is not intended to substitute any of the existing metamodeling languages like Ecore[3] or MOF[4], but rather to give an agile support for embedding metamodels into

programming languages which are common-place in given domains. In fact, a team of web developers is far more likely to embrace MDE if they are encouraged to use a familiar - albeit suboptimal – technology such as PHP[5] in order to specify their models and templates. Once the change in paradigm has been absorbed, a transition to proper MDE tooling will most likely be more smooth as developers will be in a better place to appreciate the benefits of such a transition. In this respect, in Listing 1 an implementation of the basic infrastructure is given in PHP which does not have built-in agents. Thus the function for_all and there_exists are explicitly implemented (lines 26-45), as well as data structures for model navi-gation (lines 5-8 and 51-52) which are modified by the *MetaAssociation* constructor.

As an example, let us consider the simple metamodel in Figure 5 which consists of the Entity and Field meta classes for specifying simple databases, then it can be implemented in Listing 2.

This represents an executable version of the metamodel. It also contains some *transformation rules* to generate the SQL code to create the tables corresponding to the specified entities. In par-ticular, in the method *test_entity2table* of the class *Entity* the for all *iterator* (see line 10 in Listing 3) invokes *test_field2column* over all field objects associated with the entity. In general, this kind of methods does not need to represent a complete transformation (although the technique does not have limitations in such sense) but it rather fo-cuses on significant transformation requirements which have to be validated against specific *test cases*. Consider the model in Figure 6, then it can be encoded as in Listing 3.

In particular, lines 1-5 in Listing 3 represent the model embedding, and line 7 invokes the *test_entity2table* method on the $news object whose execution produces the query in Listing 4. which is the expected result. In other words, the method test entity2table gives us the opportunity to validate whether the amount and granularity

Listing 1. Fragment of the PHP implementation of the basic infrastructure

```
1  class MetaClass {
2  var
3    $name,
4    [...]
5    $assocs,            // all associations
6    $source_assocs,          // all outgoing associations
7    $target_assocs,          // all incoming associations
8    $superType;              // parent metaclass
9
10   function MetaClass($name) {
11   $this->name = $name;
12   }
13
14   function addSource($assoc) {
15   $this->source_assocs[] = $assoc;
16   }
17
18   function addTarget($assoc) {
19   $this->target_assocs[] = $assoc;
20   }
21
22   function addAssociation($assoc) {
23   $this->assocs[] = $assoc;
24   }
25
26   function for_all($method, $assocName, $separator ="") {
27   $content = "";
28   $id = md5(uniqid(time()));
29
30   foreach($this->assocs as $assoc) {
31       if ($assoc->name == $assocName) {
32           $content.= aux::first_comma($id, $separator); 33
eval('$content.= $assoc->target->'.$method."();");
34       }
35   }
36   return $content;
37   }
38
39   function there_exists($assocClassName, $name) {
40   foreach($this->assoc as $assoc) {
41       if (get_class($assoc) == $assocClassName) {
42           [...]
```

continues on following page

Listing 1. Continued

```
43     }
44 }
45 }
46}
47
48 class MetaAssociation {
49 var
50   $name,
51   $source,
52   $target,
53
54   $isContainer = true;
55
56 function MetaAssociation($source, $target) {
57 $this->source = $source;
58 $this->target = $target;
59 $source->addSource($this);
60 $source->addAssociation($this);
61 $target->addTarget($this);
62 $target->addOwner($source);
63 if ($source>name != $target->name) {
64     $target->addAssociation($this);
65 }
66 }
67}
```

of information in the metamodel were adequate for such a scope. The advantage of the method lies in the capability of detecting an eventual failure at this level of abstraction without implementing any transformation rules at a lower level of abstraction as shown in Figure 1.

Sometimes it is not even possible to execute a test since, when new concepts are detected, the

Figure 4. Fragment of the basic infrastructure

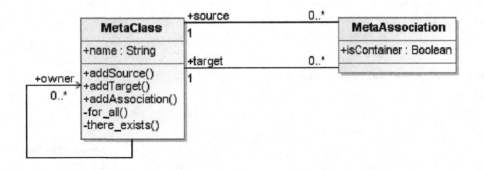

Figure 5. Model of core infrastructure for metamodeling in OOP

model is defined using them before the metamodel is extended. In essence, during the development process the models are not necessarily conforming to the current version of the metamodel since they might express a requirement (how the designer ideally conceives the modeling language) which is not yet satisfied. For instance, in the current version of the metamodel, no support to one-to-many relations is provided, and as such the following

model produces a failure since the class *Reference* does not exist (see line 13 in Listing 5).

The result of the test induces the designer to iterate and introduce a new metaclass, namely *Reference*, to capture the concept of relations among entities. Therefore, the following extension is provided in Listing 6.

After the extension, the previous model is executed again and the Reference metaclass seemingly implements the relation (as a refinement of

Listing 2. Sample metamodel

```
1  Class Entity extends MetaClass {
2
3  function Entity($name) {
4      $this->name=$name;
5  }
6
7  function test_entity2table() {
8
9      $content="CREATE TABLE {$this->name} (";
10     $content.=$this->for_all("field","test_field2column","," , ");
11     $content.=")";
12
13     return $content;
14 }
15
16 [...]
17 }
18
19 Class Field extends MetaClass {
20 var
21     $type,
22 $length;
```

continued on following page

Listing 2. continued

```
23
24   function Field($name, $type, $length = "") {
25   $this->name=$name;
26   $this->type=$type;
27   $this->length=$length;
28   }
29
30   function test_field2column() {
31   $content="{$this->name} {$this->type} {$this->length}";
32   return $content;
33   }
34   [...]
35   }
36
37   Class assoc extends MetaAssociation {
38
39   function assoc($name,$source, $target) {
40       MetaAssociation($name,$source, $target);
41   }
42   }
```

Figure 6. A simple model conforming to MM

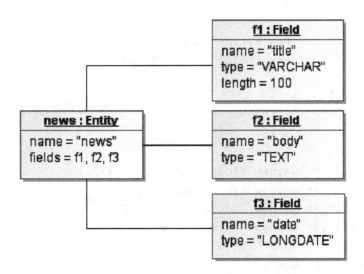

Listing 3. Encoding of the news entity

```
1 $news = new Entity("news");
2
3 new assoc("field",$news,new Field("title",VARCHAR,100));
4 new assoc("field",$news,new Field("body",TEXT));
5 new assoc("field",$news,new Field("date",LONGDATE));
6
7 $news->test_entity2table();
```

Listing 4. Sample SQL query

```
1 CREATE TABLE news (
2   title VARCHAR 100,
3   body TEXT,
4   date LONGDATE
5 )
```

the ordinary Field metaclass) by retrieving the correct typing for the category column in Listing 7.

However, depending on the SQL dialect the previous clause may not be considered valid since a reference usually points to the primary key of the referenced table. This situation clearly identifies a lack of expressiveness as the current version of the metamodel does not provide any support for the specification of primary keys. More precisely, a *failure* has been detected and a further *iteration* is prescribed in order to augment the

Listing 5. Encoding of the categories and news entities

```
1 $cat = new Entity("categories");
2
3 new assoc("field",$cat,new Field("id",INT);
4 new assoc("field",$cat,new Field("name",VARCHAR,30));
5
6 $cat->test_entity2table();
7
8 $news = new Entity("news");
9
10 new assoc("field",$news,new Field("title",VARCHAR,100));
11 new assoc("field",$news,new Field("body",TEXT));
12 new assoc("field",$news,new Field("date",LONGDATE));
13 new assoc("field",$news,new Reference("category", $cat));
14
15 $news->test_entity2table();
```

Listing 6. Encoding of the Reference metaclass

```
1 Class Reference extends Field { 2    var
3   $entity;
4
5   function Reference($name, $entity) {
6     $this->name = $name;
7     $this->type = $entity->assocs[0]->target->type;
8     $this->length = $entity->assocs[0]->target->length;
9   }
10 }
11 [...]
```

Listing 7. SQL query to create the category and news entities

```
1   CREATE TABLE category (
2     id INT,
3     name VARCHAR 100
4   )
5
6   CREATE TABLE news (
7     title VARCHAR 100,
8     body TEXT,
9     date LONGDATE,
10    category INT
11  )
```

current metamodel version (as illustrated in Figure 7) and its implementation. The extension consists of the addition of the *PrimaryKey* metaclass as a specialization of *Field*. Additionally, it is also required that the method *test_entity2table* in *Entity* is further refined as follows (see lines 7-9 in Listing 8) in order to include the primary key definition in the SQL creation clause.

Figure 7. A metamodel extension

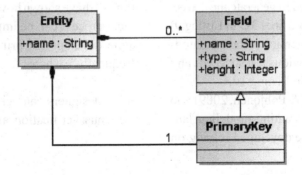

Listing 8. test_entity2table() function

```
1   [...]
2   function test_entity2table() {
3
4     $content = "CREATE TABLE {$this->name} (";
5     $content.= $this->for_all("field", "test_field2column",", ");
6
7     $pk = $this->get_all("PrimaryKey");
8     if (count($pk) > 0) {
9      $content.= ", PRIMARY KEY({$pk[0]->name})";
10    }
11    $content.= ")";
12    return $content;
13  }
```

Listing 9. test_field2column() function

```
1   [...]
2   function test_field2column() {
3   $pk = $this->entity->get_all("PrimaryKey");
4
5     $content = "FOREIGN KEY {$this->name} REFERENCE {$this->entity->name}
({$pk
        [0]->name})";
6
7   if ($this->type == VARCHAR) {
8    $content.= " {$this->length}";
9   }
10   return $content;
11  }
```

Moreover, the method *test_field2column* in *Reference* has to be adapted to generate the correct foreign key declaration. (see lines 3-5 in Listing 9)

Finally, with this new version of the metamodel implementation the previous test succeeds and generates the SQL code in Listing 10.

As discussed in (Kelly & Pohjonen, 2009), too little guidance exists in creating modeling languages and often they are developed relying on individual skills and adhoc processes. In this section, we have shown how the metamodel development process can be improved by embracing the agile development principle "deliver early and frequently", where

- Designers can achieve quick and continuous verification and validation of the ex-

Listing 10. New SQL query to create the category and news entities

```
1   CREATE TABLE category (
2     id INT,
3     name VARCHAR 100,
4
5     PRIMARY KEY(id)
6   )
7
8   CREATE TABLE news (
9     title VARCHAR 100,
10    body TEXT,
11    date LONGDATE,
12
13    FOREIGN KEY category REFERENCE category(id)
14  )
```

pressiveness of the current version of the metamodel;

- Users can focus on the available functionality step-by-step, by conveying to the implementers a more detailed and easier to interpret feedback on the expected results.

In the next section, we discuss how once a metamodel has been finalized by means of the proposed techniques, relevant information can be elicited and injected in metamodel formal specifications.

METAMODEL INJECTION

Starting from a metamodel which has been embedded and validated in a host language, its *injection* into a modeling platform can be of crucial relevance for the interoperability between the techniques presented so far and eventual model-driven environments. The injection is a powerful operation which discovers structural information in an artifact and formalizes it in a model. Several approaches for extracting models from software have been proposed even though an optimal solution which can be used in any situation does not yet exist (Izquierdo, Cuadrado, & Molina, 2008). The complexity of the problem relies on the limitation of current lexical tools which do not provide the proper abstractions and constructs to query code and generate models with respect to given metamodels (or as in this paper meta metamodels). However, interesting results can be obtained by using the BNF Converter (Forsberg & Ranta, 2004) (BNFC), a compilerconstruction tool based on the idea that from a single source grammar it is possible to generate both an abstract syntax tree definition, including a traversal function, and a concrete syntax, including lexer, parser and pretty printer. Complete definitions have so far been written for C, OCL, and Java 1.2[6].

It is worth noting that a solution for a specific language has to be developed only once in order to enable corresponding (meta)metamodel injection automation. In our case, specific *injectors* have been implemented by using traditional lexical tools, such as *sed* and *awk*, to gather proper information from PHP embeddings, and to generate the metamodel specification in KM3. These tools have been somewhat adequate so far as we only needed to parse a fragment of PHP capable of capturing the embedded meta classes and the meta associations. However, a complete PHP injection by using BNFC is under development in order to be able to extract information from those methods which validate the metamodel, e.g., *test_entity2table*, into model-to-text or model-tomodel transformation skeletons.

The result of injecting in KM3 the metamodel defined in the previous section is illustrated in Figure 8, where the PHP Entity and Field classes (left-hand side) are associated with the corresponding metaclasses in KM3 (right-hand side)[7]. All the variables of a given PHP class (e.g. type, and length in the class Field) are represented in KM3 as structural features of the induced metaclass (e.g. the attributes type, and length of the metaclass Field).

Automating the injection process is important, but even translating the embedding code into a meta metamodel in a manual way can be viable if the metamodel has been validated and has been finalized. The cost-effectiveness of these techniques are briefly discussed in Section 4.

CASE STUDY

The agile process proposed in this paper has been adopted in the context of the beContent project[8] which aims at the definition of an infrastructure for the design, implementation, and interoperability of both data-intensive and process-orientedWeb Applications (see Figure 9). The core of the project consists of the beContent metamodel (BMM), which defines the abstract syntax of the modeling languages: a diagrammatic and a textual concrete syntax, called beContent modeling language (BML) and beContent textual language (BTL), respectively, endowed with a round-tripping mechanism. The models can be edited by means of a visual and textual editor realized as Eclipse plugins (Cicchetti, Di Ruscio, et al., 2009).

A model consists of the declarative and coordinated specification of three different concerns: *data*, *content*, and *interaction*. The data view is the description of the relational model of the data, the second aspect describes the data sources and how the content is retrieved and aggregated in pages, and the latter describes how to manipulate the information entered in the forms, for instance a textual content can be edited by means of text

Figure 8. Fragment of PHP2KM3 mappings

```
Class Entity extends MetaClass {

    function Entity($name) {
        $this->name=$name;
    }
    [...]
}

Class Field extends MetaClass {
    var
        $type,
        $length;

    function Field($name, $type, $length = "") {
        $this->name=$name;
        $this->type=$type;
        $this->length=$length;
    }
    [...]
}
```

```
package metamodel {

    class Entity {
        attribute name : String;
        reference field[0-*]  container : Field;
        reference pk container :  PrimaryKey;

    }

    class Field {
        attribute name : String;
        attribute type:Integer;
        attribute lenght : Integer;
    }

    class PrimaryKey extends Field {
    }

}
package PrimaryType {
    datatype String;
    datatype Integer;
}
```

Figure 9. The beContent infrastructure

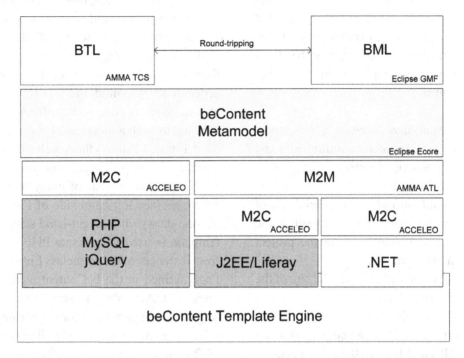

fields, text areas, or rich-text editors. Automated transformations written in Acceleo[9] starting from models like the one in Figure 10 generate a num-

ber of components including forms, CRUD operations, transactions, reporting, logs, etc.

The beContent metamodel has been defined by adopting the development approach presented

Figure 10. A simple beContent model

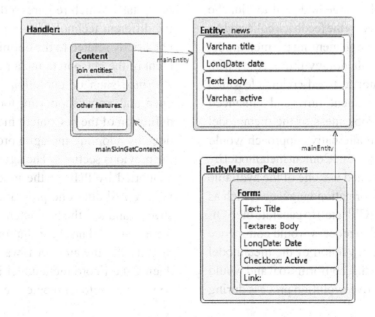

in the previous section. The outcome of the process has been a full-scale modeling language that consists of 88 meta-classes, 40 meta-associations, and 220 metaattributes. The language, has been used for designing and implementing a number of website, such as

- http://www.abruzzo24ore.tv, a news portal whose features include multimedia and rich-text content, registered users, RSS feeds, and forums;
- http://www.di.univaq.it, the official site of the Computer Science Department at the University of L'Aquila where the project has been initiated;
- http://www.univaq.it, the official site of the University of L'Aquila.

The objective of the beContent project is not limited to a PHP and MySQL10 platform generation of Web applications, but to provide a basis for other platforms as well, e.g., J2EE/Liferay. As discussed before, developing a metamodel in a more traditional way would have required to collect feedback from any layer of abstraction, primarily from model-to-model and model-to-code transformations. This is intrinsically difficult, since the abstraction distance between the platform and the metamodel is large and tend to blur the information conveyed by the feedback collected on the platform. Thus, implementing the metamodel according to our methodology provided us with the capability of a short test-and-code cycle which reduced the development time and enhanced the reliability and robustness of the metamodel implementation. An alternative approach would have been to develop the beContent metamodel by using directly Ecore and use one of the available model-to-text transformation languages (such as Acceleo, Xpand[11], EGL[12] etc.) to generate the SQL and PHP code. Such a process would commence by defining an initial version of the metamodel and a sample model that conforms to it and would then follow an iterative evolution process during which the metamodel, model and model-to-text transformations would co evolve to satisfy new requirements as they are identified.

For instance, Figure 11 shows a fragment of the beContent metamodel developed in Ecore. In order to develop model-to-text transformations, able to generate code starting from models conforming to such a metamodel, Acceleo has been used. Figure 12 shows the Acceleo project, which has been developed to generate target PHP code. Such a project consists of many transformation templates (see left-hand side of Figure 12) like the one shown on the right-hand side. The shown template is used to generate PHP code starting from instances of the metaclass EntitityManagerPage defined in the beContent metamodel (see lines 6-7). According to such a template, code fragments are generated for each instance of the referred metaclass ExtendendForm (see lines 16-26). In this case, the attribute className of such a metaclass is used (see line 17 and line 19).

As already said, metamodel modifications might affect already available artifacts defined on it. For instance, if the attribute className of the metaclass ExtendedForm is renamed, or even removed, both the existing beContent models, and the Acceleo transformation in Figure 12 are affected and need to be adapted. This is an error prone task, which requires a deep knowledge of the different technologies at hand, and which is not strictly related to the definition and enhancement of the beContent metamodel.

Since such co-evolution problems are still open, and proper supporting tools are missing, the definition of the beContent metamodel has been done by adopting the agile process described in the previous sections. The agile process has been supported by PHP as the model interpreter. So we adopted only one programming language to specify and test the beContent metamodel. Once the metamodel has been stabilized, we started to migrate the metamodel towards EMF (by producing the Ecore metamodel in Figure 11), and consequently to implement code generators by

Figure 11. Fragment of the beContent metamodel in Ecore

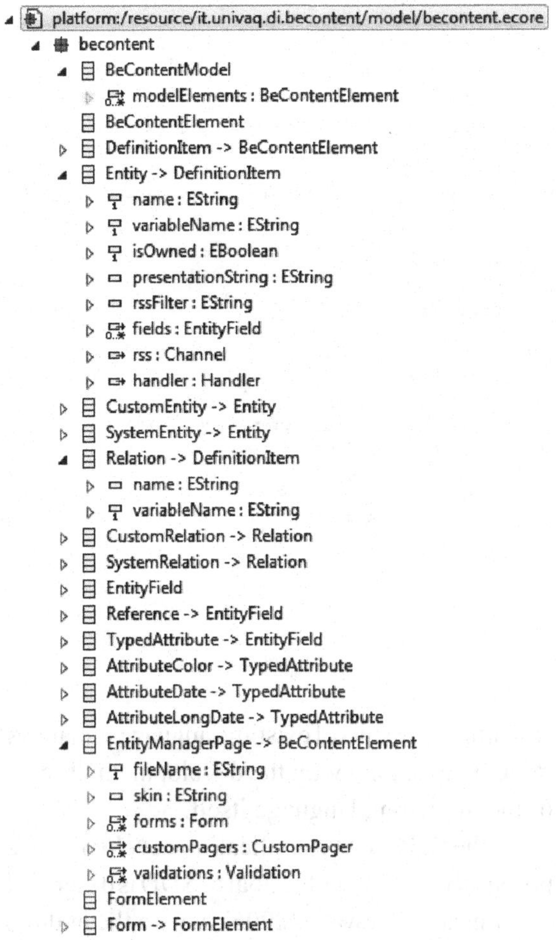

```
▲ ▶ platform:/resource/it.univaq.di.becontent/model/becontent.ecore
   ▲ ♯ becontent
      ▲ 目 BeContentModel
         ▷ ⬚ modelElements : BeContentElement
         目 BeContentElement
      ▷ 目 DefinitionItem -> BeContentElement
      ▲ 目 Entity -> DefinitionItem
         ▷ ⬚ name : EString
         ▷ ⬚ variableName : EString
         ▷ ⬚ isOwned : EBoolean
         ▷ ⬚ presentationString : EString
         ▷ ⬚ rssFilter : EString
         ▷ ⬚ fields : EntityField
         ▷ ⬚ rss : Channel
         ▷ ⬚ handler : Handler
      ▷ 目 CustomEntity -> Entity
      ▷ 目 SystemEntity -> Entity
      ▲ 目 Relation -> DefinitionItem
         ▷ ⬚ name : EString
         ▷ ⬚ variableName : EString
      ▷ 目 CustomRelation -> Relation
      ▷ 目 SystemRelation -> Relation
      ▷ 目 EntityField
      ▷ 目 Reference -> EntityField
      ▷ 目 TypedAttribute -> EntityField
      ▷ 目 AttributeColor -> TypedAttribute
      ▷ 目 AttributeDate -> TypedAttribute
      ▷ 目 AttributeLongDate -> TypedAttribute
      ▲ 目 EntityManagerPage -> BeContentElement
         ▷ ⬚ fileName : EString
         ▷ ⬚ skin : EString
         ▷ ⬚ forms : Form
         ▷ ⬚ customPagers : CustomPager
         ▷ ⬚ validations : Validation
         目 FormElement
      ▷ 目 Form -> FormElement
```

means of Acceleo (see Figure 12). In this way, since the expressiveness of the metamodel has been already validated, the code generators implementation focused only on the transformation behavior regardless of the metamodel structure and granularity. In this respect, the approach presented in this work can improve the general development process: in fact, making the metamodel a pivot artefact and its expressiveness the main concern allows to decouple the language from all the surrounding services which often pollute it with additional tool-specific information. In this way, whenever additional language features are needed corresponding maintenance can be performed through new test-and-code cycles.

RELATED WORK

Embedding a modeling language in a host language is not a novel idea, as for years developers have been implementing powerful, readable and maintainable DSLs in dynamic languages (Hudak, 1998). The goal is that domain experts can express domainspecific ideas in their language without having to learn a general-purpose language, like Java, C or UML. The work in (Izquierdo et al., 2008) extends this principle to modeling languages and to model-driven engineering; the work does not focus on the development process of metamodels and mainly emphasizes the cost-effectiveness and development time for writing model transformations by means of scripting languages. Several other works proposed language definition processes, like (Fowler, 2005 ; Kelly & Tolvanen, 2008 ; Kleppe, 2008), and a plethora of language frameworks is currently available for the generation of the tools surrounding a language definition (Budinsky, Steinberg, Merks, Ellersick, & Grose, 2003 ; Tolvanen & Kelly, 2005 ; Ledeczi et al., 2001). In general, the former works seem to consider (or assume) the metamodel definition as a linear process, without an evident need of cyclic refinements. On the contrary, our experience indicates that the complexity of language definitions unavoidably requires a stepwise definition process, in which the metamodel is continuously updated correspondingly to developer's and user's feedbacks. Moreover, even though in (Kelly & Tolvanen, 2008) the authors present a cyclic definition process, they do not specifically take into account the problem of language revisions. Finally, the existing language frameworks can be considered as supporting the subsequent phases related to the metamodel design, when the concepts have been stabilized and it is necessary to build-up the appropriate language workbench (Fowler, 2005).

Test-Driven Development (TDD) (Beck, 2000) and its integration with model-driven design, called Specification-Driven Development

Figure 12. Fragment of a model-to-text transformation in Acceleo

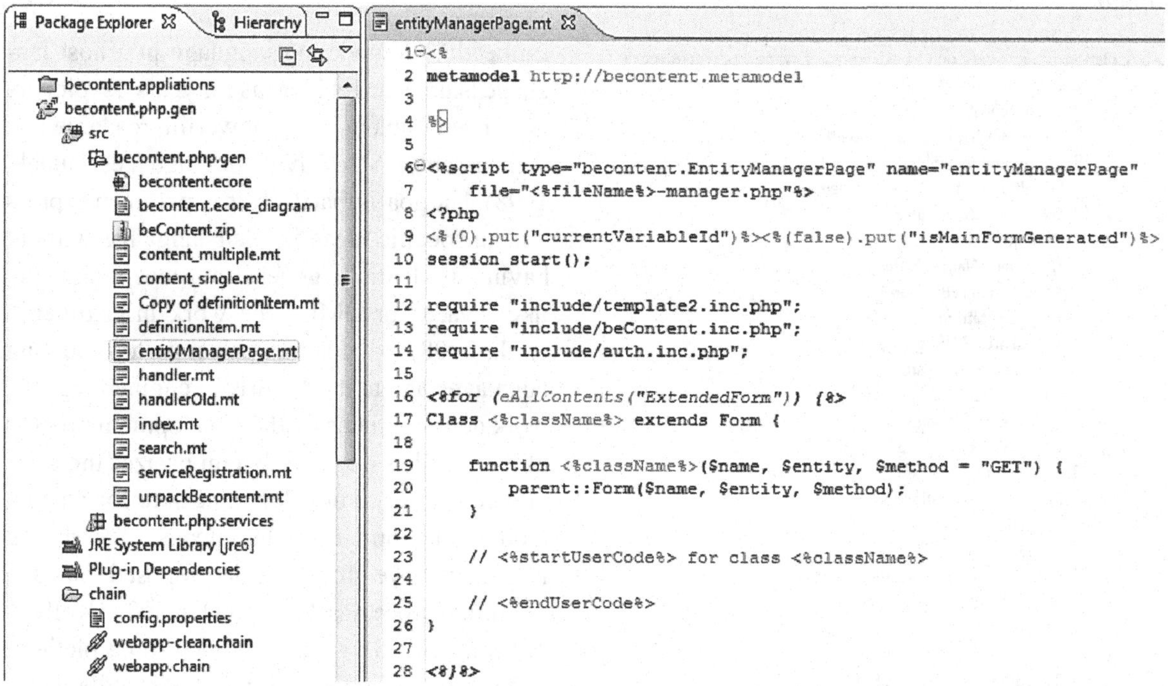

(SDD) (Paige et al., 2004), aim at providing agile methods for developing reliable, understandable and maintainable applications by incrementally adding new features to the application under realization while testing them at the same time. In particular, in (Paige et al., 2004) the authors propose executable metamodels to define and automatically check conformity constraints against model instances. The approach relies on encoding metamodels as Eiffel programs and models as test units, thus metamodels can be incrementally revisioned by adding new entities and constraints. On the contrary, in this work rapid prototyping and SSD are used to test and validate web modeling language adaptations which produce refinement and additional features to existing systems.

Recently in (Soltenborn & Engels, 2009) a test-driven approach has been proposed for the specification of language semantics. Test models are used to describe desired se mantics which trigger corresponding adaptations of the behaviour under development. Even if sharing several similarities with our proposal, such approach mainly deals with improvements of existing language semantics rather than coping with the development process of the modelling language itself.

In the field of web application development, a proposal that pursues the goal of SDD is described in (Nunes & Schwabe, 2006), where the authors illustrate HyperDe, an environment for rapid prototyping of web applications. The aim of that work is to validate the current stage of the system development through the automated generation of DSLs as Ruby extensions. However, it is neither clear whether the approach can be exploited to check the web modeling language extensions, nor a revision example is provided.

From the supporting techniques point of view, in general, a language revision requires a metamodel manipulation and the consequent migration of existing model instances. Recently, an research activity has been devoted to this issue: some works focused on the problem of metamodel matching (e.g., (Falleri, Huchard, Lafourcade, & Nebut, 2008)), while most of them concentrated on the adaptation by either assuming that change traces, for instance, are somehow available or addressing only atomic modifications (e.g., (Wachsmuth, 2007; Gruschko, Kolovos, & Paige., 2007; Herrmannsdoerfer, Benz, & Jurgens, 2008)). In this respect, we proposed a transformational approach (Cicchetti, Di Ruscio, & Pierantonio, 2009) to co-adaptation which considers complex modifications of metamodels, in contrast with current approaches (Wachsmuth, 2007; Gruschko et al., 2007; Herrmannsdoerfer et al., 2008) which tackle only atomic modifications. It is worth noting that such support is crucial, because it allows the designer to freely modify the metamodel without a) the limitation of being monotonic, and b) performing only atomic changes.

Finally, the wide exploitation of models and metamodels is causing an increasing demand for model versioning techniques specialized to deal with such abstraction levels (Lin, Zhang, & Gray, 2004). There exists a number of approaches which cope with difference calculation and representation, like (Cicchetti, Di Ruscio, & Pierantonio, 2007; Lin et al., 2007; Brand, Protic, & Verhoeff, 2010): they differ for the adopted representations mechanism, the granularity of the detected manipulations, and the ability to re-apply changes to models given as input. In this respect, we have chosen (Cicchetti et al., 2007) since it offered both support for metamodel and model difference representation, as well as the application of modifications to input models in a patching manner.

CONCLUSION AND FUTURE WORK

In this paper, we have presented an approach for rapid prototyping and proposed an agile and flexible infrastructure which can support a test-driven approach for the development of executable metamodels. In our approach, models are used to test the metamodel implementation and convey feedback to the designers as guidance for the metamodel refactoring process. This approach achieves tighter user involvement in the metamodelling process, effectively leading to shorter and more agile metamodel evolution iteration cycles. Moreover, by reusing existing and familiar - albeit suboptimal for the task - technologies, the shift in paradigm from manual to model-driven appears to be more easily engulfed by experienced developers.

The usefulness and validity of the proposed approach has been demonstrated in practice, as it has been applied for implementing the beContent metamodel which has been used for developing a number of real-world data-intensive web applications.

Future work includes the application of the approach to different domains in order to evaluate the degree to which its effectiveness depends on aspects which are tightly related to the domain of web application development. Moreover, more extensive experiments are required in the adoption of BNFC in order to be able to inject not only metamodels but also all the information encoded in the validation methods.

REFERENCES

Beck, K. (2000). *Test-driven development*. Addison Wesley.

Bezivin, J. (2005). On the unification power of models. [SoSyM]. *Jour. on Software and Systems Modeling*, *4*(2), 171–188. doi:10.1007/s10270-005-0079-0

Budinsky, F., Steinberg, D., Merks, E., Ellersick, R., & Grose, T. (2003). *Eclipse modeling framework*. Addison Wesley.

Cicchetti, A., Di Ruscio, D., Eramo, R., Maccarrone, F., & Pierantonio, A. (2009). becontent: A model-driven platform for designing and maintaining web applications. In 9th *International Conference on Web Engineering* (ICWE 2009) (vol. 5648, pp. 518-522). Berlin, Germany: Springer.

Cicchetti, A., Di Ruscio, D., Iovino, L., & Pierantonio, A. (2011). *Managing the evolution of data-intensive web applications by model-driven techniques*. Software and Systems Modeling. Retrieved from http://dx.doi.org/10.1007/s10270-011-0193-0

Cicchetti, A., Di Ruscio, D., & Pierantonio, A. (2007, October). A metamodel independent approach to difference representation. *Journal of Object Technology, 6*(9), 165–185. doi:10.5381/jot.2007.6.9.a9

Cicchetti, A., Di Ruscio, D., & Pierantonio, A. (2009). Managing dependent changes in coupled evolution. In R. F. Paige (Ed.), *Proc. 2nd International Conference on Model Transformation* (ICMT'09) (vol. 5563, p. 35-51). Zurich, Switzerland: Springer.

Falleri, J.-R., Huchard, M., Lafourcade, M., & Nebut, C. (2008). Metamodel matching for automatic model transformation generation. In *Procs. of the 11th Int. Conf. Models 2008,* Toulouse (France) (vol. 5301, pp. 326–340). Springer.

Forsberg, M., & Ranta, A. (2004). BNF converter. In *Procs. 2004 ACM Sigplan Workshop on Haskell* (pp. 94-95).

Fowler, M. (2005, Jun). *Language workbenches: The killer-app for domain specific languages?* Retrieved from http://martinfowler.com/articles/languageWorkbench.html

Gruschko, B., Kolovos, D., & Paige, R. (2007). Towards synchronizing models with evolving metamodels. In *Procs of the Work*. Modse.

Herrmannsdoerfer, M., Benz, S., & J¨urgens, E. (2008). Automatability of coupled evolution of metamodels and models in practice. In *Procs. of the 11th Int. Conf. Models 2008,* Toulouse (France) (vol. 5301, pp. 645-659). Springer.

Hudak, P. (1998). Modular domain specific languages and tools. In *Procs. Fifth International Conference on Software Reuse* (pp. 134–142).

Izquierdo, J., Cuadrado, J., & Molina, J. (2008). Gra2MoL: A domain specific transformation language for bridging grammarware to modelware in software modernization. In *Procs. Workshop on Model-driven Software Evolution.*

Jouault, F., & Bezivin, J. (2006). KM3: A DSL for Metamodel Specification. In *FMOODS'06* (vol. 4037, pp. 171–185). Springer-Verlag.

Kelly, S., & Pohjonen, R. (2009). Worst practices for domain-specific modeling. *IEEE Software, 26*(4), 22–29. doi:10.1109/MS.2009.109

Kelly, S., & Tolvanen, J.-P. (2008). *Domain-specific modeling. Wiley-IEEE Computer Society Press. Kleppe, A. (2008). Software language engineering: Creating domain-specific languages using metamodels.* Addison-Wesley Professional.

Kolovos, D. S., Di Ruscio, D., Paige, R. F., & Pierantonio, A. (2009). Different models for model matching: An analysis of approaches to support model differencing. In *Proc. 2nd CVSM'09, ICSE09 Workshop.* Vancouver, Canada. (to appear)

Kurtev, I., van den Berg, K., & Jouault, F. (2006). Evaluation of rule-based modularization in model transformation languages illustrated with ATL. In *Procs. of the 2006 ACM Symposium on Applied Computing* (pp. 1202–1209). ACM Press.

Ledeczi, A., Maroti, M., Bakay, A., Karsai, G., Garrett, J., Thomason, C., et al. (2001, 17 mai). The generic modeling environment. In *Procs Workshop on Intelligent Signal Processing*. Budapest, Hungary: IEEE.

Lin, Y., Gray, J., & Jouault, F. (2007, August). DSMDiff: A differentiation tool for domain-specific models. *European Journal of Information Systems: Special Issue on Model-Driven Systems Development, 16*(4), 349–361.

Lin, Y., Zhang, J., & Gray, J. (2004). Model comparison: A key challenge for transformation testing and version control in model driven software development. In *OOPSLA Work*. MDSD.

Mendez, D., Etien, A., Muller, A., & Casallas, R. (2010). *Transformation migration after metamodel evolution*. In International Workshop on Models and Evolution (ME'10) - ACM/IEEE Models'2010.

Nunes, D., & Schwabe, D. (2006). Rapid prototyping of web applications combining domain specific languages and model driven design. In *ICWE '06: Procs of the 6th int. Conf. on Web Engineering* (pp. 153–160). ACM.

Paige, R., Brooke, P., & Ostroff, J. (2004). Specification-driven development of an executable metamodel in Eiffel. In *Procs. of Workshop in Software Model Engineering* (WISME).

Read, R. C., & Corneil, D. G. (1977). The graph isomorphism disease. *Journal of Graph Theory, 1*(4), 339–363. doi:10.1002/jgt.3190010410

Rose, L., Etien, A., M'endez, D., Kolovos, D., Paige, R., & Polack, F. (2010). *Comparing model-metamodel and transformation-metamodel coevolution*. In International Workshop on Models and Evolutions.

Schmidt, D. C. (2006). Guest editor's introduction: Model-driven engineering. *Computer, 39*(2), 25–31. doi:10.1109/MC.2006.58

Soltenborn, C., & Engels, G. (2009). Towards test-driven semantics specification. In *Procs. of the 12th int. Conf. on Model Driven Engineering Languages and Systems* (MODELS) (pp. 378–392). Berlin, Germany: Springer-Verlag.

Tolvanen, J.-P., & Kelly, S. (2005, Octobre). Defining domain-specific modeling languages to automate product derivation: Collected experiences. In *SPLC* (vol.3714, pp. 198–209). Springer-Verlag.

van den Brand, M., Protic, Z., & Verhoeff, T. (2010). Fine-grained metamodel-assisted model comparison. In *Proceedings of the 1st International Workshop on Model Comparison in Practice* (pp. 11–20). New York, NY: ACM.

Wachsmuth, G. (2007, Juillet). Metamodel adaptation and model co-adaptation. In E. Ernst (Ed.), *Proceedings of the 21st ECOOP* (Vol. 4069). Springer-Verlag.

KEY TERMS AND DEFINITIONS

Coupled Evolution: Analogously to any software artifact, metamodels are equally prone to evolution during their lifetime. As a consequence, whenever a metamodel changes, any related entity must be consistently adapted for preserving its well formedness, consistency, or intrinsic correctness. Coupled evolution supports these adaptation activities.

Metamodel: A meta-model is a model highlighting properties of those models which conform to it. In particular, a model is said to conform to its meta-model like a program conforms to the grammar of the programming language in which it is written.

Model Driven Engineering: Model-Driven Engineering (MDE) refers to the systematic use of models as first class entities throughout the software engineering life cycle. Model-Driven Engineering (MDE) aims at rendering business logic and intellectual property resilient to technological changes by shifting the focus of software development from coding to modeling.

Model to Code Transformation: A model to code transformation is a transformation able to generate textual artifacts starting from a source model.

Model to Model Transformation: A model to model transformation is a transformation able to generate a target model starting from a source one.

Model: A model is a simplification of a system built with an intended goal in mind. The model should be able to answer questions in place of the actual system.

Test Driven Development: Test-driven development is an increasingly popular approach for building systems with reliability, understandability, and maintainability requirements.

ENDNOTES

[1]   Partially supported by the European Community's 7th Framework Programme(FP7/2007-2013), grant agreement n. 214898.

[2]   http://www.eiffel.com/

[3]   http://www.eclipse.org/emf/

[4]   http://www.omg.org/mof/

[5]   http://www.php.net/

[6]   http://antti-juhani.kaijanaho.fi/darcs/bnfc/doc/

[7]   In KM3 metaclasses are specified by means of the *class* clause.

[8]   http://www.becontent.org/

[9]   http://www.acceleo.org/

[10]   http://www.mysql.com

[11]   http://wiki.eclipse.org/Xpand

[12]   http://www.eclipse.org/gmt/epsilon/doc/egl/

Chapter 13
What is the Benefit of a Model–Based Design of Embedded Software Systems in the Car Industry?

Manfred Broy
Technical University Munich, Germany

Sascha Kirstan
Altran Technologies, Germany

Helmut Krcmar
Technical University Munich, Germany

Bernhard Schätz
Technical University Munich, Germany

ABSTRACT

Model-based development becomes more and more popular in the development of embedded software systems in the car industry. On the websites of tool vendors many success stories can be found, which report of efficiency gains from up to 50% in the development, high error reductions and a more rapid increase of the maturity level of developed functions (The Mathworks, 2010) (dSPACE 2010) just because of model-based development. Reliable and broadly spread research that analyze the status quo of model-based development and its effects on the economics are still missing. This chapter describes the results of a global study by Altran Technologies, the chair of software and systems engineering and the chair of Information Management of the University of Technology in Munich which examines the costs and benefits of model-based development of embedded systems in the car industry.

DOI: 10.4018/978-1-61350-438-3.ch013

INTRODUCTION

In the last 20 years the value chain in the car industry has changed drastically. All car producers and suppliers worldwide have worked on improvements in the area of mechanics, the improvement of quality requirements, and improvements in the logistic area. A lot of the potential in these areas is already exploited. A main differentiation factor turns out to be the electronics area, where a change from hardware to software development is carried out. The meaning electronics will have in the next years has been analyzed by a study of Mercer Management Consulting (Mercer, 2004). The study focuses mainly on the question how the cost factors in the development of a car will change until the year 2015 in comparison to the year 2002. In 2015 the costs for the development of electronics will have a value of 35% of the total car production costs. Whereas areas as power train and body have small increases, the costs for the development of electronic systems will be almost tripled. The predicted increases result from a variety of innovations which are being expected in this area. The majority of innovations are realized with embedded systems and especially with software. „90 percent of the future innovations in the car will be based on electronics and from that 80 percent will be realized by software" (Lederer, 2002). However, today's software development has big challenges to master like shortened development times for the cars in total versus longer development times for the software, high safety requirements and especially the growing complexity because of the rising number of functions and the increasing interaction between the functions. To master these challenges car producers and suppliers conduct a paradigm change in the software development from hand-coded to model-based development.

A model-based development process is specifically attractive in embedded domains like Automotive Software due to the fact that development in these domains is driven by two strong forces:

On the one side the *evolutionary* development of automotive systems, dealing with the iterated integration of new functions into a substantial amount of existing/legacy functionality from pervious system versions; And on the other side *platform-independent* development, substantially reducing the amount of reengineering/ maintenance caused by fast changing hardware generations. As a result, a model-based approach is pursued to enable a shift of focus of the development process on the early phases, supporting a function-based rather than a code-based engineering of automotive systems. Thus, the pragmatic question arises whether *a model-based approach – focusing on model of functionality as the most stable asset – is an economic approach in a domain driven by functional evolution as well as by hardware revolutions.*

On the one hand model-based development promises considerable productivity increases, improvements in quality and cost savings. On the other hand, it brings challenges since the use of model-based design results in a major process redesign. The introduction of model-based development influences established development processes, required resources and thereby also the organizational structure. In addition, high investment costs for tools and for training of the employees are necessary.

There is a controversy in the automotive industry about the benefit of model-based software development. Some companies seem to benefit of a model-based design and some don´t. Although model-based development is used by several car producers and suppliers, no major empirical investigations of the costs and benefits of model-based development have been conducted yet. Our aim is to analyze the costs and benefits of model-based development of embedded software systems in the car industry in detail, identify criteria how to optimize the costs and benefits of a model based development and give an outlook about the potential of further model-based development in development phases like requirements engineering and architecture design. In this chapter we present some of the main results of our research work.

Related Work

Statements about the benefits of model-based development in the car industry are quite rare. Most of the statements come from tool vendors, who report about successful projects their customers have conducted (The Mathworks, 2010) (dSPACE 2010). But a neutral investigation of the costs and benefits of model-based development in the car industry has not been conducted yet. Fieber at al. (Fieber, Regnat & Rumpe, 2009) have conducted an empirical study about the benefits of model-based development, but this study covers many different sectors, not only the automotive domain, and is only conducted within one single company. Results of the study have up to now not been published, but the authors present working hypothesis in their paper which result from six interviews, which they had already conducted. These are for example that:

- Models are hardly used for communication or documentation purposes but mostly for generating purposes. Most teams did not model before they introduced model driven development. The introduction of modeling activities is regarded as a necessity of the introduction of the model driven development paradigm. The terms modeling and generating are often seen as synonyms as the teams use models only for generating artifacts.
- Projects that successfully adopt the model driven development paradigm are small and agile. The paradigm is not predetermined from the organization or driven by economical considerations but is started from within the teams ("grass roots movement"). There is often one key team member pushing the adoption of the paradigm.

- The most successful adoption of modeling and the model driven development paradigm is achieved when the team members have formal qualifications (e. g. a computer science degree) and are systematically trained in (UML) modeling.
- Typical and important reasons for adopting the model driven development paradigm are raising the software quality and enforcement of consistent structures and architectures." (Fieber, Regnat & Rumpe, 2009)

(Fey & Stuermer, 2007) examined the state of the art of quality assurance (QA) methods, the pros and cons of each method and the needed effort to use them. As a result of the analysis they report that model-based development significantly improves the quality of the automotive embedded software development process. For each investigated quality assurance method like for example model reviews or automated model checks they give statements about the automation degree, the effort and the benefit. They come to the conclusion that due to the relatively high effort required to safeguard the model-based development process, it is still desirable to reduce the effort and increase the effectiveness of the applied QA methods. (Murphy, Wakefield & Friedman, 2007) have listed best practices for verification, validation and test in model-based design. The paper concludes that model-based design improves a team's ability to deploy a high-quality embedded system on time compared to traditional methods, which rely on verification, validation and testing at the end of the process. Best practices for establishing a model-based design culture like using models to generate the production code, focus on design instead on coding or that models are the sole source of truth can be found in (Smith, Prabhu & Friedman, 2007). These best practices shall help companies in adopting model-based design and achieve gains in efficiency in the development process. Asadi and Ramsin (Asadi & Ramsin,

2008) analyzed different MDA-based methodologies and found out that the methodologies are not mature enough. The majority of the methodologies have a lack when it comes to features like round trip engineering, model verification and validation or model synchronization. Another problem is that all tool-related issues are being handled by the tool vendors. As a consequence the tools are sometimes not in coherence with the proposed MDA-methodology. Dzidek et. al (Dzidek & Arisholm & Briand, 2008) conducted an empirical evaluation to analyze the impact of model-based development in software maintenance. They conducted a controlled experiment that "investigates the costs of maintaining and the benefits of using UML documentation during the maintenance and evolution of a real nontrivial system, using professional developers as subjects, working with a state-of-the-art UML tool during an extended period of time" (Dzidek & Arisholm & Briand, 2008). They found out that the UML group had on average a statistically significant 54% increase in functional correctness of changes and an insignificant 7 percent overall improvement in design quality. A much larger improvement was observed on the first change task (56 percent), at the expense of an insignificant 14 percent increase in development time caused by the overhead of updating the UML documentation.

Another interesting work is from (Mohagheghi & Dehlen, 2008) who reviewed 25 empirical studies by evaluating reasons for and effects on applying the model driven development paradigm in industrial projects. They found out that the ultimate reason for applying the model driven development paradigm in the companies are hopes to increase the productivity and thereby shorten the development time and improving quality. When having introduced model driven development, the companies sometimes report of huge productivity losses, because of immature tools and all companies report of high costs for the process redesign from classical to model-driven development. The benefits of using models is

seen in improving the understandability and communication among stakeholders. The paper ends with the result that more empirical studies have to be conducted to analyze the costs and benefits of model-based development as some companies don´t use model-based development, because of the high investment costs and the unknown benefits. Taking the results of the related work into account, the importance to analyze the costs and benefits of model-based development is confirmed by the conducted literature review.

Procedure to Analyse the Costs and Benefits of Model-Based Software Development (MBSD)

As presented in Figure 1 our approach to analyze the costs and benefits of model-based development consists of five steps. First of all a theory, which summarizes assumed changes in costs, time and quality because of model-based development was developed. The idea behind the theory is to analyze major differences between a hand-coded and a model-based development process. Therefore a couple of hand-coded and model-based development processes, which are used by car manufacturers and suppliers, were analyzed. As a result we developed a reference process for a classical software development and a reference process for a model-based software development. These two reference processes were compared and major differences were identified. To make sure that all major differences were being identified we also used the activity index of the V-Modell XT (IABG, 2010), which summaries all essential steps in a software development. The identified differences are in our opinion responsible for the changes in costs, time and quality. After identifying the differences in the development process and analyzing their influence on cost, time and quality changes, a case study was conducted to evaluate the theory (step 2). After the case study, different cost models based on the theory were developed (step 3). These cost models have been

Figure 1. Approach to analyze the costs and benefits of MBSD

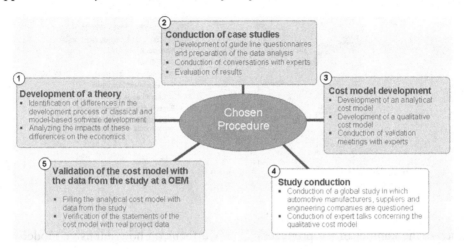

validated with experts from industry and research. As next step a global study (step 4) was conducted to get quantitative data on cost, time and quality changes in dependency of the conducted steps (degree of MBSD) in the development process like the degree of modeling and code generation or the use of test activities on models. As last step a validation of the cost model with the data of the global study at a car producer (step 5) has been conducted to see how precise the predictions of the cost model were.

In this paper we focus on the results of the global study (step 4), which we present in the following chapter.

Essential Results of the Study

The study was conducted by Altran Technologies in cooperation with the chair of software and systems engineering and the Information Management chair of the technical university in Munich. We invited more than 850 experts personally worldwide to take part in the study. We did this by contacting costumers of Altran Technologies, companies who work together with the chair of Software and Systems Engineering of TUM and companies which have published in magazines, online or at conferences about their model-based development activities. In addition we also contacted experts in business portals like LinkedIn (LinkedIn, 2011) and Xing (Xing, 2011) and made advertisements to participate in our study on the Altran Technologies website. To raise the number of participants also anonymous participation was possible. The people who answered the questionnaire anonymously only had to fill out general information about the company in our questionnaire like is the questionnaire answered from a car producer, supplier or a technology consulting company and the size of the company. About 30% of the questionnaires were answered anonymous. In total we received 67 filled out questionnaires which have been answered by almost 180 experts. The reason therefore is that the questionnaire was so comprehensive that usually 3 to 4 people of one company were needed to fill out all the questions of the questionnaire. Study participants were mainly car producers and suppliers. In addition we also involved technology consulting companies, because these companies work for the car producers and suppliers and develop a lot of software for them. Figure 2 describes the structure of the participants. It can be seen that with 58% the majority of the participants were suppliers followed by the car producers with 33%. This distribution makes sense as the number of suppliers in general

Figure 2. The structure of the study participants

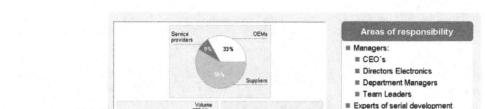

is much higher as the number of car producers. The areas of responsibility of the study participants range from experts in research departments or the serial development of the companies till directors of electronics and CEO's. The huge know-how of our study participants ensures the significance of the study results.

The study has four main pillars. First of all we want to find out the reasons why companies use model-based development. Secondly we wanted to know the positive as well as the negative experiences the companies have made with model-based design. In the following section of the study we focus on how intensive model-based design is used in each development phase (status quo of model-based design) and what effects this has on the costs of each development phase and on the total development costs. In the following pillar of the study we concentrate on the potentials of model-based development which are mainly in the area of model based requirements engineering and model based architecture design. The study ends with recommendations for action, which were derived from the results of the study. Figure 3 summaries all the aspects which are being dealt with in the study.

Figure 3. The four pillars of the study

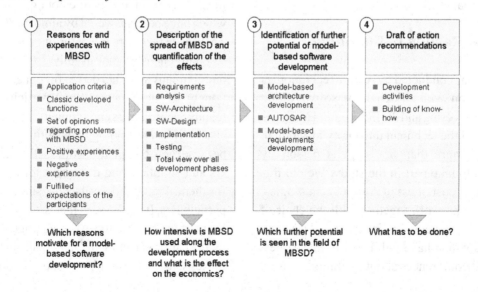

Our Understanding of Model-Based Development

The term model-based development is used so widely and has so many different meanings that we like to present our understanding of model-based development before we present the results of the study. In our understanding we speak of model-based development when the following criteria are fullfield (see also (Schätz, 2004)):

- The use of a weakly coupled tool chain
- The use of models in different development phases
- Models offer different views
- Activities are conducted with tools on the model
- Generation of code and other artifacts out of the model

In the following chapter we like to present major results of the study. First of all we present the status quo of model-based development in the car industry. Afterwards we focus on the analysis of the costs and benefits of model-based development in the development phases software design and implementation, in the total view and the impact on the maintenance costs. After presenting the results of the study we focus on potentials of further model-based development.

Status Quo of Model-Based Development in the Car Industry

The study shows that model-based development is being used for series development by the majority of the companies for more than five years. Especially in the development phases software design and implementation model-based design is used intensively. 96% of all participants use model-based development in both development phases. The other 4% have just begun using model-based development and use it only during the SW-design. 75% of the companies use model-based design

already in the requirements engineering phase by using Rapid Control Prototyping (RCP). We want to keep in mind that RCP is not model-based requirements engineering. Instead it is already designing with the modeling tool. Nevertheless the study participants report that it is an efficient method to identify missing requirements, especially while developing innovative functions. A trend can be seen that more and more companies use model-based design also in the architecture development. The aim is to increase the seamlessness in the development process and to perform early tests on the architecture model. Model-based testing (i.e. the generation of test cases out of a test model) is currently not used intensively. Only 35% of the participants use it right now, but almost 50% plan to use it in the near future.

We asked the study participants why their company uses model-based development. The top three reasons were:

- **Improvement of the product quality:** The companies hope that the frontloading of the test activities and the continuous testing during the development has a positive effect on the improvement of the product quality.
- **Development of functions with high complexity:** Functions with high complexity are difficult to design with a classical software development. The companies expect that model-based development helps them to develop high complex functions with viewer iterations and consequently less effort in the development, because of the possibility of early simulation.
- **Shorter development times:** The companies expect a more efficient development, because of the possibility to simulate early in the development process and to be able to generate artifacts like code or test cases for example. Shorter development times lead to an improvement in time to market and enable companies to present innova-

tive functions earlier on the market than the competition.

It was interesting to see that cost reductions are not within the top three reasons. It could be seen that model-based development is also used because there is a trend in the industry to use it. 83% of the participants agreed that one reason for model-based development in their company is the trend in the industry to develop model-based. Especially suppliers mentioned that car producers expect that they develop model-based. If they don´t do it, someone else, who uses model-based development gets the contract to develop the software for the car producer.

After having identified the main reasons why companies use model-based development, we asked them about their positive and also negative experiences with a model-based design.

Positive Experiences

The experts report of the simplified communication because of the use of a function model in the SW-Design. The models provide great support in the communication with other colleagues because of the graphical design. Models even ensure that colleagues from other departments or domains, who are not familiar with software development, can be involved in the software development. This helps to include extra know-how in the software development. Another positive aspect is the possibility of early simulation of the function model. Model reviews, guideline checkers, Rapid Control Prototyping (RCP) and Model in the Loop – Tests (MiL) help to find errors already in the design phase. This leads to viewer iterations in the development and thereby to cost savings. The possibility to automate is seen as a further positive effect and is a key factor for a more efficient development. Besides code generation also test cases and documentations can be generated. If the generated code isn´t changed manually after the code generation the code and the function model are consistent. This is a huge benefit for the maintenance of functions.

Negative Experiences

The main negative aspect, which was reported, is the extremely high process redesign costs, which have to be invested to develop model-based. The experts report of high efforts which are needed for the process redesign. They indicate that the main costs for the process redesign are not just costs for tools (although tool costs are a major cost factor), but also costs for defining a new development process, training costs for the employees and the regeneration of hand-coded projects. Another negative aspect is the high dependency from tool vendors. The reason therefore is that the tools do not offer interfaces to exchange models among different tools unless inside tools from the same tool vendor. Consequently if a company has decided for a modeling tool it is advisable to buy the rest of the tool chain from the same tool vendor, to maximize the seamlessness in the development process. Even if standardized interfaces would exist, the experts are still pessimistic about the dependency on tool vendors.

After having identified the main reasons for developing model-based and also the positive and negative experience the study participants made with model-based design we want to present the fullfield expectations of the study participants with a model-based design. This is an interesting question, because the use of model-based design is connected with certain expectations like better product quality, faster development times or cost savings for example. Therefore this question indicates how satisfied the study participants are. Figure 4 shows that the majority of participants report of fulfilled expectations. Nevertheless the majority also reports that there is still an enormous potential in model-based design which by now is not being exploited.

Figure 4. Fulfilled expectations

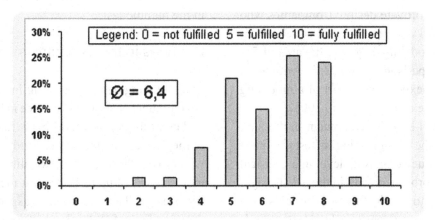

Costs and Benefits of Model-Based Development of Embedded Software Systems

As described in the introduction of this chapter we try to measure the influence of model-based development on costs, time and quality changes by interviewing companies how intensive they use model-based development (status quo) and how this has affected development costs, time and quality. We did this for all development phases from requirements engineering till testing. In addition we also focused on changes in the total development costs, total development time and product quality. This procedure enables us to analyze how the intensity of model-based design affects the economics. On the one hand we asked the participants about the intensity of their model-based development and on the other hand we asked about the effects on the economics. With the collected data we can conduct correlations between the conducted steps in the development process and the changes in the economics.

In this article we like to present the results of the development phase software design a development phase of major importance in a model-based development process, the development phase implementation, changes in the total view (costs, time and product quality) and concluding

the influence of model-based development on the maintenance costs.

Software Design

The software design is the development phase where the use of model-based development leads to many changes in the development process. The functionality for example is modeled in a function model like for instance in a Matlab/Simulink/Stateflow or Ascet SD model. During the development the engineer has the possibility to test this function model. The use of model-based design in the software design is the precondition to use code generation in the implementation.

We like to present how intensive the functions are being modeled or rather hand coded, how intensive the function models are being tested and how this (i.e. the modeling and simulation) effects the development costs, the development times and the product quality.

Status Quo

In average 73% of a total application functionality (i.e. only application software and no basis software) is already being modeled in a function model. There is a huge gap in the modeling degree if you take a look at the application period, in which the companies use model-based development in the software design. Companies who have just started with model-based development have a small modeling degree in the area of 5% to 20%. In comparison the companies with more than five years experience report of a modeling degree in the area around 90% to 100%.

Using model-based development in the SW-Design allows the "Frontloading" of test activities, which are conducted on code level in a classical hand coded approach already in the SW-Design. The possibility to test the function model is used widely in almost every company. Four test methods are used to test the function model: Model reviews, guideline checkers, Rapid Control Prototyping and Model- in the Loop tests. Figure 5 gives an overview how intensive these test methods are used.

It can be seen that all four tests methods are being used intensively. For example 41,8% of all participants use more than ten model reviews during the whole development to check the model. Another interesting result is that the majority of the participants use MiL-Tests intensively. Later on we analyze what effect the conduction

of MiL-Tests has on the number of detected errors in the module test.

Changes in the Economics

The modeling degree has a big influence on the development costs as you can see in Figure 6. The higher the modeling degree of the function model is the higher are the costs. Study participants, who model the whole functionality in a function model report of up to 100% cost increases in the SW-Design. Two other major aspects influence the costs in the SW-Design besides the modeling degree. The intensity the companies use RCP in the requirements analysis and the intensity of tests on function models. Companies, who use RCP in the requirements analysis, intensively report of a decline or almost no changes in the development costs, because they already frontloaded these development activities in the requirements analysis. This is a major reason for the high margin of derivation, which you can see in the figure.

We already mentioned that the test intensity on the function model has a major influence on the cost changes in the SW-Design. Companies

Figure 5. Overview of the intensity of tests on function model level

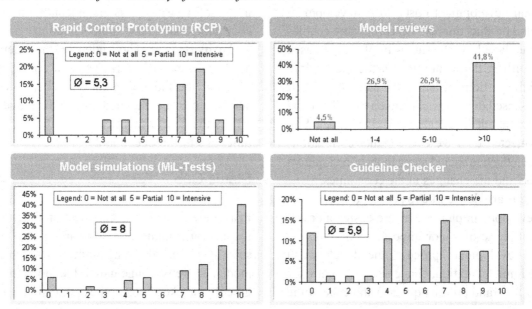

Figure 6. Correlation modeling degree in SW-Design vs. changes in costs in SW-Design

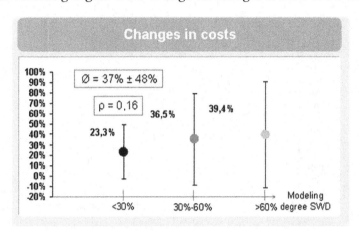

who use the possibility to test the function model intensively report of high cost risings in the SW-Design. These are usually the companies who also have a high modeling degree. Consequently we couldn´t analyze the single effect of the modeling degree and the test on function models on the cost changes during our data analysis. This makes sense, as a small modeling degree only makes it possible to test a small part of the total functionality on function model level.

Especially model reviews and MiL-tests (Model in the Loop tests) are cost intensive test methods and lead to high cost increases when conducted intensively. For example if you like to conduct MiL-tests it is advisable not just to simulate your function model with some stimuli but also to develop an environment model. Environment models have the advantage that they are more precise and complete than a selection of some stimuli. From the economic point of view you have to keep in mind that the development of an environment model is usually as expensive as the development of a function model. Consequently the development of an environment model usually only pays off, if it can be reused for different car lines. Engine models i.e. are very often used as environment models, because they are needed for the development of many functions in the car and can therefore be reused for the development of several functions from one car line and for the development of different car lines. Instead of investing the high costs to develop an environment model, lots of companies use stimuli from car tests to test the function model.

The question arises what benefit a company can have if it uses the possibility of testing on function model level. The correlation of the number of detected errors in the module test and the intensity of MiL-tests in Figure 7 shows the benefit of intensive simulations on function model level. Companies which don´t use any MiL-tests find almost 30% more errors in the module test than companies who use MiL-tests intensive. These errors have already been found and eliminated by the group which uses MiL-tests intensively on function model level (i.e. earlier error detection). The decline in the number of detected errors by the participants who don´t use MiL-tests, result from the other three possible test methods which can be used on function model level. This proves the benefit of testing on function model level. All participants use at least one of the four possible test methods on function model level and are able to reduce the number of detected errors in the module test, because they found these errors already on function model level.

In addition we also analyzed the impact of model-based development in the software design

Figure 7. Impact of MiL-tests on the number of errors found during module test

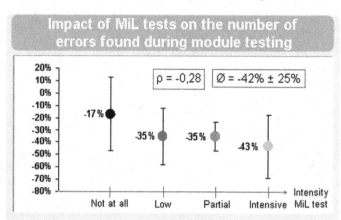

by asking how important quality criteria in the software design changed, because of a model-based development. The positive effect can be seen in Table 1. Especially in the criteria testability, correctness and clearness very positive changes are reported.

After describing the impact of model-based development in the SW-Design on the development costs for the SW-Design, on the impact of MiL-tests on the detected errors in the module test and on the quality criteria in the software design, we like to present the impact of the development phase SW-Design on the total development costs. Figure 8 shows the influence. It can be seen that the more intensive model-based development is used in the software design the higher are the reported cost savings. We define intensity as the average value of the degree of modeling and the test intensity. This is a very

interesting result, because the economic benefit of the frontloading activities in the SW-Design like modeling and testing can be shown. Figure 8 also shows the effect on changes in the product quality. We used the definition of product quality after DIN ISO 9126 (ISO, 1998), which defines the following criteria to be analyzed for product quality: functionality, reliability, usability, efficiency, maintainability and portability.

As in the correlation with the costs it can be seen that a small modeling and testing degree on function model level doesn´t bring any advantages compared to a classical hand coded development. With an intensity over 30% the companies begin to report of improvements. The improvements are especially high in companies with an intensity over 60% with a value of 0,88 which means strong improvement. It can be summarized that model-based development in the software

Table 1. Changes of the quality criteria in the software design

Quality	--	-	0	+	++
Clearness	0%	1.5%	9.1%	60.6%	28.8%
Modifiability	1.5%	1.5%	30.3%	50%	16.7%
Correctness	0%	3%	12.1%	69.7%	15.2%
Detailedness	0%	4.5%	39.4%	43.9%	12.1%
Testability	0%	1.5%	13.6%	40.9%	43.9%

Figure 8. Correlation modeling degree and test intensity vs. overall costs and vs. product quality

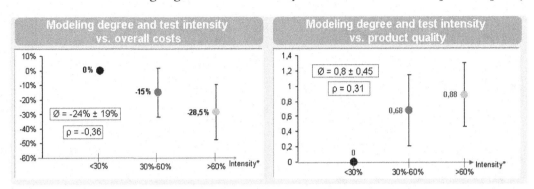

design can have a very positive effect on changes in total costs and in the product quality.

In the following we present the results for the development phase implementation.

Implementation

Before we present the effects of code generation on the costs, we present the current status quo of model-based development in the implementation phase.

Status Quo

Almost 96% of the study participants use the automatic code generation. In average 73% of the developed application software is being developed by using a code generator. However there are major differences within the companies regarding the amount of generated code. It varies between 5% and 100%. At least 40% of the participants report of a degree of generated code between 95% and 100%. What are the reasons for such high differences in the degree of generated code? The major influence on the degree of generated code has the modeling degree in the software design i.e. the degree of functionality, which has been modeled in a function model like a Matlab/ Simulink/ Stateflow or Ascet SD model. Besides the modeling degree the know-how of the employees in the use of a code generator and the

safety relevance of the developed function play a major role. Especially at high safety relevant functions the average value of the generated code with 44% is significantly smaller than for example at uncritical functions with 77%. The reason therefore is that some companies are the opinion that the current code generators are not applicable to generate high safety relevant code. Necessary qualifications or even certifications of the code generator are aligned with very high costs, which are being avoided by the companies at the moment. In addition there are many open questions concerning the code generation like which steps in the development process are obsolete, when using a certified code generator or the question if the high costs for the certification ever amortize?

In the software design the study participants put a lot of emphasize on the test on function model level. Consequently we also like to point out the current status quo of the test activities in the implementation phase. Figure 9 shows that code reviews and SiL-Tests are used intensively by the majority of the study participants. PiL-Tests are not that intensively used. The intensive use of code reviews is on the one hand surprising, because the code is generated with a code generator but on the other hand it reflects the opinion of some study participants that they don't trust the code generation process and therefore have to review the generated code.

Figure 9. Status quo of the conducted test methods in the implementation phase

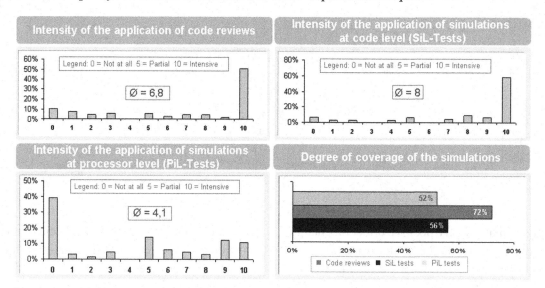

Changes in the Economics

In the following we describe how the intensity of model-based development in the implementation affects the economics. Therefore we present the results of five striking correlations.

1) Correlation degree of generated code vs. cost changes in the implementation:

Aim of this correlation is to analyze the effect of the degree of generated code on the costs for the implementation. Figure 10 shows that the higher the degree of generated code is, the higher are the cost savings in the implementation. This result is not surprising, because the code generator transforms the function model, which has been developed in the software design, automatically in C-code. Hence the cost savings are effects of the frontloading of the development activities in the software design.

2) Correlation degree of generated code vs. number of detected errors in the Implementation:

Figure 10. Correlation: Degree of generated code vs. costs in the implementation

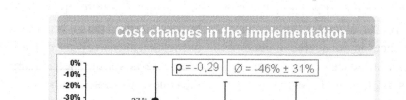

Figure 11. Correlation generated code vs. number of detected errors

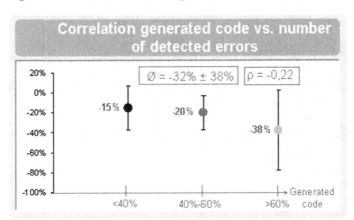

An interesting question is how the degree of generated code affects the number of detected errors in the implementation. Result of the correlation is that with a raising degree of generated code the number of detected errors decreases. Responsible therefore are especially the prevention of coding errors and the conducted tests in the software design (take also a look at the subsequent correlation).

3) Test in the software design vs. number of detected errors in the implementation:

This correlation provides a very interesting result and underlines the importance of tests on function model level. Participants, who test their function models intensively in the software design, report of significant less detected errors in the implementation than participants, who have tested sporadically. Especially strong is the delta between medium and intensive test activities with absolute 32% more detected errors. Consequently this correlation points out the importance of early testing (Keyword: Frontloading) in this case during software design.

4) Degree of generated code and test intensity vs. changes in the total costs:

Figure 12. Correlation intensity test during software design vs. detected errors in the implementation

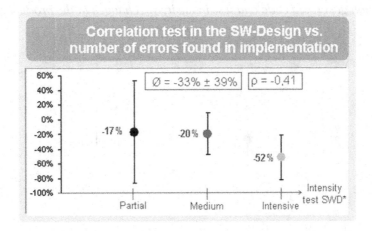

Figure 13. Correlation generated code and test intensity vs. changes in the total costs

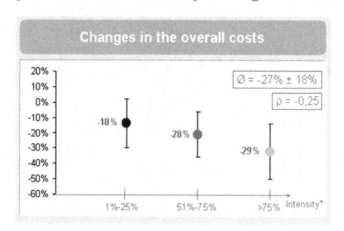

When correlating the degree of generated code and the intensity of code generation and test activities in the implementation with the total costs a trend can be seen that a raising intensity leads to a decrease in the costs.

The data analysis showed that the fundament for cost savings in the total view is laid in the software design. Participants with a high degree of generated code generally have developed a function model with a high modeling degree. For the most part these are also the participants, who have conducted intensive tests on function model level like MiL-tests and consequently also SiL-tests. The reason therefore is that conducted MiL-tests can be reused on SiL-test level, as the aim of SiL-tests is to ensure that the generated code behaves exactly the same as the function model.

5) Degree of generated code and test intensity vs. changes in the product quality criteria:

The activities in the implementation only have a small influence on the product quality. However it can be seen that even with a small intensity (<40%) strong improvements (value of 0,7) can be seen.

Total View

In average the study participants report of cost savings around –27% and time savings around -36%.

Figure 14. Correlation generated code and test intensity vs. changes in the product quality criteria

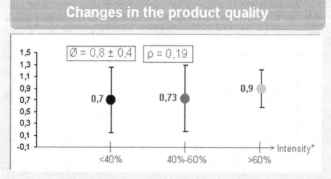

Figure 15. The top 8 identified influence factors on costs, time and quality because of model-based development

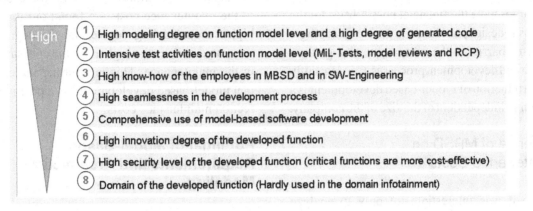

The data analysis exposed that the statements of the study participants concerning the changes in the total cost partially deviate considerably. Some study participants reported of considerable cost savings whereas others report of considerable cost increases. The answers ranged from a minimum value of -80% (cost savings) till a maximum value of +20% (cost rising). With a detailed data analysis we found out, that study participants who use model-based development since a short time only report of cost increases. These result from not well-rehearsed development processes and too little know-how of the employees in the use of the development tools. Companies with more than one year experience already report of cost savings, in general. However, also in this group there are huge differences in the statements about savings. We analyzed the reasons for these differences and found out that the cost savings depend strongly on several factors. In the following we like to present the top influence factors on the costs, time and quality changes because of model-based development.

If you like to sum it up as an elevator pitch you can say that a high modeling degree of the function model in the software design and a high degree of generated code, intensive test activities on function model level and the know-how of the employees are the three main influencing fac-

tors on the economics of model-based software development. The study participants, who have high values for these three criteria, reported of the highest total cost and time savings and the best improvements in product quality. It was interesting to see that the domain of the function doesn´t have a big influence on the costs. Except in the domain infotainment, where model-based development is currently hardly used, the statements about costs were likewise independent of the domain.

In the introduction we pointed out that our motivation is to analyze how the economics change because of model-based design and also to take the process redesign costs into account. We asked the companies if the costs for the process redesign have already amortized and if yes, how long it took? 65% of the companies report of amortized process redesign costs. In average it took them 3 ½ years. This is of course dependent on the number of conducted model-based projects. The more projects are conducted the faster the costs can be amortized.

We also asked the study participants if it is easier to introduce model-based development in a small or a large company. The majority believes that the introduction of a model-based design can be difficult independent of the size of the company. The size only plays a role because the companies face other problems. Small companies often don´t have the financial possibilities to afford the redesign costs, especially the high tool costs. Large companies have the financial possibilities for the process redesign, but face the problem that there is often a barrier in the company to change their established development processes. Consequently the introduction of model-based development is a challenge independent of the size of the company.

Influence of MBSD on Maintenance Costs

For us it was interesting not only to analyze the effect of model-based development on the development costs but also on the maintenance costs. We asked the study participants about the relevance model-based development has on the maintenance costs. 24% think that it has a very high and 67% that it has relevance on the maintenance costs. That the effect is positive can be seen when taking a look at the reported changes in the maintenance costs. In average the overall maintenance costs reduced about 15% compared to a classical development. Savings around 20% are reported when it comes to enhance the functionality of the developed function for example for a face lift of a car. One main reason therefore is that the function model can easily be added with new functionality.

When correlating the modeling degree and the degree of generated code with the changes in the maintenance costs we found out that the higher the modeling degree and the degree of generated code is the higher are the cost savings in the maintenance. This is a further indication that model-based development has a positive effect on maintenance costs.

Potential of Model-Based Requirements and Architecture Modeling

The results of the study show, that model-based development is currently used widely only in the development phases SW-Design and implementation. This was also a result of the case studies (see point 2 in figure 1), which we conducted prior to the global study. More information about the results of the case study can be found in (Kirstan & Zimmermann, 2010). This result motivated us to also include questions in the questionnaire for the global study about current challenges in requirements analysis and architecture design and the valuation of the possible benefit to also use a model-based approach in these development phases. These challenges are afterwards being mapped with the expectations our study participants have of modeling in these development

Figure 16. Influence of model-based development on the maintenance costs

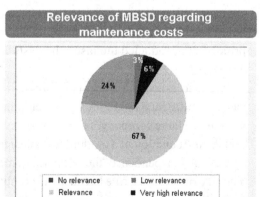
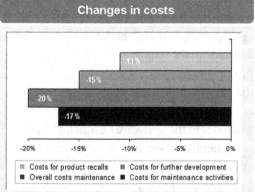

phases to see if a model-based approach can help to master the current challenges. The results are presented in the following.

Requirements Engineering

To capture the requirements right (i.e. complete and consistent) is the basis for the development of software. The study participants report that the description and the verifiability of the requirements and the reconciliation OEM – supplier are currently the biggest challenges they face in the requirements analysis. The challenges in describing the requirements are firstly to find an adequate degree of abstraction and level of detail. Secondly to control the system complexity is seen as a further challenge. Study participants report that up to 15000 requirements per function has become a normal value. Besides the question how to describe the requirements, it is also a challenge how to verify them. Text based specifications are error prone. Therefore there is a huge demand in the industry to validate them for example by tools. This can only be done if the requirements are described in a formal description language. The reconciliation between OEM and supplier is another challenge, especially in the documentation of the requirements. Not all of the requirements are documented by either the supplier or the OEM, which leads to an additional workload.

Model-based requirements engineering can be a solution to these problems. We asked the study participants which additional value they see in model-based requirements engineering. Surprisingly the answers of the participants could be grouped into the three groups, which have been reported as challenges: Description of requirements, verifiability and enhancement of the reconciliation OEM – supplier. In addition they reported some additional aspects where they also see a potential of using a model-based approach (i.e. a formal description of the requirements).

It can be seen that especially the point description of the requirements and the verifiability are strongly connected with the use of formal requirement models. Without them the verifiability of the requirements for example is difficult or even not possible.

Architecture Design

The architecture design is a very important development phase, because it has an impact on the integration, maintainability and the allocation of the work load. The challenges the companies face in architecture development can be broken

Figure 17. Expected potential of model-based requirements engineering

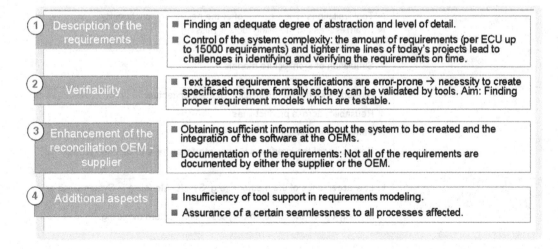

down into three points. These challenges focus also on the current modeling tools, because some study participants use them already for the series development:

- **Tool support:** There are two challenges concerning the tools. First of all the tools do not offer the necessary functionality. This is especially the case when using informal tools like PowerPoint, Excel, Visio etc.. Secondly the seamlessness to the modeling tools is missing. Consequently the results of the architecture design have to be manually transformed in a function model and that can lead to mistakes not just because there can be errors in drafting the architecture in the function model, but also that the software designer changes the architecture without notice.

- **Earlier error finding:** The participants would like to test their architecture design more intensively for example with simulations to find architecture errors earlier in the development process. This is a very important point, because usually errors in the architecture are detected in the integration phase (i.e. very late in the develop-

ment phase). To correct these errors is very cost intensive.

- **Reusability:** Strategies for the modularization of the architecture are often missing. This hampers reuse of architectures. The reuse is a main aim of the companies for example via product lines or in the field of variant management.

The question arises which improvement potential the experts see in architecture modeling? Can it handle all the challenges or at least help to solve some of them? Figure 18 summarizes the answers of the study participants. The answers could also be grouped into the same three aspects like the challenges in the architecture design.

In requirements engineering as well as in the architecture design it could be shown that the challenges and the expectations match. That means that the majority of the study participants are convinced that model-based development in these development phases can solve or at least help to master their current challenges in requirements engineering and in the software architecture design.

Figure 18. Expected potential of model-based architecture design

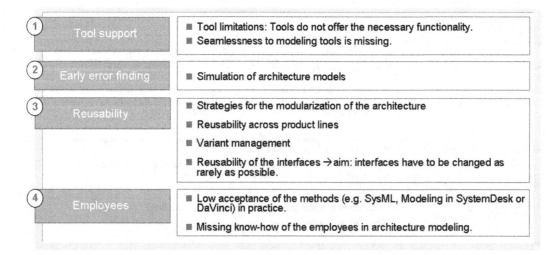

Threats to Validity

The study was conducted with highest carefulness. Nevertheless threats to validity have to be mentioned which could have influenced the results of the study.

1. The number of filled out questionnaires: We received 67 answered questionnaires. Therefore almost 180 people were involved in answering the questionnaire. In total we invited more than 850 people to take part in the study. Reasons like confidentiality and the effort to answer the questionnaire (2 hours were needed in average to answer it completely) were the main reasons why the number of filled out questionnaires were not higher. Nevertheless we were able to win several large car producers, suppliers and technology consulting companies worldwide as participants, which have a huge experience in model-based development. Their expertise ensures the validity of the study.

2. The given data by the study participants are approximations: Because a function for series development is not developed hand-coded as well as model-based the participants could only give approximations how the costs, time and quality change because of model-based development. Anyway the approximations are a good indicator, because all the companies reported about functions which they have developed hand-coded for a previous car line.

3. The design of the questionnaire: The design of the questionnaire may have influenced the answers of the study participants. We tried to minimize this thread by using best practices in the design of the questionnaire and validating the questionnaire by various experts before the questionnaire was sent to the participants.

4. The selection of the participants: The majority of the participants were personally invited to take part in the study. There is a thread that only companies took part which have a higher degree of model-based development than the industry average. By analyzing the data of the study participants we found out that the participants range from companies which have just changed their development process till companies which are using model-based development for over 10 years.

Potential of Model-Based Development in the Development Phases Requirements Engineering and Software Architecture

As we have seen in the previous sections, model-based development has proven its value for the SW-Design and Implementation phase. As a result, in domains like automotive or aeronautic systems, its application has become state of the art. This is reflected in the definition or adaptation of recent development standards like the ISO 26262 (ISO, 2010) or the up-coming DO-178C. Unsurprisingly, these standards specifically address model-based development for software unit design and implementation, adapting the required quality assurance techniques. For example, "Model Inspection" and "Model Walk-Through" are highly recommended practices in these phases.

Nevertheless, about 80% of all fatal errors and more than 50% of all heavy errors are made in the requirements specification or architecture definition phase (Jones, 1991). Consequently, these standards mentioned above already address the importance of models in the requirement specification or architecture phase. For example, (ISO, 2010) highly recommends the "use of unambiguous graphical representations" in general. Furthermore, (ISO, 2010) also highly recommends the use of "semi-formal notations" for requirements specification as well as for the software architectural design for systems with higher criticality. It specifically mentions the use of "executable models" for the verification of requirements and architecture.

Due to their general nature and their intention to define the currently achievable state-of-the-art, the recommendations provided by standards like (ISO, 2010) are not very explicit about the potential and benefits of model-based development outside SW unit design and implementation. However, current research and development has proven the following model-based techniques to be both doable and beneficial:

1. Specification of functional requirements: The current use of models in the requirements phase is often limited to structural aspects of the system under development (e.g., specification of the bus interface). The behavioural aspects are generally only described informally, using (structured) natural language, complicating their validation and verification. Here, precise requirements – in textual form of structured tables as well as graphical form like sequence diagrams – can help to establish a high quality of the requirements constructively as well as analytically (Schätz, 2009). Furthermore, such specifications also provide a basis for quality assurance in later steps, e.g., in form of test cases, which can be executed in text execution frameworks.

2. Component integration: In the current model-based development process, models are generally used to design and implement individual software components including their interfaces. However, without the use of an overall architecture, integrating all these components, issues like inconsistencies between these components and their interfaces may arise. Prominent examples like the loss of "Mars Climate Orbiter" space probe due to a conflict of metric- and imperial-based interfaces show the consequences of those inconsistencies. Here, an integrated archi-

tectural model can avoid these sources of inconsistencies (Schätz, 2009).

3. Unit integration: Component integration ensures consistency on the level of the logical architecture. However, gaps in current tool chains often leave room for inconsistencies when mapping the logical architecture to the SW level, for example when interpreting a bit-signal differently when communicated between the sender and receiver components. By using a model-based approach combining models of the logical and technical architecture as well as the deployment mapping from the former to the later, these inconsistencies can be avoided.

4. Test case generation: The use of models for the specification of system- or component-level requirements allows to immediately reuse these specifications as test cases. However, these models can even be exploited further: Using corresponding synthesis techniques, additional test cases can be generated automatically to provide a better coverage of the specified requirements or to obtain additional robustness tests.

Besides these applications, models can furthermore provide support for several additional aspects of the development of embedded systems, especially in the automotive domain. Examples for these aspects include: the *automation of the design-space exploration*, by synthesizing development artefacts like safe task and communication schedules; the *modeling of variability aspects* in function, architecture, and software as well as hardware to support the definition of product lines, and their use to generate specific product configurations from them; the provision of *model-based diagnosis*, both on-board and off-board, by deducing possible fault locations based on models of the intended behaviour; the extension of the architectural and behavioural models to include the explicit *modeling of failure assump-*

tions, supporting the construction of model-based assurance cases.

Finally, by adding explicit models of the environment to the development process, even more advanced techniques can be added, supporting, e.g., an early validation of requirements as well as a virtual commissioning of the system under development by use of simulated environment.

CONCLUSION

Main results of the study are that model-based development can bring significant cost savings, but only with a "well-chosen" model-based development and an established development process with defined interfaces and role allocations. Otherwise model-based development can be much more expensive than a hand-coded manual software development. Different factors have been analyzed which have a big impact on the changes of the development costs because of model-based development. During the development phase software design for example the intensity of testing on function model level is a major key success factor besides a high modeling degree during model-based development. The earlier the models are being tested, the earlier errors are being found. Besides the time when testing is started, the intensity of testing is very important. We found out that the more intensive function models were tested, the more savings could be achieved in the total development costs. One reason is that the study participants that tested their function model intensively report a major decline in the number of detected errors in the module and SW-SW-integration test, whereas the study participants, who only test sporadically, have just a slight decline in the number of detected errors in the module and SW-SW-integration test.

In addition we also analyzed further potentials of model-based development. Therefore we took a look at the current challenges on the development phases requirements engineering and software architecture and asked the study participants what potential they see if a model-based approach is also used in these development phases. As a result we could see that the majority of the participants see a huge benefit in using a model-based approach in both development phases.

Furthermore we presented the potential of model-based development in the development phases requirements engineering and architecture design from a theoretical point of view. Thereby we presented current research issues in this field, which can be a further potential to improve a model-based design.

It was interesting to see that the results of our study match with results of the studies presented in the related work chapter. Beginning with the motivation companies have in using model-based development till statements to productivity changes and quality improvements.

To sum it all up the study shows that model-based design has a huge benefit *in a domain driven by functional evolution as well as by hardware revolutions,* as it can bring cost and time savings in the development and in the maintenance, the quality of single development artifacts and the product quality in total improve, and in addition the developed function models can be easily reused in different car lines. With the detailed data analysis we found out that there is a huge potential within the companies to optimizes the cost and benefit ratio of their model-based design. In many companies the potential of model-based design is not fully used because they develop just punctual model-based. As a consequence they hardly see any benefit of a model-based software design. Primary the consequent use of model-based development pays off. With the extension of the model-based development also on other development phases like architecture design, requirements engineering and model-based testing there can be an additional potential to raise the economics of model-based development even more.

REFERENCES

Asadi, M., & Ramsin, R. (2008). MDA-based methodologies: An analytical survey. In Schieferdecker, I., & Hartman, A. (Eds.), *ECMDA-FA 2008, LNCS 5095* (pp. 419–431).

dSPACE. (2010). *From dSPACE: Overview TargetLink.* Retrieved from http://www.dspace.de/de/gmb/home/products/sw/pcgs/targetli.cfm

Dzidek, W., Arisholm, E., & Briand, L. (2008). A realistic empirical evaluation of the costs and benefits of UML in software maintenance. *IEEE Transactions on Software Engineering, 34*(3), 407–432. doi:10.1109/TSE.2008.15

Fey, I., & Stürmer, I. (2008). *Quality assurance methods for model-based development: A survey and assessment.* SAE 2007 Transactions Journal of Passenger Cars: Mechanical Systems. Detroit.

Fieber, F., Regnat, N., & Rumpe, B. (2009). Assessing usability of model based development in industrial projects. In T. Bailey, R. Vogel, & J. Mansell (Hrsg.), *CTIT Workshop Proceedings Series WP09-07*, (pp. 1-9). Enschede.

IABG. (2009). *From IABG: Das V-Modell XT.* Retrieved from http://v-modell.iabg.de

ISO 26262. (2010). *Road vehicles – Functional safety.*

ISO 9126. (1998). *IEEE standard for software test documentation.* New York

Jones, C. (1991). *Applied software measurement.* McGraw.

Kirstan, S., & Zimmermann, J. (2010). Evaluating costs and benefits of model-based development of embedded software systems in the car industry – Results of a qualitative case study. In *Proceedings Workshop C2M: EEMDD-From code centric to model centric: Evaluating the effectiveness of MDD.* ECMFA 2010 Paris.

Lederer, D. (2002). *The key to success: Seamless systems engineering process- An urgent task.* Elektronik Automotive. Retrieved from http://www.vectorconsulting.de/portal/medien/cmc/press

LinkedIn. (2011). *Website.* Retrieved from www.linkedin.com

Mercer Management Consulting und Frauenhofer Gesellschaft. (2004). *Future automotive industry structure 2015.*

Mohagheghi, P., & Dehlen, V. (2008). Where is the proof? - A review of experiences from applying MDE in industry. In Hartman, I. S. (Ed.), *ECMDA-FA 2008* (pp. 432–443). Berlin, Germany: Springer.

Murphy, B., Wakefield, A., & Friedman, J. (2008). Best practices for verification, validation and test in model-based design. Retrieved from www.mathworks.com/mason/tag/proxy.html?dataid=11031

Schätz, B. (2009). *Model-based development of software systems: From models to tools.* München: Habilitationsschrift, Technische Universität München.

Schätz, B., et al. (2004). *Model-based software and systems development – A white paper.* Retrieved from http://www4.in.tum.de/~schaetz/papers/ModelBased.pdf

Smith, P., Friedmann, S., & Prabhu, S. M. (2007). *(April 2007). Best practices for establishing a model-based design culture.* Sytems Engineering.

The Mathworks. (2010). *User stories from customers.* Retrieved from http://www.mathworks.com/control-systems/userstories.html

Xing. (2011). *Website.* Retrieved from www.xing.com

ADDITIONAL READING

Bowen, J. P. (2005). Ten Commandments Revisited: A Ten-Year Perspective on the Industrial Application of Formal Methods. *Proceedings of the 10 th Workshop on Formal Methods for Industrial Critical Systems (FMICS 2005)* (S. 8-16). Málaga: ACM Press.

Broy, M. (1997). Requirements Engineering for Embedded Systems. *Proceedings FemSys'97.* München.

Broy, M., Feilkas, M., Grünbauer, J., Gruler, A., Harhurin, A., & Hartmann, J. (2008). *Umfassendes Architekturmodell für das Engineering eingebetteter Software-intensiver Systeme.* München: Technical Report, Technische Universität München.

Broy, M., Feilkas, M., Herrmannsdoerfer, M., Merenda, S., & Ratiu, D. (2010). Seamless Model-Based Development: From Isolated Tools to Integrated Model Engineering Environment. *Proceedings of the IEEE, 98*(Issue 4), 526–545. doi:10.1109/JPROC.2009.2037771

Broy, M., Huber, F., Schätz, B., Philips, J., Prenniger, W., & Pretschner, A. (2004). *Model-based Software and Systems Development - A White Paper.* From http://www4.in.tum.de/~schaetz/papers/ModelBased.pdf

Broy, M., & Rumpe, B. (2007). Modulare hierarchische Modellierung als Grundlage der Software- und Systementwicklung. [München.]. *Informatik Spektrum, 30*(1), 3–18. doi:10.1007/s00287-006-0124-6

Erl, H.-P., & Kirstan, S. (2007). *Kosten- und Nutzen modellbasierter Softwareentwicklung im Automobil. Studie, Arthur D.* München: Little.

Juergens, E., Deissenböck, F., Hummel, B., & Wagner, S. (2009). Do Code Clones Matter? *ICSE '09: Proceedings of the 31st International Conference on Software Engineering,* (S. 485-495). Vancouver.

Juergens, E., Deissenboeck, F., Domann, C., Feilkas, M., Hummel, B., & Schaetz, B. (2010). Can Clone Detection Support Quality Assessments of Requirements Specifications? *ICSE '10: Proceedings of the 32nd International Conference on Software Engineering,* (S. 79-88). Kapstadt.

Kalix, E., & Bunzel, S. (2005). Integration modellbasierter Entwurfsverfahren in Softwareverifikation und –entwicklungsprozesse. *Tagungsband ASIM/GI-Fachgruppe 4.5.5 „Simulation technischer Systeme",* (S. 111-124). Berlin.

Kalix, E., & Schütte, O. (2007). Obstacles to the Adoption of Model-based Design within the Automotive Supply Industry. [Braunschweig.]. *Tagungsband des Dagstuhl-Workshops, 2007,* 29–34.

Kofler, T., Herrmannsdörfer, M., Merenda, S., Ratiu, D., & Thyssen, J. (2010). Model-based Development Tools for Embedded Systems in the Industry - Results from an Empirical Investigation. *ENVISION 2020 '10: Erster Workshop zur Zukunft der Entwicklung softwareintensiver, eingebetteter Systeme.* Paderborn.

Kramer, A. (2006). Modellbasiertes Testdesign - Ein Erfahrungsbericht. In R. B. Heinrich C. Mayr (Hrsg.), *Proceedings Modellierung 2006 LNI 82 GI 2006,* (S. 265-268). Innsbruck.

Kühl, M., & Reichmann, C. (Oktober 2007). Modellbasierte Architekturentwicklung von E/E-Systemen. *Automobil Elektronik,* S. 22-24.

Lamberg, K., & Beine, M. (2005). Test Methoden und Tools in der modellbasierten Funktionsentwicklung. *Proceedings der Jahrestagung der ASIM/GI-Fachgruppe 4.5.5 'Simulation technischer Systeme',* (S. 30-39). Berlin.

Leupers, R. (2000). Umfrage über Methoden und Techniken einer effizienten Codegenerierung zur Verbesserung der Produktivität in der Codegenerierung. *Proceedings of the 13th International Symposium on System Synthesis (ISSS'00),* (S. 173-178). Madrid.

Michailidis, A., Spieth, U., Ringler, T., Hedenetz, B., & Kowalewski, S. (2010). Test front loading in early stages of automotive software development based on AUTOSAR. *DATE '10 Proceedings of the Conference on Design, Automation and Test in Europe*, (S. 435-440). Leuven.

Mohagheghi, P., & Dehlen, V. (2007). An Overview of Quality Frameworks in Model - Driven Engineering and Observation on Transformation Quality. *Proceedings of the 2nd Workshop on Quality in Modeling Co-located with MoDELS 2007*, (S. 3-17). Nashville.

Moretti, G. (2007). *Best Practices for Adopting Model-Based Design in Electronic System Development.* From www.mathworks.com/mason/tag/proxy.html

Pretschner, A. (2005). One Evaluation of Model-Based Testing and its Automation. *Proceedings 27th International Conference on Software Engineering (ICSE'05)*, (S. 392-401). St. Louis.

Pretschner, A., & Leucker, M. (2005). Model-Based Testing – A Glossary. In Broy, M., & Jonsson, B. (Eds.), *J.-P. Katoen, M. Leucker, Pretschner, & Alexander, Model-Based Testing of Reactive Systems.* Springer Verlag. doi:10.1007/11498490_27

Schätz, B. (2009). *Model-Based Development of Software Systems: From Models to Tools.* München: Habilitationsschrift, Technische Universität München.

Schätz, B., Fleischmann, A., Geisberger, E., & Pister, M. (2005). Modellbasierte Anforderungsmodellierung in AutoRAID. *Proceedings of Informatik 2005 Workshop Modellbasierte Qualitätssicherung.* Bonn: Springer.

Schätz, B., Pister, M., & Wisspeinter, A. (2003). Von Anforderungsanalyse in der modellbasierten Entwicklung am Beispiel von AutoFocus; Vortrag bei dem GI-Treffen Fachgruppe RE, 27/12/03 - 28/12/03: http://www4.in.tum.de/~schaetz/slides/Schaetz-GI-RE-271203.pdf abgerufen

Schätz, B., Pister, M., & Wisspeintner, A. (2004). Anforderungsanalyse in der modellbasierten Entwicklung am Beispiel von AutoFocus. *Softwaretechnik-Trends 24(1)*.

Schätz, B., Pretschner, A., Huber, F., & Philipps, J. (2002). Model-Based Development of Embedded Systems. In J.-M. In: Bruel, & Z. (. Bellahsene (Hrsg.), *Advances in Object-Oriented Information Systems OOIS 2002 Workshops.* Montpellier.

Schlosser, J. (2005). *Architektursimulation von verteilten Steuergeräten, Technische Universität München.* München: Doktorarbeit.

van Lamsweerde, A. (2000). Formal Specification: a Roadmap. *Proceedings of the Conference on The Future of Software Engineering*, (S. 147 - 159). Limerick.

Vitkin, L., Dong, S., Searcy, R., & BC, M. (2006). *Effort Estimation in Model-Based Software Development.* Technical Paper, SAE Technical Paper Series, In-Vehicle Software & Hardware Systems (SP-2028), Detroit.

von der Beeck, M., Braun, P., Rappl, M., & Schroder, C. (2002). Model based requirements engineering for embedded software. *Proceedings of the 10th Anniversary Joint IEEE International Requirements Engineering Conference (RE'02)*, (S. 92). Essen.

Weber, M., & Weisbrod, J. (2003). Requirements Engineering in Automotive Development – Experiences and Challenges. *IEEE Software, 20(1), 2003*, (S. 16-24).

Wohlgemuth, F., Dziobeck, C., & Ringler, T. (2008). Von Autosar im Entwicklungsprozess: Vorgehen bei der Serieneinführung der modellbasierten AUTOSAR-Funktionsentwicklung: http://www.dspace.de

Ziegenbein, D., Freund, U., Braun, P., Sandner, R., Bauer, A., & Romberg, J. (2005). AutoMoDe - model-Based Development of Automotive Software. *Proceedings of the 2005 Conference on Design, Automation and Test in Europe (DATE)*, (S. 171-176). München

KEY TERMS AND DEFINITIONS

Cost and Benefit Analysis: The aim of a cost and benefit analysis is to analyze what an investment in a new product or technology would cost and which benefit i.e. cost savings it can bring.

Economics: We define economics as the factors of the magical triangle of the project management: Cost, time and quality.

Empirical Study: An empirical study is a survey, where companies are asked which quantitative changes they have i.e. in development costs. The data, which has been collected via the survey will be analyzed via statistical methods.

Frontloading: In our case frontloading means the possibility to shift the testing activities in earlier development phases compared to a classical hand-coded design (i.e. from module test into the SW-Design).

Function Model: The function model is the model which is being used during the SW-Design. In the function model the functional logic is being modeled. The function model will be used in the implementation phase for the code generation.

Modeling Degree: Degree of functionality which has been modeled in a function model like a Matlab/Simulink/Stateflow or ASCET-SD model.

Return on Investment: The aim of a return on investment analyses is to find out how long it takes until the investments have been amortized.

Simulation: Simulation is a technique to test i.e. the function model if it is modeled correctly.

Section 4
Miscellaneous

Chapter 14
Reusable Modelling Tool Assets:
Deployment of MDA Artefacts

Miguel A. de Miguel
Technical University of Madrid, Spain

Emilio Salazar
Technical University of Madrid, Spain

Juan P. Silva
Technical University of Madrid, Spain

Javier Fernandez-Briones
Technical University of Madrid, Spain

ABSTRACT

Model driven development attempts to resolve some common problems of current software architectures in order to reduce the complexity of software development: i) how to increase the level of abstraction by centring on software models; ii) how to automate the software development process through the use of transformations and generators; and iii) how to separate domain, technology, and technological concerns so as to avoid confusion arising from the combination of different types of concepts. Model driven development uses two basic solutions to resolve these problems: i) description of specialised modelling languages and ii) model transformations and mappings. For each domain and technology, MDSD (Model-Driven Software Development) requires specific MDA (Model Driven Architecture) artefacts for the definition of specialised languages and transformations that address specific modelling languages and platforms. The application of MDSD in a specific domain and technology combines multiple interdependent MDA technologies (e.g. MOF (Meta-Object Facilities), QVT (Query-View and Transformation), MOF2Text, UML (Unified Modelling Language) extensions, and OCL (Object Constraint Language)); MDSD combines these technologies to construct and improve tools that support the model driven development process adapted to specific domains, technologies, and platforms (e.g. e-commerce, safety-critical software systems, and SOA (Service Oriented Architecture)).

DOI: 10.4018/978-1-61350-438-3.ch014

The maintenance and evolution of software models require solutions in order to integrate all these MDA technologies and avoid dependency on their tools. The various kinds of MDA artefacts have interdependencies (e.g. model transformation and modelling language extensions), which complicate their reuse and their adaptation to new development environments. This chapter proposes solutions for the integration of all MDA technologies based on reusable modelling tool assets, and solutions for deploying artefacts so as to provide modelling tool independence. MDSD must address these problems, because in the near future, the migration of these developments to new development platforms will be as complex as current migrations from one specific run-time platform to another.

INTRODUCTION

A basic objective of model-driven software development is to place emphasis on the model when developing software. This is a change from the current situation, in that it shifts the role of models from contemplative to productive. The goal of model-driven engineering is to define a complete life-cycle method based on the use of various models automating a seamless process from analysis to code generation (Frankel 2003). This discipline puts all the software artefacts in the right place (e.g. business models, architectural models and design patterns) and actively uses them in order to produce and deploy applications.

Models provide solutions for different types of problems: i) description of problems and their concepts, ii) validation of descriptions and concepts represented through checking and analysis techniques, iii) model transformation and generation of code, configurations, and documentation.

Separation of concerns avoids the confusion generated by combining different types of concepts. Model-driven approaches introduce solutions for specialising models for specific concerns and for interconnecting concerns based on model transformations. This approach reduces the complexity of models through specialised modelling activities that are separated. It improves communications between stakeholders by using models to support the exchange of information. However, separation of concerns often requires specialised modelling languages to describe specific concerns,

and the interoperability of specialised languages requires tools integration.

MDA proposes a set of languages and technologies (Miguel et al. 2002) to construct of modelling tools that adapt MDSD to specific platforms (e.g. EJB (Enterprise Java Beans), RTSJ (Real-Time Java Specification)) and technologies (e.g. transactions, security). Standards defining such languages are: MOF (OMG 2006), QVT (OMG 2011), MOF2Text (OMG 2008a), OCL (OMG 2010b), UML (OMG 2009a), UML profiles and RAS (Reusable Asset Specification) (OMG 2005). MDSD combines these languages to create artefact infrastructures, applicable in modelling tools, to then construct MDSD environments. However the artefact's dependence on tool's infrastructures makes the artefacts tool-dependent and therefore application models are also tool-dependent. The MDA philosophy to avoid platform dependency based on PIM (Platform Independent Model) and PSM (Platform Specific Models) is not reflected in the development of MDA artefacts. For example, UML modelling-tool facilities, such as profile registration and support of stereotype applications based on modelling framework tools (e.g. EMF (Eclipse Modelling Framework)), make the profiles and the models that reuse the profiles tool dependent. When exporting the models, the profiles must be exported too, and manual adaptations must be done within the model, because the profiles installed in the target tool cannot be reused. This process requires extensive experience working with models and is not feasible for complex models.

From a conceptual view-point, this chapter addresses four important challenges of MDSD methods:

1. MDA artefact development requires significant effort and has a large number of modelling tool dependencies. Adoption of these technologies must be flexible and should not impose specific development environments. The solutions proposed in this chapter improve the *adoption of MDA artefacts in different modelling frameworks* and this improves the adoption of MDA artefacts because it does not impose specific tools.

2. MDA proposes solutions to reduce dependencies on execution platforms, but it creates dependencies on modelling tools. The solutions proposed in this chapter increase the maintainability of model-driven applications because they increase the *portability of MDA artefacts* and this avoids dependencies on modelling tools.

3. OMG has created multiple standards and languages for the specification of transformation behaviours and MDA functionality. These languages include QVT operational, QVT relational, MOF2Text, OCL and Java. No standard solutions are defined for the interoperability of these languages (e.g. invoke QVT transformations from Java or from MOF2Text). This chapter proposes solutions for handling and simplifying this *MDA behaviour artefact interoperability*.

4. *The learning curve of MDA infrastructures* for specific domains and technologies (e.g. DSL, specific transformations and generators, specific UML extensions) should be as short as possible and their application should increase productivity as much as possible. The relationships between learning duration and application benefits must be positive, and only a well planned learning curve can make this relationship positive. The solutions

introduced in this chapter pay special attention to the integration of MDA artefacts and to tool support for tutorials and documentation of domain specific MDA artefacts.

This chapter introduces the concept of Reusable Modelling Asset (RMA) and its application. RMA defines formats for interchanging assets, including MDA artefacts, to make them reusable in different modelling tools, and to support their tools' independence. This solution is based on the MDATC OMG Standard (OMG 2009d). ERMA is an implementation of this framework in *Eclipse*. Implementations of Eclipse Reusable Modelling Assets (ERMA) are available[1]. The RAS standard (OMG 2005) defines languages and infrastructures for the interchange of software assets. RMA defines an RAS profile that extends the default RAS profile to support the description of MDA artefacts that can be combined to create a specific modelling-tool asset, supporting the application of MDSD in specific domains and technologies. Figure 1 represents the general structure of an ERMA asset file. This structure is based on the RAS standard.

RMA provides solutions for interchanging and combining MDA artefacts, concentrating most modelling tool dependencies in RMA implementations; RMA makes assets reusable in different modelling tools. RMA defines services for: i) editing RMA assets and their artefacts, ii) packaging artefacts and metadata into RAS format enabling the relocation of models (e.g. UML profiles, abstract and concrete modelling language specifications) and transformations (e.g. QVT operational, and MOF2Text modules), iii) delivery of assets to RAS repositories, iv) downloading of assets, validating and relocating asset dependencies (dependencies with other assets and with external artefacts) on the target platform, v) deployment of assets and customisation for the target platform, and vi) installation/de-installation of deployed artefacts.

Figure 1. RMA file general structure

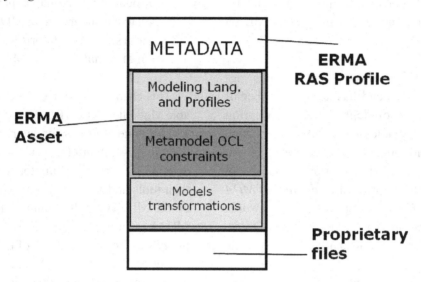

Eclipse plug-ins and features (Shavior et al. 2003), and OSGi Bundles (OSGi Service Platform 2009) are examples of software infrastructures that could be used to support RMA objectives, but they have four significant features that RMA tries to avoid: i) *Eclipse* plug-ins and OSGi Bundles are designed to support Java applications, while RMA is designed to support modelling languages and behaviour specification including languages such as QVT and MOF2Text, which are not supported in plug-ins and bundles. ii) *Eclipse* plug-ins depends on the *Eclipse* tool, while RMA attempts to avoid tool dependency as much as possible. RMA is based on OMG standards, for which there are only two important exceptions: EMF and GMF. EMF is currently the de-facto standard in defining modelling languages and *GenModel* models provide support to avoid modifications to generated code. This language specification does not have an equivalent in EMOF. Diagram Definition (DD) (OMG 2010c) is the OMG standard that supports the same concepts supported in GMF, but this standard is in the process of being finalised and there is no *Eclipse* open source implementation available yet. iii) Plug-ins and bundles are not designed to be integrated into RAS frameworks (e.g. their integration in RAS repositories and

management tools would require a wrapper asset that describes the asset, which should describe concepts such as plug-in dependencies in terms of asset dependencies). IBM has created some adaptations in asset management tools to support this approach for *Eclipse* features and plug-ins. iv) RMA is designed to be edited in RMA diagrams (a DSL (Domain Specific Language) and a diagram editor, an alternative to which could be a UML profile) that support the editing of RMA assets; XML schemas, text editors and specialised editors support the editing of plug-ins and bundle manifest files. Some UML modelling tools (e.g. RSA[2], Modelio[3] and AndroMDA[4]) provide frameworks for editing and handling modules and cartridges that integrate different kinds of artefacts, but they frequently only support a limited number of artefacts and are sometimes tool specific; we cannot interchange these modules between different tools.

IBM-Rational has done some important developments of tools (e.g. Rational Asset Manager) and methods (Ackerman et al. 2008) for the application of asset-based software development. These solutions are well integrated with UML modelling tools.

The current implementation of ERMA is based on several *Eclipse* incubation projects and is therefore in a evolving state (e.g. *QVTo* has modified the type of URI (Uniform Resource Identifier) accepted in the *modeltypes* definition in recent *Eclipse* versions; incubation versions of QVT Relations support some QVT standard packages such as *QVTRelation* and *QVTBase* but some packages, such as *QVTOperational,* are supported in neither QVT declarative nor QVT operational, and because of this, QVT abstract syntax and QVT XMI (XML Metadata Interchange) interchange are only partially integrated).

ERMA has been used in the development of multiple assets. These are assets that allow model driven support for complex kinds of development such as Safety applications and MARTE based model development environments (see the annex to this chapter). ERMA RAS repositories provide multiple assets for these two types of development environments (MARTE based development and Safe-Aware modelling systems). These assets support several kinds of MDA artefacts, such as UML profiles and model libraries, QVTo, Acceleo and Java transformations, *ecore* and *genmodel* based DSL and OCL based commands. These DSL languages integrate some analysis tools into Eclipse, such as Item Toolkit for safety analysis and MAST for real-time analysis. These assets have been developed to demonstrate the applicability of ERMA in real applications.

In the remainder of this chapter, Section 2 introduces the RMA life cycle to apply RMA concepts, Section 3 introduces the RMA specification language, Section 4 describes the design and implementation of asset deployments, Section 5 introduces future work, and finally Section 6 includes some discussion and conclusions.

GENERAL INTRODUCTION TO THE RMA LIFE-CYCLE

The development and application of RMAs are broken down into several phases. Two important kinds of modeller actors are: *RMA developer*

and *applications modeller*. The *RMA developer* designs and implements modelling infrastructures that should be reusable in different projects developed for the same domain and technologies. The *application modeller* develops the application models and reuses the assets in the RMA that are available for the construction of application models and their implementation.

Figure 2 summarises the activity phases in RMA development and application, and Figure 3 represents an example of the deployment of tools to execute these activities. These phases and activities are:

1. **Development**: The *RMA developer* carries out development activities on MDA artefacts. Development places most of the effort in the RMA life-cycle and, in particular, in the development of MDA artefacts. All activities in this phase would be executed in the *Eclipse Source Modelling Tool* node in Figure 3. The results of this phase are RMA assets that can be released.

   a. *Development of MDA Artefacts.* MDA artefacts are: UML Profiles, UML model libraries, QVT, Java and MOF2Text transformations, DSL abstract (EMF) and concrete syntax (GMF), and additional elements such as OCL and GUI (Graphical User Interface) wizards. The *RMA developer* should use specific editors such as UML profile modellers, and QVT editors.

   b. *RMA Editing.* The RMA modeller is based on the RMA specification language (introduced in Section 3). This language supports the integration of MDA artefacts into a common asset; and the RMA model defines the contents of the RMA asset and its dependencies on external artefacts. MDA artefacts are developed with a common purpose (e.g. to support the application of MDSD in technologies

Figure 2. RMA development and application phases and activities

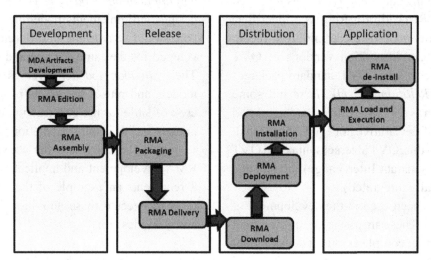

such as SOA), and different kinds of artefacts can be combined (e.g. UML extensions, DSL for configuration languages, model transformations and code generators). The RMA models combine all these artefacts into a common asset.

c. *RMA Assembly*: Frequently an RMA asset depends on other assets for several reasons: i) the input and output languages of behaviours are included in other assets, ii) the pipeline combines transformations and generators to generate target code or documents, and the generators and transformations

Figure 3. Example of distribution for RMA servers and modelling tools

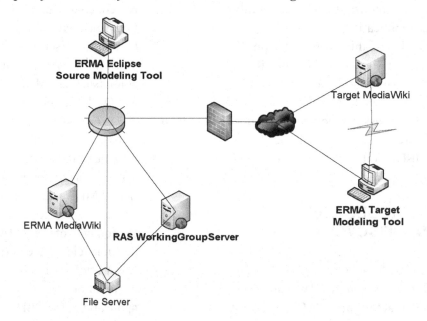

are distributed over several assets; a pipeline transformation combines all these transformations. iii) A new language is defined that extends profiles or modelling languages included in other assets, and the extension reuses behaviours included in the extended models. iv) Some general purpose assets are applicable in multiple contexts and specialised assets reuse and customise these general assets (e.g. façade assets that provide support for handling several languages, for example *ecore* and UML, with a common meta-model façade). The RMA language includes assembly dependencies, usage relationships on behaviours included in other assets, and dependencies for describing references to artefacts included in other assets or in the modelling tool (e.g. dependencies on standard languages meta-models such as OCL).

1. **Release**: The editing and assembly of an asset yields a specification of the contents and dependencies of the asset. This specification includes references to the models and files developed with MDA artefacts editors (e.g. MOF2Text modules, and Java jar files). This specification will be used to publish the asset in an RMA asset repository. To publish the asset, we must package the asset in an RAS file and deliver it to the repository:

   a. *RMA Packaging*: the packaging of assets takes into account all references from the RMA specification and packages all models and files into a single RAS (OMG 2005) file (a zip file which includes a manifest file that provides a description of the asset contents and dependencies). The packaging resolves the relocation of models; RMA packaging supports *zip* and *ras* URI schemes to reference modelling elements embedded in other RAS files. As an asset can assemble other assets, contained in the global asset; the packaging will include container and containment assets in a common RAS file. The *Eclipse Source Modelling Tool* node in Figure 3 executes the RMA packaging.

   b. *RMA Delivery*: The RAS asset includes the manifest file, and we can deliver the asset in a RAS repository that supports the ERMA RAS profile. Modelling tools can connect to the repository, search for and download assets in the repository. Delivery takes into account asset identifiers and version numbers for the identification of assets in the repository. In the deployment scenario included in Figure 3, the delivered asset will be available in the *RAS Working Group Server* repository; in the ERMA implementation, a WebSphere SOA server hosts this repository.

2. **Distribution**: An *application modeller* can reuse RMA assets for the construction of application models and for their transformation.

   a. *RMA Download*: *The application modeller* can search for assets and look through the documentation in the assets, selecting the assets to reuse it in its modelling tools and models. Downloading an asset will copy the asset from the repository and will create an asset project in the target tool for the deployment and installation of the asset. In the example depicted in Figure 3, the *ERMA Target Modelling Tool* is the target tool and it downloads the asset from the *RAS Working Group Server* while the documentation is available at the *ERMA MediaWiki* server.

   b. *RMA Deployment*: Section 4 includes a detailed description of deployment activity for the asset and its artefacts. The RMA implementation within the target modelling tool supports the deployment of assets and artefacts into the target modelling tool. The deployment reuses target tool infrastructures (e.g. plug-ins, projects, profile supports) for the integration of new artefacts into the target tool. In the example in Figure 3, the *ERMA Target Modelling Tool* executes the deployment; embedded documentation will be deployed at *Target MediaWiki*, and the remaining artefacts are deployed at the *ERMA Target Modelling Tool*.

 c. *RMA Installation*: Deployment generates artefacts for the target modelling tool, and these artefacts are installed in the target tool. This installation is tool-dependent. But in *Eclipse*-based modelling tools, installation will include plug-ins, projects and features that the deployment generates.

1. **Application**: *The application modeller reuses asset behaviour and modelling languages and extensions to construct application models.* In the example in Figure 3, the *ERMA Target Modelling Tool* executes the asset application.

 a. *RMA Loading and Execution*: The installed artefacts create new types of repositories to support new DSLs, installation registers, new UML profiles and model libraries, creating new commands that support the execution of transformations and generators. They also provide new commands to access documentation and for general asset configuration. All these new facilities support the application of MDSD techniques in the domain and technologies supported in the asset.

 b. *RMA De-install*: The target modelling tool can de-install the asset if the asset facilities are not going to be reused. De-installation removes the UML profiles and model libraries, the modelling

languages supported in the asset and the commands that provide access to transformations in the target tool.

INTRODUCTION TO THE RMA LANGUAGE SPECIFICATION

The RMA language specification is based on the MDATC (OMG 2009d) standard. The RMA language provides support for the description of MDA artefacts that are combined for a common purpose. In *Eclipse Modelling,* MDA, languages and frameworks have associated editors and run-time support for the specific languages (e.g. *ecore* modeller, QVTo editor, MOF2Text language editor); but there is no common framework for the description of integrated solutions.

ERMA use the RMA language for two main purposes: editing RMA assets to define their contents and dependencies, and generating the RAS manifest file (*METADATA* in the *ras* file in Figure 1). The ERMA framework includes an EMF-based implementation of the RMA language, a GMF based RMA diagram editor, and a QVT transformation from the RMA language to the RAS ERMA profile. Figure 4 shows the integration of the ERMA diagram editor and QVT transformation into the RAS ERMA Profile. The editor integrates ERMA models and diagrams and other MDA editors, and it also handles ERMA models (supported in an EMF repository). ERMA packaging tools integrate the QVT transformation from an ERMA model to an ERMA RAS manifest file defining the *ras* file contents. Figure 7 includes an example of an RMA diagram; this diagram represents four assets, five *assembly* relationships and three *import* dependencies. Each asset in the diagram includes some artefacts (QVT, EMF, MOF2Text and Java jar). These artefacts define new modelling languages and their associated transformations. The *Global* asset reuses transformations included in other assets and provides

Figure 4. ERMA modeller and RAS manifest file generator

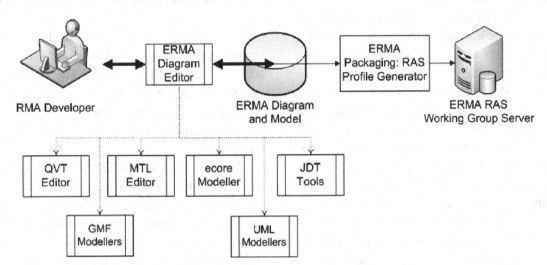

a GUI command (*GlobalCommand*) to execute the combined transformation.

The RMA Language specification is an extension of the *Constructs* package in *UML Infrastructure* (OMG 2009b). The RMA language specification merges *Constructs* and *PrimitiveTypes* packages into *UML Infrastructure* and packages that include the RMA language specification. *Constructs* is the package that merges the *Kernel* package in *UML Superstructure* (OMG 2009a) (*Kernel* is the specification core for UML class concepts in the UML 2.x *Superstructure*) and provides a minimum language for the presentation of classes, packages and simple data types. The ERMA reuses and modifies the *UML Infrastructure* standard; but the ERMA complies with the standard and only modifies the body constraints of meta-class operations and the constraint annotations of derived associations to support *UML Infrastructure* behaviours in OCL and *ecore* (operation bodies and derived associations are implemented in OCL and the code of operations and derived associations are embedded in the ERMA *ecore* meta-models). The RMA extensions to *UML Infrastructure* include constructors for the representation of MDA artefacts (Sections 3.1 and 3.2), and *interaction points* that represent functionality provided in the asset (Sec-

tion 3.3), and relationships for the description of assets and artefact dependencies (Section 3.4). RMA modelling elements include references to the following modelling language specifications: MOF2Text, QVT, GenModel, *ecore*, GMF gmf-graph, GMF gmfmap, GMF tooldef, UML *Superstructure* and OCL. The ERMA implementation of *erma* language, in *ecore*, includes references to the equivalent *ecore* meta-models.

RMA Artifacts

RMA assets are the core modelling elements in the RMA modelling language, and RMA artefacts are the main elements used to describe assets.

RMA supports three kinds of MDA artefacts: artefacts for defining modelling languages, software behaviour artefacts for handling and transforming models, and general artefacts. Table 1 depicts the different types of artefacts. Software behaviour artefacts describe transformations and other behaviours (e.g. model queries) provided in the asset. Modelling language artefacts define modelling languages to extend UML modellers and to create new DSLs. Assets can reuse elements in the modelling languages as data types (e.g. parameters, results and invocation context) to describe the provided functionalities. The RMA can contain artefacts that will be embedded in the asset, and RMA assets can reference standard artefacts available in any modelling tool (e.g. OCL meta-model and UML profile *Standard*), as well as artefacts contained in other assets.

The RMA language considers two modelling language specifications: UML modelling language extensions (based on UML profiles and UML model libraries) and DSLs (based on EMF and GMF). The RMA language specification includes four modelling elements for describing these kinds of artefacts, and each modelling element specialises in describing one artefact type.

In the RMA specification, artefact meta-classes extend the *Infrastructure::Core::Constructs::Package* meta-class and one attribute of the *UML infrastructure* packages is *visibility*. Allowed values for *visibility* are *private*, *package* and *public*. Only elements in the asset can reference *private* artefacts, other assets can reuse and extend *public* artefacts and only elements in the same RMA package[5] can include references to *package* artefacts. The relationships between artefacts depend on the languages (e.g. GMF include references to *ecore* and other GMF models, and UML profiles can include references to other UML profiles and UML model libraries), but all these references (or inheritances) must guarantee the *visibility* of the artefacts.

RMA Software Behaviour Languages

The RMA asset specifications include model handlers to transform models and to use or edit the information they contain. The *application modeller* and other asserts can use these handlers (in the case of *public* artefacts), or they can be used for local purposes only (in the case of *private* artefacts).

Software behaviour artefacts support the implementation of functional specifications (e.g. transformations, generators, GUI wizards and edition support) included in the assets. MDA languages used to represent software behaviours are QVT, MOF2Text and Java. EMF *ecore* operations can also be used in the description of software behaviours (EMF artefacts can represent modelling languages or software behaviour or both). OCL and Java can describe implementations of *ecore* operations. RMA *interaction points* (Section 3.3) specify software behaviour operations that are handled in the asset, and they are also the core elements for the specification of commands, operation calls and other asset behaviours.

Software behaviour artefacts can include dependencies: one artefact can reuse another artefact in the same language. QVT, MOF2Text and *ecore* behaviours can invoke operations in Java jar artefacts (Java jar artefacts can support QVT *black-boxes* and Java implementations of *ecore*

Table 1. Software behaviour, modelling language and general artefacts

Types of RMA Artefacts	RMA Artefacts	

Software Behavior	• EMF Meta-model
	• MOF2Text
	  o MOF2Text concrete syntax
	  o MOF2Text XMI model
	• Java Jar
		• QVT
		  o QVT Operational
		    ▪ QVTo concrete syntax
		    ▪ QVTo XMI model
		  o QVT Relational
		    o QVTr concrete syntax
		    o QVTr XMI model

Modelling Languages	• UML Profile • UML Model Library	• EMF Meta-model • GMF Diagram Definition
General	• Media Wiki documents • Icons	• Executables • Others

operations can reference Java libraries contained in other Java artefacts), and Java artefacts can invoke any kind of behaviour.

RMA Interaction Points

Many languages support MDA behaviours (in RMA they are QVTo, QVTr, MOF2Text, OCL, Java) and they are interoperable. RMA *interaction points* reduce the complexity of interaction and simplify the invocation of behaviours from one language to another.

RMA *interaction points* specify functionality that the RMA asset supports and they also specify the interfaces between behaviour artefacts. An *interaction point* has an associated set of *UML infrastructure* operations that specify the services supported at the *interaction point*. OCL body constraints or software behaviours (Java methods, *ecore* operations, QVT transformations and mappings, and MOF2Text modules) support the implementation of operations at *interaction points* (multiple artefacts can support the same *interaction point*, but an operation only has one associated artefact or one OCL value expression). The RMA language supports OCL constraints on the description of the body of operations (RMA reuses UML *Infrastructure* to describe operations). When the *interaction point* implementation is in another language, it references behaviours based on *interaction point implementation* relationships (this is a relationship between a software behaviour artefact and an *interaction point*). An *interaction point* specification can be associated with an execution context (OCL and EMF software behaviours require a context). The run-time execution of an *interaction point* operation must be performed within the context of a data type that defines the *interaction point* context. Frequently, the context references a meta-class that defines the type of modelling elements that can be used as run-time context.

The RMA asset specification includes *RMA call provided* and *RMA call required*. *RMA call required* represents language independent behaviour to be reused. Asset assembly must link *RMA call required* and *RMA call provided* to identify the asset in the target tool that will support the software behaviour. All *RMA call required* elements in an asset must be resolved before packaging. The *implementation of external interaction* modelling element represents the relationship between *call required* and *call provided* elements.

Interaction points are used for four purposes:

- *To define commands that the asset includes in GUI menus*: an asset specification can include the GUI commands provided in the asset. The command specification includes the symbolic name for the command, a reference to the icon, and a reference to the *interaction point* that specifies the behaviour. The deployment of assets generates tool-dependent code to support the command execution: the code takes the execution context into account, requests values for the operation parameters, invokes the implementation operation, and displays the execution results. *GlobalCommand* in Figure 7 is an example of a provided command; the Java implementation (*GlobalImpl*) consists of two transformations (*ModelX2Modely* and *Modely2CodeZ*).

- *To describe functionality that one asset provides to other assets*: the asset can provide services to other assets. The main purpose of *interaction points* is to reduce language dependencies among assets. When asset maintenance modifies the implementation language for an *interaction point*, and the operations have the same interface, the clients do not need to be modified. The deployment of *interaction points* that support *call provided* generates Java, and QVT and MOF2Text *black-boxes*. Software behaviour languages use generated code and the RMA run-time reflexion APIs (Application

Programming Interface) to invoke operations in a language independent way. The modelling elements *interaction point*, *RMA call provided* and *implementation of external interaction* specify the provided services. *ModelX2ModelY*, *QueryInX*, and *ModelY2CodeZ* in Figure 7 are examples of *RMA call provided* modelling elements. The *implementation of external interaction* modelling element links these elements with their implementation specification in *interaction points*.

- *Local interoperations:* software behaviour assets can invoke the execution of *private* operations implemented in some other artefact (in the same language or a different language) defined in the same asset. For local interoperations, the asset includes the specification of *interaction points* but it does not include the specification of *RMA call provided*.

- *Behaviours to execute during the installation and de-installation of assets*: Asset specifications can include the specification of *interaction points* that should be executed during the installation and de-installation of assets. In general these are *private* behaviours.

RMA Relationships

The previous subsection introduced three relationships in RMA modelling language: *implementation of external interaction, implementation of interaction point* and *implementation of external interaction*. The RMA extends *UML Infrastructure* and the RMA specification reuses and extends relationships included in the *UML Infrastructure* meta-model (e.g. *DirectedRelationship*).

Two fundamental relationships in the RMA language are:

- *External artefact references*: frequently, software behaviour assets and modelling

language artefacts extend or reuse standard behaviour and languages available in MDA modelling tools (e.g. UML metamodel, OCL model library, and Java standard libraries). The RMA *reference* relationship represents these dependencies; the dependent artefacts can extend and invoke the modelling elements and behaviours, and *interaction points* can reuse the metaclasses to define context and operation data types. The deployment of assets must take these dependencies into account.

- *Assembly of assets*: the *implementation of external interaction* and *assembly* relationships will represent these dependencies, when an asset reuses artefacts in another asset. The deployment and installation of assets will resolve these dependencies in the target platform. The RMA supports two types of *assembly* specification: embedded assembly and combined (not embedded) assembly. Embedded assembly represents the composition of assets to create a more complex asset, while combined assembly represents some aggregation dependencies (several assets can be combined into a common asset, but combiner assets do not package or deploy the combined asset). The release of an asset that embeds other assets will package, in the same asset file, the artefacts in the embedded asset and artefacts included in the container asset. The distribution of combined assets will resolve asset assembly, and the assembled asset must be available in the target tool for the distribution of assembler assets. Figure 7 includes some combined assembly relationships, where the *LanguageY* asset includes a modelling language specification (*Y*), and the *CodeZ* asset includes a generator from *Y* to *Z*. The generator can only be executed when the source language is supported in the target tool, and because of this assembly is needed. This assembly is combined and not embedded, because it would be possible to have a modelling tool that supports *Y* language and does not support the generator.

Related Work

RMA language and infrastructures depends on several OMG standards (*UML Superstructure* (OMG 2009a), QVT (OMG 2011), MOF2Text (OMG 2008a), MOF (OMG 2006) and OCL (OMG 2010b)) and three standards in particular: MDATC (OMG 2009d), *UML Infrastructure* (OMG 2009b) and RAS (OMG 2005). The implementation of these standards in *Eclipse Modelling* is the main reference for ERMA design.

Some UML modelling tools and MDA frameworks integrate modelling tool extensions solutions. These extension approaches are tool specific, and they integrate specific types of artefacts and languages to specify transformations. Some tool examples are:

- *Modelio: Modules. Modelio* is a UML modelling tool and its environment supports the installation of modules that customise the tool for specific technologies and domains. The two fundamental artefacts in modules are UML profiles and Java based transformations. Java transformations are based on a proprietary API to access repositories.
- *IBM Rational Software Architect: Pluglet.* Pluglets are Java applications that are integrated into the RSA/Eclipse modelling tool that can access the application model in the model space using EMF/UML2 interfaces. RSA still does not integrate *QVT Relational* or *Acceleo* projects.
- *AndroMDA: Cartridges.* Cartridges provide support for handling model elements, in particular, annotated elements with stereotypes or model elements that meet certain conditions. Cartridges process these

elements using template files defined within the cartridge descriptor.

RMA language and services are based on the MDATC standard, which proposes solutions for the integration of MDA artefacts and RAS. *Bendraou* and others [4,5] encourage using the MDATC concept, but they do not provide solutions for integration into RAS standards or *Eclipse Modelling* tools.

Model-Bus modelling infrastructure [2,6] look for solutions to integrate different kinds of modelling tool services. Model-Bus is centred in the model service concept. Model-Bus provides support to communicate with different model services, but is not centred on the interchange of these services between modelling tools.

IBM and other companies have developed infrastructures and tools for the application of asset-based software development. These solutions, in general, are oriented to software applications development [11,12,13]. This chapter focuses on the construction of assets for development and application of MDA artefacts. Rational Asset Manager[6] is good example of a framework for the management of assets; it provides solutions for the construction, export and import of assets, and it is well integrated with RSA modelling tool. IBM has customized these tools for the development of MDA artefacts (Ackerman et al. 2008). But IBM engineers paid special attention to RSA specific kinds of artefacts or *Eclipse* specific artefacts (e.g. JET, Java Emitter Templates, and plug-in features. See chapters 18, 19 and 20 in (Ackerman et al. 2008)) and there is no special attention to the customization of assets in alternative modelling tools (other than RSA). These solutions need improvements for the application of standards such as QVT and MOF2Text, and for the support of concrete syntaxes and DSL graphical editors. Solutions presented in this chapter, such as the integration of UML profiles in meta-model frameworks, could improve these methods and tools.

DEPLOYMENT OF RMA ASSETS

Point 3.b (*Distribution – Deployment*) in Section 2 introduces RMA deployment activity and its integration within the RMA life-cycle. This section introduces the most important challenges and their solutions using *Eclipse Modelling Tools* for the deployment of RMA assets. The challenges are broken down into several subsections, and each subsection includes a subset of the solutions. The solutions included in this chapter (ERMA) depend on implementations integrated into *Eclipse Modeling Tools*[7], *Helios Release* SR2 (build id: 20110218-0911) and the *Eclipse* EMF, MDT, M2M, M2T, and GMF projects integrated in this release.

General Issues of MDA Artifact Deployment

The deployment of an RMA asset creates new mechanisms in the target tool to support MDA artefacts. Deployment distributes and relocates models, templates, java jar files and other MDA artefacts around these new mechanisms. Relocation and redistribution in target mechanisms must resolve several general problems:

Challenge 1.1 - Relocation of internal RMA references and zip and ras URI schemes. To maintain the consistency of models and other artefacts, references must be updated during relocations. RMA relocation solutions are based on XMI (OMG 2008b) interchanging models. The URI is the most common solution to support references in XMI. RMA is also based on RAS, and RAS packages artefacts in *ras* format (*zip* files with the RAS structure and manifest files). To make both approaches compatible, deployment in the target tool must support *zip* and *ras* schemes in URI handlers. The implementation of eclipse used does not support these schemes.

Challenge 1.2 - Relocation of external RMA references. Models in *ras* files can include references to models and files embedded in other assets.

During its life cycle an asset has multiple locations and, before application, the reused-assets models are relocated into target tool mechanisms (e.g. projects, configuration files and cartridges), where references must be updated to the new locations. Relocations must be considered when deploying and installing reused assets. Relocations update the following references (targets can be both internal artefacts and reused-assets artefacts): external references in UML profiles, model libraries, EMF models, GMF models, QVT and MOF2Text XMI files, URI in QVTo *model types* and input *typed models* in MOF2Text. RMA models includes references to MDA artefacts, URL references to general artefacts such as *MediaWiki* documents and icons, and references to Java jar files.

Challenge 1.3 - Visibility of MDA artefacts. In general, the *application modeller* reuses the installed MDA artefacts (profiles, *ecore* models, transformations) embedded in an RMA asset. However, sometimes these artefacts are created for internal purposes: decomposition of transformations into several intermediate transformations, *ecore* models to represent intermediate transformations, Java jar files that support *black-boxes* for QVT and MOF2Text transformations or shape definitions for GMF canvas. *Application modeller* and other assets should only access *public* artefacts.

Challenge 1.4 - Reuse of standard models and Software Behaviours. Frequently, RMA artefacts reuse and extend standard models and artefacts such as the UML meta-model and standard profiles, the OCL meta-model, and Java standard libraries. These artefacts are not embedded in RMA assets but RMA assets can reuse them (e.g. an RMA asset that packages code generators for UML models reuses the UML *ecore* model). The location of these models and libraries is tool-dependent. The asset must specify these dependencies and the deployment must provide support to resolve model and behaviour dependencies.

Solutions in ERMA for MDA Artefacts Deployment

ERMA implements the RMA specification in *Eclipse Modelling* and the deployment creates *Eclipse* plug-ins, EMF projects, GMF projects, QVT projects and Acceleo projects. ERMA deployment generates one QVT project for each QVT artefact and one *Acceleo* project for each MOF2Text artefact. All other artefacts are deployed into a single ERMA plug-in project. This plug-in includes the models (EMF, GMF and UML models), Java jar files, and other artefacts, icons and files. The deployment of *genmodel* and *gmfgen* models can generate additional plug-ins. All projects and plug-ins include ERMA plug-in dependencies, and the ERMA plug-in project includes plug-in dependencies from other projects. The ERMA plug-in project exports non-private Java packages, and limits the visibility of Java packages when artefact *visibility* is *packaged*.

ERMA solutions for challenges included in this section are:

Solutions for Challenge 1.1 - Relocation of internal RMA references and zip and ras URI schemes. ERMA packaging services use relative path URIs for references to models and files included in the same *ras* file. The packaging service creates one folder for each embedded asset and the folder includes the artefacts in the embedded asset. EMF includes one Java class and two interfaces (and their implementations) that are fundamental for handling URIs in EMF:

a. *URI:* The URI class includes data for representing and parsing URI. URI handles schemes, fragments and other URI data, and can also handle schemes such as *zip* and *ras*. The class only represents these kinds of URIs.
b. *URIHandler:* this Java type provides information about the URI and implementations can handle specific types of URI. Zip and

ras URIs require special implementations of this interface for handling the URI.
c. *URIConverter: URIConverter* is used in the framework for two purposes: to normalise URIs (convert one URI to another) before using them to create input and output streams to access resource information (each resource is associated with the URI that locates the resource's contents).

ERMA implements *URIHandler* and *URIConverter* interfaces with special classes that support *zip* and *ras* schemes. They normalise the references between models included in the same asset file and between models located in different assets. The *URIConverter* implementation uses a mapping table to support this transformation. Zip files impose some restrictions on *URIConverter* implementation. The most important one is that two output streams for the same zip file (two zip entries) cannot be handled at the same time. An alternative solution studied is based on navigation with URI proxies. EMF supports the loading of models without remote-reference resolution (remote references can be maintained as unresolved URIs); the resolution is done explicitly (and URI can be substituted). But some generated Java code does not support this. For example, when the Java code for derived associations navigates the reference, it indirectly resolves other associations, and current implementations do not take into account unresolved remote references. The UML meta-model includes many derived associations, and UML profiles and model libraries have this same problem.

Solutions for Challenge 1.2 - Relocation of external RMA references. Model deployment considers two scenarios: referenced models that are only available in installed plug-ins (the assets were installed, but current deployments are not in the same workspace as the installed assets), referenced models are in deployed projects in the same workspace (these projects could not be installed yet). The deployment relocation must take registered assets into account to locate the first case. For the second, the deployment looks for ERMA projects in the same workspace. Depending on the situation, *URIConverter* implementations are used in different ways. References to standard models must consider the registered models to locate these models in *Eclipse* plug-ins.

Solutions for Challenge 1.3 - Visibility of MDA artefacts. ERMA deploys MDA artefacts to *Eclipse* plug-ins. Three kinds of visibility facilities for Eclipse plug-ins are handled during deployment: registrations in *Eclipse* extensions-points (EMF and GMF registration points for modelling languages, UML2 registration points for profiles, QVT transformation registrations and ERMA registration points for assets), Java exported packages and package visibility, and Java project *classpath*. Deployment of Java artefacts must take the Java exported packages, package visibility and *classpaths* into account, although these attributes of Eclipse manifest files do not support MDA specific languages such as QVT and MOF2Text. For specific MDA language packaging support validation on behaviour visibility, QVT *private* artefacts do not register transformations (*Acceleo* does not include registration facilities for MOF2Text). The Java code generated locates the transformations (*public* or *private*) in the QVT and *Acceleo* plug-ins deployed. The *Challenge 3.1 - Visibility of EMF modelling languages* discusses specific details for EMF artefacts.

Solutions for Challenge 1.4 - Reusing standard models and Software Behaviours. Another basic topic for supporting model relocation is unique and universal names (*nsURI*) for EMF packages and UML Profiles. These names are used to make universal references to XMI representation of profiles and meta-models, and these names must be employed to locate meta-models and profiles in *Eclipse* packages, which can be references to standard packages or references to models included in assets. *Eclipse Modelling* supports additional solutions based on the *pathmap* URI scheme to reduce dependencies on profile and meta-model

versions (the same *pathmap* URI can reference the specific version of meta-model or profile installed in the Eclipse tool). Frequently, *pathmap* is used to represent the prefix of namespace paths to meta-models and profiles. For example, UML2 projects, in general, use the URI *pathmap:// UML_PROFILES/Standard.profile.uml* to locate the *Standard* profile, and the two OMG *nsURI* for the two versions of *Standard* profile in UML 2.4 (OMG 2010a) are: http://www.omg.org/spec/ UML/20100901/StandardProfileL2 and http:// www.omg.org/spec/UML/20100901/Standard-ProfileL3. *Eclipse* uses some schemes and names (e.g. *platform*, *pathmap*, *plugin*, *resource*) that can create problems for model interchange and they should be avoided. Current implementations of the QVT compiler and run-time resolve *ecore* meta-models with the registered *nsURI*.

Deployment of UML Profiles and Model Libraries

The deployment of UML profiles and model libraries must consider the issues mentioned in Section 4.1. Two different UML tools can interchange Profile and model libraries in XMI format. But the deployment of XMI profiles faces the following issues:

Challenge 2.1 - Profile repositories of the target modelling tool. UML modelling tools have their own file or data base formats to represent installed profiles. The deployment must convert the XMI format to the target format.

Challenge 2.2 - References to standard and installed profiles and to modelling libraries. Profiles and model libraries can include references to elements included in other profiles and libraries located in the same asset or in external profiles (e.g. references to UML *Standard* profile or to the *UMLPrimitiveTypes* model library); UML modelling tools have specific solution for locating profiles and libraries. The deployment of profiles must resolve these external references to

XMI files inside the asset or to installed profiles and model libraries.

Challenge 2.3 - OCL constraints of profiles. UML profiles can have associated OCL constraints, and each modelling tool has specific approaches to evaluate OCL constraints.

Another important topic for the deployment of UML profiles is the technology used for applying profiles in UML modelling tools. Stereotype application requires some notation to represent these stereotype applications and the values of features defined in the stereotype. Two solutions are: i) to represent profiles with MOF models; MOF meta-classes map the stereotypes and their applications as instances of meta-classes in MOF models. The UML 2.2 *Superstructure* standard (OMG 2009a) and the revision task force for UML2.4 (OMG 2010a) (this is not normative yet) propose this solution in profile specification sections, but they are recommendations and not normative. The UML2 project in *Eclipse* uses this solution based on *ecore* models; ii) to represent stereotype applications as instances of a UML *InstanceSpecification* meta-class, or similar structures; the classifier associated with these instance specifications are the stereotypes in the profile, and MOF repositories (or MOF models) are needed to handle the profile in the tool. UML 2.3 and UML 2.4 have a mandatory interchange format for stereotype applications and these formats are oriented towards MOF-based schemas.

Challenge 2.4 - Generation of MOF models for UML profiles. In tools that support profiles with MOF models, the deployment must build the MOF models based on profile models, for the target modelling tool.

Challenge 2.5 - Application of profiles in model libraries. Model Libraries (and models in general) that apply UML profiles must represent these applications in XMI files:

a.   If the tool supports profiles with MOF, the runtime classifiers of stereotype applications are MOF elements (e.g. meta-classes), and

these versions of MOF models should be consistent with the profile model. The XMI format of stereotype applications is based on schemes that define the MOF meta-classes for the profiles.

b.   When the profile is modified, new versions of the MOF model must be created, since old applications maintain references to the old MOF models. As a result, it is common to maintain multiple versions of MOF mappings, to maintain consistent references to old versions. However in that case, the MOF models and profiles can be inconsistent.

Challenge 2.6 - Extension and references from profile to profile. For profiles supported by MOF models, when a profile references or extends another profile, the MOF model must reference or extend the appropriate MOF model. In Figure 5 a new profile extends the UML profile *Standard*. A new stereotype (*MyMetaclass*), in the new profile, extends the standard *Metaclass* stereotype in the *Standard* profile. The extender stereotype includes a reference (*related*) to the *Metaclass* stereotype in the *Standard* profile. We create a UML model that applies the *Standard* profile and the new profile (shown on the right side of Figure 5). Two UML classes are annotated with stereotypes *Metaclass* and *OneMyMetaclass*; it should be possible, during the edition of *related* property, to reference both stereotype applications. The implementation of this example in *Eclipse* project UML2 (and many other UML modelling tools based on the UML2 project), only allows the *OneMyMetaclass* stereotype application to be assigned to the *related* property. The source of the problem is the reuse of the MOF (*ecore*) model of the *Standard* profile, from the new MOF (*ecore*) profile model generated. The new MOF (*ecore*) model does not include references to the *Standard* MOF (*ecore*) model. This is a common problem of profile deployment.

Some additional problems in the deployment of profiles are:

Figure 5. Problems arising from profile representation in MOF and profile extensions

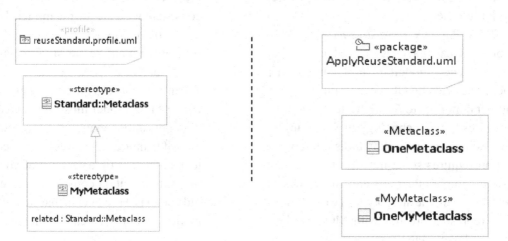

Challenge 2.7 - Profile and model library registration. The location of Profile and Model Libraries must be registered during their application. UML modelling tools have proprietary methods for profile and model library registration (UML2 project and modelling tools that reuse this software do not use the same solutions). References to external profiles must employ these registration solutions. This is a common model interchange problem. The model and its profiles must be exported because the model interchanges that reuse registered profiles is a problem that has not yet been standardised yet.

Challenge 2.8 - Registration of the profile MOF model. Registration of MOF models resolves some problems introduced in point 6. We return to the example in Figure 5; the UML2 project does not register the MOF (*ecore*) model associated with the *Standard* profile. As a result, the construction of the MOF model for the new profile cannot reference the *Standard* MOF (*ecore*) model..

Solutions in ERMA for the Deployment of Profiles and Model Libraries

ERMA solutions for challenges included in this section are:

Solutions for Challenge 2.1 - Profile repositories on the target modelling tool. The UML2 project supports UML profiles in *Eclipse Modelling*. RMA interchanges models with XMI format, and the UML2 format is based on EMF. The main difference between XMI and XML EMF formats is the annotations. Import/Export of XMI files in Eclipse Modelling must convert the EMF annotations into XMI format.

Solutions for Challenge 2.2 - References to standard and installed profiles and to modelling libraries. *nsURI* for the standard models (profiles and model libraries) should be the fundamental reference to locate standard models. The UML Profile includes the attribute *nsURI* which is used to identify instances of the profile in XMI, as the *Profile* meta-class in UML2 does not adjust using the standard. We can represent this attribute with the stereotype *Ecore::ePackage*, but it is used to identify the supporting *ecore* model and not the profile. In ERMA, we use this *nsURI* for both purposes (the same name identifies the *ecore* that supports the profile and the UML profile). There is no *nsURI* to locate the UML model library. The *ModelLibrary* stereotype in *Standard* library does not include this attribute. *UML PrimitiveTypes* is included as normative in the UML *Superstructure* standard and the universal name is http://www.

omg.org/spec/UML/20100901/PrimitiveTypes. xmi, although the model library does not include the URI. ERMA reuses UML2 registrations and proposes some additional solutions (see *Solutions for Challenge 2.7 -*).

Solutions for Challenge 2.3 - OCL constraints in profiles. UML2 supports profiles with *ecore* models (see *Challenge 2.4 -*); UML2 maps UML profiles into *ecore* models that are attached to *Profile* element; stereotype applications are dynamic instances of the *ecore* class that represent the stereotype. The UML2 run-time provides traceability between the UML profile and the generated *EPackage*, which also works with OCL constraints attached to profiles. But OCL, UML2 and EMF use non-standard notations to generate OCL validations[8] (UML2 models used as input for the generation of *ecore* models with OCL constraints must include some *Ecore* annotations). Figure 6

includes an example of UML Profile (*pp*), where this profile includes a stereotypes (*S*) that extends the *Class* meta-class. The stereotype *S* includes an OCL constraint to ensure that the name of the extended class starts with *S* (*self.base_Class. name.substring(0,0) = 'S'*). The deployment of this profile must have non-standard *Ecore* annotations attached that are included in the example (*invocationDelegates, validationDelegates, settingDelegates*). The UML2 *Define* operation on the profile will automatically create the *ecore* model that supports the profile and this operation will attach the *ecore* model to the profile. Generation includes the OCL operations for validation of constraints. The model validation will validate these constraints, but the *ecore* model must be registered (see *Challenge 2.8 -*and *Solutions for Challenge 2.8 -*).

Figure 6. Problems because of the profiles representation in MOF and profile extensions

Solutions for Challenge 2.4 - Generation of MOF models for UML profiles. As mentioned in the previous challenge, UML2 supports UML profiles with *ecore* models. Stereotype applications are dynamic instances to profile meta-models. *Ecore* models of profiles are not supported on Java generated run-time repositories; *DynamicEObject* is the Java interface that supports stereotype applications. ERMA deployment of UML profiles invokes the *define* operation for profiles in UML2. This operation generates the *ecore* model and attaches the *ecore* model to the UML profile as an *UML* annotation and the annotated profile is delivered. ERMA does not execute the *define* operation when the profile is annotated (this annotation is not standard), although some scenarios must *define* the profile during the editing of the asset. For example the MARTE standard profile includes profiles and a model library. Profiles use the model library and the model library applies some profiles. We must then define the profile during the editing of the model library.

Solutions for Challenge 2.5 - Application of profiles in model libraries. The three main references from an XMI model to an applied profile are: i) identification of the *nsURI* that locates the XML schemas for the profile, ii) the *ProfileApplication* UML modelling element includes a reference to the profile and EMF annotations can reference the *ecore* profile model. These annotations must be included as XMI Extensions but this can create portability problems, iii) Stereotype applications are represented as XML data types that define the schemas associated with *ecore* models of profiles. These are not direct references like the others, however *ecore* models of profiles are needed to represent the elements. In ERMA, we assume that a UML profile does not have more than one associated *ecore* model so as to avoid inconsistencies between *ecore* and profile models. This assumption avoids the problem of introducing a reference to the *ecore* model. ERMA proposes one solution for the registration of *Model Libraries*

(*Solutions for Challenge 2.2 -*). Models that apply this uniform name will avoid tool dependencies.

Solutions for Challenge 2.6 - Extension and references from profile to profile. UML *Superstructure* proposes two solutions for handling profile extensions: an extension based on merging the extended profile; and extension based on inheritance. The UML2 profile modeller imports the extended profiles, and the extender introduces references and inheritances from the extended stereotypes (the extended profile should not be modified). But the profile *define* operation (the transformation from profile to *ecore*) has two model generation approaches; when the extended-profile *ecore* model is not registered, the generator merges extended and extender stereotypes and the new *ecore* Class is a merger of both. At run-time, extender applications are not specialisations of the extended stereotype. In the second generation approach generation of *ecore* models from profiles requires registration of extended profiles (with inheritance or reference), and in this case generated *ecore* models reuse the *ecore* models of extended profiles.

Solutions for Challenge 2.7 - Profile and model library registration. UML2 includes the Eclipse extension-point *org.eclipse.uml2.uml.dynamic_package* but UML2 does not include registration mechanisms for model libraries. UML2 uses a URI *pathmap* to reference model libraries such us UML *PrimitiveTypes* (*pathmap://UML_LIBRARIES/UMLPrimitiveTypes.library.uml*), while other UML2 based tools use different names. *Eclipse* modelling tools that reuse UML2 have proprietary extension-points for both kinds of models (e.g. Papyrus and RSA reuse UML2 but define different extension points). ERMA registers model libraries with the *http://asset_id_LIBRARY/version/ModelLibraryName* URI, where *asset_id* is the symbolic name of the asset, and *ModelLibraryName* is the symbolic name of the *Model/Package* element, and it reuses UML2 for profile registration. These registrations include the symbolic name and the plug-in URI of the file, which include the profile or the model library. The UML standard proposes maintaining URI names for profiles: *http://prof ileParentQualifiedName>/<version>/<profile Name>.xmi* (these names should be used when editing *nsURI* of profiles). ERMA deployment generates the *pathmap://asset_id_PROFILES/* and *pathmap://asset_id_LIBRARY/* extensions of the EMF *org.eclipse.emf.ecore.uri_mapping* extension-point for URI mapping of profiles and model asset libraries.

Solutions for Challenge 2.8 - Registration of profile MOF model. The *ecore* model of the UML profile must be registered for various purposes (evaluation of OCL constraints, profile extensions and reuse of profiles in transformation languages such as QVT and MOF2Text). The main problem with this registration is that the extension-point *org.eclipse.emf.ecore.generated_package* requires the URI that represent the symbolic name and the Java class that supports the interface *Descriptor* in *EPackage* (EMF includes the extension point *dynamic_package*, but some tools do not look for registered *EPackage* in that extension, probably in the near future must of tools will take into account both kinds of registrations). UML profiles are dynamic and there is no Java code for their *ecore* model and, thus, a Java wrapper class is needed to implement the interface *EPackage. Descriptor.* ERMA run-time includes an abstract profile wrapper class that includes most of the functionality, and deployment generates a specialization of this Java class for each profile; the generated class includes the specific profile URI and the fragment for the location of the *EPackage* inside the profile. The generated wrappers and the ERMA run-time library support EMF registration for *ecore* models of profiles.

Deployment of Modelling Languages: EMF and GMF

EMF (Steinberg et al. 2009) is the most popular *Eclipse* implementation of EMOF (Essential MOF) (OMG 2006). EMF Core is a framework for constructing abstract syntaxes for modelling languages and for automatic generation of run-time support for handling and editing models. EMF uses two modelling languages to describe meta-models: the *ecore* language represents the meta-model and *EMF Codegen* (*genmodel*) supports the customisation of generated code (run-time support and editor). RMA assets reuse EMF for describing RMA artefacts that represent the abstract syntax of modelling languages. An RMA EMF artefact references the *ecore* and *genmodel* models that describe the modelling language embedded in the delivered asset, and RMA deployment reuses the target modelling tool mechanisms for the deployment of *ecore/genmodel* models. RMA uses EMF, and not EMOF, because the *genmodel* language is not part of the EMOF standard, and this language provides important facilities to deploy modelling languages. Some other important issues in EMF and GMF deployment are:

Challenge 3.1 - Visibility of EMF modelling languages. Challenge 1.3 - Visibility of MDA artefacts introduces general problems of artefacts visibility, but EMF artefact visibility poses some challenges. EMF generators are designed for constructing general modelling languages. The generated code publishes and registers the new languages and exports most of the generated Java packages. The privacy of these languages and their Java packages simplify the modelling tools and prevent software errors. An example scenario of *private ecore* models is RAS tools, which often implement the RAS profiles with *ecore* models while the manifest files are the XMI files of these *ecore*-based profiles. RAS repositories and packagers use *ecore* repositories for handling these models, but they are not used to create diagram and navigator editors, as RAS tools reuse these models internally. *Ecore* provides a simple method to construct XML schemas and handle the XML data supported by these schemas. These new types of XML files are another example of *private ecore* models.

Challenge 3.2 - ecore inter-models dependencies. The *ecore* language supports the reuse of some other *ecore* languages (based on inheritance relationships and cross-references). The generators must resolve the dependencies between *ecore/genmodel* models. The *ecore* and *genmodel* models include cross-references to the packages and classifiers that are used. The deployment must resolve cross-references between *ecore/genmodel* models, and to resolve these cross-references we must consider the implementation details of the *ecore* deployment to locate the target models (the location of the *ecore/genmodel* model in source asset models, in general, is different than the location in generated mechanisms). Cross dependencies include dependencies of standard *ecore* models such as UML, OCL, *ecore* and MOF2Text.

Challenge 3.3 - Generation of genmodel and gmfgen models. In RMA, the reference from an EMF artefact to a *genmodel* model and from a GMF artefact to a *gmfgen* model is optional. If the artefact does not include this reference, the RMA deployment uses target tool mechanisms to automatically generate the *genmodel* or *gmfgen* models, but the *genmodel* and *gmfgen* models will have default values. This approach avoids some tool dependencies and any remaining *Eclipse* dependencies are because *ecore* is not a strict implementation of the EMOF language. However, migration to EMOF modelling frameworks would be simpler. The final task force of the DD standard (OMG 2010c) does not include an equivalent to *gmfgen* language. In the future, dependencies on *gmfgen* will create *Eclipse* dependencies when specifying concrete modelling language syntaxes.

Challenge 3.4 - Generation of derived references and ecore operations. EMF generators produce most of the Java code for run-time support and navigator editors. Two exceptions are the implementation of *Operations* and some *derived* associations. EMF provides two solutions for these implementations: modifying the generated Java code and annotating the *operation* and the *derived structural feature* to generate

implementation (in OCL or in Java). The second approach has important advantages, because it is generator-independent and executing generators is simpler. An additional problem to resolve is the dependency of Java classes included in Java code modification and generation. This problem was introduced in *Challenge 1.4 - Reuse of standard models and Software Behaviours.*

Challenge 3.5 - Integration of Java code modifications. The annotations used for operation and derived references resolve the most common modifications of Java code generated in EMF. But some precise customisations require code modification. When the code in the source models is modified before packaging the asset, these modifications are lost during deployment and execution of generators.

Solutions in ERMA for the Deployment of Modelling Languages

ERMA solutions for the challenges in this section are:

Solutions for Challenge 3.1 - Visibility of EMF modelling languages. In ERMA, the deployment of *public* EMF descriptors executes the EMF generators and this will create three Eclipse plug-ins, which register the generated model and export the Java packages. We have studied two solutions for the deployment of *private* EMF artefacts: the execution of EMF generators modifies the plug-in id and reuses the asset plug-in; Java packages are not exported. The problem with this approach is the plug-in properties of EMF editors (two EMF edit projects can include the same identifier in the plug-in properties); model code can only be generated for *private* EMF artefacts. The second solution is to modify the package visibility in exported packages and to modify the extension-point of generated EMF plug-ins.

Solutions for Challenge 3.2 - ecore inter-model dependencies. The execution of generators for EMF must resolve the references to other EMF projects that support reused/extended languages.

Two scenarios are considered to locate these models and their projects: the EMF project is deployed in the same workspace, but not installed (ERMA reuses the deployed project); the EMF models are deployed, installed and registered (ERMA reuses installed plug-ins). The other cases will cause deployment errors because assembly dependency cannot be guaranteed.

Solutions for Challenge 3.3 - Generation of genmodel and gmfgen models. When EMF or GMF descriptors in *erma* models do not include a reference to *genmodel and gmfgen*, and no EMF or GMF descriptor in the same asset references the *genmodel and gmfgen* that support generation, ERMA automatically generates the generation model from *ecore* or from *gmfmap*. This is done to simplify the generation of EMF descriptors from EMOF models (or DD models in the future).

Solutions for Challenge 3.4 - Generation of derived references and ecore operations. ERMA assumes that operation code and derived associations are integrated in *ecore* models. These implementations must be Java or OCL, and the *Ecore* annotations for OCL and Java. *Genmodel* models should include all customised code supported in this model. ERMA does not support the integration of JET templates in EMF descriptors.

Solutions for Challenge 3.5 - Integration of Java code modifications. Current solutions to modify Java code generated for EMF and GMF descriptors are i) the *installation interaction points* implemented in Java artefacts (Java code executed during asset installation), and ii) modification of deployed Java code for EMF and GMF artefacts, before installation. Both are complex solutions and some tools could automate the first solution (by generating Java code that integrates the non-generated code and modifies the generated code in the target).

Deployment of Behaviour Specifications in QVT, MOF2Text and Java

In RMA we consider four languages to describe transformations or any kind of behaviour specification: OCL, Java, QVT and MOF2Text. Frequently, we can implement the same behaviour in three of these languages (e.g. we can implement the same query for a modelling language in OCL, Java or QVT). This section discusses the most important issues in deploying QVT, MOF2Text and Java. OCL expressions are attached to *ecore* models, UML profiles and *interaction points*. Challenge 1.1 - *Relocation of internal RMA references and zip and ras URI schemes* and Challenge 1.2 - *Relocation of external RMA references* introduce the general problems with relocating references. We must take these issues into account for Challenge 4.1 - *References to ecore meta-models* and Challenge 4.3 - *Dependencies of Black-Boxes* in this section. The main challenges in deploying QVT, MOF2Text and Java software behaviours are:

Challenge 4.1 - References to ecore meta-models. QVT modules and transformations reference abstract syntax meta-models with *modeltype* sentences that identify the meta-models of the modelling languages to be used in the transformation. MOF2Text includes references to the meta-model as module arguments. In both cases, the reference is the universal name URI (*nsURI*) associated with the package that represents the modelling language. This *nsURI* must be registered to locate the *ecore* model that supports the language. This can create confusion when we need to update the *ecore* model (for example to introduce some additional operations or attributes) while the transformation is being built.

Challenge 4.2 - Transformations for UML models with UML Profile applications. When we transform a UML model with profile applications, we need to reference stereotype applications. There are two solutions: i) to navigate to the stereotype applications using UML meta-model operations for handling stereotypes (most of these operations are included in the *Element* meta-class), and ii) to define the profile as a meta-model in the transformer, if the profile is run-time supported with MOF. The first solution avoids any tool dependency (the implementation of profiles with MOF is not mandatory in the OMG standard), and the second avoids many problems since UML operations use generic types (*EObject*) to resolve stereotype applications (reflexion and some additional tools are needed for handling these values).

Challenge 4.3 - Dependencies of Black-Boxes. The concrete syntax of *Black-Boxes* in QVT and some MOF2Text implementations (this is not part of the OMG standard) can invoke Java class methods. These Java classes must be embedded in some target tool infrastructure (e.g. a Java library, Java project or plug-in), and QVT or MOF2Text run-time support of target tools must locate these Java classes.

Challenge 4.4 - XMI vs Concrete Syntax Interoperability and Operational vs Relational. The MOF2Text and QVT standards propose two approaches for transformation interoperability: i) *syntax exportable models* are transformations in the concrete syntax that modelling tools use for interchange; ii) XMI exportable models are the XMI serialisations that make up the MOF meta-model (MOF2Text and QVT standards include the MOF meta-model). Both approaches are useful for different purposes and the RMA language supports both approaches. Transformation delivery and deployment should be in the concrete syntax to reuse modules and transformations in the target tool, for developing new transformations and modules.

Challenge 4.5 - Reuse of Eclipse plug-ins in Java code. Software behaviour in Java often reuses standard Java libraries (e.g. for the construction of specific wizards). *Challenge 1.4 - Reuse of standard models and Software Behaviours* and its solutions introduce general approaches to reusing Java standard libraries. *Eclipse Modelling* (Eclipse Foundation 2011) is currently used to construct

several UML modelling tools (e.g. IBM RSA[9], Magic Draw[10], Papyrus[11]) and modelling tools in general. *Eclipse* includes many reusable and extensible plug-ins. The reuse of plug-ins (e.g. general wizards and console plug-ins) would allow access to general *Eclipse* infrastructures, but their reuse limits the portability of assets to non Eclipse-based modelling tools.

Solutions in ERMA for the Deployment of Behaviour Specifications

The ERMA solutions for the challenges in this section are:

Solutions for Challenge 4.1 - References to ecore meta-models. QVTo and *Acceleo* in *Eclipse Modelling* need the *ecore* models that reference the transformations and modules to compile and execute. They dynamically locate the registered *nsURI* of the *EPackages*. They indirectly use the default *EPackage.Registration* implementation and the meta-model registry utilities in EMF. The problem is that the development of transformations would require the installation of EMF artefacts for compilation purposes. *QVTo* and *Acceleo* do not need the run-time projects of *ecore* languages, as only the *ecore* models are needed. Some additional GUI commands for *QVTo* and *Acceleo* editors can support dynamic registration of *EPackages*, and parallel development of transformations, *ecore* models (e.g. OCL implementations of *ecore* operations) and UML profiles are supported in the same workspace. *QVTo* and *Acceleo* use *nsURI* to locate the *ecore* models, which avoids dependencies arising from EMF deployment in the transformations but they are dependent on *ecore* registrations and *ecore* models. Because of this, deployment of EMF and Profile artefacts should support dynamic registration of *ecore* models to avoid compilations errors in *QVTo* and *Acceleo* deployments (this compilation is only needed to avoid installing transformations with compilation errors, although they are compiled again before execution and would run without errors if the *ecore*

EPackages are registered). An alternative solution is to use the *helper operation* and *intermediate property* in QVT transformations, but these operations and properties are handled at the QVT module level and they are not integrated into the *ecore* model for all transformations.

Solutions for Challenge 4.2 - Transformations for UML models with UML Profile applications. We can use *QVTo* and *Acceleo* in the transformation of UML models with profile applications. Two approaches are available: reuse *uml::Element* operations for stereotypes (e.g. *getStereotypeApplications, applyStereotype*), which are applicable to any UML element, or reuse the *ecore* profile model and handle with this stereotype application in the model. We use the same example for both approaches, a simplified example of *QVTo* transformation from UML+MARTE Profile to an analysis language (the *EPackage* of EMF language is *mast_mdl*). We only introduce the beginning of this transformation, as the remaining mapping can follow the same approach. Two alternative sentences in the *main* operation stereotype are shown in Exhibit 1.

In this example *mapAnalysis2* (a transformation based on *UML::Element* operations) uses *SaAnalysisContext* to select *Packages* annotated with this stereotype. An alternative is not to include the profile model type in the transformation and to use *getAppliedStereotype("SAM::SaAnalysisContext")* operation call. *mapAnalysis* (a transformation based on the *ecore* model of the profile) navigates from the stereotype application to the annotated UML elements. The reuse of the *ecore* models of the profiles has important advantages (e.g. static checking of data types for stereotype navigations), but requires the registration of the *EPackage* of the profiles, and some mappings from the UML profile to *ecore* may not be intuitive (e.g. some properties of associations). The transformations are compiled and executed for the *ecore* model and not for the UML profile model (both should be consistent).

Solutions for Challenge 4.3 - Dependencies of Black-Boxes. Black-Boxes are supported in Java jar libraries that support Java RMA artefacts. The deployment of QVT and MOF2Text models to *QVTo* and *Acceleo* projects includes the dependency of the asset plug-in that exports the Java jar files. The visibility of exported black-box packages in the plug-in asset is limited to *QVTo* and *Acceleo* projects. Currently, *QVTo* does not support black-boxes as the QVT standard proposes (in *QVTo*, Java methods must be static and the execution context should be the first argument), which can create interoperability problems. The MOF2Text standard (OMG 2008a) does not provide standard specifications for black-boxes, but *Acceleo* provides a limited implementation of Java method invocation. An alternative solution to black-boxes would be to attach Java and OCL code to operations in *ecore* models and then invoke the operations from transformations, although this solution is not possible when we use standard languages such as UML and OCL.

Solutions for Challenge 4.4 - XMI vs Concrete Syntax Interoperability and Operational vs Relational. In *Eclipse Modelling, QVTo* project supports *QVT Operational* and *QVTr* supports QVT Relations. The ERMA language supports references to QVT transformations and modules in abstract and concrete syntax, and it includes an implementation of the QVT standard in *ecore*. *QVTo* only includes an internal and proprietary version of the *ecore* model of QVT Operational, and there are not public classes for handling these models (e.g. a parser from the concrete syntax to QVT meta-model instances). Thus, it is not possible to create QVT artefacts that support QVT Operational transformations in XMI based on *QVTo* (a parser would be needed from QVT Operational concrete syntax to QVT Operational in *ecore*). *QVTr* supports QVT Relations and QVT Core in *ecore* and provides EMF editors for these models. *QVTr* is at an early stage, and ERMA requires a basic API to validate models and compile concrete syntax, to execute transformations and to analyse

Exhibit 1.

```
marte_model.rootObjects()[SaAnalysisContext]->map mapAnalysis();
marte_model.objects()[Package]->map mapAnalysis2();
```

SaAnalysisContext is a MARTE stereotype; the first sentence selects the application of this stereotype and executes the *mapAnalysis* mapping on this selection. The second sentence selects the UML *Package* elements and executes the *mapAnalysis2* mapping. The rest of the *QVTo* transformation is:

```
modeltype UML uses uml("http://www.eclipse.org/uml2/3.0.0/UML");
modeltype MARTE_SAM uses SAM("http://MARTE.MARTE_AnalysisModel/schemas/
SAM/1");
modeltype MAST uses mast_mdl("http://mast.unican.es/xmlmast/mast_mdl");
transformation MARTE2MAST(in marte_model : UML, out mast_model : MAST);
main() {

}
mapping Package::mapAnalysis2() : MAST::MASTMODELType {
    if (self.getStereotypeApplications()->
                select(oclIsKindOf(SaAnalysisContext))->size() > 0) then {
        modelName:=self.name;
    } endif;
}
mapping SaAnalysisContext::mapAnalysis() : MAST::MASTMODELType {
    if (not self.base_Package.oclIsUndefined()) then {
        modelName:=self.base_Package.name;
    } endif;
}
```

transformations and modules to identify specific properties of transformations and modules, such as the parameter types of transformations and the model types used. This means that integration of *QVTr* is also still at an early stage and *QVTo* supports this for *QVT Operational* for concrete syntax. Some functions that ERMA uses are in internal *QVTo* packages because the *QVTo* public API is very limited. For example, the public API in *QVTo* provides support for the execution of transformations[12], but not for the introspection of the data type of transformation parameters.

Solutions for Challenge 4.5 - Reuse of Eclipse plug-ins in Java code. An ERMA asset can include *reference* dependencies to external Java artefacts. The Java artefact includes the identifier for the external jar file. ERMA deployment starts looking for the jar file identifier in Java *classpath* and in Standard Java libraries (e.g. *rt.jar* and *resources. jar*). If the Java jar file is not found, ERMA deployment looks for an installed *Eclipse* plug-in with that identifier and, if the plug-in is found the deployment creates the dependency for that plug-in. This solution creates dependencies for *Eclipse* solutions, but it could be useful for RMA assets designed for *Eclipse*-based tools that reuse basic plug-ins, such as *org.eclipse.ui.console*, to access *Eclipse* console.

Figure 7. Interaction Points example

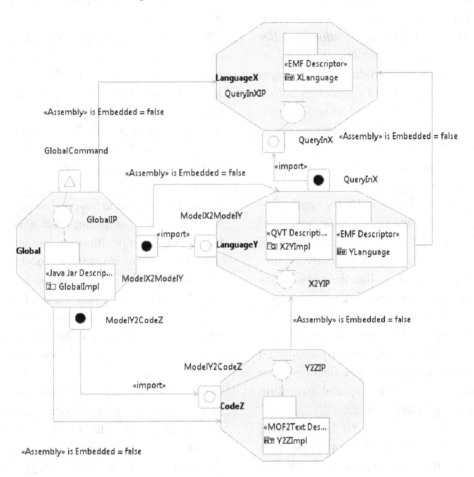

Deployment of Interaction Points

MDA has multiple languages to describe associated software behaviours, such as transformations, queries, and other functionality. RMA software behaviour languages support functionality that assets provide to *application modellers* and to some other assets. *Application modellers* can invoke this functionality, and some assets can request execution of software behaviours supported in other assets. As a result of these relationships, there are a large number of inter-dependencies between languages and it should be possible to invoke, from any language, functionality supported in the other languages. Figure 7 includes an example where the application model command *GlobalCommand*

(RMA asset *Global*) is implemented in Java and it reuses the transformations *ModelX2ModelY* in QVTO (RMA asset *LanguageY*) and *ModelYTo-CodeZ* in MOF2Text (RMA asset *CodeZ*), while *ModelX2ModelY* reuses the OCL query *QueryInX* (RMA asset *LanguageX*). The specifications of the *integration points* in this diagram (*QueryInXIP*, *GlobalIP*, *X2YIP*, and *Y2ZIP*) define the behaviour artefacts that support the operations included in the specification of each *interaction point* and provide support for the implementation of *external commands* and *ERMA calls provided*. The *import* relationships define the link from the *ERMA call required* to *ERMA call provided*, and the *assembly* dependencies define the assets required for the deployment and installation of each asset.

397

The main objective of RMA *interaction points* is to reduce the complexity of inter-asset dependencies and to simplify the *application modeller* interface with software behaviour to unify its invocation. Section 3.3 introduces the concepts that support the definition of *interaction points*. The main challenges for the deployment and run-time support of interaction points are:

Challenge 5.1 - Links from RMA Interaction Points to MDA Languages. An *interaction point* specifies a port of interaction between assets or commands provided in the GUI of the application modelling tool. An *interaction point* specification is the same for all MDA implementation languages, but the *interaction points* require particular specifications to link their operations with the functional structures in each language.

Challenge 5.2 - Inter-Language Invocation. The run-time support for *interaction points* consists of proxies for the functionality supported in the software behaviour specifications. For each language, the proxy uses special invocation methods to delegate the invocation.

Challenge 5.3 - General GUI for Command Invocation. RMA run-time support provides a uniform solution to simplify the invocation of software behaviours for all MDA languages. This simplifies the usage of RMA assets and is the common reference for defining GUI commands that invoke software behaviours.

Challenge 5.4 - Configuration of RMA Assets. Frequently, an RMA can include configuration parameters to customise the RMA asset in the concrete target tool. Examples of configuration parameters are parameters to represent input/output directories, usernames and logins to access data bases and repositories.

Solutions in ERMA for the Deployment of Interaction Points

ERMA solutions for the challenges in this section are:

Solutions for Challenge 5.1 - Links from RMA Interaction Points to MDA Languages. ERMA supports two types of implementation of *interaction point* operations: OCL and *software behaviour artefacts* (EMF, QVT, MOF2Text and Java). OCL constraints are integrated into the RMA language, since RMA extends *UML Infrastructure* and ERMA reuses OCL *Eclipse* project for compilation and execution of OCL constraints. RMA *interaction point implementation* relationships model the link from *interaction points* to *software behaviour artefacts*. The meta-class that supports relationships includes a key attribute that locates the operation implementation in the *software behaviour artefact*. For Java, the key represents the key binding to the Java methods; for QVTo and MOF2Text the key represents the qualified name for the transformation or module. One *interaction point* can have multiple associated *interaction point implementations*, because several *software behaviour artefacts* can support the same *interaction point*, but one operation must be associated with a single behaviour. The ERMA diagram editor includes a wizard for the edition of *interaction point implementation* relationships, which navigates into Java jar files, QVTo transformations and modules and MOF2Text modules for selecting the methods, transformation and mappings that implement the operation. ERMA deployment reuses this information for code generation.

Solutions for Challenge 5.2 - Inter-Language Invocation. The inter-language interaction of ERMA is based on two concepts: a run-time ERMA Java API that supports reflexion to locate and invoke *interaction points* and generate black-boxes in the deployment to be reused from MOF2Text and QVT. The generated black-boxes reuse the run-time API to invoke reused *interaction points* in Java. Figure 7 includes a Java artefact (*GlobalImpl*) that reuses *ERMA call provided* in other assets and supports the reused assets. In that example, one *ERMA call provided* (*ModelX2ModelY*) is supported in QVT and the

Exhibit 2.

```
IContainer myContainer=null;
try {
    myContainer = IContainerLocator.eINSTANCE.getContainerOfModellingAsset("Global");
    IImportedERMACall x2yCall = myContainer.getImportedERMACall("ModelX2ModelY");
    IOperationClient x2yTransformation = x2yCall.getOperationClient("x2y");
    IImportedERMACall y2zCall = myContainer.getImportedERMACall("ModelY2CodeZ");
    IOperationClient y2zGeneration = y2zCall.getOperationClient("y2z");

    List<EObject> in=new ArrayList<EObject>();
    in.add(model);
    Object[] result=x2yTransformation.invoke(null,in);

    in=new ArrayList<EObject>();
    in.addAll((List<EObject>) result[0]);
    result=y2zGeneration.invoke(null,in);
    // result[0] contains the result y2zGeneration
} catch (ERMAContainerException e) {
    // ERMA exception handler
}
```

other in MOF2Text (*ModelY2CodeZ*), but from the Java artefact the implementation language is opaque. The Java implementation would be based on the ERMA run-time reflexion API, and this implementation is (both *interaction points* are invoked with the same calls). (see Exhibit 2)

IContainer provides run-time support for the asset, and includes basic operations for introspection of *ERMA Calls* included in the asset. Other interfaces include operation to invoke *interaction point* operations. The generated ERMA run-time and code resolve execution depending on the *software behaviour language* that supports the operation. IContainer provides methods to get/set values of assets configuration parameters, and to access containers of assembled assets.

Solutions for Challenge 5.3 - General GUI for Command Invocation. RMA assets can include *External Command* specifications. ERMA deployment generates Java classes for handling the commands that delegate the operation based on the ERMA run-time API. The generated code extends *Eclipse* extension-point *org.eclipse.ui.actionSets* and creates new entries in the *Eclipse Run* Menu, creating one submenu for each asset. The submenu includes entries for executing commands, configuring asset parameters and downloading documentation artefacts. The Java code for commands introspects the operation that implement the command, requests values for parameters taking into account the modelling elements available in the active resource set, invokes the implementation of the operation and displays the results.

Solutions for Challenge 5.4 - Configuration of RMA Assets. RMA assts can have associated configuration parameters. The *application modeller* can get and set the parameters with menu entries, and *software behaviour artefacts* can get and set their values with ERMA run-time interfaces.

Deployment of Documentation Artefacts

MDSD provides innovative solutions to increase the abstraction level in software development, but MDA based tools must consider the learning process of the infrastructure supporting the MDSD process. Especially important are the DSLs. To make a new RMA asset applicable, we should consider the percentage of time required to learn a new DSL or UML profile in the application project. For example, expert UML modellers may spend several months learning a new UML profile such as MARTE (OMG 2009c). If engineers should be spending no more than one year modelling the project, the learning effort is too expensive for project development. To make the RMA asset applicable, the *RMA developer* must provide support to reduce the time for learning new languages and applying new asset commands and transformations. We must take the learning curve into account when designing a new modelling language and asset. Learning support should be integrated in the RMA asset and should reduce learning time:

Challenge 6.1 - Packaging and deployment of learning artefacts. Section 3.1 introduces artefacts for representing RMA learning documents. Two different approaches for the deployment of learning documents are: i) to maintain a single documentation server to be used from target tools; ii) to deploy the documentation to a target tool documentation server. The advantage of the first solution is centralised documentation maintenance while the advantage of the second is the independence of the target modelling environment.

Solutions in ERMA for the Deployment of Documentation Artefacts

ERMA solutions for the challenges in this section are:

Solutions for Challenge 6.1 - Packaging and deployment of learning artefacts. The use of

MediaWiki (Barrett 2008) XML files is the most common approach to support documentation artefacts in ERMA. Other types of document are supported as RAS artefact, but ERMA deployment only deploys them as files into an artefact folder. In *erma* models, *MediaWiki* artefacts are hierarchies of artefacts that can include a URI reference to a *MediaWiki* page. ERMA considers two alternative solutions for packaging *MediaWiki* artefacts: the artefacts can be embedded in the asset, or the artefact can be non-embedded. In the first case, the *MediaWiki* pages are packaged in the *ras* file, and the *ras* file includes pictures that reference the *MediaWiki* page. If other referenced *MediaWiki* pages are not embedded, the pages will maintain references to the source pages. The ERMA deployment delivers the *MediaWiki* pages to a *MediaWiki* server that can be on the same machine as the modelling target tool or on a different one (ERMA supports the configuration of a target *MediaWiki* server). If *MediaWiki* pages are not embedded, documentation menus and other code will reference the source pages. The second solution is better for sharing documentation pages and keeping all documentation updated, but it relies on Internet access. ERMA documentation commands extend the *org.eclipse.ui.actionSets Eclipse* extension-point and reuse web browsers included in the *org.eclipse.ui.browser Eclipse* plug-in to display *MediaWiki* pages. *MediaWiki* should be used to edit and maintain documentation pages, which should be independent of *MediaWiki* extensions. Packaging and deployment ERMA services are based on *import/export* functions in *MediaWiki*; *import* requires *sysop* privileges and ERMA *MediaWiki* configurations can configure user and password to be used for *MediaWiki* artefact deployments.

FUTURE RESEARCH DIRECTIONS

ERMA provides a framework to interchange modelling tools assets. A basic tool for asset interchange is RAS repositories. These repositories could be specialised for specific technologies and domains. The *ERMA RAS working group repository*[13] includes assets for the development of high integrity applications, including assets for MARTE profiles (MARTE profile modelling tools, MAST analysis tools, Ada2005 Ravenscar and Java RTSJ profile code generators), and some additional assets that support safety-aware model development: Safety & Dependability UML extensions, (FTA) Fault Tree and (FMECA) Failure mode, effects, and criticality analysis modelling languages, transformations from UML+Safety & Dependability to FTA and FMECA, and bridges from ERMA safety to Item Toolkit) (Miguel et al. 2008). OMG provides XMI models for some standards such as meta-models and profiles. Currently integration of these models into modelling tools requires experience in XMI and standard formats. Repositories that reduce customisation of these models are needed, because at present tool vendors customise these models for their tools, but do not provide open solutions, and clients depend on vendor supplied tools.

RMA supports run-time inter-asset dependency based on the *ERMA Call Provided – ERMA Call Required* relationship. Current implementations assume the execution of client and server assets in the same *Eclipse* tool. Elimination of this restriction has important advantages: to use transformation assets as remote services, to support working group modelling repositories, to learn and test assets based on remote services not installed in the working tool. The main problem in eliminating this restriction and executing client and server in different tools and on different machines would be the serialisation of parameters, context and results, and the references that the parameters can include. EMF and XMI provide serialization support for modelling objects, but the limitations are the references that these objects can include. Some alternative solutions could be based on CDO (Connected Data Objects) EMF subproject, which is a distributed shared model of EMF. In CDO, multiple modelling tools share common repositories supported in distributed data bases, and CDO run-time generated code provides transparent access to the distributed data base. CDO supports the distributed notification of model access and modifications and transactions for remote models, but there is no CDO (and Net4J integrated in CDO) solution to the problem of remote transformation execution, which would integrate CDO and transformation languages. CDO solutions are not integrated in OMG standards, and it is not currently possible for different tool vendor modelling tools to share a common modelling repository. *ModelBus* (Aldazabal et al. 2008) was another framework for the remote execution of modelling services. *ModelBus* is open source, but its problem is also standardisation.

Our current implementations of *ERMA RAS Working Group server* are based on a web server developed in *IBM WebSphere*. This web server implements a WSDL (Web Services Description Language) interface. Currently there is no RAS open source implementation for *Eclipse*. A run-time platform for the execution of RAS repositories could be *Eclipse WTP* (Web Tools Platform)[14].

CONCLUSION

Currently, complex software development based on model driven approaches are moving platform dependencies from run-time platforms and programming languages to model driven development frameworks. In the near future, similar efforts will be required to migrate current projects to new development tools. If model-driven software developments do not work on reducing the dependencies on model-driven development environments, the maintenance of these projects will require considerable future effort. RMA and ERMA represent a practical solution to avoiding modelling tools' dependencies on MDSD. The modelling tools' and MDA development environment dependencies create problems as complex as the problems of platform dependencies addressed in MDA technologies and bibliography (e.g. PIM (Platform Independent Model) to PSM (Platform Specific Model) development approaches (Frankel 2003)). MDSD should be as development environment independent as possible to reduce maintenance and development costs. However development independence require some efforts and limitations for development tools (e.g. we should avoid using proprietary development tools not based on standards, and reusing open-source and portable development tools reduces development environment dependencies).

MDSD reuses basic modelling tools such as generators, transformations and modelling languages. But these basic tools are developed in multiple languages, and combining and interoperability are complex. Learning these languages and their combined application requires extensive learning for the engineers who apply these tools. A fundamental objective of RMA is to reduce this learning period. These solutions are based on two fundamental concepts: to support the interoperability of MDA languages, and to integrate all kinds of MDA artefacts into a common framework. ERMA proposes a solution to integrate the different MDA frameworks included in *Eclipse Modelling* and to simplify their interoperability.

The interoperability of MDA models requires some improvements to standards (OMG standards in particular). UML model libraries do not include notations to represent *nsURI* in the model (e.g. *MARTE Model Library nsURI* should be included in the model), as it can only be introduced in the standard document (the MARTE standard does not include the *nsURI* of *MARTE Model Library*). The UML *Profile* meta-class includes one *nsURI* to locate the model but, in general cases, two different *nsURI* are needed: the *nsURI* for the location of the profile model (the URI used in *ProfileApplication* relationship, where the target is a *Profile*

modelling element, or the URI to be used in *PackageImport* in new profiles that extend other profiles), and the *nsURI* that locates the MOF model that supports the XMI for the profile (the URI that includes the XMI file for location of XML schemas and the URI to be used in QVT and MOF2Text transformations to reference stereotype applications). If the MOF model is embedded in the UML profile model (currently, this is not a standard solution) and there is only one MOF model attached to the profile, a single *nsURI* could be enough. But, in general cases, two different models (profile and MOF model) with two different registrations and a single universal name will require multiple registrations, and the same name will target different models in different registrations. UML profile standards do not generally include the specification of the *nsURI* for the profile (this attribute has been included in the *Profile* meta-class in recent versions of UML2) and the references to standard profiles are tool-dependent.

The learning curve is a fundamental concept in the application of MDSD technologies. For software engineers, to migrate from traditional development methods to MDA methods will require more effort than the migration to object-oriented languages and technologies some years ago. The migration from traditional development methods to MDA methods; the application of new modelling languages and transformations requires important learning effort and engineers and companies must invest time and energy. If the assets that support the new methods do not integrate education or tutorial support, it does not make sense financially to develop them. RMA includes some support for the integration of learning documents, but the development of these artefacts requires following some educational methods.

RMA design takes several steps to improve tool independency: RMA is based on MDA standards that reduce tool dependencies and software behaviour specifications in particular; ERMA implementation is based on *Eclipse* open-source projects, which simplify the interoperability of *Eclipse*-based modelling tools (ERMA adaptation to *Eclipse*-based modelling tools does not require too much effort, and most efforts will involve integrating the required projects such as *Acceleo*, *QVTo* and *OCL*); RMA defines a framework to customise a modelling tool for a specific technology and domain, so that the same basic modelling assets could customise several modelling tools, where all these tools would provide similar modelling environments.

REFERENCES

Ackerman, L., Elder, P., Busch, C., Lopez-Mancisidor, A., Kimura, J., & Balaji, N. A. (2008). *Strategic reuse with asset-based development.* IBM RedBooks.

Aldazabal, A., Baily, T., Nanclares, F., Sadovykh, A., Hein, C., Esser, M., & Ritter, T. (2008). Automated model driven development processes. In T. Ritter (Ed.), *Proceedings of the ECMDA Workshop on Model Driven Tool and Process Integration.* Stuttgart, Germany: Fraunhofer IRB Verlag.

Barrett, D. J. (2008). *MediaWiki: Wikipedia and beyond.* O'Riley.

Bendraou, R., Desfray, P., & Gervais, M. P. (2005). *MDA components: A flexible way for implementing the MDA approach.* First European Conference Model Driven Architecture: Foundations and Applications., ECMDA-FA 2005, Nuremberg, Germany, November 7-10.

Bendraou, R., Desfray, P., Gervais, M. P., & Muller, A. (2008). MDA tool components: A proposal for packaging know-how in model driven development. *Journal on Software & System Modeling*, *7*(3), 329–343. doi:10.1007/s10270-007-0058-8

Blanc, X., Gervais, M. P., & Sriplakich, P. (2005). Model bus: Towards the interoperability of modelling tools. In Hartman, A. (Ed.), *Model driven architecture, LNCS 3599.* doi:10.1007/11538097_2

Burns, A., & Wellings, A. (April 2009). *Real-time systems and programming languages* (4th ed). Ada 2005, Real-Time Java and C/Real-Time POSIX. Addison Wesley Longman.

de Miguel, M. A., Fernández Briones, J., Silva, J. P., & Alonso, A. (2008). Integration of safety analysis in model-driven software development. *IET Software*, *2*(3), 260–280. doi:10.1049/iet-sen:20070050

de Miguel, M. A., Jourdan, J., & Salicki, S. (2002). Practical experiences in the application of MDA. In J. Jezequel (Ed.), *Proceedings of Fifth International Conference on The Unified Modeling Language: UML 2002.* Springer Verlag.

Eclipse Foundation. (2011). *Eclipse modeling project.* Retrieved from http://www.eclipse.org/modeling/

Frankel, D. (2003). *Model driven architecture.* Wiley & Sons.

Goodwin, R., Ivan, A., Goh, S., Mohan, R., Srivastava, B., Mazzoleni, P., ... Rosinski, T. (2009). *Improving SAP projects with model-driven technologies for global delivery.* IBM Research, Technical Paper (RC24879).

Gurbani, V. K., Garvert, A., & Herbsleb, J. D. (2010). Managing a corporate open source software asset. *ACM Communications*, *52*(2), 155–159. doi:10.1145/1646353.1646392

International Organization for Standardization. (June 2010). *Guide for the use of the Ada Ravenscar profile in high integrity systems.* (ISO document number: ISO/IEC TR 24718:2005).

Java Community Process. (May 2009). *JSR-000282 real-time specification for Java 1.1.* (Java Specification document number: JSR 282: RTSJ version 1.1).

Larsen, G. (2006). Model-driven development: Assets and reuse. *IBM Systems Journal, 45*(3), 541–553. doi:10.1147/sj.453.0541

Object Management Group. (November 2005). *OMG reusable asset specification, Version 2.2.* (OMG document number formal/05-11-02).

Object Management Group. (January 2006). *Meta object facility (MOF) core specification, Version 2.0.* (OMG document number formal/06-01-01).

Object Management Group. (2008a). *MOF model to text transformation language, Version 1.0.* (OMG document number formal/2008-01-16).

Object Management Group. (2008b). *MOF MOF 2.0/XMI mapping, Version 2.1.1. (*OMG document number formal/2007-12-01).

Object Management Group. (2009a). *OMG unified modeling language, superstructure, Version 2.2.* (OMG document number formal/2009-02-02).

Object Management Group. (2009b). *OMG unified modeling language infrastructure, Version 2.2.* (OMG document number formal/2009-02-04).

Object Management Group. (2009c). *UML profile for MARTE: Modeling and analysis of real-time embedded systems, Version 1.0.* (OMG document number formal/2009-11-02).

Object Management Group. (2009d). *MDA tool component, Version 1.2, reviewed submission.* (OMG document number ad/2009-11-03).

Object Management Group. (2010a). *OMG unified modeling language, superstructure, Version 2.4, Revision Task Force.* (OMG document number ptc/2010-11-13).

Object Management Group. (2010b). *Object constraint language, version 2.2.* (OMG document number formal/2010-02-01).

Object Management Group. (2010c). Diagram definition, Version 1.0, Final Task Force. (OMG document number ptc/2010-12-18).

Object Management Group. (January 2011). *Meta object facility (MOF) 2.0 query/view/transformation specification, Version 1.1.* (OMG document number formal/2011-01-01).

OSGi Service Platform. (2009). *Core specification, release 4, Version 4.2.* OSGi Alliance.

Shavor, S., D'Anjou, J., Fairbrother, S., Kehn, D., Kellerman, J., & McCarthy, P. (2003). *The Java developer's guide to Eclipse.* Addison Wesley.

Steinberg, D., Budinsky, F., Paternostro, M., & Merks, E. (2009). *EMF: Eclipse modeling framework* (2nd ed.). Addison Wesley.

ADDITIONAL READING

Bendraou, R., Desfray, P., & Gervais, M. P. (2005), MDA Components: A Flexible Way for Implementing the MDA Approach. In (Ed), *Model driven architecture: foundations and applications. First European conference, ECMDA-FA* 2005, Nuremberg, Germany, November 7-10.

R. Bendraou, P. Desfray, M.P. Gervais and A. Muller (2008), MDA Tool Components: A Proposal for Packaging Know-how in Model Driven Development. *Journal on Software & System Modeling.* Springer, 7(3), 329-343

Blanc, X., Gervais, M. P., & Sriplakich, P. (2005). Model Bus: Towards the Interoperability of Modelling Tools. In Hartman, A. (Ed.), *Model Driven Architecture* (*Vol. 3599*). Lecture Notes in Computer Science. doi:10.1007/11538097_2

R. Goodwin; A. Ivan; S. Goh; R. Mohan; B. Srivastava; P. Mazzoleni; I. Naumov; R. Chopra; T. Bandyopadhyay; T. Rosinski, (2009) Improving SAP Projects with Model-Driven Technologies for Global Delivery, *IBM Research, Technical Paper (RC24879).*

Gurbani, V. K., Garvert, A., & Herbsleb, J. D. (2010). Managing a Corporate Open Source Software Asset. *ACM Communications, 52*(2), 155–159. doi:10.1145/1646353.1646392

Larsen, G. (2006). Model-driven development: Assets and reuse. *IBM Systems Journal, 45*(3), 541–553. doi:10.1147/sj.453.0541

ENDNOTES

[1] http://138.4.11.45/~erma/w/index.php/CHESS:General

[2] http://www.ibm.com/developerworks/rational/library/06/1114_kelsey/index.html

[3] http://www.modeliosoft.com/en/modules/modelio-modules.html

[4] http://www.andromda.org/docs/andromda-cartridges/index.html

[5] RMA assets can include hierarchies of packages defining RMA data types, artefacts and other RMA modelling elements

[6] http://www.ibm.com/developerworks/rational/tutorials/r-helloram/resources.html, http://www.ibm.com/software/awdtools/ram/

[7] http://www.eclipse.org/downloads/packages/eclipse-modeling-tools-includes-incubating-components/heliossr1

[8] http://wiki.eclipse.org/MDT/OCLinEcore

[9] http://en.wikipedia.org/wiki/IBM_Rational_Software_Architect

[10] http://en.wikipedia.org/wiki/MagicDraw_UML

[11] http://en.wikipedia.org/wiki/Papyrus_(software)

[12] http://wiki.eclipse.org/QVTOML/Examples/InvokeInJava

[13] http://138.4.11.45:9080/ras_erma/services/WorkGroupRepositoryServer

[14] http://www.eclipse.org/webtools/

[15] http://mast.unican.es/

[16] http://www.omg.org/spec/MARTE/20090501, http://www.omg.org/spec/MARTE/20090502

APPENDIX

ERMA Examples: ERMA Assets for MARTE Profile Application

UML Profile for MARTE: Modeling and Analysis of Real-Time Embedded Systems (MARTE) (OMG 2009c) is an OMG standard for modelling real-time systems in UML 2.x. MARTE extensions enhance UML notations for the representation of real-time specific concepts (e.g. more precise specifications of time, hardware and real-time design patterns). MARTE was designed assuming it would be integrated with analysis tools (performance and scheduling analysis for some specific) and run-time platforms. This appendix introduces five ERMA assets for the application of MARTE in MDSD tools. These assets use MARTE for two main purposes: generation of scheduling analysis models for UML MARTE models and code generation for Ada 2005 and Java. Some additional assets could support performance analysis and code generations for other real-time programming languages.

Some real-time organizations have designed profiles of platforms and programming languages for use in development of real-time applications; Ada 2005 Ravenscar profile (ISO 2010) and Java RTSJ (Java Community Process, 2009) are two examples. These profiles define libraries and run-time environments to make Ada 2005 and Java applications time predictable. These two profiles assume the application of scheduling analysis methods to make the applications time-predictable. If we use these two platforms form the execution of MARTE applications, we must take into account their specific properties and the specific details of their code generators to make time- consistent scheduling analysis results and run times. Consistency of scheduling analysis models and code generation are fundamental problems to be addressed in the assets that we introduce in this section.

This section introduces five ERMA assets examples (in Figure 8) for the support and application of MARTE:

- *MARTEBeta3*: this is an asset for the integration of MARTE into UML modelling tools. This asset includes MARTE profiles, a model library and tutorials for their application. Some additional artefacts in this asset could be used to support the VSL (Value Specification Language) and other expressions handled in MARTE.
- *MAST_RMA*: this asset integrates MAST (Modeling and Analysis Suite for Real Time Applications)[15] into general modelling tools. MAST is an open source set of tools that enables the modelling of real-time applications and the performing of timing analysis on those applications. *MAST_RMA* supports the languages in *ecore* meta-models and includes artefacts for the execution of analysis. *MAST_RMA* allows MDA languages to be used for generating and editing MAST models and for constructing additional tools, such as diagrams editors. *MAST_RMA* is independent of MARTE; MAST_RMA is an example of an asset for the support of a DSL (MAST).
- *UML2AdaRavenscar, UML2RTSJ*: these two assets generate Java and Ada code for UML models that use RTSJ and Ada Ravenscar libraries and run-time environments. They are adaptations of Java and Ada code generators in MOF2Text, which take into account the specific limitations of these programming language profiles. These assets are independent of *MAST_RMA* and *MARTE*, and they could be used as we use some others code generators, but they are adapted for Ada Ravenscar and RTSJ profiles.
- *MARTE_SA_Gen*: this asset integrates transformations of MARTE models into MAST models and UML models that use RTSJ and Ada Ravenscar libraries and run-times. The transformation

Figure 8. General diagram of MARTE assets

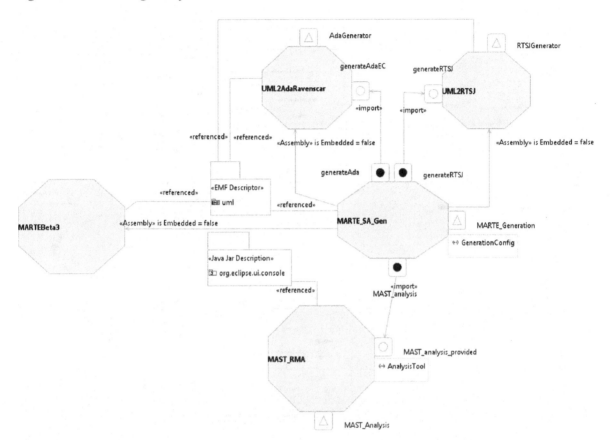

generates RTSJ or Ada Ravenscar patterns for MARTE modelling structures, and generates a MAST model taking into account MARTE::SAM profile annotations (SAM is a MARTE sub profile for the representation of scheduling analysis in UML 2.x).

Figure 8 includes five assets and their dependencies. *MARTEBeta3* supports the MARTE standard and only depends on the UML meta-model. *MAST_RMA* is the implementation of the MAST language in *Eclipse Modelling* and reuses *org.eclipse.ui.console* Eclipse plug-in for the generation of log and error messages. *MAST_RMA* includes a configuration parameter for the selection of analysis algorithm. It exports a service for the invocation of analysis from other assets, and a GUI command for the execution of analysis from modelling tool menus. *UML2AdaRavenscar* and *UML2RTSJ* depend on a UML meta-model and they provide a service for the execution of generators from other assets and from GUI commands. *MARTE_SA_Gen* depends on the other four assets (it assemblies the other assets, but they are not embedded because the others could be installed without *MARTE_SA_Gen*), and reuses the services provided in the others assets for the combined execution of analysis and code generators. Figure 9 includes a detailed ERMA diagram which includes the artefacts and interaction points for each asset.

The Beta3 version of the MARTE standard and the new version for MARTE 1.1 include two XMI models[16]: *MARTE UML profile* and *MARTE model library*. MARTE profiles use the model library and the model library applies some sub-profiles. The profile model and model library are in XMI format.

Figure 9. Detailed diagram of MARTE assets

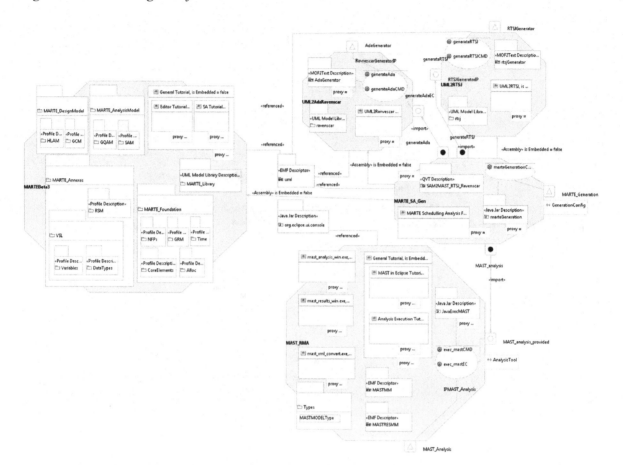

The *ecore* models are needed to represent the stereotype applications in the model library XMI file. These interdependencies create important problems in the XMI delivery of MARTE models. *The MAR-TEBeta3* asset includes the MARTE profile and the model library (the artefacts are described in Figure 9), but in this scenario we cannot delegate to ERMA the generation of MOF models for profiles, because they are needed for editing the model library, and the model library is needed for editing profiles. Similar problems occur in the *HwCommunication/HwGeneral* and *HwStorageManager/HwComputing* sub-profiles because they depend on each other (they have cross references in stereotypes in both directions) and MOF model generation requires special attention and specific solutions (*define* operations for profiles in UML2 project do not support the MOF models generations for these profiles). An alternative solution would be to merge inter-dependent profiles into a single profile, but our solutions do not modify the standards.

MARTE does not include nsURI (universal names) for the identification of profiles. We included these names in profiles with the format: http://MARTE.MARTE Packages>/schemas/<Profile Name>/1. *<MARTE Packages>* is the namespace for the profile (e.g. *MARTE.MARTE_DesignModel.HRM.Hw-Logical*). *<Profile Name>* is the name of the profile. Number 1 is the version number for the profile.

MOF2Text transformations *AdaGenerator* and *RTSJGenerator* reference several MOF2Text modules and a main module (each one is described in a single MOF2Text descriptor in Figure 9). There is a module for each design pattern and some additional modules for general Ada and Java programming structures (Burns & Wellings, 2009). The most important patterns are: *periodic, sporadic, simple, protected objects* and *passive*. They use general templates that support generation of exceptions handlers, operations and methods and guards and synchronisers. The MOF2Text modules implement the patterns in Java or Ada (e.g. instance of generics and generic classes, exception handlers and timing error handler, general execution cycles).

The *MARTE_SA_Gen* asset includes a QVTo transformation: *SA2MAST_Ravenscar_RTSJ* (Figure 9 includes the QVT artefact in the *MARTE_SA_Gen* asset). This input model for this transformation is a UML+MARTE model and it generates two output models: one MAST model and one UML model. The configuration of this asset defines what kind of UML is generated (Ada Ravenscar or RTSJ) and the generated UML models import the model library included in the *UML2AdaRavenscar* or *UML2RTSJ* assets. The output of this transformation is based on real-time design patterns (e.g. *sporadic server*, and *protected object*) and these patterns are represented with UML classes that use Ada Ravenscar libraries and run-time, and UML classes that use RTSJ libraries, and their equivalent in MAST elements. Each mapping in the transformation is applied in the same MARTE element and the mapping provides consistent outputs.

Chapter 15
The Past, Present, and Future of Model Versioning

Petra Brosch
Vienna University of Technology, Austria

Philip Langer
Johannes Kepler University Linz, Austria

Martina Seidl
Johannes Kepler University Linz, Austria

Konrad Wieland
Vienna University of Technology, Austria

Manuel Wimmer
Vienna University of Technology, Austria

Gerti Kappel
Vienna University of Technology, Austria

ABSTRACT

The evolution of software models induces a plethora of challenging research issues. Only when these problems are solved, the techniques of model-driven engineering (MDE) are able to fully exploit their potential in practice. Otherwise the advantages of MDE are relativized by time-consuming and cumbersome management tasks which are already well supported for traditional development based on textual code. One of these challenges is model versioning.

Version Control Systems (VCS) are an essential part of the software development infrastructure which (i) store the history of evolution of software artifacts, (ii) support multiple developers working in parallel, and (iii) manage different development branches. For all of these tasks, changes performed on the artifacts under version control have to be tracked. For the second and third task it is additionally necessary to detect conflicts between concurrently evolved versions of one artifact and to resolve such conflicts in order to obtain a consolidated version.

DOI: 10.4018/978-1-61350-438-3.ch015

Compared to code versioning, which works well in practice, model versioning is still in its infancy as the established approaches for code versioning may be hardly reused. However, several dedicated approaches for model versioning have been proposed. In this chapter, we review the active research field of model versioning, establish a common terminology, introduce the various techniques and technologies applied in state-of-the-art versioning systems, and conclude with open issues and challenges which have to be overcome for putting model versioning into practice.

INTRODUCTION

During the software development lifecycle, the various software artifacts under construction are subject to successive changes. Consequently, tool support for managing the evolution of these artifacts is indispensable (Estublier et al., 2005; and Mens, 2008). To this end, the discipline of Software Configuration Management (SCM) provides tools and techniques for making evolution manageable (Tichy, 1988). Amongst others, these tools include Version Control Systems (VCS) whose origins may be dated back to the early 70s. Since then, the discipline of versioning is an active research topic generating a variety of different concepts, formalisms, and technologies.

The aims of versioning approaches are three-fold. First, versioning systems maintain a historical archive of the different versions an artifact adopts during its development. With this archive, it is possible to undo harmful modifications by restoring previous development states. Second, versioning systems support handling different development branches, e.g., for building different software variants. Third, versioning approaches manage the parallel evolution of software artifacts performed by a (distributed) team of developers. In this book chapter we focus on the latter aim.

In general, two different versioning strategies exist to cope with the concurrent evolution of one artifact. When *pessimistic versioning* is applied, an artifact is locked while it is changed by one developer. Since other developers cannot perform any changes while the artifact is locked, conflicts are completely avoided with this strategy. However, the drawbacks are possible idle times

for developers waiting for the release of a locked artifact. To avoid such idle times, *optimistic versioning* allows the developers to change the same artifact in parallel and independently of each other. The typical workflow of optimistic versioning is depicted in Figure 1. Two users of the optimistic versioning system, Harry and Sally, check out the same artifact at time *t0*. Both modify the checked out Version 0 independently of each other. After Sally has finished, she checks in her modified version (Version 1) at *t1*. When Harry also tries to check in his modified version, he first has to *merge* his version (Version 2) with the latest version in the repository (Version 1). Merging, often a time-consuming and tedious task, is the price to pay, when concurrent modifications by several users are allowed. In general, the merge process may be divided into four steps: (i) identifying the differences between two concurrently modified versions, (ii) detecting conflicts between these two modifications, (iii) resolving these conflicts either automatically or manually, and finally (iv) creating a new consolidated version which, in the best case, combines all intentions behind all concurrently performed modifications.

From a technical point of view, a wealth of works have been published which contribute in solving various versioning challenges (cf. Conradi & Westfechtel, 1998 for a survey), but how versioning really works in practice when huge software applications are developed is hardly discussed. To fill this gap, in 2010 we have conducted an online survey on best practices in versioning, which has been answered by approximately 100 software engineers, software architects, and IT managers. We wanted to learn about their habits and processes when versioning software artifacts. Overall, 80% of the participants stated that they put their software artifacts under *optimistic version control*. Thus, we conclude that optimistic version control is paramountly applied in practice and of significant importance. 73% of the participants justify their preference for optimistic version control by the fact that locking specific artifacts leads to undesirable delays in software development projects.

So far, the versioning research has mainly focused on the management of textual artifacts like source code. For such artifacts, a line-oriented processing of files has largely been adopted by practitioners in the past. More fine-grained approaches, in which not lines but, e.g., words are considered as atomic units of comparison, have not gained much attention in practice. The situation is different when the artifacts put under version control are graph-based artifacts like models. Here a more precise consideration of the model elements is necessary to obtain accurate reports on the performed modifications and potential conflicts between concurrently performed changes.

With the increasing employment of model-driven engineering techniques (Schmidt, 2006)

for the development of large software systems, the call for adequate infrastructural means supporting the effective management of collaboration when working on software models grows even louder. From our online survey we learnt that 65% of the survey participants use versioning facilities also for software models (cf. Figure 2). However, 57% apply only coarse-grained versioning strategies for software models, i.e., versioning is configured to operate at the file level not considering different model elements. Consequently, a conflict is raised as soon as two users concurrently modify the same model irrespectively of the change on a specific element. In standard VCSs for code, the conflict detection is usually performed by line-oriented text comparison of files. When applied on the textual serialization of models, the result is unsatisfactory in general. Not least because of its graph-based structure, single changes on the model may result in multiple changed lines in the textual serialization like XMI[1]. Considering lines as unit of comparison, the information stemming from the graph-based structure is destroyed and associated syntactic and semantic information is lost. The majority of all survey participants disapproves this situation and would prefer more

Figure 1. The optimistic versioning process

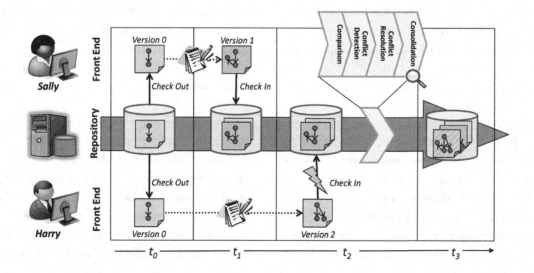

Figure 2. Survey results: artifacts under version control

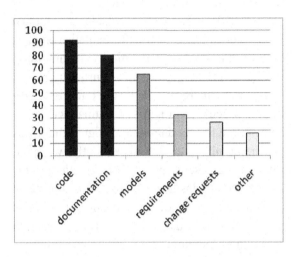

fine-grained versioning on the basis of both syntax and semantics of the model. However, fine-grained versioning of software models is only limited supported by current modeling tools.

When putting models under version control, the graph-based structure is not the only issue needing special treatment. In contrast to code, the abstract syntax of a model is separated from the layout information including the arrangement and the visualization of the dedicated model elements. Since models are normally developed and refined in a graphical syntax, fine-grained versioning considering both the model and the diagram is required, which is unfortunately not supported by current state-of-the-art VCSs. Furthermore, merging different diagram layout versions raises several challenges and open questions. No concise definition has been established yet which concurrently performed layout changes should be reported as conflicts and, furthermore, how these conflicts should be presented to the user. Consequently, the modifications and conflicts are usually presented within the tree representation of a model, abstaining from the visual information valuable for the human user. The visualization of differences and conflicts in the concrete syntax of the modeling language still remains an open

issue notwithstanding that 61% of the survey participants consider this to be one of the most important features of VCSs. The survey results reflect the call for better support when handling conflicts between two different versions of a model: according to the survey, conflict resolution causes the highest effort and most of the participants state that visual conflict resolution is desirable.

Due to all these current drawbacks, modeling mostly remains a one-(wo)man show in order to avoid model merges. This, however, is in contradiction with the term "model-driven engineering", because an engineering discipline must include – besides other important features – the ability to build software systems that are so large that they have to be built by a team or teams of engineers (Ghezzi et al., 2002). Fortunately, the urgent need for a suitable infrastructure supporting optimistic model versioning has been widely recognized and first solutions start to emerge. Barrett et al. (2008) have performed an evaluation of the versioning capabilities of commercial modeling tools and have provided an experience report. In Altmanninger et al. (2009) we have also compared different state-of-the-art tools and we have explored which kind of conflicts may be detected by recent tools. Since model versioning is urgently needed in practice, much effort is spent in this research area, resulting in a rapid evolution and maturation of model versioning approaches. New tools and approaches emerge in a very short cycle, contributing to an increase in the understanding of model versioning concepts. Based on this understanding, we aim to survey the past and present of model versioning in order to state important future challenges.

To lay out the foundations of versioning, we collect and unify important concepts, terminologies, and design possibilities regarding artifact and change representation from the *past achievements*. To get a picture of the *present situation*, we then survey state-of-the-art model versioning systems. With this background, we are able to derive *future challenges* for model versioning systems. To underpin our conjectures on potential challenges, we have not only identified these challenges from literature and from our own experiences when building a model versioning system, but we have also conducted 15 expert interviews and the aforementioned online survey which provided valuable insights on the users' requirements and expectations.

FOUNDATIONS OF VERSIONING

In the long history of active research on software versioning, diverse formalisms and technologies emerged. To categorize this variety of different approaches, Conradi & Westfechtel (1998) proposed *version models* describing the diverse characteristics of existing versioning approaches. A version model specifies the objects to be versioned, version identification and organization as well as operations for retrieving existing versions and constructing new versions. Conradi & Westfechtel distinguish between the *product space* and the *version space* within version models. The product space describes the structure of a software product and its artifacts without taking versions into account. In contrast, the version space is agnostic of the artifact's structure and copes with the dimension of evolution by introducing versions and relationships between versions of an artifact, such as, for instance, their differences (deltas). Further, Conradi & Westfechtel distinguish between extensional and intentional versioning. *Extensional versioning* deals with the reconstruction of previously created versions and, therefore, concerns version identification, immutability, and efficient storage. All versions are explicit and have been checked in once before. *Intentional versioning* deals with flexible automatic construction of consistent versions from a version space. In other words, intentional versioning allows for annotating properties to specific versions and querying the version space for these properties in order

to derive a new product consisting of a specific combination of different versions.

In this chapter, we only consider extensional versioning in terms of having explicit versions, because this kind of versioning is paramountly applied in practice nowadays. Furthermore, we focus on the *merge phase* in the optimistic versioning process (cf. Figure 1). In this section, we first outline the fundamental design dimensions of versioning systems. Subsequently, we present some representatives of versioning systems using different designs. Finally, we elaborate on the consequences of different design possibilities considering the quality of the merged version based on an example.

Fundamental Design Dimensions for Versioning Systems

Current approaches to merging two versions of one software artifact (software models or source code) can be categorized according to two basic dimensions (cf. Figure 3). The first dimension concerns the product space, in particular, the *artifact representation*. This dimension denotes the representation of a software artifact, on which the merge approach operates. Most basically, the used representation may either be *text-based* or *graph-based*. Some merge approaches operate on a tree-based representation. However, we consider a tree as a special kind of graph in this categorization. The second dimension is orthogonal to the first one and considers how *deltas are identified, represented, and merged* in order to create a consolidated version. Existing merge approaches either operate on the *states*, i.e., versions, of an artifact, or on identified *operations* which have been applied between a common origin model (cf. Version 0 in Figure 1) and the two successors (cf. Version 1 and 2 in Figure 1).

When merging two concurrently modified versions of a software artifact, conflicts might inevitably occur. The most basic types of conflicts are *update/update* and *delete/update* conflicts.

Figure 3. Categorization of versioning systems

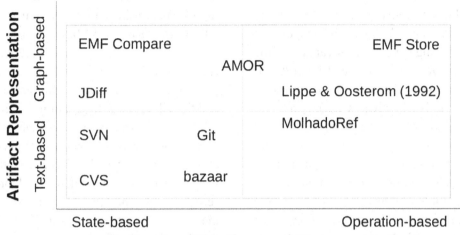

Update/update conflicts occur if two elements have been updated in both versions whereas delete/update conflicts are raised if an element has been updated in one version and deleted in the other. A profound discussion on more complex types of conflicts is given in Section *Advanced Conflicts and Future Challenges*. For more information on software merging in general, the interested reader is referred to Mens (2002).

Text-based merge approaches operate solely on the textual representation of a software artifact in terms of flat text files. Within a text file, the atomic unit may either be a paragraph, a line, a word, or even an arbitrary set of characters. The major advantage of such approaches is their independence of the programming languages used in the versioned artifacts. Since a solely text-based approach does not require language-specific knowledge it may be adopted for all flat text files. This advantage is probably, besides simplicity and efficiency, the reason for the widespread adoption of pure text-based approaches in practice. However, when merging flat files – agnostic of the syntax and semantics of a programming language – both compile-time and run-time errors might be introduced during the merge. Therefore,

graph-based approaches emerged, which take syntax and semantics into account.

Graph-based merge approaches operate on a more appropriate graph-based representation of a software artifact for more precise conflict detection and merging. Such approaches de-serialize or translate the versioned software artifact into a specific structure before merging. Mens (2002) categorized these approaches in *syntactic and semantic merge approaches*. Syntactic merge approaches consider the syntax of a programming language by, for instance, translating the text file into the abstract syntax tree and, subsequently, performing the merge in a syntax-aware manner. Consequently, unimportant textual conflicts, which are, for instance, caused by reformatting the text file, may be avoided. Furthermore, such approaches may also avoid syntactically erroneous merge results. However, the textual formatting intended by the developers might be obfuscated by syntactic merging because only a graph-based representation of the syntax is merged and has to be translated back to text eventually. Semantic merge approaches go one step further and consider also the static and/or dynamic semantics of a programming language. Therefore, these approaches may also detect issues such as undeclared variables or even infinite loops by using complex formalisms like program dependency graphs and program slicing. Naturally, these advantages over flat textual merging have the disadvantage of the inherent language dependence (cf. Mens (2002)) and their increased computational complexity. Furthermore, it is not always trivial to point the developer to the modifications that caused the conflict. If such a trace back to the causing modifications is missing or inaccurate, it might be difficult for developers to understand and resolve the raised conflicts since they are reported based on a different representation, i.e., the graph, of the artifact, and not in the textual representation the developer is familiar with.

The second dimension in Figure 3 is orthogonal to the first one and considers how *deltas are identified and merged* in order to create a consolidated version. This dimension is agnostic of the unit of versioning. Therefore, a versioned element might be a line in a flat text file, a node in a graph, or whatsoever constitutes the representation used for merging.

State-based merging compares the states, i.e., versions, of a software artifact to identify the differences (deltas) between them and merge all differences which are not contradicting with each other. Such approaches may either be applied to two states (Version 1 and Version 2 in Figure 1), called two-way merging, or to three states (including their common ancestor Version 0 in Figure 1), called three-way merging. Two-way merging cannot identify deletions since the common original state is unknown. A state-based comparison requires a match function which determines whether two elements of the compared artifact correspond to each other. The easiest way to match two elements is to search for completely equivalent elements. However, the quality of the match function is crucial for the overall quality of the merge approach. Therefore, especially graph-based merge approaches often use more sophisticated matching techniques based on identifiers and

heuristics (cf. Kim & Notkin, 2006 for an overview of matching techniques). Model matching, or more generally the graph isomorphism problem is NP-hard (cf. Khuller & Raghavachari, 1996) and therefore very expensive regarding its run-time. If the match function is capable of matching also partially different elements, a difference function is additionally required to determine the fine-grained differences between two corresponding elements. Having these two functions, two states of the same artifact may be merged with the algorithm shown in Listing 1. Please note that this algorithm only serves to conceptually clarify basic state-based merging. This algorithm is applicable for both, text-based and graph-based merging, whereas nX denotes the atomic element n within the product space of Version X.

The algorithm in Listing 1 iterates through each element $n0$ in the initial version $V0$ of a software artifact. The following two lines retrieve the elements matching with $n0$ from the two modified versions $V1$ and $V2$. However, there might be no match for $n0$ in $V1$ or $V2$ since it might have been removed. If $n0$ has a match in both versions $V1$ and $V2$, the algorithm checks if it has been modified in the versions $V1$ and $V2$. If the matching element is different from the original element $n0$, i.e., it has been modified, in one and only one of the two versions $V1$ and $V2$, the modified element is used for creating the merged version. If the matching element is different in both versions, an update/update conflict is raised by the algorithm. If the matching element has not been modified at all, the original unit $n0$ is used for the merged version. Next, the algorithm checks if there is no match for $n0$ in one of the two modified versions, i.e., it has been removed. If so, the algorithm determines whether it has been concurrently modified and raises, in this case, a delete/update conflict. If the element has not been modified, it is removed from the merged version. The element $n0$ is also removed, if there is no match in both modified versions, i.e., it has been deleted in both versions. Finally, the algo-

Listing 1. State-based merge algorithm

```
for each element n0 ∈ V0n1 := match(n0 in V1) // retrieving matching n ∈ V1 n2
:= match(n0 in V2)// retrieving matching n ∈ V2
  if hasMatch(n0 in V1) && hasMatch(n0 in V2)
    if diff(n0, n1) && not diff(n0, n2) -> use n1
    if not diff(n0, n1) && diff(n0, n2) -> use n2
    if diff(n0, n1) && diff(n0, n2) -> raise update/update conflict
    if not diff(n0, n1) && not diff(n0, n2) -> use n0
  end if
  if hasMatch(n0 in V1) && not hasMatch(n0 in V2)
    if diff(n0, n1) -> raise delete/update conflict
    if not diff(n0, n1) -> remove n0
  end if
  if not hasMatch(n0 in V1) && hasMatch(n0 in V2)
    if diff(n0, n2) -> raise delete/update conflict
    if not diff(n0, n2) -> remove n0
  end if
  if not hasMatch(n0 in V1) && not hasMatch(n0 in V2) -> remove n0
end for
for each n1 ∈ V1 | not hasMatch(n1, V0) -> add n1 to merged version
for each n2 ∈ V2 | not hasMatch(n2, V0) -> add n2 to merged version
```

rithm adds all elements from *V1* and *V2,* which have no match in the original version *V0* and which, consequently, have been added in *V1* or *V2.*

Operation-based merging does not operate on the states of an artifact. Instead, the operation sequences which have been concurrently applied to the original version are recorded and analyzed. Since the operations are directly recorded by the applied editor, operation-based approaches may support, besides recording atomic changes, also to record composite operations such as refactorings (e.g., Koegel et al., 2010). The knowledge on applied refactorings may significantly increase the quality of the merge as stated by Dig et al. (2007). The downside of operation recording is the strong dependency on the applied editor, since it has to record each performed operation and it has to provide this operation sequence in a format which the merge approach is able to process.

The directly recorded operation sequence might include obsolete operations such as updates to an element which will be removed later on. Therefore, many operation-based approaches apply a cleansing algorithm to the recorded operation sequence for more efficient merging. The operations within the operation sequence might be interdependent because some of the operations cannot be applied until other operations have been applied. As soon as the operation sequences are available, operation-based approaches check parallel operation sequences (Version 0 to Version 1 and Version 0 to Version 2) for commutativity to reveal conflicts (cf. Lippe & Oosterom, 1992). Consequently, a decision procedure for commutativity is required. Such decision procedures are not necessarily trivial. In the simplest yet least efficient form, each pair of changes within the cross product of all atomic changes in both sequences are applied in both possible orders to the artifact and both results are checked for equality. If they are not equivalent, the changes are not commutative. After checking for commutativity, operation-based merge approaches apply all non-conflicting (commutative) changes of both sides to the common ancestor in order to obtain a merged model.

In comparison to state-based approaches, the recorded operation sequences are, in general, more precise and potentially enable to gather more information, e.g., change order and refactorings, than state-based differencing. In particular, state-based approaches do not rely on a precise matching technique. Moreover, state-based comparison approaches are—due to complex comparison algorithms—very expensive regarding their run-time in contrast to operation-based change recording. However, these advantages come at the price of strong editor-dependence. Furthermore, one part of the computational complexity which was saved in contrast to state-based matching and differencing is lost again due to operation sequence cleansing and non-trivial checking for commutativity. Nevertheless, operation-based approaches scale for large models from a conceptual point of view because their computational effort mainly depends on the length of the operation sequences and—in contrast to state-based approaches—not on the size of the models (Koegel et al. (2010)).

Anyhow, the border between state-based and operation-based merging is sometimes blurry. Indeed, we can clearly distinguish whether the changes are recorded or differences are derived from the states, however, some *state-based* approaches derive the *applied operations* from the states and use operation-based conflict detection techniques. But this is only reasonable if a reliable matching function is available, for instance, using unique identifiers. On the contrary, some *operation-based* approaches derive the *states* from their operation sequences to check for potentially inconsistent states after merging. Such an inconsistent state might for instance be a violation of the syntactic rules of a language. Detecting such conflicts is often not possible by solely analyzing

the operation sequences. Eventually, the conflict detection strategies conducted in state-based and operation-based approaches are very similar from a conceptual point of view. Both check for direct or indirect concurrent modifications to the same element and try to identify illegal states after merging, whether the modifications are explicitly given in terms of operations or are implicitly derived from a match between two states.

Selected Representatives

In Figure 3, we cited some representatives for each combination of the two dimensions in the domain of source code versioning as well as model versioning. In the following, we briefly introduce and compare the representatives listed in Figure 3. For a more detailed description of existing model versioning approaches we kindly refer to Section *State-of-the-Art Model Versioning Systems*.

The combination of *text-based and state-based merge approaches* are probably the most adopted ones in practice. For instance, traditional central Version Control Systems such as *CVS*[2] and *SVN*[3] use state-based three-way merging of flat text files. The smallest indivisible unit of merging in these systems is usually a *line* within a text file, as it is the case for the Unix *diff* utility (Hunt & McIlroy (1976). Lines are matched across different versions by searching for the Least Common Sub-sequence (LCS). For efficiency, usually only *completely equal* lines are matched and, therefore, no dedicated difference function for deriving the actual difference between two lines is required: A line is simply either matched and therefore equal, or unmatched and therefore considered to be added or removed at a certain position in a text file. Consequently, parallel modifications to *different* lines can be merged without user intervention as long as they are at different positions. As soon as the same line is modified in both versions (Version 1 and Version 2) or modified and concurrently deleted, a conflict is annotated in the merged file. As stated earlier, due to their syntax and semantics unawareness, compile-time and run-time errors might be introduced by the merge. The same applies to the Distributed Version Control Systems (DVCS) *git⁴* and *bazaar⁵* since they are also state-based and line-based. The major difference to SVN and CVS is their distributed nature. DVCS disclaim a single central repository and take a peer-to-peer approach instead. Developers commit their changes to a local repository, i.e., a peer, and push them to other remote peers as they wish. Besides several other organizational advantages, this enables a higher commit frequency since a commit does not immediately affect other developers. Changes might therefore be grouped into *atomic commits* and pushed to other peers more easily which is a step towards operation-based merging.

MolhadoRef (Dig et al., 2008), a representative for *text- and operation-based approaches*, aims at improving the merge result by also considering refactorings applied to object-oriented (Java) programs. Applications of refactorings are recorded in the development environment. When two versions are merged, all recorded refactorings are undone in both modified versions, then the versions, excluding the refactoring applications, are merged in a traditional text-based manner, and, finally, all refactorings are re-applied to this merged version. This significantly improves the merge result and avoids unnecessary conflicts in many scenarios. However, as already mentioned, a strong dependency to the applied editor is given because the editor has to provide operation logs. Furthermore, handling refactorings requires language-specific knowledge encoded in the merge component.

Several *state-based approaches* exist which operate on a *graph-based representation* of the versioned software artifact. In Figure 3, we cite two representatives for graph-based and state-based approaches – one for source code, namely *JDiff* by Apiwattanapong et al. (2007), and one for software models, namely EMF Compare⁶. *JDiff* is a graph-based differencing approach for Java source code. Corresponding classes, interfaces

and methods are matched by their qualified name or signature. This matching also accounts for the possibility to interact with the user in order to improve the match of renamed but still corresponding elements due to the absence of unique identifiers. For matching and differencing the method bodies, the approach builds enhanced control-flow graphs representing the statements in the bodies and compares them. By this, JDiff can provide information that accurately reflects the effects of code changes on the program at the statement level. *EMF Compare* is a model comparison framework for EMF based models. It facilitates heuristics for matching model elements and can detect differences between matched elements on a fine-grained level (metamodel features of each model element). The matching and differencing is applied on the generic model-based representation of the elements.

There are several purely *operation-based* approaches which record changes directly and apply merging on a *graph-based representation*. The first publication which introduced operation-based merging was elaborated by Lippe & Oosterom (1992). They proposed to record all changes applied to an object-oriented database system. After the precise change-sets are available due to recording, they are merged by re-applying all their changes to the common ancestor version. In general, a pair of changes is conflicting if they are not commutative. *EMF Store* (Koegel et al. (2010)) is an operation- and graph-based versioning system for software models. *AMOR* (Brosch et al., 2010a) is depicted in the center of state-based and operation-based approaches which apply graph-based merging. In AMOR, differences are obtained from the states; however, explicit operations including composite operations such as refactorings are inferred from the differences which build the basis for its operation-based conflict detection and resolution.

Since EMF Compare, EMF Store, and AMOR are representatives of model versioning systems, they are further elaborated on in Section *State-of-the-Art Model Versioning Systems*.

Consequences of Design Decisions

To highlight the benefits and drawbacks of the four possible combinations of the versioning approaches based on Figure 3, we present a small versioning example depicted in Figure 4 and conceptually apply each approach for analyzing its quality in terms of the detected conflicts and derived merged version.

Consider a small language for specifying *classes*, its *properties*, and *references* linking two classes. The textual representation of this language is depicted in the upper left area of Figure 4 and defined by the EBNF-like Xtext[7] grammar specified in the box labeled *Grammar*. The same language and the same examples are depicted in terms of graphs in the lower part of Figure 4. In the initial version (Version 0) of the example, there are two classes, namely Human and Vehicle. The class Human contains a property name and the class Vehicle contains a property named carNo. Now, two users concurrently modify Version 0 and create Version 1 and Version 2, respectively. All changes in Version 1 and Version 2 are highlighted with bold fonts or edges in Figure 4.

Figure 4. Versioning example

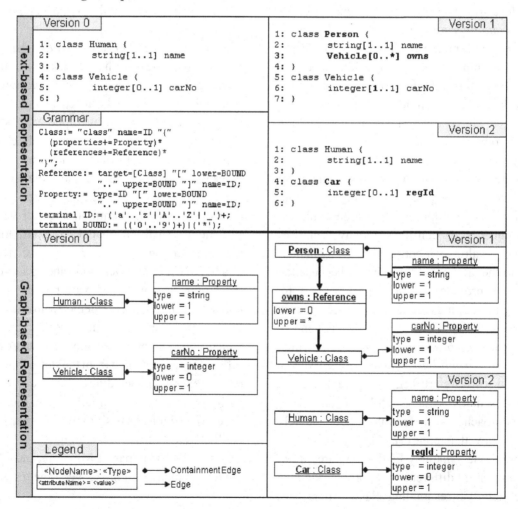

The first user changes the name of the class Human to Person, sets the lower bound of the property carNo to 1 (because every car must have exactly one number) and adds an explicit reference owns to Person. Concurrently, the second user renames the property carNo to regId and the class Vehicle to Car.

Text-Based Versioning

When merging this example with *text- and state-based* approaches (cf. Figure 5(a) for the result) where the artifact's representation is a single line and the match function only matches completely equal lines (as with SVN, CVS, Git, bazaar, etc), the first line is correctly merged since it has only been modified in Version 1 and remained untouched in Version 2 (cf. Listing 1). The same is true for the added reference in line 3 of Version 1 and the renamed class Car in line 4 of Version 2. However, the property carNo represented by line 5 in Version 0 has been changed in both Versions 1 (line 6) and Version 2 (line 5). Although different features of this property have been modified (lower and name), these modifications result in a concurrent change of the same line and, hence, a conflict is raised. Furthermore, the reference added in Version 1 refers to class Vehicle, which does not exist in the merged version anymore since it has been renamed in Version 2. We may summarize that text- and state-based merging approaches provide a reasonable support for versioning software artifacts. They are easy to apply and work for every kind of flat text file irrespectively of the used language. However, erroneous merge results may occur and several "unnecessary" conflicts might be raised. The overall quality strongly depends on the textual syntax. Merging textual languages with a strict syntactic structure (such as XML) might be more appropriate than merging languages which mix several properties of potentially independent concepts into one line. The latter might cause tedious manual conflict and error resolution.

One major problem in the merged example resulting from text-based and state-based approaches is the wrong reference target (line 3 in Version 1) caused by the concurrent rename of Vehicle. *Operation-based approaches* (such as MolhadoRef) solve such an issue by incorporating knowledge on applied refactorings in the merge. Since a *rename* is a refactoring, MolhadoRef would be aware of the rename and resolve the issue by re-applying the rename after a traditional merge is done. The result of this merge is shown in Figure 5(b).

Graph-Based Versioning

Applying the merge on top of the *graph-based representation* depicted in Figure 4 may also significantly improve the merge result because the representation used for merging is a node in a graph which more precisely represents the versioned software artifact. However, as already mentioned, this advantage comes at the price of language dependence because merging operates either on the language specific graph-based representation or a translation of a language to a generic graph-based structure must be available.

Figure 5. Text-based versioning example: (a) state, (b) operation

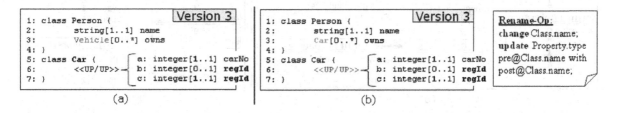

Graph- and state-based approaches additionally require a match function for finding corresponding nodes and a difference function for explicating the differences between matched nodes. The preciseness of the match function significantly influences the quality of the overall merge. Assume matching is based on name and structure heuristics for the example in Figure 4. Given this assumption, the class Human may be matched since it contains an unchanged property name. Therefore, renaming the class Human to Person can be merged without user intervention. However, heuristically matching the class Vehicle might be more challenging because both the class and its contained property have been renamed. If the match does not identify the correspondence between Vehicle and Car, Vehicle and its contained property carNo is considered to be removed and Car is assumed to be added in Version 2. Consequently, a delete/update conflict is reported for the change of the lower bound of the property carNo in Version 1. Also the added reference owns refers to a removed class which might be reported as conflict. This type of conflict is referred to as *delete-use* or *delete-reference* in literature (cf. Taentzer et al. (2010), Westfechtel (2008)). If, in contrast, the match relies on unique identifiers, the nodes can soundly be matched. Based on this precise match, the state-based merge component can resolve this issue and the added reference owns correctly refers to the renamed class Car in the merged version. However, the concurrent modi-

fication of the property carNo (name and lower) might still be a problem since purely state-based approaches usually take the element's changes of only one version to construct the merged version. Some state-based approaches solve this issue by conducting a more fine-grained difference function to identify the detailed differences between two elements. If these differences are not overlapping – as in our example – they can both be applied to the merged element. The result of a graph-based and state-based merge without taking identifiers into account is visualized in Figure 6(a).

Purely *graph- and operation-based approaches* are capable of automatically merging the presented example (cf. Figure 6(b)). Between Version 0 and Version 1, three operations have been recorded, namely the rename of Human, the addition of the reference owns and the update concerning the lower bound of carNo. To get Version 2 from Version 0, class Vehicle and property carNo have been renamed. All these atomic operations do not interfere, i.e., they are commutative, and therefore, they all can be re-applied to Version 0 in order to obtain a correctly merged version.

To sum up, a lot of research activity during the last decades in the domain of traditional source code versioning has lead to significant results. Approaches for merging *software models* draw a lot of inspiration from previous works in the area of *source code* merging. Especially graph-based approaches for source code merging form

Figure 6. Graph-based versioning example: (a) state, (b) operation

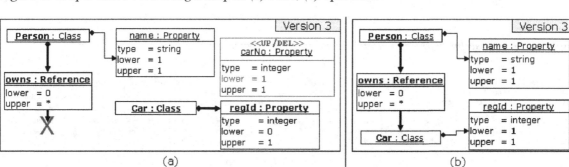

the foundation for model versioning. However, several challenges still have to be addressed in future. First, the same trade-off as in traditional source code merging has to be made regarding editor- and language-independence versus preciseness and completeness. Model matching, comparison and merging, as discussed above, can significantly be improved by incorporating knowledge on the used modeling language. On the other hand, model versioning approaches are also forced to support several languages at once because even in small MDE projects several modeling languages are usually combined. Therefore, a generic infrastructure which may be adapted for several modeling languages is as valuable as it is challenging to design. Second, software models are usually created and maintained using a (textual or graphical) concrete syntax rather than using the abstract syntax. When model versioning approaches solely work on the graph-based abstract syntax representation, a huge gap accrues between the representation used for merging and the representation which developers use and consequently are familiar with. This hinders developers to efficiently grasp identified differences and raised conflicts. Moreover, the graphical representation of a model carries a lot of additional information, which has been discussed, e.g., by Misue et al. (1995). These considerations are mostly ignored by recent model versioning approaches.

STATE-OF-THE-ART MODEL VERSIONING SYSTEMS

In the previous section, general versioning concepts have been introduced without putting special emphasis on *model* versioning. These general concepts which are the result of intensive research efforts provide the basics for dedicated model versioning systems, which are urgently required in times when model-driven engineering technologies mature and find their way from academia into industry. In this section, we review the status-quo in the active research landscape on model versioning and discuss the current achievements and advancements.

Overview

Over the years, several graph-based versioning systems for software models have been proposed, which are shortly introduced in the following. We consider approaches which provide differencing and merging facilities as well as complete model versioning systems including a repository, and we highlight their distinguishing features.

Approach of Alanen and Porres

One of the earliest works on the versioning of UML models was the paper by Alanen & Porres (2003), who presented various metamodel independent algorithms for difference calculation, model merging as well as conflict resolution. They identified seven elementary operations which are grouped into positive and negative operations. Whereas positive operations add model elements and can therefore be used to represent any model, negative operations have the opposite effect and remove model elements. For calculating the differences between the original version and the modified version, first an unambiguous mapping is created which allows the calculation of the necessary changes to obtain the new version from the old version. For the mapping, unique identifiers of the model elements are required. For the merge, different situations are considered. Conflicts are reported if an updated element is deleted or two ordered features are added. Then manual intervention is necessary for conflict resolution. Finally, metamodel-aware automatic conflict resolution is suggested in order to repair the model in such a manner that broken well-formed rules are again obeyed.

Approach of Oda and Saeki

The version control support proposed by Oda & Saeki (2005) builds upon the facilities offered by a meta-CASE tool which allows the construction of modeling editors for arbitrary modeling languages. Together with the typical functionalities also versioning features like the calculation of differences are included into a modeling editor built from a given metamodel. The generated tool offers a menu for performing check-in, check-out, and update operations on the repository. When a model is changed within such an editor, the modifications are recorded and stored to the central repository. Since the modeling editors are newly built by the meta-CASE tool, the necessary functionality is included as required. Model elements are assigned a unique identifier and model specific operations may be defined. Also layout information is considered within the versioning process.

Approach of Ohst, Welle, and Kelter

Within their merge algorithm, Ohst et al. (2003) put special emphasis on the visualization of the differences. They offer a preview to the user which contains all modifications even if they are contradicting. The diagram shown in the preview may be modified, conflicts may be manually resolved, and automatically applied merge decisions may be undone. For the merge, unique identifiers of the model elements are required. Considered conflicts are update/update and delete/update conflicts. For indicating the modifications, the different model versions are shown in a unified document containing the common parts, the automatically merged parts, as well as the conflicts. For distinguishing the different parts, different colors are used. In the case of delete/update conflicts, the deleted model element is crossed out and decorated with a warning symbol to indicate the modification.

Approach of Mehra, Grundy, and Hosking

The approach of Mehra et al. (2005) also focuses on visualization support for comparison and merging tasks in CASE tools. Therefore, they provide a plugin for the meta-CASE tool Pounamu, a tool for the specification and generation of multi-view design editors. The diagrams are serialized in XMI, which are converted into a Java object graph for comparison. The obtained differences are translated to Pounamu editing events which have been applied on the model. Differences cover not only modifications performed on the model, but also modifications performed on the visualization, e.g., editing events like ResizeShape. The differences between various versions are highlighted in the concrete syntax, i.e., in the diagram view, presented to the modeler who may accept or reject modifications. When a modification is accepted it is applied on the model and stored within the repository.

Approach of Cicchetti, Di Ruscio, and Pierantonio

Cicchetti et al. (2008) propose a domain-specific language to specify conflicts and conflict resolution patterns. Conflicts are defined based on a proprietary difference model which describes the modifications performed on subsequent versions of one model. To this end, the authors are able to establish an extendable set of conflicts, represented as forbidden difference pattern. By this means, the realization of a customizable conflict detection component is possible. The difference model conforms to a difference metamodel which is dedicated to the used modeling language. This difference metamodel is automatically generated from the metamodel of the modeling language. When two different versions of a common base model evolve, then the merged version may be obtained by composing the two difference models. The result of the composition of two difference models is again a difference model containing the minimal difference set, i.e., only these modifications are included, which have not been overwritten by other operations. When the modifications are conflicting, this conflict has to be reported or resolved by applying a dedicated reconciliation strategy defined for the conflict pattern.

ADAMS

Beside versioning features, the Advanced Artifact Management System ADAMS offers process management functionality, coordination of multiple modelers, and the management of traceability information (De Lucia et al., 2006). ADAMS may be integrated via specific plug-ins into various modeling environments to realize model management and context-awareness, i.e., every modeler knows who else is working on the same model element. De Lucia et al. (2009) present an ADAMS plug-in for versioning ArgoUML models. For ArgoUML, XMI files with the diagram information, and additional files with layout information and meta information about the models are considered and transformed into an internal format to be stored within the model repository. If a model is checked-out or updated, the model stored in the repository is again converted back to the tool specific format. On the client-side, the deltas are calculated when the model is modified based on the assumption that unique identifiers are available. Only the deltas are committed to the central versioning server where the merge process is performed. In ADAMS it is possible to configure the unit of comparison. Changes to uncorrelated elements are automatically merged, whereas for conflicting modifications manual intervention is necessary. For newly introduced model elements, simple matching heuristics are applied to check whether another modeler has introduced the same element. If a potential duplication is detected, it is reported to the modeler and like in a conflict situation manual intervention is necessary. In ADAMS, the layout information is

also considered as a model and is therefore also set under version control.

AMOR

The model versioning system AMOR presented by Brosch et al. (2010a) implements a conflict detection component for Ecore models which reports not only conflicts resulting from atomic changes, but also from composite changes. These composite changes are not tracked following an operation-based approach, but they are recalculated based on the versions of one model which are potentially conflicting. Due to this state-based approach, the conflict detection of AMOR is independent of any modeling environment. For handling the conflicts, AMOR offers two different approaches: (i) immediate conflict resolution and (ii) living with inconsistencies. If the conflicts shall be resolved immediately, a conflict resolution recommender guides the modeler during the conflict resolution process by suggesting potential, automatically executable resolution patterns. In some situations, it might be preferable, to defer the conflict resolution to a later point in time. AMOR offers a mechanism to incorporate the changes of any modeler into one model which is annotated with information about the conflicts (Brosch et al., (2010c)).

CoObRA

The Concurrent Object Replication framework CoObRA developed by Schneider et al. (2004) realizes optimistic versioning for the UML case tool Fujaba[8]. CoObRA records the changes performed on the model elements and aligns incremental changes into groups. The change protocols are committed to a central repository. When other modelers want to update their local models, these changes are fetched from this repository and replayed on the local model. To identify equal model elements, unique identifiers are introduced and the model elements are enhanced with versioning information. Conflicting changes are not applied (also the corresponding local change is undone) and finally presented to the user who has to resolve these conflicts manually. Repair mechanisms to fix model inconsistencies resulting from the merge are shortly reported.

EMF Compare

The open-source, Java-based component EMF Compare, which is part of the Eclipse Modeling Framework Technology (EMFT) project[9], supports generic model comparison and model merging. EMF Compare reports differences between Ecore models based on two-way or three-way comparison approaches. Within the Eclipse environment, the differences are indicated on a tree-based representation of the models where conflicting changes are highlighted in a dedicated color. Programmatic access of EMF Compare is also possible. For comparing two models, EMF Compare distinguishes two phases: a matching phase and a differencing phase building a Match Model as well as a Diff Model. The matching phase relies on four metrics based on type, name, value, and relationship similarity. The Diff Model provides information about inserted, deleted, and updated elements. The comparison and merge algorithms are kept generic in order to make them applicable for any Ecore-based modeling language, but the adaption to language-specific features is explicitly intended.

IBM Rational Software Architect (RSA)

The RSA[10], a UML modeling environment built upon the Eclipse Modeling Framework, provides two-way and three-way merge functionality for UML models. During the merge, not only syntax and the low-level EMF semantics are considered, but even the semantics of UML elements is taken into account. The differences are shown either in a tree-editor, or directly in the diagram. If the later view on the differences is chosen, then modified elements are highlighted. Conflict resolution must be done by the modeler manually, by either rejecting or accepting changes. Furthermore, the RSA offers a model validation facility which checks the conformance of the merged version to the UML metamodel.

EMF Store

The model repository EMF Store presented by Koegel et al. (2010), which has been initially developed as part of the Unicase[11] project, provides a dedicated framework for model versioning of EMF models. When a copy of a model is checked out, changes are tracked within the client and committed to the repository. With this operation-based approach, an efficient and precise detection of composite changes is possible coming along with the drawback that composite operations like refactorings are only detectable if they are explicitly available within the modeling editor. Changes obtained from the head revision of the repository and the changes of the local copy, which have not been checked in so far, are considered. Having the two lists of the performed changes, two kinds of relationships are established: "requires" and "conflicts". Whereas the former relationship expresses dependencies between operations, the later emphasizes contradicting modifications. Since the exact calculation of requires and conflicts relationships would be too expensive, heuristics are applied to obtain an approximation. To keep the conflict detection component flexible, a strategy pattern is implemented, which allows the adaption to specific needs. For example, in Koegel et al. (2010), the FineGrainedCDStrategy is proposed, which works on the attribute and reference level. Basically, two changes are conflicting, if the same attribute or the same reference is modified. All operations are classified to a few categories for obtaining potentially problematic situations. Furthermore, the authors introduce levels of severity to classify conflicts. They distinguish between hard conflicts and soft conflicts referring to the amount of user support necessary for their resolution. Whereas hard conflicts do not allow including both conflicting operations within the merged model, for soft conflicts this is possible (with the danger of obtaining an inconsistent model). A wizard guides the merge process.

Odyssey-VCS

The version control system Odyssey-VCS by Oliveira et al. (2005) is dedicated to versioning UML models. For each project, behavior descriptors may be specified which define how each model element should be treated during the versioning process. For the conflict detection, it may be specified which model elements should be considered atomic. If an atomic element is changed in two different ways at the same time, a conflict is raised. Behavior descriptors are expressed in XML and therefore, Odyssey-VCS is customizable for different projects. In the merge algorithm, all possible scenarios are considered, and the resulting actions, such as safely adding both operations, reporting a conflict, doing nothing, etc., are taken. A validation of the resulting model is not provided. Odyssey-VCS may be used either with a standalone client or with arbitrary modeling tools. The communication with the server is realized with Web services. More recently, Odyssey-VCS 2 by Murta et al. (2008) has been released which is built on top of Ecore resulting in a gain of flexibility concerning reflective processing of the model elements. Consequently, the conflict detection and merge algorithm is expressed in a more generic manner. Additionally, Odyssey-VCS is capable of both, pessimistic versioning and optimistic versioning. In the latter case, explicit branching is performed for storing not only the merged version, but also the working copies the merge is based on.

SMOVER

The semantically-enhanced versioning system SMOVER by Reiter et al. (2007) aims at reducing the number of falsely detected conflicts resulting from syntactic variations of one modeling concept. Furthermore, additional conflicts shall be identified by using knowledge about the modeling language. This knowledge is encoded by the means of model transformations which rewrite a given model to so-called semantic views. These semantic views provide canonical representations of the model which makes certain aspects of the modeling language more explicit. Consequently, more precise information about potential conflicts might be obtained when the semantic view representation of two concurrently evolved versions are compared.

Features

When considering the model versioning systems above, it becomes obvious that the individual systems set different focus on the challenges they tackle although all of them follow the same goal of providing sophisticated versioning facilities for software models. Table 1 provides an overview of the distinguished features offered by the various systems grouped into four categories which we discuss in the following. Applicable features are indicated with the checkmark symbol (✓); partly applicable features are marked with the tilde symbol (~). Empty boxes state that the specific feature is not applicable to the approach.

Physical Model Management (MM)

At some point in time, it is necessary to physically store the model versions. Therefore, a repository is required as well as a format in which the model versions may be accessed by the versioning system.

Table 1. State-of-the-art evaluation

	MM		Differences			Conflicts				Flexibility					
	Repository	*Standard Format*	*Operation Tracking*	*Matching Heuristics*	*Difference Model*	*Conflict Model*	*Graphical Visualization*	*Automatic Resolution*	*Layout Information*	*Modeling Language*	*Editor*	*Unit of Comparison*	*Detectable Operations*	*Detectable Conflicts*	*Resolution Strategies*
Alanen and Porres								✓		✓	✓				
Oda and Saeki	✓		✓						✓	✓					
Ohst et al.	~						✓		✓						
Mehra et al.			✓	·	·		✓	·	✓	✓	✓	·	·		·
Cicchetti et al.					✓	✓		✓		✓		✓	✓	✓	✓
ADAMS	✓		✓	✓					✓			✓	✓	✓	
AMOR	~	✓	·	✓	✓	✓	✓	✓	✓	✓	✓		✓	✓	✓
CoObRA	✓		✓					✓							
EMF Compare		✓		✓	✓	✓				✓	✓				
RSA	~	✓			✓	✓									
EMF Store	✓		✓		✓	·		✓		✓	✓	✓	✓	✓	
Odyssey-VCS	~	✓								✓	✓	✓			
SMOVER	~	✓								✓	✓	✓	✓	✓	

Repository

Whereas some systems offer a complete solution with an integrated *repository* where the historical information of the artifacts is stored, other approaches realize only the model merge component and rely on available repositories, which administrate files of arbitrary kinds.

Standard Format

The models may either be serialized in a standard format, i.e., XMI, or a format specific for the editor/versioning system. Consequently, transformations might be necessary before the versioning system may be used. If a direct import and processing of the XMI serialization, like it is the case in AMOR and Odyssey-VCS, versioning might be performed independently of any modeling editor.

Differences

The various systems follow different approaches how differences are obtained and represented, which are the basis for the calculation of conflicts.

Operation Tracking

Overall, the differences are either calculated retrospectively by a state-based algorithm or directly tracked during the modeling activity in operation-based approaches. Concerning the latter, more information is available, but a tighter coupling to the editors is given. All approaches belong to one of these two categories, only AMOR is a special case as discussed in the previous section. In AMOR, the atomic changes are obtained by a state-based comparison, from which composite changes might be retrospectively recovered.

Matching Heuristics

All approaches use unique identifiers to match elements occurring in all versions. EMF Compare and ADAMS additionally apply certain heuristics when no identifiers are available and to be able to match newly introduced elements.

Difference Model

Some approaches like EMF Compare, AMOR, and Cicchetti et al. represent differences as model. The differences are described in terms of operations from which, when applied to the origin model, the revised model may be recreated.

Conflicts

When modifications are contradicting, conflicts have to be reported. The various systems follow different paradigms to represent, to report, and finally to resolve conflicts.

Conflict Model

Some approaches like EMF Compare, AMOR, and Cicchetti et al. consider conflicts as first-class citizens and encode them not only implicitly within the algorithms. In these approaches, dedicated conflict models are specified. The explicit specification of a conflict model allows the serialization and an extended processing of conflicts.

Graphical Visualization

Most approaches report conflicts not using the concrete model syntax, but a tree representation, only. For the human user, much information is lost this way. Some approaches are able to decorate the models with the information about conflicts in the concrete syntax. Only a few approaches exist which highlight changes using coloring techniques as proposed by Ohst et al. (2003) and Mehra et al. (2005). However, these approaches require the implementation of special editor extensions. Thus, to the best of our knowledge,

Brosch et al. (2010b) started the first attempts of tackling these challenges using UML Profiles which will be integrated into the AMOR model versioning system.

Automatic Conflict Resolution

Most approaches require manual conflict resolution. In AMOR and the approach of Cicchetti et al. (2008), automatically executable conflict resolution patterns are defined which are recommended to the modeler in charge of the conflict resolution. In EMF Store, hard and soft conflicts may be defined. Soft conflicts do not require any user intervention and only a warning is shown.

Layout Information

When models are modified, also the layout of the diagram is potentially changed. Some systems like the approaches of Oda and Saeki (2005) and Mehra et al. (2005) also consider layout information to be put under version control. In most versioning systems, however, this information is neglected and no dedicated merging actions are provided.

Flexibility

The versioning systems often put special emphasis on being independent from any modeling language and modeling editor and being extensible with respect to the detectable operations, the detectable conflicts, and the automatically applicable resolution patterns.

Modeling Language

The versioning systems which foster language independence, require the modeling languages whose models shall be put under version control to be specified either in MOF or in Ecore. Other approaches consider one language only, for example, CoObRA is implemented for models formulated in Fujaba, only.

Editor

Whereas some versioning systems are tightly integrated with a modeling editor, other versioning systems aim for tool independence. Even operation-based systems might be designed in such a way that they may be used with different editors – then customized plugins have to be implemented, like in ADMAS and EMF Store.

Unit of Comparison

Some versioning systems, such as Odyssey-VCS and ADAMS, allow the configuration of the granularity level. It is possible to specify which model elements are considered as atomic and which have to be further decomposed. This configuration directly influences the number of reported conflicts.

Detectable Operations

In most versioning systems, the set of detectable operations is fixed. In some versioning systems, this set may be extended. For example in AMOR, this extension is supported by the means of operation specifications. In this way, AMOR may be extended to detect composite operations without programming effort.

Detectable Conflicts

In most versioning systems, the detectable conflicts are hardcoded into the conflict detection algorithm. AMOR's conflict detection uses the information stored in the pre- and postconditions of the operation specifications. With the addition of new operation specifications, additional conflicts are therefore detectable. Cicchetti et al. propose to describe conflict patterns by the means of models. The set of conflict patterns is extensible. Thus, further conflicts than the simple update/update and delete/update conflicts may be described and detected. A detailed discussion of these further potential conflicts is given in the next section.

Resolution Strategies

Only few versioning systems provide automatic conflict resolution facilities. In some versioning systems, rudimentary rules stating how to react on a certain conflict are hard coded. AMOR and the approach of Cicchetti et al. allow specifying conflict-specific resolution strategies.

Discussion

Whereas for some approaches deployable software or even the source code is available, others are still subject to ongoing development work. However, all of them contribute important ideas and concepts for building reliable model versioning systems. When we consider the time of publication, the majority of the systems has been presented in the last few years. This might be closely related with the maturity of the Eclipse Modeling Framework, which offers a sophisticated environment for the development of such model manipulation tools.

As we have seen, the different versioning systems tackle very manifold challenges of the versioning process and therefore it is kind of difficult to directly compare the systems, or even perform a competitive evaluation.

In most systems, differences and conflicts are not explicitly stated as first-class citizens, but they are hard-coded within the corresponding algorithms. Interestingly, the notion of "conflict", a very central concept when building a versioning system, is hardly explicitly discussed. Conflicts are mainly reduced to update/update and delete/update conflicts. Concerning the model correctness and consistency after the merge process, all current approaches refer to external solutions which for example ensure the conformance to the metamodel.

ADVANCED CONFLICTS AND FUTURE CHALLENGES

As discussed in the previous sections, one key element in model versioning is a *conflict*. However, the term *conflict* is strongly overloaded and differently co-notated. In the case of metamodel violations, the term conflict is used synonymously to the term inconsistency. Current model versioning systems mainly focus on single changes that are directly contradicting as they may be detected in an efficient and language independent way. Nevertheless, there is a multitude of further problems which could occur when merging two independently evolved models. Therefore, in this section we first present a comprehensive categorization of conflicts based on our previous work (Brosch et al., 2010b, Brosch et al., 2010d), followed by 10 research questions highlighting technical challenges contributing to more precise conflict detection and higher merge quality, as well as organizational challenges, demanding for better usability and support for true collaboration.

Conflict Categorization

The practical application of versioning systems depends on the quality of the merge component, especially on model comparison and conflict detection. In general, merge conflicts on models may occur either if one change invalidates another change, or if two changes do not commute (Lippe & Oosterom, 1992). In order to better understand the notion of conflicts, different categories were set up to group specific issues. In the field of software merging, *textual*, *syntactic*, *semantic*, and *structural conflicts* were surveyed by Mens (2002). While textual conflicts are detected by a line-based comparison of the program (cf. Section *Foundations of Versioning*), syntactic merging operates on the parse tree or abstract syntax graph, and thus, ignores conflicts resulting from textual reformatting. A syntactic-aware merging component takes the programming language's syntax into account and reports conflicts causing parse errors. Semantic merging goes one step further and reflects the semantic annotation of the parse tree, as done in the semantic analysis phase of a compiler. Here, static semantic conflicts like undeclared variables or incompatible types are detected. A structural conflict occurs due to changes overlapping with restructured and refactored parts of the program. Then, it is not decidable where to integrate the changes.

First attempts to apply this conflict categorization to model versioning failed. In fact, the term semantics itself is in the field of modeling heavily overloaded (Harel & Rumpe, 2004), referring to language semantics and real-world semantics. The assignment to a certain category is often based on objective preferences and, consequently, ambiguous. Already in small models, a separation between syntactic conflicts and semantic conflicts quickly blurs, especially when the metamodel is enriched with additional constraints such as OCL constraints in the case of UML. For instance, two modelers are working on a UML class diagram consisting of the two classes Circle and Ellipse. Each of them adds an inheritance relationship between the two classes. Unfortunately, both modelers disagree regarding the direction of the generalization and introduce a new inheritance relationship in the opposite direction. As a result, the merged model contains an inheritance cycle. This conflict may be either referred to as syntactic since such cycles are forbidden by the UML metamodel, or as semantic, since it is not clear how to interpret the case, that a class is subclass of its own subclasses. Further, even, if such conflicts could be clearly assigned to those categories, it would not provide any insights on how to detect and resolve that kind of conflicts.

From the analysis of many conflict scenarios, we learned that the number of reasons *why* a conflict might occur is limited in regards to the existing language definitions. We identified two main groups of conflicts, namely *overlapping changes* and *violations* (cf. Figure 7).

Figure 7. Conflict categorization

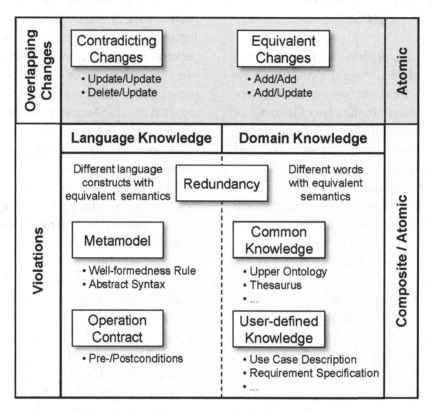

Overlapping Changes

Overlapping Changes refer to two opposite atomic changes (*add, delete, update*) on an overlapping part of the model with respect to the unit of comparison, e.g., a feature of a model element or a container element. We further distinguish between two types of overlapping changes, namely *contradicting changes* and *equivalent changes*. While conflicts of the first category arise due to directly competing changes, the latter category covers parallel changes leading to an equivalent result.

Contradicting Changes

Such changes find their expression in *update/ update* and *delete/update* conflicts. Update/update conflicts occur when an existing element of the common ancestor model is changed in both versions differently (cf. the multiplicity in Figure 8

(a)). Delete/update conflicts emerge either due to the concurrent update and deletion of the same element, or due to an update of an element and the deletion of the container element, e.g., a property is added and the corresponding class is deleted, like in the example in Figure 8 (b).

Equivalent Changes

If parallel update/update, delete/delete and add/ add changes are the "same", they are referred to as equivalent changes and only one of the two changes has to be integrated into the merged version to completely reproduce the intention of both modelers. In the case of add/add changes, no common ancestor of the affected model element is available, but redundant elements are added to the merged versions if all changes are naively merged. If the duplicate elements are deep equal, i.e., all features and containments have the same

Figure 8. Conflict examples

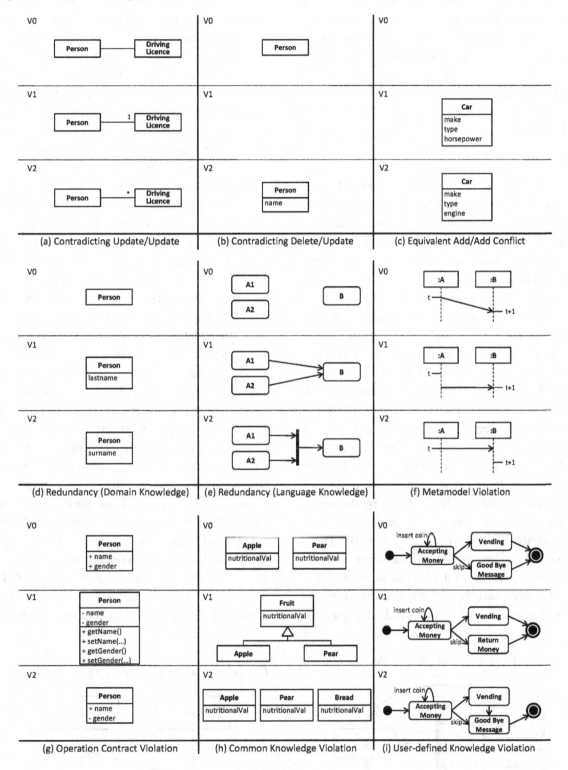

(a) Contradicting Update/Update

(b) Contradicting Delete/Update

(c) Equivalent Add/Add Conflict

(d) Redundancy (Domain Knowledge)

(e) Redundancy (Language Knowledge)

(f) Metamodel Violation

(g) Operation Contract Violation

(h) Common Knowledge Violation

(i) User-defined Knowledge Violation

values, only one of the elements should be inserted in the merged model and no conflict should be reported. However, if there are slight differences like the properties horsepower and engine in the classes Car of Figure 8 (c), an add/add conflict should be raised.

Violations

Besides the directly competing changes which are overlapping in terms of editing the same element in the "materialized" model, also combinations of changes in different elements may lead to an inconsistent model. This kind of conflict is harder to detect, as additional knowledge is necessary. This knowledge regards the underlying modeling language and the modeled domain.

Redundancy may be introduced to a model either by equivalent modeling concepts or variations in natural language expressing equivalent facts. Figure 8 (d) shows a redundancy conflict, as both modelers add the properties lastname and surname to the class Person in parallel, which are synonyms. Different modeling concepts may also express equivalent semantics. For example, the actions A1 and A2 of the UML activity diagram depicted in Figure 8 (e) may trigger the execution of action B using an implicit join by modeling a simple control flow, or by modeling the synchronization explicitly using a join node. Thus, Version 1 and Version 2 have equal semantics, i.e., the execution of A1 and A2 is required to execute B. However, naively merging these two variants would result in a redundant model (cf. Figure 9).

Metamodel violations may also be caused by concurrent changes, which do not overlap, but lead to an inconsistent model with respect to formal language constraints like the metamodel itself or additional OCL constraints. For an example of a metamodel violation, consider a UML sequence diagram with a message taking one time unit to be sent (cf. Figure 8 (f)). Both modelers change the message to be sent without taking time. However, they do not agree on the point in time, when the message will be sent and change the sendEvent and receiveEvent, respectively, which do not syntactically overlap. A naive merge (not taking language knowledge into account) would produce a message going back in time (cf. Figure 10), which is technically not realizable.

Operation contract violations denote conflicts where a composite operation applied on one version is invalidated by a change of the other version. A composite operation is a set of associated atomic changes necessary to perform a larger change like a refactoring. Each composite operation formulates a contract in terms of pre- and postconditions, e.g., requiring the existence or non-existence of specific elements, or specific values for features. Only the union of all atomic changes reflects the intention of the change and therefore, if a change of the opposite version violates the contract, a composite operation should not be divided and partially applied. Figure 8 (g) shows an example for an operation contract violation. One modeler applies an encapsulate field refactoring to all public properties, i.e., name and gender, of class Person. The refactoring sets the

Figure 9. Naive merge of example (e) of Figure 8

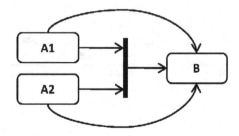

Figure 10. Naive merge of example (f) of Figure 8

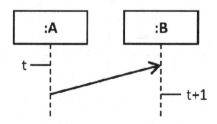

properties to private and generates public getter and setter methods. A parallel change setting the property gender to private invalidates the operation contract and a conflict should be reported.

Common knowledge available in upper ontologies, thesauri, or other kinds of knowledge bases may be used to detect violations of real-world semantics. Consider two classes Apple and Pear with a common property nutritionalVal (cf. Figure 8 (h)). While one modeler applies a pull up field refactoring to shift the common property to a newly created superclass named Fruit, the other modeler adds a new class Bread with the same property to the class diagram. A refactoring aware merge would include the newly introduced class into the pull up field operation, resulting in a Bread of type Fruit, which does not reflect reality.

User-defined knowledge from use case descriptions, requirement specifications and other models restricts the modeled domain and therefore may be used to detect further violations. With such information available, conflicts like the one depicted in Figure 8 (i) may be detected. A simple vending machine, expressed as UML state machine, containing the three states accepting money, vending, and Good Bye Message is refined by two modelers in parallel. One modeler changes the state Good Bye Message to Return Money, to express the fact, that in case of aborting the vending process, the inserted money should be returned. Concurrently, the other modeler changes the flow going from Vending to the final state to show the Good Bye Message in between. In the merged version depicted in Figure 11, the vending machine would return the money after vending, which may contradict requirement specifications.

Figure 11. Naive merge of example (i) of Figure 8

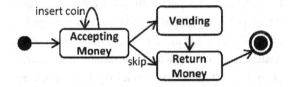

To draw short conclusions, detecting conflicts is a hard undertaking. Categorizing conflicts in homogeneous groups assists to better understand why such conflicts occur and to focus on one problem after another. If conflicts arise due to syntactically overlapping changes, they may be detected in a generic and language independent way, such as already done by several tools (cf. Section *State-of-the-Art Model Versioning Systems*). In order to increase the quality of the merged model, it is not sufficient to regard overlapping changes only, but to consider associated changes in a broader context. However, this may only be achieved by language specific conflict detection incorporating external knowledge, like the metamodel, refactoring contracts, equivalence statements, etc.

Ten Challenges for Model Versioning Systems

To outline the future of model versioning, we present 10 challenges for realizing efficient and reliable model versioning systems in the following. The first five challenges are derived from the afore presented conflict categorization, in particular, from conflict kinds which are only limited supported by the current systems. To compliment these five technical challenges, we elaborate on five further challenges which have been derived from an empirical study. In this study, we have interviewed 15 experts working as software engineers, software architects, or IT managers in different domains in large enterprises. The focus of the interviews has been on organizational and usability aspects.

Challenge 1: Consistency-Aware Versioning

When merging two independently evolved versions of one model, it might occur – even if both versions are consistent on their own – that the merged version violates consistency rules of, e.g., the underlying modeling language. In order to produce consistent models only, changes leading to inconsistencies should be specially treated in the merge process. Unfortunately, those inconsistent changes might not be overlapping and therefore harder to detect. Consider, for instance, the metamodel violation example depicted in Figure 8 (f). In this example, the sendEvent and the receiveEvent of a message are changed in both versions of the UML sequence diagram, eventually leading to a message going back in time. Beside language constraints, also user-defined constraints, stated in requirements documents or in additional models, might be violated during the merge. For example, the naively merged version of the UML state machine depicted in Figure 8 (i) may violate the postcondition of the corresponding vending process in a UML class diagram, expressing the requirement of incoming payment.

These violations are hardly detectable until the merged version is produced. Thus, the challenge is to trace back to the relevant changes causing the violation. For doing this, first, the model elements have to be identified where the evaluation of a consistency rule fails. Second, changes operating on those model elements have to be selected from the complete change set, and third, if several changes have been performed on these elements, the relevant subset of changes has to be distinguished which actually is producing the violation. First promising approaches for defining relationships between models to detect inconsistencies are already available (Lopez-Herrejon & Egyed, 2010).

Challenge 2: Intention-Aware Versioning

When merging two concurrently modified versions, ideally the merged version should constitute a combination of *all intentions* each modeler had in mind when performing their changes. Merging intentions is often more than just naively combining all non-conflicting atomic changes of both

sides. Changing a model is realizing a certain goal rather than simply modifying some parts of it. However, capturing the modeler's intention from a set of changes is a major challenge. First steps in this direction aim at treating *composite operations* such as *model refactorings* as first-class entities, because composite operations are more than the set of atomic changes applied in a certain sequence. Usually, they consist of preconditions and an intended final state (i.e., the operation contract). Therefore, detecting applications of well-defined composite operations and regarding their conditions during the merge is a first valuable step towards intention-aware versioning which is, for instance, done by Dig et al. (2007) for code versioning.

Challenge 3: Semantics-Aware Versioning

Current model versioning systems mainly facilitate matching and differencing algorithms operating on the syntactic level only. As the UML activity diagram presented in Figure 8 (e) demonstrates, syntactically different changes might be semantically equal. To avoid unexpected properties of the merged model (e.g., i), deadlocks, etc.), a combination of syntactic and semantic comparison of two model versions is highly valuable. In order to automatically compute if change-sets or (parts of) two models have the same semantics, the modeling language's semantics have to be defined formally in terms of a mapping between the modeling language and a semantic domain. However, currently no commonly agreed formal semantics exists for widespread employed modeling languages like UML. Even worse, the semantics of semantic is heavily discussed within the modeling community (Harel & Rumpe, 2004). First attempts for performing semantic differencing on models publish promising results (Nejati et al., 2007; Maoz et al., 2010). As these approaches focus only on two-way comparison and operate on a restricted set of modeling languages and constructs, the application of semantic differencing techniques in model versioning systems is not directly possible. The definition of a formal semantics for a comprehensive set of the UML, including intra-model dependencies, is a challenge on its own. Furthermore, as models may be used as sketch in the early phases of software development, as well as for specifying systems precisely to generate code, a satisfactory compromise has to be found to do justice to the multifaceted application fields of modeling.

Challenge 4: Conflict Dependencies

Especially with operation-based merging, changes within a sequence of changes might be interdependent. For instance, if a new element is introduced and an existing element is moved into the new element, the move operation can only be done after the addition has been performed. Since changes are interdependent, also conflicts might have dependencies among each other. An example is depicted in Figure 12: Assume that element z has to be deleted in order to allow the addition of an element x. Dependent on that element, y can be moved to x. In parallel, element z is updated and element y is deleted independently of the first change sequence. Thus, the changes Delete(z) and Update(z) are conflicting. Now, it depends on the resolution of this conflict, whether

the changes Move(y→x) and Delete(y) also lead to a conflict. Because, if the user decides to omit to merge Delete(z) and applies Update(z) instead, the dependent changes Add(x) and Move(y→x) are obsolete and, consequently, Delete(y) may be applied without a conflict. This example shows that change dependencies are a valuable but only first ingredient for grouping conflicts as well as for finding best resolution paths for resolving dependent conflicts. This idea was introduced by Lippe & Florijn (1991) and, more recently, has been picked up by Koegel et al. (2010) and Küster et al. (2009) for model versioning. However, it is still an open challenge, how to efficiently and precisely detect dependencies also between more complicated changes such as refactorings as well as detecting dependencies between more complicated conflicts such as the aforementioned violations. Furthermore, for computing an optimal order for resolving conflicts more efficiently, a precise change impact forecast is required. This, however, poses a challenge on its own.

Challenge 5: Adaptable Versioning System

Existing model versioning systems are often inflexible with respect to the trade-off between generic applicability and proper versioning support (cf. Table 1). The systems are either generic,

Figure 12. Conflict dependency example

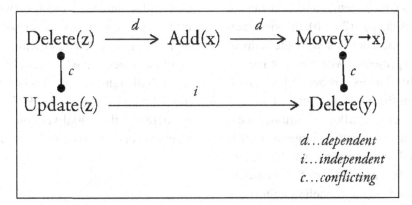

i.e., applicable to any modeling language, being however, characterized by limited versioning support, or, to exhibit enhanced versioning support, bound to a specific modeling language. This inflexibility is even worse because of the rapidly growing number of domain-specific modeling languages (DSMLs), entailing either the straightforward application of an existing generic system or requiring big efforts in developing a dedicated VCS from scratch. Thus, a big challenge in model versioning is to develop a framework which on the one hand may be used out of the box in a generic sense, and on the other hand, may be adapted for a certain modeling language on basis of a set of meaningful and well-defined extension points.

Challenge 6: Conflict Resolution in Concrete Syntax

In our interviews, a recurring practical need has been mentioned, namely to have versioning support within the concrete syntax of the models. Of course, this result is not unexpected, because modelers are usually familiar with the concrete graphical syntax but not with computer internal representations like XMI or abstract syntax graphs. Some dedicated approaches have been proposed for visualizing differences of models (cf. Mehra et al., 2005; Ohst et al., 2003). They construct a dedicated view using the concrete syntax, which combines and highlights changes of both models using coloring techniques. However, these approaches require for special extensions of the modeling editors which seems to be a barrier for adoption. In Brosch et al. (2010b), the visualization of changes and conflicts with the help of UML Profiles is presented which do not require for heavy-weight editor extensions. When visualizing conflicts in the concrete syntax it should, of course, improve the conflict resolution process even when the model is getting large to quickly find changes and to understand which changes have led to a certain conflict. For this, some interactive techniques in the modeling editors are needed to understand changes and conflicts within the concrete syntax. In addition, for concentrating on the resolution of one conflict, the computation of a specialized conflict view which only incorporates one conflict as well as the necessary context to understand the model fragment seems to be a way to go.

Challenge 7: Diagram Versioning

Not only the visualization of changes and conflicts has to be tackled by model versioning systems, but also the diagram layout information has to co-evolve with the model. Thus, the diagram layout information has to be put under version control. Due to the fact that diagram information is nowadays also represented in terms of models, model versioning features may be reused. However, this approach neglects the nature of 2D diagram layout by representing only x/y coordinates as Integer values. Thus, for larger models, this approach seems to be not accessible for modelers. For providing appropriate diagram versioning support, the following sub-challenges arise. First, means for visualizing changes of the layout information are needed within modeling editors by, e.g., interactively showing the changes by animation techniques. Ohst et al. (2003) and Mehra et al. (2005) have proposed first approaches going in this direction. Second, no general notion has been established yet which concurrently performed layout changes are in fact contradicting changes,.e.g., also considering the inconvenience of small unintended changes when a modeler moves an element one pixel without intending it. Third, appropriate resolution mechanisms for layout conflicts have to be established. Here, the most challenging question is how to preserve the mental map (Misue et al., 1995) of both modelers between the initial version, the two parallel changed versions, and the finally merged version.

Challenge 8: Tolerating Conflicts

In contrast to code, models are often used in an informal manner for sketching ideas and discussing design alternatives in the early phases of software development. One major benefit of models in this phase is to manage and improve communication among team members by establishing common domain knowledge. In this context, it is desirable to keep all or at least many of the model changes, even if they are conflicting. The reason for this is that conflicts may not only be seen as negative result of collaborative development, but rather as necessary means for identifying aspects of systems which need further analysis or which need to reflect different viewpoints of different stakeholders. Thus, conflicts may help to develop a common understanding of the requirements for to be developed systems. A versioning system for tolerating conflicts should allow to explicitly representing and persisting conflicts as well as to allow tracking conflicts to resolve them later on. A promising resource for learning how to tolerate conflicts is the field of multi-perspective development, where inconsistencies can be compared with conflicts in the area of versioning. Originally, the need for inconsistency-aware software engineering emerged in the field of programming languages, especially when very large systems are developed by a team (cf. Schwanke & Kaiser, 1988; Balzer, 1989; Finkelstein et al., 1994; and Nuseibeh et al., 2001). In Brosch et al. (2010c), a first step in tolerating conflicts in the context of versioning systems for UML has been made.

Challenge 9: Avoiding Conflicts

An alternative to pessimistic versioning through locking for avoiding conflicts is to have a synchronous development environment (Dewan & Hegde, 2007). Here the hypothesis is that conflicts can be avoided through awareness. Consider for example that when one modeler is working on a certain model fragment and another modeler is also opening this model fragment, both modelers are informed that they are concurrently working on a certain part of the model. Then they have the possibility to consolidate their planned changes with the help of collaborative tool features such as chats. Developing such collaborative modeling environments would allow for new ways of collaborative modeling in general and poses the first sub-challenge. For making synchronous modeling effective, appropriate model partitioning techniques are necessary as a prerequisite. Here again, the distinction has to be made for which purpose models are used. For example, when models are used for implementation of object-oriented systems, object-orientation provides a perfect separation of concerns into packages, classes, operations and so on. However, in the requirement phase of a project, where the goal is to find the structure for the system to implement, further partitioning techniques and design approaches are needed. An alternative paradigm would be not to design one model, but to express the different concerns in separate models and then try to integrate these different models to form the whole system. In the field of aspect-oriented requirements engineering, there exist promising approaches separating different parts of a systems by concerns, which could be adopted for model partitioning in the context of model versioning. Finding appropriate separation of concerns techniques for the different phases of software development poses the second sub-challenge in the context of conflict avoidance.

Challenge 10: Model/Code Versioning

The long term vision of model-driven engineering is to employ only models for software development, but currently a mixture of models and code is used. Thus, roundtrip engineering raises the challenge of synchronizing models and code if changes are allowed on both levels. Inconsistencies arise if not all artifacts are consistently updated after a change is performed. A first approach for tackling this problem is presented in Estublier et al. (2010), who propose to employ dedicated consistency constraints in combination with evolution policies. However, in the context of model versioning, parallel modifications on code level and on model level by different developers raises a big challenge, especially when the granularity used on the model level does not match the granularity on the code level which is quite likely. In addition, it seems to be promising to use models for versioning large code repositories in case several conflicts between different versions occur. Here the hypothesis, which has to be verified in the future, is that the higher-level of abstraction of models helps for detecting and resolving conflicts. However, a prerequisite for model-based code versioning is to have appropriate reverse engineering techniques (Chikofsky & Cross, 1990) available for producing comprehensibly models out of the code.

Overall, we conclude this book chapter with the observation that the research area of model versioning still offers a multitude of tough challenges despite the many achievements which have been made until today. These challenges must be overcome in order to obtain solutions which ease the work of the modelers in practice. The final aim is to establish methods which are so well integrated in the development process that the modelers themselves do not have to care about versioning tasks and that they are not distracted from their actual work by time consuming management activities. Therefore, different facets of the modeling process itself have to be reviewed to gain a better understanding of the inherent dynamic. Versioning is about supporting team work, i.e., about the management of people who work together in order to achieve a common goal. Consequently, versioning solutions require not only the handling of technical issues like adequate differencing and conflict detection algorithms or adequate visualization approaches, but also the consideration of social and organizational aspects. Especially in the context of modeling, the current versioning approaches have to be questioned and eventually revised. Here the requirements posed on the versioning systems may depend on the intended usage of the models. Models are not always created with the intention to obtain an exact representation of the world, but to obtain a shared understanding on a very specific aspect. This desired fuzziness may not be eliminated by the versioning process, because valuable information might get lost. Besides the graphical visualization and the separation of concerns which is carried to extremes by the means of different views like in the various diagrams of UML, this fuzziness is a feature which sets models apart from mere source code of traditional, textual programming languages demanding new methods for the management of collaborations.

ACKNOWLEDGMENT

This work has been partly funded by the Austrian Federal Ministry of Transport, Innovation, and Technology and the Austrian Research Promotion Agency under grant FIT-IT-819584, by the Vienna Science and Technology Fund (WWTF) under grant ICT10-018, and by the fFORTE WIT Program of the Vienna University of Technology and the Austrian Federal Ministry of Science and Research.

REFERENCES

Alanen, M., & Porres, I. (2003). Difference and union of models. *Proceedings of the Conference on the Unified Modeling Language (UML), volume 2863 of LNCS*, (pp. 2-17). Springer

Altmanninger, K., Seidl, M., & Wimmer, M. (2009). A survey on model versioning approaches. *International Journal of Web Information Systems, 5*(3), 271–304. doi:10.1108/17440080910983556

Apiwattanapong, T., Orso, A., & Harrold, M. J. (2007). JDiff: A differencing technique and tool for object-oriented programs. *Automated Software Engineering, 14*(1), 3–36. doi:10.1007/s10515-006-0002-0

Balzer, R. (1989). Tolerating inconsistency. *Proceedings of the 5th Int. Software Process Workshop* (ISPW), (pp. 41-42). IEEE Computer Society.

Barrett, S., Chalin, P., & Butler, G. (2008). Model merging falls short of software engineering needs. *Proceedings of the 2nd Workshop on Model-Driven Software Evolution @ MoDELS'08.*

Brosch, P., Kappel, G., Seidl, M., Wieland, K., Wimmer, M., Kargl, H., & Langer, P. (2010a). Adaptable model versioning in action. *Proceedings of the Modellierung, GI,* (pp. 221-236).

Brosch, P., Kargl, H., Langer, P., Seidl, M., Wieland, K., Wimmer, M., & Kappel, G. (2010b). Representation and visualization of merge conflicts with UML profiles. *Proceedings of the International Workshop on Models and Evolution (ME) @ MoDELS'10,* (pp. 53-62).

Brosch, P., Langer, P., Seidl, M., Wieland, K., & Wimmer, M. (2010d). Colex: A web-based collaborative conflict lexicon. *Proceedings of the 1st International Workshop on Model Comparison in Practice (IWMCP),* (pp. 42-49). ACM Press.

Brosch, P., Langer, P., Seidl, M., Wieland, K., Wimmer, M., & Kappel, G. (2010c). Concurrent modeling in early phases of the software development life cycle. *Proceedings of the 16th Collaboration Researchers' International Working Group Conference on Collaboration and Technology (CRIWG),* (pp. 129-144). Springer.

Chikofsky, E., & Cross, J. H. (1990). Reverse engineering and design recovery: A taxonomy. *IEEE Software, 7,* 13–17. doi:10.1109/52.43044

Cicchetti, A., Di Ruscio, D., & Pierantonio, A. (2008). Managing model conflicts in distributed development. *Proceedings of the 11th International Conference on Model Driven Engineering Languages and Systems (MoDELS), volume 5301 of LNCS,* (pp. 311-325). Springer.

Conradi, R., & Westfechtel, B. (1998). Version models for software configuration management. *ACM Computing Surveys, 30*(2), 232–282. doi:10.1145/280277.280280

De Lucia, A., Fasano, F., Oliveto, R., & Tortora, G. (2006). ADAMS: Advanced artefact management system. *Proceedings of the 10th European Conference on Software Maintenance and Reengineering,* (pp. 349-350). IEEE.

De Lucia, A., Fasano, F., Scanniello, G., & Tortora, F. (2009). Concurrent fine-grained versioning of UML models. *Proceedings of the 2009 European Conference on Software Maintenance and Reengineering* (CSMR '09), (pp. 89-98). IEEE Computer Society.

Dewan, P., & Hegde, R. (2007). Semi-synchronous conflict detection and resolution in asynchronous software development. *Proceedings of the 10th European Conference on Computer-Supported Cooperative Work,* (pp. 159–178). Springer.

Dig, D., Manzoor, K., Johnson, R., & Nguyen, T. N. (2007). Refactoring-aware configuration management for object-oriented programs. *Proceedings of the 29th International Conference on Software Engineering* (ICSE), (pp. 427-436). IEEE Computer Society.

Dig, D., Manzoor, K., Johnson, R., & Nguyen, T. N. (2008). Effective software merging in the presence of object-oriented refactorings. *IEEE Transactions on Software Engineering, 34*(2), 321–335. doi:10.1109/TSE.2008.29

Estublier, J., Leblang, D., van der Hoek, A., Conradi, R., Clemm, G., Tichy, W., & Wiborg-Weber, D. (2005). Impact of software engineering research on the practice of software configuration management. *ACM Transactions on Software Engineering and Methodology, 14*(4), 383–430. doi:10.1145/1101815.1101817

Estublier, J., Leveque, T., & Vega, G. (2010). Evolution control in MDE projects: Controlling model and code co-evolution. *Proceedings of the Conference on Fundamentals of Software Engineering* (FASE), (pp. 431-438). Springer.

Finkelstein, A., Gabbay, D. M., Hunter, A., Kramer, J., & Nuseibeh, B. (1994). Inconsistency handling in multiperspective specifications. *IEEE Transactions on Software Engineering, 20*(8), 569–578. doi:10.1109/32.310667

Ghezzi, C., Jazayeri, M., & Mandrioli, D. (2002). *Fundamentals of software engineering* (2nd ed.). Prentice Hall PTR.

Harel, D., & Rumpe, B. (2004). Meaningful modeling: What's the semantics of "semantics"? [IEEE.]. *Computer, 37*(10), 64–72. doi:10.1109/MC.2004.172

Hunt, J. W., & McIllroy, M. D. (1976). *An algorithm for differential file comparison*. Technical Report 41, AT&T Bell Laboratories Inc.

Khuller, S., & Raghavachari, B. (1996). Graph and network algorithms. *ACM Computing Surveys, 28*(1), 43–45. doi:10.1145/234313.234334

Kim, M., & Notkin, D. (2006*)*. Program element matching for multi-version program analyses. *Proceedings of the 2006 International Workshop on Mining Software Repositories* (MSR '06), ACM.

Koegel, M., Herrmannsdoerfer, M., Wesendonk, O., & Helming, J. (2010). Operation-based conflict detection on models. *Proceedings of the International Workshop on Model Comparison in Practice (IWMCP) @ TOOLS'10*.

Küster, J., Gerth, C., & Engels, G. (2009). Dependent and conflicting change operations of process models. *Proceeding of the Conference on Model Driven Architecture - Foundations and Applications (MDAFA), volume 5562 of LNCS,* (pp. 158-173). Springer.

Lippe, E., & Florijn, G. (1991). Implementation techniques for integral version management. *Proceedings of the European Conference on Object Oriented Programming* (ECOOP), (pp. 342-359).

Lippe, E., & van Oosterom, N. (1992). Operation-based merging. *Proceedings of the 5th ACM SIGSOFT Symposium on Software Development Environments* (SDE), (pp. 78-87). ACM.

Lopez-Herrejon, R. E., & Egyed, A. (2010). Detecting inconsistencies in multi-view models with variability. *Proceedings of the European Conference on Modelling Foundations and Applications* (ECMFA), (pp. 217-232). Springer.

Maoz, S., Ringert, J. O., & Rumpe, B. (2010). A manifesto for semantic model differencing. *Proceedings of the International Workshop on Models and Evolution* (ME2010) @ MoDELS'10.

Mehra, A., Grundy, J. C., & Hosking, J. G. (2005). A generic approach to supporting diagram differencing and merging for collaborative design. *Proceedings of the 20th IEEE/ACM International Conference on Automated Software Engineering* (ASE), (pp. 204-213). ACM.

Mens, T. (2002). A state-of-the-art survey on software merging. *IEEE Transactions on Software Engineering, 28*(5), 449–462. doi:10.1109/TSE.2002.1000449

Mens, T. (2008). Introduction and roadmap: History and challenges of software evolution. In Mens, T., & Demeyer, S. (Eds.), *Software evolution* (pp. 1–11). Springer. doi:10.1007/978-3-540-76440-3_1

Misue, K., Eades, P., Lai, W., & Sugiyama, K. (1995). Layout adjustment and the mental map. *Journal of Visual Languages and Computing, 6*(2), 183–210. doi:10.1006/jvlc.1995.1010

Murta, L., Corrêa, C., Prudêncio, J. G., & Werner, C. (2008). Towards Odyssey-VCS 2: Improvements over a UML-based version control system. *Proceedings of the International Workshop on Comparison and Versioning of Software Models (CVSM) @ ICSE'08*, (pp. 25–30). ACM.

Nejati, S., Sabetzadeh, M., Chechik, M., Easterbrook, S., & Zave, P. (2007). Matching and merging of statecharts specifications. *Proceedings of the 29th International Conference on Software Engineering* (ICSE), (pp. 54-64). IEEE.

Nuseibeh, B., Easterbrook, S. M., & Russo, A. (2001). Making inconsistency respectable in software development. *Journal of Systems and Software, 58*(2), 171–180. doi:10.1016/S0164-1212(01)00036-X

Oda, T., & Saeki, M. (2005). Generative technique of version control systems for software diagrams. *Proceedings of the 21st IEEE International Conference on Software Maintenance (ICSM)*, (pp. 515-524). IEEE Computer Society.

Ohst, D., Welle, M., & Kelter, U. (2003). Differences between versions of UML diagrams. *Proceedings of the 9th European Software Engineering Conference*, (pp. 227-236). ACM.

Oliveira, H., Murta, L., & Werner, C. (2005). Odyssey-VCS: A flexible version control system for UML model elements. *Proceedings of the 12th International Workshop on Software Configuration Management*, (pp. 1-16). ACM.

Reiter, T., Altmanninger, K., Kotsis, G., Schwinger, W., & Bergmayr, A. (2007). Models in conflict - detection of semantic conflicts in model-based development. *Proceedings of the 3rd International Workshop on Model-Driven Enterprise Information Systems (MDEIS) @ ICEIS'07*, (pp. 29-40).

Schmidt, D. C. (2006). Guest editor's introduction: Model-driven engineering. *IEEE Computer, 39*(2), 25–31.

Schneider, C., Zündorf, A., & Niere, J. (2004). CoObRA - A small step for development tools to collaborative environments. In *Proceedings of the Workshop on Directions in Software Engineering Environments.*

Schwanke, R. W., & Kaiser, G. E. (1988). Living with inconsistency in large systems. *Proceedings of the Workshop on Software Version and Configuration Control,* (pp. 98-118).

Taentzer, F., Ermel, C., Langer, P., & Wimmer, M. (2010). Conflict detection for model versioning based on graph modifications. *Proceedings of the 5th International Conference on Graph Transformations, Springer LNCS 6372,* (pp. 171–186).

Tichy, W. F. (1988). Tools for software configuration management. In J. F. H. Winkler (Ed.), *Proceedings of the International Workshop on Software Version and Configuration Control,* (pp. 1–20). Teubner Verlag.

Westfechtel, B. (2010). A formal approach to three-way merging of EMF models. *Proceedings of the 1st International Workshop on Model Comparison in Practice* (IWMCP), (pp. 31-41). ACM.

ENDNOTES

[1]   XML Metadata Interchange
[2]   http://www.cvshome.org
[3]   http://subversion.tigris.org
[4]   http://git-scm.com
[5]   http://bazaar.canonical.com
[6]   http://www.eclipse.org/emft/projects/compare
[7]   http://www.eclipse.org/Xtext/documentation/1_0_1/xtext.html#grammarLanguage
[8]   http://www.fujaba.de
[9]   http://www.eclipse.org/modeling/emft
[10] http://www.ibm.com/developerworks/rational/library/05/712_comp/index.html
[11] http://www.unicase.org

About the Contributors

Jörg Rech is a Senior Scientist and Project Manager at SAP Research Center Karlsruhe. He received his PhD from the University of Hildesheim, Germany and his BSc (Vordiplom) and his MSc (Diplom) in computer science from the University of Kaiserslautern, Germany. Previously, he worked for Fraunhofer IESE in Kaiserslautern and the University of Kaiserslautern. His research mainly concerns model-driven software development, quality defect diagnosis, refactoring, software analysis, intelligent assistance, semantic technologies, and knowledge management. He has published a number of papers, mainly on software engineering and knowledge management topics.

Christian Bunse is currently with the University of Applied Sciences Stralsund, working in the field of software systems. He received his PhD in computer science from the Technical University of Kaiserslautern, Germany and his BSc (Vordiplom) and Msc (Diplom) in Computer Science with a minor in medicine from the Technical University of Dortmund, Germany. His research interests are in the area of model-driven development, resource-aware software systems, and energy efficiency. Christian authored several international journal articles, books, book chapters, and refereed conference papers that focus on software engineering, model-based development, and quality assurance. In addition, Christian served as a PC member and organizer of international workshops and conferences. He is a member of the German Computer Society (GI) and works actively in several of the GI's working groups.

* * *

Berthold Agreiter is a Research Assistant at the Institute of Computer Science at the University of Innsbruck, Austria. He graduated at the Institute of Computer Science in Innsbruck and is currently working on his Ph.D. in the field of model-driven security configuration. His further research interests include model engineering, model-driven testing, software evolution, and IT-landscape modeling. Berthold Agreiter collaborates in the EU-funded project SecureChange whose objective it is to develop techniques and tools that ensure "lifelong" compliance to evolving security, privacy, and dependability requirements for a long-running evolving software system. Additionally, he is responsible for a project within the QE LaB competence center about the maintenance of IT-landscape models.

Colin Atkinson is the leader of the Software Engineering Group at the University of Mannheim (since April 2003). Before that he held a joint position as a Professor at the University of Kaiserslautern and Project Leader at the affiliated Fraunhofer Institute for Experimental Software Engineering. From 1991 until 1997 he was an Assistant Professor of Software Engineering at the University of Houston - Clear

Lake. His research interests are focused on the use of model-driven and component based approaches in the development of dependable computing systems. He received a Ph.D. and M.Sc. in computer science from Imperial College, London, in 1990 and 1985, respectively, and received his B.Sc. in Mathematical Physics from the University of Nottingham 1983.

Florian Barth is a member of the Software Engineering Group at the University of Mannheim (since October 2009). His research interests are focused on the verification and validation of software systems and test definition languages. He played a major role in developing the Testsheets testing technology and has applied it in various application scenarios such as component-based computing systems in the context of dependability assessment, socio-technical enterprise information systems dealing with information flow security, as well as requirements engineering in complex systems with focus on acceptability testing. He received his Diploma in business information systems at the University of Mannheim in 2009.

Ruth Breu is full Professor at the University of Innsbruck, Institute of Computer Science, since 2002 and head of the research group Quality Engineering. Prior to that she worked for several years as software engineering consultant for companies in the finance and telecommunication sector and passed her academic degrees at Technische Universität München and Universität Passau, Germany. Ruth Breu has long year experience in the areas of model-driven software development, requirements engineering, quality management, and security engineering. She is co-author of three books and over hundred publications in international journals and conferences. Since 2009 Ruth Breu is scientific head of QE LaB, a private-public partnership competence center. QE LaB focuses on continuous quality management of collaborative systems.

Javier Fernández Briones received his degree as Ingeniero de Telecomunicación at the Universidad Politécnica de Madrid (MsC EAC/ABET accredited) in 2001. After two years working as software engineering in different companies, he joined the Real-Time Systems and Telematic Services Architecture to work as a researcher. He has been awarded with several grants funded by the Ministerio de Educación y Ciencia and the Universidad Politécnica de Madrid and worked in IST-funded projects such as ARTIST and MODELWARE. Currently, he is pursuing his PhD in the topics of software architecture, dependable systems, and model-driven engineering.

Petra Brosch received a Master's degree in Business Informatics in 2006. Since then, she is a Research Assistant at the Business Informatics Group of the Vienna University of Technology. She gained experience in national and international funded research projects in the field of service engineering and model-driven engineering. Her main research focus is model versioning with special emphasis on conflict resolution and retaining the concrete syntax of the models.

Manfred Broy studied Mathematics and Computer Science at the Technische Universität München. He graduated in 1976, 1980 he received his Ph. D. and 1982 he completed his Habilitation Thesis at the Faculty of Mathematics at the Technische Universität München. From 1983 till 1989 he worked as a full Professor for computer science and founding dean at the Faculty of Mathematics and Computer Science at the University of Passau. In October he became a full Professor for Computer Science at the Faculty of Computer Science the Technische Universität München (former chair of Professor F.L. Bauer). His research interests are software and systems engineering comprising both theoretical and applied aspects including system models, specification, and refinement of system components, specification techniques, development methods, and verification. Professor Broy is a member of the European Academy of Sciences and a Member of the Deutsche Akademie der Naturforscher "Leopoldina." In 1994 he received the Leibniz Award by the Deutsche Forschungsgemeinschaft and in 2007 the Konrad Zuse Medal by the Gesellschaft für Informatik.

Antonio Cicchetti is a Research Assistant in the Innovation, Design, and Engineering Department at the Mälardalen University, Sweden from 2008. He got his Ph.D in Computer Science in 2008 at the University of L'Aquila with the thesis entitled "Difference Representation and Conflict Management in Model-Driven Engineering" under the supervision of Prof. Alfonso Pierantonio. His research interests include techniques for model differencing and version management in current model-engineering platforms, domain-specific modeling languages, (bidirectional) model transformations, and model weaving. Moreover, he is involved in implementation of MDE techniques for the development of component-based embedded systems in industrial applications.

Serge Demeyer is a Professor at the University of Antwerp and the spokesperson for the ANSYMO (Antwerp System Modeling) Research Group. He directs a research lab investigating the theme of "Software Reengineering" (LORE - Lab On REengineering). His main research interest concerns software reengineering, more specifically the evolution of object-oriented software systems. He is an active member of the corresponding international research communities, serving in various conference organization and program committees. He has written a book entitled "Object-Oriented Reengineering" and edited a book on "Software Evolution." He also authored numerous peer-reviewed articles, many of them in highly respected scientific journals. He completed his M.Sc. in 1987 and his PhD in 1996, both at the "Vrije Universiteit Brussel." After his PhD, he worked for three years in Switzerland, where he served as a Technical Coordinator of a European research project. Switzerland remains near and dear to his heart; witness the sabbatical leave during 2009-2010 at the University of Zürich in the research group SEAL.

Iwona Dubielewicz received MSc degree and PhD degree in Computer Science in 1972 and 1977, respectively, both from the Wroclaw University of Technology, Poland. Her PhD dissertation was associated with the use of formal languages in software engineering. Since 1977 she has been working as an Assistant Professor at the Institute of Informatics, Wroclaw University of Technology. Her main scientific interests include, but are not limited to software development methodologies, modeling languages, and quality of the software systems and processes. She is a member of Polish Committee for Standardization. Since 1994 she has been involved in the development of several international standards for Polish Comittee. Iwona Dubielewicz has over 40 publications in the international journals and conference proceedings from different areas of software engineering.

Qurat-ul-ann Farooq is a doctoral student in Ilmenau University of Technology, Ilmenau, Germany. She is working in the field of model-based and model-driven development and testing. She earned her Master's degree in systems and software engineering in 2007 from Mohammad Ali Jinnah University, Islamabad, Pakistan. From 2007 to 2009 she also worked as a Lecturer at the University of Arid Agriculture, Islamabad, Pakistan. At present, her research focuses particularly on model-based regression testing to support software evolution. One of her core research interests is model transformations for model-driven test generation. Her other research interests include traceability and impact analysis to support model-based software evolution.

Liliana Favre is a full Professor of Computer Science at Universidad Nacional del Centro de la Provincia de Buenos Aires in Argentina. She is also a Researcher of CIC (Comisión de Investigaciones Científicas de la Provincia de Buenos Aires). Her current research interests are focused on model driven development, model driven architecture, and formal approaches, mainly on the integration of algebraic techniques with MDA-based processes. She has been involved in several national research projects about formal methods and software engineering methodologies. Currently she is research leader of the Software Technology Group at Universidad Nacional del Centro de la Provincia de Buenos Aires. She has published several book chapters, journal articles, and conference papers. She has acted as Editor of the book *UML and the Unified Process*. She is the author of the book *Model Driven Architecture for Reverse Engineering Technologies: Strategic Directions and System Evolution*.

Michael Felderer is a Research Assistant at the Institute of Computer Science at the University of Innsbruck, Austria. He holds Ph.D. and M.Sc. degrees in computer science. His research interests are model-driven testing, risk-based testing, model engineering, software evolution, and requirements engineering. Michael Felderer leads the research projects Telling TestStories and MATE to define a model-driven testing approach for service-centric systems, and contributes to other research projects. Additionally, he transfers his research results into practice as consultant and speaker on industrial conferences.

Frederic Fondement is a Research and Teaching Assistant in the computer science and control department of the ENSISA engineering school. His area of interest includes model- and language- driven software engineering. He received in 2007 his PhD from the Swiss Federal Institute of Technology in Lausanne (EPFL) for his work on concrete syntaxes for modeling languages, and in 2000 his engineering degree from the University of Mulhouse. In 2002 he was a Research Engineer at INRIA Rennes where he developed a model transformation language. In 2000-2001 he was part of the research and development team of ObjeXion Software where he developed a web application modeler.

Juan Pedro Silva Gallino is a Telecommunications Engineer by the Universidad ORT Uruguay. He then joined the Sistemas de Tiempo Real y Arquitectura de Servicios Telemáticos (STRAS) group, at the Universidad Politécnica de Madrid (UPM) as a Researcher, in pursuit of his doctoral degree. Currently, his research is principally focused on the fields of model-driven development, non-functional characteristics of software, service-oriented architectures, and web services.

Jeff Gray is an Associate Professor in the Department of Computer Science at the University of Alabama. His research interests include model-driven engineering, aspect orientation, code clones, and generative programming. Jeff received a Ph.D. in Computer Science from Vanderbilt University and both the BS and MS in Computer Science from West Virginia University. He is a member of the ACM and a Senior Member of the IEEE.

Charles-Georges Guillemot is a PhD student (3° year) in the MIPS Laboratory of the Haute Alsace University under the supervision of the Professor Michel Hassenforder, and Frederic Fondement. His thesis focuses on the area of ontologies and their contributions to the construction of intelligent scientific workflows. In 2003, he received a two-year diploma from the University Institute of Technology of Belfort-Montbeliard in Computer Sciences, and in 2008 his Master's degree in Software Engineering from the University of Franche-Comte. Since 2009, he teaches in the GEII department of the University Institute of Technology of Mulhouse and in 2011, he will teach at the ENSISA Engineering School.

Ignacio García-Rodriguez de Guzmán is Assistant Professor at the University of Castilla-La Mancha and belongs to the Alarcos Research Group at the UCLM. He holds the PhD degree in Computer Science from the University of Castilla-La Mancha. His research interests include software maintenance, model-driven development, and software modernization.

Michel Hassenforder was appointed Professor in 1998 following an accreditation to supervise research. Since 2008, he leads the Software Engineering group of the MIPS laboratory which brings together seven people including four teachers on the theme of the Model Driven Engineering. He was member of the IPC of conferences such as IDM'06, IDM'08, LMO'10, and reviewer for MODELS conference between 2004 and 2006. He is author and co-author of a software patent, two collective works, 7 international publications in journals with peer review, and 32 papers in refereed conferences. He participated in six industrial contracts for very diverse amounts and is currently involved in a EUREKA project. His personal work is rooted in the model driven engineering with the problem of the textual representation of models and metamodels (Sintaks), and more recently, in the area of ontologies and their contributions to the construction of intelligent scientific workflows.

Andrea Herrmann has 15 years of working experience: six years in software projects (as a consultant and project manager), and nine years in science and teaching. The focus of her research is decision-making for software engineering, specifically elicitation and modeling of non-functional requirements, prioritization, risk estimation, agile development, and distributed software engineering. She works as a Research and Innovation Manager at Infoman AG (Germany) and is lecturing at the University of Heidelberg. She is active in the German Informatics Society (Gesellschaft für Informatik) as the vice speaker of the Requirements Engineering group and as the leader of two special interest groups ("Requirements engineering and project management" and "Softskills required!").

Bogumila Hnatkowska received MSc degree and PhD degree in Computer Science in 1992 and 1997 respectively, both from the Wroclaw University of Technology, Poland. Her PhD dissertation was associated with the use of formal methods in software engineering. Since 1998 she has been working as an Assistant Professor at the Institute of Informatics, Wroclaw University of Technology. Her main scientific interests include, but are not limited to software development processes, modeling languages, model driven development, model transformations, and quality of the software products. She is a member of program committees of several international conferences. Bogumila Hnatkowska has over 60 publications in international journals and conference proceedings from different areas of software engineering.

Zbigniew Huzar received the M.Sc., Ph.D., and habilitation degrees in Computer Science from Wrocław University of Technology, Poland, in 1969, 1974, and 1990, respectively. During 1978-1984 he was Deputy Director of Computer Center; from 1984-2003 he served as a head of Informatics Center, from 2004- 2008, as director of the Institute of Applied Informatics, and since 2008, as director of the Institute of Informatics, Wrocław University of Technology, Poland. The scope of his scientific interests concerns software engineering, and in particular, covers methods of formal specification and design of real-time systems, and model-based software development. He is author and co-author of 10 books. He is a member of the Polish Information Processing Society and editor-in-chief of the e-Informatica Software Engineering Journal.

Sheridan Jeary is a Senior Lecturer at Bournemouth University and has research interests that span software development methods, business and software process improvement, and the alignment of Information Technology with business (strategy and process). She had several years of management and systems experience across a variety of domains before moving into academia. She was the BU Project Manager for the EU funded VIDE project on model driven development has just completed a secondment in Poland in a software development company as part of a EU Marie Curie funded project - INFER.

Gerti Kappel is a Full Professor at the Institute of Software Technology and Interactive Systems at the Vienna University of Technology, heading the Business Informatics Group. Until 2001, she was a Full Professor of Computer Science and head of the Department of Information Systems at the Johannes Kepler University of Linz. She received the MS and PhD degrees in Computer Science and Business Informatics from the University of Vienna and the Vienna University of Technology in 1984 and 1987, respectively. From 1987 to 1989 she was a visiting researcher at the Centre Universitaire d'Informatique, Geneva, Switzerland. Her current research interests include model engineering (model transformation, model versioning), Web engineering (ubiquitous Web technologies, model-driven Web engineering), as well as process engineering (business process modeling and transformation).

Anne Keller received her Diploma in Media Systems in 2006 from the Bauhaus-University, Weimar. She did her thesis on "Optimizing Abstract Data Types in Embedded Applications at Modeling Level" at IMEC VZW, Leuven. She is currently pursuing a PhD at the University of Antwerp. Her research interests include model-driven engineering, with a particular focus on inconsistency management, inconsistency resolution, and change impact analysis.

Sascha Kirstan is external Ph.D. student at the chair of software & systems engineering at the Technische Universität München (Prof. Broy) and Engineering Consultant at Altran Technologies. He studied computer science at the Technische Universität München. His research interest is model-based development of embedded software systems in the car industry and especially the analysis of the costs and benefits of model-based software development. He was responsible for the conduction of the global study for Altran Technologies and the evaluation of the collected data.

Dimitrios S. Kolovos is a lecturer in Enterprise Systems in the Department of Computer Science of the University of York. He has published more than 50 articles in international journals, conferences, and workshops in the field of model driven engineering, and is currently leading the development of the Epsilon open source MDE platform (http://www.eclipse.org/gmt/epsilon). In the past, Dimitrios has participated in several collaborative projects on MDE including the ModelWare and ModelPlex EU IP projects, and the MADES EU STREP project, and is currently a co-investigator in the COMPASS project which is funded by the EU under the SESAR-JU initiative.

Helmut Krcmar holds the Chair for Information Systems at the Department of Informatics at Technische Universität München (TUM) since 2002. He is a member of the Department of Informatics and the Faculty of Business Administration as well as a member of the "Carl von Linde-Akademie." Since 2004, he is a member of the Program Faculty of the Elite Graduate Program "Finance and Information Management (FIM)" in the Elitenetzwerk Bayern. Until May 2007, he was Academic Director of the Executive Training Program ¡Communicate! Since January 2004, he is Board Member of the Center for Digital Technology and Management (CDTM) at Technische Universität München. Krcmar is founder of Informations- und TechnologieManagement Beratungsgesellschaft (ITM) and co-founder of several spin-offs out of the academic environment. His research interests include information and knowledge management, IT-enabled Value webs, service management, computer supported cooperative work, Information Systems in health care, and eGovernment.

Philip Langer studied at the Vienna University of Technology from 2003 to 2009 and received a Master's degree in Business Informatics with an topical emphasis on Model-Driven Engineering. During that time, he was also involved in several industry projects as a freelancing software and web developer. Since 2009, he is researcher at the Department of Telecooperation at the Johannes Kepler University as well as at the Business Informatics Group of the Vienna University of Technology. His research focus is model versioning and model transformations in the course of the research project AMOR (http://www.modelversioning.org).

Liliana Martinez is an Assistant Professor in Computer Science area at the Facultad de Ciencias Exactas, Universidad Nacional del Centro de la Provincia de Buenos Aires (UNCPBA), Tandil, Argentina. She is a member of the Software Technology Group, which develops its activities at the INTIA Research Institute at the UNCPBA. She has a Master's degree in Software Engineering from Universidad Nacional de La Plata, Argentina. Her research interests are focused on system modernization, reverse engineering, and refactoring in particular. She has been member of the program committee of international conferences related to software engineering.

Miguel A. de Miguel is an Associate Professor at the Universidad Politécnica de Madrid since 2002. He has a large experience in research activities of model driven development of safety-aware applications, and QoS middleware. These activities include the analysis of software models with high integrity analysis techniques and code generation for real-time software platforms. He has been the Chairman on some OMG standardization process. He is involved in several committees of real-time and model driven symposiums. Miguel A. de Miguel finish is PhD on 1997 and he has been Post-doc at University of Illinois at Urbana-Champaign and Research Engineer at INRIA-IRISA and Thales-TRT.

Ayse Morali is currently employed as an operational risk Consultant at Ascure N.V. - Belgium. After achieving her Bachelor's degree in Business Information Systems at the Marmara University - Turkey,

Ayse completed her MSc. degree in Computer Science and Business Administration at the Technische Universität Darmstadt - Germany. She acquired the PhD title from the University of Twente - The Netherlands, with her thesis titled "IT architecture-Based Confidentiality Risk Assessment in Networks of Organizations." During her PhD Ayse has analyzed the practical IT security risk management problems of industrial partners of her research project, provided them with practical yet effective solutions and tested these solutions on real-world case studies.

Dima Panfilenko received the Bachelor's degree in Economics at Kiev National University in Ukraine and his Master's degree in Information Systems at University of Saarland in Germany. He is a Researcher and a PhD student at the Institute for Information Systems (IWI) at German Research Center for Artificial Intelligence (DFKI). He has experience from a number of European and national research and software development projects including VIDE, R4eGov in FP6, and SHAPE in FP7. His main research interests include enterprise architectures, model-driven development, domain specific languages, semantic business process modeling and interoperability, as well as semantic service engineering.

Claudia Pereira is an Assistant Professor in Computer Science area at the Facultad de Ciencias Exactas, Universidad Nacional del Centro de la Provincia de Buenos Aires (UNCPBA), Tandil, Argentina. She is a member of the Technology Software Group at the INTIA Research Institute at the UNCPBA. She has a Master's degree in Software Engineering from Universidad Nacional de La Plata, Argentina. Her main research interests are focused on system modernization, reverse engineering, and refactoring in particular. She has been member of the program committee of international conferences related to software engineering.

Ricardo Pérez-Castillo holds the MSc degree in Computer Science from the University of Castilla-La Mancha, and he is currently a PhD student in Computer Science. He works in Alarcos Research Group at the University of Castilla-La Mancha. His research interests include architecture-driven modernization, model-driven development, and business process recovery.

Keith Phalp originally read for a first degree in Mathematics (completed 1986), at the University of Kent, which he then taught for a few years, before completing a Master's in Software Engineering (1991), followed by Ph.D. in Software Process Modeling (1994) both at Bournemouth University. He then spent three years as a post-doctoral research fellow at the University of Southampton, before returning to Bournemouth to take a lectureship, and has been there ever since in a variety of roles. He has been an Associate Dean within the School of Design, Engineering & Computing, since 2007, and he is also Head of Computing and Informatics. His research interests are broad, and he has published in both software engineering and applications of artificial, though he is particularly interested in the upstream areas of software development, such as business and IT alignment, specification, and software modeling.

Mario Piattini is full Professor at the UCLM. His research interests include software quality, metrics, and maintenance. He holds the PhD degree in Computer Science from the Technical University of Madrid, and leads the Alarcos Research Group at the Universidad de Castilla-La Mancha. He is CISA, CISM, and CGEIT by ISACA.

Alfonso Pierantonio is Associate Professor in computer science at the University of L'Aquila (Italy) where he is currently Director of the Master in Web Technology degree program. His current research interests include Model-Driven Engineering and in particular the theory and practice of model versioning/ evolution with a specific emphasis on coupled evolution. In particular, he investigated the problem of co-evolution between metamodels and other artifacts in order to define the basis for their (semi) automatic adaptation. He has been and is currently part of program and organization committees of conferences and has been among the initiators and in the steering committee of the International Conference on Model Transformation (ICMT). He co-edited several special issues on model transformations, which appeared on *Science of Computer Programming* and are going to appear on the *International Journal of Software and Systems Modeling*. Additional information can be found on his webpages: http://www. di.univaq.it/alfonso.

Matthias Riebisch is currently working as Assistant Professor at the Ilmenau University of Technology, Ilmenau, Germany. He is leading a research group on software architectural design methods, software evolution, and model-based design. He spent three years in leading positions in industry as project leader and architect of large software projects. Previously, during his career in academia he worked in several international and national projects in a strong collaboration with industry. In 2004 he earned a Habilitation degree and in 1993 a doctoral degree in computer science from the Ilmenau University of Technology. He received a diploma degree in automation engineering from Dresden University of Technology, Germany, in 1988. His research has spanned a range of topics in the fields of software engineering, systems engineering, software processes and quality, reusability, and software architectures. He has also worked on software evolution and traceability, especially for model-based design.

Davide Di Ruscio is Assistant Professor in the Computer Science Department of the University of L'Aquila. His research interests include code generation, methodologies for Web development, model driven engineering, and more specifically model differencing and model evolution. He published several papers in journals and international events in these topics. He has been in the PC of several workshops and conferences, and reviewer of many journals like *Science of Computer Programming*, and *Software and Systems Modeling*. Additional information can be found on his webpages: http://www.di.univaq. it/diruscio.

José Emilio Salazar completed his Computer Engineering studies in Universidad Politécnica de Madrid (UPM), on September 2008. Since September 2008, Emilio is undergoing his PhD studies at the UPM Ingeniería de Sistemas Telemáticos (DIT) department. From September of 2008 he participated in EU 7th FP projects such as MORE and CHESS. In these projects, he is focused on the automatic code generation from modeling languages and profiles such as UML and MARTE models using MDA languages such as QVT and MTL.

Bernhard Schätz received his Ph.D. in computer science at the TU München in 1998. He holds a Lecturer position at TU München and acts as Deputy General Manager as well as heads the department for Software and System Engineering at the Fortiss Research and Transfer Institute. His work focuses at the development and application of methods for the engineering of reliable embedded software systems, especially by means of CASE tools for model-based development. He is the organizer of several regular events on model-based techniques. Besides his academic activities he works as a Consultant in the domain of embedded systems and model-based development; furthermore, he is co-founder and member of the advisory board of the Validas AG.

Christian Seel was born in 1979. He holds a Bachelor and Master of Science degree in Information Systems (MScIS) from the University of Münster. From 2004 till 2008 he worked at the "Institut für Wirtschaftsinformatik" (IWi) in the German Research Center for Artificial Intelligence (DFKI) in Saarbrücken, where he led several national and European founded research projects in the areas of model-driven architecture (MDA), model-driven development (MDD), business process management (BPM), and business rules. Afterwards he worked for IDS Scheer AG and Software AG as Senior Software Engineer in research and development of the ARIS product line. In 2009 Christian Seel received his Ph.D. from the Saarland University. Since October 2011 he is holding a professorship for Information Systems at the University of Applied Science in Landshut. His research is focused on information systems, process management, model-driven software development, and mobile computing.

Martina Seidl holds a PhD in computer science and works at the Business Informatics Group of the Vienna University of Technology and the Institute for Formal Models and Verification of the Johannes Kepler University Linz. Her research interests include various topics from the area of model evolution and model versioning, automated reasoning with special focus on the evaluation of quantified Boolean formulas, as well as software verification.

Yu Sun is a Ph.D. candidate in the Department of Computer and Information Sciences at the University of Alabama at Birmingham (UAB) and member of the SoftCom Laboratory. His research interests include domain-specific modeling, domain-specific languages, and model transformation techniques. He received his BS in Computer Science from Zhengzhou University, China and MS in Computer Science from UAB. He is a student member of the ACM.

Lech Tuzinkiewicz received MSc degree and PhD degree in Computer Science in 1976 and 1982, respectively, both from the Wroclaw University of Technology, Poland. His PhD dissertation was associated with the automation of the design process of industrial electrical networks and electrical equipments - formalization issues. Since 1983 he has been working as a Assistant Professor at the Institute of Informatics, Wroclaw University of Technology. His main scientific interests include, but are not limited to: databases, data warehouses, data modeling, software development processes, modeling languages, model driven development, model transformations, and quality of the software products. Lech Tuzinkiewicz has over 70 publications in international journals and conference proceedings from different areas of software engineering.

Jules White is an Assistant Professor at Virginia Tech. He received his BA in Computer Science from Brown University, his MS in Computer Science from Vanderbilt University, and his Ph.D. in Computer Science from Vanderbilt University. Dr. White's research focuses on applying a combination of model-driven engineering and constraint-based optimization techniques to the deployment and configuration of complex software systems. Dr. White is the project leader for the Generic Eclipse Modeling System (GEMS), an Eclipse Foundation project.

Konrad Wieland studied Business Informatics at the Vienna University of Technology from 2003 to 2009. During that time he was working as a Teaching Assistant at the "Information & Software Engineering Group" (IFS, TU Wien). Since the beginning of 2009 he is working at the BIG as Research Assistant. His research interests comprise Collaborative Modeling supported by Model Versioning Systems as developed within the research project AMOR (http://www.modelversioning.org).

Manuel Wimmer is working as a Senior Researcher at the Business Informatics Group at the Vienna University of Technology. In his PhD thesis he has been working on several model-based tool integration topics such as automatically extracting metamodels out of legacy CASE tools as well as providing interoperability between domain-specific modeling languages and UML. His current research interests comprise Web engineering and model engineering; in particular model transformations based on formal methods, generating transformations by-example, as well as applying model transformations to deal with model (co-)evolution.

Index